Food Science

Food Science

SECOND EDITION

Helen Charley

Professor Emeritus of Foods and Nutrition
Oregon State University

MACMILLAN PUBLISHING COMPANY
New York

COLLIER MACMILLAN PUBLISHERS
London

Copyright © 1982, by Macmillan Publishing Company,
a division of Macmillan, Inc.
Earlier copyright © 1971, by John Wiley & Sons, Inc.

Macmillan Publishing Company
866 Third Avenue, New York, New York 10022
Collier Macmillan Canada, Inc.

Library of Congress Cataloging in Publication Data:

Charley, Helen.
  Food science.

  Includes index.
  1. Food.   2. Nutrition.   3. Cookery.   I. Title.

TX354.C47   1982   641.3   81-11366
ISBN 0-02-321940-8   AACR2

Printed in the United States of America

Printing   10   11   12   13   Year   7   8   9   0

ISBN 0-02-321940-8

Preface

This edition of *Food Science* is essentially an updated version of the original. The sequence of chapters is unchanged. The emphasis remains on the presentation of scientific concepts as a basis for understanding foods as complex chemical systems. The bibliographies with their numerous additions are still annotated.

Knowledge in particular areas covered in the book has expanded tremendously in the decade since the original publication. I have distilled information from the literature and integrated the new material into the text so that it is comprehensible to the scientifically oriented beginning student of foods. The sections of several chapters have been rewritten not only to incorporate pertinent new material but also to clarify original presentations. Some of the chapters are reorganized with the aim of presenting the subject matter more logically so that the students may comprehend it more readily. In the present edition, more emphasis is given to handling foods so that they are safe to eat, to cooking as it affects nutritive value and palatability, and to alternate uses of food resources in a hungry world.

My purpose is to present concepts as accurately and completely as the current state of knowledge allows. Gaps in knowledge exist, however, some of which I noted in the text. Our understanding of some issues necessarily remains incomplete, perhaps even erroneous, a situation that can only be remedied by a diligent perusal of forthcoming literature related to the science of foods.

I value the helpful suggestions for improvement of the present book from users of the first edition. I express appreciation to authors and publishers for permission to use illustrations that supplement and reinforce the words of the text.

Carlisle, Indiana   Helen Charley

Preface to the First Edition

Knowledge of food science, which draws upon a number of disciplines, is expanding rapidly. Even so, some aspects of the subject remain more art than science. The complex nature of foods and of the changes in them which occur naturally and as a result of handling and manipulating are major factors contributing to the imperfect state of our knowledge. Where we know too little, we can draw tentative conclusions only, and must await the results of further research for more satisfactory answers.

This book emphasizes the scientific aspects of the study of foods. It is designed to serve as a college text for a basic course for students who have had at least general college chemistry or the equivalent and have some knowledge of elementary nutrition.

The basic sciences and the literature in food science are drawn upon to give a fundamental understanding of both theoretical and practical aspects of the subject. Background information needed for a better grasp of individual topics precedes or parallels the subject itself. Effort has been made to present technical material in a clear and comprehensible manner. Hopefully the book will provide intellectual stimulation and challenge for the serious student of food science.

Emphasis throughout the text is on the reasons for procedures and phenomena, not just what to do and how to do it. To minimize chances of failure for the student with limited experience, crucial steps in the preparation of basic foods are given in detail. Such directions are reinforced whenever possible by reasons for the steps recommended or the precautions to be taken. The presentation should be comprehensible to all students, although the explanations of phenomena to be observed will often mean more to the student with the better background.

For students who wish fuller coverage or more details on specific topics, a selected and annotated list of references is included with each chapter.

I wish to thank Oregon State University for granting a sabbatical leave, part of which was spent writing the manuscript for this text. I also wish to thank Pauline Douglas, whose blue pencil eliminated a plethora of introductory prepositional phrases and similar offenses; Mary E. Bell, who in typing the manuscript deciphered a wandering and wayward script; and the students in my classes, who, as the lectures evolved on which the manuscript for this text was based, listened, questioned, and challenged. Finally, I wish to include a special word of appreciation to those authors and publishers who generously permitted the use of photographic, photomicrographic, and other illustrative material and to Wilbur Nelson, photographer of those illustrations prepared by the author while on the Home Economics Staff at West Virginia University.

Corvallis, Oregon
August 1970

Helen Charley

Contents

ONE

Evaluation of Food

One of the objectives of a study of foods is to develop the ability to prepare and serve more palatable foods. In many cases food of poor quality is eaten because none better is available. The burden of improving the standards of acceptability for foods rests mainly on the homemaker, who selects, prepares, and serves food for the family. Quality of foods served in the home does much to set the standards of taste in the country.

A good cook is able to evaluate food from a quality standpoint and do so objectively. In evaluating a food one must know what characteristics to look for and have a vocabulary adequate for differentiating quality in foods. The vocabulary for characterizing foods is neither as complete nor as precise as might be wished.

SENSORY ASSESSMENT OF FOOD QUALITY

When the quality of a food product is assessed by means of human sensory organs, the evaluation is said to be sensory, or subjective. Most judgments of food quality are of this type. Every time food is eaten a judgment is made. Consciously or otherwise the eater decides that the food in question is or is not of acceptable quality, that it shall or shall not pass!

APPEARANCE OF FOOD

The size and shape of pieces of food, the brownness of the crusts of breads and pies, and the brightness and trueness of the color of fruits and vegetables are judged by eye. Sight also plays a part in the assessment of the lightness as well as the structure of foods like bread and cakes.

VISUAL PERCEPTION

Perception of the size, shape, and color of foods and of such characteristics as transparency, opaqueness, turbidity, dullness, and gloss is mediated by the organs of sight (1).* We see an object when radiant energy from it impinges upon the retina of the eye. The retina contains two types of receptors of radiant

*Numbers in parentheses identify individually the references given at the end of each chapter.

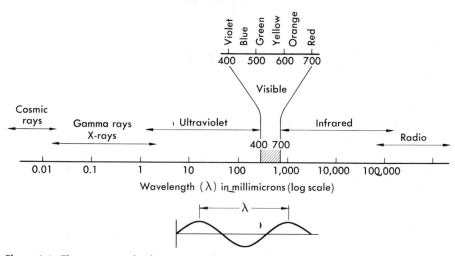

Figure 1-1. The spectrum of radiant energy plotted on a logarithmic wavelength scale. (From *Life of the Green Plant* by Arthur Galston, 2nd edition, © 1964 by Prentice-Hall, Inc., Englewood Cliffs, N. J. p. 4. Reprinted by permission of Felix Cooper.)

energy, categorized by their shapes as rods (long and slender) and as cones (tapering). An estimated 110 to 130 million rods and 6 to 7 million cones are found in the human retina. Radiant energy absorbed by pigments in these receptors, in some fashion not clearly understood, triggers nerve impulses which are transmitted to the brain by way of the optic nerve. The visual sensation which results is light, upon which perception of the form and the color of objects depends. What is perceived (seen) is a conscious response to stimulation of the visual apparatus.

The rods and cones are sensitive to those rays which vary in wavelength from approximately 400 to 700 millimicrons (1 millimicron, abbreviated mμ, equals 0.000001 or 10^{-6} millimeter), a very narrow segment of the entire electromagnetic spectrum. (See Fig. 1-1.) The rods, which are more sensitive to light than are the cones, make possible the perception of the form of objects in dim light. Nerve impulses in the rods are initiated when light bleaches the pigment, rhodopsin, for the generation of which vitamin A is essential. The cones require a stronger stimulus to initiate nerve impulses, which here result in the perception of fine details of form and the perception of color. (Dining by candlelight does not enhance the *visual* perception of food.)

COLOR OF FOODS

The individual waves which make up white light can be separated into all the colors of the rainbow by passing the light through a prism (21). An object which reflects all these rays appears white; one which absorbs all the components of white light appears black. The eye (together with the brain) is able to distinguish among the waves which constitute white light. Those rays with the shortest wavelengths (near one end of the visible spectrum) elicit the response called "violet," and the longest waves at the other end the response called "red." Objects appear colored because the light from them which reaches the eye contains only a part of the waves from the visible portion of the spectrum. Spinach is green because it absorbs part of the radiation which makes up white light but reflects those rays which elicit the response to which the term "green" is given.

Electromagnetic waves somewhat shorter than the 400 millimicrons of the violet region are in the category called ultraviolet. Gamma rays, x-rays, and cosmic rays are progressively shorter in wavelength. The last are measured in fractions of an angstrom (1 angstrom, abbreviated Å, equals 10^{-7} millimeter). Those electromagnetic waves somewhat longer than the longest visible ones in the red region make up the infrared rays. Beyond these are the much longer radar and radio waves.

The color of foods contributes immeasurably to one's esthetic appreciation of them. For example, visualize these three menus: (1) steamed halibut, mashed potatoes, buttered cauliflower, apple salad and, for dessert, ice cream and angel cake; (2) roast beef, buttered carrots, Harvard beets, sliced tomato, and shredded red cabbage salad and, for dessert, cherry pie; and (3) roast beef, mashed potatoes, buttered carrots, tossed salad of lettuce, spinach, cauliflower, and green pepper, and for dessert, orange ice and angel cake. There is not much question which of the three has more eye appeal.

In addition to giving pleasure, the color of foods is associated with other attributes. For example, the ripeness of fruits such as bananas and strawberries is judged by color. Color is used as an index to the quality of a number of foods. Dried apricots which are a clear, bright orange in color have more sales appeal than do those that are dark and dull, in part because of the superior flavor expected in the former. The strength of coffee and tea is judged in part by the color of the beverages. The color of roast beef is used as an index to doneness. Toast which is too brown is likely to be rejected in anticipation of a somewhat scorched, bitter taste.

FLAVOR OF FOODS

Once food passes the "sight test," sensory organs in the nose and mouth are utilized to obtain additional information about the quality of a food. These sensations are included under the heading of "flavor." The flavor of a food has three components: odor, taste, and a composite of sensations known as "mouthfeel." Although food scientists and technologists are interested in sensory evaluation of the flavor of foods, physiologists and psychologists in the main have been the ones who have attempted to ascertain how flavor sensations are perceived.

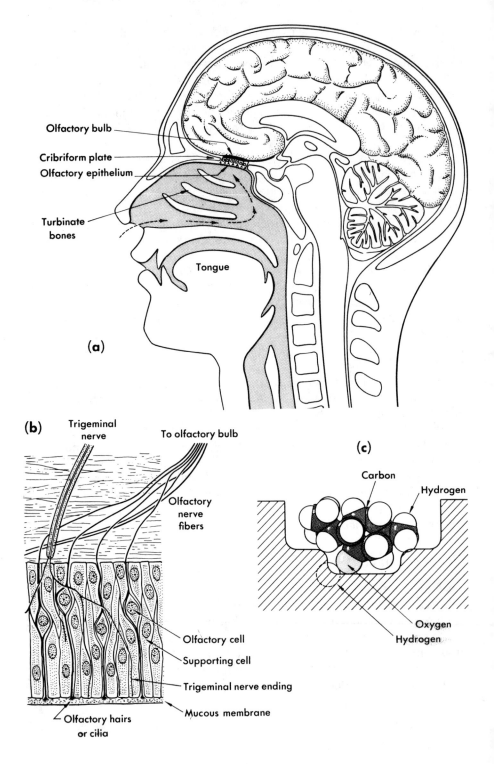

(a)

(b)

Trigeminal nerve

To olfactory bulb

(c)

Carbon

Hydrogen

Olfactory nerve fibers

Olfactory cell

Supporting cell

Trigeminal nerve ending

Mucous membrane

Olfactory hairs or cilia

Oxygen

Hydrogen

Olfactory bulb

Cribriform plate

Olfactory epithelium

Turbinate bones

Tongue

ODOR

The odor of a food contributes immeasurably to the pleasure of eating. Odor, like appearance, may be a valuable index to the quality of a food and even to its wholesomeness and edibility.

SENSORY ORGAN FOR DETECTING ODOR. Information regarding the odor of food is obtained through the olfactory epithelium, a yellow pigmented area about the size of a postage stamp, located in the upper part of the nasal cavity and above the turbinate bones. (See Fig. 1-2a.) Olfactory cells (from 10 to 20 million in humans *vs.* 100 million in the rabbit) through which odors are detected are located in this area. Each olfactory cell terminates in a number of hairlike projections or extensions of the cell wall, called "cilia," which extend into the mucous lining of the olfactory epithelium. Nerve endings from the first cranial nerve (also called the olfactory nerve) make contact with nerve fibers from the olfactory cells by way of the olfactory bulb, which is just above the odor-detecting area and separated from it by the perforated cribriform plate. The nose is also innervated with fibers from the fifth cranial (or trigeminal) nerve, which senses pain, a fact that accounts for the sensitivity of the nose to pepper. The simplified drawing of the microscopic appearance of a section of the olfactory epithelium in Figure 1-2*b* shows olfactory cells with their terminal hairs and the nerve fibers which serve the area.

Normally, most of the inhaled air flows past the olfactory area but does not impinge directly upon it. However, in the act of swallowing a slight vacuum is formed in the nasal cavity and as food starts down the esophogus a small gust of odor-laden air from the food is drawn up into the olfactory area. Sniffing to better sense an odor also draws air up to this organ.

ODOR DETECTION. There are many unsettled questions as to how odors are sensed, but there are two points on which there is general agreement. A substance which produces odor must be volatile, and the molecules of the substance must make contact with receptors in the epithelium of the olfactory organ. To perceive an odor, information is picked up at the terminal ends of the sensory organ (the cilia) and transmitted as electrical impulses by the nerves to the brain, where the message is decoded. How contact of an odorous molecule initiates the impulse which results in the sensation of odor is not known. Even more of a mystery is how these electrical impulses which reach

---

Figure 1-2. (a) Nasal cavity, showing location of the olfactory area above the turbinate bones, with the olfactory bulb above and the olfactory epithelium below the cribriform plate. (b) Simplified drawing of a section of the olfactory epithelium showing olfactory cells with nerves leading to the olfactory bulb and with terminal hairs projecting into the mucous lining of the epithelium. Also shown are supporting cells and trigeminal nerve. (c) According to the stereochemical theory, the odor of a molecule depends on its size and shape or its charge, which in turn determines on which slots or pits of the olfactory nerve endings it will fit. A molecule that fits the "pepperminty" cavity is shown. (From "The Stereochemical Theory of Odor" by J. E. Amoore, J. W. Johnston, Jr., and M. Rubin. Copyright © 1964 by Scientific American, Inc. All rights reserved.)

the brain are decoded. The concentrations at which substances can be detected in air are incredibly low. One odorous substance, vanillin, can be sensed when the concentration is only 2×10^{-10} (0.0000000002) milligram per liter of air, a low concentration indeed. Methyl mercaptan added to the gas supplied to a kitchen range to give it a noticeable odor is said to be detected with only 1 milligram in 25 million liters of gas; what is more, only about a tenth of a liter of air is inhaled at each breath and not more than 2 percent of this contacts the olfactory organ.

It is estimated that the olfactory sense of humans has the capacity to distinguish 16 million odors. However, the vocabulary to differentiate among the many odors perceived through the sensory organ is woefully inadequate. Analogy is employed in an attempt to verbalize differences which can be distinguished nasally. For example, odors may be characterized as nut-like, fruity, oily, or minty.

ODOR STIMULI.   An early attempt to define odors in terms of a few basic elements was that of Crocker and Henderson. They proposed (7) that any odorous substance has four components: fragrant, also described as flowery or fruity; acid or sharp; burnt or tarry or scorched; and caprylic or goatlike. Theoretically, no two odors will be identical in intensity for each of these basic elements. A nine-point scale was proposed (from 0 to 8) to indicate the magnitude of each of the four components in a particular odorous substance. A 0 indicates the absence of any one component and 8 denotes maximum intensity. A substance rated 0000 would have no odor and one that rated 8888 would be as intensely fragrant, acid, burnt, and goaty as possible. According to the Crocker-Henderson system, the odor of a damask rose can be expressed as 6523 and that of coffee as 7683. The aroma of coffee differs from the odor of a damask rose mainly in the greater intensity in coffee of the burnt component, the proposed standard for which is a compound called guaiacol.

Just why a molecule provokes a certain odor sensation has interested a number of investigators. Attempts have been made to single out the group or groups of atoms that confer on a molecule its characteristic odor. Compounds which differ markedly in structure may have similar odors; conversely, small differences in structure may give molecules with markedly different odors. One intriguing scheme attempts to relate the contour of the molecule to the particular odor sensation which it provokes (2). According to this theory, there are seven primary-odor receptor sites and as many different types of odorous molecules, one to fit each type of olfactory receptor. Molecules which are quite different in chemical makeup but which are similar in size or shape will provoke the same odor sensation. (A molecule which fits into more than one receptor can produce more than one basic odor sensation.) According to this theory, the geometry of the molecule is of primary importance so far as odor is concerned.

Molecules which are responsible for the primary odor called *ethereal* are small, thin, and rod-shaped; those with a *camphoraceous* odor are hemi-spherical and near 7 angstroms in diameter. Molecules with a *musky* odor are somewhat larger, near 10 angstroms, and resemble a flat disk. The shape rather than the size is important for those molecules with a *floral* and for those with a *minty* odor. Molecules which elicit a floral odor are shaped like a keyhole and those with a minty odor are wedge-shaped. The electronic status is the important factor for compounds with a *pungent* and for those with a *putrid* odor. Molecules of the former carry a negative charge and those of the latter a positive charge. The relation of molecular contour or geometry and odor sensation as proposed in this scheme is shown graphically in Figure 1-3.

A recent refinement suggests that the odor of a compound depends not only on the proportions of the molecule, but also on the ease with which the molecule can pass from the air to the moisture on the surface of the olfactory receptors and from there to the lipid layer underneath. Instead of a few primary odors, this theory envisions a spectrum of odors, as shown in Figure 1-4.

Another theory suggests that vibrations of molecules of an odorous compound cause them to collide in a specific manner with the olfactory surface and thus elicit the olfactory response (33). According to this theory, many receptor sites could be contacted by a single molecule, thus accounting for the great sensitivity of the sense of smell. And still another theory proposes that odorous compounds migrate through the olfactory mucosa in a manner analogous to thin layer chromatography and that one odor is distinguished from another by its speed of passage (18).

Most of the odors that assault the nose are composite impressions. Like chords of music, most are combinations of simpler "notes." Pleasant odors are those in which there is a harmonious balance. Pleasing combinations are subtle rather than either monotonous or jarring.

TASTE

Important as odor is in the sensory evaluation of foods, few people would be content just to smell food before swallowing it. We value food for its taste, in the restricted sense of the word.

ORGANS FOR DETECTING TASTE.   Taste is sensed by the taste buds, which are located in the papillae (bright-pink spots) on the tongue. Young children have taste buds on the hard and soft palate and the pharynx as well as on the tongue. This may account for their propensity to roll food in the mouth. The location of papillae on the tongue can be seen in Figure 1-5. Nerves to the back part of the tongue, exposed by dissection, are also shown.

Taste buds are located in the epithelium and on parts of the tongue which food contacts most during chewing and swallowing. Fungiform papillae and the taste buds they contain are found on the dorsal surface and toward the front of the tongue, as are the filiform papillae. The latter contain no taste buds, but are sensitive to touch. Foliate papillae are found on the sides of the

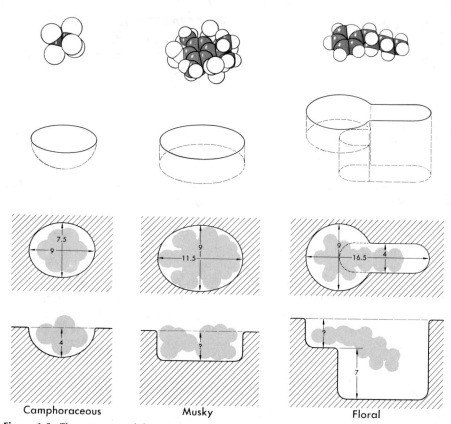

Camphoraceous   Musky   Floral

Figure 1-3. The geometry of the primary odors and their receptor sites. The shapes of the first five sites are shown in perspective and (with the molecules silhouetted in them) from above and the side; dimensions are in angstrom units. Molecules that are pungent or putrid are so because

tongue and the few (7-10) circumvallate papillae across the back, arranged in a V-shape. The central surface of the tongue contains no taste buds.

Some papillae contain more taste buds than do others. The diagram in Figure 1-6 shows papillae (much enlarged) of the tongue and taste buds located in one circumvallate papilla. A taste bud is made up of a number of cells grouped in a knoblike cluster microscopic in size and surrounded by a depression, called a "pore," in which the saliva collects. A simplified diagram of a taste bud is shown in Figure 1-7. Cells which make up a bud are of two types, supporting cells and taste cells. Each elongated, gustatory (i.e., taste-sensing) cell terminates in a microvillus, a hairlike projection into the pore, much as cilia project from olfactory cells. To be tasted, a substance must be dissolved in the saliva and make contact with the microvilli. Nerve fibers which make contact with the taste cells are from the seventh (chorda tympani) and ninth (glossopharyngeal) cranial nerves, and from a branch of the tenth (vagus), as shown in Figure 1-8.

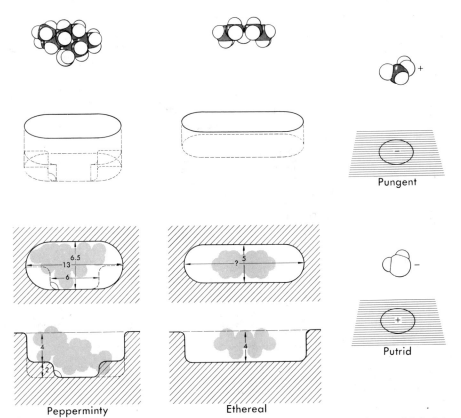

Pungent

Putrid

Pepperminty

Ethereal

of charge, not shape, according to this theory. (From "The Stereochemical Theory of Odor" by J. E. Amoore, J. W. Johnston, Jr., and M. Rubin. Copyright © 1964 by Scientific American, Inc. All rights reserved.)

The number of taste buds in humans is estimated at 9,000 to 10,000, much fewer than the number reported in such animals as the antelope. Cells which constitute a taste bud degenerate and are replaced over a seven-day period. As an individual grows old the number of taste buds declines. Atrophy of the papillae begins when one is about forty-five.

TASTE STIMULI.   Taste sensations which the taste buds register are categorized as sweet, salt, sour, and bitter (12). Taste buds in the different areas of the tongue are not equally sensitive to all taste stimuli, and at least some taste cells respond to more than one stimulus. Taste buds near the tip of the tongue are more sensitive to sweet and salt, those on the sides to sour, and those near the back to bitter.

The sensation known as *sour* is associated with hydrogen ions supplied by acids such as vinegar, by those found in fruits and vegetables, and by acid salts such as cream of tartar, which is commonly found on the kitchen shelf.

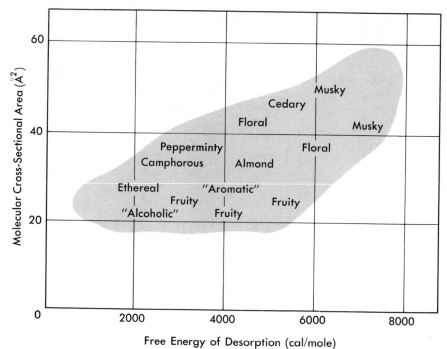

Figure 1-4. The odor spectrum lends support to the theory that the odor of a molecule depends on its cross-sectional area and the ease with which it can pass from air to water to lipid. (From J. T. Davies, *Journal of Theoretical Biology* **8:** 6, 1965. Copyright © by Academic Press, Inc., New York.)

The intensity of the sour sensation produced by an acid depends more upon the hydrogen-ion concentration than upon the total acidity; however, sourness and hydrogen-ion concentration do not run exactly parallel.

Salt taste is due to ions of salts. Those of sodium chloride (table salt) are the most common source of the salt sensation in foods. Sodium chloride is said to be the only salt with the pure salt sensation; even so, in dilute concentration it is frequently identified as sweet.

Substances which elicit the *sweet* sensation are primarily organic compounds. Alcohols, certain amino acids, and aldehydes such as cinnamic aldehyde (found in cinnamon) taste sweet. Glycerol (glycerine) tastes mildly sweet. Sugars, however, are the main source of sweetness in foods.

According to a current concept, molecules that taste sweet have functional groups which comprise an AH-B system, the AH a proton donor and the B a proton acceptor (26). The two components of the system must be positioned in such a way that they can hydrogen bond to a similar system AH-B at a receptor site on a taste bud, shown schematically (27):

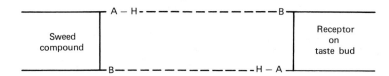

When this occurs, the membrane of the taste receptor is depolarized, initiating a nerve impulse which results in the sensation of sweetness. The oxygens of the two glycol groups $-\overset{|}{\underset{\overset{|}{OH}}{C}}-\overset{|}{\underset{\overset{|}{OH}}{C}}-$ are thought to be the A and B of sweet-tasting sugars (25) and a protein on the taste bud to provide the AH and B at the receptor site (10). A sweet-sensitive protein, with a high content of the amino acid lysine, has been isolated from the taste buds of bovine tongue.

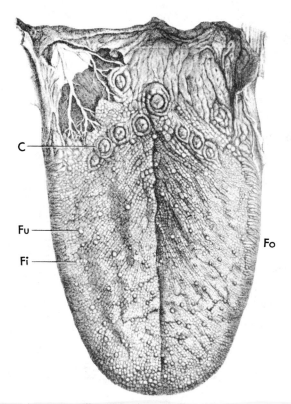

Figure 1-5. Tongue, showing papillae. Taste buds are found in the circumvallate (C), the fungiform (Fu), and the foliate (Fo), but not in the filiform (Fi) papillae (from Wenzel). (From H. C. Warren and L. Carmichael, *Elements of Human Psychology.* Copyright © 1930 by Houghton Mifflin Company, Boston. Reprinted by permission.)

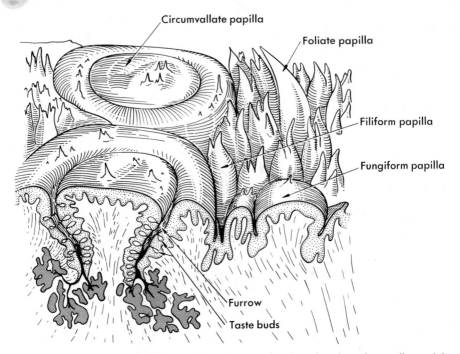

Figure 1-6. Mucous membrane covering the tongue much enlarged to show the papillae and the taste buds in one circumvallate papilla. (Reprinted by permission of Macmillan Publishing Co., Inc., from *The Human Body: Its Structure and Physiology,* 4th edition, by Sigmund Grollman. Copyright © 1978, Sigmund Grollman.)

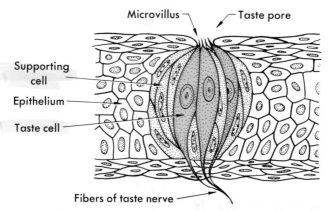

Figure 1-7. Diagram of a taste bud. Taste cells with their nerve fibers and with their microvilli projecting into the taste pore are shown, as are supporting cells. (Adapted from Fred D'Amour, *Basic Physiology,* University of Chicago Press, Chicago, 1961, p. 623.)

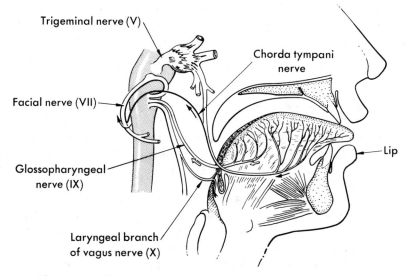

Figure 1-8. The tongue with the nerves that transmit taste sensations to the brain. (Reprinted by permission of Macmillan Publishing Co., Inc., from *The Human Body: Its Structure and Physiology*, 4th edition, by Sigmund Grollman. Copyright © 1978, Sigmund Grollman.)

The strength of the complex between this protein (the $-NH_2$ and the $>C=0$ of lysine possibly supplying the AH and B) and sugars decreased with decreasing sweetness of the sugars (fructose, sucrose, glucose, galactose, and mannose) (9). The stereochemical position of the $-OH$ groups on a molecule of sugar influences the ability of the molecule to elicit the sweet sensation (26). If the effective distance between two such groups is too great, they are unable to bond to active groups on the taste bud, and, if too close, they form intramolecular bonds. In either case, sweetness is diminished. The somewhat greater sweetness of the alpha form of D-glucose (see "Starch Chemistry" in Chapter 8) compared to the beta form (20) is attributed to hydrogen bonding between groups in the latter.

Sugars have been ranked in descending order of sweetness as follows: fructose, sucrose, glucose, galactose and mannose, maltose, and lactose (24). Numerical values assigned to each sugar (1.15, 1.00, 0.64–0.61, 0.59, 0.46, and 0.30, respectively, for the sugars above) may be misleading. The relative sweetness depends on whether the sugar is in the form of crystals or in solution, on the concentration of the solution, on the age of the solution and the extent to which the sugar has mutarotated (20), on the temperature of the solution, and, in foods, on the presence of acids, salts, and other constituents. For example, fructose dissolved in water at low concentration was ranked more than one and one-half times as sweet as sucrose. In acidic beverages and at higher concentration, however, the sweetening power of the two sugars was essentially the same, as was true when they were compared in white cake, sugar cookies, and vanilla pudding (4,13). In one study in which three sugar alcohols and three simple sugars were compared with sucrose for sweetness, the values were for sucrose 1.00, fructose 1.24–1.32, glucose 0.56–0.83, xylose 0.57–0.87, sorbitol 0.50–0.82, xylitol 0.96–1.18, and mannitol 0.51–0.62 (34).

Although sugars are important food sweeteners, there are circumstances where noncaloric sweeteners are desired (8). For this reason, certain tropical plants with sweet taste-modifying characteristics are of interest (14), as is a dipeptide (trivial name aspartame), which is many times sweeter than sucrose (5). Dihydrochalcones derived from certain flavonoid pigments were once considered promising (15).

Saccharin is a noncaloric substance which has been used for many years to elicit the sweet sensation. As a sweetener, it is usually marketed as a sodium salt. Saccharin in this form is 300 times sweeter than sucrose. The ammonium salt of saccharin called "sucramine" is 700 times sweeter. Cyclamic acid and its calcium and sodium salts, known as "cyclamates," are 30 times sweeter than sucrose, or one-tenth as sweet as saccharin. Cyclamates were withdrawn from the market because of the possible hazards to health in their unrestricted use and the advisability of indiscriminate use of saccharin has been questioned.

A number of different types of compounds taste *bitter*. Alkaloids such as caffeine and theobromine (for formulas see "Constituents in the Coffee Bean, Chapter 7), nicotine, quinine, and strychnine are bitter. So are glycosides of phenolic compounds, such as naringin in grapefruit (0.75 percent of the peel), and a miscellaneous group of substances including bile salts and the salts of magnesium (magnesium sulfate is epsom salts), ammonium, and calcium. Synthetic sweeteners may leave a bitter aftertaste, especially in high concentrations.

Although the significance of the observation is not known, it is of interest that a drug, gymnemic acid, renders the taste buds insensitive to sweet and bitter but not to salt and sour. A berry grown in Africa, known as the "miracle fruit," when eaten makes sour foods like lemons, limes, rhubarb, and strawberries taste sweet. Apparently the active substance coats the taste buds, which interferes with their ability to sense sour stimuli. These and similar observations show that there are many gaps in our understanding of the sense of taste.

TASTE BLINDNESS.   Some individuals, approximately one-fourth of the population, are said to be "taste blind": they are unable to taste the compound

phenylthiocarbamide and related compounds, which contain the $-N-\overset{\displaystyle S}{\overset{\displaystyle \|}{C}}-$

group. In "tasters," such compounds produce an unpleasant, bitter sensation. Taste blindness is specific for these compounds and is inherited as a Mendelian recessive trait.

Rather than say a food "tastes" good, in most instances one probably should say it "smells" good. Although a person with a cold complains that food has no taste, the sensitivity of the olfactory organ—not of the taste buds—is impaired. It is the ability to detect odors that is missing and missed. The pleasant sensations in eating come more from odor than from taste.

TASTE SENSITIVITY.   The concentration of a substance (in saliva) required to trigger the sensation of taste is much higher than the concentration of a substance (in air) required to provoke the sensation of odor. The four primary tastes are not sensed with equal ease. Time is one factor. Salt on the tongue is sensed in a fraction of a second, whereas a bitter substance may require a full second after it contacts the tongue before it is sensed by the taste buds. Once perceived, bitter sensations tend to linger, however. Most bitter substances are only slightly soluble in water. Concentration is a second factor. The concentration needed to bring about a sensation varies with the substance in question. That concentration required for identification is known as the "threshold" for that particular substance. Individuals differ in their sensitivity to the four taste sensations, and the threshold for each of the four primary tastes is usually not at the same level in any one individual. For a discussion of the effect of temperature on ability to taste, see the section on mouthfeel in this Chapter.

TASTE INTERACTION.   Because foods contain mixtures of substances which elicit all four taste sensations, the possibility of their interacting has been investigated (12). Results which have been reported are not always in agreement. For some individuals at least, salt in subthreshold concentrations reduces the tartness of acid. The effect is greater with malic and tartaric than with acetic and citric acids. Subthreshold concentrations of salt also increase the apparent sweetness of sucrose. These effects of salt may account for the preference of some individuals for a sprinkling of salt on grapefruit and for the fact that a small amount of salt improves the flavor of fruit pies, lemon pie filling, and Harvard beets. Conversely, acids in subthreshold concentration intensify the saltiness of sodium chloride, so it is easy to oversalt tart foods. Sugar in subthreshold concentration reduces the saltiness of sodium chloride, so a pinch of sugar may improve vegetable soup or chili that has been oversalted. Sugar also reduces the sourness of acids and the bitterness of caffeine.

The effects of suprathreshold concentrations of sweet, salt, sour, and bitter have been studied, also, again with conflicting results (22). For example, decrease in the apparent sweetness of sucrose both by salt and acid (citric) and decrease in the apparent saltiness of salt by sugar (sucrose) have been reported. But an increase in apparent sweetness of sucrose and in apparent bitterness of caffeine by acid have also been reported, as has an increase in the apparent sourness of acid by caffeine and a decrease in the apparent sourness of acid and in the apparent bitterness of caffeine by sugar. Possibly the level of the test substance above the threshold influences the results. As everyone is aware, a lemonade that is too tart can be made acceptable by adding more sugar, and coffee with sugar is not so bitter as that without.

FLAVOR POTENTIATORS.   Flavor potentiators are substances which add to or improve the flavor of foods, primarily through their effect on taste. One potentiator which has been in use for some time is monosodium glutamate, the sodium salt of glutamic acid. It is odorless, but in dilute solutions it produces either a salty or a sweet sensation. Monosodium glutamate in a high-protein food appears to balance and blend the taste complex and to produce a sensation described as "mouth-filling." The flavor appeal of mushrooms, alone or with other foods, may stem in part from their high glutamic acid content. The use of monosodium glutamate as a food additive has been approved by the Food and Drug Administration. The 5'-nucleotides, disodium 5'-inosinate and disodium 5'-guanylate, are two flavor potentiators that were approved as food additives in 1962. They are more potent enhancers of meat flavor than is monosodium glutamate.

MOUTHFEEL

The third aspect of the composite sensation known as "flavor" has to do with the way food feels in the mouth, termed "mouthfeel." The color, odor, taste, and mouthfeel of a food all influence its acceptability. Even though color, odor, and taste are acceptable, a food may still be rejected on the basis of mouthfeel. When foods are acceptable, mouthfeel will play an important part in the sensory pleasure of eating. Nerve fibers from the trigeminal (fifth cranial) nerve (see Fig. 1-8) are the means by which mouthfeel is sensed. Fibers from this nerve are sensitive to pain, to heat and cold, and to tactile sensations.

PAIN.   Pepper stimulates the pain-sensing fibers inside the mouth as well as in the nose. A little pepper "pain" is pleasant; a trifle too much is actually painful. The sensation is described as hot or burning.

TEMPERATURE.   Hot and cold are sensations that contribute to the composite flavor of a food. Such expressions as hot chocolate, piping hot soup, chilled salad, iced tea, ice cold watermelon, and frosted sherbet all attest the importance of temperature in one's appreciation of food.

Temperature of food per se is an important aspect of quality. In addition, temperature influences the volatility of compounds which elicit odor and affects the ability of taste buds to pick up taste sensations. Taste sensations are less intense as the temperature of a food is lowered below 20°C (68°F) and raised above 30°C (86°F). Variations within this temperature range apparently make little difference in the intensity of taste sensations. Thus really hot coffee is not so bitter as that which has cooled in the cup; iced coffee is not so bitter as that which is warm but not really hot. Melted ice cream tastes unpleasantly sweet, although in the frozen state it is acceptable. The diminished taste of cold foods may be due in part to the fact that molecules of substances which provoke sensations are more sluggish when cold, although no doubt very cold substances anesthetize the taste buds, too. Foods hot enough to "burn" the tongue diminish or destroy the sensitivity of the taste buds to taste stimuli. The cells in an injured taste bud are regenerated, but several days are required.

TACTILE SENSATIONS.   Mouth, tongue, and jaws can assess the shape, form, and feel of a food, that is, its tactile character. This makes up a part of the sensory impressions associated with eating. One reason carbonated beverages are popular is that the bubbles of carbon dioxide are liberated from the liquid with enough force to stimulate the tactile nerve fibers in the mouth. A child's characterization of carbonated beverages as "tickle water" recognizes the tactile stimuli.

In some instances the tactile properties of a food are part of a composite known as *texture,* to be discussed in a separate section.

With some foods *consistency* makes an important contribution to tactile sensations. Fondant and fudge, ices and ice creams may be too hard, too soft, or desirably firm. Gravies, sauces, and syrups range in consistency from thick to thin. Temperature may affect markedly the consistency of foods. Cold syrup is thick, or viscous; hot syrup is much thinner. Cheese, at room temperature an elastic solid, when heated becomes liquid enough to flow or pour. A food may be a slightly viscous fluid as is broth in which less tender meat or poultry has been cooked, or it may be an elastic solid as is the same broth after it has been refrigerated for some time. The consistency of a soft custard, besides being thick or thin, may be smooth or curdled, that of cream soups and gravies may be smooth or lumpy. Mashed potatoes may be mealy or pasty. Gels made with gelatin, with fruit pectin, or with eggs as in a baked custard may be rubbery or friable, weak or firm. Particles of cooked cereal should be separate and distinct but, improperly cooked, the cereal may be pasty. All of the characteristics enumerated above relate to consistency, some to texture.

Chewiness is one aspect of the mouthfeel of certain foods. A food that resists chewing stimulates receptors for pressure around the teeth. Muscles of the tongue and jaw are stimulated. Chewy foods may be tender, tough, or just moderately chewy. The tactile sensations derived from eating a raw apple harvested on a cool day in early fall contrast with those experienced when a cooked apple is eaten. Although the teeth must exert enough pressure to fracture cells in a raw apple, much less force is needed to cleave (separate) cells along the middle lamella (see Chapter 27, on fruits) in cooked tissue. Fruits, vegetables, and meats are cooked to make them tender. "Tenderness" in fruits and vegetables depends on how easily the cells separate; in meats ease of separation of the lean tissue is involved, but so is the elasticity of the separated constituents of the meat. "Tenderness" in pastry is another matter. It is assessed by the ease with which the crisp crust breaks and is actually friability or brittleness. Nibbling on a pastry crust is one way to evaluate its "tenderness." A shortometer that measures the force needed to break the crisp pastry is another. (See Fig. 15-3.)

Astringency makes an important contribution to the tactile sensations of some foods. It is a dry, puckery sensation believed to be due to precipitation of proteins in the saliva and in the mucous membrane lining of the mouth, which deprives them of their lubricating character. Astringent substances may also constrict the ducts leading from the salivary glands to the mouth. The pleasure from drinking cider derives in part from its being mildly and pleasantly astringent. In contrast, unripe persimmons are excessively and unpleasantly astringent.

INFLUENCE OF MOUTHFEEL ON TASTE SENSATIONS. The mouthfeel of a food influences its acceptability. In addition, it affects the taste of a food (16,17). The taste of a watery food is more pronounced than that of one which is thick or viscous. Flavorful tomato juice may seem less so when served molded as an aspic. Sweetness and tartness in an orange ice stand out more than they do in an orange sherbet made from the same mix, but with the addition of gelatin or egg white to the latter.

TEXTURE OF FOODS

The tactile characteristics of a food may constitute one aspect of texture, but we apprise the texture of foods through more than the sense of touch. Structural components of foods confer on them a wide range of properties referred to collectively as texture (29,30). Which particular aspect of texture predominates varies from food to food.

Graininess is one aspect of texture. Texture in ice cream and fudge, which depends upon the size of the crystals and how they feel on the tongue, is characterized as "coarse" or "fine." Coarse-textured crystalline products are said to be "grainy." In muffins, biscuits, yeast bread, and cake, texture depends upon the character of the crumb around the cells or holes. The latter are referred to as the "grain" of a baked product assessed by sight as well as by mouthfeel. Lean meats are described as having "fine" or "coarse" texture (sometimes also called "grain"). In this instance the size of the structural units which make up the lean is involved.

The *brittleness* of food is another aspect of texture. Tissues in a raw vegetable or fruit are somewhat brittle or crunchy. The cells offer moderate resistance to fracture by the pressure of the teeth. The textural quality of a raw apple is augmented if the fruit or vegetable is crisp, that is, is turgid with water. Raw celery and raw carrot sticks are valued for their crispness and crunchiness. An apple may be crisp but so may a cracker, the one because it has an abundance of water, the other because it has little. The crispness or crunchiness of toasted, flaked cereal, crisp cookies, and well-baked pie crust contributes to the pleasure derived from eating them. With all four, moisture reduces crunchiness. Crispness is judged to be primarily accoustical (32).

The texture of food is important not only per se, but also because of the effects of texture on taste. Fudge candies made from two portions of the same syrup, one beaten while the syrup is still hot and the other after it has cooled, do not taste exactly alike because of differences in texture. Ice creams from the same mix, half of which is frozen so that the product is coarse and the other half fine, have different flavors.

SENSORY ASSESSMENT OF TEXTURE AND CONSISTENCY

Both texture and consistency and the words used to designate each are imprecise terms used to characterize foods. Because precise terms are lacking, analogy is often used to describe texture. Thus the word "creamy" is used to indicate texture in fudge or consistency in cream sauce, neither of which is commonly made with cream. "Velvety" is another such word used to characterize the mouthfeel of ice creams and some cakes. "Rubbery" is used to describe some gels and the white of an egg that has been boiled rather than hard cooked.

A recent attempt to classify and define more precisely the terms used to indicate textural qualities of food is a step in the right direction (29). In this scheme, four of the primary characteristics proposed are hardness, cohesiveness, viscosity, and elasticity, all of which are influenced by the attraction between constituents which make up a food. Adhesiveness, the fifth characteristic, applies to the attraction between surfaces. Secondary characteristics of food texture include brittleness, chewiness, and gumminess.

A rating scale for each textural characteristic, with one food product as a standard for each step on the intensity scale has been proposed (31). A nine-point scale for hardness is proposed with cream cheese at the lower end and uncooked carrots, peanut brittle, and rock candy typifying the three highest points. On the seven-point scale for brittleness, a commercial brand of corn muffins at the lower end and ginger snaps and peanut brittle at the other end are the standards suggested. Rye bread (crumb) and Tootsie rolls mark the extremes of the seven-point scale for chewiness; for adhesiveness, hydrogenated vegetable shortening and peanut butter mark the extremes of the five-point scale. Food standards on the eight-point viscosity scale range from water and light cream with low viscosities to condensed milk with high viscosity.

PSYCHOLOGICAL FACTORS AND FLAVOR

In addition to color, odor, taste, and mouthfeel, certain psychological factors contribute to the acceptability of a food. Pleasant associations increase the likelihood that a food will be liked, unpleasant associations that it will be rejected. One's reaction to a particular food or to the way a food has been prepared is conditioned by association. Cinnamon flavor in "mint" candy wafers tinted green comes as a surprise, as does vanilla flavor in strawberry-pink ice cream. Many such subtle factors contribute to one's assessment of the "taste" of foods.

SENSORY TESTING OF FOODS

Sensory methods may be used to evaluate the quality of a food. Individuals of a food-testing panel are asked to use the senses of sight, taste, smell, feel, and hearing to assess the character of a food. Objectives of sensory testing fall into two general categories. The experimenter may wish to learn whether the panelists prefer a product or to learn of its potential for acceptability by the consuming public. On the other hand, the experimenter may wish to know if there is a detectable difference between or among samples or to learn the nature of any such differences. The former is called acceptance or consumer testing and the latter difference or discrimination testing. Panels appropriate for performing the two functions differ. Differences between the two are reflected in the number of judges that constitute a panel, in the qualifications of its members, and in what the panelists are asked to do.

DIFFERENCE OR DISCRIMINATION TESTING

This type of food-testing panel is used as an instrument to assess differences in color, odor, taste, texture, and other aspects of food quality. For difference testing a small group of panelists is used. Actually one extremely discriminating, painstaking, and unbiased individual would suffice. But the human instrument is frequently uneven in its ability to discriminate different aspects of food quality, and daily variations in physical condition may cause variations in operating efficiency. A cold, for example, may render a panelist useless for days. Psychological factors such as preoccupation, worry, and other stresses may prevent a judge from operating effectively, as may environmental factors such as distracting noises, extraneous odors, and uncomfortable temperature. Furthermore, it is not always easy for the experimenter to know when a judge is not in optimum adjustment for the job of food-difference testing. For these reasons, a panel of judges is used, with three to five discriminating and conscientious individuals sufficing.

Judges may be asked to indicate differences among foods in any one of the following ways (11). In the *paired* test, judges are given two samples and are asked to indicate the one which has more or less of the attribute under consideration (6). Three samples, two exactly alike, are presented to the judge in the *triangle* test, and the judge is asked to indicate the different or odd sample. Judges may be asked to *rank* in order three or more samples for specified characteristics. Alternately, they may be asked to score each sample on a scale from 1 to 5 up to 1 to 10. The assignment may be to check the samples against a scale of descriptive terms such as none, slight, moderate, strong, and extreme that could apply to a number of attributes for foods, or against such terms as waxy, slightly mealy, moderately mealy, and very mealy for potatoes or such terms as not present, just recognizable, slight, moderate, and strong for vanilla flavor in ice cream. When more than two samples are involved, ranking is the simplest technique.

ACCEPTANCE OR CONSUMER TESTING

A fairly large number of individuals, representative of the public or a large market segment of it, is essential for acceptance testing if results are to be valid. Panelists require little preliminary training. Typically they are asked to record their reactions on a 9-point scale that ranges from like extremely to dislike extremely. They may also be asked to indicate the extent to which or the frequency with which they anticipate using the product. Commercial enterprises use food-testing panels as they develop a new product to learn how the public might react to it before the company attempts to put it on the market.

Recent work in food testing has centered on obtaining the panelists' assessment of a food in such a way as to learn not just that there are detectable differences, but more importantly the magnitude of any differences. Some progress has been made toward this goal. It is hoped that if sensory attributes can be quantified, a number of advantages will accrue. For example, if the manufacturer of a sweetened drink could learn from a panel the magnitude of a sensory response to each increment of sweetener, he or she would be in a better position to assess the point of diminishing returns and make a judgment about the cost/sensory benefit ratio of the sweetener.

OBJECTIVE ASSESSMENT OF FOOD QUALITY

RHEOLOGICAL CHARACTERISTICS OF FOODS

Some of the characteristics of foods discussed above under texture and consistency have to do with fundamental rheological properties of matter (23). Rheology, defined as the science of the deformation and flow of matter, has three aspects: elasticity (or springiness), viscous flow, and plastic flow. Elementary models have been proposed to aid in visualizing (or understanding) each of the three fundamental aspects of the flow properties of materials. In Figure 1-9, elasticity is envisioned as a coiled spring attached to a fixed sup-

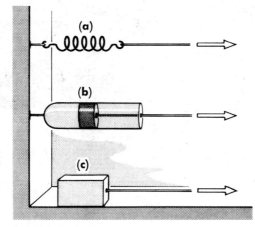

Figure 1-9. Rheological models for the three aspects of the flow properties of matter. The spring (a) represents the elastic element, the dashpot (b) viscous flow, and the block which resists being pulled (c) the plastic property of matter. (From ''The Flow of Matter'' by Marcus Reiner. Copyright © 1959 by Scientific American, Inc. All rights reserved.)

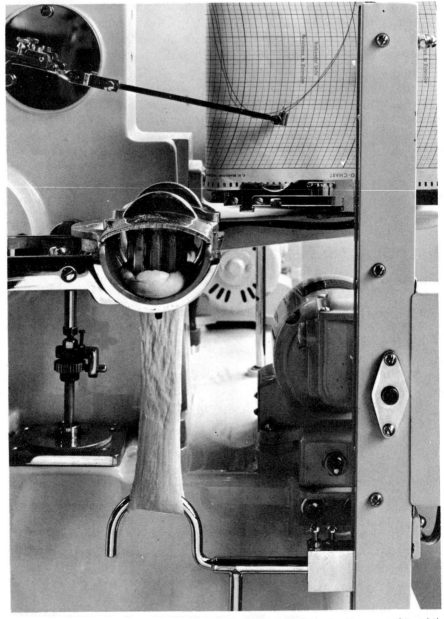

Figure 1-10. The ability of yeast dough to stretch (measured here in an extensograph) and the quality of the baked bread are related. (Print courtesy of C. W. Brabender Instruments, Inc., South Hackensack, N. J. Credit: David Linton, *Scientific American*.)

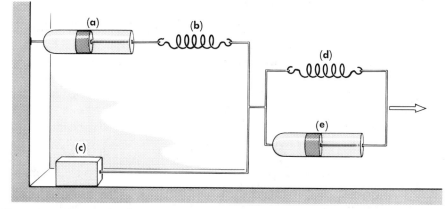

Figure 1-11. The complex flow of dough is represented by this combination of rheological models. A viscous element (a) in series with an elastic element (b) is joined in parallel with a plastic element (c); the combination is united in series with an elastic element (d) in parallel with a viscous one (e). (From "The Flow of Matter" by Marcus Reiner. Copyright © 1959 by Scientific American, Inc. All rights reserved.)

port. Viscous flow is pictured as a dashpot, which consists of a column of liquid inside a tube and, fitting inside the tube, a stopper with a plunger attached. Material that exhibits plastic flow behaves like a stationary object which moves only after a certain minimum force is applied.

The flow characteristics of a food are usually quite complex. For example, dough for yeast bread, shown stretched in the extensograph in Figure 1-10, is pictured as containing the combination of the three elementary mechanisms in Figure 1-11.

If bread dough is stretched, but not too far, it will spring back. To the extent that it does, the dough is elastic. Elasticity is a characteristic of importance in baked products, too. The crumb of sponge cake is elastic, particularly when the cake is still hot, which is one reason a sponge cake is allowed to cool in an inverted pan. Elastic deformation is reversible; plastic flow is not. A material that exhibits plastic flow resists changing position until a minimum force is applied. This is a desirable characteristic in a cake frosting. A soft frosting is desired, but it should stay in place and not run down the sides of the cake. Such phenomena as a concentrated gelatin sol climbing the spindles of an egg beater as the blades are rotated and the behavior of catsup as described in the verse "Going to Extremes"*

> Shake and shake
> The catsup bottle.
> None will come,
> And then a lot'll.

are in the realm of rheology.

*From Light Armour *by Richard Armour, copyright ©1954 by Richard Armour. Used with the permission of the McGraw-Hill Book Company.*

OBJECTIVE TESTS FOR FOODS

Objective tests for food quality include all those that do not rely mainly on human sensory organs. Instead of assessing the color of cooked carrots or cooked green beans by eye, the carotene content of the former and the chlorophyll content of the latter can be determined by chemical means or by an instrument which measures color in "just noticeable differences." Instead of comparing three samples of lemon juice for tartness, their hydrogen-ion concentrations can be measured (indirectly) with a pH meter, just as the concentration of sugar in a syrup can be measured by a refractometer. Study of the structure in the cells of plants and in the fibers of the lean of meat, as well as of the distribution of ingredients in cake batter, requires the aid of a microscope. A number of the aspects of food texture can be measured by instruments (28). The texturometer, devised to measure aspects of the texture of foods, is an instrument made of moving parts which simulate the motion of the teeth in chewing. It is attached to a source of power to activate the parts and a device for measuring and recording the force-distance of each "bite" the texturometer makes into a food. From the resulting curve, called a "texture profile," information regarding the hardness, cohesiveness, elasticity, and adhesiveness of a food may be obtained.

In certain instances a food lends itself to measurement of one or more of its fundamental rheological properties by an instrument which is available. For example, the viscosity or resistance to flow of a liquid like an oil can be determined by a viscosimeter equipped with a rotating spindle, by a falling-ball apparatus, or by a capillary tube through which its rate of flow can be measured. A simplified version of the latter is the Jelmeter (see pectin gel formation, Chapter 29), which is used to measure the flow time of a fruit pectin extract to be used for making jelly.

Many objective tests used to assess food textures (28,29) are empirical in nature. Although the information provided may not be of a fundamental, rheological character, it is a valid and meaningful index to the texture of a food. Measuring the force needed to break crisp pastry or cookies with a shortometer (see Fig. 15-3) or the resistance of a molded gelatin or of cooked vegetables to penetration by the needle or cone of a penetrometer are examples of empirical tests for food texture.

One aspect of the tenderness of meat may be assessed by a penetrometer, but a shearing device is more commonly used. A hydraulic press is sometimes used to measure the expressible liquid from cooked meats. A hand-held pressure tester is used to determine the optimum stage of maturity for picking such fruits as pears. A line spread test (see milk cookery, Chapter 17) may be used to measure differences in the consistency of batters, puddings, and sauces. A compressimeter is used to measure the firmness or staleness of bread. A sophisticated instrument, the Instron Universal Testing Machine, is now widely used to measure a number of aspects of the textural properties of foods (3).

REFERENCES

1. Amerine, M. A., R. M. Pangborn, and E. B. Roessler. 1965. *Principles of the Sensory Evaluation of Food.* New York: Academic Press. Pp. 220–227. Vision and the appearance of foods.

2. Amoore, J. E., J. W. Johnston, Jr., and M. Rubin. 1964. The stereochemical theory of odor. *Sci. American* **210**(2): 42–49. Size and shape of molecules as related to odor.

3. Breene, W. M. 1975. Problems in instrumental analysis of texture in foods. *J. Texture Studies.* **6:** 53–82. Technical discussion of instrumentation.

4. Cardello, A. V., D. Hunt, and B. Mann. 1979. Relative sweetness of fructose and sucrose in model solutions, lemon beverage and white cake. *J. Food Sci.* **44:**748–751. Effects of concentration and acidity.

5. Cloninger, M. R., and R. E. Baldwin. 1970. Aspartylphenylalanine methyl ester: A low-calorie sweetener. *Science* **170:** 81–82. Sweetening power compared to sucrose.

6. Cover, S. 1959. Scoring for three components of tenderness to characterize differences among beef steaks. *Food Research* **24:** 564–573. An attempt to refine organoleptic testing of foods.

7. Crocker, E. C. 1945. *Flavor.* New York: McGraw-Hill. P.15. Odor standards in the Crocker-Henderson system.

8. Crosby, G. 1976. New sweeteners. CRC *Critical Reviews in Food Science and Technology* **7:** 293–323. Status of "new" sweeteners; taste, stability, and toxicity.

9. Dastoli, F. R. 1968. The chemistry of taste. *New Scientist.* **37:** 465–467. Initiation of the neural message.

10. Dastoli, F. R., and S. Price. 1966. Sweet-sensitive protein from bovine taste buds: Isolation and assay. *Science* **154:** 905–907. Interaction of the protein with sugars.

11. Dawson, E. H., and E. H. Dochterman. 1951. A comparison of sensory methods of assessing differences in food qualities. *Food Technol.* **5:** 79–81. Comparison of paired and triangle taste tests, ranking and scoring.

12. Fabian, F. W., and H. B. Blum. 1943. Relative taste potency of some basic food constituents and their competitive and compensatory action. *Food Research* **8:** 179–193. Effects of subthreshold concentrations of taste substances on discernment of others.

13. Hardy. S. L., C. P. Brennand, and B. W. Wyse. 1979. Fructose: Comparison with sucrose as sweetener in four products. *J. Am. Dietet. Assoc.* **74:** 41–46. Lemonade, sugar cookies, white cake, and vanilla pudding.

14. Inglett, G. E. 1974. Sweetness in perspective. *Cereal Science Today.* **19**(7): 258–261, 292–295. Miracle fruit, katemfe, and serendipity berry included.

15. Inglett, G. E., L. Krbechek, B. Dowling, and R. Wagner. 1969. Dihydrochalcone sweeteners—Sensory and stability evaluation. *J. Food Sci.* **34:** 101–103. Taste potency and disadvantages as sweeteners.

16. Mackey, A. O., and P. Jones. 1954. Selection of members of a food tasting panel. Discernment of primary tastes in water solution compared with judging ability in food. *Food Technol.* **8:** 527–530. Four primary taste substances in water, in applesauce, in pumpkin, and in mayonnaise.

17. Mackey, A. O., and K. Valassi. 1956. The discernment of primary tastes in the presence of different food textures. *Food Technol.* **10:** 238–240. Liquids, gels, and foams compared.
18. Mozell, M. M. 1970. Evidence for chromatographic model of olfaction. *J. Gen. Physiol.* **56:** 46–63. Another attempt to account for olfaction.
19. Pangborn, R. M. 1963. Relative taste intensities of selected sugars and organic acids. *J. Food Sci.* **28:** 726–733. Four sugars and four acids compared.
20. Pangborn, R. M., and S. C. Gee. 1961. Relative sweetness of α- and β-forms of selected sugars. *Nature* **191:** 810–811. Effects of mutarotation.
21. Photographic Essay: The Science of Color. *Life* **17**(1): 39–50. July 3, 1944. Vision and the nature of color, profusely illustrated.
22. Pilgrim, F. J. 1961. Interaction of suprathreshold taste stimuli. In *Physiological and Behavioral Aspects of Taste*. Morley R. Kare and B. P. Halpern, eds. Chicago: University of Chicago Press. Pp. 66–78. Effects of the level of taste stimuli on the perception of others.
23. Reiner, M. 1959. The flow of matter. *Sci. American* **201**(6): 122–132, 135–136, 138. Rheology in simplified and graphic terms.
24. Schutz, H. G., and F. J. Pilgrim. 1957. Sweetness of various compounds and its measurement. *Food Research* **22:** 206–213. Sugars compared.
25. Shallenberger, R. S. 1963. Hydrogen bonding and the varying sweetness of sugars. *J. Food Sci.* **28:** 584 –589. An attempt to account for differences in sweetness.
26. Shallenberger, R. S., and T. E. Acree. 1967. Molecular theory and sweet taste. *Nature* **216:** 480–482. Stereochemistry of vicinal OH groups.
27. Shallenberger, R. S., T. E. Acree, and C. Y. Lee. 1969. Sweet taste of D- and L-sugars and amino acids and the steric nature of their chemoreceptor site. *Nature* **221:** 555–556. The AH-B concept.
28. Szczesniak, A. S. 1963. Objective measurements of food texture. *J. Food Sci.* **28:** 410–420. Equipment and its use, with illustrations.
29. Szczesniak, A. S. 1972. Texture measurement. *Food Technol.* **20:** 1292–1296, 1298. Sensory and instrumental assessment of textural qualities of foods.
30. Szczesniak, A. S. 1977. An overview of recent advances in food texture research. *Food Technol.* **31**(4): 71–75, 90. Progress in refining the concept of texture; sensory and instrumental measurements.
31. Szczesniak, A. S., M. A. Branst, and H. H. Friedman. 1963. Development of standard rating scales for mechanical parameters of texture and correlation between the objective and the sensory methods of texture evaluation. *J. Food Sci.* **28:** 397–403. Lists of foods illustrating gradations in textural characteristics.
32. Vickers, Z., and M. C. Bourne. 1976. A psychoaccoustical theory of crispness. *J. Food Sci.* **41:** 1158–1164. The essential nature of crispness.
33. Wright, R. H. and A. Robson. 1969. Basis of odor specificity: Homologues of benzaldehyde and nitrobenzene. *Nature* **222:** 290–292. The vibrational theory of odor specificity.
34. Yamaguchi, S., T. Yoshikawa, S. Ikeda, and T. Ninomiya. 1970. Studies on the taste of some sweet substances. Part I. Measurement of the relative sweetness. *Agr. Biol. Chem.* **34:** 181–186. Three simple sugars, three sugar alcohols, and sucrose compared.

TWO

Measures and Weights

In the preparation of many foods, success depends in part upon correct proportions of ingredients. This does not mean that slight variations in proportions of ingredients in a product such as cake will cause it to be a failure. But it does mean that, to duplicate a product, the proportions of ingredients which go into the product must be duplicated. This may be achieved by weighing, the practice in a number of European countries, or by measuring, as is customary in the United States. Weighing has advantages, provided that balance or scale is accurate and is sufficiently sensitive for the amount being weighed (7). In the United States practically all recipes give measures rather than weights, so ingredients are combined on the basis of volume. But duplicate volumes of the same ingredient do not always provide the same weight. In many instances weighing is faster than measuring, also. To be sure of obtaining the correct amount of each ingredient by measure, two things are essential—accurate utensils for measuring and correct use of these utensils.

MEASURING UTENSILS

CAPACITIES

One set of household measuring utensils which has been in use for many years (see Fig. 2-1) is based on the standard quart measure (3). In this system a standard one-cup measure holds one-fourth of a quart, or 236.6 milliliters. The volume is 8 fluid ounces, English measure. Each tablespoon holds one-sixteenth of a cup, so one fluid ounce equals two tablespoons. Most measuring cups are subdivided into the following fractions of a cup: ¾, ⅔, ½, ⅓, ¼. In addition to the cup measure with its subdivisions, metal and plastic fractional measures with capacities of 1, ½, ⅓, ¼ cup are available in sets. For quantities less than ¼ cup, measuring spoons should be used. One tablespoon, one teaspoon, with a capacity one-third that of the tablespoon, and two fractional teaspoons, ½, and ¼, comprise a set of measuring spoons.

Currently, measures based on the metric or SI system are being introduced on a voluntary basis. Volumes of the measuring utensils in this system are based on the liter. In addition to 1000 mL and 500 mL volumes, 250, 125, 50, 25, 15, 5, 2, and 1 mL volumes have been recommended (2). The 250 and the 125 mL metric measures have capacities approximately equal to the one-

Figure 2-1. Conventional measuring utensils. A glass measuring cup for liquids, a set of fractional cup measures for dry ingredients and fat, and a set of measuring spoons. (Photograph by Zoe Ann Holmes.)

cup and the ½ cup measures, respectively, and the 15 and 5 mL metric measures the volumes of the tablespoon and the teaspoon, respectively.

TOLERANCES

Some years ago the American Home Economics Association (A.H.E.A.), in cooperation with the American Standards Association,* formulated a set of standards and proposed tolerances for household measuring utensils (3). The capacity of a standard measuring cup is 8 fluid ounces or 236.6 milliliters. A deviation of 5 percent from this precise volume is considered an allowable, or tolerable, amount. For the one-cup measure, this tolerance amounts to 11.8 milliliters. The capacity of a standard tablespoon is 14.8 milliliters and of a standard teaspoon 4.9 milliliters, with tolerances of three-quarters and one-quarter of a milliliter, respectively. With a 5 percent tolerance, the 250 mL metric measure could range in volume from 237.5 to 262.5 mL. Insisting on greater precision would add to the cost of manufacture of the measuring utensils, whereas a deviation greater than 5 percent could make an appreciable difference in the proportion of ingredients and in the quality of the finished product.

ACCURACY

Unfortunately, not all measuring utensils on the market meet this minimum tolerance. Two items, tap water and a graduated cylinder, suffice to test the accuracy of a measuring utensil. The capacity of the graduated cylinder should be equal to or slightly greater than the capacity of the measuring utensil being tested. To check the accuracy of a measuring utensil, it is filled with water to

*Now the American National Standards Institute.

the mark which indicates the fraction of the cup measure being tested. This water is then transferred, without spilling, to a graduated cylinder and the volume read in milliliters. Two precautions should be observed. Both the measuring utensil and the graduated cylinder should be on a level surface, and the eye should be level with the water level at the bottom of the meniscus (the lowest level of the surface of the liquid). An alternate way to test the accuracy of a measuring utensil is illustrated as follows: to check a ¼-cup measure, for example, it is filled level-full four times and the liquid is transferred to the one-cup measure or filled twice to see if the water level comes to the one-half cup mark. If it does not, then one of the measures is inaccurate, assuming of course, that the ¼-cup measure was filled level-full and no water was spilled in the transfer.

A word of caution. Suppose on three successive tries a metric measure that holds exactly 250 mL was filled with liquid. On all three occasions the volume of the liquid remeasured in a graduated cylinder was 230 mL. The precision of the activity would be remarkable, to say the least, but the accuracy leaves something to be desired. Filling a teaspoon three times instead of a tablespoon once or a 5 mL measure three times instead of a 15 mL once gives three times the chance for error in measuring technique.

MEASURING TECHNIQUES: ACCURATE

Accurate measuring utensils are essential for obtaining exact quantities of ingredients, but the method used to measure an ingredient is as important as the accuracy of the measuring utensils (4). Method of measuring involves two considerations: choosing the right utensil for the particular ingredient, and using the correct technique for handling each.

LIQUIDS

Liquid ingredients are the easiest to measure. Causes of inaccurate measurement are over- or underfilling or insufficient drainage of the measuring utensil. A measure with subdivisions and with headspace above the top mark is recommended for liquids which flow readily. The smallest measuring utensil that will hold the volume desired should be used. For example, a half-cup of liquid should be measured in a cup measure, not in a pint one with subdivisions.

With a glass measure it is possible to read the level of the liquid at the bottom of the meniscus. A measure with a pouring spout minimizes the chances of spilling liquid when it is transferred to the mixing or cooking utensil. Fractional measures are satisfactory for measuring liquids which are sufficiently viscous, such as molasses and honey. Surplus liquid can be removed from the top of the measure by rapidly moving a spatula with a straight edge across the top of the utensil. A rubber scraper should be used to remove thick liquids from the measuring utensil.

FATS

Fats are more accurately weighed than measured. When measured, a fractional measuring utensil should be used. It is practically impossible to level a half-cup of fat in a one-cup measure. Fat at room temperature is easier to measure than fat which is cold and hard. There is less chance of trapping air when it is packed in the utensil, and it is easier to level the fat in the measure when it is soft. A flexible rubber scraper or a *clean* finger may be used to transfer the fat from the measuring utensil. Butter or margarine marketed in quarter-pound units need not be measured. One pound measures 2 cups. If a recipe calls for one half-cup of butter, a one-quarter pound stick may be used without measuring. A cup of whipped butter or margarine weighs only two-thirds of the regular form (1), and a cup of hydrogenated fat weighs less than a cup of oil from which it was made because of incorporated gas bubbles.

SUGAR

Granulated sugar and certain other dry ingredients which do not pack appreciably may be measured in fractional measures or in a one-cup measure with subdivisions. No special precautions need be taken in measuring granulated sugar. Coarser crystals do not pack as well as fine ones, so the weight of a cup filled with coarse sugar may be less than standard weight.

Unlike granulated sugar, crystals of brown sugar have a film of syrup on the surface which prevents them from sliding past each other freely. Brown sugar should be packed into the measure firmly enough to hold the shape of the utensil when it is turned out. Special free-flowing brown sugar is measured as is granulated sugar. A cup of this special sugar weighs one-fourth less than a cup of regular brown sugar (1). Much of the syrup found on the surface of particles of conventional brown sugar is held within the spongelike pores of free-flowing brown sugar. This reduces stickiness of the surface. Confectioner's sugar has a tendency both to lump and to pack. Lumps should be rolled or mashed and the sugar sifted and measured as for flour.

FLOUR

Measuring flour presents more problems than measuring liquids or fats. Particles of flour vary widely in shape and particularly in size (See Fig. 10-4.) As a result, flour shows a marked tendency to pack (6). For this reason, there is no absolute value for the weight of a cup of flour. However, most recipes assume a certain weight. The object in measuring flour is so to manipulate it that the filled measure holds the standard weight, and the technique should be such that variation in weight with subsequent measurings is minimal. The former is a matter of accuracy and the latter of precision.

Flour is best measured in a fractional measure. There are two commonly accepted techniques for measuring flour. In one, small portions of flour (not more than two or three cups) are sifted. Then this loosened, aerated flour is transferred to the measuring utensil which is filled to overflowing without packing the flour. The surplus is removed from the measure with the straight edge of a spatula.

A second technique calls for sifting the flour directly into the measure until the flour overflows slightly. Then the excess flour is removed with the straight edge of a spatula. Sifting the flour directly into the measure has the advantage of taking less time and fewer operations and so is more efficient. The weight of a cup of flour so filled varies little with repeated fillings. However, it may average one teaspoon less than a cup of flour measured by sifting the flour and then transferring it to the measure.

For certain recipes where an exact amount of flour is unnecessary, stirring the flour in the container before measuring may be sufficient (4,5). Agglomerated flour has fairly large particles of uniform size. (See Chapter 10.) Because this flour does not pack, measuring it presents no special problem, and sifting it before it is measured is unnecessary.

Whole wheat flour and cornmeal should be stirred before being spooned into the measuring utensil. Flours differ in density; a cup of sifted cake flour weighs just under 100 grams, and the accepted value for pastry flour is 100 grams per cup (1). The value of 115 grams per cup of all-purpose flour reflects its greater density.

Occasionally a recipe may call for amounts of dry ingredients less than the capacity of any measuring utensil. To measure ⅛ teaspoon of a dry ingredient, the procedure is to fill the ¼-teaspoon measure level-full and then divide the ingredient in half, removing the unwanted portion. For ¹⁄₁₆ teaspoon the process is repeated on the ⅛ teaspoon remaining in the spoon. Baking powder, soda, and spices should be aerated by stirring before they are measured.

A publication is available which gives the average weight of a measured cup of a number of foods (5).

MEASURING TECHNIQUES: APPROXIMATE

Experienced and talented cooks may produce first-rate products without standard measuring utensils and without apparent regard for the techniques of handling ingredients. Such cooks have trained their eyes to see and their fingers to feel when a product has the right amount of each ingredient. This ability requires practice and perseverance. It also involves a number of failures and many indifferent successes. Accurate measuring utensils properly used make it possible to have precise quantities of ingredients on the first or second try. Thus, accurate measuring utensils and the proper manipulation of the ingredients during measuring are actually a short cut to success in food preparation in those instances where success depends upon having ingredients in a certain proportion. How precisely measured ingredients are manipulated is usually as important as how much of each is used. Problems of manipulation for different foods will be discussed in the appropriate chapters.

REFERENCES

1. A.H.E.A. 1975. *Handbook of Food Preparation*. Washington, D.C.: American Home Economics Association. Pp. 37, 65, 83. Weight per cup of fats, sugars, flours.
2. A.H.E.A. 1977. *Handbook for Metric Usage*. Washington, D.C.: American Home Economics Association. Pp. 10–11.
3. A.S.A. 1963. *American Standard dimensions, tolerances, and terminology for home cooking and baking utensils*. A.S.A. Z 61.1-1963. New York: American Standards Association, Inc.
4. Arlin, M. L., M. M. Nielson, and F. T. Hall. 1964. The effect of different methods of flour measurement on the quality of plain two-egg cakes. *J. Home Econ.* **56:** 399–401. Sifted *vs.* unsifted flour compared.
5. Fulton, Lois, Evelyn Matthews, and Carole Davis. 1977. Average Weight of a Measured Cup of Various Foods. *Home Economics Research Report* 41. Washington, D. C.: U.S. Department of Agriculture. Pp. 1–26.
6. Matthews, R. H., and O. M. Batchelder. 1963. Sifted *vs.* unsifted flour: Weight variations and results of some baking tests. *J. Home Econ.* **55:** 123–124. Effects on muffins and cakes.
7. Miller, B. S., and H. B. Trimbo. 1972. Use of metric measures in food preparation. *J. Home Econ.* **64**(2): 20–25. Advantages of the metric system and of weighing over measuring.

THREE
Heating and Cooling Foods

Energy, either its application or its removal, is involved at many points in the preparation of foods. For example, heat is utilized to remove excess moisture from frostings and jellies, to alter the texture and flavor of potatoes, to decrease the bulk of a vegetable such as spinach, to inactivate microorganisms in or on the surface of foods, to alter consistency and form 'the texture of breads, to change the fluid mixture for a custard into a gel, and to improve the flavor and alter the consistency of cereals. In other instances, removal of heat rather than its application is desired. Many foods remain safe to eat and palatable for a longer time if they are kept cool. For example, refrigeration reduces the rate at which microorganisms present in milk or on the surface of meats multiply; it retards the rate at which butter, salad oil, nuts, and other fat-rich foods become rancid; it retards ripening of fruits and senescence of fresh vegetables; and it can convert a mixture for a gelatin salad or dessert into a gel. Cooled to still lower temperature and maintained in the frozen state, meats and fruits and vegetables can be preserved for periods varying from 3 months to a year.

Instances where the input or removal of energy and the achievement or maintenance of a certain temperature are critical in the preparation of individual foods will be given in the chapters that follow. General principles of heating and cooling foods are emphasized in this chapter.

HEATING FOODS

When a substance is heated, the molecules are set in motion or become agitated. If heating is done with a gas burner, the energy which sets and keeps the molecules in motion is obtained from the combustion of the fuel. Resistance to the passage of an electric current by the coils of the heating element is the source of heat in an electric range. In either case the energy came originally from the sun.

INTENSITY OF HEAT

Intensity of heat, that is, the extent to which energy has set molecules into motion, is measured in degrees by a thermometer. Two scales are in common use (2), the Celsius (or centigrade) and the Fahrenheit, with a third scale, the Kelvin (or absolute), used for scientific purposes.

A listing of commonly used temperatures together with their descriptive designations follows:

Temperature		
°C	°F	**Verbal Designation**
−18	0	Maximum temperature for holding frozen foods
0	32	Freezing point (pure water)
4–7	40–45	Refrigerator temperature
20–25 ±	68–77 ±	Room temperature
37	98.6	Lukewarm (body temperature)
65 ±	149 ±	Scalding (liquid)
85	185	Simmering (water)
100	212	Boiling (water)
115	240	Boiling (water) Pressure 10 pounds per square inch (psi) or 69 Kilopascals (kPa)

Although a range of temperatures is given for the refrigerator, the lower one is preferable because this minimizes the growth of microorganisms (present in or on food) and other undesirable changes. Scalding temperature given is approximate only because scalding temperature varies with the material in question. Different temperatures are required for water to scald peaches or tomatoes to make the skins slip, to scald chickens and turkeys to loosen feathers, to scald dishes to inactivate microorganisms on the surface, and to scald milk to make custard with improved flavor, or to make yeast bread dough of better handling properties and baked products of better quality.

An assortment of thermometers (jelly, candy, deep fat frying) is on the market. One ordinary, mercury-filled, glass-stemmed thermometer, with degrees from −10° to 200°C (14° to 392°F) etched in the glass, is adequate for all household needs except meat cookery, where a short (approximately 6 inches) mercury-filled, glass-stemmed thermometer is needed. The one disadvantage of the chemical thermometer is that there is no way to fasten it to the side of a pan. However, the all-glass is easier to keep clean than is the metal backing that is found on many household-type thermometers. Too, if the metal slips, the thermometer is useless.

QUANTITATIVE ASPECTS

When a substance is heated, the amount of energy involved depends not only upon how agitated the molecules of a substance are (the temperature), but also upon the number of molecules in motion. In two pans of boiling water, one containing one cup and the other one gallon, the intensity of heat is the same. However, the amount of energy needed to bring the gallon of water to a boil is greater. Two units have been used to express the amount of energy. One is the calorie, which is the amount of energy expended in raising the temperature of one gram of water 1° Celsius (from 14.5°C to 15.5°C) or the large calorie, which is the energy needed to raise the temperature of one kilogram of water one degree centigrade. This calorie is the unit used to express the energy value of foods. The second unit is the British thermal unit, abbreviated Btu, which is the amount of energy required to raise the temperature of one pound of water from 63°F to 64°F. This unit is commonly used to specify the heating potential of fuels. Both the calorie and the British thermal unit will be replaced in the SI system by a unit called the joule, or more commonly by the kilojoule (1).

ENERGY TRANSFER

Foods are cooked on conventional ranges powered by gas or electricity or, more recently, in electronic ranges. In the latter, energy in the form of high-frequency radio waves (microwaves) is used to heat the food (3).

Most food is still cooked on conventional ranges. A discussion of the way heating is accomplished and the factors that affect the transfer of energy is pertinent. Energy gets from the source to the food which is heated by radiation, conduction, or by convection currents (5). More than one method of transfer is involved in most instances.

RADIATION

Units of energy, known as "quanta," which travel as electromagnetic waves or rays, are one source of heat. These infrared rays are longer than those of visible light, but shorter than radio and sound waves. (See Fig. 1-1.) When energy is transmitted by radiation, it goes directly from the source to the object heated, unassisted by an intervening medium (10). In fact, an intervening surface only reduces the amount of energy transmitted by radiation. Energy that reaches the earth from the sun does so by radiation. Radiation is a rapid method of heating, for radiant energy travels with the speed of light (186,000 miles per second). Although the rays of energy travel in a straight line, they do fan out from the source. The farther an object from the source of radiant energy, the fewer rays it receives and the less it is heated. Sources of radiant energy used in cooking include the broiler on a range, the toaster, and the glowing coals of a campfire. Once coils on the surface of an electric range are hot enough to glow, they radiate energy as does a gas flame.

CONDUCTION

When heat travels by conduction, kinetic energy or agitation is transmitted from molecule to molecule (5). A cold object is heated by conduction only when in direct contact with a source of heat. Heat is transmitted to a saucepan by conduction where the pan contacts the coils of an electric unit. Heat moves from the bowl of a spoon resting in boiling liquid to the end of the handle by conduction. Conduction is a comparatively slow method of transferring heat, although some materials are better conductors than others. Metals are good conductors. Water conducts heat more rapidly than air, which is a poor conductor (5,17). Foods cook even more rapidly in hot fat because fat can be heated to temperatures much above that of boiling water.

CONVECTION CURRENTS

A third method of energy transfer is by convection currents. The energy that does the heating arrives via air, water, or liquid fat. When a gas or a liquid is heated, it becomes less dense than its cold counterpart. Hot gases and liquids rise and cold ones flow downward to where the heat is applied. This sets up a flow from bottom to top and then from top to bottom. This circular flow of convection currents tends to keep the temperature somewhat uniform throughout the medium. Although currents of hot water, hot fat, and hot air can circulate rapidly to the object being heated, the energy must pass from the hot medium to the object by conduction. Where convection currents are involved, heating is accomplished more rapidly than by conduction alone, but much slower than by radiation. Convection currents are involved in cooking food in a saucepan of water, in deep fat frying, and in baking in an oven.

HEATING FOODS WITH A CONVENTIONAL RANGE

The source of the energy, the utensil used, and the nature of the food influence the transfer of energy when a food is heated. In most instances the transfer of energy is complicated.

IN AN OVEN

The heating unit in an oven is placed at the bottom for a good reason. As the lower layer of air is heated, it becomes less dense and rises, whereas the colder, heavier air flows to the bottom of the oven where it, in turn, is heated. (See Fig. 3-1.) This sets up circulating currents of air in the oven which tend to make the temperature uniform. Heating is more uniform in the center of an oven. Temperatures tend to be hotter at the top and bottom of an oven and at the back and sides. When more than one pan is placed in an oven, pans should be staggered so that the circulation of air and passage of radiant energy will not be impeded (Fig. 3-2).

A high proportion (two-thirds to three-fourths) of the heating effected in an oven is due to radiation (13). The material from which a baking pan is made influences how fast the contents of the utensil heats. Although metals are good conductors, a container made of bright shiny metal is disadvantageous when transmission of radiant energy is involved because it blocks the passage of electromagnetive rays. Materials with dark or dull surfaces are much more emissive, that is, permit the passage of radiant energy. For efficient

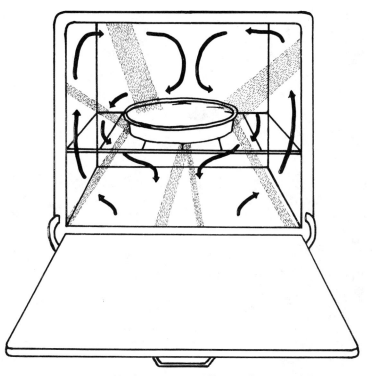

Figure 3-1. Heating in an oven. Circulating currents of hot air flow around the container of food. Energy that reaches the food in this way passes from the hot air through the utensil and into the food by conduction. Electromagnetic waves of radiant energy that pass the lining of the oven from the source (gas flame or glowing electric coils) go directly to the utensil or its contents. Part of this energy is deflected by the utensil; the remainder reaches the food and heats it. Utensils differ in their ability to transmit radiant energy.

heating, the emissivity of a baking utensil is more important than its ability to conduct heat from the currents of hot air in an oven (6,8). Metal utensils with dark, dull surfaces shorten the baking period. Baking utensils made from glass transmit radiant energy and in this respect are comparable to highly emissive metal pans (10). It is for this reason that a lower baking temperature is recommended for glass baking utensils. Thus baking time varies not only with the oven temperature and the size of the utensil, but also with the material from which the utensil is made. Adjustment of the baking temperature can compensate in part for differences in the efficiency of baking utensils, although there is still a residual pan effect. Metal skewers in baking potatoes or in a roast speed the conduction of heat from circulating currents of hot air.

A utensil made of material that conducts heat or transmits radiant enegy too rapidly may allow food to brown excessively or unevenly in the oven. A dark or dull baking sheet may not be the best choice for thin, rich cookies or pastry for this reason.

Figure 3-2. When a single baking utensil is used in an oven, the rack should be adjusted so that the utensil is centered in the oven. If more than one utensil is used, racks and utensils should be positioned to facilitate circulation of hot air and to provide for uniform exposure to radiant energy. (Courtesy of Robertshaw Controls, New Stanton Division, Youngwood, Pennsylvania.)

In a viscous substance such as cake batter, much of the heat penetrates from the bottom and outer edges of the cake to the top-center by conduction, but still part of the heating is effected by convection currents. (See Fig. 21-7.)

With its one high-output heating element at the bottom, with a lining that absorbs much of the radiant energy, coupled with shiny, reflective baking utensils to prevent overheating at the bottom and sides of the food being baked, the oven in a conventional range is wasteful of energy (12). Lining the oven with material that reflects rather than absorbs radiant energy, replacing the single high-output heating element with a lower output one and adding a second low-output one at the top of the oven, and using emissive rather than reflective baking utensils could increase the efficiency of the baking process, making possible energy savings as high as 75 percent.

IN A SAUCEPAN ON A SURFACE UNIT

Heat from a gas burner reaches a saucepan by means of convection currents of hot air and as radiation from the flame of the burning gas. A utensil used on a gas burner should be able not only to transmit by conduction the heat brought to it by the convection currents of hot air, but also to transmit radiant energy. On a surface unit of an electric range where part of the heat is transmitted by conduction, a utensil with a flat bottom to make good contact with the coils or with the heated area on a smooth top range is desirable as is the ability of the material to conduct heat (8,15). A pan made from highly emissive material will permit maximum transmission of radiation from glowing coils or from a gas flame.

When the liquid which is next to the bottom and sides of a saucepan becomes hot, convection currents are established that tend to equalize the temperature throughout. Solid foods such as potatoes in boiling water or doughnuts in hot fat are heated by conduction from the hot liquid.

If the material from which a saucepan is made transmits heat too efficiently, localized heating spots may cause the food to scorch even when there is ample water in the pan. Glass, ceramic ware, enameled iron, and stainless steel utensils are vulnerable to this defect. A copper bottom on a stainless steel pan eliminates this disadvantage. A pan too small for the unit wastes heat regardless of the method of heat transfer.

Liquid in a saucepan is a better conductor of heat than is air in an oven. For this reason one can reach into a hot oven to remove food without getting burned by hot air but not into a pan of boiling water. For the same reason less time is required to cook a potato in boiling water (212°F) than to bake one in a hot oven (400°F), and it takes as long to bake biscuits in a hot oven (425°F) as to cook the same dough as dumplings in boiling liquid (212°F). Differences in conductivity account for the fact that removing a baking pan from a hot oven with a bare hand causes a blister but taking biscuits from the same pan does not; water at room temperature feels cooler than air at the same temperature.

IN A DOUBLE BOILER

Some foods are best heated in a double boiler. A stirred custard is one example. Consider the barriers to energy transfer with this utensil. Assume the double boiler is of a shiny aluminum and the source of heat the coils of an electric range. Most of the radiation from the glowing coils is deflected by the shiny surface of the aluminum. Had the double boiler been made of glass, much of the radiant energy would be transmitted by the utensil. What was not absorbed by the water would reach the contents of the top of the double boiler. Where the bottom of the aluminum utensil contacts the coils, heat passes through the metal by conduction and so warms the layer of water next to the pan. This sets up in the water convection currents by which the heat reaches the bottom of the upper part of the double boiler. Heat from the hot

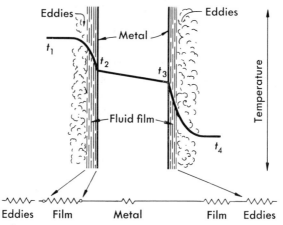

Figure 3-3. Thermal resistances encountered when heat is transferred from one fluid to another through metal (as in the top of a double boiler), shown schematically. (From James B. Austin, *The Flow of Heat in Metals.* Copyright © 1942 by the American Society for Metals, Metals Park, Ohio. Reprinted by permission.)

water is transmitted through this surface, again by conduction, and warms the layer of liquid on the bottom of the pan. This layer, being lighter, rises, and colder layers descend, and in this way the entire volume of the liquid is heated. Stirring hastens equalization of temperature throughout the contents of the top of the double boiler. The metal of the pan is a good conductor, as shown by the small drop in temperature (t_2 to t_3) in the diagram in Figure 3-3. Heat transfer into the contents of a double boiler would be more rapid were it not for the tightly adhering films of water on the surfaces of the utensil and the adjacent eddies of liquid.

Because the temperature in the top of a double boiler never quite reaches 100°C (212°F), foods in the top will not stick or scorch. This is one reason for the use of the double boiler. Cooking a food in the top of a double boiler eliminates the need for continuous stirring, an advantage in cooking flaked cereal. Water in the bottom part of a double boiler helps cushion the contents of the upper part from the intense heat of the unit because of the specific heat of water (see Chapter 4) and because the temperature of water in the bottom part is limited by the fact that it boils. In some cases water in the bottom of a double boiler should not reach the boiling point. For instance, custard heated above simmering temperatures usually curdles, so the water surrounding it should not be above simmering.

Cooking foods in a double boiler has distinct advantages, but it is necessary to keep in mind the limitations. Starchy foods which must be heated to or near the boiling point to effect gelatinization of the starch require an excessively long time to cook entirely in the double boiler. The cooking time can be shortened by heating the product to the boiling point directly on the hot unit and then completing the cooking in the top of a double boiler over boiling water.

HEATING FOODS IN A MICROWAVE OVEN

Foods cook in an electronic range without being exposed to heat. A magnetron in the oven generates electromagnetic waves (microwaves), with wavelengths longer than infrared rays of the electromagnetic spectrum (Fig. 1-1) and in the region of short radio waves. In the electromagnetic field generated in the oven, there is a rapid reversal of charge (at either 915 or 2450 megahertz or million cycles per second). When microwaves penetrate a food, the dipolar molecules of water that are present oscillate about their axes in response to this reversal of charge. Heat is generated in the food itself as a result of this rapid oscillation. The interior of a microwave oven remains cool, as does the container which holds the food. Any rise in temperature of the latter is the result of contact with the heated food. Because heat is generated within the food, the surfaces of most foods do not brown. Foods can be cooked faster in a microwave oven than with a conventional range. For example, four medium-sized potatoes require 8 to 12 minutes in an electronic oven as compared with 45 minutes to 1 hour in a conventional oven; and a pork loin roast which requires 3 hours in a conventional oven cooks in less than 30 minutes in an electronic oven. The cooking time varies with the load in the oven and with the moisture content of the food. Uneven heating as some foods cook may necessitate their being turned during the cooking period. Covering the food with a plastic wrap that does not stretch, stick, or melt may result in more uniform heating (4).

Controls on a microwave oven consist of a master switch, a button to start the cooking, and a timer. The latter is important because a difference in cooking time of only a few seconds may make a great difference in the doneness of most foods. Recently microwave ovens have been made with magnetrons which have an on-and-off cycle. This permits control of the rate of heating not possible with the first microwave ovens marketed, in which cooking time only could be varied. Utensils that transmit microwaves and are not themselves heated are used in microwave cooking. Satisfactory utensils are made from glass, paper, china without metallic trim, ceramics, and some plastics. Utensils made from metal reflect microwave energy, not only deflecting it from the food to be heated, but also risking damage to the magnetron. A glass of water kept in an otherwise empty oven will protect the magnetron should the oven be turned on accidentally.

Rapid heating by microwaves has an advantage in serving precooked frozen foods when the serving period extends over 3 hours. Frozen entrees heated to serving temperature by microwaves retained more (93.5 percent) of the thiamine of the freshly prepared product than did those heated by infrared rays (90 percent) or those thawed by immersion in hot water (86 percent). The advantages of microwave thawing are even greater in view of the retention of thiamine when freshly prepared entrees were kept at serving temperature for 1 hour (78 percent retention), 2 hours (74 percent retention), and 3 hours (67 percent retention) (9). Microwave cooking of vegetables, meats, and other foods will be discussed in later chapters.

Although probably not as saving as some undocumented claims, microwave cooking may utilize electrical energy somewhat more efficiently than does cooking on a conventional electric range (16). In a recent study the use of a microwave oven along with a conventional electric range or a smooth top electric range, one with and one without thermostatic control, to prepare one week's meals for a family of four decreased the total energy used by approximately 24 to 35 percent (11).

Body tissue that is exposed to microwaves can be damaged by the heat that is generated (14), so the oven door should fit securely to prevent leakage of the microwaves. Damage to the seal around the door should be avoided, and the seal should be kept free of spatters and spills and scrupulously clean. Staying at arm's length from the door of the oven when it is in operation minimizes the hazards should stray electromagnetic waves escape.

TESTS FOR DONENESS OF COOKED FOODS

There are a number of ways to tell when foods are done, few of which are precise end points. Most of them work reasonably well for the experienced. A thermometer can be used to determine more or less precisely the doneness of some foods. Boiling point of candy and jelly and internal temperature of roast meat and broiled steaks can be used to assess doneness. Less precise and more subjective criteria for doneness include judging the doneness of stirred custard by the way it coats the spoon (see Fig. 19-6), of a soft pie filling by its thickness, of a poached or fried egg by the opaqueness of the white, of a baked product such as cake by its springiness when touched by a finger, and of fruits, vegetables, and meats by the ease with which they are pierced by a fork. The brownness of a baked product may be, but sometimes is not, a good index to doneness. A loaf of bread, for example, usually gets brown some time before the center of the loaf gets hot enough to set the crumb. Time tables are useful guides to approximate cooking times, and most recipes give approximate cooking or baking time.

COOLING AND REFRIGERATING FOODS

Discussion to this point has centered on heating foods. In many instances a food needs to be cooled instead. How fast a food cools depends on the cooling medium, on the material of the container, and the nature of the food itself. Cooked foods are cooled in air or in water. If cooled in air, the conductivity of the container is not of primary importance because the low density of air makes it a poor conductor. Foods cool in air more rapidly in a utensil that permits the passge of radiant energy from the hot food to the surrounding air. Pans made of glass, enameled iron, or anodized aluminum transmit radiant energy from hot food to cooler air more rapidly than do pans made from shiny metal, just as they transmit radiant energy more readily into the food as it is heated. Putting very hot food into a refrigerator wastes energy. During the first

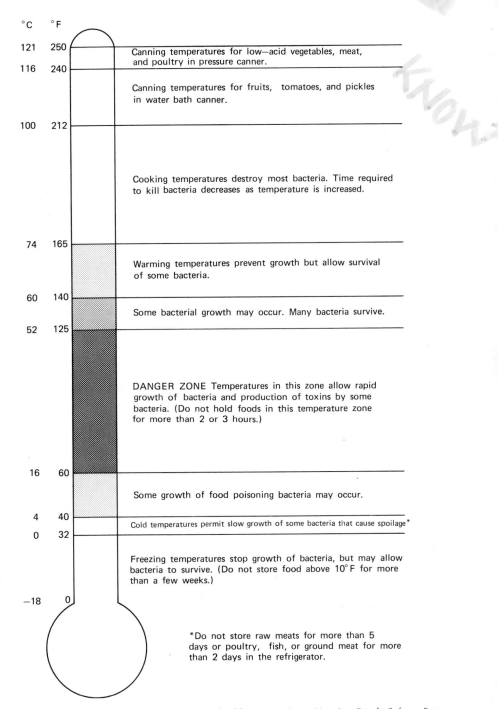

Figure 3-4. Temperature of foods for the control of bacteria. (From *Keeping Foods Safe to Eat,* Home and Garden Bulletin No. 162, sl. rev. 1978.)

few minutes the temperature of the food may drop slightly faster in the cooler air in the refrigerator, but the refrigerator will be forced to operate longer to dissipate this heat.

A hot food will cool much faster in cold water at 20°C than in the cold air in a refrigerator at 5°C. When a food is cooled in water, the ability of the container to conduct heat is of primary importance, and for this metals are superior. Water is a good coolant; it is denser than air and its specific heat is high. Stirring the water surrounding the metal container speeds the cooling. A mixing bowl made of pottery, which is not a good conductor, is a poor choice of container if rapid cooling is desired.

Solid foods cool more slowly than do liquid ones because much of the heat must pass from the interior to the surface by conduction, a slow process. Convection currents that form in cooling liquids speed the cooling by exposing more of the hot material to the cooler surface of the utensil. Stirring the hot liquid hastens cooling.

Perishable foods keep longer when held in a refrigerator until they are eaten. And many perishables must be held at refrigerator temperature to prevent rapid spoilage and, in some instances, to keep them safe to eat. This applies to most cooked foods which should be served while still hot or cooled promptly to room temperature and then refrigerated. Holding highly perishable foods at temperatures that are neither hot nor cold (Fig. 3-4) may make the food unsafe to eat even if not unpalatable. A refrigerator should be cold enough to hold foods just above the freezing point, with 5°C the highest temperature recommended.

Convection currents operate in a refrigerator as in an oven, except that the cooling coils are at the top in a refrigerator and the source of heat at the bottom in an oven. Heat from the warmer air that rises in a refrigerator and flows past the coils is absorbed by the refrigerant. This cooled, denser air flows to the bottom of the refrigerator. Overcrowding a refrigerator (an oven, also) interferes with the circulation of air which is essential for maintaining the temperature and keeping it more or less uniform throughout.

REFERENCES

1. A.H.E.A. 1977. *Handbook for Metric Usage*. Washington, D.C.: American Home Economics Association. Pp. 5, 28. Conversion of calories and Btu to joules.
2. A.H.E.A. 1975. *Handbook of Food Preparation*. Washington, D.C.: American Home Economics Association. Pp. 14, 15. Temperature conversions; oven temperatures.
3. Anon. 1971. *The ABC'S of Microwave Cooking*. Microwave Energy Applications Newsletter. P.O. Box 241, Amherst, N.H. 03031. Nontechnical do's and don'ts.
4. Armbruster, G., and C. Haefle. 1975. Quality of foods after cooking in 915 MHz and 2450 MHz microwave appliances using plastic film cover. *J. Food Sci.* **40:** 721–723. Three wraps compared; advantages of a satisfactory wrap.

5. Austin, J. B. 1941. *The Flow of Heat in Metals*. Cleveland, Ohio: American Society for Metals, Pp. 3–17, 84. Nature of heat: explanation of the high heat conductivity of metals.

6. Cornehl, B., and V. N. W. Swartz. 1931. Speed and efficiency of oven utensils. *J. Home Econ.* **23:** 464–467. Aluminum, china, glass, cast iron, enameled iron, and stainless steel compared.

7. Fenton, F. 1957. Research on electronic cooking. *J. Home Econ.* **49:** 709–716. Microwave compared to conventional heating; effects of former on selected foods.

8. Gartell, B. M. 1930. A study of the effect of different materials and finishes on thermal efficiency of pans. M.S. thesis (available in library). Ames: Iowa State College. Aluminum, copper, enameled iron, glass, steel, and tin compared on both surface units and in an oven.

9. Kahn, L. N., and G. E. Livingston. 1970. Effects of heating method on thiamine retention in fresh and frozen prepared foods. *J. Food Sci.* **35:** 349–351. Microwave, infrared, and hot water thawing compared.

10. Littleton, J. T., and C. J. Phillips. 1932. Electric range oven performance *Elect. World* **100:** 527–529. Heating efficiency as affected by character of baking utensil and by oven temperature.

11. Lovingood, Rebecca P., and Rosemary C. Goss. 1980. Electric energy used by major cooking appliances. *Home Economics Research J.* **8:** 234–241. Comparison of family meals cooked in a microwave oven, a conventional electric range, and a smooth top electric range.

12. Peart, M. Virginia, Susan T. Kern, and David P. DeWitt. 1980. Optimizing oven radiant energy use. *Home Economics Research J.* **8:** 242–251. Development of an oven system more efficient than those currently available.

13. Phillips, J. C., and M. L. Nordberg. 1934. Ovenware and fuel economy. *J. Home Econ.* **26:** 37–41. Heat transfer in gas and in electric ovens.

14. Rosén, Carl-Gustov. 1972. Effect of microwaves on food and related materials. *Food Technol.* **26**(7): 36–37, 39–40, 55. Technical evaluation of suspected adverse effects of microwaves.

15. Sater, V. E., and L. J. Peet. 1933. Thickness of an aluminum utensil as a factor in its thermal efficiency when used in surface cookery on an electric range. *J. Home Econ.* **25:** 324–326. Heating efficiency in pans of five thicknesses compared on open, closed, and Calrod units.

16. Voris, Helen H., and Frances O. VanDuyne. 1979. Low wattage microwave cooking of top round roasts: energy consumption, thiamin content and palatability. *J. Food Sci.* **44:** 1447–1450, 1454. Microwave roasting at low power and conventional roasting compared.

17. Worthington, R. 1928. Heat conductivity of metals as factors in heat transfer. *Chem. Met. Eng.* **35:** 481–482. Effects of air and water films on heat conductivity of metals.

FILM

1. *The Nature of Heat.* 11 min. Coronet. Heat and its transfer.

FOUR
Water

Water is a ubiquitous substance with a number of unique characteristics that are often taken for granted. Water influences the appearance, texture, and flavor of foods and it performs a number of important functions in food preparation.

Water can exist as a fluid, solid, or a gas, depending on temperature and pressure. It is useful in cooling as well as in heating foods. Water makes possible ionization of acids and bases which can then react. Such a reaction occurs when biscuits, muffins, and shortened cake are leavened with baking powder. With acid present, water can hydrolyze table sugar to simpler sugars, a reaction desired in fondant, brown sugar fudge, fruit pectin jellies, and yeast bread dough.

All living things, including foods of plant and animal origin, are made mainly of water. The high moisture content gives to raw fruits and vegetables their crisp, crunchy texture and to meats their turgor. Even seemingly dry foods such as dried beans, dried fruits, cereal, and flour contain appreciable quantities of moisture, although much less than when these foods were immature. The moisture content of a food cannot be judged by appearance. Strawberries appear to have more moisture than cabbage, milk more than green beans, and "dry" flour seems devoid of moisture. See Table 4-1.

Not only is water an integral part of all foods, but many of the changes

Table 4-1   Moisture content of common foods

Raw tomatoes	94%	Cream, coffee	72%
Watermelon	93	Round steak	67
Cabbage	92	White bread	36
Strawberries	90	Dried prunes	28
Green beans	90	Butter	15
Broccoli	89	All-purpose flour	12
Peaches	89	Dried beans	11
Whole milk	87	Rolled oats	8

SOURCE: U.S. Dept. Agr. Handbook No. 456. *Nutritive Value of American Foods in Common Units.* Issued November 1975.

that take place when foods are combined or cooked do so only because of the presence of water. An aqueous medium makes possible hydrophobic interactions between nonpolar molecules, and proteins are denatured only when in contact with water. Water serves as a means of dispersing ingredients, and it gives coherence to the flour in batters and doughs. In the absence of water, flour would not cook; instead it would scorch or even char. The water-holding capacity of muscle influences the color and also the tenderness of the meat. Foods high in moisture are readily spoiled by microorganisms unless means are used to limit their access to the water. And not least, water is a good cleansing agent for both the foods themselves and for utensils and dishes used in the preparation and serving of food.

NATURE OF WATER

THE MOLECULE

Before considering the role of water in food preparation, a brief discussion of the nature of water and its many unique properties is pertinent. Chemically, water consists of one atom of oxygen united to two atoms of hydrogen. An atom of oxygen has a nucleus with eight protons, an inner electron shell which contains two electrons, but only six electrons and a deficiency of two in the outer shell. A hydrogen atom has a nucleus with one proton and an inner electron shell with only one electron. A stable molecule of water is formed when each of the two atoms of hydrogen shares its one electron with the oxygen atom and the oxygen shares two of its electrons, one with each of the two hydrogen atoms (5). (See Fig. 4-1.) Thus a molecule of water contains two pairs of electrons shared covalently. The two hydrogens are so positioned relative to the oxygen as to form an angle of approximately 105°.

Overall, a molecule of water is electrically neutral. However, the distribution of charges in the molecule is such as to make one side (the oxygen side) slightly more negative and the side where the two hydrogens are located slightly more positive. A water molecule is envisioned as occupying the center of a tetrahedron (8), a solid with four faces, each of which is defined by an equilateral triangle, with the charges oriented as shown in Fig. 4-2.

HYDROGEN BONDING AND THE STATES OF WATER

A water molecule with its positive and negative poles is permanently dipolar. Unlike charges attract, so a water molecule is attracted to other substances that carry either a positive or a negative charge. This includes other water molecules (16). Attraction between a positive pole of one water molecule and a negative pole of another leads to association of water molecules through a

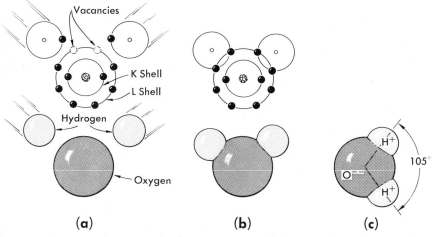

Figure 4-1. Formation of a water molecule. (a) Two atoms of hydrogen and one of oxygen, shown schematically, unite. (b) Each hydrogen atom shares with the oxygen a pair of electrons, shown in equilibrium position. (c) Unequal distribution of positive and negative charges makes the water molecule permanently dipolar. (Illustrations from *Water: The Mirror of Science* by K. S. Davis and J. A. Day. Copyright © 1961 by Educational Service, Inc. Reproduced by permission of Doubleday and Company, Inc.)

type of secondary valence bond, known as a "hydrogen bond," as shown:

$$H—O \text{-----} H—O$$

Hydrogen bond

A hydrogen bond is much weaker than the covalent or shared bond that joins the hydrogen to the oxygen within the molecule of water. Each water molecule has the potential for uniting by hydrogen bond with four adjacent water molecules, two by way of the oxygen and one each by way of the two hydrogens. The ability of water to form hydrogen bonds gives it many of its unique properties. Water can exist in three states depending on the extent to which the molecules are hydrogen bonded.

WATER IN THE LIQUID STATE

Water is a liquid at temperatures between 0°C and 100°C at normal atmospheric pressure. The flow properties are due to hydrogen bonds which link adjacent molecules of water. Otherwise, under these conditions water would be a gas because of the small mass of the molecule. In the liquid, molecules associate in small clusters which break up and reassociate continuously. These clusters move about freely and there is much hydrogen-bond interchange (3,8).

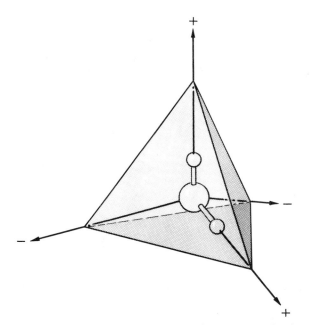

Figure 4-2. Orientation of charges around a molecule of water gives it the shape of a tetrahedron. (From O. Fennema and W. D. Powrie, *Advances in Food Research* **13:** 223. Copyright © 1964 by Academic Press Inc., New York. Reprinted by permission.)

WATER IN THE CRYSTALLINE STATE

When the temperature of water is lowered, the motion of the molecules in the liquid is slowed. The volume of the water shrinks slightly as it cools. Hydrogen bonding within the clusters persists longer as the temperature drops. By the time water is cooled to 4°C, the water molecules have begun to associate via hydrogen bonding in a precise arrangement. This continues as the temperature drops from 4°C to 0°C, and the volume of the water begins to expand. If additional heat is withdrawn from water after it reaches 0°C, crystals appear, and as ice water changes to ice crystals expansion is abrupt. This liquid ice water becomes crystalline and solid, that is, ice. The angle at which the bonding in the crystal lattice takes place is such as to leave unfilled spaces which are hexagonal in shape. (See diagram in Fig. 4-3.) These spaces are so positioned as to give rise to innumerable channels which pervade ice. As a result, ice occupies 1/11 more space than the water from which it was formed. Ice, less dense than water, floats to the surface.

When water molecules crystallize from the vapor state, single crystals are obtained as snowflakes with the typical hexagon shape. The reverse of the condensation of water vapor as snowflakes is the change from ice crystals to water vapor without the ice melting. This phenomenon is known as subli-

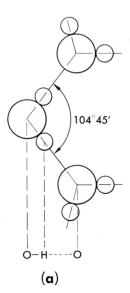

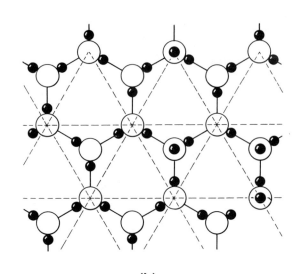

(a)

(b)

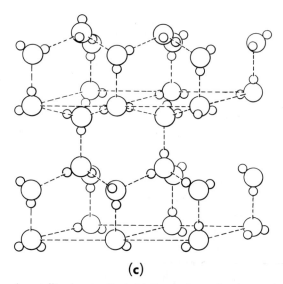

(c)

Figure 4-3. Lattice of crystallized water (ice). (a) Two water molecules, each hydrogen bonded to a third with a bond angle of approximately 105°. (b) Water molecules bonded to form crystals leave hexagon-shaped spaces in ice. (c) Three-dimensional model of crystallized water. (From A. Frey-Wyssling and K Mühlethaler, *Ultrastructural Plant Cytology,* copyright © 1965, p. 23, by Elsevier Publishing Company, Amsterdam. Reprinted by permission of authors and publisher.)

mation. Freezer burn during the storage of frozen foods is the result of sublimation; and moisture is removed from freeze-dried foods by sublimation. Such dried foods rehydrate better than ordinary dried foods because structural components remain in place and excessive hydrogen bonding between components of the food itself is eliminated.

WATER IN THE GASEOUS STATE

In addition to existing as a liquid and as a solid, water may exist also in the gaseous state as either water vapor or steam. If a container of water is left uncovered and exposed to the air for some time, the level of water will gradually lower and the container will eventually become empty. For this evaporation to take place, individual molecules of water must have attained sufficient kinetic energy because of random motion (2) so that they can escape into the atmosphere. This involves breaking hydrogen bonds that are essential for the liquid state. The rate of evaporation varies with temperature and humidity of the air. Had the container been covered instead of open, molecules of water vapor would have accumulated above the surface. As the number of molecules of water vapor increases so, too, do their chances of contacting the surface of the liquid and reuniting with it. After a time an equilibrium would be reached, with the number of molecules leaving the liquid as vapor balanced by the number returning to it. At equilibrium, the pressure exerted by the molecules of water vapor on the surface of the liquid below represents the *vapor pressure* of the water.

BOILING OF WATER

CHANGES OBSERVED AS WATER IS BROUGHT TO A BOIL

When cold tap water is heated, small bubbles can be observed in the water where it contacts the bottom and sides of the pan. These bubbles form because air is less soluble in hot water than in cold. When water reaches simmering temperature, larger bubbles, which form mainly on the bottom of the pan, float lazily to the surface of the water before they break. In this instance the bubbles are of water vapor. When water reaches the state of boiling, the bubbles not only form rapidly but they also break before they reach the surface and as they leave the water the surface is agitated. When water boils, the molecules leave the liquid as steam, not singly but in battalions. For water molecules to change to water vapor, in the phenomenon known as boiling, both the force of attraction between water molecules and the atmospheric pressure must be overcome. The latter is due to the weight of the air resting on the surface of the liquid. At sea level the standard value for the weight of the column of air is equal to 760 mm of mercury, or 15 pounds per square inch (103 kPa). At sea level and with standard barometric pressure, pure water boils at 100 °C (212°F).

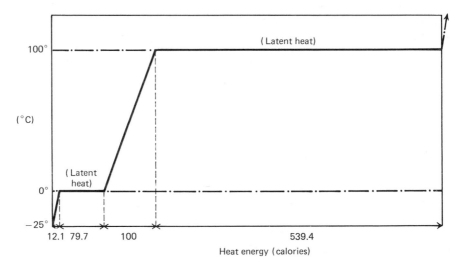

Figure 4-4. The latent heats of water are plotted on this graph. One gram of water (ice) at the melting point absorbs approximately 80 calories and changes to the liquid state without a rise in temperature. One gram of water at the boiling point absorbs approximately 540 calories before it changes to steam and before the temperature begins to rise again. (Illustration from *Water: The Mirror of Science* by K. S. Davis and J. A. Day. Copyright © 1961 by Educational Service, Inc. Reproduced by permission of Doubleday and Company, Inc.)

SPECIFIC HEAT. The graph in Figure 4-4 shows the energy involved at strategic points in the heating of water from 0° Kelvin to 100°C. The figures given are for 1 gram (1 ml) of water. As the graph shows, 273 calories are required to bring the temperature of 1 gram of water from 0°K to 273°K (0°C). This is 1 calorie for each 1 degree rise in temperature or a *specific heat* of 1 (derived from the ratio of the two). Water has a higher specific heat than most substances. This characteristic is utilized in the kitchen to cushion or protect certain foods against a too rapid rise in temperature. Examples are heating a food in a double boiler instead of putting the pan in direct contact with the hot unit and placing the container with a custard or soufflé in a pan of water when it is put into the oven to bake. The high specific heat of water accounts in part for the fact that it is a good coolant. Fats, also used to transmit heat in food preparation, have a much lower specific heat than water. Olive oil, for example, has a specific heat of 0.471. A pan of oil will heat to temperature more than twice as fast as a pan of water, the input of energy being the same. The specific heat of air of 0.3329 is less than that for fat. Lower still are the specific heats of two metals from which cooking utensils are made, 0.214 for aluminum and 0.119 for cast iron.

LATENT HEAT. Referring again to Figure 4-4, the graph shows that although it takes 273 calories to raise the temperature of 1 gram of water (ice) from 0°K to 273°K (0°C), the temperature then remains at 0°C until 80 (approximately) additional calories have been absorbed. The 80 calories are called *latent heat* because the input of energy is not accompanied by a rise in temperature. These 80 calories are needed to melt or fuse the 1 gram of ice by disrupting the hydrogen bonds which maintain the orderly arrangement of molecules in the crystals of ice. The result at this point is 1 gram of ice water still at 0°C. Only after the ice melts does the temperature again begin to rise and again 1 degree for each calorie absorbed.

Thus 100 calories will bring the temperature of 1 gram of ice water (at 0°C) to 100°C, but the water still remains in the liquid state. It is estimated that approximately 40 percent of the water molecules are still hydrogen bonded. To change 1 gram of water at the boiling point (100°C) to vapor requires an additional 540 calories. Again *latent heat* is involved, this time heat of vaporization. The 540 calories are a measure of the energy required for the water molecules to overcome the force of atmospheric pressure and the attraction of the hydrogen bonds which remain in water at the boiling point.

Latent heat of vaporization of water in addition to its high specific heat gives a factual basis for the observation that "a watched pot never boils." A steam burn is so severe because of the 540 calories of latent heat of vaporization which are released when the steam condenses. Water may be used to keep foods cool because of latent heat of vaporization. Without refrigeration, foods may be kept reasonably cool by storing them in a cloth that is kept damp. Spraying fruits and vegetables on display in a produce department with a fine mist of water not only prevents wilting, but it also helps to keep the food cool as the water evaporates from the surface. Latent heat of fusion explains why ice is a good coolant. And the country practice of putting a tub of water in a cellar on a cold night to keep fruits and vegetables from freezing worked because each gram of water which was converted to ice released 80 calories.

FAST VERSUS SLOW BOILING.   Once water is hot enough to boil, the temperature will go no higher no matter how hot the heating unit. The water will be more agitated as it boils and it will evaporate faster. Sometimes this is desired. Evaporation of water from the syrup is the chief object of cooking candies and fruit pectin jellies. A rapid boil may be used to eliminate residual cooking water around certain vegetables to conserve nutrients. But when the object is to heat foods, not to evaporate water, rapid boiling only wastes energy and does not speed cooking. And excessive evaporation when foods are cooked at a rapid boil may result in their being scorched. Foods high in starch are more likely to boil dry because starch absorbs water when it is gelatinized. Dried foods that absorb moisture as they cook may become dry and scorch. Meats, fruits, and most vegetables contribute water to that added to the utensil in which they are cooked.

If foods are to be cooked in a small amount of water, a heavy pan with a tight-fitting lid is essential. A pan with a small diameter reduces the rate at which water evaporates. A lid on the pan serves to condense steam and as this water returns to the pan the loss of water by evaporation is slowed. The intensity of heat must be controlled to limit evaporation when a small amount of water is used.

FACTORS AFFECTING THE BOILING POINT OF WATER

ALTITUDE.   Water does not always boil at 100°C (212°F). The weight of the column of air which rests on the surface of water varies with altitude, and this affects the temperature at which water boils. For each 960-foot increase in altitude above sea level, the boiling point of water is lowered by 1°C. As a consequence of this reduction, a longer time is required to cook foods at higher altitudes. This effect of altitude was noted by Marco Polo as he, his father, and his uncle traveled the land route from their home in Venice to the land of the great Kublai Khan. He recorded this observation as they made their way along the top of the world:

So great is the height of the mountains, that no birds are to be seen near their summits; and however extraordinary it may be thought, it was affirmed, that from the keenness of the air, fires when lighted do not give the same heat as in lower situations, nor produce the same effect in dressing victuals [i.e., cooking foods]!*

Foods not only may need to cook longer at higher elevations but the proportions of ingredients, especially water, may need to be altered because of the lower boiling point. Modifications of recipes and of cooking times have been developed for high altitude regions that occupy approximately one-third of the United States (15).

BAROMETRIC PRESSURE.   Even at the same altitude atmospheric conditions change frequently, and this causes fluctuations in the temperature at which water boils. If barometric pressure is low, water boils below 100°C and evaporates faster.

When the weather is changing from clear to cloudy, barometric pressure is usually low (air is less dense) so the boiling point of water is lower. A change from cloudy conditions to bright is usually accompanied by high barometric pressure (more dense air) and an elevation in the boiling point. The boiling point of water should be determined and adjustment made prior to using a thermometer to assess the doneness of boiling syrup of candy and fruit pectin jellies.

STEAM PRESSURE.   The boiling point of water may be raised above 100°C in a pressure saucepan or a pressure canner. When water boils in either of these utensils once they are sealed, the steam that forms is confined within the container.

*The Travels of Marco Polo the Venetian, by Marco Polo, Everyman's Library Text, Ernest Rhys, editor. Copyright © 1926 by E. P. Dutton & Co., Inc. Reprinted by permission of E. P. Dutton & Co., Inc.

One volume of water can give rise to 1600 to 1800 volumes of steam (one teaspoon of water can yield approximately 2 gallons of steam). When this steam is confined within the space formerly occupied by the air, the pressure builds rapidly. As the pressure rises more heat must be applied to the water to give the molecules sufficient energy to escape as steam. As the steam pressure rises so does the boiling point; and it will continue to do so as more heat is applied, converting more water to steam. At 5 pounds steam pressure (34 kilopascals) water boils at 109°C (228°F); at 10 pounds (69 kilopascals) it boils at 115°C (240°F); and at 15 pounds (103 kilopascals) it boils at 121°C (250°F). The pressure in a pressure saucepan or pressure canner may be increased 1 pound (7 kilopascals) for each 2000-foot increase in altitude to compensate for the effect of altitude on the boiling point of water.

As steam under pressure exerts much force, the pressure saucepan or canner and the closure must be built to withstand the pressure. When steam is confined in such utensils, it is dangerous to try to remove the lid without first cooling the utensil to reduce the steam pressure to zero. The petcock should be opened to make certain no steam is confined.

Unless the petcock is opened or the pressure gauge removed when the steam pressure reaches zero, a partial vacuum forms. Should this happen, the contents of the cooker or canner may begin to boil again even though the temperature has dropped below 100°C (212°F). This is one cause of loss of liquid from jars in canning. When a partial vacuum forms, less than the usual amount of pressure is exerted on the surface of the water and the boiling point is lowered. For instance, when sealed fruit jars are removed from a pressure canner, a partial vacuum may form in the jars which permits the liquid to boil after the jars are cool enough to be handled comfortably.

SALT AND SUGARS.   Salt and sugar, two common ingredients in food preparation, elevate the boiling point of water (see Chapter 6) and depress its freezing point (see Chapter 5). Presence of either of these two substances in water dilutes the water molecules and so lowers the vapor pressure of the water (2). To compensate for this reduced vapor pressure the water that contains sugar or salt must be hotter before it can boil.

FUNCTIONS OF WATER IN FOOD PREPARATION

A MEDIUM FOR THE TRANSFER OF HEAT

One important function of water in preparing foods is that it serves as a medium for the transfer of energy from heating unit to food. If a saucepan were placed over a lighted gas burner or on a hot electric unit with food but no water in the pan, pan and food would be hottest where the pan was contacted by the flame or where the pan rested on the hot coils. The food would scorch where it contacted the pan before the remainder of the food had a chance to become warm. Water in the pan absorbs the heat which sets up convection currents that equalize the temperature throughout. Water is a good conductor of heat, that is, it readily gives up heat to food in contact with it. A more detailed discussion of the role of water in the transfer of heat was given in Chapter 3.

A DISPERSING MEDIUM

Water serves as a means of dispersing many constituents present in foods and used in food preparation. For some constituents it acts as a solvent. Others are dispersed colloidally, as an emulsion, or as suspended matter.

SOLUTIONS

Water dissolves such substances as salt, sugars, water-soluble vitamins and minerals, and flavoring substances such as those extracted from tea leaves and coffee beans.

Solutions are of two types, ionic or molecular. In a crystalline material such as table salt the sodium ion has donated one electron in its outer shell to a chlorine atom which lacks one electron in its outer shell, as shown in Figure 4-5. Two oppositely charged ions, a positive sodium ion and a negative chloride ion, are the result. In a crystal of sodium chloride (Fig. 4-6) these two types of ions are bonded to each other by electrostatic forces. Water reduces the attractive force between oppositely charged sodium and chloride ions to approximately 1 percent of what it was in the crystal of sodium chloride (3). The ions become hydrated (Fig. 4-7) and as such are towed away by water molecules. In this way solution of the crystal is effected. Acids and bases, like salts, ionize in water. Because of this the acid and base in baking powder react and give off the gas which helps to leaven quick breads. (See Chapter 11.) Molecules or ions in solution are known as the "solute," and the liquid in which they are dissolved the "solvent."

Molecules of many compounds in foods are associated through hydrogen bonds. Molecules of sucrose in a sugar crystal are an example. When a crystal of sugar comes in contact with water, water molecules unite by hydrogen bonds to polar groups on sucrose molecules on the surface of the crystal. Hydrated sucrose molecules are removed layer by layer from the surface of the crystal. Heating the water reduces the attraction of water molecules for each other and gives them enough energy to overcome the attraction of sugar molecules for each other. Solubility of substances such as sugar, where hydrogen-bond interchange is involved, increases with an increase in the temperature of the water. Thus sugars are more soluble in hot water than in cold.

COLLOIDAL DISPERSIONS

A number of constituents found in foods do not form true solutions but can still be dispersed by water. Colloids constitute one such group. A colloidal dispersion differs from a true solution in the larger size of the molecules or

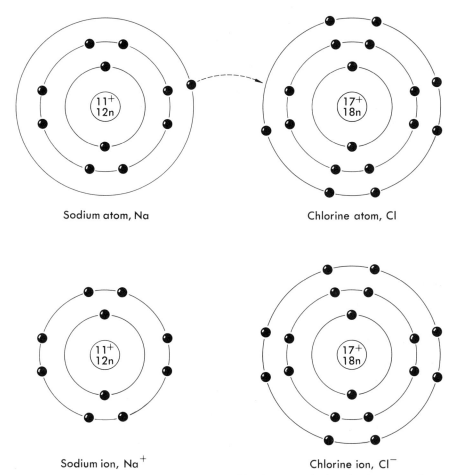

Sodium atom, Na   Chlorine atom, Cl

Sodium ion, Na$^+$ Chlorine ion, Cl$^-$

Figure 4-5. A positive sodium ion and a negative chloride ion result when a sodium atom donates an electron to a chlorine atom. (From Brownlee, Fuller, Hancock, Sohon, and Whisit's *Elements of Chemistry* revised by Paul J. Boylan. Copyright © 1962 by Allyn and Bacon, Inc. Reproduced by permission of Allyn and Bacon.)

particles involved and their relatively larger surface areas. Colloids are not so large that they settle out and not so small that they form true solutions. Proteins as a group form colloidal dispersions (or sols). An example is gelatin which disperses colloidally in hot water. Many colloidal dispersions are unstable because of the size of the particles involved. The curdling of milk, for example, is due to the instability of the colloidal casein micelles.

Constituents in foods may unite with molecules of water by hydrogen-bond formation, that is, become hydrated, without being dispersed. The starch and proteins of flour are hydrated when ingredients are combined for quick breads, yeast bread, cakes, and pastry. Unless the flour is hydrated by the liquid, ingredients will not adhere to form a batter or dough.

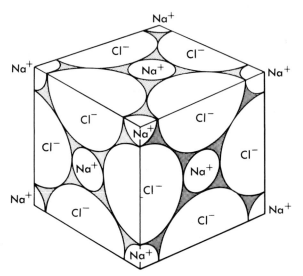

Figure 4-6. Sodium and chloride ions in the sodium chloride crystal lattice. (Reprinted by permission from *Chemical Systems* by Chemical Bond Approach Project. Copyright © 1964 by Earlham College Press, Inc. Published by Webster Division, McGraw-Hill Book Company.)

EMULSIONS

Another type of dispersion in foods where water is involved is an emulsion. Although both water-in-oil and oil-in-water emulsions are possible, the latter type predominates in foods. Mayonnaise, cream, homogenized milk, and shortened cake batters contain fat in emulsified form. Discussion of emulsions is included in Chapters 16, 17, and 21, which deal with these foods.

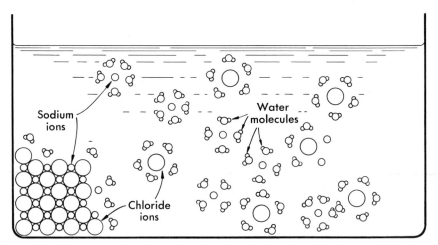

Figure 4-7. Polar water molecules weaken ionic bonds. A sodium chloride crystal dissolves as sodium and chloride ions become hydrated. (From H. C. Metcalfe et al., *Modern Chemistry,* copyright © 1962 by Holt, Rinehart and Winston, Inc., New York. Reprinted by permission.)

SUSPENSIONS

Still another type of dispersion is a suspension. Here the particles of the substance are so large or so complex that they can neither dissolve nor be colloidally dispersed in water. A common example of such a suspension is that of starch grains in cold water. When cornstarch is used to make a thickened pudding or soft pie filling, the starch grains are suspended in cold liquid and the temporary suspension is stirred and heated until the starch grains are swollen sufficiently to remain permanently suspended throughout the pudding.

DISPOSITION OF WATER IN FOODS

FREE AND BOUND WATER

Water makes up a major portion of many foods, constituting from near 70 percent to more than 90 percent of fruits, vegetables, and meats (Table 4-1). Part of this water is readily separated from other constituents present, as happens when fresh fruits and vegetables are sliced, diced, or shredded. However, part of the water is separated with difficulty. The former is referred to as *free* and the latter as *bound* water (13). Bound water, in contrast to that which is free, is characterized in a number of ways. It does not act as a solvent for such constituents as salts, sugars, and acids, it can be frozen only at very low temperature, it exhibits essentially no vapor pressure, and its density is greater than that of free water. The proportion of bound water in a food varies somewhat with the technique used to measure it (7), and especially with the amount of energy expended by the method. In fact, part of the water may be on the borderline between bound and free (6).

Water may be present in foods as water of crystallization, as in monocalcium phosphate monohydrate ($CaH_4(PO_4)_2 \cdot H_2O$), the acid ingredient used in fast-acting baking powder. Water molecules may be bound to polar groups on such macromolecules as starches, pectins, hemicelluloses, and on gelatin and other proteins or attracted to ionic sites. The first layer of bound water molecules is held the most firmly and the second layer bonded to the first only slightly less so, with additional layers less and less ordered until the association typical of bulk water prevails (6). Much of the water in such high moisture foods as fruits, vegetables, and meats is free but unable to flow because it is trapped in spaces formed by structural elements that make up the tissues. Many gels such as baked custard, molded gelatin salads and desserts, fruit pectin jellies, and puddings or pie fillings thickened with starch or vegetable gums have a high water content, but it is immobilized by the capillary spaces or the amorphous network formed by the gelling agent.

ACTIVITY OF WATER

The presence of dissolved substances in the fluid within the cells of fresh fruits and vegetables and in the muscle fibers of meat enables the tissues of these foods to take up and retain water and so maintain crispness or turgor. The passage of water across semipermeable membranes is called osmosis and is discussed in Chapter 27. In addition to influencing the water-holding capacity of tissues, solutes lower the activity of water (10). Activity of water (A_w) is defined as the ratio of the vapor pressure of water in a solution (P_s) to the vapor pressure of pure water (P_w):

$$A_w = \frac{P_s}{P_w}$$

The lowered activity is attributed to dilution of water by solutes (2). The activity of water is high in fruits, vegetables, and meats because of the high moisture and the low concentration of solutes. Bacteria, yeasts, and molds grow and multiply readily at high A_w, so these foods are susceptible to spoilage by microorganisms (4,18). Some methods of food preservation are successful because they lower the A_w sufficiently so that microorganisms are unable to grow. Decrease of moisture in tissues by dehydration or freezing, use of sugar in high concentration as in jams and jellies, and use of a concentrated solution of salt as in brining are effective in the main because they lower the activity of water enough so that it can no longer support growth of microorganisms which cause food spoilage (10,14). Salt lowers the activity of water more effectively than does sugar. A 10 percent solution of sodium chloride has an A_w of 0.93 (vs. 1.00 for pure water); a 10 percent solution of sucrose has an A_w of 0.994 (14). Bacteria require a higher A_w for growth, and molds can tolerate a lower A_w than do yeasts. The food poisoning organism, Staphylococcus aureus, was unable to produce toxin at A_w's below 0.93 to 0.91 (19).

Whether a food exposed to the air dehydrates or takes on moisture depends on the relationship between the A_w of the water in the food and the relative humidity of the air. Relative humidity is the ratio of the vapor pressure of the moisture in the air to that of pure water at the same temperature. Because it is customarily expressed as percent, $RH = A_w \times 100$ (4). A raw apple exposed to air in a warm kitchen for several days will lose moisture, eventually becoming spongy and shriveled, but dried fruit (in which the sugar has been concentrated) left in an open container in the same kitchen may absorb moisture from the air.

The ability of a substance to bind water and its ability to lower the activity of water do not necessarily go hand in hand, as was demonstrated in a study comparing sodium chloride, glycerol, and sodium caseinate (12). With sodium chloride, the higher the concentration (from 5 to 20 percent) the higher the percentage of bound water and the greater the lowering of A_w. Glycerol, a polyhydric alcohol, lowered the activity of water but behaved essentially like water in regard to hydrogen bonding. Sodium caseinate, a large molecule derived from a protein of milk, did bind water but it had no appreciable effect on the A_w. In systems with multiple components, however, the presence of a substance such as sodium chloride which decreases A_w also results in a decrease (not necessarily linear) in the amount of water bound by a macromolecule (12,17).

CHARACTERISTICS OF WATER THAT AFFECT ITS USE

HARDNESS OF WATER

The quality of water used in food preparation is important. When a community boasts of a pure water supply, reference is made to the absence of harmful bacteria, which have been filtered from the water or destroyed by chemicals. But water may contain dissolved substances that make it impure in a chemical sense. One such substance is air, which consists of nitrogen, oxygen, and carbon dioxide. When water is boiled, the dissolved air is removed and as a result boiled water tastes flat. As water filters through the soil microorganisms are removed but it may dissolve various substances, some of which affect the taste of water, others the ability of water to extract solubles from such things as tea and coffee, and still others that make the water hard.

TYPE AND DEGREE OF HARDNESS

Hardness of water is due to the presence of calcium or magnesium ions (5). These may make the water temporarily or permanently hard, depending on whether they are present in the form of soluble carbonates or sulfates, respectively. If calcium bicarbonate, $Ca(HCO_3)_2$, or magnesium bicarbonate, $Mg(HCO_3)_2$, is present, the water is said to be temporarily hard. Permanently hard water contains either calcium sulfate, $CaSO_4$, or magnesium sulfate, $MgSO_4$. Hardness of water is expressed in parts per million or in units called "grains," with one grain equivalent to 0.064 gram of calcium carbonate. Based on the grains of carbonate per gallon, water is classified as follows:

Soft	1 to 4 grains per gallon
Medium	5 to 10 grains per gallon
Hard	11 to 20 grains per gallon

SOFTENING HARD WATER

One way to soften temporarily hard water, that is, eliminate the calcium and magnesium ions, is to boil the water. Heat converts soluble bicarbonates into insoluble carbonates and so removes the unwanted calcium or magnesium ions from the water. A grayish-tan layer of sediment accumulates in a utensil in which temporarily hard water is boiled day after day, due to the deposition of these insoluble carbonates. Permanently hard water cannot be softened by boiling. Some type of chemical water softener must be used to eliminate the calcium or magnesium ions. (Temporarily hard water may be softened by the addition of the same chemicals used to soften permanently hard water.) Some water softeners react with calcium and magnesium ions in hard water to form insoluble salts. Washing soda, Na_2CO_3, which is the alkaline salt formed by the reaction of strongly basic sodium hydroxide and weakly acidic carbonic acid, is one such chemical that may be used to precipitate the unwanted ions as insoluble calcium or magnesium carbonate. Polyphosphate salts soften water by binding calcium or magnesium ions.

Ion exchange is an alternate way of removing unwanted ions from hard water. In this method the water is allowed to percolate over a bed of insoluble, granular material which removes calcium or magnesium ions from the water in exchange for sodium or hydrogen ions. When zeolites (hydrous silicates) are used, sodium ions from the zeolite are exchanged for calcium or magnesium ions of the water. When the chemical can bind no more calcium ions, the complex is regenerated by flushing it with a solution of sodium chloride which removes the calcium or magnesium ions and replaces them with sodium ions. When resins are used instead of zeolite, hydrogen ions rather than sodium ions replace the calcium and magnesium ions.

HARD WATER IN COOKING

Hardness of water is of concern when foods are cooked. Calcium or magnesium ions in water may interfere with the tenderizing of certain foods during cooking. For example, it is difficult to cook dried beans, peas, and lentils in extremely hard water. Hardness of water is a disadvantage in making beverages. To make iced tea, it is customary to brew tea extra strong to allow for dilution by melting ice. If the water used to make tea is hard, the beverage is more likely to become clouded. Sodium ions frequently present in softened water increase the time during which water remains in contact with coffee grounds when the beverage is made by the drip method. (See Chapter 7, on brews and infusions.)

pH OF WATER

Aside from being soft or hard, water may be acidic, alkaline, or neutral. Water at a pH of 7 is neutral. Tap water may be neutral but is likely to be adjusted to be slightly alkaline (pH 7.5 to 8.5) Within this pH range both corrosion of water pipes and deposition of carbonates in the pipes are at a minimum. The boiling of water removes carbon dioxide which has dissolved in it from the air, making the water more alkaline.

WATER AS A CLEANSING AGENT

Water is a cleansing agent of importance in the preparation and serving of food. Water removes soil and some of the microorganisms which are present on the surface. It removes food particles and a good share of the microorganisms from cooking utensils and work surfaces with which food comes in contact during preparation. It does the same for dishes and silver used in the serving of foods. Soap or detergent increases the cleansing power of water.

When soap is used with unsoftened, hard water, it must first react with any calcium or magnesium ions present before it can perform its function of lowering the surface tension of water, that is, "making the water wetter." This not only wastes soap, but the curds so formed deposit as a film on dishes and glassware and interfere with the cleansing action of water.

Detergents lower the surface tension of water without having to react with any calcium or magnesium ions present; because of this advantage, they have largely replaced soap. Many dishwashing detergents are so formulated that their cleansing action is not impaired by the presence of either type of calcium or magnesium salt. Some detergents do not make water foam as soap does. Soap left in the waste water when it returns to the soil is decomposed by microorganisms. This was not true of early detergents, now replaced by biodegradable types, that is, can be decomposed by microorganisms.

REFERENCES

1. A.H.E.A. 1975. *Handbook of Food Preparation*. Pp. 3–5, 96–99. Altitude and boiling; altitude and steam pressure.
2. Andrews, F. C. 1976. Colligative properties of simple solutions. *Science* **194:** 567–571. Vapor pressure of solutions, boiling point elevation, freezing point depression, and entropy; thermodynamic treatment.
3. Buswell, A. M., and W. H. Rodebush. 1956. Water. *Sci. Amer.* **194**(4): 76–89. Water as a solvent and the freezing of water at elevated temperatures.
4. Christian, J. H. B. 1963. Water activity in the growth of microorganisms. *Recent Advances in Food Science: Biochemistry and Biophysics in Food Research* **3:** 248–255. J. M. Leitch and D. N. Rhodes, eds.
5. Davis, K. S., and J. A. Day. 1961. *Water: The Mirror of Science*. Anchor Books S 18. Garden City, New York: Doubleday. Pp. 24–36, 90–102. Simplified account of some of the unique properties of water.
6. Drost-Hansen, W. 1971. Role of water in cell-wall interactions. *Fed. Proc.* **30**(5): 1539–1548. Structure of water at solid interfaces; a review.
7. Fennema, O. 1976. Water and ice. In *Principles of Food Science*. Part I. *Food Chemistry*. O. R. Fennema, ed. New York, N.Y.: Marcel Dekker, Pp. 13–39.
8. Fennema, O., and W. D. Powrie. 1964. Fundamentals of low temperature food preservation. *Advances in Food Research* **13:** 221–229. Proposed structures for water and for ice.
9. Fox, B. A., and A. G. Cameron. 1970. *Food Science—A Chemical Approach*. London: University of London Press. Pp. 224–231. Some facts about the physical characteristics of water.
10. Garner, R. G. 1966. Water activity in relation to foods. *Agricultural Science Review* **4**(3): 17–23. Water activity and stability of foods.
11. Gur-Arieh, C., A. I. Nelson, and M. P. Steinberg. 1967. Studies on the density of water adsorbed on the low-protein fraction of flour. *J. Food Sci.* **32:** 442–445. Levels of adsorbed water of 0–7 percent, 7–14 percent, and 14–26 percent compared.

12. Karmas, E., and C. C. Chen. 1975. Relationship between water activity and water binding in high and intermediate moisture foods. *J. Food Sci.* **40:** 800–801. Effects of caseinate, glycerol, and sodium chloride.

13. Kuprianoff, J. 1958. Bound water in foods. In *Fundamental Aspects of the Dehydration of Foodstuffs*. London: Society of Chemical Industry. Pp. 14–23. Forms of water in foods.

14. Labuza, T. P. 1974. Sorption phenomena in foods. In *Theory, Determination and Control of Physical Properties of Food Materials*. C. Rha, ed. Dordrecht, Holland: D. Reidel Pub. Co. Pp. 197–219.

15. Lorenz, K. 1975. High altitude food preparation and processing. CRC *Critical Reviews in Food Technology* **5:** 403–441. A review of many aspects including boiling of water.

16. Matz, S. A. 1965. *Water in Foods*. Westport, Conn: Avi Publishing Co. Pp. 1–9. Technical treatment of the nature of water.

17. Ross, K. 1978. Differential scanning colorimetry of nonfreezable water in solute-macromolecule water systems. *J. Food Sci.* **43:** 1812–1815. Relationship of bound water and water activity.

18. Scott, W. J. 1957. Water relations of food spoilage microorganisms. *Advances in Food Research* **7:** 83–127. Water and the keeping quality of foods.

19. Troller, J. A., and J. V. Stinson. 1975. Influence of water activity on growth and enterotoxin formation by *Staphylococcus aureus* in foods. *J. Food Sci.* **40:** 802–804. Two strains of the microorganism compared in two media.

FILMS

1. *Chemistry of Water*. 14 min. Color. Chemical and physical properties. Sutherland.
2. *Structure of Water*. 14 min. "Basic Chemistry Series." Hydrogen bonding and the effects of heat and cold on water. McGraw-Hill.

FIVE
Ice Crystals and Frozen Desserts

This chapter is concerned with the effects of cold (the absence of heat) on water in ices, fruit and milk sherbets, and ice milk and ice creams. Such frozen desserts are crystalline substances. The crystals are those of ice. For the smooth, creamy texture desired in frozen desserts crystals must be small. The role of constituents present in the mix as it is frozen and of the techniques of freezing the mix as they affect ice crystal size are discussed in this chapter. Also considered are factors which affect the consistency of the frozen product. For a discussion of how and why ice crystals form see Chapter 4.

FACTORS AFFECTING ICE CRYSTAL FORMATION

COMPONENTS OF THE MIX

An essential ingredient in a frozen dessert is water, either as such or supplied by milk, cream, or fruit juice. Sugar is included, so a mix for a frozen dessert is actually a syrup. The sugar is usually the disaccharide, sucrose, at least in part. A frozen product consists of crystals of ice floating or suspended in syrup in which air bubbles have been incorporated (1). A frozen dessert is a solution, a suspension, and a foam. If the mix contains cream, an emulsion is involved, too. The structure of a frozen dessert viewed with a light microscope is shown in Figure 5-1. Additional constituents in the syrup differentiate ices, sherbets, and ice creams. Some of these constituents affect the size of the ice crystals formed.

SUGAR

Sugar in the freezing syrup affects ice crystal formation in two ways. For one, it lowers the freezing point of water. When sugar molecules are present, the water molecules must be slowed down more, that is, must have more heat removed, before ice crystals begin to form. It is possible that orientation of water molecules around hydrated sugar molecules makes more difficult participation of these water molecules in the ice crystal lattice. Each gram-mo-

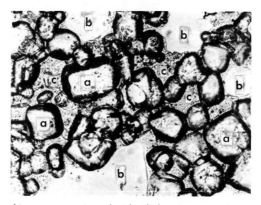

Figure 5-1. Structure of ice cream as viewed with a light microscope: (a) ice crystals, (b) air cells, and (c) unfrozen material. Magnification X 250. (From Wendell S. Arbuckle, Missouri Agricultural Experiment Station Research Bulletin 320, 1940. Reproduced by permission.)

lecular weight of sugar (342 grams of sucrose, or 1¾ cups) per liter (approximately one quart) of water lowers the freezing point by 1.86 Celsius degrees. The proportion of sugar in ices and sherbets is approximately twice that in ice creams and ice milks to compensate for the acids in the first two. This means that for an ice to begin to freeze the temperature must be lowered more than for ice cream.

A second effect of sugar in a mix for a frozen dessert is that the sugar helps keep the size of the crystals small. Evidence available appears to indicate that sugar restricts crystal size by increasing the amount of liquid which remains unfrozen (1). When milk and cream are used in a mix to be frozen, they contribute some sugar in the form of lactose. The amount of this disaccharide desirable in ice cream is limited because of its low solubility in cold water and its tendency to precipitate (17). Lactose crystals (called "sandiness") are likely to form when a high proportion of dried milk solids is used in a frozen dessert. A frozen dessert contains more sugar than its sweetness suggests because of the effect of low temperature on taste buds.

FAT

A number of substances used in frozen desserts which have no effect on the freezing point of the mix help keep ice crystals small, too. Presumably, these substances do so because they act as mechanical barriers to the deposition of water molecules on ice crystals. Water molecules slowed down sufficiently by the removal of heat to unite to water molecules already immobilized in the crystalline state are unable to do so when a foreign molecule or particle intervenes. Instead of an ice crystal already started becoming larger by the addition of molecules of water to its surface, new crystals begin to form. Hence, more—but smaller—crystals form in the presence of interfering substances.

One such substance is fat supplied by milk or cream. Other factors being the same, an ice cream made from cream with 18 percent milk fat will have smaller crystals (finer texture) than a frozen product made from whole milk with a lower fat content. Homogenized milk or cream is even more effective in limiting the size of ice crystals because of the much greater number of fat globules formed as the result of homogenization. Frozen desserts made with evaporated milk have a finer texture than those made with fluid milk (10). In part, this effect arises because the fat has been homogenized. Fats influence the texture of ice cream in another way. In two frozen products with ice crystals of equal size, the one with the higher fat content will seem finer in texture. This phenomenon is attributed to the lubricating effect of the fat droplets on the ice crystals (8).

NON-FAT MILK AND OTHER SOLIDS

Milk solids limit the size of ice crystals more effectively than do fat droplets. The greater concentration of milk solids in undiluted evaporated milk is another reason it makes fine-textured ice creams. These solids increase the viscosity of the mix and favor the incorporation of air bubbles as the mix is agitated during freezing.

Because of the milk solids, milk sherbets are usually finer textured than those made with a water base. Also, the acid from the fruit juice brings about changes in the milk protein which cause the milk to thicken perceptibly. This thickening interferes with the development of large ice crystals. In addition, the viscous mix allows the incorporation of many air bubbles. Delay in freezing the mix for a milk sherbet may result in curdled milk, particularly if the fruit juice is decidedly tart. Thickening milk with eggs as for custard or setting the milk with rennin before it is frozen favors the formation of smaller ice crystals. The gel structure may possibly interfere mechanically with the formation of large ice crystals.

A sherbet that contains egg white or gelatin is finer in texture than an ice made from water, fruit juice, and sugar only. Such sherbets increase in volume more than ices. The difference in volume between an unfrozen mix and the frozen product is known as "overrun." Part of overrun is due, of course, to the expansion of water as it crystallizes, but more is due to air bubbles incorporated by the rotating dasher. Some overrun is desirable to keep the finished product from being too compact. An overrun of 50 percent will give an acceptable product, although commercially an overrun of 100 percent is common. If overrun is excessive, the frozen mix tends to be frothy and to lack flavor. Fat in the mix tends to decrease overrun owing to rupture of air bubbles as the mix is agitated in the course of freezing.

EMULSIFIERS

Ice cream made at home usually contains fat already in emulsified form. The level of milk solids in commercial ice cream is sufficient to emulsify the fat when the mix is homogenized (11). The greater dispersion of fat that results favors the formation of more and so smaller ice crystals. Emulsions and emulsifiers are discussed in Chapter 16. Incorporation of additional emulsifier in commercial ice cream has been the practice for a number of years. The beneficial effects on the quality of the frozen product were recognized, although how emulsifiers accomplish this was far from clear (12). Emulsifiers, together with milk solids, were known to promote incorporation of air bubbles and foaming of the mix. The current concept is that emulsifiers have dual and opposing roles in ice cream. They are essential for emulsification of fat in the unfrozen mix, but they are just as essential for partial destabilization of the emulsion as the mix freezes. The importance of fat in the structure of ice cream has been known for some time (5,16). The air bubbles in ice cream are surrounded by an aqueous film containing the dispersed milk proteins and in which are distributed emulsified fat and ice crystals. Fat freed by destabilization migrates to the air/liquid interface of the foam (6). Some de-emulsification of fat confers dryness, stiffness, and melt resistance on the frozen product, but destabilization must be controlled (14). If excessive, clustering of fat and a buttery mouthfeel results, as well as breakdown of the foam and appearance of whey. Mono- and diglycerides and polyoxyethylene sorbitan esters of fatty acids are emulsifiers used in commercial ice creams. The latter are the more effective destabilizers (11). Soft serve ice cream is extruded from the freezer at a lower temperature than conventional (hard) ice cream so the mix is agitated longer. An emulsifier attracted more to the fat than to the aqueous phase of the mix is less likely to result in excessive de-emulsification (13,15).

AGITATION AND ICE CRYSTAL FORMATION

In most frozen desserts, reliance is not on interfering substances alone to form small crystals of ice. Agitation of the mix when it reaches the temperature at which it begins to freeze favors the development of many small crystals. As the temperature of the mix is lowered from room temperature to near freezing, it is agitated slowly to equalize the temperature throughout. If the mix has a high proportion of cream, rapid agitation during this preliminary cooling may cause the fat droplets to unite (16). Ice cream with a greasy texture is the result. This is less likely to happen if the cream is homogenized.

When the temperature is lowered enough for ice crystals to begin to form, vigorous agitation with the blades of the dasher of the freezer initiates the growth of innumerable crystal nuclei. Construction of the dasher influences the effectiveness of the freezing process in forming small ice crystals. Agitation should be uninterrupted as the temperature drops through the zone of maximum deposition of water molecules in the crystalline state. As ice crystals form and water is removed from the syrup, the concentration of sugar in the syrup increases and the temperature at which the remaining water crystallizes becomes progressively lower. As the temperature is lowered the ratio of crystals to syrup increases, and the frozen product becomes thicker or stiffer.

HARDENING OF FROZEN DESSERTS

A mix used for a frozen dessert will become too difficult to manipulate in a freezer before enough of the water has been converted to ice for the frozen product to have a desirable consistency for serving. For this reason, the partially frozen mix is held in contact with a coolant and allowed to continue to freeze and harden without agitation. How hard the frozen product becomes depends on how low the temperature goes and also on the proportion of sugar in the mix. The two factors are interrelated. Because of the higher proportion of sugar, ices and sherbets must be brought to a lower temperature than ice creams and ice milks before the ratio of ice crystals to syrup is high enough to give a desirable consistency for serving. Letting a frozen dessert stand for a short time after it is frozen will mellow and improve the flavor as well as harden it.

Commercially frozen desserts are hardened at or near a temperature of $-15°C$ ($5°F$). At this temperature they are too cold and firm to serve because too much water (more than three-fourths) has been converted to ice crystals. The consistency of such a product is analogous to that of overcooked fondant and fudge. (See Chapter 6.) However, the hardness of ice cream is temperature produced and temperature dependent. If a frozen product is brought to the temperature of the ice-cube compartment of the refrigerator, the crystals melt enough to increase the proportion of syrup and give a more desirable firmness. Most ices and ice creams have a desirable consistency at a temperature of $-12°$ to $-10°C$ (14 to $10°F$). Frozen products are more flavorful at the higher temperature.

STABILIZERS IN FROZEN DESSERTS

Once small crystals form in a frozen dessert, the object is to keep them small. During frozen storage some of the smaller ice crystals melt; at the same time, water molecules unite with larger ice crystals. Growth of larger ice crystals at the expense of smaller ones during storage tends to make the frozen product coarse. The growth of ice crystals can be minimized by storing the frozen product at a low temperature and preventing fluctuations in the storage temperature.

Even under optimum conditions, frozen desserts that contain no stabilizer become coarse in texture when stored for an extended period. Inclusion in the mix of one or more ingredients which prevent ice crystals from growing larger is essential if the frozen dessert is to be stored for more than a few hours. Such stabilizers include a number of vegetable gums (acacia, agar, alginate, carrageenan, furcelleran, guar, karaya, locust bean, tragacanth), gelatin, and sodium carboxymethylcellulose (3). Stabilizers enable frozen desserts to better withstand "heat shock" or fluctuations in temperature with alternate thawing and freezing. The effects of wide fluctuation in storage temperature on ice cream (3) are shown in the photomicrograph in Figure 5-2. One theory as to

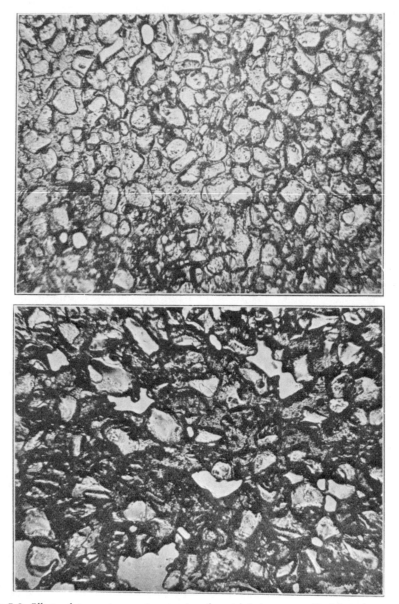

Figure 5-2. Effects of storage temperature on size of crystals in ice cream. (Top) Stored at constant low temperature. (Bottom) Stored at fluctuating temperature for 5 days. Magnification X 100. (From W. C. Cole, *Journal of Dairy Science* **15:** 432, 1932. Reproduced by permission.)

the mode of action of a stabilizer such as gelatin is that it binds water and thus prevents its deposition on existing crystals during the hardening and subsequent holding period. Such stabilizers also aid in the formation of small ice crystals during the initial freezing. Stabilizers not to exceed 0.5 percent of the finished weight are permitted in commercially frozen desserts.

FREEZING DESSERTS IN AN ICE CREAM FREEZER

A mix for a frozen dessert freezes due to the withdrawal of heat. For agitated desserts this process takes place in an ice cream freezer. Essential parts of a freezer include (1) a metal can to hold the mix to be frozen, because metal is a good conductor, (2) a dasher which fits into the can, preferably one with construction to give triple action, which does a more efficient job of agitating the mix as it freezes and which incorporates more air into the mix, and (3) a bucket to hold both the metal can and the freezing mixture, one of wood, preferably, as it is a relatively poor conductor of heat.

THE FREEZING MIXTURE

A freezing mixture has three components: ice, salt, and brine. Ice alone cannot freeze water, owing to the latent heat involved (see Chapter 4), much less the mix for a frozen dessert with its dissolved substances which lower the freezing point. In the freezing mixture, the salt added to the ice dissolves in the water on the surface of the melting ice and lowers its freezing point. This means that the resultant brine can give up more heat to the unmelted ice and get colder without freezing than can ice water alone.

Salt depresses the freezing point of water more effectively than sugar for two reasons. As a molecule of salt gives rise to both sodium and chloride ions, the freezing point of water is depressed twice 1.86 Celsius degrees for each gram-molecular weight of salt (58 grams, or 3⅓ tablespoons) per liter of water. Also, a gram-molecular weight of salt is less than a gram-molecular weight of sugar, so gram for gram salt makes it possible to get a colder brine than does sugar. How cold it is possible for the brine to get depends on the concentration of salt, but how cold the brine actually becomes depends also upon the amount of ice that melts. The solubility of salt in water limits the lowest temperature attainable by a mixture of ice and salt to $-21°C$, a minimum achieved by combining 29 parts salt with 71 parts ice.

The three parts of a freezing mixture work together as follows. The brine is colder than ice and is the part that actually withdraws heat from the mix through the walls of the metal container. Freezing does not begin until the brine forms and gets cold enough to lower the temperature of the mix to its freezing point. As the ice melts, it absorbs heat from the brine and so lowers its temperature. Salt, as it dissolves, maintains the concentration of the brine. The resultant depression of the freezing point of the water makes it possible for melting ice to absorb more heat from the brine. The freezing mixture is thus a dynamic combination of brine which is colder than ice and actually absorbs heat from the mix, ice which as it melts keeps the brine cold, and salt, which, as it dissolves, keeps the brine concentrated.

To prepare the freezing mixture for ice creams, ¼ cup of rock salt for each quart of chipped ice (1 part salt to 8 parts ice by weight) will give a brine cold enough to effect the freezing in a reasonable time. A coarse salt is recommended because finer salt tends to cake. A higher proportion of salt to ice,

⅓ cup per quart or 1 part to 6 by weight, is used for ices because of the higher proportion of sugar in the mix. Lower ratios of salt to ice increase the time needed to freeze a mix. Ratios of salt to ice which are too high waste salt and ice and drop the temperature of the mix so fast that it hardens before air is incorporated. Keeping the temperature of the brine low as freezing continues is dependent upon having ice to continue to melt, and to absorb 80 calories for each gram that does melt, and salt to continue to dissolve.

MANIPULATING THE FREEZER

Preliminary chilling of the mix shortens the freezing time. With the mix to be frozen in the metal container and the freezing mixture of ice, salt, and brine around it, agitation of the mix should begin. The freezer should be cranked, slowly at first (for approximately 3 minutes), until the temperature of the mix is lowered by the brine to the point at which the mix begins to freeze. Once crystallization begins, the freezer should be cranked rapidly (160 revolutions per minute) until the temperature of the mix drops through the zone of maximum ice crystal formation (approximately 6 minutes). This is essential if ice crystals are to be small. After that, cranking should continue but at a slower rate until it is too hard to turn the crank. When 60 percent or more of the water in the mix is frozen, the freezer can no longer be cranked because the mix is too stiff. The frozen dessert at this point should stand with brine around the metal container for one-fourth to one-half hour. During this time the ratio of ice crystals to unfrozen mix increases until the product attains a desirable consistency for serving.

Bacterial contamination is a hazard in making ice cream (9). Parts of the freezer should be scrupulously clean. In addition, contamination of the frozen dessert with the mixture used to freeze it should be avoided.

STILL-FROZEN DESSERTS

THE MIX

In the absence of agitation to aid in the formation of small crystals in a frozen dessert, a higher proportion of interfering substances is needed in the mix (2). Mixes for still-frozen products rely heavily on a high proportion of fat droplets and the incorporation of innumerable small bubbles of air, before the mix is frozen, to keep the crystals small. Whipped gelatin, whipped cream, whipped evaporated milk, and beaten egg white are used to introduce air bubbles into still-frozen desserts. Faster freezing also aids in the formation of small crystals. For this reason a high proportion of sugar in a mix to be still-frozen is a disadvantage. Two products that may be satisfactorily still-frozen are mousses and parfaits.

FREEZING THE MIX

The mix should be chilled before it is put to freeze. Still-frozen desserts may be frozen by surrounding the mix with a freezing mixture of 1 part salt to 3 or 4 parts ice by measure. An alternative is the freezing compartment of a refrigerator. The thermostat should be set as low as possible a half hour or so before the mix is put to freeze. Good contact between the bottom of the freezing tray which contains the mix and the cooling surface of the refrigerator aids in rapid withdrawal of heat from the mix. A film of water between the two insures good contact and eliminates air, which is a poor conductor. Rapid drop in temperature favors the formation of many ice crystal nuclei, which helps keep the crystals small.

QUALITY CHARACTERISTICS OF FROZEN DESSERTS

In addition to flavor, three main characteristics by which the quality of a frozen dessert may be assessed are texture, consistency, and body. Texture refers to the feel of the frozen dessert on the tongue. It may be coarse or fine, depending on the size of the ice crystals. When crystals are small (less than 35 μm), the ice cream is very smooth. Somewhat larger crystals, 35–55 μm in size, yield a smooth textured product. Frozen products with crystals larger than 55 μm are coarse textured (4). Crystals from mixes with a high proportion of fat seem finer than they actually are, presumably because fat lubricates the crystals.

Consistency refers to the hardness or softness of a frozen dessert. Frozen products should be firm enough to hold their shape. This characteristic is influenced mainly by temperature but also, to some extent, by the viscosity of the syrup which remains unfrozen. A typical mix extruded from the freezer near $-5°C$ has approximately half the water in the form of ice crystals; stored at $-11°C$ three-fourths, and hardened at $-30°C$ more than nine-tenths of the water is in crystalline form (5).

Aside from texture, which depends on the size of the ice crystals, and consistency, which depends upon the ratio of ice crystals to syrup, the way a frozen dessert behaves when it warms and begins to melt is a characteristic of consequence in determining quality. The body of a frozen dessert may be too viscous and spongy on the one hand or too watery and compact on the other. Body is influenced primarily by the characteristics of the liquid in which the crystals are suspended.

REFERENCES

1. Arbuckle, W. S. 1940. A microscopic and statistical analysis of texture and structure in ice cream as affected by composition, physical properties and processing method. *Missouri Expt. Sta. Res. Bull.* **320:** 25–32. Effects of fat, sugar, serum solids, and gelatin on structure and texture; illustrated with photomicrographs.

2. Bentley, L., and B. M. Watts. 1939. Use of stabilizers in unagitated ice cream. *Food Research* **4:** 101–111. Effectiveness of agar, pectin, rennin, gelatin, starch, egg yolk and dried skim milk in controlling crystal size.

3. Berger, K. G. 1976. Ice cream. In *Food Emulsions*. Stig Friberg, ed. New York: Marcel Dekker, Inc. Pp. 141–213. An overview of the subject.

4. Berger, K. G., B. K. Bullimore, G. W. White, and W. B. Wright. 1972. The structure of ice cream—Part 1. *Dairy Industries* **37**(8): 419–425. Air cells, fat globules, and ice crystals.

5. Berger, K. G., B. K. Bullimore, G. W. White, and W. B. Wright. 1972. The structure of ice cream—Part 2. *Dairy Industries* **37**(9): 493–497. Fat/mix, air/mix, and ice/mix interfaces in ice cream.

6. Berger, K. G. and G. W. White. 1971. An electron microscopic investigation of fat destabilization in ice cream. *J. Food Technol.* **6:** 285–294. The role of destabilization.

7. Cole, W. C. 1932. A microscopic study of ice cream texture. *J. Dairy Sci.* **15:** 421–433. Illustrated with photomicrographs.

8. Cole, W. C., and J. H. Boulware. 1940. Influence of some mix components upon the texture of ice cream. *J. Dairy Sci.* **23:** 149–157. Effectiveness of butterfat *vs.* milk solids.

9. Foltz, V. D., and W. H. Martin. 1941. A study of homemade ice cream. *Food Research* **6:** 31–38. Bacterial contamination and possible sources.

10. Given, M. 1928. Texture of ice cream as influenced by some constituents. *Ind. Eng. Chem.* **20:** 966–968. Effects of gelatin, egg (custard), and evaporated milk.

11. Govin, R., and J. G. Leeder. 1971. Action of emulsifiers in ice cream utilizing the HLB concept. *J. Food Sci.* **36:** 718–722. The importance of controlled de-emulsification.

12. Kloser, J. J., and P. G. Keeney. 1959. A study of some variables that affect fat stability and dryness in ice cream. *Ice Cream Review* **42**(10): 38–41, 56–60. An early attempt to elucidate the role of emulsifiers.

13. Knightly, W. H. 1963. Surfactants in food manufacturing. 2. Applications and mode of action. *Food Mfg.* **38:** 661–666. Functions of emulsifiers in frozen desserts.

14. Leeder, J. G. 1971. A new concept about the function of emulsifiers in ice cream. *Am. Dairy Rev.* **33**(10): 28 B,D. Importance of the HLB of the emulsifier.

15. Lin, P., and J. G. Leeder. 1974. Mechanism of emulsifier action in an ice cream system. *J. Food Sci.* **39:** 108–111. An attempt to account for the destabilizing action.

16. Sherman, P. 1965. The texture of ice cream. *J. Food Sci.* **30:** 201–211. The effects of freezing on the fat globules of ice cream.

17. White, G. W., and S. H. Cohebread. 1966. The glassy state in certain sugar-containing food products. *J. Food Technol.* **1:** 73–82. Control of sandiness in ice cream.

FILMS

1. *Crystals*. 24 min. "PSSC Physics Series." Modern Learning Aids or Eductional Services Inc. Growth of crystals viewed under the microscope.

2. *Structure of Water*. 14 min. "Basic Chemistry Series." McGraw-Hill. Hydrogen bonding and the freezing of water.

SIX
Sugars, Sugar Crystals, and Confections

Sugars are valued for the sweet taste they impart to foods. The relative sweetening power of common sugars was given in Chapter 1. The sweetness of ripe fruits comes from the sugars present. Sucrose, fructose, and glucose account for most of the carbohydrates found in fruits (Chapter 27), but such minor sugars as xylitol, xylose, and sorbitol are widely distributed (6). Honey is a concentrated solution of fructose and glucose (near 80 percent) (3). Bees manufacture honey from the nectar of flowers which contains fructose, glucose, and sucrose. Much of the latter is changed by the enzyme invertase secreted by the bee to glucose and fructose, so honey contains less than 2 percent sucrose. Corn syrups are manufactured from cornstarch. They contain varying proportions of glucose (dextrose), maltose, and dextrins, all products of the hydrolysis of the starch (see Chapter 8). High fructose corn syrup is now on the market. Corn syrup in which dextrose predominates is treated with an isomerase which converts part of the dextrose to the much sweeter levulose (fructose) (7). The most widely used sugar is sucrose. Its functions and that of other sugars in quickbreads, yeast breads, cakes, and pectin jelly will be discussed in subsequent chapters.

Sugar and sugar crystals, particularly in making candies and frosting, are considered in this chapter. Such confections are either crystalline, as in fondant, fudge, and panocha, or noncrystalline as in caramels, brittles, glacés, and chewy taffies, or have a special texture, as in gum drops (a gel), marshmallows (combination of foam and gel), and divinity and 7-minute frosting (combination of foam and crystals). Crystalline candies are sugar crystals surrounded by and suspended in saturated sugar syrup.

Fundamental material on ice crystal formation in frozen desserts (Chapter 5) also applies to sucrose crystal formation in crystalline confections. A noncrystalline candy such as caramels is just a very thick syrup. Certain noncrystalline candies, such as brittles and lollipops, have a low moisture content (1–2 percent) and are hard and glasslike.

A brief discussion of sugar (sucrose) precedes consideration of the details of manipulating it in making candies.

Figure 6-1. Enlarged model of a representative crystal of sucrose. (Courtes of California and Hawaiian Sugar Company, San Francisco, Calif.)

SUGAR

SOURCE

Sucrose is the crystalline ingredient (see Fig. 6-1) from which candies and other confections are made. It is obtained from the cell sap of the sugar cane or the sugar beet. The methods of manufacture of the white granulated sugar of commerce from the two sources differ in detail, but the main steps are similar. Stalks of sugar cane from which the leaves have been removed are crushed between heavy rollers to express the juice; sugar beets are shredded and the sugar extracted with hot water. The thin juice, which contains from 10 to 15 percent sugar, is treated with lime, and the impurities are removed by filtration. The treated juice is then evaporated under vacuum until the sugar is concentrated sufficiently for crystallization to take place. The light molasses, separated from the crystals by spinning in a centrifuge, is concentrated a second and a third time, the last yielding blackstrap molasses, a good source of calcium, iron, and potassium. The brown crystals of sucrose so formed are coated with molasses. Removal of the molasses and other impurities to produce white granulated sugar is called "refining." Crystals are washed and centrifuged to remove adhering syrup, and then dissolved in warm water. All but traces of impurities which remain in the syrup are removed by precipitation and filtration, and the syrup is made crystal clear by passage over charcoal. The syrup is then concentrated in vacuum pans at a low temperature to precipitate the sugar. When the crystals reach the desired size, the adhering syrup is removed by centrifugation. After the last traces of moisture are removed from the crystals, they are separated by sieve according to size. The granulated sugar so obtained is dry and the crystals are rather coarse (see Fig. 6-2), two characteristics that make it unpalatable. The size of the crystals can be altered by changing the conditions under which the sugar crystallizes. Crystals of refined white sugar contain not more than 0.05 percent impurities. Brown sugars are made by adding cane molasses to refined sugar, and so are sources of calcium, iron, and potassium.

CHEMISTRY

Sugars belong to a class of compounds known as carbohydrates. "Saccharide" is a term that denotes sugar, or substances derived from sugar. Monosaccharides are simple or single sugars; disaccharides are derived from monosaccharides and when hydrolyzed, yield two molecules of simple sugar; and molecules containing several sugar residues such as starches and cellulose are known as polysaccharides.

Sucrose is a disaccharide which is formed by the union of one molecule of the monosaccharide glucose (dextrose) with one of the monosaccharide fructose (levulose) through carbons 1 and 2 and with the loss of one molecule of water:

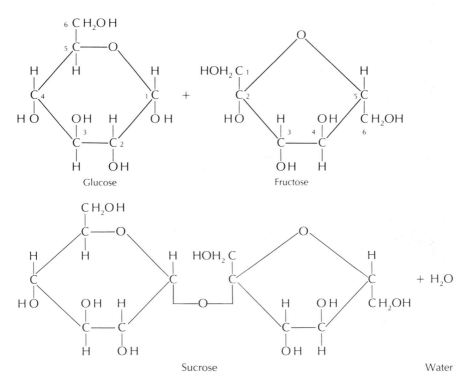

Glucose

Fructose

Sucrose

Water

(a)

(b)   (c)

(d)   (e)

(f)   (g)

Figure 6-2. Relative sizes of sugar crystals commonly available: (a) topping sugar, (b) medium granulated, (c) extra-fine granulated, (d) fruit-fine granulated; powdered sugars made by grinding or pounding granulated sugar and usually containing 3 percent cornstarch added to prevent caking in (e) standard powdered and (f) 6X powdered; (g) clusters of crystals of brown sugar. (From J. A. Dunn and J. R. White, *Cereal Chemistry* **14:** 792, 794, 1937. Reproduced by permission.)

Thus sucrose is made from and can give rise to one molecule of glucose and one of fructose.

SOLUBILITY OF SUGAR

The first step in making candies and frostings is to dissolve the dry, coarse crystals of granulated sugar in water. An excess of water is used to ensure complete solution. Sucrose is highly soluble in water, more so than glucose, but less so than fructose. Lactose is least soluble of the common sugars. The solubility of any sugar in water increases with an increase in temperature. Table 6-1 gives the solubility of sucrose in water at various temperatures. When the amount of sucrose specified in the table is dissolved in 100 grams of water at a given temperature, a saturated solution is developed. At 20°C (68°F) a 67 percent sucrose solution (203.9/303.9) is saturated; at 115°C the concentration of sucrose in a saturated solution is 87 percent. Solubility of fructose at two temperatures and of sodium chloride at three temperatures is also given.

Hydroxyl groups on sugar molecules confer on them their solubility in water. Elevating the temperature makes little difference in the solubility of sodium chloride where ionic bonds are involved, but a marked difference in the solubility of sugar where hydrogen bonds are involved.

The high solubility of sucrose in water is an advantage in making candies and frostings but a disadvantage when the candy absorbs moisture from the atmosphere and becomes sticky or soft. Those candies with a high proportion of fructose are especially likely to take up moisture. A difference of 1 percent in relative humidity when a candy is made may affect the consistency of the finished confection.

Table 6-1 Effect of temperature on solubility of sucrose, fructose, and sodium chloride (grams per 100 grams of water)

Temperature (°C)	Sucrose[a] (grams)	Fructose (grams)	Sodium Chloride (grams)
0	179.2		35.6
10	190.5		
20	203.9	375.0	36.0
30	219.5		
40	238.1	538.0	
50	260.4		
100	487.2		37.8
115	669		

[a]SOURCE: C. A. Browne, *A Handbook of Sugar Analysis,* copyright © 1912 by John Wiley & Sons, Inc., New York, p. 649.

Table 6-2 Effect of concentration of sucrose on boiling point of syrup

Sucrose (percent)	Boiling Point (°C)
0	100 (water)
10	100.4
20	100.6
40	101.5
60	103.0
80	112
85[a]	114 (soft ball stage for candies)
90.8	130
100	160 (molten sugar)

[a]Approximate.

SOURCE: C. A. Browne, *A Handbook of Sugar Analysis,* copyright © 1912 by John Wiley & Sons, Inc., New York, p. 651.

EFFECT OF SUCROSE ON THE BOILING POINT OF WATER

A substance like sugar that dissolves in water elevates the boiling point. Each mole of sucrose (342 grams) dissolved in a liter of water elevates the boiling point 0.52°C. A mole of salt (58 grams) per liter of water elevates the boiling point twice this much or 1.04°C because each molecule of salt ionizes to give one sodium and one chloride ion. Table 6-2 gives the boiling points for sucrose solutions of different concentrations. Notice the steep rise in the boiling point after the concentration of the sucrose in the syrup reaches 80 percent.

The boiling point of a sucrose syrup is an index to its concentration. One can measure indirectly the concentration of sugar in a syrup by measuring the temperature at which the syrup boils. By this means it is possible to determine when a sugar syrup has reached the concentration desired. Allowance must be made for variations in barometric pressure, for the presence of other sugars, and for altitude.

MELTING AND CARAMELIZATION OF SUGAR

As the water in a solution of sucrose evaporates and the concentration of the sucrose increases, the temperature of the syrup (the boiling point) rises and will continue to do so until all of the water has boiled away. When this happens, the liquid that remains is molten sugar. The melting point of sugar is 160°C (320°F). Sugar crystals can be melted by putting dry sugar in a heavy frying pan, placing the pan over low heat and shaking it so that sugar on the bottom does not overheat before the remainder has a chance to reach the melting point. Molten sugar, removed from the source of heat and left undisturbed, supercools. It then becomes a clear, glassy, noncrystalline brittle solid.

If molten sugar is heated a few degrees above the melting point (to 170°C or 338°F), the sucrose begins to caramelize. Caramelized sugar is used to make "burnt sugar" frostings. The decomposition of sucrose by heat gives rise to a complex mixture of aldehydes and ketones in which 5-hydroxymethyl furfural and furfural are prominent constituents. The products of the pyrolysis of sucrose include, in addition, a mixture of cresols, eight of which have been identified (5). When soda is added to caramelized sugar, the heat plus the acids present release carbon dioxide, bubbles of which inflate the molten mass. When cooled it is porous and brittle. When a syrup of sucrose and water is heated to the soft crack stage (so named for the sound the hot syrup makes when a small amount of it is spooned into cold water), it takes on a *pale* amber tint. This is not due to caramelization, but is attributed to liberation of furfural from the sugar by the high temperature followed by the formation of polymers which tint the syrup.

CANDIES

DETERMINING DONENESS OF CANDIES

BOILING POINT OF THE SYRUP

Once sucrose is in solution, the next step is to boil away the right amount of excess water which was added originally to ensure solution of the large sugar crystals. One of the problems in making any confection is to know how long to cook the syrup, that is, how much water to boil away to give a product of the desired consistency. The chief factor that determines consistency in the finished product is the concentration of sugar in the syrup. For this the temperature of the boiling syrup is an index. For either noncrystalline or crystalline products, a thermometer can be used to determine when the boiling syrup is done. A thermometer will not give a true reading unless the syrup is boiling, the bulb of the thermometer is submerged in the boiling syrup but not touching the pan, and the eye is level with the top of the column of mercury when the temperature is read.

For noncrystalline candies such as caramels, the object is to concentrate the syrup so that it will be neither too thin nor too thick when it has cooled to room temperature. The syrup should be just viscous enough that the pieces when cut will hold their shape and can be handled. Almost all the water is evaporated from syrup for brittles, glacé, and toffee. The high proportion of interfering substances permits these supersaturated syrups to supercool and form candies which are vitreous.

For crystalline candies the object is to obtain in the finished product the correct ratio between sucrose crystals and remaining saturated syrup. The following example will explain how this is accomplished. When sucrose syrup boils at 115°C, each 100 grams of water in the syrup has dissolved in it 669 grams of sucrose. When this syrup is cooled to 40°C, each 100 grams of water at this temperature can dissolve only 238 grams of sucrose. The liquid thus holds more solute than it can dissolve at that temperature and is said to be *supersaturated*. The difference between the amount of solute which the 100 grams of water holds and the amount which it could dissolve at 40°C (669 minus 238, or 431 grams) is a measure of how supersaturated the syrup is. This extra sucrose is held precariously in solution, and with a little encouragement it will precipitate as crystals until the remaining syrup is just saturated. The higher the boiling point, the more supersaturated the syrup when it has cooled and the more sucrose precipitated. The more sucrose that crystallizes, the less the amount of syrup that remains, and the firmer the candy.

The boiling point is not a true index to the concentration of sucrose when other sugars are present with sucrose in a syrup, because they contribute to the elevation of the boiling point, too. When other sugars are present, the syrup must be cooked to a higher temperature to concentrate the sucrose sufficiently. A second point needs to be considered, too. Ingredients other than sugar may not affect the boiling point, yet their presence in the syrup makes it more viscous. With a more viscous syrup less sucrose needs to precipitate to give the candy the desired consistency. This means that when milk solids, cocoa or chocolate, fat, or dextrins are present, the sucrose in the syrup need not be so concentrated. Thus syrup for fudge reaches the soft ball stage at a slightly lower boiling point than fondant (see Table 6-3).

Formulas for different candies and the temperature to which each should be brought are given in Table 6-3.

CONSISTENCY OF THE SYRUP (COLD WATER TEST)

A second index to the doneness of a candy syrup which takes into account these factors, as well as the concentration of sucrose, is the consistency of the cooled syrup. This should be tested near the end of the cooking period. The pan containing the syrup should be removed from the heat while the test is made. A small amount of the candy syrup is poured into *cold* water and its behavior noted.

For example, syrup which is at the soft ball stage can be collected from the bottom of the container of cold water, but it is so soft that it runs through the fingers. Syrup cooked to the soft ball stage is really soft. An end point that is so subjective is liable to errors in judgment. Syrups for both fudge and fondant are sometimes overcooked when this method of assessing doneness is used. Too often the syrup for fudge is cooked beyond this stage to the firm or even the hard ball stage. Table 6-4 gives the stages of doneness of a sugar syrup as assessed by its consistency in cold water. Included in the table is the approximate boiling point necessary to give syrup of each consistency and the uses of syrups cooked to the different stages.

Table 6-3 Formulas for candies

	Crystalline		Amorphous or Noncrystalline				Special Textures	
	Fondant	Fudge	Caramels	Taffy	Toffee	Lollipops	Divinity	Marshmallows
	1 cup Sugar	1 cup Sugar	1 cup Sugar	1 cup Sugar	1 cup Sugar	1 cup Sugar	1 cup Sugar	1 cup Sugar
	1 tbsp Corn syrup	1 tbsp Corn syrup	1 cup Corn syrup	1/4 cup Corn syrup	1 tbsp Corn syrup	1/3 cup Corn syrup	2 tbsp Corn syrup	1 tbsp Corn syrup
	or							
	1/16 tsp Cream of tartar							
		1 tbsp Butter	1/4 cup Butter		3/4 cup Butter		1 Egg white	1 tbsp Gelatin
	1/2 cup Water	1/2 cup Milk	1 cup Cream *or* Evaporated milk	1/3 cup Water	1/4 cup Water	1/2 cup Water	1/4 cup Water	1/4 cup Water
	114°C (237°F)	112°C (234°F)	120°C (248°F)	127°C (261°F)	149°C (300°F)	154°C (310°F)	122°C (252°F)	120°C (248°F)
	Soft ball	Soft ball	Firm ball	Hard ball *or* 135°C (275°F) Soft crack	Hard crack Hard crack	Hard crack	Hard ball	Firm ball

Table 6-4   Consistency, boiling point, and uses for syrups

Consistency	Temperature Range[a]		Behavior	Uses
	(°F)	(°C)		
Thread	230–236	110–113	Forms a 2-inch thread as it leaves the spoon	Syrup
Soft ball	234–240	112–116	Forms in cold water a ball too soft to retain its shape	Fondant, fudge, panocha
Firm ball	244–250	118–121	Forms in cold water a ball firm enough to hold its shape	Caramels
Hard ball	250–266	121–130	Forms in cold water a hard ball which can be deformed by pressure	Divinity, marsh-mallows
Soft crack	270–290	132–143	Forms hard threads in cold water	Butterscotch, taffy
Hard crack	300–310	149–154	Forms brittle threads in cold water	Brittles, glacé, toffee
Molten sugar	320	160	Clear, viscous liquid	Barley sugar
Caramel	320–348	160–177	Brown, viscous liquid	Flavor and color for confections

[a] Temperatures indicate concentration at sea level. Subtract 1 Fahrenheit degree for each 500 feet above sea level or 1 Celsius degree for each 900 feet above sea level.
SOURCE: Adapted from A.H.E.A. *Handbook of Food Preparation,* copyright © 1975, p. 81. American Home Economic Association, Washington, D.C.

INTERFERING AGENTS AND SUCROSE CRYSTAL FORMATION

FUNCTIONS OF INTERFERING SUBSTANCES

The proportion of interfering substances present in a candy syrup influences the amount of sugar, if any, which crystallizes from the syrup as well as the size of the sucrose crystals.

Under the appropriate conditions, sucrose molecules in a syrup can align themselves in a manner unique to the sugar molecule to form crystals. Forces holding the molecules together in the crystals are hydrogen bonds between hydroxyl groups on contiguous molecules. A molecule of any sugar other than sucrose has a different shape, is foreign, and will interfere with sucrose molecules in solution joining or adding to sucrose crystals already started. This is

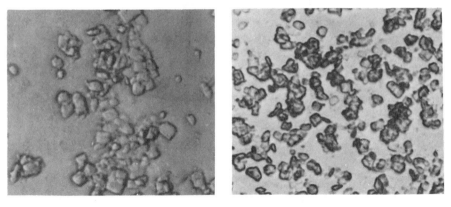

(a)   **(b)**

Figure 6-3. Effect of invert sugar on sucrose crystal formation. (a) Crystals from sugar and water fondant. (b) Crystals from sugar, water, and cream of tartar fondant. Invert sugar formed as the latter cooked contributed to the formation of numerous, small crystals. Magnification approximately X 200. (From E. G. Halliday and I. T. Noble, *Hows and Whys of Cooking,* 1946, University of Chicago Press, Chicago, Ill. Reproduced by permission of Isabel Noble.)

true for molecules of glucose and fructose even though they are part of the sucrose molecule itself. When interfering sugars, such as glucose and fructose are present in a syrup, many sucrose crystals tend to form instead of only a few which grow exceedingly large. Thus foreign sugars favor the formation of more (and smaller) crystals in crystalline candies. (See Fig. 6-3a and b.) Aside from foreign sugars, other substances may interfere with the formation of large sucrose crystals in crystalline candies. In fact, a high proposition of interfering substances in a candy syrup may prevent crystallization altogether which makes possible noncrystalline candies.

PROPORTIONS OF INTERFERING SUBSTANCES

Two methods are employed to ensure the optimum concentration of interfering substances in candies. The interfering substances may be added to the syrup or they may be formed from sucrose as the candy cooks.

When interfering substances as such are added, the quantity should be measured with care. This is particularly true for crystalline candies. A common way to provide interfering sugars is to use corn syrup. Corn syrup is made from cornstarch. When molecules of starch are hydrolyzed, dextrins, maltose, and finally glucose are formed. Either acid and heat or enzymes catalyze the reaction:

$$\text{Starch} + \text{Water} \quad \underset{\text{Acid plus Heat}}{\overset{\text{Enzymes}}{\text{— or }\longrightarrow}} \quad \text{Dextrins} + \text{Maltose} + \text{Glucose}$$

Enzyme-hydrolyzed corn syrup is marketed under the trade name of Sweetose.

If starch has been converted to glucose completely, the syrup has a dextrose equivalent (DE) of 100 percent; syrups with lower DE have more dextrins and maltose and less glucose. For each cup of sugar used to make fondant and fudge, 1 tablespoon of corn syrup will provide enough interfering substances to control effectively the size of the crystals. Honey, which contains both glucose and fructose, may be used to provide interfering sugars in candies.

Interfering sugars, instead of being added in a definite quantity, may be formed from some of the sucrose molecules as the candy syrup is boiled. Sucrose molecules will react with water molecules when the syrup is heated in the presence of acid. For each molecule of sucrose hydrolyzed, one molecule each of glucose and fructose is obtained:

$$Ch_{12}H_{22}O_{11} + H_2O \xrightarrow[\text{Sucrase}]{\text{Acid plus Heat or}} C_6H_{12}O_6 + C_6H_{12}O_6$$

$$\underset{\text{Sucrose}}{} \qquad \underset{\text{Water}}{} \qquad\qquad\qquad \underset{\text{Glucose}}{} \qquad \underset{\text{Fructose}}{}$$

$$\text{L- Invert sugar -}$$

This reaction (the reverse of that shown earlier in the section on chemistry) may be catalyzed by the enzyme sucrase also. The equimolar mixture of glucose and fructose which results is known as invert sugar.

When acid is added to candy syrup to help form invert sugar, the amount added is even more critical than in the case of corn syrup. The amount of sucrose converted to invert sugar depends upon the concentration of hydrogen ions (amount of acid) present when the candy syrup is cooked (8). The alkalinity of the water and its neutralizing value must be taken into consideration when acid is used to hydrolyze the sucrose (2). One way to control the amount of acid in fondant is to use a carefully measured amount of cream of tartar. This compound, $KHC_4H_4O_6$, is the acid salt of tartaric acid. Vinegar, used in some recipes for taffy, serves the same purpose, as does acid present in the syrup around the crystals of brown sugar used to make panocha, which is similar to fudge.

When acid is used in candy, the length of the cooking time is critical (1). A cooking time that is too short gives insufficient invert sugar and a candy that is likely to be coarse and grainy. Some invert sugar is desired in candy to keep crystals small or the texture fine, but prolonged cooking will yield too much invert sugar. In this case, too little sucrose crystallizes and the candy is too soft to handle. One reason for this is that invert sugar increases the solubility of sucrose. With 6 percent invert sugar the solubility of sucrose at room temperature is increased from 67 percent to 80 percent. At any given concentration of sucrose, fewer crystals would be expected to precipitate in the presence of invert sugar than in its absence. In addition, the two molecules that make up the invert sugar formed elevate the boiling point twice as much as does the sucrose from which it was derived. This means that the boiling point of the syrup in the presence of excess invert sugar is not a true index to the concentration of sucrose and hence to the doneness of the syrup. From 6 to 15 percent invert sugar in fondant is sufficient to keep the crystals small (8); more than this (16–23 percent) gives a candy semifluid in consistency.

A soft fondant has an advantage if it is to be melted and used to make mint wafers or as a coating for bonbons. A firmer fondant is needed for molding cream centers to be dipped in melted fondant or melted chocolate. Chocolate-covered bonbons which are semifluid in consistency are made by incorporating the enzyme sucrase in the fondant centers before they are dipped in chocolate. This enzyme converts enough of the sucrose to invert sugar during storage so that the sucrose crystals partially dissolve.

EFFECT OF INTERFERING SUBSTANCES ON CONSISTENCY

Some interfering substances influence the consistency of a candy as well as the size of the sucrose crystals. Fat globules and the proteins from milk, as well as the solids from cocoa and chocolate, influence the viscosity of the syrup. When the syrup is more viscous because of the presence of these constituents, the crystal-to-syrup ratio need not be so high. It is for this reason that the boiling points for fondant and fudge differ. The final temperature for the syrup for the fondant recipe given in Table 6-3 is 114°C, while that for fudge is 112°C. Both syrups reach the soft ball stage and so have the same consistency or flow properties when tested in cold water, and the candies should have the same consistency. Fondant will have a higher ratio of sucrose crystals to saturated syrup; in fudge the milk solids, the butter, and the solids from the cocoa contribute enough thickness to the syrup to compensate for the lower ratio of crystals to syrup. Both fondant and fudge differ from the original sugar in that the sucrose crystals are smaller and are now suspended in syrup.

PREVENTION OF CRYSTAL FORMATION

A high proportion of interfering substances in a candy syrup may prevent crystallization of sucrose altogether. This is desired in amorphous or noncrystalline candies such as caramels, taffy, toffee, and brittles. Compared with fondant and fudge, taffy has a high proportion of corn syrup, toffee a high proportion of fat, and caramels a high proportion of both. See Table 6-3 for the proportions of ingredients in different candies. Noncrystalline candies are either very thick syrups or hard and glasslike. Their consistency depends chiefly on how much the syrup was concentrated before it was removed from the heat. Syrups for noncrystalline candies are sufficiently concentrated that they will not flow at room temperature. Syrup for toffee, a brittle candy, is heated to the hard crack stage, that for taffy to the soft crack or the hard ball stage, depending on whether a brittle or a chewy product is desired. Syrup for caramels which have a chewy consistency is heated to the firm ball stage. The brown color and characteristic flavor of caramels and toffee are attributed to a reaction between protein and sugar brought about by the high temperature.

Aside from their use in candies, interfering sugars are useful in preventing crystallization of sucrose in syrups. Syrup for preserves is cooked until the sucrose concentration is near 65 percent. Slight overcooking gives a super-saturated syrup and the likelihood of large sucrose crystals forming eventually unless acid is present to invert some of the sucrose as the preserves cook. For this reason lemon juice is added to watermelon preserves. In most fruit pectin jellies the sucrose concentration must be at or close to 65 percent. Jellies made with pectin concentrate have such a short boiling period (usually one minute) that very little invert sugar is produced and sucrose crystals may form in the jelly during storage.

AGITATION AND SUCROSE CRYSTAL FORMATION

FONDANT AND FUDGE

The texture of a crystalline candy or frosting is influenced not only by the proportion of interfering agents present but also by the number of crystal nuclei that form once crystallization begins. If syrup for fondant or fudge is beaten while still hot, too few crystals are initiated and these grow larger as the syrup cools, the result being coarse, grainy candy. On the other hand, when fondant syrup is allowed to stand undisturbed, eventually a few crystals begin to form, initiated by dust or lint, or possibly seeded by sucrose crystals from syrup splashed on the sides of the pan. These few grow exceedingly large because the other sucrose molecules that precipitate do so on the crystals that first form. The crystals become so large that they can be seen by the unaided eye and their dimensions measured by a ruler. Crystals need not be this large for the graininess of crystalline candies to be detected, however. Crystals no larger than 45 microns across (1 micron equals 0.0001 or 10^{-4} centimeter) make fondant seem grainy on the tongue (8). In fact, crystals which are more than 25 microns across make fondant detectably crystalline; those no larger than 20 microns seem fine and creamy. This means that the tongue can detect a difference in the size of crystals of only 6 microns!

To obtain a large number of crystal nuclei, the syrup should be sufficiently supersaturated before any crystals begin to form. Crystals should be wiped from the sides of the pan as the syrup for fondant cooks. Syrup for fondant is cooled to 40°C (1) and that for fudge, in which more interfering substances are present, is cooled to 50°C. Syrup for fudge is usually cooled in the pan; that for fondant is poured from the pan onto a flat surface to cool. (See Fig. 6-4.) The syrup is drained—not scraped—from the pan, and the thermometer is in position before the syrup is poured. Such syrups, as they cool, are unstable and should be undisturbed. Any agitation will start crystal formation before the syrup is sufficiently supersaturated. When a few crystals form before the syrup has cooled enough to be sufficiently supersaturated, these crystals grow larger as the syrup continues to cool instead of new crystals forming. The result is large crystals, as shown in Figure 6-5.

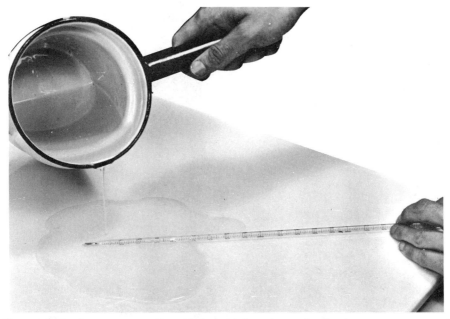

Figure 6-4. Fondant syrup spread in a thin layer is allowed to cool and so become supersaturated prior to beating. (Photograph by Wilbur Nelson.)

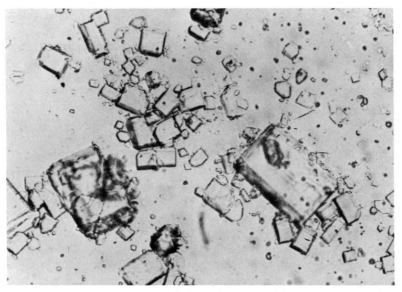

Figure 6-5. Crystals from fondant syrup beaten while it was still hot (103°C). Original magnification approximately X 200. Compare with the crystals in Figure 6-3a, which formed in syrup cooled to 40°C (and so supersaturated) before it was beaten. (From E. G. Halliday and I. T. Noble, *Hows and Whys of Cooking,* 1946, University of Chicago Press, Chicago, Ill. Reproduced by permission of Isabel Noble.)

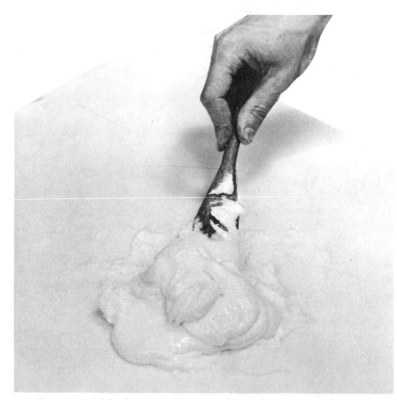

Figure 6-6. Supersaturated fondant syrup beaten until crystallization is nearly complete. Beating the syrup continuously is essential for the formation of fine crystals of sucrose. (Photograph by Wilbur Nelson.)

Once the syrup is supersaturated sufficiently and beating begins, it should be *continuous* until crystallization is complete, as shown in Figure 6-6. As beating proceeds, the moving surfaces of the spoon provide the stimulus that initiates the formation of innumerable crystal nuclei. If beating stops, no new crystals begin to form. Instead, sucrose molecules deposit on existing crystals. This makes them larger and the candy coarser. Thus sucrose crystals grow larger by the addition of sucrose molecules at the expense of the formation of many new and smaller sucrose crystals. Too, large crystals form if no interfering agent is present, if syrup is not cooled to make it supersaturated, and if cooled syrup is not beaten continuously as crystals form.

Agitation of the syrup incorporates air bubbles which make fondant opaque, rather than transparent like the syrup. Pulling taffy accomplishes the same thing. Air beaten into syrup for fudge lightens the color. The formation of sucrose crystals contributes to the opaqueness of fondant and the lighter color of fudge, too. Fondant made with cream of tartar is snowy white, in contrast to that made with corn syrup which is creamy white. Impurities in the water may give the fondant a grayish cast. Fondant stored for 12 to 24 hours in a closed container becomes softer and more pliable. This ripening is due to the solution of extremely small crystals and the reduction in surface area to which the syrup can adhere.

DIVINITY

Syrup for divinity is cooked to the hard-ball stage because it will be diluted by water from the egg white. The hot syrup is beaten into the films of liquid around the air bubbles of beaten egg white. Beating the hot syrup favors the growth of large sucrose crystals. The formula for divinity calls for twice as much corn syrup per cup of sugar as does that for fondant and fudge. This is to counteract the effect of beating the hot syrup as it is added to the egg white. In addition, the protein of the egg white serves as an interfering agent.

Even after the hot syrup is beaten into the egg white, divinity should be beaten continuously until crystallization has proceeded sufficiently for the candy to hold its shape. As this stage approaches, the candy temporarily loses its gloss as the spoon moves through it. At this point, the candy should be transferred to an oiled surface to harden. When divinity finally hardens, the egg white foam has been immobilized by the deposition of sucrose crystals in the films of syrup around each air bubble.

Another indication that crystalline candies have reached the stage of maximum sucrose crystal formation is a slight softening of the candy. Heat was required to dissolve the sugar in the first place and as sugar recrystallizes this heat is liberated. The trick is to stop beating a crystalline candy such as fudge and panocha and pour it from the pan after it softens and just before it crystallizes enough to set. Fondant should be kneaded after it hardens. For noncrystalline candies and confections such as caramels, brittle, and toffee, agitation of the syrup once it is removed from the heat is to be avoided.

AMORPHOUS CANDIES

Some amorphous or noncrystalline candies are soft and chewy, for example, marshmallows, gum drops, and jellies. Marshmallows resemble divinity in that both are foams, but in the former the liquid which encloses the air bubbles is the syrup which contains gelatin. The gelatin prevents sucrose in the syrup from crystallizing. When the foam stands, the gelatin sets, or gels the liquid around the air bubbles (see Chapter 25, on gelatin). When marshmallows are toasted (heated), the gel liquefies. In gum drops and similar candies, starch or pectin converts the syrup to a gel. As was pointed out earlier, caramels are a very thick syrup with a high proportion of interfering substances. Toffee and lollipops are amorphous candies so concentrated that they are hard rather than chewy.

Candies with a high proportion of invert sugar absorb water when exposed to moist atmosphere. The surface becomes sticky and grainy (4). To prevent this, pieces of candy are wrapped in moisture-vapor-proof wrap. A wrap such as paper with a high number of —OH groups in the cellulose is avoided, because candies adhere tenaciously to such materials. Instead, waxed paper or other wrap incapable of participating in hydrogen-bond formation is used.

COMPARISON OF CANDIES AND FROZEN DESSERTS

Fondant and fudge, like ices and ice creams, are a two-phase system of crystals in syrup—sucrose crystals in candy and ice crystals in frozen desserts. Both frozen desserts and fondant and fudge depend on the presence of interfering substances to limit the size of the crystals. Interfering substances in frozen desserts include milk solids, fat droplets, air bubbles, and sugars, plus stabilizers like gelatin and vegetable gums. In crystalline candies, the simple sugars, glucose and fructose, fat droplets, milk solids, and solids from cocoa and chocolate aid in the formation of small sucrose crystals.

Agitation of the mix as crystals form increases the number and decreases the size of ice crystals in frozen desserts and of sugar crystals in candies. Like amorphous candies, still-frozen desserts have a high ratio of interfering substances. However, interfering substances other than sugar should be increased in still-frozen desserts, as a high level of sugar depresses the freezing point and so makes freezing slower. This favors the formation of large crystals when the mix is not agitated as it freezes. Still-frozen desserts contain crystals of ice, unlike amorphous candies, which contain no crystals of sucrose. Air bubbles are incorporated in both crystalline candies and in frozen desserts by agitation of the syrup or of the mix. Preliminary incorporation of air bubbles in a whipped cream, beaten egg white, or liquid thickened by gelatin serves as a means of introducing air into still-frozen desserts.

Temperature of the boiling syrup for fondant and fudge and of the frozen dessert influences the ratio of crystals to syrup and so the consistency of the product. The ratio of crystals to syrup in frozen desserts is altered with alterations in temperature.

REFERENCES

1. Carrick, M. S. 1919. Some studies in fondant making. *J. Phys. Chem.* **23:** 589–592. Variables studied were amounts of water, cooking time, and temperature of syrup when beating started.
2. Daniels, A. L., and D. M. Cook. 1919. Factors influencing the amount of invert sugar in fondant. *J. Home Econ.* **11:** 65–69. Effects of varying proportions of water and cream of tartar.
3. Doner, L. W. 1977. The sugars of honey—A review. *J. Sci. Food Agric.* **28:** 443–456. Minor as well as major sugars; sources and formation.

4. Heiss, R. 1959. Prevention of graininess and stickiness in stored hard candies. *Food Technol.* **13:** 433–440. Technical treatment of the problem.
5. Johnson, R. R., E. D. Alford, and G. W. Kinzer. 1969. Formation of sucrose pyrolysis products. *J. Agr. Food Chem.* **17:** 22–24. Aldehydes, ketones, and cresols identified.
6. Mäkinen, K. K., and E. Söderling. 1980. A quantitative study of mannitol, sorbitol, xylitol, and xylose in wild berries and commercial fruits. *J. Food Sci.* **45:** 369–371, 374. Nineteen fruits and two wines analyzed.
7. Newton, J. M., and E. K. Wardrip. 1974. High fructose corn syrup. In *Symposium: Sweeteners.* G. E. Inglett, ed. Westport, Conn.: Avi Publishing Co. Pp. 87–96. Brief account of its development; advantages and uses.
8. Woodruff, S., and H. van Gilder. 1931. Photomicrographic studies of sucrose crystals. *J. Phys. Chem.* **35:** 1355–1367. Level of acid (citric, tartaric, hydrochloric, and cream of tartar), invert sugar, and size of crystals in fondant.

FILMS

1. *Crystals.* 24 min. "PSSC Physics Series." Educational Services, Inc., or Modern Learning Aids. Shows crystals growing from solution and also the melting of crystals.
2. *Properties of Solutions.* 28 min. Coronet. Effect of temperature on solubility; effect of solutes on the boiling point; supersaturated solutions.

SEVEN
Beverages

Coffee and tea beverages are consumed for their appealing flavor and for their stimulating effect. Served hot, as coffee usually is, or iced, as tea frequently is, they provide desirable temperature contrasts with meals. More coffee than tea is consumed. Chocolate and cocoa beverages occupy a different place in the diet because they are made with milk.

COFFEE

Coffee is the most popular hot beverage in this country. A per capita consumption of approximately 8 pounds of coffee as coffee beans was forecast for 1979 (19). Assuming a yield of 50 cups of beverage for each pound of coffee, the coffee beverage consumed in the United States totals billions of cups, an impressive volume.

Brazil is the source of approximately half the world's coffee. Colombia, which is the second most important source, along with other Latin American countries, supplies one-fourth. African countries, including Ghana, Kenya, and Ethiopia, supply one-sixth of the world's coffee.

CHARACTERISTICS OF THE BEVERAGE

Whoever prepares and serves coffee would do well to heed the admonition of Brillat-Savarin to "let the mistress of the house see to it that the coffee is excellent." First-rate coffee beverage is clear and has a high aroma. The color, which may range from deep amber to rich brown, depends on the strength of the brew and the degree of roast. Good coffee has a silky feel on the tongue. It has a mellow taste and is slightly astringent rather than either flat or excessively bitter. Coffee should be served piping hot. Some of the factors which influence the quality of coffee brew are discussed in the section that follows.

CONSTITUENTS IN THE COFFEE BEAN (GROUNDS)

The coffee used to make the beverage is ground, roasted beans (seeds) of the coffee tree. Climatic conditions in the country where the coffee is grown influence the character of the green coffee bean; the quality is modified by blending beans from different areas and by the roasting process.

EFFECTS OF ROASTING

Roasting brings about two kinds of changes in the green coffee berry. Structural changes are effected by tiny bubbles of steam that form as the green berry is heated. These make the roasted bean light and porous. This porosity makes possible greatly increased contact between water and ground coffee beans when the beverage is brewed. Even more important are the chemical changes. Some of these liberate or form compounds in the bean which influence the taste, the aroma, and the appearance of the brew. The color of the bean, which depends on the degree of roasting, varies from a light cinnamon to dark brown. The degree of roasting of course, affects the color of the beverage. Caramelized carbohydrates contribute to the color of the brew.

CAFFEINE

The roasted coffee bean contains 1.2 percent caffeine, a bitter constituent which gives the brew its stimulating effect. It is also a diuretic. Caffeine has the formula

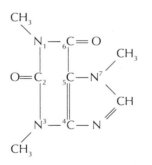

Caffeine (1,3,7-trimethylxanthine or methyl theobromine)

Theobromine differs from caffeine in that the former has a hydrogen instead of a methyl group at position 1. The caffeine content of coffee beverage varies with the method of brewing. For example, coffee made in a percolator, automatic or nonautomatic, averaged just over 100 milligrams per 5-ounce cup (150 ml). This contrasts with coffee made by the drip method which averaged appreciably more (142 mg and 151 mg per cup for nonautomatic and automatic drip coffee makers, respectively (1). The average caffeine content of instant freeze dried coffee (5 brands) was roughly two-thirds that of percolated coffee (66 mg per 5-oz cup). The caffeine content of cola beverages ranged from 32 mg to 65 mg per 12-ounce can. Values for decaffeinated coffee were 1 to 3 mg per cup for instant and 2 to 6 mg per cup for brewed decaffeinated (8).

CARBON DIOXIDE

Another constituent in roasted coffee that contributes to the quality of the beverage is carbon dioxide. This gas, which collects in the spaces in the coffee bean formed by the pockets of steam, is responsible for ground coffee floating when it first comes in contact with water. Some of the zip in the taste of the brew comes from the carbon dioxide.

ORGANIC ACIDS

Two of the acids found in roasted coffee are phenolic compounds. One of these is caffeic acid. The other (which contains caffeic acid) is chlorogenic acid, which has this formula.

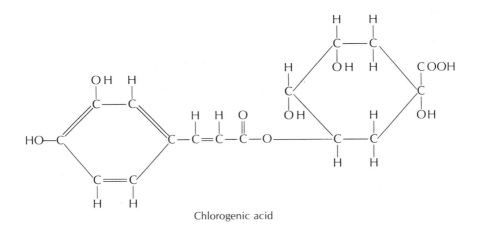

Chlorogenic acid

Chlorogenic acid is the main soluble constituent in coffee. It accounts for more than 4 percent of the weight of the roasted coffee bean and approximately two-thirds of all acid in coffee beverage. It is a somewhat sour and slightly bitter substance. Because of the quantity present it no doubt makes an appreciable contribution to the taste of the brew.

Other organic acids found in roasted coffee include citric, malic, tartaric, and somewhat smaller amounts of oxalic. These acids are readily extracted from roasted coffee, which explains why the taste of weak coffee is predominantly sour.

TRIGONELLINE

Another constituent, which makes up approximately 5 percent of the water-soluble material in roasted coffee, is trigonelline (the methylbetaine of nicotinic acid); its formula is

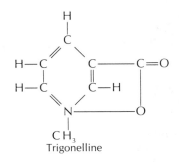

Trigonelline

Trigonelline is approximately one-fourth as bitter as caffeine. During the roasting of coffee, part of the trigonelline is converted to nicotinic acid so that coffee beverage averages 0.5 milligram of niacin per cup.

A number of volatile constituents are formed during roasting, and these interact with each other and with the breakdown products of carbohydrates to yield substances that contribute to the aroma of coffee (20).

COFFEE AROMA

The aroma of coffee has been more difficult to analyze than has the taste. More than 100 compounds have been identified in the volatiles from coffee. Several volatile organic acids are present, with acetic the main one. A number of aldehydes and ketones, including diacetyl, acetylmethyl carbinol, and furfural, are present. Pyridine, apparently formed from trigonelline during roasting, is present, as are guaiacol and p-vinyl guaiacol. The last two, together with carbon dioxide, are decomposition products of chlorogenic acid. Guaiacol is a brown, oily substance with a burnt or tarlike odor. The unsaturated nature of these compounds is illustated by the formulas given for two, furfural and guaiacol:

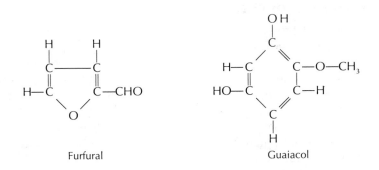

Furfural   Guaiacol

Recently furan and 2-methyl furan have been isolated from roasted coffee in appreciable amounts, as has dimethyl disulfide. No one of these constituents predominates in the aroma of coffee and the unique combination of substances essential for the characteristic aroma still is unknown. The presence of phenolic substances and of sulfur-containing compounds appear to distinguish the aroma of coffee from that of coffee substitutes.

PREPARING THE BREW

Although instant coffee has gained wide acceptance because of speed, convenience, and cost, it has not replaced brewed coffee. This section deals with some of the fine points of brewing the beverage.

A number of factors influence the concentration in the beverage of the various constituents from the ground coffee bean. Proportion of ground coffee to water and the freshness of the roasted coffee used to make the brew determine the amounts of these constituents available. The grind, the method used to brew the coffee, the temperature of the water, and the length of time it is in contact with the grounds influence the percentage of available constituents actually extracted and in the brew. All these factors affect the strength of coffee.

GRINDS

Grinds of coffee on the market are designated by such terms as fine, drip, flaked, electric percolator, and regular. The size of particles within any one grind varies greatly and difference in size of particles between grinds is not great. Terms used to designate the different grinds are confusing or inadequate. "Fine" refers to the size of the particles; "flaked" denotes shape; "drip" and "electric percolator" refer to methods for making coffee; "regular" has no obvious association. In general, the finer the grind, the smaller is the proportion of coffee to water needed to yield brews of comparable strength. The effect of the grind on the overall quality of the brew is an unsettled question, as is the issue of which grind is best for each type of coffee maker.

PROPORTIONS OF COFFEE TO WATER

The proportion of ground coffee to water initially determines the potential strength of the beverage. When 1 tablesoon of coffee per cup of water is used, the brew is weak, with 2 tablespoons a brew of medium strength is obtained, and with 3 tablespoons per cup of water the coffee is strong. The preferred strength of brewed coffee differs from one part of the country to another as well as from individual to individual. To ascertain the number of servings from a given amount of water and grounds, two points need to be considered. Coffee grounds retain a part of the water added and a full measuring cup of brew makes 1½ cups (servings) of coffee.

BREWING TEMPERATURE AND TIME

Hot water is applied to coffee grounds to make the brew: the hotter the water, the more solubles extracted (6). Substances responsible for the aroma are readily extracted, as are carbon dioxide and caffeine. The temperature of the water when it is in contact with the grounds should be at least 85°C (185°F) to extract enough soluble solids to give desired body. At this temperature nearly three-fourths of the caffeine is extracted. The maximum temperature recommended for the water when it is in contact with the grounds is 95°C (203°F). Water which is hotter than this extracts such a high proportion of soluble constituents as to make the beverage excessively bitter. Loss of carbon dioxide and of aroma from the beverage occurs, too. When the temperature of the water is at or near the maximum recommended and all of the hot water is in contact with the grounds at once, desirable proportions of the various constituents are extracted in 2 minutes' brewing time. Approximately 80 percent of the caffeine and of the trigonelline, nearly 70 percent of the chlorogenic acid, just under three-fourths of the total soluble solids, and somewhat more than half the color are extracted under these conditions (6). When coffee is made in a percolator, only a small amount of the water comes in contact with the grounds at any one time so percolation time needs to be longer. If contact time is too brief or if the water is not hot enough, the brew is flat and insipid and is predominantly sour. If brewing time is too long, the brew is likely to be unpalatably bitter and astringent.

The best beverages are those for which the brewing temperature and time are such as to extract 18 to 22 percent of the weight of the grounds. Overextraction (22 to 30 percent) gives a beverage that is excessively bitter. Connoisseurs of coffee have indicated a preference for coffee beverage which contains from 1.21 to 1.25 percent soluble solids. Substances dissolved in the brew affect the specific gravity, and measuring the specific gravity is a precise way to assess the strength of brewed coffee (17).

EFFECT OF WATER ON COFFEE BEVERAGE

The water used to brew coffee influences the quality of the beverage. Naturally soft water is best. Water may be brought to the boiling point before it is applied to the grounds, but it should not continue to boil. Boiled water tastes flat because of loss of dissolved air. Coffee made with such water also tastes flat. Substances dissolved in water which affect its taste are likely to influence the taste of the brew, too. Carbonate or bicarbonate ions in the water prolong the time water remains in contact with grounds, as does the presence of sodium ions in water softened by ion exchange.

METHODS FOR MAKING COFFEE

STEEPED COFFEE

There are four methods for brewing coffee. Steeping, popular for picnics and camping, is a simple method for which no special equipment is needed. The coffee grounds (regular grind usually recommended) are held in contact with hot water (above simmering but below boiling) for 2 to 4 minutes. The brew

Figure 7-1. Steeping method for making coffee. (From P. B. Potter and A. H. Fuller, Virginia Agricultural Experiment Station Bulletin 367, 1945. Reproduced by permission.)

is then decanted into a preheated pot. Steeped coffee can be very good indeed, but this method can also produce a most unpalatable brew. It is difficult to control the temperature during both the steeping period and that required for convection currents to settle the fine particles in the brew. If the grounds are mixed with egg white before they are put in the hot water, the coagulating egg white traps and carries down the fine particles. Steeped coffee prepared in this way is clear and mild in flavor. For steeping large quantities, the grounds may be tied loosely in a bag of cheesecloth or other porous fabric. See Figure 7-1.

PERCOLATED COFFEE

For coffee made in a percolator (Fig. 7-2), water near the boiling point is applied in small jets to grounds (regular grind usually recommended) in the perforated coffee basket. Steam, which exerts pressure on the surface of the water under the dome that is attached to the tube which supports the coffee basket, forces water up the tube and onto the coffee. Thus a percolator acts as a steam-jet pump. Once percolation begins, the heat should be adjusted so that the jets of water hit the lid of the percolator gently and approximately every 2 seconds. Percolation time, which depends on the speed of percolation, varies from 8 to 15 minutes. A perforated cover on top of the coffee basket spreads the water. The pot should be at least two-thirds full when the brew is made. When percolation stops, the grounds should be removed because they absorb aroma.

With this method of making coffee the temperature of water when it

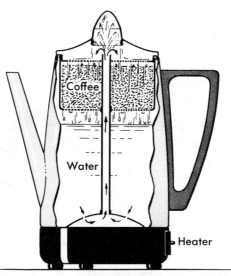

Figure 7-2. Sectional view of a percolator (valveless type). (From P. B. Potter and A. H. Fuller, Virginia Agricultural Experiment Station Bulletin 367, 1945. Reproduced by permission.)

contacts the grounds tends to be too high. All of the brew is at or near the boiling point for the entire period of percolation. For this reason much of the desirable aroma of the beverage is boiled away. In the case of a percolator with a valve, only that portion of the brew in the depression over which the valve fits boils before each jet of water. Some electric percolators are equipped with a valve.

COFFEE IN A VACUUM COFFEE MAKER

A third method of making coffee is in a vacuum coffee maker. Steam confined in the base of a vacuum coffee maker exerts pressure on the surface of the boiling water (see Fig. 7-3). This forces the water, against gravity, up the tube of the coffee maker and onto the coffee grounds (fine grind usually recommended). If the coffee maker is assembled before the water boils, the water will rise to the grounds before it is hot enough to give good extraction. A layer of water remains in the base to maintain steam and to keep the base from cracking or warping. Steam is essential for the working of a vacuum coffee maker just as it is with a percolator. The heat should be lowered to give just enough steam to hold the water in contact with the grounds for from 2 to 4 minutes. The dry grounds will float, so to ensure good contact with water the grounds should be stirred.

When the coffee maker is removed from the heat, the steam condenses. As a vacuum begins to form the beverage is drawn down into the lower part. If the seal between the upper and lower parts of a vacuum coffee maker is broken, a vacuum will not form; the beverage will remain in the funnel part

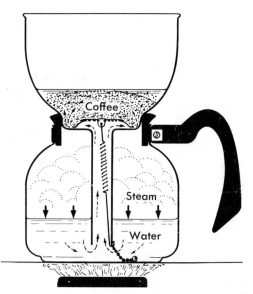

Figure 7-3. Sectional view of a vacuum coffee maker. (From P. B. Potter and A. H. Fuller, Virginia Agricultural Experiment Station Bulletin 367, 1945. Reproduced by permission.)

with the grounds. Should this happen, the funnel should be adjusted so the seal forms and the coffee maker returned to the hot unit until the lower part again is filled with steam. When this condenses, a vacuum forms and the beverage will be pulled to the lower part. Coffee made this way usually has good flavor because the beverage never boils.

COFFEE IN A DRIP COFFEE MAKER

The fourth method for brewing coffee is in a drip coffee maker, automatic or nonautomatic (Figs. 7-4 and 7-5). Freshly boiling water is poured into the water receptacle or the cold water is heated in it. From this the hot water drips or flows to the ground coffee in the basket below (drip grind usually recommended). From the grounds the brew drips (again by gravity) through the perforated bottom of the coffee basket and into the preheated pot below. A filter in the bottom of the coffee basket holds back fine particles and ensures a clear brew. The number and size of the holes in the water basket control the rate at which the water flows onto the grounds. The number and size of the holes in the coffee basket influence how fast the beverage leaves the grounds. Efficiency of extraction depends mainly on construction of the drip coffee maker and the fineness of the coffee used. Regardless of the brewing method, the grounds should be removed from the coffee maker at the end of the extraction period, as they absorb aroma from the beverage. A filtered coffee maker works on the same principle as a drip coffee maker.

Figure 7-4. Sectional view of a drip coffee maker. (From P. B. Potter and A. H. Fuller, Virginia Agricultural Experiment Station Bulletin 367, 1945. Reproduced by permission.)

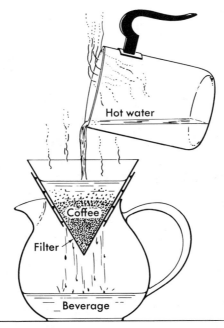

Figure 7-5. Another type of drip coffee maker. (From P. B. Potter and A. H. Fuller, Virginia Agricultural Experiment Station Bulletin 367, 1945. Reproduced by permission.)

MATERIAL FROM WHICH THE COFFEE MAKER IS MADE

A coffee maker of nonmetal is preferable because metals affect the flavor adversely. Utensils of glass or pottery are good from this standpoint. The oily guaiacol, plus fats, oils, and waxes, make it hard to keep a metal coffee pot clean. Utensils should be washed thoroughly with hot water containing soap or detergent to remove the oily film that collects. They should be rinsed just as thoroughly, because traces of soap or detergent spoil the taste of the brew.

EFFECTS OF HOLDING ON BREWED COFFEE

Coffee is improved if it is held at serving temperature for a few minutes (3 to 5) before it is served. Individual constituents merge and blend and the brew becomes more mellow in flavor during this ripening period. If coffee beverage is held longer, some loss of flavor results (15). Interaction of constituents in the brew or loss of volatile substances may account for deterioration. If the beverage must be held for an hour, a holding temperature of 93°C (200°F) is preferred to lower temperatures. Brews held for longer times deteriorated less at lower holding temperatures (15). Color and clarity are not so good if the brew is held much longer than 1 hour.

STALING OF COFFEE

CHANGES INVOLVED

Constituents in the green coffee bean are quite stable. When the bean is roasted, this is no longer true. Once it is ground and exposed to the air, the roasted bean has an even more limited storage life. The staling of coffee is accompanied by a loss of carbon dioxide. In addition, the guaiacol becomes oxidized, and changes in the unsaturated volatile compounds alter their odor and possibly make them less soluble in water. Coffee brewed from stale grounds tastes flat and lacks aroma.

SUGGESTIONS FOR RETARDING STALING

Freshness of ground coffee is maintained commercially by sealing it in a container under a vacuum. Once a container of vacuum-packed coffee is opened, it should be handled in such a way as to minimize staling. Storing the grounds in a cool place will delay the onset of staleness. A storage temperature of 4.4°C (40°F) is superior to 18°C (65°F) or higher (1). Even more detrimental to freshness than heat is moisture (3). Were it possible to keep moisture-laden air away from ground coffee, it would remain reasonably fresh up to six weeks. From a practical standpoint, this is not possible. Once a can of coffee is opened, contact with moist air should be kept to a minimum and the contents of the can kept cool.

For those who like a hot beverage without the stimulating effect of caffeine, decaffeinated coffee is available. However, some of the full coffee flavor is removed along with the caffeine. Instant coffee is made by removing the moisture from brewed coffee. In the process some of the aroma of the brew is lost. This loss is minimized in freeze-dried coffee. Coffee substitute is made from a blend of toasted cereals.

TEA

Tea is the most universally used beverage. It is prepared from the dried shoots of an evergreen shrub, *Thea sinensis,* a camellia. The main tea-producing areas are India, China, Sri Lanka (Ceylon), Japan, and Taiwan. In the United States, standards for purity, quality, and fitness for consumption of imported tea are maintained under the authority of the Tea Importation Act of 1897.

KINDS OF TEA

High quality tea comes from the bud and the first two leaves of the growing shoot, although more mature leaves are used in some teas. The quality of tea beverage is influenced by the climate where the tea plant is grown. Teas also differ because of the way the leaves are treated before they are dried (12). For green tea, the fresh leaves are heated or steamed to inactivate enzymes before they are rolled and dried. For black tea, the leaves are allowed to wither before they are rolled. Then they are held a few hours before they are heated and dried. During this holding period enzymes in the green leaf catalyze the oxidation of constituents which results in changes in color, taste, and aroma. Such tea is described as fermented, although the changes are due mainly to oxidation. Oolong tea is only partly fermented and a brew from Oolong tea has some of the characteristics of both green and black tea. More than nine-tenths of the tea consumed in the United States is black tea. Tea is dried to a moisture content of approximately 3 percent.

QUALITY OF THE BEVERAGE

Tea beverage of high-quality is clear and bright. A flavorful cup of tea has a quality known as "briskness," and a distinct but subtle aroma. Some astringency is inherent in tea, but green tea is more astringent than black. The strength of the beverage determines whether the taste of the tea is mild or robust. Green tea is pale, greenish yellow, and the black tea is a deep amber color.

CONSTITUENTS IN TEA

CAFFEINE

Tea beverage, as with coffee, is valued for the stimulating effect of the caffeine which it contains. Tea leaves contain more caffeine (2.7 to 4.6 percent of the dried green tea leaf) than does roasted coffee, but the concentration in the beverage averages somewhat less in tea. Values found in the literature include 70 mg, per cup of beverage (type of tea and details of steeping unspecified) (8) and 28 mg, 44 mg, and 47 mg per cup for black tea in bags (three brands) steeped 1, 3, and 5 minutes, respectively (1). Comparable values given for loose black tea were 31 mg, 38 mg, and 40 mg per cup of beverage. Green and Oolong tea beverages, bagged or loose, contained less caffeine than black tea. Tea contains, in addition to caffeine, small amounts of two other methyl xanthines, theobromine and theophylline, dimethyl and monomethyl xanthine, respectively (12).

PHENOLIC CONSTITUENTS IN GREEN TEA

Tea leaves are extraordinarily rich sources of a group of compounds known as polyphenolic substances, which account for almost one-third of the weight of dried leaf (11). The color of the beverage and much of its taste, especially astringency, is attributed to these polyphenolic compounds, or to their oxidation products in black tea. Green tea contains a number of flavonols with the basic structure

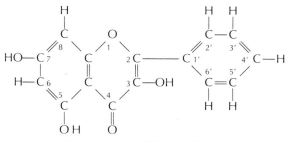

Basic structure of flavonols in tea

Specific flavonols found in tea include myricetin (hydroxyls at carbons 3', 4', and 5'), quercetin (hydroxyls at positions 3' and 4'), and kaempferol (hydroxyl at position 4'), and their glycosides.

Other phenolic compounds found in tea in even greater concentration than the flavonols are the flavanols. This group constitutes 80 percent of the total polyphenols in tea. These include catechin and gallocatechin (hydroxyls at positions 5' as well as at 3' and 4' as in catechin), their esters with gallic acid, catechin gallate, and gallocatechin gallate, and their epimers. The formulas for these phenolic compounds are

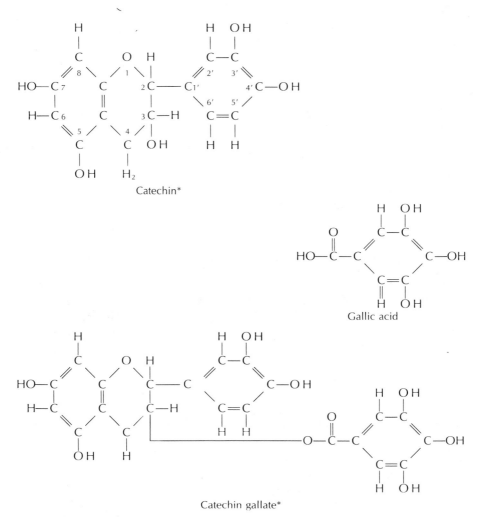

Catechin*

Gallic acid

Catechin gallate*

*Gallocatechin and gallocatechin gallate have an −OH at carbon 5'.

*Epi*gallocatechin gallate is the main flavanol in dried green tea. The catechins are responsible for the slightly astringent, metallic taste of green tea beverage. They are involved also in browning and other types of discoloration in foods of plant origin. (See Chapters 27 and 28.) Another phenolic constituent in tea, theogallin, accounts for approximately 1 percent of the dry weight of the leaf. Chlorogenic acid, also a phenolic compound, is a minor constituent in tea.

PHENOLIC CONSTITUENTS IN BLACK TEA

More than three-fourths of the polyphenolic constituents of tea may be extracted after the leaves are fermented. In addition to those compounds found in green tea, new ones appear in black tea (12). Rolling the leaves prior to fermentation permits the polyphenolase enzyme to come in contact with the phenolic substrates and catalyze their oxidation. Theaflavins which are formed when flavanols are oxidized make up approximately 2 percent of the weight of dried black tea. Alone, they are very astringent, and the amount of caffeine in tea should make it very bitter. It appears that theaflavins modify the bitterness of caffeine and caffeine the astringency of theaflavins, giving the beverage its characteristic briskness (7,11).

A second group of substances which appear in fermented tea are the thearubigins, the structures of which are still questioned (12). These constitute from 7 to 20 percent of the weight of dried black tea. The bright orange theaflavins give sparkle to tea and the rusty brown thearubigins depth to the color. As fermentation proceeds the thearubigins increase and the theaflavins decrease.

The concentration of phenolic substances is greatest in the bud and the first leaf of the harvested tea shoot, is progressively less in leaves 1 to 3 and is least in the stem. A high phenolic content gives a tea with a high color. Tea leaves are separated into classes according to size and so marketed. The terms "orange pekoe," "pekoe," and "souchong" denote progressively larger leaves of black tea. The prefix "broken" inserted before each term indicates that the leaves are not intact. Smaller pieces of tea leaves are known as "fannings" and fragments which are finer still are designated "dust." These are used in tea bags.

AROMA

The aroma of tea contributes to its appeal. The volatile compounds responsible have been referred to as essential oils. Approximately 30 compounds have been identified in the aroma of green tea, the major ones being benzyl alcohol, phenylethyl alcohol, a hexenol, linalool, geraniol, and methyl salicylate (21). The aroma of black tea is more complex. More than 300 compounds are present, half of which have been identified and none of which alone gives a unique black tea aroma (14). The breakdown of amino acids which occurs as the flavanols are oxidized gives rise to aldehydes in black tea aroma (3). Theanine, the ethyl amide of glutamic acid, is the main amino acid in the fresh leaf (2) and contributes 1 to 2 percent of the dried weight, but other amino acids arise during the early part of the processing. *Trans*-2-hexenal formed from linolenic acid is a major component of the aroma (5). Other constituents are thought to come from the oxidation of carotenoids of the leaf (13).

PREPARING TEA BEVERAGE

STEEPING TEMPERATURE AND TIME

Desired soluble constituents, some of which are volatile, are extracted from tea leaves by steeping the leaves in hot water. The temperature of the water when it is in contact with the leaves is as important in making tea as it is in making coffee. Water which has just come to a rolling boil, not boiled water which makes flat-tasting tea, should be added at once to tea leaves in a pre-heated pot. Unless the pot is very hot, the temperature of the water will drop too low during steeping for the best extraction. A lid on the pot as the tea steeps helps prevent loss of heat and escape of steam and aroma from the beverage.

A steeping period of 5 minutes with water at 88°C (190°F) is required to give tea of the same strength as that steeped 3 minutes at a temperature of 93°C (200°F) (10). Minimum temperature of the water when it is in contact with tea leaves is simmering (85°C, or 185°F), and at this temperature (which should be maintained for the entire period of extraction) the time required to steep tea is 6 to 7 minutes. Extracting caffeine from the tea leaves is not a problem because a high percentage of it is removed in 2 minutes by water at 85°C (185°F). Thearubigins are more readily extracted than theaflavins (16). If water boils when it is in contact with tea leaves, a high proportion of poly-phenolic compounds are extracted. These make the hot beverage excessively astringent.

The tea pot should be made of a material other than metal. This is even more important for tea than for coffee because of the high proportion of poly-phenolic substances in tea.

EFFECT OF ACID ON COLOR OF BLACK TEA

The color of black-tea beverage is influenced by the hydrogen-ion concentration of the water. Thearubigins in tea brew are weak acids that ionize. The anions are highly colored. If the water used to brew tea is alkaline, the color of the beverage is deeper, an effect due to greater ionization of thearubigins. If acid is added to tea, the hydrogen ions depress the ionization of thearubigins, which makes the beverage lighter. This accounts for the effect of lemon juice on the color of tea. Theaflavins are not involved in the change in color of tea associated with a change in acidity.

CLOUDY TEA

Under certain conditions chilled tea beverage becomes cloudy or turbid. Formation of a complex between caffeine and theaflavins and thearubigins is believed to be responsible. The caffeine carries a positive charge and the thearubigin ions a negative charge. When the concentration of the two is high, a precipitate forms. The stronger the tea, the more likely is the complex to form. It is most likely to occur if the water is allowed to boil when it is in contact with the leaves. Iced tea is more likely to become cloudy than hot tea. This complex can be broken by adding hot water or acid to the beverage.

STORAGE OF TEA

Staleness of tea is not as obvious as is staleness of coffee, but loss of flavor does occur as tea is stored (18). Oxidation of fatty acids and theaflavins and loss of theanine and volatile aldehydes occur. High moisture (6.5 to 7.5 percent) is particularly detrimental. Tea should be stored in a closed container at a temperature below 30°C.

CHOCOLATE MILK AND COCOA

Chocolate and cocoa beverages which are made with milk occupy a somewhat different place in the diet from coffee and tea. Chocolate (cooking and baking) is the solidified liquor formed when fermented cacao beans are pulverized. Cocoas are made by removing much of the fat, called cocoa butter, from the liquor and then pulverizing the remaining solids. Chocolate and cocoa beverages have one thing in common with coffee and tea. All contain methyl xanthines, but theobromine predominates over caffeine in chocolate and cocoa (22). The theobromine content of hot chocolate made from five cocoa mixes currently available averaged 65 mg per 5-oz cup and the caffeine content 4 mg per cup. Values for chocolate milk (four different mixes) averaged 58 mg theobromine and 2 mg caffeine for an 8-oz glass.

REFERENCES

1. Bunker, M. L., and M. McWilliams. 1979. Caffeine content of common beverages *J. Am. Dietet. Assoc.* **74:** 28–32. Coffee, instant and brewed; tea, loose and in bags; cola beverages.
2. Cartwright, R. A., E. A. H. Roberts, and D. J. Wood. 1954. Theanine, an amino-acid N-ethyl amide present in tea. *J. Sci. Food Agric.* **5:** 597–599. The main amino acid, accounting for 1–2 percent of the dried leaf.
3. Co, H., and G. W. Sanderson. 1970. Biochemistry of tea fermentation: Conversion of amino acids to black tea aroma constituents. *J. Food Sci.* **35:** 160–164. Source of part of tea aroma.
4. Farber, I. 1959. Volatile reducing substances and the evolution of the aroma of coffee. *Food Research* **24:** 72–78. Effect of storage temperature on loss of volatile constituents.
5. Gonzales, J. G., P. Coggon, and G. W. Sanderson. 1972. Biochemistry of tea fermentation: Formation of *t*-2-hexenal from linolenic acid. *J. Food Sci.* **37:** 797–798. A major constituent in tea aroma.
6. Merritt, M. C., and B. E. Proctor. 1959. Extraction rates for selected components of coffee brew. *Food Research* **24:** 735–743. Effects of time and temperature on extraction of main constituents.
7. Millin, D. J., D. J. Crispin, and D. Swaine. 1969. Non-volatile components of black tea and their contribution to the character of the beverage. *J. Agr. Food Chem.* **17:** 717–721. Constituents that contribute to the taste of black tea.
8. Nagy, M. 1974. Caffeine content of beverages and chocolate. *J. Amer. Med. Assn.* **229:** 337. Brewed, instant, decaffeinated coffee, and cola drinks.
9. Prescott, S. C., R. L. Emerson, and L. V. Peakes, Jr. 1937. The staling of coffee. *Food Research* **2:** 1–19. An attempt to analyze the staling of coffee; effect of humidity on staling.

10. Punnett, P. W. 1955. The role of temperature in tea brewing. *Tea and Coffee Trade J.* **109:** 73–74. Effect of temperature on brewing time and on quality of tea beverage.

11. Roberts, E. A. H. 1958. Chemistry of tea manufacture. *J. Sci. Food. Agr.* **9:** 381–390. Phenolic constituents in both green and black tea.

12. Sanderson, G. W. 1972. The chemistry of tea and tea manufacturing. In *Recent Advances in Phytochemistry.* V. C. Runeckles, ed. New York: Academic Press. Vol. V: 247–315. A review.

13. Sanderson, G. W., H. Co, and J. G. Gonzales. 1971. Biochemistry of tea fermentation: the role of carotenes in black tea aroma formation. *J. Food Sci.* **36:** 231–236. Beta-carotene as a source of odorous compounds.

14. Sanderson, G. W., and H. N. Graham. 1973. On the formation of black tea aroma. *J. Sci. Food Agric.* **21:** 576–585. A summary.

15. Segall, S., and B. E. Proctor. 1959. The influence of high holding temperature upon the components of coffee brew. *Food Technol.* **13:** 266–269. An attempt to pinpoint causes for deterioration of flavor in the brew. Technical.

16. Smith, R. F., and G. W. White. 1965. Measurement of color in tea infusions. II. Effects of methods of preparation on the color of tea infusions. *J. Sci. Food Agric.* **16:** 212–219. Effects of water quality and steeping time on extraction of theaflavins and thearubigins.

17. Sprague, E. 1925. Studies of coffee making by precise methods. *J. Home Econ.* **17:** 206–211. An early attempt to assess objectively the strength of coffee brew.

18. Stagg. G. V. 1974. Chemical changes during the storage of black tea. *J. Sci. Food Agric.* **25:** 1015–1034. Importance of low moisture.

19. United States Department of Agriculture. *National Food Review.* Economics, Statistics, and Cooperatives Service A. 1980 (Winter). NFR-9, p. 51. Per capita consumption of major foods.

20. Viani, R., and I. Horman. 1974. Thermal behavior of trigonelline. *J. Food Sci.* **39:** 1216–1217. Products of pyrolysis.

21. Yamanishi, T., T. Kiribuchi, M. Sakai, N. Fugita, Y. Ikeda, and K. Sasa. 1963. Studies on the flavor of green tea. Part V. Examination of the essential oil of the tea leaves by gas liquid chromatography. *Agr. Biol. Chem.* **27:** 193–198. Major components of the approximately 30 identified.

22. Zoumas, B. L., W. R. Kreiser, and R. A. Martin. 1980. Theobromine and caffeine content of chocolate products. *J. Food Sci.* **45:** 314–316. Cocoa, chocolate, and chocolate beverages analyzed.

EIGHT
Starches and Vegetable Gums

Starch is an important constituent in many foods. It helps achieve the desired consistency in such products as tapioca and cornstarch puddings, gravies and sauces, and soft pie fillings. Starch plays a role in the quality of both cooked potatoes and rice. In terms of quantity, it is the main constituent in flour and an important one in products that contain flour, such as biscuits, muffins, bread, pastry, and cake. The role of starch in each of these products is discussed in subsequent chapters. Starch as a thickening agent and the factors that affect its thickening power are emphasized in this chapter.

At the outset it is well to keep in mind that the term "starch" is used with two different meanings. Certain types of molecules are referred to as starch. In the cells of plants these starch molecules are organized into microscopic packages or granules. These granules or grains are referred to as starch, too. When a recipe specifies a quantity of starch, it is starch in the granular form that is meant. The functional properties of granular starch in foods stem from the nature of the starch molecules and their unique organization within the granule. To understand the fundamental role of starch in food preparation, some knowledge both of starch molecules and of their arrangement within the granule is essential.

STARCH CHEMISTRY

GLUCOSE

Molecules of starch are polymers of the simple sugar (or monosaccharide), glucose. Glucose is a hexose, that is, a sugar with 6 carbon atoms in the molecule. The cluster of atoms which make up each glucose molecule is tightly packed. Molecules of glucose in solution exist in both the aldehyde and the pyranose (ring) structures, as shown on the following page. The ring structures of glucose predominate (15). The two ring structures, α-D-glucose and β-D-glucose, differ only in the orientation of the hydroxyl group at carbon 1. In the alpha, (α) form, this hydroxyl group is oriented in the same direction

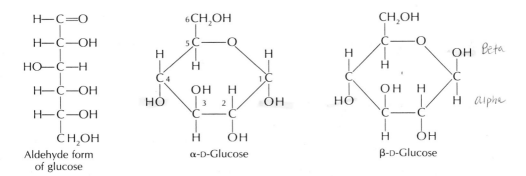

| Aldehyde form of glucose | α-D-Glucose | β-D-Glucose |

as the hydroxyl at carbon 4. In the beta (β) form the hydroxyl groups at carbons 1 and 4 are oriented in opposite directions. A starch molecule is made of glucose with the pyranose structure, and in the alpha rather than the beta form.

MALTOSE

Two α-D-glucose molecules linked through carbon 1 of one molecule and carbon 4 of the other (with a glycosidic linkage and the elimination of one molecule of water) give rise to a molecule of the disaccharide, maltose, as shown:

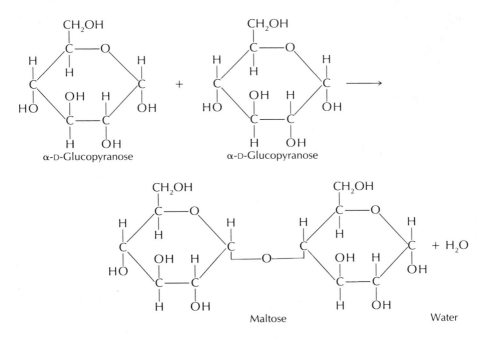

Three glucose molecules joined by this maltose-type linkage form a triose. A chain of several such glucose residues is called a dextrin.

STARCH MOLECULES

When the glucose units in a molecule exceed a certain number, the resulting high polymer is called "starch." Estimates of the number of glucose residues in molecules of starch vary from 400 to 4000 in some to several hundred thousands in others. The fewer the glucose residues, the more soluble is the compound. Maltose with two residues is soluble, as are most dextrins. But when the polymer is long, as in starch, molecules are too large to form true solutions.

Two types of starch molecules are synthesized by plants. In some molecules all the glucose residues are united through the 1,4-linkage as in maltose. Such a linear starch molecule is called "amylose," a fragment of which is shown:

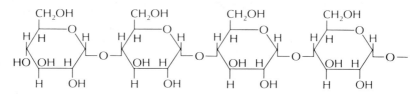

Unlike linear amylose, molecules of amylopectin are branched. Branching occurs at intervals of 15 to 30 glucose residues. The linkage is between carbon 1 of the branch and carbon 6 of the glucose residue to which the branch is attached, as shown:

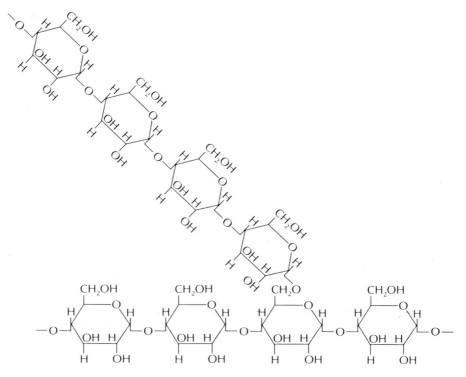

Such branching gives a bushy shrub effect to molecules of amylopectin and tends to make them less readily dispersible in water.

Molecules of starch and especially amylose exist in water as random coils (1). In the presence of certain fatty substances or molecules of iodine, starch assumes the shape of a helix, with 6 to 7 glucose residues comprising each coil. The space inside each coil accommodates a molecule of iodine, and this complex makes possible the iodine test for starch. The color of the complex depends on the length of the helix and thus on the number of iodine molecules involved. If the helix is long, the iodine-starch complex is blue; if short, the complex is red.

OTHER POLYSACCHARIDES

Glycogen, a polymer of glucose synthesized by animals, is more highly branched than is amylopectin. Cellulose is also a polymer of glucose, but glucose in the β-pyranose form. Two molecules of β-D-glucose united through carbons 1 and 4 give rise to the disaccharide, cellobiose, as shown:

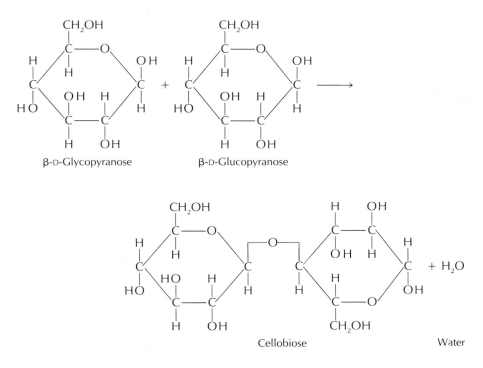

β-D-Glycopyranose   β-D-Glucopyranose

Cellobiose   Water

This compound is analogous to maltose. When a sufficient number of such units are joined, the resulting polymer is cellulose. Thus both starch and cellulose are polymers of glucose in the pyranose (ring) form. The marked differences in the chemical and physical properties of starch and cellulose are attributed to the presence of the α-1,4-linkage in the former and the β-1,4-linkage in the latter.

STARCH GRANULES

SIZE AND SHAPE

As starch molecules are formed by the plant, they are deposited in the amyloplasts of the cell. These eventually become the starch grains or granules. (See Fig. 28-4.) Starch grains from different plants have characteristic sizes and shapes. Diameters vary from 2 to 150 microns. Those from rice are the smallest of the grains of starch produced by plants; they average 3 to 8 microns in diameter and are polygonal in shape. Tapioca from the root of the cassava plant and cornstarch from the endosperm cells of corn average 12 to 25 microns. The former are round and the latter are either round or polygonal. Wheat starch grains are of two types. The small, spherical ones average 10 microns in diameter and the larger lentil- or discus-shaped ones are approximately 35 microns in diameter. Potato starch grains which are large (starch grains from canna are the largest) can be identified by their oyster shell shape and by the appearance of distinct concentric rings or striations. Photomicrographs of starches from different sources are shown in Figure 8-1. One pound of cornstarch contains an estimated 800 billion starch grains. A scanning electron micrograph of wheat starch is found in Figure 8-2.

INTERNAL ORGANIZATION

The starch grains of most plants consist of approximately one-fourth amylose molecules and three-fourths amylopectin molecules. However, certain plants have the ability to make starch grains which contain a high proportion of either amylose or amylopectin molecules. The coupling of glucose residues by the 1,4-linkage depends on the presence in the plant of one specific enzyme, that of the 1,6-linkage on a second enzyme (15,17). The relative amounts of the two types of starch molecules which a plant makes is attributed to the ratio of the two enzymes in the plant, an inherited characteristic determined by the genes. The proportion of the two types of starch molecules within starch grains influences their behavior in cooking.

A special type of cornstarch has been on the market for a number of years which contains amylopectin molecules only (18). This is known as waxy or nongelling cornstarch and is marketed under the trade names of Amioca and Clearjel. Branched amylopectin molecules predominate in Chinese glutinous rice, also. A corn plant has been developed by selective breeding which produces starch that is predominately amylose. This high-amylose cornstarch lends itself to the formation of transparent, edible packaging films.

Microscopic examination of starch grains provides clues to the arrangement of the starch molecules within. For microscopic examination, an easily available source of fresh starch grains is a slice of potato. Starch grains readily wash from the cut cells. For observation under the microscope, the starch grains can be mounted in either water or glycerine. Concentric striations visible on the surface of some granules are beautifully illustrated in the photo-

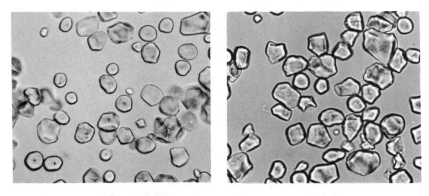

(a)   (b)

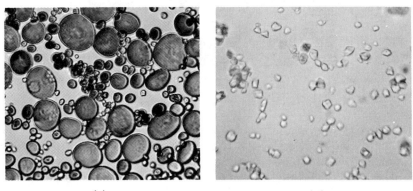

(c)   (d)

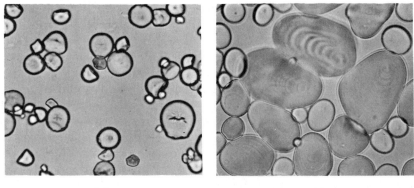

(e)   (f)

Figure 8-1. Photomicrographs of starch grains from different plants: (a) corn, (b) waxy corn, (c) wheat, (d) rice, (e) tapioca, (f) potato. Original magnification X 500. (Courtesy of R. J. Dimler, USDA Northern Regional Research Center, Peoria, Ill.)

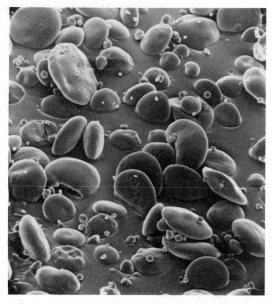

Figure 8-2. Scanning electron micrograph of wheat starch grains. (From R. C. Hoseney, W. A. Atwell, and D. R. Lineback, *Cereal Foods World* **22**(2): 57, 1977. Reprinted by permission.)

micrograph of starch grains from the potato berry shown in Figure 8-3. These same starch grains viewed under crossed nicol prisms are shown in Figure 8-4. As polarized light is transmitted through a starch grain, the granule appears to be divided into brilliantly colored quadrants. One pair of opposite quadrants is one color, the other pair a second color. This is a characteristic of highly ordered material.

Starch grains which have been partially digested either by acid or by enzymes show that all areas of the grains are not equally resistant to attack. Concentric striations and radial cracks and fractures which give rise to pie-shaped fragments are observed (15,17). (See Fig. 8-5.) These indicate that the starch molecules within a granule are not deposited in a uniform manner or that the bonding forces differ. Even so, the order within the granule is evident. The granules are believed to be made of starch molecules laid down in concentric rings which in cross section look like the rings in a slice of onion. Starch molecules which make up a layer are deposited in a radial fashion and more or less parallel to each other. Certain parts of each ring are believed to be in a compact, highly ordered crystalline state. These radially arranged crystallites are linked by amorphous areas in which the starch molecules are deposited in a less orderly fashion (Fig. 8-6). Presumably, hydrogen bonds are the forces which hold starch molecules together in the less ordered regions as well as in the crystalline areas. Information about the submicroscopic organization of the starch grain is obtained from x-ray and electron-microscopic studies. The close packing and orderly arrangement of starch molecules within

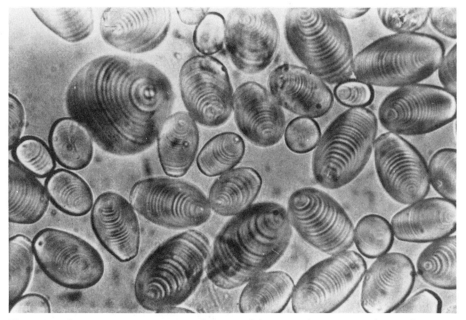

Figure 8-3. Concentric striations on starch grains of the potato berry. Original magnification X 750. (From C. T. Greenwood and S. MacKenzie, "An Investigation of the Starch of the Fruit of the Potato *Solanum tuberosum*," *Die Stärke* **15**: 251, 1963. Reproduced by permission.)

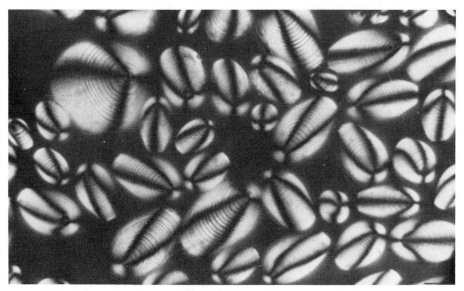

Figure 8-4. Photomicrograph of starch grains (of Figure 8-3) under polarized light, showing crosses that suggest a sphero-crystalline structure. (From C. T. Greenwood and S. MacKenzie, "An Investigation of the Starch of the Fruit of the Potato *Solanum tuberosum*," *Die Stärke* **15**: 251, 1963. Reproduced by permission.)

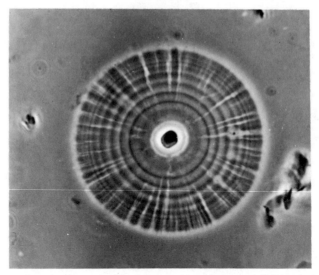

Figure 8-5. A starch grain digested with alpha-amylase, showing radial cracks and concentric laminations. (From R. M. Sandstedt, *Cereal Science* Today **10:** 312, 1965. Reprinted by permission.)

granules are believed to account for some of the functional properties of starch in food preparation.

STARCH AS A THICKENING AGENT

REVERSIBLE SWELLING OF STARCH

Starch grains are formed in a watery medium inside the living cells of plants. The starch of commerce consists of starch grains from which most of the moisture has been removed. As the grain dries, molecules of starch pack more closely and the grain shrinks. When uncooked and undamaged starch grains are put into cold water, they absorb water and swell (15). However, the amount of water absorbed and the swell are limited. The small increase in volume which takes place in water at room temperature is a true swelling and is reversible. Crystallinity and birefringence of the granules are unchanged. The uptake of water is exothermic.

PASTING OR GELATINIZATION

Starch grains can be induced to swell enormously by heating them in excess water. This pasting, commonly referred to as gelatinization, is irreversible. The water may be in the food itself, as in a potato as it bakes, or it may be combined with the starch as a liquid in a pudding or sauce.

NATURE OF THE PROCESS.   When the kinetic energy of the water molecules in contact with the starch grains becomes great enough to overcome the attraction between the hydrogen bonded starch molecules within the granule,

Figure 8-6. Organization of starch molecules within a granule, as originally conceived by the botanist, Arthur Meyer, in 1895. Branching trichitic crystals are pictured in radial orientation, with concentric layers in the granules attributed to alternate shells of dense and loose packing. (From T. J. Schoch, *Brewer's Digest* **37**(2): 43, 1962. Reprinted by permission.)

water molecules can penetrate the starch grain, first in the less dense areas and, as the temperature rises, in the crystalline areas. The two diagrams in Figure 8-7 may help to visualize what happens inside a starch grain as it is pasted (17). The diagram on the left represents the compact arrangement of starch molecules in a section of one concentric ring of a grain of starch before it is gelatinized; that on the right represents the less dense, water-inflated structure of a section of a gelatinized starch grain. The network has expanded but remains, held together by the crystallites.

The uptake of water by starch grains begins at a temperature that varies with the source of the starch. As it occurs, the milky suspension becomes less

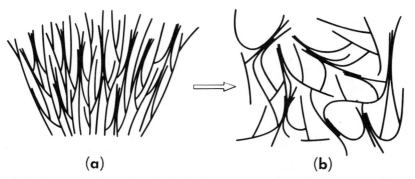

(a)   **(b)**

Figure 8-7. A segment of a starch grain showing the mechanism of pasting, as visualized by high-polymer chemist, K. H. Meyer (1940). (a) Unheated segment is held together by crystalline micelles (shown as thickened areas). These consist of sections of linear chains of amylose associated by hydrogen bonding with linear branches of amylopectin. (b) Hydration, which occurs as pasting proceeds, results in more micellar spaces. The network of starch molecules within the pasted granule, although expanded, remains because of the micelles that persist. (From T. J. Schoch, *Brewer's Digest* **37**(2): 45, 1962. Reprinted by permission.)

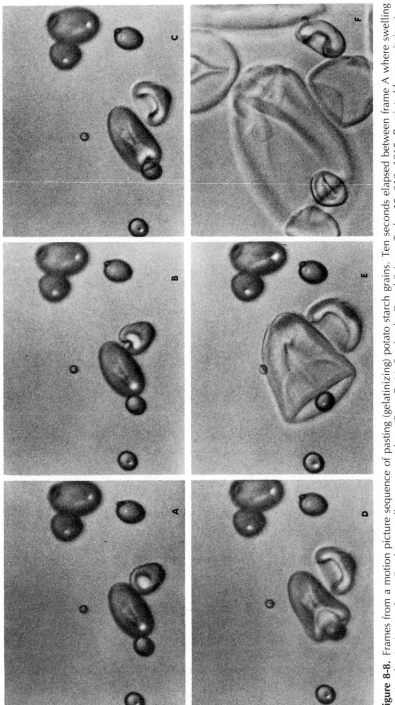

Figure 8-8. Frames from a motion picture sequence of pasting (gelatinizing) potato starch grains. Ten seconds elapsed between frame A where swelling was just beginning, to frame F, where swellng was complete. (From R. M. Sandstedt, *Cereal Science Today* **10**: 312, 1965. Reprinted by permission.)

opaque and more translucent and the swelling grains lose their birefringence and initiate thickening of the liquid. The enlarged frames from a motion picture sequence of the pasting of potato starch grains shown in Figure 8-8 are instructive (15). Only 10 seconds elapsed from frame A, where swelling is just beginning, to frame F, where it is complete. Note both the increase in size and the increase in translucency of the gelatinizing grains and, in frame E and especially in frame F, the folding of the swollen grains. The increase in translucency is because the refractive index of the swollen grains is near that of water. Because of the great number of hydroxyl groups on starch molecules, starch grains can absorb large amounts of water. Such water-inflated grains behave as elastic, fragile blobs of jelly.

Even when the grains have lost their birefringence and swollen the maximum, thickening is incomplete because additional heating of the suspension results in additional thickening (10). Thus the pasting of starch is now considered to occur in stages, the final increase in thickness as heating continues attributed to an exudate from the swollen grains. (See Fig. 8-9.) Peak viscosity of a cooked paste coincides with release of the exudate and folding (deformation) of swollen starch grains. The grains are now less dense and so remain suspended in the liquid and are assisted by the presence of the exudate which is considered responsible for most of the thickening.

Gelatinized starch grains can be dried, but they do not return to their original condition. The pasted dried grains do retain the ability to reabsorb large amounts of water. This characteristic of pasted starches (referred to as pregelatinized) is utilized to make such convenience foods high in starch as instant rice, instant mashed potatoes, and instant puddings (20).

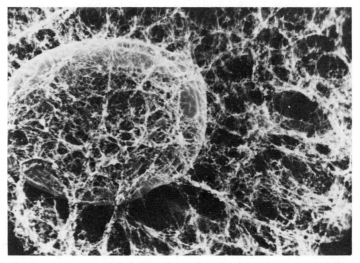

Figure 8-9. Exudate from a pasted (gelatinized) starch grain shown in a scanning electron micrograph (X 1200). (From B. S. Miller, R. I. Derby, and H. B. Trimbo, *Cereal Chemistry* **50**: 279, 1973. Reprinted by permission.)

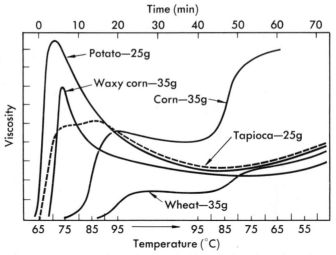

Figure 8-10. Changes in viscosity during heating, holding, and cooling of starch pastes. Concentration of starch in grams per 450 milliliters of water. (Reprinted from T. J. Schoch and A. L. Elder, "Starches in the Food Industry," in *Uses of Sugars and Other Carbohydrates in the Food Industry,* Advances in Chemistry Series No. 12, p. 24, 1955. Copyright © 1955 by the American Chemical Society and reprinted by permission of the copyright owner.)

EFFECT OF TEMPERATURE.   All starch grains from a single plant source are not pasted at the same temperature. The larger grains tend to swell at a lower temperature. The range in gelatinization temperature varies for different starches. The increase in viscosity as a suspension of starch grains in water is heated is a convenient way to assess the progress of pasting.

Changes in viscosity during the heating of five commonly used starches are plotted in Figure 8-10. The left-hand side of each curve shows the viscosity for each pasting starch as a function of time and temperature. The viscosity of a potato, waxy corn, or tapioca (from cassava or manioc) starch suspension begins to increase at a lower temperature than does that of other starches. Potato starch paste reaches peak viscosity at a very low temperature, the viscosity dropping abruptly as temperature continues to rise. Tapioca never reaches the maximum thickness of potato starch paste. A suspension of tapioca starch grains continues to thicken up to 85°C (185°F), but additional heating causes a decrease in viscosity. Waxy cornstarch shows a sharp peak near 75°C (167°F). The rapid drop thereafter is similar to that which occurs in potato starch. At its maximum, waxy cornstarch paste is not as viscous as that of potato starch.

Wheat starch as well as corn needs to be heated to a higher temperature before thickening begins than do the other three starches. Thickening is gradual for a while, shows a steeper increase, and again levels off. This break in the viscosity curves is typical of cereal starches. Presumably it indicates that more than one type of bonding force is involved within the granule.

Thus root starches and waxy cornstarch reach maximum viscosity at lower temperatures than do the cereal starches. Gelatinization is complete in most starches at a temperature no higher than 95°C (203°F). From a practical standpoint, when starches from corn, wheat, and rice are heated to the boiling point, pasting is complete. Gelatinization is complete in root starches such as potato and tapioca (cassava) at lower temperatures. In tapioca the process is complete near simmering (85°C or 185°F) and this starch is sometimes overcooked as a consequence. Presence of surfactants, such as monoglycerides delay pasting (7).

Cooked potato and tapioca starch grains are elastic and readily deformed. This gives to the cooked paste a cohesiveness and stringiness not observed in pastes thickened with wheat or cornstarch. Once starch grains are completely pasted, unnecessary stirring should be avoided. Manipulation at this stage breaks swollen granules into smaller fragments and thins the paste.

UNEQUAL SWELLING OR LUMPS

When starch is used as a thickening agent, a uniformly thickened liquid without lumps is desired. First the starch grains must be separated before they are heated in the liquid. This may be accomplished by suspending them in a small quantity of the cold liquid. This is made easy by the fact that starch grains carry a negative charge and so repel each other in water. When conventional flour is used as a source of starch, separation is more difficult. Instantized flour, however (see Chapter 10), disperses readily in cold liquid. Alternately, starch grains or flour particles may be separated with grains of sugar or with a coating of fat, either melted or plastic. This last is sometimes referred to as a *roux*.

Separating the starch grains is only the first step in getting a smooth starch-thickened paste. It is equally important that each starch grain swell independently of every other grain. When dry starch grains are blended with cold water, the grains remain suspended as long as the water is agitated. The temporarily suspended grains settle and pack when stirring stops. Heating must be slow so that the suspension can be stirred fast enough to keep the starch grains suspended and the temperature uniform. In this way no grains take up more than their share of water, none less. Otherwise, grains will swell unevenly and some will adhere. Lumps are the result.

Flavor of gelatinized starch is improved by cooking the paste an additional five minutes directly on the hot unit. The alternative is to heat the paste over boiling water an additional 10 to 15 minutes. Pastes cooked directly on the unit need to be stirred occasionally; those cooked over boiling water should be covered to prevent evaporation and the formation of a skin.

SETTING OR GELATION OF A COOKED STARCH PASTE

Some of the starch molecules, chiefly amylose, which are dispersible in hot water escape from the swollen granules and into the surrounding liquid. Thus a cooked hot starch paste consists of swollen granules suspended in hot water in which are dispersed molecules of amylose. The ability of starch grains to thicken a hot paste such as gravy or sauce is one thing; the ability of the cooked, cooled paste to set so that it holds its shape when unmolded as in puddings and pie fillings is another.

RETROGRADATION OF AMYLOSE

The amylose molecules which have leached from the pasted grains stay dispersed in the liquid of a cooked paste as long as it remains hot. The hot paste retains its ability to flow, that is, it is viscous but not rigid. When the paste cools, the kinetic energy is no longer great enough to counteract the marked tendency of the amylose molecules to reassociate. The amylose molecules rebond to one another and to starch molecules on the outer edges of granules. Thus they unite swollen starch grains in a network. This occurs provided the swollen grains are relatively close together and enough amylose molecules have escaped from the granules (3). The recrystallization of gelatinized starch is known as "retrogradation." Not all cooked starch-thickened mixtures exhibit this phenomenon. Differences among starches are shown in Figure 8-10. The right-hand sides of the curves show the changes in viscosity of the five cooked pastes as they cool. Those for potato, tapioca, and waxy cornstarch show gradual and low increases. This is what one would expect of most systems as they cool. However, viscosity curves for wheat and especially for cornstarch show sharp increases as the temperature drops. This abrupt rise is attributed to the structure of the gel formed by the retrograding amylose.

Waxy starches do not set or gel a liquid. Only those starch grains that contain amylose are effective agents for setting or immobilizing liquid. Five parts of cornstarch (by weight) can immobilize 95 parts water. The gel that forms holds its shape when turned from a mold and it cuts with a sharp edge. Amylose molecules of an intermediate size favor gel formation. Those with too few glucose-unit residues are too short to bridge the gaps between swollen starch granules. Those with too many residues tend to be too sluggish for optimum orientation.

DISPOSITION OF WATER IN A GEL

Part of the water still outside the swollen granules in a cooked, cooled starch paste is bonded firmly to starch molecules on the surface of the swollen grains and to the amylose molecules which link the swollen grains. Part of the remaining water is bonded to the first layer of firmly bound water. The bulk of the water in the cooked paste is free, held in the spaces formed by the network of swollen starch grains and precipitated amylose. When a gel is cut or even as it ages, some of the liquid will seep from the interstices. This leakage of liquid from a gel is known as "syneresis." In soft pie fillings the gel should not be too stiff. The filling should not flow, but the gel should be weak enough that the filling bulges when a piece of pie is cut.

The structural framework responsible for the setting of a cooked starch paste as it cools can be demonstrated by freezing a portion of the paste and

Figure 8-11. Cooked starch pastes after freezing and thawing show the structural framework responsible for the setting of a cooled, cooked paste: (a) a coarse textured starch sponge, originally magnified 7½ times; (b) similar view of a fine textured sponge. (From G. E. Hilbert et al., *Food Industries* **17:** 878, 1945. Courtesy of the Northern Regional Research Center, Peoria, Ill. Reprinted by permission of Food Engineering.)

then allowing it to thaw. (See Fig. 8-11.) When a cooked starch paste freezes, water bonded to the starch and held in the network is converted into ice crystals. The starchy framework remains intact. When the ice crystals melt, the water regains its fluidity, but it is unable to reassociate with the starch as it was prior to freezing. The water now can be squeezed from the starch grain-amylose sponge and the sponge can reabsorb the water when pressure is released. The structure of a starch sponge is quite fragile and the sponge must be handled with care.

A frozen paste made from 2 tablespoons of cornstarch per cup of liquid yields a good sponge, that from 1 tablespoon of cornstarch a fragile one, but a paste made from 2 tablespoons of waxy cornstarch has no structure at all. This shows that, for setting to take place, swollen starch grains must be sufficiently close to each other and that amylose molecules must be present to leach from the swollen grains.

LOSS OF TRANSLUCENCY

Most cooked starch pastes lose some of their translucency upon cooling, owing to the precipitation or crystallization of amylose. Exceptions are tapioca and waxy cornstarch. When waxy cornstarch is used, the hot paste will thicken but the cold paste will not set or gel. This is due to the absence of amylose molecules in these starches. The translucency of the juice in fruit pies thickened with such starches has eye appeal. The greater opaqueness of a hot liquid thickened with flour instead of with ordinary cornstarch is due to the non-starchy constituents in the flour. Opaqueness increases as a cooked paste made with nonwaxy starch cools and the amylose retrogrades.

FACTORS AFFECTING THE CHARACTER OF COOKED STARCH PASTES

PROPORTIONS OF STARCH

The viscosity of a hot cooked starch paste and the stiffness of a cooled cooked paste are influenced by a number of factors. An important one, of course, is the proportion of starch to liquid. One tablespoon of flour per cup of liquid gives a thin sauce, 2 tablespoons a medium one, and 3 tablespoons a thick sauce. In puddings, sauces, and gravies, the amount of liquid is sufficient to permit gelatinization of the starch. In some batters and doughs the proportion of liquid to flour is usually too low to permit complete gelatinization of the starch (4,8).

TYPES OF STARCH

Starches vary in their thickening power. Cornstarch, which is almost pure starch, has approximately twice the thickening power of flour, which is the finely cracked endosperm of wheat. Flour that has been browned as for making gravy has less thickening power than unbrowned flour, because some of the starch molecules in the starch grains of flour have been converted to dextrins. Cornstarch and tapioca have approximately the same thickening power although a liquid thickened with tapioca does not set. In fact, tapioca is used in fruit pies to thicken the juice because it does not form a rigid gel. Although both regular and waxy cornstarch have thickening power, the latter attains a higher peak viscosity at a lower temperature (see Fig. 8-10), but the cooked paste also thins more with subsequent heating and stirring. The inflated grains of cooked starch are fragile and easily ruptured, root starches more so than cereal starches. Liquids thickened with potato, tapioca, or waxy cornstarch are more elastic than those thickened with cereal starches.

Starches in their natural form are limited in their usefulness. Starches modified chemically to eliminate some of their defects are now widely used by the food industry (21). For example, waxy cornstarch can be made to resist thinning when the cooked paste is stirred if it has been cross-bonded. The starch is reacted with phosphate or some other compound which forms ester links with OH groups on adjacent starch molecules. Only limited cross-bonding is needed to strengthen the granule so that it can not only resist breakdown when stirred, but also can withstand the high temperature used to sterilize foods and resist thinning due to acid (see below). To eliminate undesired association of amylose leading to loss of clarity and syneresis when starch-thickened foods are refrigerated or frozen (13), another type of modification is used. Certain mono-functional groups are substituted at OH groups on individual starch molecules. These bulkier groups in place of the hydrogen prevent the amylose which has escaped from the swollen granule from associating.

SUGAR

Other ingredients added to a liquid to be thickened by starch may affect the thickness of the hot paste and its rigidity when cooled. The effect depends on the particular ingredient and the proportions of that ingredient. Sugar (sucrose), except in low concentrations, in starch-thickened puddings and soft pie fillings decreases the thickness of the cooked product. It decreases the stiffness of the cooled product even more. Presumably sugar limits the swelling of the starch grains by competing with them for water (6). In addition, sugar elevates the temperature at which starch grains begin to thicken a liquid. It also makes the swollen grains more resistant to mechanical rupture after they are gelatinized. High levels of both sucrose and lactose affect the pasting of starch more than other sugars (2,16).

ACID

Acid, in the form of vinegar, or lemon juice or other fruit juice, is often used in starch-thickened foods. Acid reduces the thickness of the hot starch paste and the firmness of the cooled paste (5). The effect of acid is more pronounced than that of sugar. However, with acid the decrease in thickness and stiffness has been attributed in part to fragmentation of swollen granules rather than to reduced swelling (2). Acid and heat catalyze the hydrolysis of molecules of starch to dextrins (see section on proportion of interfering substances, Chapter 6). Reduction in the thickening power of starch that results could be due to alteration of the exudate as well as to fragmentation of swollen starch grains. For starch-thickened dishes that contain acid, such as lemon pie filling, Harvard beets, and fruit pie fillings, the effect of the acid as well as the sugar on the thickening power of starch must be taken into account when the recipe is formulated. Adding acid at the end of the cooking period minimizes the hydrolysis of starch. Apparently there is no advantage in waiting until a cooked starch paste is cool before the lemon juice is added. In fact, disturbing the filling once the gel starts to form makes the gel somewhat weaker (12). The acid of the lemon juice, if added after the filling is cooked, does not affect the consistency. Both sugar and acid tend to make the cooked paste clearer. Salts of phosphoric acid, usually disodium phosphate, hasten the cooking of starch and are used in quick-cooking macaroni and cereals and in packaged starch-thickened puddings.

When wheat starch (flour) is used as a thickening agent, the liquid will be thicker if the flour is put into hot fat rather than dispersed in cold liquid.

Heat inactivates the alpha-amylase of the flour, which would otherwise bring about some hydrolysis of the starch (19). And a soft pie filling must be heated sufficiently after the egg yolk is added or it will thin upon standing (11).

VEGETABLE GUMS

Plant polysaccharides in addition to starch and pectin (Chapter 29) are now widely used in the fabrication of many commercial foods, as the reading of a few labels will attest. These polysaccharides include gum arabic, gum karaya, gum tragacanth, locust bean gum, gum guar, and seaweed-derived algin, agar, and the carrageenans. These vegetable gums are complex polymers of various sugars and sugar-derived uronic acids (14). All are hydrophilic. Some yield clear, viscous sols; others are valued for their gelling properties. The particular gum used depends on the special quality the manufacturer wishes to impart to the food. Vegetable gums are used as thickeners and emulsifiers in French dressings that do not separate. They are used to stabilize suspended matter in chocolate milk, to give body to such foods as cream cheese, to keep evaporated milk free-flowing, to prevent crystallization, and to form gels. Sodium carboxymethylcellulose (CMC), made by chemical modification of cellulose, is used extensively in the food industry.

REFERENCES

1. Banks, W., C. T. Greenwood, and D. D. Muir. 1973. The structure of starch. In *Molecular Structure and Function of Carbohydrates.* G. G. Birch and L. F. Green, eds. London: Applied Science Publishers, Ltd. Pp. 177–194.
2. Bean, M., and E. M. Osman. 1959. Behavior of starch during food preparation. II. Effect of different sugars on the viscosity and gel strength of starch pastes. *Food Research* **24:** 665–671. Dextrose, fructose, invert syrup, sorbitol, lactose, maltose, and sucrose compared.
3. Campbell, A. M., and A. M. Briant. 1957. Wheat starch pastes and gels containing citric acid and sucrose. *Food Research* **22:** 358–366. Effects of the added substances on gelatinization temperature, thickness of pastes, and firmness of gels.
4. Derby, R. I., B. S. Miller, B. F. Miller, and H. B. Trimbo. 1975. Visual observation of wheat-starch gelatinization in limited water systems. *Cereal Chem.* **52:** 702–713. Moisture levels of 33 to 60 percent compared.
5. Hansuld, M. K., and A. M. Briant. 1954. The effect of citric acid on selected edible starches and flours. *Food Research* **19:** 581–589. Thickening and gelling of pastes, made with cornstarch, wheat starches, and flours, compared.
6. Hester, E. E., A. M. Briant, and C. J. Personius. 1956. The effects of sucrose on the properties of some starches and flours. *Cereal Chem.* **33:** 91–101. Thickness of hot pastes and rigidity of cold pastes from cornstarch, wheat starches, and flour.

7. Langley, R. W., and B. S. Miller. 1971. Note on the relative effects of mono-glycerides on the gelatinization of wheat starch. *Cereal Chem.* **48:** 81–85. Length of fatty acid chain and delay in pasting.

8. Lineback, D. R., and E. Wongsrikasem. 1980. Gelatinization of starch in baked products. *J. Food Sci.* **45:** 71–74. Effects of sugar on gelatinization; birefringence and scanning electron micrographs.

9. Meyer, K. H. 1952. The past and present of starch chemistry. *Experientia* **8:** 405–420. A comprehensive review.

10. Miller, B. S., R. I. Derby, and H. B. Trimbo. 1973. A pictorial explanation for the increase in viscosity of a heated starch-water suspension. *Cereal Chem.* **50:** 271–280. Evidence for presence of exudate.

11. Murthy, G. K. 1970. Thermal inactivation of alpha-amylase in various liquid egg products. *J. Food Sci.* **35:** 352–356. Whole egg and egg yolk compared; effects of salt and sugar.

12. Nielsen, H. J., J. D. Hewitt, and N. K. Fitch. 1952. Factors affecting consistency of a lemon pie filling. *J. Home Econ.* **44:** 782–785. Effects of cooking time after addition of yolks, of cooling time before addition of lemon juice, and of acidity of lemon juice.

13. Osman, E. M., and P. D. Cummisford. 1959. Some factors affecting the stability of frozen white sauces compared. *Food Research* **24:** 595–604. Influence of the kind of starch and other ingredients on freeze-thaw stability.

14. Rees, D. A. 1972. Polysaccharide gels. A molecular view. *Chem & Ind.* Aug. 19, pp. 630–636. Technical presentation.

15. Sandstedt, R. M. 1965. Fifty years of progress in starch chemistry. *Cereal Sci. Today* **10:** 305–315. Clear comprehensible presentation with many excellent photomicrographs.

16. Savage, H. L., and E. M. Osman. 1978. Effects of certain sugars and sugar al-cohols on the swelling of cornstarch granules. *Cereal Chem.* **55:** 447–454. Three monosaccharides, three disaccharides and two sugar alcohols compared at levels of 5, 20, and 50 percent of the weight of the water.

17. Schoch, T. J. 1962. Recent developments in starch chemistry. *Brewers Digest* **37**(2): 41–46. Starch molecules and their biosynthesis; enzymatic breakdown; starch granule structure.

18. Schopmeyer, H. H. 1945. Amioca—the starch from waxy corn. *Food Ind.* **17:** 1476–1478. Characteristics and functional properties.

19. Trimbo, H. B., and B. S. Miller. 1971. Factors affecting the quality of sauces (gravies). *J. Home Econ.* **63**(1): 48–53. Effects of the alpha-amylase of the flour.

20. Waldt, L. M. 1960. Pregelatinized starches for the food processor. *Food Technol.* **14:** 50–53. Nature and functional properties of pregelatinized starches.

21. Wurzburg, O. B., and C. D. Syzmanski. 1970. Modified starches for the food industry. *J. Agr. Food Chem.* **18:** 997–1001. Advantages of cross-bonding and stabilizing.

NINE
Cereals

The word "cereal" derives from the name of the Roman grain or harvest goddess, Ceres (usually depicted with ears of barley braided in her hair). Cereals are the seeds of grasses. The plants from which cereals come are wheat, rice, corn, rye, oats, and barley. A limited quantity of wild rice, *Zizania aquatica*, is marketed in the United States. It is a cereal and more like barley than like ordinary rice (16). Unlike the other cereals which evolved in nature, triticale, a wheat-rye hybrid, was crossed intentionally. Cereal products made from grain include breakfast foods, rice, flours, and macaroni products. Discussion of flours and macaroni products is deferred to the chapter which follows.

CONSUMPTION OF CEREALS

For human consumption, wheat is the main cereal in the United States and Canada; rice the main cereal in China, Japan, and India; rye the chief one in Russia and in Central Europe. Corn is used in Mexico, South America, and the United States. Oats are used to a limited extent for human food.

Not only does the main cereal consumed vary from country to country, but so does the importance of cereals as a whole in the diet. The proportion of total calories which comes from cereals is low in the United States (21 percent), in contrast to parts of the Far East where the proportion is much higher (64 percent) (17). The reason for these extremes is that in this country the resources (land, climate, money, machinery, and agricultural know-how) for the production of food in relation to the number of people to be fed are high; in the Far East they are low. Where the food supply is inadequate for the population, grains must be eaten to prevent starvation. Fruit and vegetables do not begin to approximate the calories contained in cereals from the same amount of land and labor. Furthermore, to produce milk, eggs, and meat, primary agricultural products are fed to animals, which convert them into a more desirable form, but in the process waste much potential food for human beings.

The following comparison gives a rough idea of the effects of alternate uses of our land resources. The estimated yield from 10 acres of land devoted to growing cattle is enough beef (in pounds) to feed one individual for one year (11). But the 10 acres of land could be used to produce enough wheat to feed 15 people for a year or enough rice to feed 24. The corn plant is an especially valuable food producer. It is one of the most efficient trappers of the sun's energy, sugar cane being another (20). Of course, filling an individual is not the sole function of food. But when one is hungry, getting enough food is an immediate objective.

Cereals provide almost half (47 percent) of the dietary protein worldwide (12), and they could make a greater contribution. In the United States we feed roughly 90 percent of our production of edible (for humans) plant proteins from cereals, legumes, and vegetables to animals, and for each unit of animal protein obtained approximately five units of plant protein are fed. Consumption of cereal foods directly represents a more efficient use of arable land, fossil energy, and labor. Each hectare (2.47 acres) of corn planted in the United States will yield enough utilizable protein to feed 12 people 60 grams of protein per day for one year. For rice the figure is 10 and for wheat 8. True, cereals do not compare with animal foods for either quantity or quality of protein. Cereals are especially deficient in the essential amino acid lysine. Even so, yields of both protein and of essential amino acids per acre of cultivated land are several times greater from corn when the seed is used directly as food rather than from animals fed the same amount of corn (1). Calculated yield of protein from corn is 234 pounds per acre, and of essential amino acids 80 pounds per acre. Were this corn fed to animals, calculated yields of protein in pounds per acre are 87 for milk, 82 for broilers, 60 for eggs, 56 for hogs, 49 for chickens, and 26 for beef. Yields of essential amino acids in pounds per acre range from 37 for milk to 10 for beef. Interestingly, the yield of protein which can be extracted from the leaves of green corn is at least as great as that from the mature seed.

The utilization of cereals has declined in the United States. The consumption of wheat forecast for 1979 was 112 pounds per capita (18), three-fourths of it as flour and most of that white flour. This compares with an annual per capita consumption of 309 pounds 60 years ago (17). A number of things have contributed to this change in our food pattern. Refrigeration makes available fresh, perishable foods the year around and eliminates dependence upon nonperishable cereals for a large part of the winter's food supply. Too, people have more money and with a high standard of living shift from economy foods such as cereals and potatoes to more expensive ones. Another possible reason for the shift from cereals is that many people do not lead such active lives as in previous times and so do not need as much energy. For example, providing butter for the family table in many homes 50 years ago necessitated first milking the cow, straining the milk, cooling the milk, separating the cream, churning it, carrying the butter to the spring or a milk house to keep it cool, and finally making a trip for it just before the meal. Today, providing butter involves a trip in an automobile to the nearest supermarket, lifting the parchment-wrapped sticks from the refrigerator, and driving home, where the butter is

Table 9-1 Composition and energy value of selected cereals (100-gram edible portion)

Cereal	Water (%)	Calories[a]	Protein (g)	Carbohydrates Total (g)	Fiber (g)	Fat (g)	Calcium (mg)	Phosphorus (mg)	Iron (mg)	Vitamin A Value (I.U.)	Thiamine (mg)	Riboflavin (mg)	Niacin (mg)	Ascorbic Acid (mg)
Bran flakes (40%), added thiamine	3.0	303	10.2	80.6	3.6	1.8	71	495	4.4	(0)	.40	.17	6.2	(0)
Corn flakes, added nutrients	3.8	386	7.9	85.3	.7	.4	17	45	1.4	(0)	.43	.08	2.1	(0)
Corn grits, degermed unenriched, yellow[b]	12.0	362	8.7	78.1	.4	.8	4	73	1.0	440	.13	.04	1.2	(0)
Corn meal, degermed unenriched, yellow[b]	12.0	364	7.9	78.4	.6	1.2	6	99	1.1	440	.14	.05	1.0	(0)
Farina, regular unenriched[b]	10.3	371	11.4	77.0	.4	.9	25	107	1.5	(0)	.06	.10	.7	(0)
Macaroni, unenriched[b]	10.4	369	12.5	75.2	.3	1.2	27	162	1.3	(0)	.09	.06	1.7	(0)
Oats, rolled[b]	8.3	390	14.2	68.2	1.2	7.4	53	405	4.5	(0)	.60	.14	1.0	(0)
Rice, brown, raw	12.0	360	7.5	77.4	.9	1.9	32	221	1.6	(0)	.34	.05	4.7	(0)
Rice, white unenriched, raw	12.0	363	6.7	80.4	.3	.4	24	94	.8	(0)	.07	.03	1.6	(0)

Table 9-1 Composition and energy value of selected cereals (100-gram edible portion) Cont'd

Cereal	Water (%)	Calories[a]	Protein (g)	Carbohydrates Total (g)	Carbohydrates Fiber (g)	Fat (g)	Calcium (mg)	Phosphorus (mg)	Iron (mg)	Vitamin A Value (I.U.)	Thiamine (mg)	Riboflavin (mg)	Niacin (mg)	Ascorbic Acid (mg)
Flour, all purpose enriched	12.0	364	10.5	76.1	.3	1.0	16	87	2.9[c]	(0)	.44[c]	.26[c]	3.5[c]	(0)
Flour, whole wheat	12.0	333	13.3	71.0	2.3	2.0	41	372	3.3	(0)	.55	.12	4.3	(0)
Wheat, puffed, added nutrients	3.4	363	15.0	78.5	2.0	1.5	28	322	4.2	(0)	.55	.23	7.8	(0)
Wheat, rolled[b]	10.1	340	9.9	76.2	2.2	2.0	36	342	3.2	(0)	.36	.12	4.1	(0)
Wheat, shredded	6.6	354	9.9	79.9	2.3	2.0	43	388	3.5	(0)	.22	.11	4.4	(0)
Wheat, whole meal[b]	10.4	338	13.5	72.3	2.2	2.0	45	398	3.7	(0)	.51	.13	4.7	(0)

NOTE: Zeroes in parentheses indicate values too small to measure.

[a]1 kilocalorie = 4.185 kilojoules.

[b]Dry form.

[c]Minimum level of enrichment.

SOURCE: U.S. Dept. Agr. Handbook No. 8. *Composition of Foods. Raw, Processed, Prepared.* Revised 1963.

placed in a refrigerator until mealtime. Too, the current emphasis on slenderness may have some bearing on the decrease in the use of grain for human food. Such starchy foods as cereals and breads as well as potatoes are considered fattening. None of these is inherently fattening. The sugar, cream, butter, and other fats eaten with such foods or combined with them in recipes often contribute more calories than the cereals or potatoes themselves.

COMPOSITION OF CEREALS

Table 9-1 gives the composition and the energy value of representative cereal products. Cereals as a group are approximately 75 percent carbohydrates, 10 percent protein, 1 to 2 percent fat, 10 percent moisture, and 1 to 2 percent ash. The main carbohydrate in cereals is starch. A second carbohydrate is cellulose. Cereals contain protein of a quality somewhat lower (10) than that found in animal foods such as meat, milk, and eggs. Cereals as a group are deficient in lysine, and low in tryptophan and methionine. The level of these essential amino acids can be increased in cereals by the introduction of certain mutant genes. High lysine corn was developed some years ago. Two genes, opaque-2 and floury-2, enable the corn plant to synthesize more lysine and also more tryptophan (4) than the typical hybrid corn. Genes are available for improving the quality of the proteins in rice, barley, and wheat, too (20). Unfortunately, this genetic engineering which results in a higher lysine content also may result in lower total protein and lower yield. Functional properties of the cereal in food preparation are altered, too. The liming of corn in the preparation of such foods as tortillas paradoxically decreases a number of nutrients in the corn, at the same time improving its overall nutritive value by producing a better balance of amino acids (7). Triticale, the rye-wheat hybrid, is higher than wheat in lysine and in protein but the yield per acre is lower (14).

STRUCTURE OF CEREAL GRAINS

THE CELL

The cell is the basic structural unit of cereals as of all foods of plant origin. (See Fig. 27-5.) A plant cell is bounded by a cell wall which encloses the protoplasm or actual living part of the plant. The cell wall contains celluloses and hemicelluloses. The protoplasm consists of water (in large quantities in the living plant), protein, starch grains, fat globules and, in solution, water-soluble minerals, vitamins, and pigments.

PARTS OF A CEREAL GRAIN

Not all cells in a cereal grain are alike. Because of this, cereal grains can be separated into three different parts: the bran, the germ or embryo, and the endosperm. The parts of a wheat kernel are shown diagrammatically in Figure

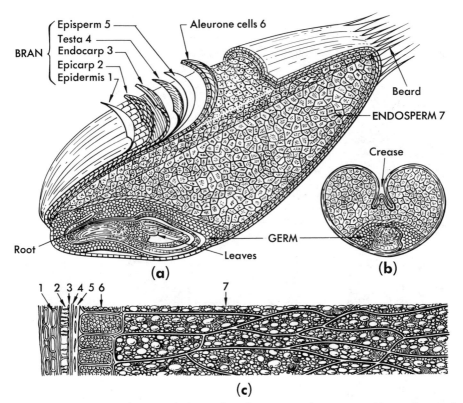

Figure 9-1. (a) Diagram of a grain of wheat enlarged approximately 17 times, with a wedge equal to approximately one quarter of the grain cut away. Layers 1 to 5 constitute the bran, separated from the endosperm by a layer of aleurone cells. (b) A cross section through the lower end of the kernel, the crease somewhat spread apart. (c) A section near the periphery of the grain enlarged approximately 238 times to show starch grains embedded in a protein matrix in the cells of the endosperm. Compare with Figure 9-2. (From J. Storck and W. D. Teague, *Flour for Man's Bread: A History of Milling,* University of Minnesota Press, Minneapolis. Copyright © 1952 by the University of Minnesota.)

9-1. The bulky bran consists of the outermost layer of cells of the grain. These cells have thick walls made mainly of cellulose and hemicellulose. The main constituent in the bran of cereals is this indigestible material, which gives bulk to the diet. The bran also contains minerals, chiefly iron. Water-soluble vitamins, which include thiamine, niacin, and riboflavin, together with some protein, are found in the bran. The bran accounts for about 5 percent of the entire grain. A single layer of cells (called the "aleurone") separates the bran from the rest of the grain.

The germ or embryo makes up 2 to 3 percent of a cereal grain. Cells in this part of the grain are rich in unsaturated fat, the molecules of which are not too stable. (See Chapter 14 on fats.) The germ is removed from many of the cereal products on the market to prevent them from becoming rancid.

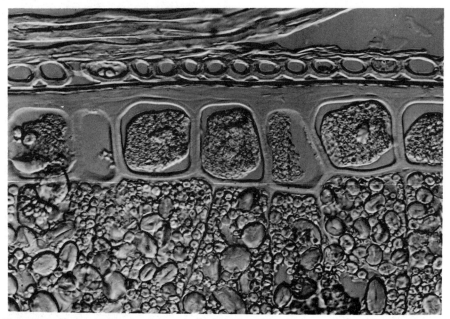

Figure 9-2. Photomicrograph of the outer layers of a grain of wheat. Note the layer of starch-filled endosperm cells. Original magnification X 1,000. (Photograph by R. I. Derby, General Mills, Inc.)

Cells making up the germ also contain protein, iron, niacin, thiamine, and riboflavin.

The endosperm is the major portion of a cereal grain. It is made up of starch-storing cells. These cells are packed full of starch grains, which are embedded in a matrix of protein. The walls of the cells of the endosperm are quite thin so there is less cellulose in this part of the grain. The two nutrients of any quantity in the endosperm of cereals are starch and protein. Cells in different parts of the endosperm vary somewhat in composition. However, differences among these cells are not so pronounced as between cells of different parts of the grain. See Figure 9-2 for a photomicrograph of cells of endosperm, aleurone layer, and inner layer of bran.

PROCESSING CEREALS FOR THE MARKET

MILLING

Although it is possible to cook and eat the whole cereal grain, this is not customarily done (9). Cereals do not keep as well with the germ left in, and many people consider them more palatable without the outer, branny layer. Also, the cooking time required for the whole grain is long. For these reasons cereals are milled before they are put on the market. Milling may involve subdivision of the grain. As an example, the entire wheat kernel may be subdivided into coarse cracked wheat, fine granular wheat (wheatena), and still finer whole wheat flour. Corn endosperm, from which the pericarp has been removed by soaking in alkali, is marketed whole as hominy, cracked as grits, and ground as cornmeal.

Instead of subdividing the whole grain in milling, it may be separated into the three parts. Subsequently the endosperm may be subdivided. From rice the bran may be removed by abrasion. This yields white, or polished, rice. Bran is removed from barley in the same way. This gives pearl barley used in some canned vegetable soups and in Scotch broth.

To separate the bran and germ from the endosperm of wheat, the kernels are passed between rollers operating at high speed. Heat from the rollers causes the fat in the germ to melt and the germ and bran then come off in flakes. These are separated from the endosperm by a combination of sifting plus air currents to remove pieces of the lighter bran. Then the endosperm is passed between rollers set closer and closer together, each one further subdividing the endosperm. After each passage through the rollers, the material is sifted. Pieces of endosperm which resist cracking most are used either directly as breakfast cereal, such as farina, or to make breakfast cereals. When the bran and germ are removed, along with them go a high proportion of the nutrients, except starch and protein. Cereals from which the bran and germ have been removed by milling are called refined cereals (3).

HEAT TREATMENT

Some cereals are marketed without any heat treatment, but a number are partially or completely precooked. Wheat products that have not been heated include cracked wheat, farina, and bran. For one type of wheat flakes which are partially cooked, the pieces of kernel are steamed, flattened, and toasted before they are marketed. Precooked and ready-to-serve wheat products include puffed wheat, shredded wheat, and wheat flakes (whole wheat cooked, flattened, and dried). Steel-cut oatmeal has had no heat treatment, unlike both regular and quick-cooking rolled oats which are heated before they are flattened into flakes. Regular rolled oats are made from the entire kernel; quick-cooking oats are made of pieces of the kernel. Hominy grits and cornmeal from corn are uncooked, but cornflakes are ready to serve. Brown rice, polished rice, and wild rice are unheated. Converted (parboiled) rice has been steamed under pressure to force water-soluble nutrients from the bran and germ into the endosperm. After this treatment the rice is dried and then polished as for white rice. Quick-cooking rice on the market has been partially cooked, and both instant and puffed rice are precooked. The latter is ready to serve; and instant rice requires no cooking, only to have hot water added (6). When cereals are subjected to high temperature, as in puffing and toasting, the heat may destroy some thiamine and lower the nutritive value of the protein.

NUTRITIVE VALUE OF CEREALS

WHOLE GRAIN VERSUS REFINED

Cereals are inexpensive sources of energy, furnishing from 1600 to 1700 calories per pound. Whole grains are good sources of iron, thiamine, and niacin and fair sources of riboflavin. They are fair sources of protein. Although the protein is of better quality than that from the endosperm alone, it still needs to be supplemented with the proteins of milk, eggs, meat, or legumes. Whole-grain cereals are good sources of cellulose, which furnishes bulk in the gastrointestinal tract. Refined cereals yield mainly energy from the starch and some incomplete protein.

ENRICHED CEREALS

Cereals may be enriched by restoring to them the main nutrients removed by milling. Iron, thiamine, niacin, and riboflavin are the nutrients which must be added or returned to a refined cereal when it is enriched. Addition of calcium and vitamin D is optional. Federal standards for the level of each nutrient in an enriched product have been established (under the authority of the Federal Food, Drug and Cosmetic Act) for white flour, farina, white bread, corn meal, grits, macaroni products, and rice. If a cereal is enriched, it must be so labeled in compliance with the labeling requirements of the act. Enrichment of white flour and white bread is required by law in 29 states and in Puerto Rico. Enrichment of degerminated corn meal and grits is mandatory in some states; at least two require the enrichment of whole corn meal, too. One state has required the enrichment of white rice since 1956. Polished rice may be enriched by returning to the surface of the kernels or grains a mixture of those nutrients removed along with bran and germ. For this reason polished cereals should not be washed before they are cooked. Parboiled rice (called converted rice) retains a high proportion of the nutrients which are removed when white rice is polished.

COOKING OF CEREALS

PURPOSES

Cereals are cooked to increase their digestibility and their palatability. Chewing uncooked cereal is wearing on the molars. Cooking softens the cellulose, but mainly cooking increases the palatability of cereals by its effect on the major component, starch. From 2 to 6 volumes of water are required to cook one volume of cereal because of the uptake of water by the gelatinizing starch.

PRECAUTIONS

One of the problems in cooking cereals, as with using starch itself in cooking, is to avoid having lumps. When the dry cereal is added to boiling water, it should be stirred in with a fork, but only enough to prevent the formation of lumps. Excessive agitation, either stirring or allowing the water to boil vigorously, results in an inferior product.

When the cereal is milled, the cells of the grain are fractured and some of the embedded starch grains are exposed on the surfaces of the individual particles. If the cereal is agitated during cooking, many of these starch grains are dislodged. These thicken the liquid around the individual particles of cereal. This gives a cooked cereal with individual pieces embedded in a thick starch paste, a gooey consistency that many find unpalatable. Cooked cereal has a better consistency if the starch grains remain in place on the surface of the pieces of cereal. Flaked cereals are particularly susceptible to disintegration by agitation during cooking because flakes are inherently more fragile than granules. Effects on consistency aside, if the heat is too high under the cereal, it is likely to scorch.

PROPORTIONS OF LIQUIDS

Proportion of water to cereal depends in part upon the size of the particles and their ability to absorb water. Fine granular cereals require 5 to 6 times their volume of water, coarse cracked cereals 4 times, and flaked cereals 2 times. The amount of water needed to cook a cereal is an indication of the approximate amount it will swell. However, rice increases more than twice in volume, even when it is steamed in only twice its volume of water. When this low proportion of water is used, the rice grains absorb all of it and the swell is limited. A pan with a tight-fitting lid and low heat should be used. If rice is cooked with a higher proportion of water, the increase in volume will be greater. The product will be more moist, also. Long-grain rice tends to swell more than short-grain rice; converted rice swells less than the same type polished. Brown rice swells somewhat less than polished. When cooked in milk, cereals swell more than when cooked in water. (Possibly phosphates from the milk are involved.)

AMOUNT OF SALT

Approximately one teaspoon of salt per cup of dry cereal will season all except fine cereals, for which somewhat more salt (1½ teaspoons per cup) is suggested.

COOKING TIME

A number of factors influence how long a cereal needs to be cooked. Size of the fragments (how much the grain is subdivided) and prior heat treatment are two such factors. Cereals have a better flavor when cooked beyond the point at which starch is gelatinized. To verify this, one has only to compare the flavor of cereal cooked only until the product thickens with some of the same cereal which has had additional cooking.

Cooking time needed beyond gelatinization varies from a minimum of 5 to 10 minutes on direct heat to 10 to 15 minutes over boiling water. When cooking is completed over boiling water, more than 15 minutes' additional cooking does no harm. It is usually impractical to cook cereals for the entire time over boiling water because it takes so long to get the cereal hot enough to gelatinize the starch.

The cooking time of rice depends upon the variety. Some need be cooked only 15 minutes, but others may require up to 30. Quick-cooking rolled oats cook in less time than do regular rolled oats because the pieces are smaller. Directions on the package specify a cooking time of 5 minutes over direct heat for regular rolled oats and one minute for quick-cooking rolled oats. Flavor in both is improved by additional cooking.

A number of quick-cooking cereal products, including rice, farina, and macaroni, have had disodium phosphate, Na_2HPO_4, added to them. This phosphate salt speeds the cooking by enabling starch grains to reach gelatinization temperature sooner. The cereal may reach the consistency desired in less time, but as with untreated cereal, additional cooking is needed for best flavor. Because of the current emphasis on saving time, directions on packages frequently give the minimum rather than the optimum cooking time.

EFFECT OF ALKALINE COOKING WATER

Polished rice or refined cereal may be cream colored or yellow tinted when cooked in alkaline water because of the presence of flavonoid compounds. A small amount of acid (vinegar, lemon juice, or cream of tartar) added to the cooking water, preferably late in the cooking period, will keep the pigments in colorless form.

CHARACTERISTICS OF COOKED CEREAL

Pieces of cooked flaked cereal should be separate and distinct. They should be moist but not sticky. Cooked granular cereal should be free from lumps. It should not be so thin that it pours readily, but it should flow enough to assume the shape of the dish in which it is served. The cereal should not have a pasty consistency. The flavor of all cooked cereal should be mild and nutlike.

On the basis of cooked quality, rice falls into two categories. Most varieties of long-grain rice are slender and translucent and yield fluffy, dry grains which remain separate. Most medium- or short-grain varieties are soft and chalky and when cooked are moist and sticky and tend to adhere. A number of factors that might account for differences in the cooking quality of rice have been investigated. These include the amount of moisture the rice absorbs as it cooks, its gelatinization temperature, the amylose content of the starch, and the anatomy of the kernel, particularly the amount and distribution of components which could limit the swelling of the starch (8). All of these factors point directly or indirectly to the starch component. When seven cooking methods were compared, the quality of the cooked rice appeared to stem more from characteristics inherent in the rice than from the cooking method used (2).

USES OF LEFTOVER CEREAL

Leftover cooked cereal need not be wasted. Cooled in a mold and cut into strips, the cereal can be browned in fat and served in the place of toast for breakfast or in place of a starchy vegetable for lunch or dinner. Leftover cereal can be used to make scrapple, which is cornmeal mush mixed with cooked leftover meat and then allowed to cool. This is a heritage from a less sophisticated era when hogs were butchered on farms and there were quantities of meat scraps to dispose of without waste. Leftover cereals can be used to make polenta or tamale pie, as a topping for meat pies, or as a lining for a casserole made from leftover stew or creamed meat.

POPCORN

Popcorn is a cereal, but in a category of its own. The kernels are inflated by steam produced from moisture within the vitreous endosperm. The volume of corn may increase 20 to 30 times when it pops. Corn pops satisfactorily only when the moisture content is within a narrow range (11–14 percent) (15); a content near the upper end of the range (13½ percent) is optimum. Popping expansion depends upon gelatinization of the starch and presumably on the horny endosperm which allows steam pressure to build (13). After the steam is released from the expanded grains, the hollow shells are dried and form a three-dimensional network. Quality popcorn has had the moisture content adjusted before it is put on the market, and it is sold in a moisture-vapor-proof package. Once a package is opened, popcorn should be stored in a sealed container.

The temperature to which the popper is preheated is another factor that influences the yield from popcorn (5). Optimum temperature varies somewhat with the size of the popper, its ability to hold heat, and the amount of corn popped at one time. If the popper is too hot, the corn scorches, and if not hot enough, the corn dries before it pops. Temperature inside the popper when the corn is popping should range from 173° to 198° C (343° to 388° F). The popper, itself, needs to be at a higher temperature (243° to 299° C or 470° to 570° F). A practical guide is to adjust the heat so that the corn begins to pop in 1 to 3 minutes after it goes into the popper. If, once popping begins, all the grains pop within 2 minutes, the yield of popped corn will be maximum. Properly engineered electric corn poppers eliminate the guesswork from attempts to maintain optimum temperature.

Thirty-six compounds have been identified in the volatiles from popped corn (19). Those considered important contributors to the aroma were pyrazines, furans, pyrroles, carbonyls, and substituted phenols. The odor of corn popped in a microwave oven did not differ materially from that popped conventionally in oil, but it did differ in tactile character.

REFERENCES

1. Akeson, W. R., and M. A. Stakmann. 1966. Leaf protein concentrates: A comparison of protein production per acre of forage with that from seed and animal crops. *Econ. Botany* **20:** 244–250. Alternate uses of natural resources for food production.
2. Batcher, O. M., M. G. Staley, and P. A. Deary. 1963. Palatability characteristics of foreign and domestic rices cooked by different methods. *Rice J.* **66**(9): 19–24; **66**(10): 13–16. Seven methods compared.
3. Calhoun, W. K., F. N. Hepburn, and W. B. Bradley. 1960. The distribution of the vitamins in wheat in commercial milled products. *Cereal Chem.* **37:** 755–761. Water-soluble vitamins in whole wheat, bran, shorts, clear flours, patent flour, and farina.
4. Christianson, D. D., U. Khoo, H. C. Nielsen, and J. S. Wall. 1974. Influence of opaque-2 and floury-2 genes on formation of proteins in particulates of corn endosperm. *Plant Physiol.* **53:** 851–855. High-lysine mutants.
5. Huelsen, W. A., and W. P. Bemis. 1954. Temperature of the popper in relation to volumetric expansion of popcorn. *Food Tech.* **8:** 394–397. Yields of popcorn at different temperatures.
6. Instant rice—from an idea to the perfected product. 1947. *Food Ind.* **19:** 1056–1061. Readable account of how one precooked cereal was readied for the market.
7. Katz, S. H., M. L. Hediger, and L. A. Valleroy. 1974. Traditional maize processing techniques in the new world. *Science* **184:** 765–773. Effects of liming on nutritive value.
8. Little, R. R., and E. H. Dawson. 1960. Histology and histochemistry of raw and cooked rice kernels. *Food Research* **25:** 611–612. Cooking quality of rice and anatomy of the kernel.
9. Matz, S. A. 1959. Manufacture of breakfast cereals. In *The Chemistry and Technology of Cereals as Food and Feed*. S. A. Matz, ed. Westport, Conn.: Avi Publishing Co. Pp. 547–568. Farina, rolled oats, and flaked, shredded, and puffed cereal.
10. Mertz, E. T., and L. S. Bates. 1964. Mutant gene that changes protein composition and increases lysine content of maize. *Science* **145:** 279–280. Improvement in the nutritive value of corn.
11. Milne, L., and M. Milne. 1964. *Water and Life*. New York: Atheneum. P. 42.
12. Pimentel, D. W., J. K. Dritschilo, J. Krummel, and J. Kutzman. 1975. Energy and land constraints in food protein production. *Science* **190:** 754–761. Options for meeting the world's food needs.
13. Reeve, R. M., and H. G. Walker. 1969. The microscopic structure of popped cereals. *Cereal Chem.* **46:** 227–241. Structural changes when popped.

14. Ruckman, J. E., F. P. Scheile, and C. O. Qualset. 1973. Protein, lysine, and grain yield of triticale and wheat as influenced by genotype and location. *J. Agr. Food Chem.* **21:** 697–700. Improved nutritive value of the hybrid.
15. Smith, G. M., and A. M. Brunson. 1947. *Hybrid Popcorn in Indiana*. Purdue University Agr. Exp. Sta. Bull. No. 510. 18 pp. Popping expansion; optimum moisture content.
16. Tames wild rice. 1953. *Food Eng.* **25**(3): 94, 152, 154. Harvesting and preparing wild rice for the market.
17. United States Department of Agriculture, Economic Research Service. *National Food Situation.* NFS-115, February 1966. Per capita consumption of major foods in different countries.
18. United States Department of Agriculture. *National Food Review.* Economics, Statistics and Cooperatives Service A. 1980 (Winter). NFR-9, p. 51. Per capita consumption of common foods.
19. Walradt, J. P., R. C. Landsay, and L. M. Libbey. 1970. Popcorn flavor: Identification of volatile compounds. *J. Agr. Food Chem.* **18:** 926–928. Popped conventionally in oil and dry by microwaves; aroma and tactile quality.
20. Woodbury, W. 1972. Biochemical genetics and its potential for cereal improvement. *Bakers Dig.* **46**(5): 20–24, 27, 63. Protein quality; photosynthetic efficiency.

TEN
Flour

Wheat is the primary cereal used to make flour, although a limited amount of flour is made from rye. Although the proteins of wheat flour are superior for making bread, nutritionally they are incomplete. The limiting amino acid is lysine. Development of the wheat-rye hybrid, triticale, has yielded a grain with a lysine content higher than that of the parent wheat. Some information is available on the performance of triticale flour in bread making (25,42). Work has been done also on the feasibility of using oil seed flours to supplement the proteins of wheat flour. Early work emphasized the use of soybean flour because of its high lysine as well as high protein content. More recently attention has focused on other flours including cottonseed, cowpea, field pea, peanut, safflower, sesame, and sunflower (28,38). Most will yield acceptable bread if the amount of wheat flour replaced is limited, if the formula is modified, and in some cases if the manipulation is altered (41). Bread made with wheat flour is the standard against which breads made with nonwheat flours are measured.

Wheat flours differ from uncooked wheat cereal primarily in the extent to which the grain has been subdivided or milled. Milling fractures many of the cells of the endosperm, exposing their contents. All wheat flours are not alike. Success in baking depends in part upon using the best type of flour for the product, so some consideration of how and why flours differ is pertinent.

TYPES OF FLOUR

KIND OF WHEAT

Flours are classed according to the type of wheat (26) from which they are milled. There are three common species of wheat grown in the United States. Two, the common (*Triticum aestivum*) and club (*Triticum compactum*) wheats, are used to make flour. The third, durum wheat, is used to make macaroni products. Wheats grown for flour can be classed according to color of the surface of the kernel (white or red), season when planted (winter or spring), and whether they are hard or soft. Red wheat varieties, some soft and others hard, predominate. Soft red wheat is planted in the fall so is referred to as winter wheat. Hard red wheat is planted in either spring or fall, depending on the growing conditions in the area. The endosperm of hard wheat shows greater resistance to cracking during the milling process. The difference between soft and hard wheat had been attributed solely to the higher ratio of protein to starch in the latter. Recent evidence indicates, however, that the hardness of hard wheat comes from greater continuity of the protein matrix within the cells and the tighter bonding of starch granules to this matrix (19,39). These differences are shown in the scanning electron micrographs (Fig. 10-1) of particles of flour milled from the two types of wheat. The protein matrix in the soft wheat lacks continuity and the structure appears more open. Many starch grains are exposed and some dislodged. Starch grains in hard wheat flour appear firmly embedded in a continuous protein matrix so that fracture of endosperm cells is more likely to crack starch grains. Soft wheat flour feels soft and powdery; hard wheat flour feels gritty.

EFFECTS OF MILLING

Flours differ not only in the kind of wheat from which they are made, but also in the way they are milled (40). Whole wheat flours are made from the entire kernel. White flours come from the endosperm. White flour accounts for 97 percent of the total flour consumed. When the endosperm of wheat is reduced by milling to pieces of a size to qualify as flour, usually a maximum of 72 percent of the grain is utilized (45). The other 28 percent constitutes shorts which includes bran and germ, much of which is used as food for animals. A 72-percent-extraction flour is known as "straight flour." However, millers do not put the last and more crush-resistant pieces of endosperm into high-quality flour. Those flours that are made of less than the entire endosperm are known as "patent flours." The remainder of the endosperm yields lower-grade clear flours. The part of the endosperm from which clear flours come is also used to make breakfast cereals.

Long patent flours contain a high proportion of the endosperm. Short patent flours contain relatively less, with a higher proportion of the endosperm left as clear flour. The diagram in Figure 10-2 shows the percentage of the wheat kernel found in the different fractions of flour. That portion of the endosperm which most resists cracking is higher in protein and lower in starch. Thus longer patent flours have a higher percentage of protein than shorter patent flours made from the same type of wheat.

Air classification can be used to separate a flour into fractions with different ratios of protein to starch. A controlled flow of air is used to separate the particles of flour according to size and weight. Because heavier pieces are higher in protein, this technique provides flours from the same wheat differing widely in protein content (46). Before this innovation, the protein content of the flour had to be controlled by the kind of wheat used and to a lesser extent by the proportion of endosperm crushed to make the flour. By means of air classification, flours that vary in protein content over a range of from 5 to 20 percent can be obtained from the same wheat. White flour averages 65 to 70 percent starch and 8 to 13 percent protein. Moisture content ranges from 12

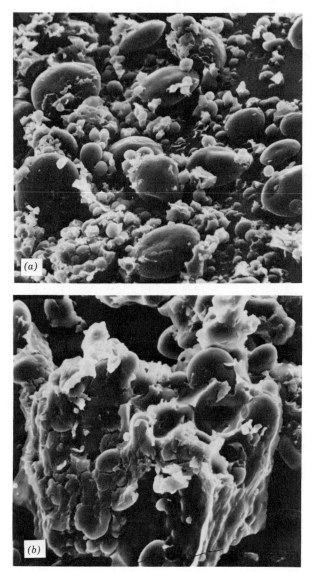

Figure 10-1. Scanning electron micrograph of (a) soft winter wheat flour and (b) hard red winter wheat flour. Magnified X 800. (From R. C. Hoseney and P. A. Seib, *Bakers Digest* **47**(6): 28. Reprinted with permission from the December 1973 issue of *Bakers Digest,* Chicago, Ill.)

to 15 percent. It can vary with the relative humidity of the air to which the flour is exposed. Flour contains approximately 2 percent pentosans and 1 to 2 percent lipids.

PARTICLE SIZE. Pieces of endosperm in patent flour must be small enough so that 98 percent pass through a sieve with a mesh of 210 micrometers. (See

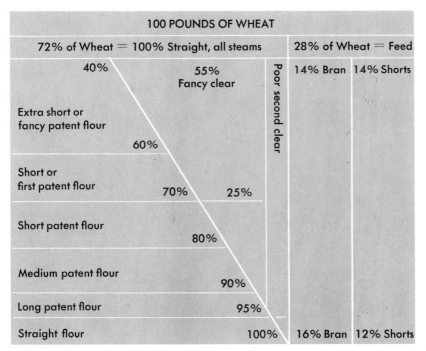

Figure 10-2. Milling of flour: yields of milled fractions from 100 pounds of wheat. (From C. O. Swanson, *Wheat Flour Quality,* copyright © 1938, Burgess Publishing Company, Minneapolis, Minn.)

Fig. 10-3.) This is specified in the standard of identity for white wheat flour as promulgated by the Food and Drug Administration. But the range in size of particles is great. The heterogeneous character of conventional flour is shown in Figure 10-4a. Such flour packs and does not pour readily. In addition, its wettability is poor. Individual particles are too small to overcome the surface tension of water. The mass tends to float when combined with water, buoyed up by air trapped in the spaces between the finer particles. Uneven access of individual particles of flour to water results in lumps. To eliminate these disadvantages of conventionally milled flour, instantized flours (also called instant-blending or instant-mixing flours) have appeared on the market (29). Two types of instantized flour are available. One is made of cracked endosperm too coarse to be classed as regular flour, but too fine for farina. The second is a coarse flour made from regular flour by a process known as "agglomeration." Particles of conventional flour are brought into contact with moisture so that they adhere. These clumps are then dried. The particles of instantized flour must pass through a sieve with a mesh of 840 micrometers. Only 20 percent of the flour particles can be small enough to pass a mesh of 74 micrometers. Particles of instantized flours are not only larger than ordinary flour, but they are more uniform in size, as the illustrations in Figure 10-4 show.

Figure 10-3. Photomicrograph of 16 xx mesh silk bolting cloth with particles of flour adhering. Original magnification X 160. (Photograph by R. I. Derby, General Mills, Inc. From *Cereal Science Today,* October 1957. Reprinted by permission.)

Such flours do not pack, but pour easily and blend readily in cold liquid because each particle is heavy enough to sink. Instantized flours absorb moisture more slowly than conventional flour and they can tolerate more mixing without making the product tough (8,27).

CLASSED BY USE

A third classification of flours is according to use, as bread flour, all-purpose or family flour, pastry flour, and cake flour. Milled in the conventional way, bread flour is a long extraction of hard wheats. Cake flour, at the other end of the scale, is a short patent of soft wheats. Although the particles for all conventionally milled flours must fall within a certain size range, some flours are finer than others. Bread flour is coarse and gritty compared with cake flour, which is fine and powdery, with a greater tendency to pack. To obtain particles as small as those of cake flour, extensive crushing of the endosperm is required so that the pieces of flour pass a very fine sieve. Family or all-purpose flour is, as the latter term implies, an intermediate type, not as coarse as bread flour or as fine as cake flour. In a cup of all-purpose flour there are an estimated one hundred billion (10^{11}) pieces of endosperm. Pastry flour is not quite as short a patent as cake flour, but it resembles cake flour more than all-purpose flour in composition and in baking properties.

(a)

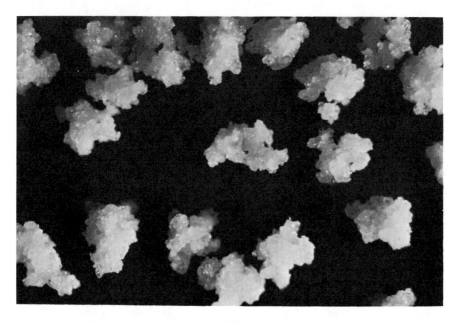

(b)

Figure 10-4. Photomicrographs of (a) conventional flour, showing unevenness of size of particles, and (b) instantized (agglomerated) flour, with particles of uniform size. (Photographs by R. I. Derby, General Mills, Inc.)

Bread flour is eminently suited to making yeast breads. All-purpose flour makes biscuits, muffins, waffles, gingerbread, coffee cake, and even yeast bread of high quality. Recipes for muffins, biscuits, and pastry especially adapted for soft wheat flour have been developed. Large quantities of soft wheat flour are used by the packaged mix industry. Oilseed flours lack the dough-forming potential of wheat flour proteins.

As a consequence of differences in composition, flours vary in density. A cup of bread flour weighs more than a cup of all purpose flour which in turn weighs more than a cup of cake flour. (See the A.H.E.A. *Handbook of Food Preparation* or U.S. Dept. Agr. Handbook No. 456, *Nutritive Value of American Foods in Common Units* for the weights per cup of different flours.) Actually, a cupful of two brands of all-purpose flour may not weigh exactly the same. The weight of a cup of all-purpose flour of the same brand may differ slightly from year to year from variations in supply of wheat available to the miller. For substituting one flour for another, weight rather than measure is a better basis.

Durum wheat is harder than the hardest of hard wheats. When the endosperm of this type of wheat is milled, the product is called "semolina." A paste of semolina and water is used to make all high-quality macaroni products (macaroni, spaghetti, noodles). Macaroni can be made from hard wheat bread flour, but the quality of the product is poor. Noodles differ from macaroni in that egg is added to the mix for the former.

FORMATION OF DOUGH FROM FLOUR

The conversion of wheat flour into bread dough is a complex process still poorly understood, as the many scientific papers appearing on the subject attest (10,15,20,23,36). When particles of flour are wetted and then manipulated, a coherent mass of dough forms, the visco-elastic character of which is attributed to the development of a colloidal complex called gluten. The proteins of flour participate in the formation of gluten in bread dough, but other constituents of the flour including flour lipids and water-soluble pentosans and glycoproteins are involved, too. And the presence of water is necessary.

HYDRATION

Bread dough contains 40 percent or more of water so the affinity of flour for water is great. Flour and water begin interacting the instant they are combined. When a drop of water came in contact with a particle of flour on a microscope slide, films of protein which separated into fibrils were observed emerging from the fractured surface of endosperm cells (3). As these fibrils streamed from the cells, carrying with them grains of starch, they united to form a network. (See Fig. 10-5.) It was suggested that protein molecules may be deposited in the protein bodies of endosperm cells of wheat in laminar fashion (4) similar to that of starch molecules within the granule.

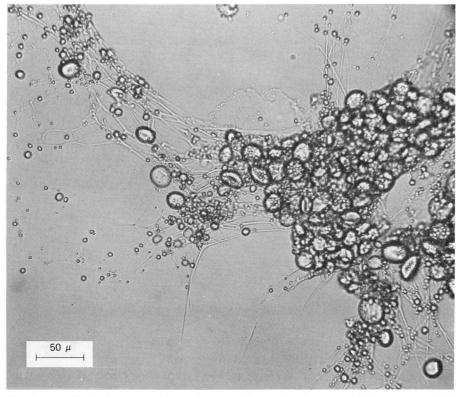

Figure 10-5. Fibrils of protein (with starch grains adhering) that have emerged from a particle of flour wetted with a drop of water on a microscope slide. (From J. E. Bernardin and D. D. Kasarda, *Cereal Chemistry* **50:** 531, 1973. Reprinted by permission.)

When water is combined with flour to form a dough, part of the water is bound by constituents of the flour, chiefly starch and protein (1). Exposed surfaces where the water may contact the starch and protein of the flour are very great. Estimates are as high as 235 square meters of surface per gram of flour (6). The first layer of water molecules is firmly adsorbed. Succeeding layers are less and less firmly bound until the water is free to flow (43). Flour can adsorb or bind firmly slightly more than one-fourth its weight of water (1). Dough that contains only bound water is stiff, inelastic, and lifeless. Only that portion of water not required to meet the hydration capacity of the flour is free to contribute to the mobility of the flour-water mixture. The optimum ratio of water to flour in a dough varies with the flour, with those flours from harder wheats having a greater water-holding capacity. It is in this aqueous milieu that flour is converted to bread dough with desirable rheological properties (14). Bread dough is elastic. When stretched, it recovers, in part at once and in part slowly. Bread dough is viscous and will gradually flow and so fit into containers of any shape. Elasticity and viscosity are attributed to the devel-

Figure 10-6. Three stages in the development of gluten: (left) dough immediately after water was stirred into the flour; (center) gluten incompletely developed; (right) satiny surface of dough in which gluten is fully developed. (Courtesy of the Wheat Flour Institute.)

opment of gluten. Dough also has an element of plasticity, that is, force is needed to initiate flow. Hydrated starch grains which comprise slightly less than half the volume of unrisen yeast dough confer on it the plastic quality. Models have been devised to help visualize the complex rheological character of bread dough (14). (See Fig. 1-11.)

DEVELOPMENT OF GLUTEN

Gluten is developed by manipulating hydrated particles of flour. Figure 10-6 shows three stages in the development of a dough. At the left is shown dough immediately after water is stirred into the flour. In the center is dough with gluten incompletely developed. The satiny surface of the dough on the right denotes well-developed gluten. If the ratio of water to flour is so high that the dough is too soft and sticky to be manipulated with the hands, gluten can be developed by stirring the dough with a spoon or with the blades of an electric mixer operating at low speed. If the mass is not too sticky to handle, it may be kneaded on a bread board or other suitable surface. Kneading involves a gentle stretching and folding of the hydrated mass. The object is to move fibrils past each other and align them so that they bond at strategic points to form gluten. Dough that is kneaded the optimum amount is elastic and springy yet extensible. These qualities are essential in dough if it is to yield high-quality bread. The film of gluten that covers starch grains in the dough shown in the scanning electron micrograph of Figure 10-7 is typical of gluten films present in well-developed dough such as that illustrated in Figure 10-6.

Harder wheat flours require more manipulation and yield doughs that are more elastic and extensible than softer wheat flours. In fact, doughs made from all-purpose flour differ in this respect. Dough from rye flour lacks the visco-elastic quality of wheat flour dough; its prominent characteristic is plasticity. The combination of rheological models in Figure 1-11 only hint at the complex visco-elastic character of bread dough. Differences in the gluten-

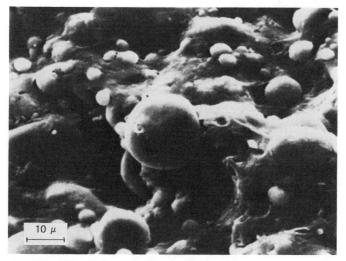

Figure 10-7. A veil-like film of gluten covers starch grains in this scanning electron micrograph of dough mixed to optimum development. (Reprinted from L. G. Evans, T. Volpe, and M. E. Zabik from the *Journal of Food Science* **42:** 71, 1977. Copyright © by Institute of Food Technologists.)

forming potential of three types of flour—bread, all-purpose, and cake—are illustrated in the mixograms in Figure 10-8. These curves were made by an instrument that measures and records on a moving graph the force needed to manipulate flour and water as gluten develops in a dough. The length of each vertical line in the curve indicates the resistance of the developing dough to the movement of the working parts of the instrument as they oscillate in the dough. The sharper the angle of the left side of the curve, the faster the gluten develops; the higher the peak, the stronger the gluten. On the right, the steeper the slope, the faster the gluten in the dough weakens with overmanipulation.

Once gluten is developed in a dough it can be separated from other constituents of the flour, mainly starch grains and water solubles, by washing in cold water. The starch grains that are adhering to the gluten are dislodged by the water. The grayish mass that remains is crude gluten, which may still contain small adhering grains of starch and which is approximately two-thirds water. Harder wheat and longer patent flours yield more gluten than do softer wheat and shorter patent flours. (See Fig. 10-9.) The yield of gluten from cake flour is small.

The ability of dough to retain gases and expand as they accumulate is due to gluten. When crude gluten is shaped into a ball and put into an oven and baked, it increases in volume several-fold (Fig. 10-9). The pressure of the expanding gas, coupled with the ability of the gluten to stretch and confine the steam, is responsible for the marked expansion of the gluten as it bakes. Once the gluten is inflated, pressure of the expanding steam maintains its volume until heat has had time to set the protein. If the gluten is removed from the oven before it has set, the steam condenses and the inflated gluten col-

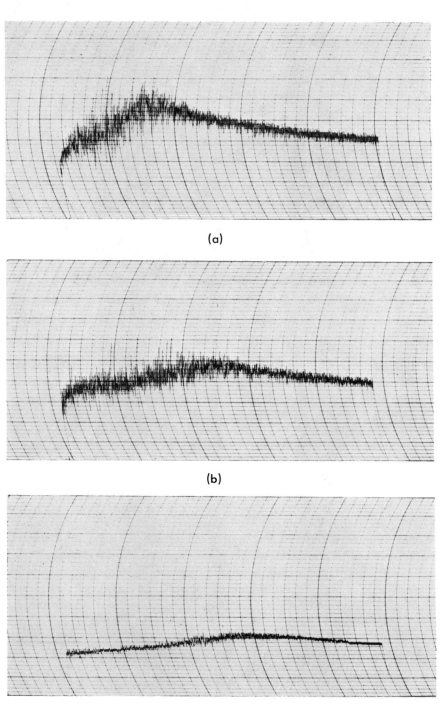

Figure 10-8. Mixograms showing the development and breakdown of gluten as flour and water are manipulated: (a) baker's hard wheat flour; (b) all-purpose or family flour; (c) cake or soft wheat flour.

156

Figure 10-9. Gluten balls from different flours before and after baking: (left) cake flour; (center) all-purpose flour; (right) bread flour. (Courtesy of the Wheat Flour Institute.)

lapses. When the optimum volume has been reached or the gluten has expanded as much as it will or can, the oven temperature is lowered to avoid burning the exterior before the interior has had time to get hot enough to set. The interior of a baked ball of gluten shows pockets where bubbles of steam were once trapped by films of gluten.

Different flours may yield the same amount of raw gluten, yet the volumes after baking may differ. Glutens from different flours differ in their ability to stretch with increasing pressure of trapped and expanding gas. Gluten from flours best suited to making yeast dough is very elastic and expands more during baking.

Much research effort has been expended to learn just how the constituents of wheat flour interact to form gluten. Although much has been learned about many of the bits and pieces of the puzzle, still there are gaps in our knowledge and uncertainty about how all the known pieces fit together. One worker in the field candidly stated that we still do not know just how the proteins of flour participate in the formation of gluten (15). Reviews of papers on various aspects of the subject appear regularly. The discussion that follows attempts to summarize briefly some pertinent information.

PROTEINS.   The assortment of amino acids that makes up the proteins of gluten is unique (9,24). (The chemistry of proteins is discussed in Chapter 17.) A single amino acid, glutamic, makes up more than 40 percent of the total. Most of this amino acid is present, not with its second carboxyl group free, but as an amide, and as such it is available for hydrogen bonding with the oxygens of hydroxyl, carboxyl, and carbonyl groups of proteins and other molecules. Next in quantity is the amino acid proline which makes up approximately 14 percent of the total amino acids in gluten. The presence of proline puts constraints on the shape that a polypeptide can assume. The low percentage of basic amino acids and the even lower content of acidic ones result in a low net charge on most of the molecules in the gluten complex. A fair proportion of the amino acids present are such as to favor hydrophobic or Van der Waals bonding between protein molecules when they are in an aqueous medium such as dough. Approximately 2 percent of the amino acids of gluten are cystine, molecules of which contain the disulfide bond. Without doubt, many of the special characteristics of gluten come from its unique amino acid makeup.

Although the proteins of flour are known to be required for the formation of gluten, the water-soluble albumins and the salt-soluble globulins that constitute 15 percent of the total are not essential. Of the remaining proteins, which do participate in the formation of gluten, approximately half are soluble in 70 percent alcohol, and these molecules constitute the gliadin fraction. The other half, the alcohol-insoluble molecules of protein, comprise the fraction known as glutenin. It is the glutenin fraction that confers on bread dough its elastic properties, whereas the gliadins are fluid and sticky (9). (See Fig. 10-10.) A proper balance of elastic and viscous elements is essential in dough if it is to yield high-quality bread. The gliadin proteins are thought to be single polypeptide chains maintained in compact, ellipsoidal shape by intramolecular disulfide (-S-S-) bonds (32). The glutenins are a more varied assortment of molecules. These alcohol-insoluble glutenins can be separated into a fraction which is soluble in dilute acetic acid and a fraction which is insoluble in this medium (33). One scheme devised to help visualize how the two subgroups of glutenin might be arranged is shown in Figure 10-11 (23). Insoluble glutenin (glutenin II of the scheme) is made of polypeptide subunits, each held in compact shape by intramolecular disulfide bonds. These subunits are linked, in turn, in more or less linear fashion by interpolypeptide disulfide bonds (11). Subunits of acetic acid-soluble glutenins (glutenin I of the scheme) are believed to be united to each other and to glutenin II polypeptides by secondary bonds such as hydrogen, hydrophobic, and Van der Waals linkages. In this scheme, glutenin II would contribute elasticity, and the mobile linkages of glutenin I would contribute the viscous element to gluten. The ratio of the two in a flour would in large measure determine the rheological characteristics of the dough. The fibrous character of glutenin is shown in the scanning electron micrograph of Figure 10-12.

LIPIDS. Lipids account for only a fraction of the weight of flour, but they are essential in breadmaking (30). (See Chapter 14 for a discussion of the chemistry of lipids.) Most of the lipids of flour can be removed by a nonpolar solvent. But once flour is formed into a dough, much of the fat can no longer be extracted (7). So dough formation involves the binding of lipids. The lipids of flour are known to be a complex mixture (30,35,37). Flour lipids are classed on the basis of solubility as either free lipids or bound, and the two groups are present in roughly equal proportions. A high proportion of the bound lipids are polar and a high proportion of the free lipids are nonpolar. The free non-

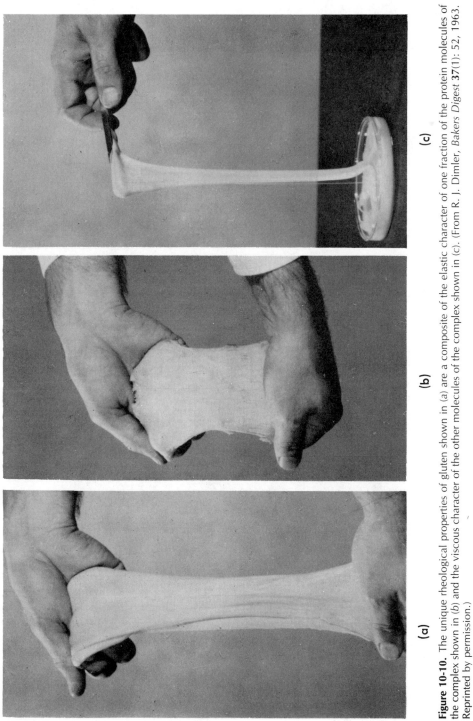

(a)   (b)   (c)

Figure 10-10. The unique rheological properties of gluten shown in (a) are a composite of the elastic character of one fraction of the protein molecules of the complex shown in (b) and the viscous character of the other molecules of the complex shown in (c). (From R. J. Dimler, *Bakers Digest* **37**(1): 52, 1963. Reprinted by permission.)

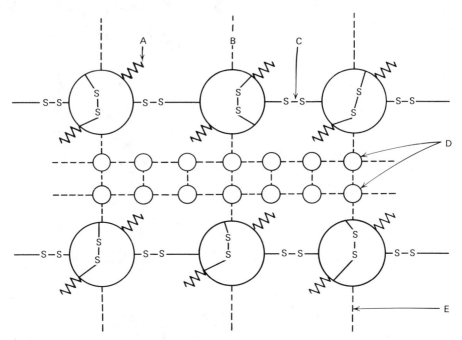

Figure 10-11. Model of glutenin: a scheme to account for its functional properties. (A) Glutenin II subunit with (B) intrapolypeptide disulfide bond and (C) interpolypeptide disulfide bond, (D) glutenin I subunits, and (E) secondary bonds (e.g., hydrogen bonds and hydrophobic interactions). (From K. Kahn and W. Bushuk, *Bakers Digest* **52**(2): 19. Reprinted with permission from the April, 1978, Issue of *Bakers Digest*, Chicago, Ill.)

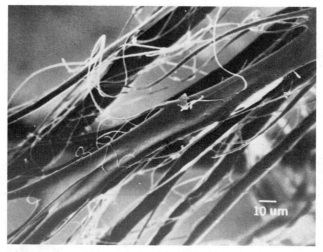

Figure 10-12. Scanning electron micrograph of purified glutenin from a gluten ball made from hard red spring wheat shows its fibrous character. (From R. A. Orth, B. L. Dronzek, and W. Bushuk, *Cereal Chemistry* **50:** 700, 1973. Reprinted by permission.)

polar lipids are mainly triglycerides. The main polar lipids are phospholipids (i.e., have phosphoric acid as part of the molecule) and galactolipids (i.e., have the sugar, galactose, as part of the lipid molecule). For a time the phospholipids were considered the essential fraction of flour lipids for the formation of gluten. In fact, one model for the structure of gluten that was widely accepted envisioned these polar phospholipid molecules arranged in bimolecular layers with these layers interspersed among layers of platelets of protein (13). Currently, the digalactosyl diglycerides are the polar lipids considered important in the formation of gluten (30,35). There is evidence that free polar lipids unite with gliadins by hydrogen bonds and with glutenins by hydrophobic interaction and Van der Waals forces (16). Thus in unfractionated gluten, polar lipids could bind simultaneously with both gliadins and glutenins, possibly contributing to the gas-holding capacity of the gluten complex. The loaf-volume potential has been attributed to the gliadin fraction (17), but also to the glutenins of dough (33). Although galactolipids are associated with gluten in dough, in bread the major portion is shifted to and complexed with gelatinized starch (44). Galactolipids or surfactants with similar properties can be added to counteract the damaging effects on bread of high levels of soy or oilseed flours (35).

EFFECTS OF SUGAR AND OF FAT ON DEVELOPMENT OF GLUTEN

Sugar and fat are two ingredients commonly found in recipes for baked products that contain flour. Included in high proportions, they limit the amount of gluten that can be developed in a flour. Sugar does this because it is even more avid for water than flour (2), and fat because it coats the particles of flour and thus prevents water from making contact with them. Fat is a more effective inhibitor of the development of gluten than is sugar.

OXIDIZING OR MATURING AGENTS FOR FLOUR

Oxidizing or maturing agents are added to flour so that dough will have the desired rheological properties. Dough should not be so tight and inextensible that gas bubbles are unable to expand, or so weak that the dough gives too easily and leaks gas. Current thinking is that disulfide bonds in the molecules of glutenin give elasticity to dough (31) and enable it to resist expansion, and that sulfhydryl groups weaken dough by disrupting disulfide bonds (5). Some sulfhydryl-disulfide interchange may be desirable as dough is mixed so that protein fibrils may be stretched as they are aligned to form gluten. Once gluten is developed, however, sulfhydryl groups are detrimental to dough by depolymerizing the molecules that formed the gluten. Sources of sulfhydryl groups in dough are small peptides in the water-soluble constituents of flour, substances released as the result of fermentation, unheated milk, wheat germ, and sulfhydryl groups formed by mechanical scission of disulfide bonds when dough is made (21).

Oxidizing agents permitted in flour include acetone peroxides, benzoyl peroxide, chlorine: (in cake flour), chlorine dioxide, nitrosyl chloride, and oxides of nitrogen (21). All of the above bleach the pigments (mainly xanthophylls) of flour, too. Flours so treated are labeled "bleached." Some unbleached flour is on the market. Bleached flour is snowy white instead of the natural cream color of the endosperm. The improver effect of oxidizing agents is attributed to their elimination of unwanted sulfhydryl groups. Two other compounds which are used as flour improvers are ascorbic acid and potassium bromate, and although they are effective improvers, just how they act is still unclear (18,22).

ENRICHMENT OF FLOUR

Most of the wheat consumed as human food is in the form of flour and the major portion is refined white flour. Because enrichment of flour is mandatory in more than half of the states, practically all millers, because of competition, voluntarily enrich their flour. As a result, most of the flour on the market is enriched. Enriched flour is so labeled, and the inclusion of four nutrients—thiamine, riboflavin, niacin, and iron—is mandatory. Inclusion of calcium and vitamin D is optional.

PASTAS

Macaroni and other pastas are made from a flour-water dough which has been extruded in characteristic shapes after which the pasta is dried. High-quality products are made from the crushed endosperm (called semolina) of durum wheat, although bread wheat is sometimes used to make these pastas. Usually from 1 to 1½ ounces of uncooked pasta are allowed per serving.

Macaroni products may be cooked in either a minimum or an excess of water. With the former, twice as much water as macaroni product is used and the pasta is steamed as for rice. Nutrients are not discarded with surplus cooking water when this method is used. The flavor of the product is more pronounced and it is chewier. Danger of scorching is greater with this method. Using a heavy pan with a tight-fitting lid and turning the unit low once the product reaches cooking temperature minimize this hazard. When a macaroni product is cooked in excess water, the cooking time is reduced somewhat, the product swells more, and the pieces are less likely to adhere. Rinsing the cooked product with hot water removes starch from the surface of the pieces so they do not adhere when cool. Macaroni products should be cooked until the pieces are tender and no raw taste remains. Overcooking will cause the pieces to fall apart. Macaroni products made from durum flour hold their shape better than do those from bread flour. Directions on the package for quick-cooking macaroni products call for a very short cooking time. Although the presence of phosphate salt speeds the gelatinization of a starch, somewhat longer cooking than is suggested improves the flavor.

REFERENCES

1. Baker, J. C., H. K. Parker, and M. D. Mize. 1946. The distribution of water in dough. *Cereal Chem.* **23:** 30–38. Bound and free water in dough and their relation to flow properties.
2. Baxter, A. J., and E. E. Hester. 1958. The effect of sucrose on gluten development and the solubility of proteins of soft wheat flour. *Cereal Chem.* **35:** 366–374. An attempt to account for the effects of sucrose on baked products made with flour.
3. Bernardin, J. E., and D. D. Kasarda. 1973. Hydrated protein fibrils from wheat endosperm. *Cereal Chem.* **50:** 529–536. Microscopic evidence for the formation of fibrils when flour is wetted.
4. Bernardin, J. E., and D. D. Kasarda. 1973. The microstructure of wheat protein fibrils. *Cereal Chem.* **50:** 735–745. Noncovalently linked fibrils as a basis for elasticity and viscous flow.
5. Bloksma, A. H. 1975. Thiol and disulfide groups in dough rheology. *Cereal Chem.* **52:** 170r–183r. Proposal that viscous flow is due to thiol disulfide interchange.
6. Bushuk, W., and I. Hlynka. 1964. Water as a constituent in flour, dough and bread. *Bakers Digest* **38**(6): 43–46, 92. The role of water in dough formation and in baking.
7. Chiu, C. M., and Y. Pomeranz. 1966. Changes in the extractability of lipids during breadmaking. *J. Food Sci.* **31:** 753–758. Binding of lipids during mixing and baking.
8. Claus, W. S., and E. M. Brooks. 1965. Some physical, chemical, and baking characteristics of instantized wheat flours. *Cereal Sci. Today* **10:** 41–43, 52, 62. Comparison of layer cake, angel cake, and bread made with conventional and instantized flours.
9. Dimler, R. J. 1963. Gluten—The key to wheat's utility. *Bakers Digest* **37**(1): 52–57. Chemical makeup and physical properties.
10. Ewart, J. A. D. 1972. Recent research in dough visco-elasticity. *Bakers Digest* **46**(4): 22–28. Proteins of flour and the properties of dough.
11. Ewart, J. A. D. 1979. Glutenin structure. *J. Sci. Food Agric.* **30:** 482–492. Disulfide-bonded linear structure reemphasized.
12. Fleming, S. E., and F. W. Sosulski. 1978. Microscopic evaluation of bread fortified with concentrated plant proteins. *Cereal Chem.* **55:** 373–382. Effects of soy flour and sunflower, fava bean, and field pea concentrate compared.
13. Grosskreutz, J. C. 1961. A lipoprotein model of gluten structure. *Cereal Chem.* **38:** 336–339. An attempt to account for the formation and the structure of gluten.
14. Hlynka, I. 1970. Rheological properties of dough and their significance in the breadmaking process. *Bakers Digest* **44**(2): 40–41, 44–46, 57. Rheological models for behavior of dough; factors affecting flow properties.
15. Hoseney, R. C. 1979. Dough forming properties. *J. Am. Oil Chemists' Soc.* **56:** 78A–81A. The gluten complex.
16. Hoseney, R. C., K. F. Finney, and Y. Pomeranz. 1970. Functional (breadmaking) and biochemical properties of wheat flour components. VI. Gliadin-lipid-glutenin interaction in wheat gluten. *Cereal Chem.* **47:** 135–140. Evidence for the complex.

17. Hoseney, R. C., K. F. Finney, Y. Pomeranz, and M. D. Shogren. 1969. Functional (breadmaking) and biochemical properties of wheat flour components. III. Characterization of gluten protein fractions obtained by ultracentrifugation. *Cereal Chem.* **46:** 126–135. Importance of gliadin to loaf volume.

18. Hoseney, R. C., K. F. Finney, and M. D. Shogren. 1972. Functional (breadmaking) and biochemical properties of wheat flour components. X. Fractions involved in the bromate action. *Cereal Chem.* **49:** 372–378. Effectiveness of bromate.

19. Hoseney, R. C., and P. A. Seib. 1973. Structural differences in hard and soft wheat. *Bakers Digest* 47(6): 26–28, 56. Shown by electron micrographs.

20. Huebner, F. R. 1977. Wheat flour proteins and their functionality in baking. *Bakers Digest* **51**(5): 25–28, 30–31, 154. Characterization of gliadin and glutenin.

21. Jackel, S. S. 1977. The importance of oxidation in breadmaking. *Bakers Digest* **51**(2): 39–43. Approved oxidants and their action; effects of over and under oxidation.

22. Johnston, W. R., and R. E. Mauseth. 1972. The interrelations of oxidants and reductants in dough development. *Bakers Digest* **46**(2): 20–22. Current concepts; emphasis on the role of ascorbic acid.

23. Kahn, K., and W. Bushuk. 1978. Glutenin: Structure and functionality in breadmaking. *Bakers Digest* **52**(2): 14–16, 18–20. Physico-chemical character; a working model.

24. Krull, L. H., and J. S. Wall. 1969. Relationship of amino acid composition and wheat protein properties. *Bakers Digest* **43**(4): 30–34, 36, 38–39. Properties and interaction of component amino acids.

25. Lorenz, K. J., R. Welsh, N. Normann, and J. Maga. 1972. Comparative mixing and baking properties of wheat and triticale flour. *Cereal Chem.* **49:** 187–193. Water absorption, mixing tolerance, and handling properties compared.

26. Mangelsdorf, P. C. 1953. Wheat. *Sci. American* **189**(1): 50–59. Origin and development of wheat: varieties.

27. Matthews, R. H., and E. A. Bechtel. 1966. Eating quality of some baked products made with instant flour. *J. Home Econ.* **58:** 729–730. Adjustment recommended when instant flour is used in baked products.

28. Matthews, R. H., E. J. Sharp, and W. M. Clark. 1970. The use of some oilseed flours in bread. *Cereal Chem.* **47:** 181–189. Cottonseed, peanut, safflower, and soy flours compared.

29. Miller, B. S., H. B. Trimbo, and R. I. Derby. 1969. Instantized flour—physical properties. *Bakers Digest* **43**(6): 49–51, 66. Structure, physical properties, and ease of dispersion in water.

30. Morrison, W. R. 1976. Lipids in flour, dough and bread. *Bakers Digest* **50:** 29–34, 36, 47. In-depth summary of various aspects.

31. Nielsen, H. C., G. E. Babcock, and F. R. Senti. 1962. Molecular weight studies on glutenin before and after disulfide bond splitting. *Arch. Biochem. Biophys.* **96:** 252–258. Importance of disulfide bonds in elastic and cohesive properties.

32. Nielsen, H. C., A. C. Beckwith, and J. S. Wall. 1968. Effect of disulfide bond cleavage on wheat gliadin fractions obtained by gel filtration. *Cereal Chem.* **45:** 37–47. Evidence of intramolecular disulfide bonds only.

33. Orth, R. A., and W. Bushuk. 1972. A comparative study of proteins of wheat of diverse baking qualities. *Cereal Chem.* **49:** 268–275. Protein fractions and loaf volume.

34. Orth, R. A., B. L. Dronzek, and W. Bushuk. 1973. Studies of glutenin. IV. Microscopic structure and its relation to breadmaking quality. *Cereal Chem.* **50:** 688–696. Fibrous character of glutenin from washed gluten of different flours.

35. Pomeranz, Y. 1971. Glycolipid-protein interaction in breadmaking. *Bakers Digest* **45**(1): 26–31, 58. Evidence for interaction; mechanisms; role in protein-enriched breads.

36. Pomeranz, Y. 1980. Molecular approach to breadmaking: An update and new perspectives. *Bakers Digest* **54**(1): 20–27; **54**(2): 12, 14, 16–18, 20, 24–25. Summary of current knowledge of flour components and their interaction in breadmaking.

37. Pomeranz, Y., and O. K. Chung. 1978. Interaction of lipids with proteins and carbohydrates in breadmaking. *J. Am. Oil Chemists' Soc.* **55:** 285–289. Characterization of the lipids and evidence for their interaction.

38. Rooney, L. W., C. B. Gustavson, S. P. Clark, and C. M. Cater. 1972. Comparison of the baking properties of some oilseed flours. *J. Food Sci.* **37:** 14–18. Cottonseed, peanut, sesame, and sunflower compared.

39. Stenvert, N. L., and K. Kingswood. 1977. The influence of the physical structure of the protein matrix on wheat hardness. *J. Sci. Food Agric.* **28:** 11–19. Importance of continuity of the matrix and its bonding with starch.

40. Storck, J., and W. T. Teague. 1952. *Flour for Man's Bread: A History of Milling.* Minneapolis: University of Minnesota Press. 382 pp. Profusely illustrated.

41. Tsen, C. C., and W. J. Hoover. 1973. High-protein bread from wheat flour fortified with full-fat soy flour. *Cereal Chem.* **50:** 7–16. Modifications that yield acceptable bread.

42. Tsen, C. C., W. J. Hoover, and E. P. Farrell. 1973. Baking quality of triticale flours. *Cereal Chem.* **50:** 16–20. Three triticale flours compared.

43. Webb, R. J., Y. Heaps, P. W. Russell, P. W. R. Eggitt, and J. M. B. Coppock. 1970. A rheological investigation of the role of water in wheat flour doughs. *J. Food Technol.* **5:** 65–76. Free and bound water in yeast dough.

44. Wehrli, H. P., and Y. Pomeranz. 1970. A note on autoradiography of tritium-labeled galactolipids in dough and bread. *Cereal Chem.* **47:** 221–224. Localization of galactolipids.

45. Wheat Flour Institute. *From Wheat to Flour.* Chicago: The Institute. 75 pp. The wheat plant and its culture; milling of wheat and the kinds of flour.

46. Wickser, F. W. 1958. Baking properties of air classified flour fractions. *Cereal Sci. Today* **3:** 123–126. Photomicrographs of flour fractions and photographs of bread, layer cake, and angel cake made from each.

ELEVEN
Leavens

The palatability of most baked products depends in part upon their being porous and light. The extent to which this is achieved depends upon the elasticity and the gas-holding capacity of the liquid-and-flour paste. Equally important is the availability of gas to inflate the elastic mass. Baked products made from flour would be heavy and compact without gas to leaven them. Air, steam, and carbon dioxide are the leavening gases. Most bakery products are leavened with more than one of the three gases. Some air bubbles are incorporated in all bakery products. Because all contain liquid, some steam is formed in all. Not all baked products are leavened with carbon dioxide, however.

STEAM AS A LEAVEN

As was pointed out in the preceding chapter, steam leavens a gluten ball when it is baked. The interior of a baked gluten ball contains thin films of gluten which once surrounded pockets of steam. Gluten balls do not appear on menus, but baked products leavened mainly by steam do. Cream puffs and popovers are hollow shells inflated by steam as the batter bakes. Yorkshire pudding is popover batter baked in a different shape. The flakes in pie crust result from blisters caused by steam that forms in the dough as it bakes. Steam, also, causes the blisters on the surface of Norwegian lefse and Indian chapati.

PROPORTIONS OF WATER TO FLOUR

When steam is the chief leaven, the proportion of water to flour must be high enough so that not all of the water is bound by the dry ingredients. The volume of liquid should equal the volume of flour. (See Chapter 12, on quick breads.) Vaporization of part of the liquid gives enough steam to make the product rise. This high ratio of water to flour gives a mixture with a fluid consistency which pours easily. Baked products leavened mainly by steam are baked in a hot oven for the first few minutes to convert the water to steam.

GAS-HOLDING PROPERTIES OF A BATTER OR DOUGH

Although gluten washed free of starch has the ability to trap sufficient steam to make it rise (see Fig. 10-9), the gluten in popovers and cream puffs is not concentrated enough for this purpose. It is too diluted with starch. However, both popovers and cream puffs contain eggs, and part of the ability of these two batters to trap steam is due to the protein supplied by the eggs, particularly the proteins of egg white. In baked products in which steam is not the main leaven it still contributes some leavening action.

AIR AS A LEAVEN

When ingredients are combined for baked products, some air bubbles are incorporated incidentally. In fact, it appears to be impossible to avoid trapping some air. This is fortunate because air appears to be an essential leaven in baked products (5). This point is illustrated in the pound cakes in Figure 11-1. The ingredients (fat, sugar, flour, milk, and eggs) for the cake on the left were combined by a standard method which incorporates much air. The cake on the right was made in the same way, but all the air was evacuated before the cake was baked. The cake on the left rose; that on the right had essentially the same volume as the batter before it was baked. Thus the presence of air bubbles appears to be essential for the functioning of steam as a leaven. When the ingredients were combined for the cake in the center, precautions were taken to keep the incorporation of air to a minimum. However, the cake rose to a limited extent, presumably because some air was incorporated unintentionally.

Usually, attempts are made to incorporate air into baked products. In cakes made with fat, air is incorporated into the fat deliberately (see Chapter 21, on shortened cakes). Beating air into egg white is another means of introducing air into shortened cake. A high proportion of beaten egg is used in angel and sponge cakes. These two products are leavened by air and by steam. Air incorporated into beaten eggs provides the leaven (along with steam) in such foods as soufflé, fondue, and puffy omelet.

CARBON DIOXIDE AS A LEAVEN

SOURCE OF CARBON DIOXIDE

The third leavening gas used to make baked goods rise is carbon dioxide (CO_2). Carbon dioxide produced by microorganisms is utilized in yeast dough (see Chapter 13, on yeast breads). Alternately, it may be liberated from sodium bicarbonate ($NaHCO_3$), baking soda.

When sodium bicarbonate is heated, some carbon dioxide is released from the molecule. Washing soda is formed concurrently. The reaction is

$$2NaHCO_3 \xrightarrow{\text{Heat }(\Delta)} Na_2CO_3 + CO_2 + H_2O$$

| Sodium bicarbonate | Washing soda | Carbon dioxide | Water |

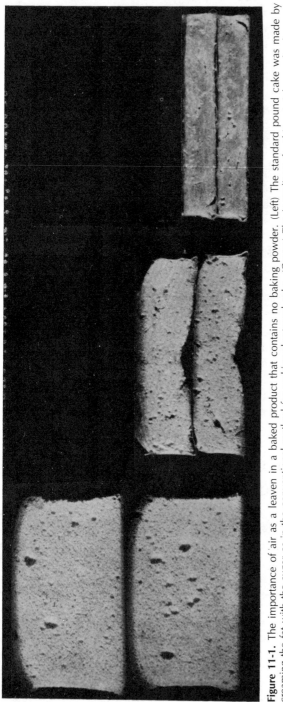

Figure 11-1. The importance of air as a leaven in a baked product that contains no baking powder. (Left) The standard pound cake was made by creaming the fat with the sugar as in the conventional method for making shortened cake. (Center) The ingredients for this special pound cake were combined so as to minimize introduction of air into the batter. (Right) For this cake, part of the same batter for the standard cake was subjected to a vacuum to remove the air. (From J. A. Dunn and J. R. White, *Cereal Chemistry* **16:** 96, 1939. Courtesy of Lever Brothers Company. Reprinted by permission.)

The washing soda that is formed is markedly alkaline. It imparts to baked products an unpleasant, soapy taste, bitter if present in excess, and a yellowish color (attributed to the effect of the alkali on the flavonoid pigments of the flour). Thiamine is more susceptible to decomposition by heat when in an alkaline medium. Another reason soda alone is undesirable as a source of carbon dioxide is that the gas is liberated too late in the baking period to be most effective as a leaven.

Ammonium bicarbonate is another source of carbon dioxide. In addition, it yields ammonia and water which can be converted to steam. The reaction is

$$NH_4HCO_3 \xrightarrow{\text{Heat}} NH_3 + H_2O + CO_2$$

The use of ammonium bicarbonate as a source of leavening gas is limited to low moisture baked products such as cookies and crackers which do not retain the ammonia (7).

RELEASE OF CARBON DIOXIDE FROM SODA BY ACID

Sodium bicarbonate, as a salt of a strong base (sodium hydroxide) and a weak acid (carbonic), is alkaline. Because of this it reacts with acids. In solution, acids ionize, freeing hydrogen ions (H^+). Sodium bicarbonate in solution also ionizes, freeing sodium ions (Na^+) and bicarbonate ions (HCO_3^-). The positive sodium ion unites with the negative ion supplied by the acid to form the sodium salt of the acid. The positive hydrogen ion from the acid unites with the negative bicarbonate ion to give carbonic acid (H_2CO_3). The reaction, illustrated with hydrochloric acid, is

$$\underset{\substack{\text{Baking}\\\text{soda}}}{NaHCO_3} + \underset{\substack{\text{Hydrochloric}\\\text{acid}}}{HCl} \xrightarrow{H_2O} \underset{\substack{\text{Sodium}\\\text{chloride}}}{NaCl.} + \underset{\substack{\text{Carbonic}\\\text{acid}}}{H_2CO_3}$$

Sodium chloride, an acceptable ingredient in baked products, is the salt formed. The carbonic acid dissociates to give carbon dioxide and water, as follows:

$$\underset{\substack{\text{Carbonic}\\\text{acid}}}{H_2CO_3} \underset{\longleftarrow}{\longrightarrow} \underset{\text{Water}}{H_2O} + \underset{\substack{\text{Carbon}\\\text{dioxide}}}{CO_2}$$

This method of obtaining carbon dioxide as a leavening gas was first patented in 1837 by Dr. Whiting in England (1).

Hydrochloric acid is not used in baked products, but ingredients such as sour milk, vinegar, honey, and molasses, which contain one or more acids in solution, are used. Sour milk and buttermilk contain lactic acid, which is produced from the sugar in milk by certain bacteria. Vinegar contains 5 percent acetic acid and the main acid in honey is gluconic acid in equilibrium with gluconolactone (12). Molasses contains aconitic acid chiefly. The reaction that occurs when soda comes in contact with the acid in sour milk is typical although a different salt results with each acid.

$$NaHCO_3 + CH_3CHOHCOOH \xrightarrow{H_2O} CH_3CHOHCOONa + H_2O + CO_2$$

| Sodium bicarbonate | Lactic acid | Sodium lactate | Water | Carbon dioxide |

BAKING POWDER

When any food which contains acid already in solution is combined with soda, the soda dissolves in the cold liquid and the acid rapidly releases the carbon dioxide from the soda. A salt of the acid is formed along with the gas. Unless both the acid and the soda are in solution and ionized, however, the two do not react. Baking powder, which is a mixture of dry soda and dry acid, takes advantage of this fact: it is stable in a closed container because both reactants are dry. The first baking powder was marketed in 1853 in the United States (1). A selling point used to promote this new product was that it would decrease baking failures and so reduce "nervous tension."

YIELD OF CARBON DIOXIDE

The yield of carbon dioxide from baking powder is set by law at a minimum of 12 percent, although most baking powders are formulated to yield 14 percent. This means that every 100 grams of baking powder must yield at least 12 grams of carbon dioxide. Because soda is the source of this CO_2, all baking powder contains at least this minimum of soda, which amounts to approximately ¼ teaspoon of soda in each teaspoon of baking powder.

To formulate a baking powder, sufficient acid is added to neutralize the soda. The amount of acid needed for each teaspoon of baking powder depends on the combining weight of the acid with the soda. The difference between the volume of soda plus the dry acid and one teaspoon is made up by an inert powder which serves as a means of standardizing the baking powder. Baking powder made with an acid that has a high combining weight will take less inert material to standardize it. Cornstarch, which is inert, tasteless, and inexpensive, or calcium carbonate ($CaCO_3$) is commonly used. Cornstarch absorbs moisture and so keeps the reactants dry. If one runs short of baking powder, ¼ teaspoon of soda and ½ teaspoon of cream of tartar may be used for each teaspoon of baking powder the recipe calls for. Flour to which has been added sufficient soda and acid for leaven and enough salt for flavor is called "self-rising flour." This product, which has been on the market for many years, is the prototype of today's array of packaged mixes.

In products leavened by carbon dioxide small bubbles of air trapped in the batter seem to be essential for a proper leavening. It appears that adequate distribution of carbon dioxide depends upon numerous air cells previously incorporated in the batter, illustrated by observation of cake batter which contained a source of carbon dioxide as it baked on a microscope slide (2). It was noted that few if any new gas cells formed. The evolving gas appeared to collect in the existing air cells.

The relative importance of the three leavening gases—air, steam, and carbon dioxide—was studied in shortened cake (6). The percentage of the total leavening gas contributed by air was small, but essential (for reasons given above). Carbon dioxide made the major contribution to leavening action, but a considerable part of the expansion during baking was due to steam. In angel cake, which contains no source of carbon dioxide, one-third to one-half of the total expansion of ingredients is due to steam formed during baking and the remainder to air incorporated during mixing and its expansion during baking.

TYPES OF BAKING POWDER

Differences among baking powders are due to the kinds of acid used (3,7,11) to formulate them. At one time three types of baking powder were readily available to the home baker. One, a phosphate baking powder, has been off the market for a number of years, and another, a tartrate baking powder, was withdrawn more recently. Two acids, tartaric and potassium acid tartrate (cream of tartar), were used to formulate tartrate baking powder. Both phosphate and tartrate baking powders were classed as *quick-* or *single*-acting because the acids involved dissolved and a high proportion of the carbon dioxide was liberated when the baking powder came in contact with cold liquid. Cream of tartar, the potassium acid salt of tartaric acid,

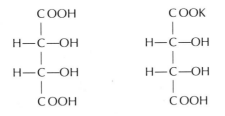

is available and can be combined with soda to yield a homemade baking powder. The reaction when this acid releases carbon dioxide from soda is

$$NaHCO_3 \ + \ KHC_4H_4O_6 \ \xrightarrow{\ H_2O\ } \ KNaC_4H_4O_6 \ + \ CO_2 \ + \ H_2O$$

Sodium   Potassium   Sodium   Carbon   Water
bicarbonate   acid tartrate   potassium tartrate   dioxide

The only type of baking powder now available to the home baker is a slow or double-acting type. It is formulated with two acid-reacting ingredients, one of which is monocalcium phosphate monohydrate. An equation for one of several reactions believed to occur when this acid reacts with soda is

$$3CaH_4(PO_4)_2 + 8NaHCO_3 \rightarrow Ca_3(PO_4)_2 + 4Na_2HPO_4 + 8CO_2 + 8H_2O$$

| Monocalcium phosphate | Sodium bicarbonate | Tricalcium phosphate | Disodium phosphate | Carbon dioxide | Water |

Monocalcium phosphate monohydrate is readily soluble in cold water.

The rates at which carbon dioxide is liberated from soda by this acid and by cream of tartar are shown in Figure 11-2. As the graph shows, almost 70 percent of the available carbon dioxide is evolved during the first two minutes. The hydrated form of monocalcium phosphate can react with soda and liberate a high proportion of the carbon dioxide as a batter or dough is mixed. When soda alone is used in a biscuit type dough, one-fifth of the CO_2 is released (Fig. 11-2) by the acidic constituents in the flour and milk (7).

The second acid-reacting ingredient used in double-acting baking powder is sodium aluminum sulfate (abbreviated SAS). This ingredient is not an acid. However, it reacts with *hot* water to form sulfuric acid according to the following reaction:

$$Na_2Al_2(SO_4)_4 + 6H_2O \xrightarrow{\text{Heat}} 2Al(OH)_3 + Na_2SO_4 + 3H_2SO_4$$

| Sodium aluminum sulfate | Water | Aluminum hydroxide | Sodium sulfate | Sulfuric acid |

This sulfuric acid then liberates carbon dioxide from the soda left unneutralized by the calcium acid phosphate, as follows:

$$3H_2SO_4 + 6NaHCO_3 \xrightarrow{H_2O} 3Na_2SO_4 + 6H_2CO_3$$

| Sulfuric acid | Sodium bicarbonate | Sodium sulfate | Carbonic acid |

Double-acting baking powder which contains both SAS and monocalcium phosphate monohydrate (usually in a ratio of 2:1) is known as SAS-phosphate baking powder. The double action refers to the sequential release of CO_2, first in the dough by the cold-water soluble calcium acid phosphate and later during baking by the acid derived from sodium aluminum sulfate. This means that some CO_2 is released during mixing, but that the major portion is released only after the product is heated in the oven and the acid is formed.

A number of leavening acids are available commercially, each tailored to meet stringent requirements for release of carbon dioxide (7,11). Packaged mixes, packaged doughs, frozen batters, doughnuts from automatic doughnut

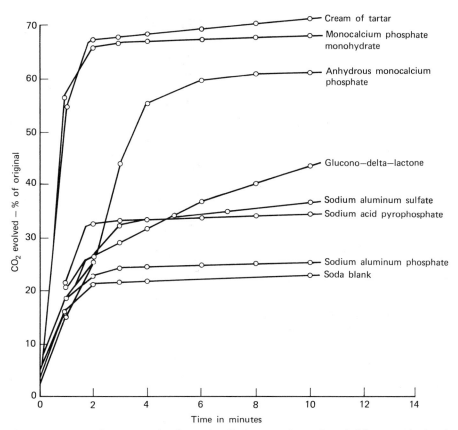

Figure 11-2. Rate of reaction in dough at 27°C of baking powder made with different acids (dough stirred 3 minutes). (From T. P. Kichline and J. F. Conn, *Bakers Digest* **44**(4): 37. Reprinted with permission from the August, 1970, issue of *Bakers Digest,* Chicago, Ill.)

machines, and bakery cake batters made in large batches all require specially formulated leavens.

The anhydrous form of monocalcium phosphate is less soluble in cold water than the monohydrate, made so in part by a coating of an insoluble material. The delay in release of CO_2 during the first few minutes of mixing means less loss of leavening gas from the batter and so greater mixing toler-ance. Sodium acid pyrophosphate, $Na_2H_2P_2O_7$, is used commercially as a leavening acid. Forms of the acid that dissolve at different temperatures during baking are available. Sodium aluminum phosphate, $NaH_{14}Al_3(PO_4)_8 \cdot 4H_2O$, is a third acid-reacting ingredient with limited solubility in cold liquid. A high proportion of the self-rising flour on the market contains this compound as one of the acid-reacting ingredients. These three acids, anhydrous monocal-cium phosphate, sodium aluminum phosphate, and sodium acid pyrophos-phate, alone or in combination are used in packaged mixes.

The use of the acid, glucono-delta-lactone, with baking soda as a source of carbon dioxide was introduced in the early 1940's (9). This acid is the lactone of gluconic acid, a derivative of glucose. Quick bread leavened with this combination of soda and acid has the appearance, volume, grain, and texture of yeast bread (but not the flavor). No fermentation time is needed, but the batter can stand up to 50 minutes before it is baked.

EFFECTS ON BAKED PRODUCTS

The faster acting the baking powder, the less the tolerance of a batter or dough to mixing. With fast acting leaven, nearly three-fourths of the available carbon dioxide is released in the cold batter or dough, whereas with SAS-phosphate type just over one-third is released (10). Only 20 to 30 percent of the carbon dioxide liberated in cold batter or dough is retained at the end of the mixing period to leaven the product. For this reason, unnecessary stirring of flour mixtures leavened with soda and sour milk or cream of tartar should be avoided. The percentage of carbon dioxide retained varies with the thickness of the unbaked mixture. The amount of baking powder used in quick breads usually varies from 1 to 2 teaspoons per cup of flour. Less is needed to leaven a product when a large amount of air is incorporated into a batter or dough. A lower proportion of baking powder is required in cake batter in which air is incorporated by means of fat.

Davies, who studied the influence of a number of variables on the quality of cakes, including leavens, used 5 grams of tartrate baking powder per 100 grams of flour for a basic formula (4). In measure this is 1¼ teaspoons per cup of flour. Increasing the baking powder by 50 percent (to 1.9 teaspoons per cup) made the grain of the cake coarse and the texture slightly harsh. Decreasing the baking powder 50 percent (to 0.64 teaspoon per cup of flour) gave a cake with a fine, close grain but a tight, slightly soggy texture.

The type of baking powder used influences the pH of the batter or dough (8). Batters and doughs made with tartrate baking powder are more acid than are those made with phosphate baking powder. The latter yields more acid batter than does the SAS-phosphate type. For example, biscuit dough made with tartrate, with phosphate, and with SAS-phosphate baking powder had pH values of 6.4, 6.7, and 7.0, respectively (8). With more acid batters, the crumb tends to be finer; with less acid ones it tends to be more open. Batters that are more acid yield baked products with a whiter crumb and a sweeter taste.

Aside from causing differences in the volume and in the pH of baked products, different baking powders leave different salts as residues. For example, if hydrochloric were used, the salt would then be sodium chloride; with sour milk the salt is sodium lactate; with tartaric acid the salt is sodium tartrate; with cream of tartar it is sodium potassium tartrate; with calcium acid phosphate the salts include tricalcium phosphate and disodium phosphate; with sodium aluminum sulfate, both sodium sulfate and aluminum hydroxide are left in the baked product. Salts produced when soda is neutralized by the various acids influence the taste of the baked product. Difference in taste is more difficult to detect in muffins than in blander-tasting biscuits. However, differences in taste due to the type of baking powder can be detected in cakes.

The ions from the leavening acids influence viscosity and elasticity of batters and doughs and the grain, resiliency, and moistness of the crumb of quick breads (7). This can be observed when biscuit dough made with soda and cream of tartar is compared with dough made with SAS baking powder. Cracks are more likely to appear along the sides of biscuits made with double-acting baking powder because of the greater elasticity and viscosity of the dough caused by the aluminum ions (3). The late release of part of the carbon dioxide during baking may be a contributing factor (1).

SODA AND SOUR MILK

When soda and sour milk or buttermilk are used in place of sweet milk and baking powder, the difficulty is in estimating the amount of acid present in the milk. One cup of very sour milk or buttermilk has enough lactic acid to neutralize and so release the carbon dioxide from ½ teaspoon of baking soda. If there is any question as to the sourness of the milk, the amount of soda per cup of milk should be limited to ¼ teaspoon. If a recipe calls for 1 cup of sour milk and only sweet milk is available, the equivalent of the sour milk is made by adding 1¼ teaspoons of cream of tartar to 1 cup of sweet milk. Or sour milk may be made by using 1 tablespoon of vinegar or lemon juice and enough milk to fill a 1-cup measure. However, baking powder (and no soda) can be used with sour milk as well as with sweet, eliminating the danger of having unneutralized soda in the baked product. The small amount of acid in slightly sour milk will do no harm; in fact, the crumb will be whiter, finer, and more moist, as can be demonstrated by adding ⅛ to ¼ teaspoon of cream of tartar per cup of flour to biscuits made with baking powder and sweet milk. A disadvantage of this addition is that the crust does not brown as readily. Phosphated flours tolerate recipes with high proportion of soda because of the neutralizing effect of the phosphate.

One cup of fully sour milk together with ½ teaspoon of soda will yield carbon dioxide equivalent to the amount obtained from 2 teaspoons of baking powder. This amount of soda and sour milk in a batter or dough which contains two or more cups of flour will not yield enough carbon dioxide to leaven the product. For this reason many recipes using sour milk call for baking powder as well as soda. For example, to leaven 2 cups of flour, as in biscuits, 4 teaspoons of single-acting baking powder may be used. If one cup of very sour milk is used with ½ teaspoon of soda, 2 teaspoons of baking powder are needed in addition. To change a recipe from sour milk and soda to sweet milk requires an additional teaspoon of baking powder for each ¼ teaspoon of soda omitted. When soda is used, it should be sifted with the dry ingredients. If it is added to the sour milk instead, the lactic acid will release the carbon dioxide into the atmosphere instead of within the batter where it is needed. Excess soda in quick breads should be avoided because of greater destruction of thiamine in more alkaline products.

REFERENCES

1. Barackman, R. A. 1954. Chemical leavening agents. *Trans. Am. Assoc. Cereal Chemists.* **12:** 43–55. Leavening power and side effects of the various acids. Brief account of the introduction of the various acids.
2. Carlin, G. T. 1944. A microscopic study of the behavior of fats in cake batter. *Cereal Chem.* **21:** 189–199.
3. Conn, J. F. 1965. Baking powders. *Bakers Digest* **39**(2): 66–68, 70. Desirable features in leavening agents: neutralizing value, leavening rate, and the effects of various leavening acids.
4. Davies, J. R. 1937. The effect of formula and procedure variables upon cake quality. *Cereal Chem.* **14:** 819–833. Major ingredients including leavens.
5. Dunn, J. A., and J. R. White. 1939. The leavening action of air included in cake batter. *Cereal Chem.* **16:** 93–100. Effects of evacuation of the batter and of modified mixing method on volume of pound cake.
6. Hood, M. P., and B. Lowe. 1948. Air, water vapor, and carbon dioxide as leavening gases in cakes made with different types of fats. *Cereal Chem.* **25:** 244–254. Relative contribution of each type of leaven.
7. Kichline, T. P., and J. F. Conn. 1970. Some fundamental aspects of leavening agents. *Bakers Digest* **44**(4): 36–40. Neutralizing value and special characteristics of the various leavening acids.
8. McKim, E., and H. V. Moss. 1943. Observations on the pH of chemically leavened products. *Cereal Chem.* **20:** 250–259. The pH of biscuit dough, biscuits, cake batter, and cake made with common leavening agents.
9. Miller, J. A., C. S. McWilliams, and S. A. Matz. 1959. Development of the leavening system for an instant bread mix. *Cereal Chem.* **36:** 487–497. Use of glucono-delta-lactone.
10. Noble, I. T., and E. G. Halliday. 1931. A quantitative measurement of the carbon dioxide evolved in and lost from simplified muffin batters. *Cereal Chem.* **8:** 165–167. Carbon dioxide evolved from three types of baking powder in water only and with three combinations of ingredients used in batters.
11. Reiman, Herbert M. 1977. Chemical leavening systems. *Bakers Digest* **51**(4): 33–34, 36, 42. Emphasis on leavens for commercial products.
12. White, Jonathan W., Jr. 1978. Honey. *Adv. Food Research* **24:** 304–305. Acids present.

TWELVE
Quick Breads

Numerous baked products are made with flour. In the preparation of bakery products, flour is combined with liquid in such ratios as to form either a batter or a dough. Pour batters used for popovers and cream puffs have a ratio of liquid to flour of 1:1 and are, as the term implies, thin enough to pour. A drop batter has 2 parts flour and 1 part liquid, as for muffins. Doughs are stiff enough to handle. Soft doughs have 3 parts flour to 1 part liquid, as for biscuits and yeast bread. A higher ratio of flour to liquid yields a stiff dough as for cookies, pastry dough, and noodles. Most batters and doughs and the baked products from them are foams. The size and shape of the gas cells determine the grain of the baked product. The texture is influenced mainly by the character of the material which defines and surrounds the gas cells.

INGREDIENTS IN QUICK BREADS AND THEIR FUNCTIONS

FLOUR

Flour gives to batters and doughs stretch or elasticity, a characteristic enabling them to hold leavening gas or gases. Flour also contributes structure or rigidity to baked products. This rigidity is due to gluten, which is coagulated by heat, and to starch, which is gelatinized. Flours differ in the amount and quality of the gluten they yield and these, in turn, affect the moisture-holding or -binding capacity of the flour. (For a discussion of the differences among flours, see Chapter 10.)

LIQUID

A liquid ingredient is essential to dissolve sugar, salt, and the soda and acid in baking powder. In water, the soda and the acid ionize, after which they can react to release carbon dioxide. Water hydrates the protein of flour, a preliminary to the development of gluten. It also hydrates the starch and makes possible its gelatinization during baking. Water converted to steam serves as a leavening agent.

SALT

Salt is used in quick breads to improve the taste, but it also influences rate and degree of hydration of the flour. The usual proportion is ½ teaspoon per cup of flour unless the recipe includes a high proportion of salted table fat. The recipe for cream puffs (see Table 12-1) specifies less than this amount of salt because of the large amount of butter or margarine. If unsalted butter or hydrogenated shortening is substituted, the amount of salt should be increased. It is possible to make a breadstuff from flour, salt, and water. Water is necessary to make the particles of flour adhere and salt to make the flour palatable. These three ingredients are basic to any quick bread.

LEAVEN

Included in a batter or dough for a baked product is either a gas or a source of gas which can expand during baking and cause the product to rise. Air may be beaten into the batter directly or may be incorporated as beaten egg white. Steam, in addition to air trapped incidentally, can provide sufficient leaven if surplus water is available in the mixture. Steam contributes some leavening action in all baked products. Soda used with an acid already in solution (as in sour milk, honey, or molasses) or soda combined with dry acid (as in baking powder) is a source of leaven in most quick breads.

Leaven not only increases volume but is responsible in part for the grain of a baked product. The gas forms holes or pockets in a batter or dough and converts it into a foam. The amount and distribution of the leavening gas determine whether the holes in the crumb are big or little and round and intact or large and exploded. Of course the ability of the dough to stretch and also to retain the leavening gas as it is liberated and as it expands when heated is as important in determining both volume and grain of the baked products as is the amount of leaven that goes into the batter.

FAT

Fat is included in batters and doughs to tenderize the product. It accomplishes this in part by waterproofing the particles of flour. It thus limits the ease with which gluten is developed. Fat also lubricates the gluten strands already formed and permits them to slip past each other more readily. The function of fat as a tenderizing agent will be treated more fully in Chapter 15 on pastry.

SUGAR

Aside from the obvious function of contributing sweetness, sugar is included in batters and doughs because it, too, contributes to the tenderness of baked products. Sugar decreases the uptake of water by flour and so interferes with the development of gluten, although to a lesser extent than does fat. Sugar serves also as a means of incorporating air into fat and so into the batter. This role of sugar is of primary importance in shortened cakes, for which the sugar is creamed extensively into the fat. Another reason for including sugar in baked products is that it aids in browning. The color is attributed to a reaction between reducing sugars and protein. In the absence of sugar, browning results from dextrinization of starch. More acidic batters brown slowly. One popular homemade quick bread mix includes cream of tartar, which is added to delay the onset of rancidity. (See Chapter 14.) Cream of tartar makes the mix more acid than were baking powder only included. A small amount of sugar is included in the mix (9) to compensate for the retarding effect of the acid on browning.

EGGS

Beaten eggs serve as a means of incorporating air into batters and doughs. Eggs contain protein, which contributes elasticity to the batter and structure to such baked products as muffins, popovers, and cream puffs. Cream puff batter contains twice as many eggs as does popover batter for the same amount of flour and liquid (see Table 12-1). More eggs are needed in cream puffs because of the high proportion of fat they contain. Egg yolk contains a fatlike material which can tie together or emulsify two incompatible liquids, water and melted fat.

PROPORTIONS OF INGREDIENTS IN QUICK BREADS

BALANCING INGREDIENTS

Ingredients in any baked product need to be in reasonable balance. Structural ingredients, such as flour and egg, are balanced against tenderizing ingredients or those which weaken structure, such as fat and sugar. In addition, liquid ingredients, milk, egg, and fat, are balanced against dry ingredients, mainly flour. For example, when sugar, fat, or both are increased in the basic muffin recipe, the egg is increased to compensate. After these modifications are made, the recipe approaches that for a shortened cake. Ingredients do not need to be in perfect balance, a fact which makes possible the infinite number of "new" recipes. There is a range in the proportions of ingredients over which a recipe will still give an acceptable product. But a good start toward success in baking is to have ingredients in good proportion, and the most practical means of doing so is to start with a balanced recipe. Unfortunately, not every recipe that is printed is good, and many are printed without being tested! Proportions of ingredients in batters and doughs may need to be altered for altitudes above 2500 to 3000 feet (1,2,8).

MEASURING INGREDIENTS

Assuming a recipe in which the ingredients are reasonably well-balanced, success in baking may hinge upon the accuracy with which the ingredients are measured. (For discussion of measuring, see Chapter 2.) Accurate measures are essential only for those ingredients for which the proportions are critical. If a recipe for muffins gives a range for the amount of sugar, there is little reason for leveling the utensil when the sugar is measured. There would be even less justification for measuring *precisely* the grated cheese to go into cheese biscuits, because perfectly good biscuits can be made without cheese. Baking powder is one ingredient that should be measured accurately because the ratio of this ingredient to flour is important. Of course, if a lighter and coarser baked product is desired, overmeasuring the leavening would produce the desired effect; to make the product more compact, skimping the leaven might be indicated. But to produce a finished product exactly like the recipe, ingredients need to be measured accurately.

MANIPULATION OF INGREDIENTS FOR QUICK BREADS

When ingredients for a batter or dough are combined, a number of factors have a bearing on the success of the operation. Techniques used to prepare quick breads should be appropriate for the ingredients used and for the results desired. Bowls and other utensils should be of appropriate size and shape. The distribution of ingredients brought about by manipulation and the resultant chemical and physical changes in or interaction among them are important factors. Each of these points is discussed below.

TECHNIQUES

A number of terms with fairly precise meanings are used in the directions for manipulating batters and doughs. To *beat* means to combine with a regular over-and-over or circular motion, either to make smooth (as for popover batter) or to incorporate air (as for beaten egg white). To *blend* means to combine thoroughly (as for melted chocolate in a batter). To *cream* applies to sugar and fat. The sugar crystals are worked into the fat to incorporate air which results in a foam (as for shortened cakes). To *cut* applies to fat and flour, with the fat progressively subdivided and coated with particles of flour (as for pastry). To *fold* means to use a knife, a spatula, or a rubber scraper to incorporate one ingredient within another (as beaten egg white into waffle batter, soufflés, or angel cake). Because the inexperienced have difficulty with this technique, it is given in detail. In folding, the edge of the implement leads. The first movement is down to the bottom of the bowl; the handle is rotated in the hand a quarter of a turn and the implement is moved across the bottom of the bowl; the handle is rotated another quarter turn and the spatula brought up through the mix, the edge of the implement leading; and finally the handle is given another quarter turn and the implement is moved across the top of the mixture. (See Figure 12-1.) Using the utensil as a paddle should be avoided when ingredients are folded. To *knead* means to stretch, fold, and press dough gently to form and arrange strands of gluten (as for biscuit or yeast bread dough). To *mix* means to distribute ingredients using any technique suitable to the ingredients involved. To *stir* means to combine, usually with a spoon, with a circular motion. Liquid and dry ingredients are combined by stirring. To *whip* means to beat rapidly for the purpose of incorporating air.

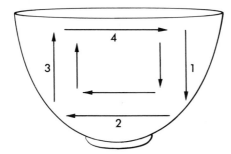

Figure 12-1. Technique of folding. Diagram shows the direction of movement of the implement used.

UTENSILS

Success in mixing batters and doughs depends in part on having utensils of good construction; price is not always an indication of quality. Using the best utensil for the work at hand is equally important.

BOWLS. Mixing bowls should have sides with a gentle slope such as that shown in Figure 16-5 rather than exhibit a pronounced curve. Although the base of the bowl should be wide enough to eliminate the danger of its overturning, the inside of the bowl at the base should be narrow. Otherwise it is difficult to combine ingredients thoroughly without much waste motion, and parts of some ingredients may be incompletely incorporated even after extensive mixing. The size of the mixing bowl or other utensil used to hold ingredients should be chosen with a view to what one intends to accomplish in manipulation. If the container is too large, ingredients are difficult to corner; if too small, ingredients are inadequately manipulated. If the volume of ingredients increases during manipulation, allowance must be made when selecting the container.

SPOONS. Spoons shaped more like paddles than the conventional shape are superior for creaming and mixing batters. Some metal spoons used for stirring foods in aluminum pans discolor or give a peculiar taste to the food. Stainless steel and wooden spoons do not, but the latter are considered unsanitary by some.

BEATERS. Hand beaters of different types—rotary, wire whip, and coiled spring—are available. (See Fig. 12-2.) The size of the handle on a rotary beater is important, as is its positioning. A handle either too large or too small or set at a wrong angle will cause the hands to cramp and tire quickly. Blades made from thin metal and whips made from thin wire will incorporate smaller bubbles of air and so produce finer foams. A spring-type whip is convenient for beating small volumes of liquids or for blending egg with milk. Too, it is easier to wash than the large rotary beater. A turbine-type beater has an advantage over a rotary type for beating small amounts of liquid. If gears on rotary beaters

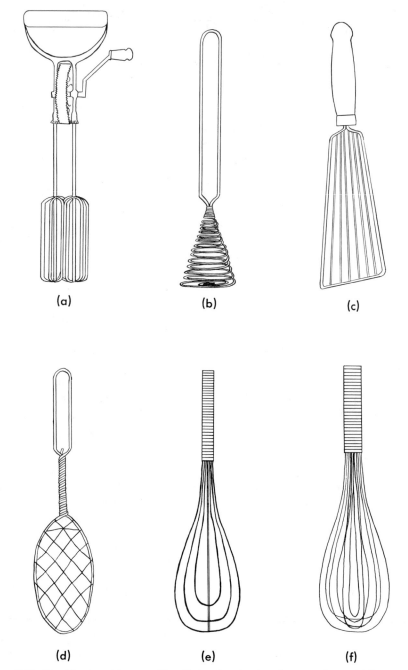

Figure 12-2. Hand beaters: (a) rotary; (b) coiled spring; (c, d, e) flat wire whips of different types; (f) chef's whip.

are exposed, they are easier to keep clean, dry, and free from rust. The blades of the beater should be washed and rinsed after use, but it is poor practice to submerge the gears of a rotary beater in dishwater. If food does get on this part of the beater, it must be washed, of course. After it is washed the beater should be rinsed in very hot water and the exposed surfaces wiped dry. The gears should be rotated rapidly for a few seconds to remove moisture. A small drop of lubricant applied to the working parts when they are dry makes the handle turn easily.

Electric mixers are either hand-held or stationary. The working parts of a hand-held electric mixer work like a hand-operated rotary beater, with electricity replacing muscle power. Stationary electric mixers are of two types. In one the bowl revolves around the rotating blades. In the other the bowl is stationary and the blades, wire whip, or dough hook attachment move in a hypocycloidal or "planetary" fashion. The attachment not only rotates, but it also moves in an orbit around the inside of the bowl.

SCRAPERS AND SPATULAS. A flexible rubber scraper is the next best thing to a *clean* finger for getting the last of the batter out of a mixing bowl, for transferring the last bits of food from one utensil to another, and for otherwise eliminating waste. A rubber scraper is useful also for folding and for some stirring operations. It is a good implement for scraping plates and other dishes preparatory to washing.

A metal spatula is helpful for folding beaten egg whites into batters, for turning pancakes, and for removing cookies from a baking sheet. The blade should be flexible enough to bend to form a right angle. Unless the blade is flexible, a kitchen knife would do almost as well; this would eliminate one more item cluttering the cutlery drawer.

FORKS AND BLENDERS. Pastry forks and pastry blenders are utensils made primarily for cutting fat into flour for biscuits and pastry. Both are dispensable, because the same operation can be performed with a kitchen fork, two table knives, two spatulas, or the fingers.

PURPOSES

A number of things need to be accomplished when the ingredients for batters and doughs are combined. One object is to achieve uniform distribution of the leavening gas throughout the batter. This objective is achieved by sifting the leaven with the flour and other dry ingredients. A second object is to distribute the fat uniformly throughout the flour. Plastic fat can be cut in for biscuits and pastry and for muffins made by the biscuit method. It can be creamed with sugar as for cakes. Finally, it can be melted or an oil used and added to the flour along with the liquid ingredients. The distribution of fat by this last method is the least uniform of the three, but it is speedy. It is the way fat is incorporated in batters made by the muffin method. A third object of the manipulation of batters is to achieve a uniform distribution of liquid. Liquid and dry ingredients are stirred to distribute the water. This also helps to dissolve the salt, the sugar, and the acid and soda in baking powder. Stirring gives cohesiveness to the mixture and actually forms the batter or dough. This should be accomplished with the minimum loss of leavening gas and without making the mixture too viscous.

Knowing how much to manipulate a batter or dough requires experience. Directions such as "stir until the ball of dough leaves the sides of the pan," "barely dampen the ingredients," or "cut until the mixture resembles coarse corn meal" require subjective criteria that can come only from experience. And it is not possible to specify in directions the precise number of strokes to produce the best product. The optimum amount of manipulation is influenced by the volume of the mix, the size and shape of the bowl, the effectiveness of the mixing utensil, and whether the strokes are vigorous or weak. Specifying the number of strokes is preferable to specifying a time, as the number of strokes by hand in a given time varies. However, strokes are not equally vigorous. Even with a hand-operated rotary beater and the same number of strokes, the speed at which the beater is turned will make some difference in the results. The extent of manipulation may be duplicated by timing with an electric mixer, but bowls, beaters, and the efficiency of mixers differ.

BAKING QUICK BREADS

CHANGES EFFECTED IN BATTERS AND DOUGHS

Early in the baking period the fat begins to melt if it is not already liquid. The mix becomes more fluid. Substances soluble only in hot water begin to dissolve. Baking powder continues to form carbon dioxide. Heat causes both carbon dioxide and air in the batter to expand. Proteins of flour and eggs, if present, begin to set as the temperature in the mix rises. The starch begins to gelatinize. Part of the water is converted to steam which provides additional leaven and further inflates the product. When the heat penetrates the interior, the structure of the baked product is set because of the coagulation of the protein and the gelatinization of the starch. Finally, evaporation of water from the surface slows and the surface gets hot enough to brown.

BAKING TIME AND TEMPERATURE

Before an oven is used, the accuracy of the setting of the thermostat should be checked by means of an oven thermometer. Directions for adjusting the thermostat are usually included in the operating instructions which come with the range. The temperature is likely to be most uniform in the center of the oven, although household ovens are not precision instruments and small variations in temperature are to be expected.

Placement of the racks should be checked before the oven is turned on. (See Fig. 3-2.) The baking utensil (not the rack) should be centered in the oven to assure uniform heating. If the utensil is deep, the rack should be placed below the center position. Usually only one rack is used in an oven. If the other is stored in some place outside the oven, only one rack will need to be cleaned when it is necessary to clean the oven. It is not always necessary to preheat an oven before putting in the product to bake. In some cases success depends upon having the oven hot, but other foods may be placed in the oven at the time it is turned on.

Most quick breads are baked in a hot oven, at least during the early part of the baking period. Aside from oven temperature, the baking time depends upon the material from which the baking utensil is made (see Chapter 3) and upon the size and shape of the utensil. Heat from convection currents, which is transmitted by the baking pan, moves to the center of the product mainly by conduction, a slow process at best, further slowed down by the innumerable bubbles of gas in the batter or dough. The temperature in the interior of a baked product is approximately that of boiling water even though the food is baked in a hot oven.

CLEANING BAKING PANS

Baking pans are usually oiled to keep food from sticking. Removing this fat presents a problem. Probably the most important thing is to have very hot water, because hot water itself will remove much of the fat. However, a thin film of fat will adhere tenaciously to the surfaces of the utensil. Detergent or soap in the water helps wash away most of this adhering fat. Vigorous scrubbing also helps.

Only that part of a baking utensil which will be in contact with the baked product should be oiled. Fat on exposed surfaces of the pan gets so hot that it polymerizes. The result is a thick, gummy layer. Scouring will remove this or the utensil may be soaked in hot water to which ammonia has been added. However, soaking with ammonia will discolor utensils made of aluminum. *Teflon** (a fluorocarbon resin) and similar coatings on baking utensils eliminate the need for oiling. The lining fills the pits in the metal which otherwise would cause baked products to stick.

INDIVIDUAL QUICK BREADS

FORMULAS

Formulas for five quick breads—popovers, cream puffs, muffins, biscuits and waffles—are given in Table 12-1.

*Registered trademark for Dupont's Teflon TFE nonstick finish.

Table 12-1   Formulas for quick breads

Ingredient	Popovers	Cream Puffs	Muffins	Biscuits	Waffles
Flour[a]	1 cup	1 cup	1 cup	1 cup	1 cup cake flour
Salt	½ tsp	¼ tsp	½ tsp	½ tsp	¼ tsp
Baking powder[b]	—	—	2 tsp	2 tsp	2 tsp
Liquid	1 cup	1 cup	½ cup	⅓ to ⅜ cup	⅝ cup
Fat	1 tbsp	½ cup	1-2 tbsp	2½ tbsp	¼ cup
Eggs	2	4	½	—	1
Sugar	—	—	1-2 tbsp	—	—

[a]All-purpose except where cake flour is specified.
[b]Single acting.

POPOVERS

PROPORTIONS

Equal parts flour and liquid used in popovers give a thin or pour batter. Such a batter can be used to make timbale cases and Yorkshire pudding as well as popovers or as a cover for apple fritters or French fried onion rings. (See Chapter 14, on fats.) Crêpes are made from a similar batter except that the proportion of egg is slightly higher. The proportion of ingredients in popovers is far more critical than the technique of combining them. The protein of egg white is the ingredient which is essential if popovers are to "pop," so size of the eggs is important. Proportion of liquid to flour is also important. Too much liquid produces a batter so weak that the protein is unable to hold the steam. Too little liquid yields a tight batter with insufficient steam to inflate it. Too much fat, either added to the batter or used to oil the baking utensil, will weaken the batter and cause loss of steam and poor volume.

MANIPULATION

No special technique or precautions are necessary to make popover batter. A spoon, a spring whip, or a rotary beater may be used to combine the ingredients to form a smooth batter.

BAKING

Special baking utensils are unnecessary for popovers. Muffin tins or custard cups may be used. The depth of the cup which holds the batter is important. This influences the amount of popover that the steam can support above the top of the utensil. Popovers baked in shallow utensils do not pop well.

A hot oven is used during the first part of the baking period to vaporize the water and inflate the batter. Then the heat is reduced to moderate to coagulate the protein and gelatinize the starch and so set the batter without unduly browning the popovers. Popovers will collapse if the oven is opened and the steam is permitted to condense before the batter gets hot enough to set. The oven need not be preheated for popovers if it comes to temperature within 5 minutes. The photographs in Figure 12-3 illustrate six stages in the conversion of popover batter to the baked product.

CHARACTERISTICS

Popovers are golden-brown, tender, crisp shells. The interior is divided by fairly thin, slightly moist, but thoroughly cooked partitions.

CREAM PUFFS

PROPORTIONS

Cream puffs are made with the same ratio of liquid to flour as popovers but contain eight times as much fat. The high proportion of fat makes cream puffs more tender and richer than popovers just as extra fat and sugar make a cake more tender and richer than muffins. More eggs are required in cream puffs than in popovers because of the large amount of fat in the former. Less salt is added to cream puffs to allow for the salt contributed by the large amount of salted table fat.

MANIPULATION

To make the paste for cream puffs, the flour is added to the rapidly boiling water–melted fat mixture in a sauce pan. The flour does not lump because the melted fat which floats on the surface of the water coats the flour before it comes in contact with the boiling water. When the liquid and flour are cooked to make cream puff paste, the mixture becomes thick, due to the gelatinization of the starch in the flour. The same thing happens in the thin popover batter when it is baked. Although cream puff paste does not have lumps, it does have a curdled appearance at this stage because the fat does not blend with the water. After the eggs are beaten into the cooked paste, the batter takes on a smooth, glossy appearance. Egg yolk contains emulsifier, mainly lipoproteins, molecules of which have an affinity for both water and fat and so effectively unite the two. Instead of being in two phases, the gelatinized starch-in-water phase and the melted fat scattered-about-in-lakes phase, the two are intimately combined through the intermediary supplied by the egg yolk. The main emulsifiers belong to a class of fats known as phospholipids (see Chapter 16, on emulsions). In addition to emulsifier, eggs contribute protein, which confers on the cooked paste the ability to stretch (11) under the pressure of the evolving steam formed during baking. The proteins of egg white are particularly effective for this purpose.

If too much water is boiled away when cream puff paste is cooked, the flour will absorb most of the remaining water. This gives a paste that is too

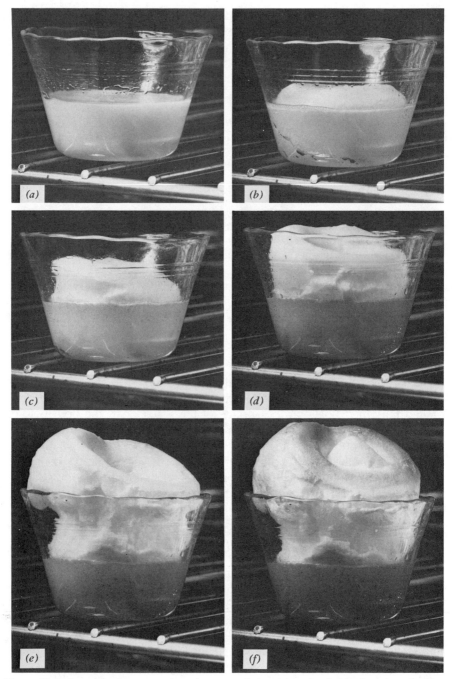

Figure 12-3. Stages in the conversion of popover batter (a) to the finished product (f). (From *Sunset*, May 1963. Darrow M. Watt, Photographer, 188 Felton Drive, Menlo Park, CA.)

stiff, with little water free to form steam to leaven the product. As a result, the cream puff paste does not puff during baking. Failure of the batter to lose its curdled appearance after the egg is added is an indication that too much water has been evaporated. To remedy this, hot water should be stirred in gradually until the paste appears glossy. Fat oozing from the paste during baking is another indication of a deficiency of water in the batter as is failure of the cream puffs to rise.

Too much water in the paste keeps it from rising, also, because the paste is too fluid to retain the steam. After the eggs are beaten into the cooked paste, it should be stiff enough to be transferred to the baking sheet with a spoon and should not flatten on the baking sheet. The proportion of fat is important, too. Fat enables the paste to give with pressure; with too little fat the paste cannot expand, whereas with excess fat too much steam escapes. Either way the paste fails to rise sufficiently.

BAKING

Cream puffs, like popovers, are baked in a very hot oven for a few minutes so they will rise. Baking then continues in a slow oven to complete coagulation of the protein and gelatinization of the starch. Like popovers, cream puffs will collapse if the steam that inflated them condenses before the structure is set.

CHARACTERISTICS

Cream puffs of high quality, like popovers, are hollow shells. The crust is crisp and more tender than that of popovers due to a large amount of finely dispersed fat. Interior partitions are thin, tender, and crisp.

MUFFINS

PROPORTIONS

Muffins are made from a drop batter of two parts all-purpose flour to one of liquid. A basic recipe contains 1 egg for each 2 cups of flour. Proportions of fat and sugar increase from a lean to a rich muffin. Most recipes call for 1½ to 2 teaspoons of baking powder (depending on the type) for each cup of flour. Muffins made from cake or pastry instead of all-purpose flour should have the proportions of flour increased or the milk reduced, or both (5).

MANIPULATION

The baking powder should be sifted with the flour or stirred in thoroughly to ensure uniform distribution. This is essential for uniform gas cells, that is, grain, in the crumb of the baked muffin. The egg and milk should be blended thoroughly but without beating up a foam. The protein of the egg is needed primarily as a binding or structural ingredient and not as a means of incorporating air. If the egg is not blended thoroughly with the milk, it will be unevenly distributed and the crumb around part of the gas cells will be thick and tough. The muffin method of combining ingredients calls for the addition to the dry ingredients of fat in the liquid state at the same time that the milk and egg mixture is added. Alternately, plastic fat may be cut into the sifted dry ingredients before the liquids are added.

The ratio of liquid to flour in muffin batter is ideal for the development of gluten, especially when all-purpose flour is used. It is easy to overstir muffin batter and develop more gluten than is desirable. Muffins made from soft wheat flour (pastry or cake) tolerate more mixing and are still fine grained and tender. Muffin batter low in fat or sugar should be stirred only enough to barely dampen the dry ingredients. It will still be lumpy. Otherwise, too much gluten will be formed and the batter will be too elastic. Bubbles of carbon dioxide trapped in a too elastic batter will be retained and become very large. Confined by the walls of the muffin pan, the only way the bubbles can expand is upward. Thus they tend to be oriented from the bottom to the top of the muffin. These elongated gas cells are called "tunnels" (Fig. 12-4). When they form inside a muffin, it has a peaked top. Sometimes the unbaked batter pushes through the top crust which has begun to set.

Because both fat and sugar interfere with the development of gluten, rich muffin batter not only can tolerate more manipulation but actually needs more. Muffin batter needs some gluten to give gas-retaining properties essential for a good volume in the baked product. It is an art to know by the look and feel of muffin batter at which stroke to stop stirring. The best way to acquire this art is to remove from the mixing bowl enough batter for a muffin, at successive stages in the mixing of the liquid and dry ingredients, and relate the charac-teristics of the baked muffin with those of the batter from which it came.

Once the muffin batter has been mixed, it should be transferred to oiled or Teflon-lined baking cups at once; otherwise, more of the carbon dioxide liberated in the batter will be lost during the transfer. The batter can stand in the baking utensil for a few minutes before baking without detriment to the quality of the baked product.

BAKING

Muffins are baked in a hot oven (425°F, or 218°C). The baking time depends on the size of the muffin cups as well as the material from which the utensil is made. The small diameter of the cups of a muffin pan and the high baking temperature may contribute to the formation of tunnels (10).

Muffins can be removed from the pan more easily if they are allowed to stand for a minute or two after they come from the oven. The steam that condenses facilitates their removal. Leaving them in the tins too long, how-ever, will cause them to be soggy. It is to avoid condensation of moisture as well as cooling that muffins and other hot breads are served on a plate or tray lined with a cloth napkin.

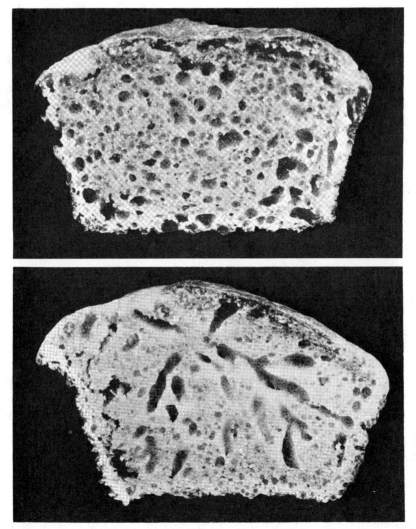

Figure 12-4. Structure of the crumb of muffins from batter stirred the optimum (top) and from overstirred batter (bottom). (From E. G. Halliday and I. T. Noble, *Hows and Whys of Cooking*, 1946, University of Chicago Press. Reprinted by permission of Isabel Noble.)

CHARACTERISTICS

Muffins should have a thin, uniformly golden-brown crust. The top should be symmetrical, with a contour similar to a head of cauliflower. (See center muffin in Fig. 12-5.) The holes in the crumb should be round and medium sized and the cell walls fairly thin, like the upper muffin shown in Figure 12-4. The richer the batter, the smaller are the gas cells and the thinner the walls. The muffin should be light and the crumb tender. Indications of an understirred

Figure 12-5. The cauliflower-shaped top of the muffin in the center indicates optimum manipulation and optimum amount of liquid in the batter. The rough top and lower volume of the muffin on the left indicates a deficiency of liquid or of manipulation. Overmanipulation or too much liquid could cause the slick top of the muffin on the right. The peak suggests overmanipulation. (Courtesy of Andrea Mackey and the Oregon Agricultural Experiment Station.)

muffin are low volume, coarse crumb, flat, ricey top, and brown specks from undissolved soda. Tunnels, a peaked top, and pale, slick crust are indicative of overstirred muffin batter.

BISCUITS

PROPORTIONS

Biscuits are from a soft dough, made with three parts flour to one of liquid. Aside from leaven and salt, biscuits contain from 2⅓ to 3 tablespoons of fat per cup of flour. For biscuits, a plastic fat apparently is a better shortening than a liquid fat (7). The ratio of liquid to flour in biscuits is a critical one. The softer the dough the better, provided the dough can be kneaded. Variations in the moisture-absorbing capacity of flours make it impossible to state in a recipe the precise amount of liquid. The exact amount of milk per cup of all-purpose flour falls between ⅓ cup and ⅜ cup. The kind of milk makes some difference (4).

MANIPULATION

For biscuits as for muffins, the baking powder is sifted with the flour to obtain a uniformly fine grain. Plastic fat is cut into the dry ingredients until the mixture resembles coarse cornmeal. A pastry fork, pastry blender, two knives, or fingers may be used to cut in the fat. Milk is added next, all at once, in the optimum amount for the moisture-absorbing capacity of the flour. The milk should be dispersed in the dry ingredients at once, with a fork. Stirring should continue until the mixture stiffens perceptibly. Stirring helps dissolve the salt and the acid and soda in the baking powder, dampens the flour, and forms the dough. For a dough made with 2 cups of flour approximately 20 to 30 strokes are necessary. The exact number depends on the size and shape of the mixing bowl, the quantity of dough, the kind of milk used, and the effectiveness of the stirring strokes.

Once the dough stiffens and loses some of its stickiness, it may be turned onto a *lightly* floured bread board or other suitable surface and kneaded (stretched and folded gently) 10 to 20 times to develop the desirable amount of cohesiveness. Because of the low ratio of liquid to flour in biscuit dough, gluten is slow to develop. Unlike muffin batter, where the common fault is overstirring, biscuit dough is likely to be undermanipulated. Biscuit dough not only tolerates but requires more manipulation. It is the total that counts. If biscuit dough is understirred in the bowl, it should be kneaded more.

The technique for handling biscuit dough is harder to acquire than is that for muffin batter. The ability to recognize when biscuit dough has been manipulated the optimum amount comes with experience. This can be achieved by removing a biscuit at a time from the dough as kneading proceeds. Again the object is to associate the characteristics of the baked biscuit with the way the dough handles and looks.

The kind of baking powder used in a dough will influence its handling characteristics (3). Dough made with SAS-phosphate baking powder tends to be less sticky than that made with phosphate or with tartrate baking powder. Biscuit dough made with double-acting baking powder is compact; that made with soda and cream of tartar is spongy.

Biscuit dough with a high proportion of fat requires more manipulation, as does that slightly deficient in liquid. If the amount of milk is skimpy for the quantity of flour or for its moisture-absorbing capacity, the dough will be stiff. A stiff dough requires more manipulation to develop the desired amount of gluten. The dough is too tight to stretch, the biscuit does not rise as much as it should and cracks appear on the sides. The crumb of the biscuit is dry, compact, and crumbly. Brown specks are likely to appear in the crust of the biscuit. The more milk in biscuit dough, the quicker the optimum amount of gluten develops. A slight excess of milk is preferable to too little. With too much liquid, the dough may be too sticky to handle. In this case, it may be stirred more in the bowl instead of kneaded and the dough dropped by the spoonful onto an oiled baking sheet.

Unless the dough is stirred and kneaded sufficiently, all of the soda and acid may not dissolve and some soda may be unneutralized. When soda is heated during baking, washing soda is formed. This results in yellow spots in the crumb and brown spots on the crust.

When the dough is kneaded sufficiently, biscuits can be cut and placed on a baking sheet and allowed to stand at least 15 minutes before they are baked. Standing for this length of time at room temperature does no harm, and if held in the refrigerator the quality of the biscuits may be improved (6). They are not so likely to have brown spots on the crust, attributed to the reaction between undissolved monocalcium phosphate from the baking powder and carbohydrates in the flour. Unbaked biscuits should be covered with a cloth or waxed paper to prevent the surface from becoming dry.

BAKING

Biscuits are baked in a hot oven (425°F, or 218°C) for 12 to 15 minutes. Alternately, dough may be dropped in boiling liquid and steamed, in which case the product is called dumplings. The liquid may be meat broth, soups such as tomato and mushroom, or cooked fruit such as cherries, berries, or a medley of cooked, dried fruit.

CHARACTERISTICS

If biscuits are made with sour milk and baking powder, the crumb in the interior will be snowy white, owing to the lowered pH, and it will be fine and moist. With an excess of soda the crumb of the biscuit is yellow; it tends to be coarse and have a slightly soapy taste because of the washing soda produced from the unneutralized baking soda. Excess soda causes the crust to be too brown. A biscuit made with a high proportion of fat has a fine grain and a tender crumb. Biscuits made with SAS-phosphate baking powder frequently have deep cracks along the side (3), indicating some inability of the dough to stretch during baking.

A biscuit of high quality has a golden-brown crust without brown specks. The biscuit is symmetrical, with a smooth, level top and straight sides. (See Fig. 12-6a.) The crust is crisp and tender. The crumb should be white to creamy white, fine grained, moist and fluffy, and should peel off in layers. A dry, crumbly crumb results from too little liquid or too little manipulation or both. In any case, the biscuit is likely to be low in volume. With too much liquid, the biscuit is likely to have a rounded top, which also may result from too much manipulation.

GRIDDLE CAKES AND WAFFLES

A pour batter is used for griddle cakes and waffles. Usually the ingredients are combined as for muffins. Frequently the beaten egg whites are folded into the batter at the end of the mixing. The same batter may be used for both griddle cakes and waffles. For the former, the batter is poured onto a preheated griddle, 2 tablespoons or more, depending on the diameter of the cake desired. The iron is hot enough to cook the griddle cakes when a drop of cold water snaps as it contacts the iron. If the batter contains fat, oiling the iron is unnecessary. Griddle cakes should be turned when the gas cells on the upper surface break. Griddle cakes should have a smooth, evenly browned surface with few pits. The crumb should be fine grained, moist, tender, and light.

Waffles should be baked in a preconditioned iron. The grids on a new waffle iron usually are preconditioned. Should batter stick to the grids, they should be removed, soaked in hot water, and then washed, rinsed, and dried. To recondition the grids, the waffle iron is heated and the grids brushed with unsalted fat. The iron is closed, heated to baking temperature, and left on for approximately 10 minutes. Heating polymerizes the fat which has filled the

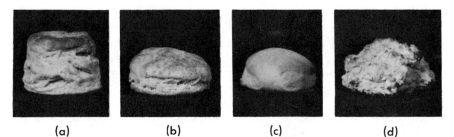

(a)   (b)   (c)   (d)

Figure 12-6. Variations in the quality of biscuits as affected by manipulation. (a) Optimum manipulation gives a biscuit with a flat top, straight sides, and good volume. (b) Low volume and rounded but rough top characterize biscuits from undermanipulated dough. (c) A biscuit with low volume and a smooth, rounded top results from overmanipulation of the dough, especially if a slight excess of liquid has been used. (d) Drop biscuits made intentionally or becuase the dough is too sticky to handle have a rough exterior and a crunchy crust. (Courtesy of the United States Department of Agriculture).

pores in the iron. This keeps the batter from sticking. The iron is allowed to cool naturally, after which it is ready for use. A griddle iron may be conditioned in the same way except that the iron is heated in a moderately hot oven for approximately 10 minutes.

The temperature of most waffle irons is thermostatically controlled. When the light on the preheated waffle iron indicates "Bake," batter is poured into the center of each section, with enough space around the edges for expansion of the batter as it bakes. The waffle should bake in approximately 3 minutes. It is done when steam no longer escapes from the iron. Waffles may stick to the iron if there is insufficient fat in the batter or if the waffle iron is either too hot or too cold when the batter is poured in. If the hinge on the iron is too stiff, the waffle will tend to be soggy. If the knobs on the iron are high and close together, the waffle tends to be crisp; shallower knobs far apart produce a softer waffle. Gingerbread batter, biscuit dough, and French toast may be cooked on a waffle iron.

REFERENCES

1. Bowman, F., and E. Dyar. 1951. *Quick mixes for high-altitude baking.* Colorado Agr. Exp. Sta. Bull. 415-A. 34 pp. Recipes adapted for 5000, 7500, and 10,000 feet.
2. Boyd, S., and M. C. Schoonover. 1965. *Baking at high altitude.* Wyoming Agr. Exp. Sta. Bull. No. 427. 71 pp. Cakes, cookies, and quick breads for 5000 and 7000 feet.
3. Briant, A. M., and M. R. Hutchins. 1946. Influence of ingredients in thiamine retention and quality in baking powder biscuits. *Cereal Chem.* **23:** 512–520. Effects of different types and levels of baking powder on hydrogen-ion concentration of biscuits, on quality of dough, and on retention of thiamine.

4. Kirkpatrick, M. E., R. M. Mathews, and J. C. Collie. 1961. Use of different market forms of milk in biscuits. *J. Home Econ.* **53:** 201–205. Effects of the kind of milk on manipulation necessary for optimum hydration of dough and for desirable characteristics in biscuits.

5. Mackey, A., M. Strauss, and J. Stockman. *Soft wheat flour muffins.* Oregon Agr. Exp. Sta. Circ. Inf. 547.

6. Maclay, E. 1926. The effect of delayed baking on biscuits. *J. Home Econ.* **18:** 157. Effects of holding temperature and time on unbaked biscuits and of holding time on refrigerated dough.

7. Matthews, R. M., and E. H. Dawson. 1963. Performance of fats and oils in pastry and biscuits. *Cereal Chem.* **40:** 291–302. Tenderness and flavor of products made with five levels each of three oils and three fats.

8. Peterson, M. W. 1930. *Baking flour mixtures at high altitudes.* Colorado Agr. Exp. Sta. Bull 365. 180 pp. Report of experimental work on baking from the high-altitude laboratory; recipes for elevations of 3000 to 11,000 feet.

9. Sunderlin, G. 1952. *Master mix.* Purdue University Agr. Ext. Bull. 344. 16 pp. Proportions for the mix and recipes for its use.

10. Trimbo, Henry B., and Byron S. Miller. 1973. The development of tunnels in cakes. *Bakers Digest* **47**(4): 24–26, 71. Contributing factors.

11. Wheeler, F. G. 1946. Cream puff troubles are overcome by test studies. *Food Ind.* **18:** 88–90. Functions of ingredients; common faults and their causes.

FILMS

1. *Quickbreads. Part I: Biscuit Method.* Color. Forty-three frames. Wheat Flour Institute.

2. *Quickbreads. Part II: Muffin Method.* Color. Thirty-nine frames. Wheat Flour Institute.

THIRTEEN
Yeast Bread

Yeast breads are made from soft dough leavened with carbon dioxide formed by microorganisms. Yeast dough is a foam. Bubbles of carbon dioxide are surrounded by or trapped in the dough. The ingredients, their proportions, and the way they are handled all interact to influence the characteristics of the dough in which the bubbles of gas are generated. These, in turn, influence the quality of the baked product.

INGREDIENTS AND THEIR FUNCTIONS

Flour, liquid, yeast, and salt are essential ingredients in yeast dough. Sugar and fat, although not absolutely necessary, are usually included. Eggs are optional.

YEAST

Yeast for bread is made of cells of selected strains of the microorganism *Saccharomyces cerevisiae*. (See Fig 13-1.) Fresh, active yeast cells are available as compressed cakes or dry pellets. If compressed cake yeast is held at room temperature, the cells soon die. Even in the refrigerator, compressed yeast will remain fresh and the cells viable for only a few days. If fresh compressed yeast is frozen and held in frozen storage, the yeast cells will live and the cake of yeast will stay fresh for 3 to 4 months (26). Active dry yeast in pellet form can be held without refrigeration for several weeks. The secret of its stability at room temperature is that the moisture content (29) of the suspension of yeast cells has been reduced to approximately 8 percent *vs.* near 70 percent for compressed cake yeast. The pellets (7 grams, or ¼ ounce) are sealed in the package to prevent absorption of moisture after the contents are flushed with nitrogen gas to further prolong shelf life. If a package of pellet yeast is opened, the unused portion should be stored in a closed container in the refrigerator. The useful life of pellet yeast is indicated by an expiration date stamped on the package.

Yeast is included in bread dough because, as the cells metabolize fermentable sugars, under anaerobic conditions which prevail in the dough, they give off carbon dioxide as a waste product. This waste product of the metabolism of yeast cells is utilized in dough as a leaven. Yeast cells are able to

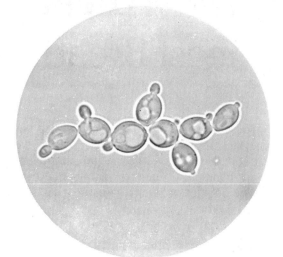

Figure 13-1. Bakers yeast *(Saccharomyces cerevisiae).* A cluster of yeast cells giving rise to new cells by budding. Note the large vacuoles in older cells. Original magnification X 1200. (Courtesy of Fleischmann Laboratories, Standard Brands, Inc.)

ferment four sugars: glucose, fructose, sucrose, and maltose; they are unable to utilize the sugar from milk. The biochemical changes which take place when sugars are fermented by yeast are complex (15,20). The main overall reaction, ignoring a number of intermediate steps, for the production of CO_2 with glucose as the sugar can be expressed by the Gay-Lussac equation

$$C_6H_{12}O_6 \rightarrow 2C_2H_5OH + 2CO_2$$

Glucose   Ethyl alcohol   Carbon dioxide

Yeast cells also possess the enzyme invertase (sucrase) on or near the cell wall, which acts as a catalyst for hydrolysis of the disaccharide, sucrose, to simple (and fermentable) sugars in the following reaction:

$$C_{12}H_{22}O_{11} + H_2O \xrightarrow{\text{Sucrase}} C_6H_{12}O_6 + C_6H_{12}O_6$$

Sucrose   Water   Glucose   Fructose

Maltose is fermented only after the supply of glucose and fructose is exhausted. Even then fermentation proceeds slowly. Yeast cells not only produce carbon dioxide which inflates the dough, but also (and by a secondary biochemical pathway) substances which modify the elasticity, the stickiness, and the flow properties of the dough. All of this contributes to the way the dough handles. Fermentation products of yeast contribute to the aroma of bread.

FLOUR

Bread flour produces bread of superior grain and texture and maximum volume, especially when made under commercial conditions. All-purpose flour makes excellent yeast breads or rolls when these products are made at home. Quality of the gluten which a flour can yield, as well as the quantity, is important. Oxidizing and maturing agents are added to flour to improve its dough- and bread-forming potential (10). (See Chapter 10.) Leavening gas is produced over a period of time, and the dough must be able to withstand stress for a considerable period. The weaker the gluten, the less stress the dough can stand. The fermentation period for bread dough from flour which yields weak gluten should be short (6). A higher proportion of yeast and one rising are indicated for yeast breads made with such flour. At no time should the dough be allowed to become overly light.

Although the gluten-forming potential of wheat flour is emphasized in bread making, the importance of the starch should not be overlooked. In fact, satisfactory bread has been made experimentally by replacing the proteins of flour with ingredients that mimic their functional properties, but no satisfactory replacement has been found for the starch in flour. The starch grains from wheat and those from rye and barley appear uniquely suitable for the formation of yeast dough and bread (9). Starch grains in bread dough are embedded in or trapped between the films of gluten that surround the gas cell. In the baked bread, these starch grains, now gelatinized, give rigidity to the crumb. Starch has another role in breadmaking. It is the source of fermentable sugar.

Yeast cells need sugar to produce carbon dioxide, but too much sugar (above 10 percent based on the weight of the flour) in the dough at one time retards fermentation (3). Yeast cells do best with a continuously replenished supply of fermentable sugar. Ability of flour to support fermentation depends upon the presence of two starch-hydrolyzing enzymes, alpha-amylase and beta-amylase (15). Most wheats contain sufficient beta-amylase. This enzyme frees molecules of the disaccharide, maltose, by catalyzing the hydrolysis of the α-1,4 glycosidic linkages, beginning at the reducing end of the starch polymer (15). Once the branching points are reached in amylopectin, hydrolysis by beta-amylase, known as an exo-enzyme, stops. The resulting polymer, a stubbier, shrubby-looking residue, is called limit dextrin. Alpha-amylase, unlike beta-amylase, can attack undamaged starch grains, but the amount of alpha-amylase in flour is variable and insufficient. When flour is milled, it is tested for alpha-amylase activity (gassing power) and a sufficient quantity of this enzyme from malted grain is added. Both amylases catalyze the hydrolysis of the α-1,4 glycosidic linkage but alpha-amylase does so at random in both amylopectin and amylose molecules. Beta-amylase can then hydrolyze molecules of maltose from the amylopectin fragments. Alpha-amylase thus makes more of the starch available for fermentation by yeast. Cooked potato starch is readily attacked by amylases, which explains why water in which potatoes have been cooked is sometimes used in making yeast dough. Other nutrient substances leached from cells of the potato favor fermentation, too. The flour itself provides nutrients needed by the yeast.

LIQUID

Water may be used as the liquid in yeast dough, although milk, which is 87 percent water, is usually used. Milk increases food value and also delays staling of bread. Liquid dissolves salt and sugar and aids in dispersing the yeast cells through the flour. It also serves as a means for transporting food to yeast through cell membranes. Water is essential for the hydrolysis of both starch and sucrose.

Water hydrates both starch and protein of the flour and is essential for the development of gluten as the dough is manipulated (see Chapter 10). Although hydration of the constituents of flour is essential, so is the presence of unbound water. The free water in dough influences its extensibility (30). Too much and the dough is sticky and too soft; too little and it is stiff and resists stretching. The consistency of the dough influences the extent to which the films of gluten around the gas bubbles resist the pressure of accumulating carbon dioxide during fermentation and the pressure of expanding gases during baking. The volume of the bread and the texture of the crumb are affected. Water is essential for the gelatinization of starch when the dough is baked (4), and the steam it provides contributes to expansion in the oven.

SALT

Salt has more important functions in yeast dough than improving the taste of the baked product. Some salt in yeast dough favors the action of amylases and thus helps to maintain a supply of maltose as food for the yeast. Also, salt affects the character of the dough itself by inhibiting the action of proteases (protein splitting enzymes) of the flour. Yeast dough without salt is sticky and hard to handle. The weakened gluten permits gas cells to overexpand during fermentation. Additional expansion of the cells and extensive rupture as the dough bakes give a moth-eaten appearance to the bread. Salt does, however, slow the production of carbon dioxide by the yeast. Presumably it is an osmotic effect that limits the net flow of water into the yeast cells (5). For this reason a lower proportion of salt to flour is used in yeast dough compared with quick breads. If yeast dough rises very rapidly and the same dough is sticky and hard to handle, that salt was omitted is a possibility. However, both stickiness and rapid rising may result from allowing the dough to rise at too high a temperature. Tasting the dough is one way to pinpoint the trouble. Bread made without salt for people on a salt-free diet is inferior in grain and texture.

SUGAR

Sugar is included in dough for yeast bread mainly to serve as a readily available source of fermentable sugar (5). Flour contains only a small amount of sucrose (approximately 1 percent). During the first few minutes after a dough is mixed a high percentage of the sucrose is hydrolyzed to invert sugar (3,20). In the absence of added sugar, production of cabon dioxide by yeast cells is limited and delayed, pending hydrolysis of starch in the flour to maltose by amylases (5). Reducing sugars which remain in the dough when it goes into the oven aid in browning and also flavor the product.

FAT

Adding fat to yeast dough is optional because good bread can be made without it. Fat does make the product more tender and the crust brown better. The increase in volume of bread when fat is included is attributed to the fat plugging holes in the walls of dough around the gas cells. This enables them to expand more before they rupture and leak carbon dioxide. For this purpose, plastic fat is superior to liquid fat (17). Glycolipids of the flour are essential for the formation of gluten. (See the section on gluten formation in Chapter 10.)

EGGS

Many yeast breads are made without eggs. When eggs are included in dough, they make the product look and taste richer. The protein of the egg gives additional stretchability to the dough without making it sticky.

PROPORTIONS OF INGREDIENTS

FLOUR TO LIQUID

Approximately three volumes of flour to one of liquid are used to make the soft dough for yeast breads. The optimum amount of flour depends upon its moisture-holding capacity. Bread dough contains approximately 40 percent water (30). Doughs from strong flours can carry more liquid than can those from weak flours. If the milk from yeast dough is measured before it is scalded, the amount of liquid actually used to make the dough is an unknown quantity. The amount of water lost by evaporation calculated in percent may be considerable. Two tablespoons of water evaporated from one-half cup of milk as it is scalded (not an unlikely amount) means a 25 percent loss in volume. In this event, the flour should be reduced to compensate. A dough that contains too much flour is stiff and inelastic and slow to rise. Expansion of the dough during baking is limited. Cells in the bread are small with thick cell walls. The volume is small as a consequence. The higher the ratio of liquid to flour the better, provided the dough is not too sticky to handle.

SALT AND SUGAR

For reasons explained earlier, the ratio of salt to flour is critical in yeast dough. Less salt per cup of flour is used in yeast dough than in quick breads. The amount of salt usually does not exceed 2 percent of the weight of the flour (5).

When only the small amount of fermentable sugar supplied by the flour is available to the yeast, fermentation is slow to start. As the amount of sugar added to dough is increased, up to 10 percent of the weight of the flour, fermentation proceeds more rapidly. Yeast dough made with ½ tablespoon of sugar per 1½ to 1¾ cups of flour (a half-pound loaf of bread) has approximately 4 percent of sugar. For rolls the amount of sugar may be doubled, and for sweet rolls it may be quadrupled. When the level of sugar in yeast dough exceeds 10 percent, the production of carbon dioxide by the yeast is inhibited (3). Dough for sweet rolls is slow to rise. This explains why starch-hydrolyzing enzymes are essential in bread flour. Presumably a high concentration of sugar limits the entry of water and nutrients into the yeast cells by an osmotic effect. Reducing the amount of salt in a very sweet dough will help to compensate for the effects of high levels of sugar (greater than 10 percent of the weight of flour) on the rate of fermentation. Increasing the yeast is another means of maintaining a desirable rate of fermentation in sweet dough. A high proportion of sugar in dough delays the uptake of water by flour (3). Sweet doughs should be mixed or kneaded longer as a consequence. Fat may be increased in yeast dough without prolonging fermentation unduly.

YEAST

A certain amount of carbon dioxide is needed to make dough rise. The more yeast cells added to the dough, the sooner will the required amount of carbon dioxide be produced. The amount of yeast used for each ½ cup of milk (approximately 1½ cups of flour) may vary from ⅓ to 1⅓ cakes or packages. Apparently the number of yeast cells in a dough increases when a small proportion of yeast is used to make the dough. When one cake or one package of pellet yeast is used with ½ cup of milk and 1½ cups of flour, dough needs approximately 1 hour to rise the first time and approximately ½ hour after it has been shaped and placed in the baking pan. (See fermentation schedule in Table 13-1.)

Table 13-1   Approximate Fermentation Schedule at 27°C (80°F)

Yeast	Liquid	First Rising	Second Rising[b]	Rising in Pan
⅓ Cake or package yeast[a]	½ cup	2 hr	1 hr	1 hr
⅔ Cake or package yeast	½ cup	1½ hr	45 min	45 min
1 Cake or package yeast	½ cup	1 hr	15 min	35 min
1⅓ Cakes or packages yeast	½ cup	25 min	5 min	30 min

[a]1 package of pellet yeast weighs 7 grams.
[b]Omit for soft wheat flour; optional for all-purpose flour; recommended for hard wheat flour.
SOURCE: Adapted from Belle Lowe, *Experimental Cookery*, (Copyright © 1955 by John Wiley & Sons, Inc., New York), p. 435. Reprinted by permission.

Too little yeast and the dough takes a long time to rise; too much yeast and the dough is inflated before other essential changes take place in the dough. An excess may make the product taste yeasty. A higher proportion of yeast is used when the time available for making yeast bread is limited. Time permitting, less yeast and a somewhat longer fermentation time makes better bread unless the flour yields weak gluten. Cells from the cake of compressed or pellets of active dry yeast do not produce carbon dioxide as readily at the start of fermentation. Dough is slow to rise at first, but it picks up momentum as fermentation proceeds because the cells are more active. A higher proportion of yeast is indicated in sweet dough to compensate for the effect of high concentrations of sugar on rate of fermentation.

MANIPULATION OF YEAST DOUGH

BASIC METHODS

Ingredients for yeast dough may be combined by the straight-dough, the sponge, or the no-knead method. When bread is made by the straight-dough method, all of the ingredients are combined and the dough is kneaded before it is allowed to rise. Yeast bread made by the no-knead method has a high proportion of liquid so that the gluten can be developed by stirring rather than by kneading. When dough is made by the sponge method, the yeast, dispersed in the liquid, and part of the flour are combined. Addition of part of the sugar is optional. This batter is allowed to rise until it becomes spongy and light. The remainder of the ingredients are stirred into the sponge and the dough is then kneaded and allowed to rise as in the straight-dough method. The yeast cells while they are in the sponge adjust to fermenting maltose.

SCALDING THE MILK

Milk used to make yeast dough should be scalded; otherwise, the dough is slack and sticky and the bread is coarse and of poor volume. One or more constituents of the serum proteins of milk are believed to be responsible (11), but neither the loaf-depressant factor nor the protein(s) responsible for the slackness of dough have been identified unequivocally (29). (For discussion of milk proteins, see Chapter 17.) Scalding may be accomplished by heating milk to a high temperature for a short time (92°C, or 198°F, for 1 minute) or for a longer time at a lower temperature (85°C, or 185°F, for 7 minutes) (14). Insufficient heating of milk for bread making does more harm than good (11). Sugar and salt dissolve more quickly while the milk is hot and the fat melts more readily. Scalded milk should be cooled at least to near lukewarm and, preferably, to near 27°C (80°F) before the yeast is added, because the cells are quite sensitive to heat. Yeast cells are unable to survive a temperature of 54.4°C (130°F), known as the "thermal death point."

DISPERSING THE YEAST

One objective in combining ingredients for yeast dough is to distribute the cells of yeast evenly through the dough. To this end, the yeast, compressed cake or pellet, is put in liquid to separate the cells, which can then be distributed via the water. The liquid should be no hotter than lukewarm when compressed yeast is used. Pellets of active dry yeast are put in water instead of milk to permit the cells of yeast to rehydrate. Yeast cells have an outer membrane which encloses the living protoplasm. When the moisture content of the yeast cells in the pellet is reduced to 8 percent, the permeability of this membrane is altered so that it will let out of the cell certain constituents which make the dough soft and sticky (21). The temperature of the water used to rehydrate active dry yeast is critical. Directions on the package specify a range in temperature of 105° to 115°F (40° to 46°C) for the water. This range is optimum for returning to the cell membrane its normal and original permeability. Water much hotter will harm the yeast. If the water is cooler than 40°C (105°F), a substance detrimental to the quality of the dough diffuses from the cells. The offender appears to be glutathione, a reducing substance which contains sulfhydryl groups. Dead yeast cells from compressed yeast cake held too long or at too high a temperature affect dough in the same way as does pellet yeast hydrated below 40°C (104°F). The greater compactness of whole wheat bread is attributed at least in part to the presence of glutathione in the germ. This is in addition to the shearing action on the gas cells of the coarse bran in whole wheat flour, which tends to lower loaf volume and crumb quality as well.

ADDING THE FLOUR

After the suspension of yeast cells is distributed in the liquid, a portion of the flour is added. The mixture is stirred or beaten to distribute the flour and form a batter, as shown in Figure 13-2. For the sponge method this batter is allowed to rise, as shown in Figure 13-3. For the straight-dough method, enough of the remaining flour is added to the batter (without allowing it to rise) to give a dough that is as soft as possible without being too sticky to handle (Fig. 13-4). Too much flour produces a stiff, lifeless dough. Each of the last portions of flour should be stirred in thoroughly to avoid an excess. If dough is permitted to stand for 5 minutes after the last addition of flour, it will lose some of its stickiness. The constituents of flour take up water at different rates. Until particles of flour are hydrated, there is little point in starting to knead the dough. A very sweet dough should be stirred extra long for the flour to absorb the optimum of water. The less flour added, the faster a dough rises. The minimum of flour produces superior bread with fine grain and texture and large volume.

A soft dough at the mixing stage is no advantage if much flour is worked into the dough as it is kneaded. The surface on which the dough is to be kneaded should be floured *lightly*. When the dough is turned from the utensil in which it was mixed (see Fig. 13-4), the dough should be rolled in flour until

Figure 13-2. Mixing yeast bread dough. Part of the flour is combined with the liquid in which the yeast cells are dispersed. The curdled appearance is due to wispy strands of gluten. (Photograph by Wilbur Nelson.)

Figure 13-3. Batter for yeast bread made by the sponge method is allowed to ferment until it becomes foamy and light. (Photograph by Wilbur Nelson.)

Figure 13-4. Yeast dough ready for kneading. The last portions of flour should be added cautiously to avoid an excess, and each addition should be stirred in thoroughly. With the optimum amount of flour and adequate mixing, little dough adheres to the mixing bowl. (Photograph by Wilbur Nelson.)

the surface is completely coated before kneading is started. This keeps the ball of dough from being too sticky to handle and helps prevent its sticking to the board. Should dough stick to the fingers, rubbing dry flour onto them will remove it. Water should not be used, because dough will adhere to a damp surface. Scraping all of the dough from the pan or bowl before kneading is started eliminates waste and makes it possible to put the dough to rise in the same utensil in which it was mixed, thus eliminating one washing of the utensil.

KNEADING

Adequate development of gluten in dough is essential for a high-quality bread. Some gluten is developed in yeast dough as flour is stirred into the liquid. However, dough that is stiff enough to be shaped later cannot be stirred with a spoon sufficiently for this purpose. Gluten can be developed in dough with an electric mixer. But a mixer with a dough hook attachment should be used and the speed of the mixer regulated to prevent overload on the motor. Alternately, the dough may be kneaded by hand. The dough needs to be worked to form numerous gas cell nuclei by the inclusion of air (1) and to give the dough elasticity and gas-holding capacity. Gas leaks from cells in both under- and overworked dough and the cells coalesce. In the one instance elasticity is underdeveloped, and in the other the dough is worked so much it can no longer hold the gas. Much stretching and folding is required but done so gently and in such as way that strands of gluten already formed are not broken. (See

Fig. 13-5.) Firm, short, rhythmic strokes with time between each for the dough to relax are best to develop springiness in the dough. When gluten is sufficiently developed, the dough loses its stickiness and becomes stretchy yet elastic (8). Numerous tiny bubbles appear just below the surface. Obvious changes which take place in yeast dough when it is kneaded properly are convincing evidence that there is indeed ''some magic in the stretching of dough'' (1).

It is possible to overwork yeast dough so that the gluten loses its cohesiveness and springiness, the cells leak gas, and they coalesce. Kneaded by hand, more dough is ruined by incorrect kneading than by excessive kneading done skillfully. A common fault when dough is kneaded by hand is for the bread maker to tire before the gluten is developed. Increasing the kneading time or the number of strokes 50 to 100 percent above what one considers optimum is not likely to harm, and frequently improves, the quality of the product.

It is important to learn to recognize signs which indicate that a dough has been adequately kneaded. A quantity of dough can be kneaded until the gluten seems sufficiently developed (10 to 15 minutes). One-third of the dough can then be removed and put to rise. The remainder of the dough may be kneaded 50 percent more and half of this put to rise. The third portion can then be

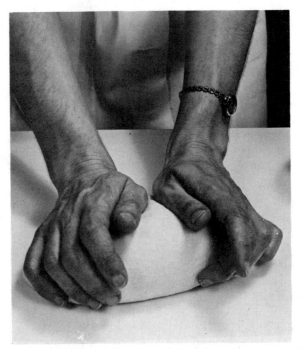

Figure 13-5. Yeast dough is kneaded by stretching and folding with short, firm, rhythmic strokes. (Photograph by Wilbur Nelson.)

kneaded for an additional 50 percent before it is put to rise. At no time should the dough be handled roughly. No flour should be put on the board when the last two portions of the dough are kneaded. Should the dough stick to the board, oiling the board lightly should eliminate the problem. In this way one may learn to associate characteristics of feel and appearance in the dough with a satisfactory baked product. If as kneading proceeds the surface of the dough looks rough and lumpy, it probably means that the dough is being mistreated and that gluten strands are being broken instead of developed and arranged in an orderly fashion.

FERMENTATION OF YEAST DOUGH

After the dough is kneaded it is ready to rise. It should be put into a utensil with a tight-fitting lid to keep the surface from drying. Alternately, the surface may be oiled lightly and the dough covered with waxed paper or a clean towel.

TEMPERATURE

Temperature of the dough as it ferments influences markedly the speed of fermentation and the quality of the final product. When the temperature is increased from 20°C (68°F) to 30°C (86°F) the fermentation rate increases threefold and the rate is twice as great at 55°C (95°F) as at 25°C (77°F) (20). Below 24°C (75°F) fermentation is slow and the dough is slow to rise. Optimum temperature for the growth and reproduction of yeast ranges from 24°C (75°F) to 35°C (95°F). For fermentation of bread dough the optimum range in temperature is narrower, lying between 25°C (78°F) and 27.7°C (82°F). Yeast dough at 37°C (98.6°F) rises rapidly, but the dough may become light before it has a chance to mellow, and undesirable by-products of fermentation may give a soured or off odor. Furthermore, dough that is too warm is soft and likely to be sticky and hard to handle. Directions to ferment yeast dough in a warm place should not be taken literally. Ideally, the temperature of the liquid, the flour, and the room should be at or near 27°C (80°F). Because the optimum temperature is lower than body temperature, the dough should feel cool to the touch.

Fermentation of yeast dough may be retarded by chilling the dough. However, there are problems attendant upon holding yeast dough in the refrigerator. The dough cools slowly, and as long as it is warm fermentation continues. Unless the dough is punched periodically, it will get too light. Yeast cells may die if they exhaust the nutrients in their immediate vicinity in the dough. Contents of dead cells bring about changes in the dough which lower volume as well as quality of the crumb. A rich dough, especially one high in sugar (to retard fermentation and to maintain a supply of sugar for the yeast) is recommended for dough for refrigerated storage. A limited increase in salt may also prove beneficial. Refrigerated dough should be used within 3 or 4 days.

PRODUCTION OF ACID

During fermentation there is much activity within the dough, both chemical and physical. Yeast cells produce acids along with carbon dioxide. The main acids are lactic and acetic, in a ratio of approximately 3:1. Part of the carbon dioxide dissolves in water to form carbonic acid. Acids produced during fermentation lower the pH of yeast dough from near 6.0 to 5.6 to 5.0. Production of some acid in the dough is desirable because it favors both fermentation and the action of amylases. Increasing the acidity of the dough will contribute to making the dough less sticky. Acid will shift the pH nearer to the isoelectric point (see section entitled "Unique R Groups," Chapter 17) of gluten so the gluten is less soluble, less sticky, and more elastic. Yeast dough of good quality is easier to handle after it has fermented.

INFLATING AND STRETCHING THE DOUGH

When dough is first put to rise, the gluten is tight and resists stretching. Carbon dioxide liberated by yeast collects in bubbles which convert the dough into a foam. Expansion of these bubbles stretches the films of gluten surrounding them; this stretching is essential if the dough is to expand as it should during baking. The extent to which the dough needs to be stretched varies with the flour that supplies the gluten. Dough from harder wheat flour can rise more than that from softer wheat flour without unduly weakening the gluten.

Yeast dough should never be allowed to become overlight. Once gluten strands are overstretched, like rubber bands stretched beyond their elastic limit, they are unable to recover their original elasticity. Dough allowed to become overlight before it is punched is unable later to retain as well the gas produced by the yeast. Such dough is slow to rise the second time and does not regain the volume it had at the end of the first rising. The result is a heavy, compact loaf of low volume and poor texture.

Dough is sufficiently light when it has approximately doubled in bulk. Slightly less is better for dough from all-purpose flour and somewhat more is better for hard wheat flour. A second criterion for lightness is that the dough barely springs back when punched lightly with the finger. The time required for yeast dough to rise depends mainly on the proportion of yeast in the dough and on the fermentation temperature (see schedule in Table 13-1). The proportion of salt and of sugar and the stiffness of the dough are contributing factors.

PUNCHING THE DOUGH

When the dough is sufficiently light, it should be punched down gently. Lifting the dough, now an inflated foam, from the sides of the utensil will cause it to collapse. Dough made from hard wheat flour may be allowed to rise and be punched a second time. Should a dough become light sooner than anticipated, it should be punched and allowed to begin rising again, not allowed to become too light. The dough can be shaped any time and does not have to reach its full volume a second time. A second rising needs no more than half the time for the first rising. (See Table 13-1.) After the dough is punched, it should be manipulated but handled in such a way as to avoid tearing or matting the gluten strands which have been separated by bubbles of carbon dioxide. One object of punching dough is to keep the films of gluten around gas cells from being overstretched. A second object is to subdivide the gas cells which have enlarged during the fermentation period. Working the dough at this stage divides and increases the number of gas cells (1). The larger the number of gas cells, the better is the distribution of carbon dioxide in the dough and the more even the grain in the baked product. Apparently, carbon dioxide produced by yeast collects in gas cells formed in the dough as it was mixed, kneaded, and shaped. New gas cells do not form. As fermentation proceeds, the yeast cells use the nutrients in the immediate vicinity. Punching the dough replenishes the supply. Also, if the yeast cells have multiplied, manipulating the dough distributes these cells more uniformly throughout. Heat is evolved during fermentation, so another reason for punching yeast dough is to equalize the temperature. The dough is warmer in the interior than on the surface. This condition is not so noticeable with a small quantity of dough, but with a large quantity, as in a bakery, the amount of heat evolved is appreciable and means must be provided to dissipate it. The optimum amount of manipulation of the dough at this stage can be determined in the same way as the optimum amount of kneading.

When the dough has been punched sufficiently, it is ready to be shaped. Dough is easier to shape if it is allowed to rest for a few minutes after it is punched. To produce bread with a good contour, the dough should be so manipulated that the strands of gluten are made parallel. Shaping should be done with the minimum of tearing and matting of gluten strands. If the dough has a tendency to stick, the surfaces with which it comes in contact may be oiled. Unfermented flour should not be used at this stage to keep the dough from sticking.

PROOFING

After the dough is shaped and in the baking pan, it is proofed, that is, allowed to rise again, this time so the baked product will be light. (See Fig. 13-6.) Temperature of the dough during proofing should be near 27°C (80°F) or possibly a few degrees higher at this stage. Proofing should be terminated when the dough again has approximately doubled in bulk and when it holds a slight depression if punched gently with a finger.

BAKING

TEMPERATURE

Yeast dough is put to bake in a hot oven at 400° to 425°F (204° to 218°C). Temperature may be lowered after the first 10 to 15 minutes if the crust appears

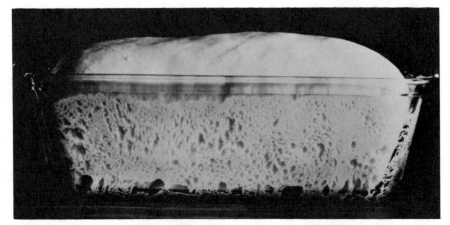

Figure 13-6. Yeast dough at the end of proofing. Bubbles of carbon dioxide trapped in strands of gluten convert the dough into a foam. (Courtesy of the Wheat Flour Institute.)

to be getting too brown. Rich dough which browns readily may be baked in a moderate oven, 350° to 375°F (177° to 190°C).

CHANGES EFFECTED

The volume of bread dough increases rapidly during the first few minutes in the oven. This phenomenon, known as "oven spring," may be observed if the oven has a glass window. The increase in volume may approach 80 percent in good dough from hard wheat flour. A number of factors contribute to this marked increase in volume. The quality of the dough as it goes into the oven influences oven spring. As the temperature of the dough begins to rise it becomes more fluid. The amylase enzymes are more active and the rapid conversion of starch to dextrins makes the dough more fluid. As a result, the dough is less able to resist the pressure of expanding gases. Production of carbon dioxide is temporarily accelerated and heat causes gases within the dough to expand. The ability of the films of gluten to retain gases is important at this stage. As the gas bubbles expand, the starch grains are oriented in the films of protein which enclose them (22,23). The cohesive gluten which forms a lining for the gas bubbles gives a silky sheen to the cells of bread.

Oven spring is most rapid when the interior of the loaf approaches 60°C (131°F), after which expansion is reduced. As the dough nears this temperature, translocation of water from protein to starch begins (16), making possible gelatinization of the starch. The structural integrity which in dough depends primarily on protein is shifted during baking to gelatinized starch in bread. Baking converts an elastic and somewhat mobile foam into rigid but deformable bread crumb (16,23). The appearance of bread crumb as seen under the microscope is shown in Figure 13-7. Good dough of optimum lightness expands just enough before it sets and the cells begin to leak gas to give very thin cell walls and a fine grain in the baked product. The temperature in the dough should rise fast enough to stop the production of carbon dioxide by

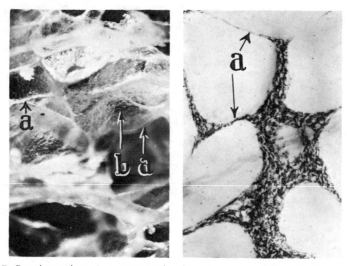

Figure 13-7. Bread crumb as it appears under the microscope: (left) untreated crumb; (right) embedded and stained crumb. Areas marked "a" are cuts across films of crumb that define gas cells; those marked "b" are surface views. Original magnification X 30. (From R. M. Sandstedt, L. Schaumburg, and J. Fleming. *Cereal Chemistry* **31**: 45, 1954. Reprinted by permission.)

yeast, to inactivate the amylase enzymes which soften the dough, and to set the crumb so cells begin to leak gas before overinflation of the foam ruins the grain and texture of the bread. Rupture of cells and rigidity of the crumb occur at 90° to 95°C (194° to 203°F) (16).

If dough is overlight when it is placed in the oven to bake, oven spring is magnified. The baked product will have large cells, some of which will have exploded. This gives the crumb a moth-eaten appearance. The top tends to flatten and to balloon over the sides of the pan. Insufficient salt and an oven temperature too low also cause excessive oven spring. If the dough is underlight when it is put to bake, the gas cells will be underinflated when the dough sets. This gives a baked product with thick cell walls and low volume. Tightness of the dough and inability of the gas cells to leak carbon dioxide, alcohol, and water vapor cause pressure to build as the gases accumulate and expand. As a result, the top crust separates from the lower crust with a wide tear rather than a fine shred as in dough that is at optimum lightness.

DONENESS

At the end of the baking period the temperature in the interior of bread is approximately that of boiling water. Evaporation of moisture from the surface of the bread keeps it cool during the early part of the baking period. When the surface dries, the temperature rises and may go as high as 150°C (302°F). Heat effects the formation of a complex between reducing sugars and protein which causes browning of the crust. Doneness of bread is difficult to assess, and brownness is not always a criterion. And a loaf of bread may sound hollow when thumped, even when it is not done. Baking for a specified time is probably the best way to assess doneness, but the size of the loaf influences baking time. Doubling the size of the loaf does not double the baking time, because the distance from the outside to the center of the loaf is not doubled.

THE BAKING PAN

The shape of the pan in which bread is baked influences the product. A shallow pan is preferred, because a deep one appears to put maximum strain on the dough. The comparative shallowness of muffin tins may explain why rolls baked in them have better grain and texture than does a loaf of bread baked from the same dough. Possibly, faster heat penetration in the muffin tins contributes to the better quality of the rolls, too. Of course, more extensive manipulation of the dough and the formation of many more gas bubbles as the dough is shaped for rolls may be contributing factors.

QUALITY OF BREAD

AROMA

The aroma of baking and freshly baked bread is appreciated by everyone. Fermentation by yeast appears to be essential for the development in bread of substances which contribute to aroma. Bread made to rise by an excess of oxidizing agent with no time for fermentation lacks aroma. Because a ferment of water, yeast, and sugar has the characteristic aroma of bread, sugar appears to be essential, too. Sugar contributes to aroma in another way. Bread cooked in such a way that it has no crust lacks aroma. Apparently odorous compounds are formed in the crust as it browns and these diffuse into the crumb. The mixture of compounds which contributes to the odor of baked yeast products is complex. More than 60 volatile components are considered as possible contributors to the aroma of bread (12). Included are organic acids, alcohols, and esters as well as carbonyl compounds from the crust. It appears that a combination of volatiles is responsible for the tantalizing aroma of freshly baked bread. Gas chromatography should prove a useful tool for identifying the essential constituents in the aroma of bread.

OTHER CHARACTERISTICS

Quality yeast bread is light without being overinflated. The top crust is well rounded and symmetrical. The crust is thin and a uniform golden brown. The crumb is moist and resilient. Films of baked dough that constitute the cell walls are thin and the surfaces have a silky sheen. (See Fig. 13-8.) The flavor is pleasant and nutlike without traces of soured or yeasty odor.

STORAGE OF BREAD

STALING

The characteristics enumerated above are those of freshly baked bread. Once out of the oven, bread begins to stale. The cause of the staling of bread has

Figure 13-8. Fine texture, even grain, and good volume characterize homemade bread at its best. From *Sunset,* October 1962. Darrow M. Watt, Photographer, 188 Felton Drive, Menlo Park, Calif.

long been a puzzle (18). The symptoms are clear enough. The crust becomes tough and leathery; the crumb becomes rigid, harsh, and crumbly. These changes occur in bread even though it is sealed in a moisture-vapor-tight wrap. A number of factors, including the role of lipids, proteins, and pentosans and the migration of moisture within the crumb, have been investigated for possible roles in bread staling, with no clear-cut answers (13,18). Staling does involve the retrogradation of starch, but whether it is the amylose or the amylopectin or both that recrystallizes is still unsettled. The presence of a surfactant such as glycerol monostearate or stearoyl-2-lactylates helps maintain softness of the crumb (18,31). Decreased swelling of starch grains and less soluble starch leached from the grains have been observed in bread made with certain surfactants.

The development of off flavor in yeast bread is another aspect of staling. Oxidation has been suggested as a contributing factor.

STORAGE TO DELAY STALING

Fresh bread will stay fresh longer if it is held at 60°C (140°F) or above. Stale bread can be refreshed by heating it to this temperature, but precautions must be taken to prevent drying. Bread is likely to mold at high storage temperatures unless it contains a compound such as calcium propionate which retards the growth of mold. An alternate way to prevent staling is to freeze fresh bread and store it at −18°C (0°F) (19).

SOUR DOUGH BREAD

Sour dough bread is a special type that has been made and appreciated on the West Coast for many years. The dough is propagated by a starter or sponge from a previous bake. Recently the organisms responsible for sour dough bread have been identified (24,25). One, a rod-shaped bacillus, *Lactobacillus sanfrancisco,* utilizes maltose preferentiallly to form lactic and acetic acid. The latter may account for as much as 50 percent of the total acid in sour dough. The second organism is a yeast, *Saccharomyces exiguus,* which can grow in the presence of the antibiotic elaborated by the bacillus but which is unable to metabolize maltose. This yeast thrives at the low pH of sour dough (3.8–4.5) and at the high concentration of acetic acid, conditions in which baker's yeast cannot survive. Although lactic and acetic are the major acids, six minor acids, propionic, butyric and two of its modifications, isovaleric, and valeric, also contribute to the flavor of sour dough bread (7).

REFERENCES

1. Baker, J. C., and M. D. Mize. 1941. The origin of the gas cell in bread dough. *Cereal Chem.* **18:** 19–34. Effects of mixing, punching, molding, and oxidizing agents on crumb structure.
2. Baker, J. C., H. K. Parker, and M. D. Mize. 1946. The distribution of water in dough. *Cereal Chem.* **23:** 30–38. Bound and free water in dough and their relation to flow properties.
3. Bohn, R. T. 1959. How sugar functions in high sugar yeast dough. *Cereal Sci. Today* **4:** 174–176. Effects of sugar on fermentation and on water uptake by dough.
4. Bushuk, W., and I. Hylinka. 1964. Water as a constituent of flour, dough, and bread. *Bakers Digest* **38**(6): 43–46, 92. The role of water in dough formation and in baking.
5. Cooper, E. J. and G. Reed. 1968. Yeast fermentation—effect of temperature, pH, ethanol, sugars, salt, and osmotic pressure. *Bakers Digest* **42**(6): 22–24, 26, 28–29, 63. Summary of pertinent facts.
6. Davis, E. M., and J. A. Kline. 1926. Making light bread from Missouri soft wheat flour. *Cereal Chem.* **3:** 411–419 Basic information on optimum proportions and handling of yeast dough from soft wheat flour.

7. Golal, A. M., J. H. Johnson, and E. Varriano-Martson. 1978. Lactic and volatile (C_2–C_5) organic acids of San Francisco sourdough French bread. *Cereal Chem.* **55:** 461–468. Minor acids present.
8. Halton, P., and G. W. Scott Blair. 1937. A study of some physical properties of flour doughs in relation to their bread-making qualities. *Cereal Chem.* **14:** 201–219. Nature and significance of the rheological characteristics of bread dough; a complicated topic clearly presented.
9. Hoseney, R. C., K. F. Finney, Y. Pomeranz, and M. D. Shogren. 1971. Functional (breadmaking) and biochemical properties of wheat flour components. VIII. Starch. *Cereal Chem.* **48:** 191–201. Effects on loaf volume and bread crumb of starches from various sources.
10. Jackel, S. S. 1977. The importance of oxidation in breadmaking. *Bakers Digest* **51**(2): 39–43. Approved oxidants and their action; effects of under and over oxidation.
11. Jenness, R. 1954. Milk proteins. Effect of heat treatment on serum proteins. *J. Agr. Food Chem.* **2:** 75–81. Discussion of the loaf-depressant factor in unheated milk. Or see R. Jenness. 1954. Recent work on the effects of milk in bread. *Bakers Digest* **28:** 87–91, 103.
12. Johnson, J. A., and C. R. S. Sanchez. 1973. The nature of bread flavor. *Bakers Digest* **47**(5): 48–50. Constituents involved.
13. Kim, S. K., and B. L. D'Appolonia. 1977. The role of wheat flour constituents in bread staling. *Bakers Digest* **51**(1): 38–42, 44, 57. Conflicting evidence summarized.
14. Larson, R. A., R. Jenness, and W. F. Geddes. 1949. Effect of heat treatment of separated milk on the physical and baking properties of doughs enriched with dry milk solids. *Cereal Chem.* **26:** 189–200. Heat treatment required for milk used to make yeast bread.
15. Magoffin, C. D., and R. C. Hoseney. 1974. A review of fermentation. *Bakers Digest* **48**(6): 22–23, 26–27. Utilization of sugars; starch and the function of amylases; effects on dough development.
16. Martson, P. E., and T. L. Wannan. 1976. Bread baking—the transformation from dough to bread. *Bakers Digest* **50**(4): 24–28, 49. A review of chemical and physical changes.
17. Morrison, W. R. 1976. Lipids in flour, dough, and bread. *Bakers Digest* **50**(4): 29–34, 36, 47. Starch lipids, lipoxygenase, lipid binding, crumb softeners, and antistaling agents.
18. Osman, E. M. 1975. Interaction of starch with other components of food systems. *Food Technol.* **29**(4): 30–32, 34–35, 44. Theories of bread staling; effects of sugar, surfactants.
19. Pence, J. W., N. N. Standridge, T. M. Lubisich, D. K. Mecham, and H. S. Olcott. 1955. Studies on the preservation of bread by freezing. *Food Technol.* **9:** 495–499. Optimum temperatures for maintaining freshness.
20. Pomper, S. 1969. Biochemistry of yeast fermentation. *Bakers Digest* **42**(2): 32–33, 36–38. Effects of pH, temperature, and osmotic pressure on carbohydrate metabolism by yeast.
21. Ponte, J. G. Jr., R. L. Glass, and W. F. Geddes. 1960. Studies on the behavior of active dry yeast in breadmaking. *Cereal Chem.* **37:** 263–279. Effect of rehydration temperature on functional properties.

22. Sandstedt, R. M. 1961. The function of starch in the baking of bread. *Bakers Digest* **35**(3): 36–43. Importance of starch reviewed.
23. Sandstedt, R. M., L. Schaumburg, and J. Fleming. 1954. The microscopic structure of bread and dough. *Cereal Chem.* **31:** 43–49. Illustrations and interpretation.
24. Saunders, R. M., H. Ng, and L. Kline. 1972. The sugars of flour and their involvement in the San Francisco sour dough French bread process. *Cereal Chem.* **49:** 86–91. Substrates for the yeast and for the bacillus.
25. Sugihara, T. F., L. Kline, and L. B. McCready. 1970. Nature of the San Francisco sour dough French bread process. II. Microbiological aspects. *Bakers Digest* **44**(2): 51–53, 56–57. Bacillus and yeast identified.
26. Thiessen, E. J. 1942. The effect of temperature upon the viability and baking properties of dry and moist yeast stored for varied periods. *Cereal Chem.* **19:** 773–784. Loss of activity during frozen and refrigerated storage.
27. Thorn, J. A., and G. Reed. 1959. Production and baking techniques for active dry yeast. *Cereal Sci. Today* **4:** 198–200, 213. Production (brief) and use in baking.
28. Tu, C. C., and C. C. Tsen. 1978. Effects of mixing and surfactants on microscopic structure of wheat glutenin. *Cereal Chem.* **55:** 87–95. Photomicrographic evidence of formation and then breakdown of sheetlike structure as mixing proceeds.
29. Volpe, T., and M. E. Zabik. 1975. A whey protein contributing to loaf volume depression. *Cereal Chem.* **52:** 188–197. A proteose-peptone identified.
30. Webb, R. J., J. Y. Heaps, P. W. Russell, P. W. R. Eggitt, and J. M. B. Coppock. 1970. A rheological investigation of the role of water in wheat flour doughs. *J. Food Technol.* **5:** 65–76. Disposition of water in dough.
31. Zobel, H, F. 1973. A review of bread staling. *Bakers Digest* **47**(5): 52–53, 56, 61. Role of starch; action of surfactants.

FILM

1. *The Trick of Yeast Rolls and Coffee Cake.* Sixty frames. Color. Wheat Flour Institute. Steps in making a basic dough; its use in a variety of rolls and coffee cakes.

FOURTEEN
Fats and Oils

Fats are an integral part of almost every food. They contribute tenderness to pastry crust, shortened cakes, and cookies. By aerating batters or doughs, they help establish texture in baked products. Fats contribute to or modify the flavor of foods and influence their mouthfeel. Most salad dressings contain high proportions of fat in emulsified form. Fats are used as a medium for the transfer of heat to fried foods.

Some of the fats used in food preparation are obtained from animals, others from plants. Crude fat is either expelled under pressure, extracted with suitable solvent or, in the case of lard, rendered from fat tissue by heating until the melted fat drains from the cells. Crude fat or oil so obtained undergoes a series of manufacturing processes before it is marketed. These include treatment with alkali to remove certain impurities, removal of pigments by adsorption on clay or carbon, deodorization by steam distillation, hydrogenation if a plastic fat is desired instead of an oil, and plasticizing to give fat a creamy smoothness.

Some knowledge of the chemistry of fats is essential for an understanding of their functional properties in food preparation. Fats of special interest in food preparation are classed on the basis of their chemical makeup as phospholipid, glycolipids, and neutral lipids. Phospholipids, important in forming emulsions, occur in egg yolk, milk fat, and in the seeds of plants. They will be discussed in subsequent chapters. The glycolipid group, of which galactosyl glycerides are members, are important in the development of gluten (see Chapter 10). The neutral fats make up the bulk of food fats. This group is discussed in this chapter.

CHEMISTRY OF FATS

Chemically, fats belong to the class of organic compounds known as esters (7), which are formed by the reaction of an alcohol with organic acids. The alcohol that participates in the formation of each molecule of fat is the water-soluble trihydric glycerol:

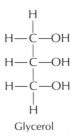

Glycerol

The acids are the fatty acids.

FATTY ACIDS

Fatty acids, like all organic acids, characteristically contain a carboxyl group:

In addition, each fatty acid contains a radical made up of a chain of carbon atoms. Radicals are denoted in chemical shorthand by the symbol R. Thus,

represents any fatty-acid molecule. What the R stands for is the feature that distinguishes one fatty acid from another. The particular fatty acids found in the molecules of a fat influence the chemical and physical properties of the fat and its functional properties in food preparation.

Molecules of most fatty acids contain an even number of carbon atoms, from 4 to 24. Some are saturated, that is, each carbon atom with a valence of 4 is linked to 2 other carbon atoms and to 2 atoms of hydrogen

Other fat molecules are unsaturated, that is, one or more carbon atoms are linked to a second carbon by a double bond, thus:

Unsaturated fatty acids differ in the number and position of the double bonds. They also differ from saturated fatty acids in the overall shape of the molecule. Saturated fatty-acid molecules are linear in shape as shown diagrammatically for stearic acid:

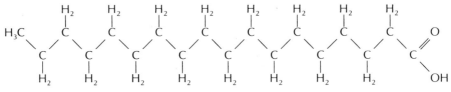

Linear form of a saturated fatty acid (stearic)

Unsaturated fatty acids usually exist in the *cis* form, instead of a more linearity of the molecule linear (*trans*) disrupted at the double bond, as shown:

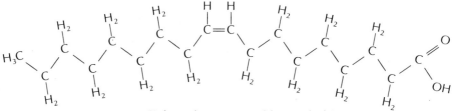

Cis form of an unsaturated fatty acid (oleic)

The fatty acid with the shortest chain, 4 carbons, is butyric. When the carbon chain is so long that it is tedious to write all the —CH_2 groups, a shorthand form, $CH_3(CH_2)_xCOOH$, may be used. The x may stand for two such groups, as in butyric acid, or 14, as in palmitic acid. Stearic acid, $CH_3(CH_2)_{16}COOH$, is a characteristic acid of the molecules of fat of land animals. Another fatty acid with the same number of carbon atoms in the chain is oleic acid. It is distinguished from stearic by a double bond in the center of the molecule between carbons 9 and 10, with the carboxyl carbon numbered 1. The formula for oleic acid is $CH_3(CH_2)_7CH{=}CH(CH_2)_7COOH$.

Some fatty acids and their chemical makeup follow:

Butyric	$CH_3CH_2CH_2COOH$
	also written $CH_3(CH_2)_2COOH$
Caproic	$CH_3(CH_2)_4COOH$
Caprylic	$CH_3(CH_2)_6COOH$
Capric	$CH_3(CH_2)_8COOH$
Lauric	$CH_3(CH_2)_{10}COOH$
Myristic	$CH_3(CH_2)_{12}COOH$
Palmitic	$CH_3(CH_2)_{14}COOH$
Stearic	$CH_3(CH_2)_{16}COOH$

Oleic	$CH_3(CH_2)_7CH{=}CH(CH_2)_7COOH$
Linoleic	$CH_3(CH_2)_3(CH_2CH{=}CH)_2(CH_2)_7COOH$
Linolenic	$CH_3(CH_2CH{=}CH)_3(CH_2)_7COOH$
Arachidonic	$CH_3(CH_2)_3(CH_2CH{=}CH)_4(CH_2)_3COOH$

GLYCERIDES

Glycerides are esters of fatty acids and the polyhydric alcohol, glycerol. One fatty acid united with a molecule of glycerol yields a monoglyceride, as shown:

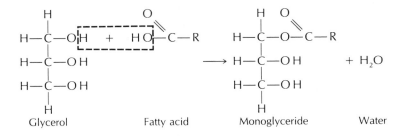

The unesterified part of the glycerol retains its water-soluble character, whereas the fatty acid radical confers on the monoglyceride the ability to unite with fat. When three fatty acids are esterified to the same molecule of glycerol, a molecule of fat (a triglyceride) results, as shown:

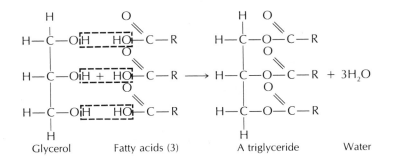

Many different molecules of fat are possible, depending on the fatty acids involved and their position of attachment on the glycerol. If all three fatty acids are alike (which is rare), a simple triglyceride results. All may be different (which is rarer) or two may be alike and one different, the usual pattern. In either of the last two cases, the fat molecule is a mixed triglyceride. With two fatty-acid radicals alike, the odd one may be attached to the middle carbon, designated 2 or beta (β) which gives a symmetrical molecule, as shown:

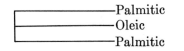

Or the odd fatty-acid radical may be attached at either the alpha (α) or alpha prime (α') carbon, as the end carbons are designated, which gives rise to an unsymmetrical molecule, thus:

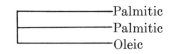

A triglyceride with stearic acid radicals only is called (tri)stearin, with palmitic only (tri)palmitin, and with oleic only (tri)olein. Mixed triglycerides such as palmityl diolein, oleyl dipalmitin, or dipalmityl stearin are more common.

Considering food fats as a whole, the most abundant and widely distributed saturated fatty acid is palmitic, although fats of animal origin, in contrast to those from plants, have appreciable quantities of stearic acid. Oleic acid is the most ubiquitous unsaturated fatty acid. Most fats of vegetable origin contain appreciable amounts of linoleic acid. Natural fats like olive oil, lard, and corn oil are mixtures of mixed triglycerides.

The formula for a triglyceride molecule is customarily written as shown above. Due to steric hindrance when all three fatty-acid radicals are oriented in the same direction, a tuning fork arrangement, with the fatty acid at the middle carbon positioned in the opposite direction from the fatty acids on the end carbons,

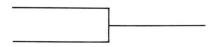

has been proposed. Alternately a chair arrangement

with the fatty acid on the alpha carbon oriented in a direction opposite the other two has been suggested.

CRYSTALS OF FAT

When liquid fat is cooled, removal of heat slows down the movement of the molecules. When they approach within 5 angstroms, they are attracted to each other by van der Waals forces (14). Such attraction has been likened to a zippering effect. If the molecular chain is long enough, as in the higher fatty acids, the cumulative attractive forces may be appreciable. As a result of this

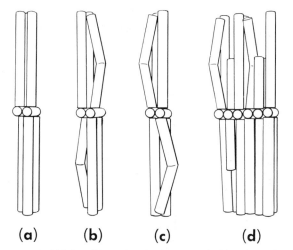

(a)   **(b)**   **(c)**   **(d)**

Figure 14-1. Arrangement of triglyceride molecules in a crystal of fat, shown by models. (*a*) Close packing of fatty acid chains in a triglyceride such as palmitin. (*b, c*) Unsaturated fatty acids on the central or on the terminal carbon atoms of glycerol interfere with the close packing shown in (*a*). (*d*) Variations in the chain length and presence of *cis* forms make crystal formation more difficult. (From C. W. Hoerr and D. F. Waugh, *Journal of the American Oil Chemists' Society* **32:** 40, 1955. Reprinted by permission.)

attraction, fatty-acid radicals in fat molecules are aligned in parallel fashion, the molecules overlapping thus (14):

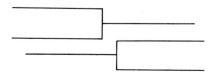

and they bond to form crystals.

Symmetrical molecules and those with fatty acids that are similar in chain length can align themselves more readily to form crystals. (Compare the close packing of a saturated triglyceride such as palmitin in Figure 14-1*a* with that of less symmetrical molecules in *b, c,* and *d.*) Fats that contain such asymmetrical molecules have low melting points.

POLYMORPHISM

Most fats are polymorphic, that is, they can exist in more than one of four crystalline forms (13). If a fat is chilled very rapidly, it forms small, transparent alpha crystals. Alpha crystals of most fats seldom last. Instead, they change rapidly to the beta prime form which exists as delicate needles not more than one micrometer long. Those fats, the beta-prime crystals of which are stable, remain fine-grained. The beta-prime crystals of other fats change into the intermediate form, 3 to 5 micrometers in size, and finally transform to the coarse beta crystals. The latter range from 25 to 30 micrometers up to 100 micrometers in length (13). Figure 14-2 shows photomicrographs of three of the polymorphic forms in which crystals of fats may exist. The particular polymorphic form in which a fat exists depends on the conditions under which the crystals were formed, the treatment of the fat after crystallization, and the fatty-acid makeup of the fat molecules.

Rapid cooling and agitation, which favor the formation of small crystals in frozen desserts and candies, promote the formation of small alpha crystals in fats. Slow cooling of melted fat favors the formation of coarser crystalline forms. For example, butter, with crystals so small that one is unaware that they exist, when melted and allowed to cool, forms crystals so large they are readily seen. The butter is not only coarser, but it appears oily because the few large crystals have much less surface area for the unsolidified phase to coat. This same butter can be made fine-grained again by melting it, cooling it rapidly, and agitating it as it cools.

The fatty acid makeup of the triglycerides of a fat influence which crystalline form will be stable. The more heterogeneous the fatty acid makeup of the individual triglycerides, the more likely are the crystals to stabilize in the beta-prime crystalline form and the texture of the fat remain fine-grained. Acetoglycerides (acetic acid radicals replacing one or two fatty acid radicals in a molecule) stabilize in the alpha crystalline form (21).

Homogeneity in the molecules which make up a fat favors transformation to coarser crystalline forms. Crystals in lard readily transform to the coarse beta form which tends to associate in large clusters as the fat is stored. The instability of the finer crystalline forms in lard is attributed to the high proportion of molecules which are similar in chemical makeup. More than one-fourth of the molecules of lard contain one unsaturated fatty-acid radical (usually oleic), one stearic acid radical, and one palmitic acid radical, the last attached at the central carbon of the glycerol.

MELTING POINTS

The melting point of a fat is a measure of the strength of the bonding forces between fatty-acid radicals within the crystals. The greater the attraction between molecules, the less they need to be slowed down (by removal of heat) in order to crystallize. Fats that contain such molecules have high melting points. Those fatty acids that do not fit so well must have more heat removed before they crystallize. Much less energy in the form of heat is needed to melt the crystals of the latter; that is, they have a lower melting point. The melting points of the triglycerides which make up a fat determine whether the fat will be a liquid, a plastic solid, or hard and brittle at room temperature. The consistency of a fat influences its functional properties in preparation. Characteristics of fatty acids which influence the attractive forces between adjacent molecules of fat (within the crystal) are the length of the carbon chain, the

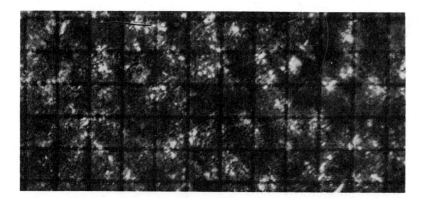

Beta prime

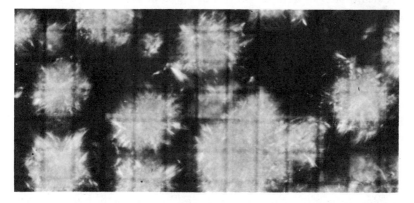

Intermediate

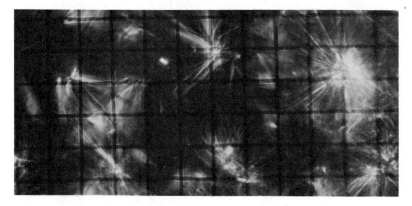

Beta

Figure 14-2. Photomicrographs (in polarized light) of polymorphic forms of crystals of fat. Original magnification X 200. Grid lines represent 18 microns. (From C. W. Hoerr, *Journal of the American Oil Chemists' Society* **37:** 542, 1960. Reprinted by permission.)

number of double bonds in the chain, and whether the unsaturated fatty acid is in the *cis* or *trans* form.

The longer the carbon chain, the higher is the melting point of the compound.

Fatty Acid	Number of Carbons	Melting Point, °C (5)
Butyric	4	−4.5
Stearic	18	71.2

Butyric acid liquefies at a temperature below the freezing point of water, yet stearic acid is still in crystalline form at room temperature.

The melting point decreases with an increase in the number of double bonds. Unsaturated fatty acids do not fit together well enough for maximum attraction because of the bends in the carbon chain at the double bonds. The greater the number of double bonds, the poorer is the fit.

Fatty Acid	Number of Double Bonds	Melting Point, °C
Stearic	0	71.2
Oleic	1	16.3
Linoleic	2	−5
Linolenic	3	−11.3

The *trans* form of a fatty acid has a higher melting point than the *cis* form. Linear molecules are more readily "zippered" into crystals than are molecules which are bent.

Fatty Acid	Geometrical Form	Number of Double bonds	Melting Point, °C
Elaidic	*trans*	1	45.0
Oleic	*cis*	1	16.3

The melting point of a triglyceride is conditioned by the melting point of the component fatty acids. Monoglycerides have higher melting points than the corresponding triglycerides.

Saturated	Melting Point, °C	Unsaturated	Melting Point, °C
Stearic acid	71.2	Oleic acid	16.3
Glyceryl monostearate	81.0	Glyceryl monooleate	35.0
Tristearin	73.0	Triolein	5.5

The melting point of a fat increases with each shift in polymorphic form from alpha crystals to beta. For example, the melting point of alpha crystals of tristearin is 55°C; for the beta form the melting point is 73°C.

CONSISTENCY OF FATS

The consistency of a fat influences its functional properties in food preparation. Fats are either liquid at room temperature (oils) or they are plastic (so-called solid fats). Plastic fats are a two-phase system, as are fondant, fudge, and ice creams. The solid phase consists of crystals of fat surrounded by a liquid phase of oil. The consistency of a plastic fat depends mainly on the ratio of the volume of crystals to the volume of oil. As the temperature of a plastic fat rises, the crystals melt. Those formed from triglycerides with lower melting points melt first. The fat softens and eventually becomes liquid. Cooling a liquid fat may cause crystals to form. Salad oil placed too near the freezing coils of the refrigerator may appear milky if the temperature of the oil is below the melting point of some of the fat molecules. Most salad oils have been chilled to remove those molecules that would crystallize at refrigerator temperature, a process called "winterizing" (19). A heat-oxidized saturated fat, oxystearin, has been approved as a crystal inhibitor for salad oils by the Food and Drug Administration.

Fats with a wide plastic range have some glycerides that remain in the crystalline form at elevated temperatures and others that remain liquid at low temperatures. A wide plastic range and small crystals (15) are desired in fats that are to be creamed, as for shortened cakes. On the other hand, one of the desirable attributes of butter as a table spread is its mouthfeel as it melts and this is due to its narrow plastic range. This characteristic is a disadvantage when butter is served on a very warm day. Manufacturers of margarine have found it difficult to produce a product with the unique melting characteristics of butter. Some of the crystals in the fat of beef and lamb have high melting points. Such fats which melt above body temperature are said to be tallowy.

The fat in chocolate has a unique melt-down. A high proportion of the triglyceride molecules in cocoa fat are identical, that is, they contain palmitic, oleic, and stearic acid radicals, with oleic positioned at the central carbon of glycerol (POS) (22). Oleoyldistearin (SOS) is another major component. These two triglycerides in their stable crystalline form have melting points within a few degrees of each other and just below body temperature (22). This gives to chocolate its sharp melting point and freedom from chewiness. Cocoa butter is "solid" below 31°C (88°F). Heated above 34°C (93°F), it melts sharply (15). Chocolate for dipping is first melted and then cooled and agitated so as to develop many crystal nuclei in the stable beta form. If unstable crystals are present in chocolate used to coat a center, these eventually melt and this fat migrates to the surface where it recrystallizes. These crystals dull the chocolate coating which is said to "bloom." Coconut fat with its high percentage of two short-chain saturated fatty acids, lauric and myristic, has a sharp melt-down, too.

Crystal size, as well as ratio of crystals to oil, also influences the consistency of a fat. In hydrogenated fat (see below) the crystals may be only 2 to 3 microns long; those in lard may measure 20 to 30 microns. Hydrogenated fats have more than 100 times the number of crystals that lard does, with the ratio between the volumes of crystals and liquid in both fats the same. When crystals of fat are large, so are the spaces between crystals. Spaces that are too large are unable to hold the liquid portion of the fat, which tends to leak from the pores between the crystals. Such fats are coarse and oily, and they are softer than fats with the same ratio of solid to liquid glycerides, but which contain many smaller crystals. A fat may be plastic (workable) at room temperature when the solid phase accounts for as little as 5 percent of the total or as much as 35 percent, depending mainly on the size and type of crystals involved.

Fat molecules, unlike water molecules, are more dense in the crystalline form. When a fat melts, it increases in volume. A cup of melted fat weighs less than a cup of solid fat. It should be noted, however, that a cup of most commercial hydrogenated shortenings weighs less than a cup of the same fat melted because 10 to 12 percent of the volume of the shortening is due to gas incorporated during manufacture (29).

COMPOSITION OF FOOD FATS

Most of the so-called visible fats which are consumed are pure fats. In this group are lard (rendered from the fatty tissue of pork), vegetable oils (coconut, corn, cottonseed, olive, peanut, safflower, sesame, soya and sunflower), and hydrogenated vegetable shortenings. Butter and margarine are approximately 80 percent fat. Water and milk solids account for the other 20 percent. "Invisible" fats are consumed in larger quantities than visible ones. A number of foods contain appreciable quantities of invisible fat. Included are meats, poultry, certain fish, whole milk cheese, chocolate, egg yolk, avocados, as well as pastries, cakes, cookies, salad dressings, nuts, and fried foods.

The fatty-acid makeup of some of the more common food fats is given in Table 14-1. Fats from beef and butter contain a higher proportion of saturated fatty acids and those from plants (chocolate and coconut excepted) a higher proportion of unsaturated fatty acids. Chicken fat has a higher proportion of unsaturated fatty acids than does the fat from beef or pork. Aside from chocolate, stearic acid is found in greatest concentration in beef, pork, and butter fat. Linoleic, an unsaturated fatty acid with two double bonds, predominates over oleic acid in safflower (one type), sunflower, corn, cottonseed and soy bean oil, and in the fat from English walnuts and from wheat. In other fats oleic acid predominates. The oil from sunflowers grown in northern states has

Table 14-1   Fatty acid content of selected food fats (grams per 100 grams of ether extract or crude fat)

Food Source	Saturated			Unsaturated			
	Palmitic	Stearic	Total	Oleic	Linoleic	Linolenic	Total
Meats							
Beef	24.9	18.9	49.8	36.0	3.1	0.6	45.8
Lamb	21.5	19.5	47.3	37.6	5.5	2.3	48.4
Chicken	21.6	7.6	29.8	37.3	19.5	1.0	65.6
Fats							
Butter	21.3	9.8	50.5	20.4	1.8	1.2	26.4
Cocoa butter	25.4	33.2	59.7	32.6	2.8	0.1	35.9
Lard	23.8	13.5	39.2	41.2	10.2	1.0	56.3
Margarine,[a] hard	10.9	8.6	19.8	32.0	23.6	1.5	57.1
Margarine,[a] soft	7.2	4.9	12.8	16.1	47.6	0.4	64.1
Shortening[a]	14.1	10.6	25.0	44.5	24.5	1.6	70.6
Oils							
Coconut	8.2	2.8	86.5	5.8	1.8	—	7.6
Corn	10.9	1.8	12.7	24.2	58.0	0.7	82.9
Cottonseed	22.7	2.3	25.9	17.0	51.5	0.2	69.7
Olive	11.0	2.2	13.5	72.5	7.9	0.6	82.1
Palm	43.5	4.3	49.3	36.6	9.1	0.2	46.3
Peanut	9.5	2.2	16.9	44.8	32.0	—	78.2
Safflower[b]	6.2	2.2	9.1	11.7	74.1	0.4	86.6
Safflower[c]	4.8	1.3	6.1	75.3	14.2	—	89.5
Sesame	8.9	4.8	14.2	39.3	41.3	0.3	81.4
Soybean	10.3	3.8	14.4	22.8	51.0	6.8	81.2
Sunflower	5.9	4.5	10.3	19.5	65.7	—	85.2
Walnuts	7.0	2.0	9.1	22.2	52.9	10.4	86.1
Wheat germ	16.6	0.5	18.8	14.6	54.8	6.9	76.8

Source: U.S. Dept. Agr. Handbook No. 8-4. *Composition of Foods. Fats and Oils. Raw, Processed, Prepared.* 1979.

[a]Varies widely with the fats used in manufacture.
[b]High linoleic acid.
[c]High oleic acid.

a higher proportion of linoleic to oleic acid than does that from plants grown in a warmer climate (3,26). Oleic acid makes up three-fourths the total fatty acids in olive oil. Chicken fat contains a higher proportion of linoleic acid than does beef or pork. Soybean oil and the fat from English walnuts contain appreciable amounts of linolenic acid.

MODIFICATION OF NATURAL FATS

Plants supply the raw material from which not only salad and cooking oils are made, but the bulk of shortenings and margarines also. Soybeans are the chief source of oil, but cotton, corn, peanut, palm, safflower, and sunflower seed are other sources (33). For plastic shortenings and margarines, the oils are hardened.

HYDROGENATION

Oils that are fluid at room temperature can, by a process known as hydrogenation (6,29), be changed to fats that are plastic and workable. Fat which contains unsaturated fatty-acid radicals is exposed to hydrogen gas in the presence of a catalyst. Double bonds in the fatty-acid radical open, and one atom of hydrogen unites to each of the two carbon atoms formerly joined by a double bond. If the fatty acid is oleic, stearic acid results, in a reaction as shown:

$$CH_3(CH_2)_7CH{=}CH(CH_2)_7COOH \ + \ 2H \rightarrow CH_3(CH_2)_7CH_2CH_2(CH_2)_7COOH$$

Oleic acid   Hydrogen   Stearic acid

Double bonds not only decrease in number but also migrate during hydrogenation. In the case of polyunsaturated fatty acids, only certain of the double bonds may become saturated. As a result, isomers of unsaturated fatty acids which do not occur naturally are formed. Temperature, pressure, and amount of agitation during hydrogenation influence which unsaturated fatty acid and which double bonds on polyunsaturated acids will be saturated.

During hydrogenation some of the unsaturated fatty acids change from the *cis* to the *trans* form (25). This shift, in addition to a decrease in unsaturated fatty acids, accounts for the conversion of an oil to a plastic fat. *Trans* fatty acids are found in hydrogenated shortenings and margarines. Of the 10 margarines analyzed in one study (both hard and soft types represented), 8 had more than 15 percent mono-unsaturated fatty acids in the *trans* configuration and 9 of the 10 contained smaller amounts (less than 5 percent) of di-unsaturated fatty acids in the *trans* form (4). In another study, seven samples of margarine had mono-unsaturated fatty acids which ranged from 25 to 64 percent, 6 to 33 percent of which were in the *trans* configuration (25). Butter fat may contain up to 10 percent *trans* unsaturated acids, formed by bacteria in the rumen of the cow from *cis* forms of fatty acids in the cow's feed.

After an oil has been hydrogenated but while it is still in liquid form, it is charged with nitrogen gas under pressure. The fat is cooled rapidly to 18°C (65°F), at which point it is agitated for a few minutes to effect crystallization (29). With the sudden release in pressure, the gas is dispersed throughout the mass of plastic fat. The fat is then tempered, that is, warmed sufficiently so that the crystals first formed change over to the most stable crystalline form. After a hydrogenated fat has been tempered, the crystals are stable and the consistency of the fat does not change appreciably even though the storage temperature may fluctuate from 4°C (40°F) to 32°C (90°F). Hydrogenated shortenings are superior to butter or regular lard in this respect.

An alternate method of producing a plastic fat from a vegetable oil is to add highly hydrogenated fat to the oil. Fats so formed are called "compound" shortenings in contrast to the former, known as "hydrogenated all-vegetable" shortening.

REARRANGEMENT

When fat is heated under nitrogen and in the presence of a suitable catalyst, the fatty-acid radicals migrate and recombine with the glycerol in a more random fashion (14,16). As a result of this shuffling of fatty-acid radicals, new glycerides form. Molecules of a fat after such interesterification are more heterogeneous. For example, lard, normally quite coarse and grainy, after rearrangement contains smaller crystals. Photomicrographs of crystals of lard before and after rearrangement are shown in Figure 14-3. Rearrangement alters the consistency of a fat, and it remains plastic over a wider range of temperature.

ACETYLATION

When acetic acid radicals replace fatty-acid radicals in a fat molecule, acetylated or acetin fats are formed (21). Acetin fats may be liquid or plastic at room temperature, depending on the fatty acids present in the molecule. Oils advertised as edible lubricants are acetin fats. The presence of acetic acid radicals in triglycerides has the advantage of lowering the melting point, as does an unsaturated fatty acid, without the instability of the latter. A second advantage is that acetin fats crystallize and remain in the alpha form. Acetin fats appear translucent and waxy rather than grainy when they crystallize. The crystals form a ribbonlike, unordered but interlocking network, as shown in Figure 14-4. Acetin fats are considered safe and currently are permitted in edible fats. Acetin fats form flexible films and are used as coating agents for such foods as dried raisins, prepared meats, cheese, and nuts (21).

SUPERGLYCERINATION

A number of shortenings now on the market contain from 2 to 3 percent glyceryl monostearate (34) (which is usually accompanied by smaller amounts of the diglyceride). Fats which contain monoglyceride, referred to as "superglycerinated fats," are advantageous in cake making. (See Chapter 21, on shortened cakes.)

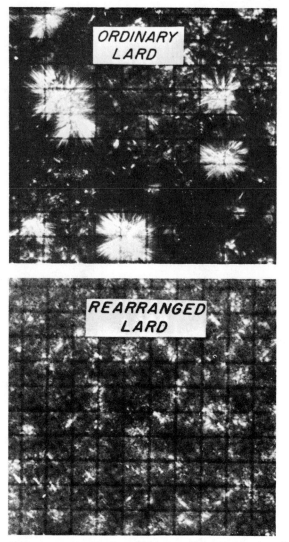

Figure 14-3. Effect of rearrangement (interesterification) on the size of the crystals of lard. Original magnifiction approximately X 200. (From C. W. Hoerr and D. F. Waugh, *Journal of the American Oil Chemists' Society* **32:** 37, 1955. Reprinted by permission.)

DETERIORATION OF FATS

ABSORPTION OF ODORS

Fats absorb odors because they dissolve odorous gases to which they are exposed. This type of spoilage is quite obvious when fat is held in an open container in a refrigerator in which cantaloupe is stored. But there are many more subtle instances of spoilage of fat due to absorption of odors.

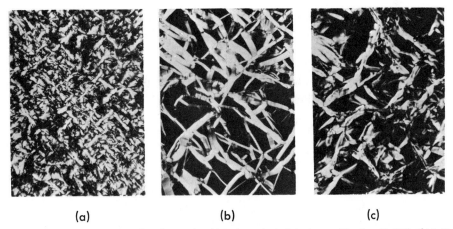

(a)   (b)   (c)

Figure 14-4. Photomicrographs of crystals of (a) tristearin (original magnification X 405); (b) 1,2-diaceto-3-stearin (original magnification X 150); and (c) 1-aceto-3-stearin (original magnification X 150). Translucency of acetin fats is due to alpha-tending crystals; the waxiness comes from the feltlike layering of the crystals. (From R. O. Feuge, *Food Technology* **9**: 315. Copyright © 1955 by the Institute of Food Technologists.)

RANCIDITY

Fats may spoil because they have become rancid. Rancidity in fats is due to either hydrolysis or oxidation (9). In hydrolytic rancidity, the triglyceride reacts with water and for each molecule of water involved one molecule of fatty acid is released. When a molecule of fat reacts with three molecules of water, glycerol and three fatty acids are formed, as shown below:

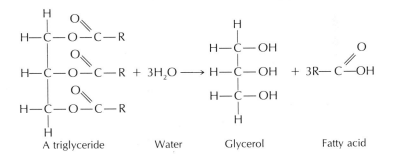

A triglyceride   Water   Glycerol   Fatty acid

Heat acts as a catalyst for this reaction, so hydrolysis takes place in a kettle of fat used for deep fat frying. Cold, wet food placed in hot fat favors hydrolysis of the fat. If the molecule of fat reacts with the base NaOH instead of water, glycerol and three molecules of the sodium salt of the fatty acid are formed. The latter, of course, is soap. Ammonium hydroxide will react with fat in the same way as the stronger base. It is for this reason that ammonia in hot dishwater effectively removes fat from the surface of utensils and an open container of ammonia placed in a hot oven in which fat has been spattered aids in its removal.

Fat-splitting enzymes known as "lipases," when present in foods, act as catalysts for the hydrolysis of fats, too. For example, butter becomes rancid when stored in a warm place, which favors the activity of the enzyme. Keeping fats cold delays the beginning of hydrolytic rancidity. The odor of rancid butter comes from butyric acid, which has been liberated according to the reaction above. Aged whipping cream, particularly that which clings to the edges of the container, may have a bitter taste from the butyric acid liberated by hydrolysis.

Molecules of fat which contain unsaturated fatty-acid radicals are subject to oxidative rancidity. The unpleasant odor of such rancid fats is attributed to the formation and subsequent breakdown of hydroperoxides (9,27). According to the theory held currently, a hydrogen on a carbon adjacent to one carrying a double bond is displaced by a quantum of energy to give a free radical:

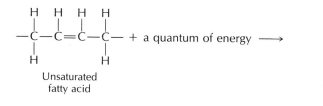

Both heat and light are common sources of the energy that gives rise to free radicals. Molecular oxygen can unite with the carbon which carries the free radical to form an activated peroxide as follows:

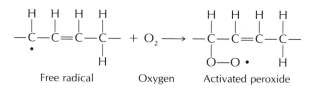

The energy from this activated peroxide can displace a hydrogen from another unsaturated fatty acid and thus activate it. The latter becomes a free radical.

The displaced hydrogen unites with the activated peroxide to form a hydroperoxide. This part of the reaction is

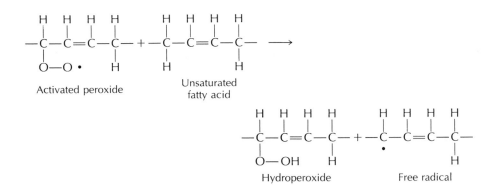

Activated peroxide

Unsaturated fatty acid

Hydroperoxide   Free radical

In this way the energy that catalyzes the oxidation of a fatty acid is not squandered but is passed on to another fatty acid where it repeats the process. A free radical is particularly troublesome becaues it is the beginning of a self-perpetuating reaction whereby the oxidation of many unsaturated fatty-acid radicals is catalyzed. A hydroperoxide is very unstable, decomposing into compounds with shorter carbon chains. These include fatty acids, aldehydes, and ketones, which are volatile and which contribute to the unpleasant odor of rancid fat.

The more unsaturated the fatty acid, the greater is its susceptibility to oxidative rancidity. Hydrogenation makes a fat more stable in this respect. Hydrogenated fats after extended storage, especially at elevated temperatures, however, undergo a change called reversion. An aldehyde, 6-nonenal, has been identified as responsible for the off-odor. Oxidation of two isomers of linoleic acid, formed during hydrogenation, gives rise to the aldehyde (18).

Because of the prooxidant effect of light, fats should be stored in a dark as well as a cold place. Printed on potato chip packages are directions to avoid placing the package where sunlight can reach it. Certain frequencies of the light spectrum, especially the ultraviolet, are more harmful than others. Certain metals also catalyze the reaction leading to oxidative rancidity in fats. Both copper and iron are prooxidants (9). For this reason stainless steel or aluminum utensils are preferred for fats. Oxidation of unsaturated fats may be catalyzed by the enzyme lipoxygenase (32) as well as by heat, light, and certain metals. Iron freed from the pigment hemoglobin catalyzes rancidity in cooked meats. Reactions similar to those outlined above for autocatalytic oxidative rancidity occur in unsaturated fats when the enzyme lipoxygenase is present (9,32). Less energy is needed for the reaction so low temperatures are less effective in preventing lipoxygenase-catalyzed than autocatalytic rancidity (9).

ANTIOXIDANTS

Substances that delay the onset of oxidative rancidity in fats have been sought because of the unpalatability of rancid fats. These substances are known as "antioxidants." One of them was known to the pioneers, who added the bark of the slippery elm tree to pork fat when lard was rendered. A substance derived from the inner bark acted as an antioxidant. Lard so rendered could be stored longer before it became rancid.

Most of the antioxidants in use today are phenolic compounds (30). Three phenolic antioxidants approved for use in fats are butylated hydroxyanisole (BHA), butylated hydroxytoluene (BHT), and propyl gallate. Labels on containers for margarine and many rich crackers indicate the presence of one or more of these antioxidants. Flavonoid compounds with a minimum of two hydroxyl groups in the *ortho* position (on adjacent carbons) or *para* position (on carbons opposite each other) are good antioxidants. Many oils derived from seeds of plants contain tocopherols, naturally occurring antioxidants. The delta or gamma isomers are more effective antioxidants than the alpha form, which is the more potent biologically. Vegetable oils keep as well as they do at room temperature because of the presence of this naturally occurring antioxidant.

A molecule of an antioxidant functions by replacing an unsaturated fatty acid as the source of labile hydrogen to unite with a free radical or an activated peroxide. The molecule of antioxidant is oxidized instead of another fatty acid. In the process, the antioxidant siphons off the energy which would otherwise be available for the formation of a new fatty acid free radical and which would perpetuate the chain reaction that occurs in the autoxidation of fats. The phenolic hydroquinone illustrates how the more elaborate molecules of phenolic antioxidants act as hydrogen donors:

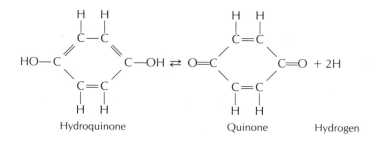

Hydroquinone   Quinone   Hydrogen

Certain organic acids which act as synergists may be added to fats along with a phenolic antioxidant (30). A synergist is a substance that increases the effectiveness of the primary antioxidant. Di- or tricarboxylic acids are effective because they bind or sequester metal ions. A molecule of citric acid used as a synergist may bind prooxidant iron thus:

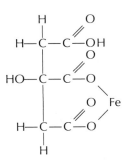

Ethylenediaminetetraacetate (EDTA) is a metal-sequestering agent used in some salad dressings.

In one homemade quick bread mix, cream of tartar is included to act as a synergist and increase the effectiveness of the tocopherol present in the vegetable oil from which the fat was made. Other synergists keep the primary antioxidant in reduced form and thus maintain its ability to act as a hydrogen donor. The effectiveness of one antioxidant may be increased by using it in combination with another. A combination of butylated hydroxyanisole and propyl gallate is more effective than the sum of the effectiveness of the two used separately. Use of antioxidants and synergists in foods that contain fat are responsible for improved keeping qualities of many foods.

Cereals, especially whole grain ones, are likely to become rancid from the polyunsaturated fat they contain. Baked products such as crackers and cookies and fried foods are subject to oxidative rancidity. For these and similar foods, an antioxidant which is stable at the high temperatures used in baking and frying is desirable. One such antioxidant with high "carry over" is butylated hydroxyanisole. Sugar cookies that contain a small amount of the reducing sugar glucose, in addition to sucrose, resist rancidity more than do cookies made from sucrose alone (11). The greater stability of the former is attributed to the antioxidant properties of the products of the sugar-amine reaction which contribute to browning of the cookies.

FATS AS A MEDIUM FOR THE TRANSFER OF HEAT

Foods are cooked in hot fat by sautéing or by deep fat frying. A fat used for frying should be odorless and bland tasting, a neutral medium for the transfer of heat. A number of food fats qualify. When fats and oils are prepared for market, they are decolorized and deodorized (29). Some are more difficult to purify than others.

Liquid fat is a good conductor of heat, with the advantage that the temperature attained by the fat is not self-limiting due to boiling, as is true of water. Foods heated in fat are not only cooked, but the surface is browned due to caramelization of sugars and to reducing sugar-protein reaction. Because it is desired to brown fried food, the fat used must be able to withstand high temperatures. Frying temperatures recommended vary from 177°C to 201°C (350° to 395°F). A thermometer suspended in the fat permits a close check of the temperature. The crisp surface of fried foods adds to their appeal, as does their flavor. Unsaturated gamma-lactones have been identified as contributing to the flavor of deep fat fried foods (23).

A number of changes take place in the hot fat, some of which influence the quality of the fried food (28). The color of the fat changes from light yellow through amber to varying shades of brown, the smoke point of the fat is lowered, the fat becomes more viscous and begins to foam, and the amount of fat absorbed by the food increases.

SMOKE POINT OF FATS

When a fat is overheated, the glycerol which accumulates because of hydrolysis is decomposed and the fat gives off a blue gas which is irritating to the mucous membranes. The glycerol is dehydrated, and the unsaturated aldehyde, acrolein, results.

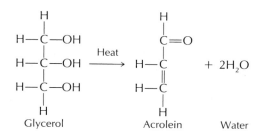

A desirable characteristic of fats used for frying is a high smoke point (the temperature to which they can be heated before the appearance of acrolein) (2). The smoke point of a fat depends on the percentage of free glycerol in the fat or the ease with which the molecules are hydrolyzed to free glycerol (20). Monoglycerides hydrolyze more readily than triglycerides. Fats with added monoglycerides are likely to smoke when used for frying. Of course, fatty acids accumulate as well as glycerol. Free fatty acids can be titrated with base, and this provides an index to the amount of glycerol present.

Fats which have been used previously smoke at a lower temperature because hydrolysis of some fat molecules has already occurred. Fats should be heated no hotter and no longer than necessary, to minimize hydrolysis. The surface area of the container will influence the smoke point also; the smaller the diameter, the hotter the fat can get before it begins to smoke (2).

ABSORPTION OF FAT

Absorption of fat during frying should be kept to a minimum because fat-soaked foods are less palatable and carry more calories. Keeping to a minimum both the contact time and the surface of the food exposed to the fat reduces absorption, as does coating the surface of the food with egg. The fat should be kept at optimum temperature during the entire period. Overloading the kettle causes the temperature of the fat to drop and prolongs the cooking time. Batters cause more rapid deterioration of the fat used for deep frying than do French fries (1). The smoking point is lower and the fat discolors more rapidly when batter is fried. Baking powder, egg, and milk are responsible for the greater decomposition. Doughnuts from leaner dough absorb less fat, but those from richer dough are more tender (7). Absorption of fat was greater in dough-nuts with more lecithin and in those made with tartrate rather than with SAS-phosphate baking powder (24).

Molecules of a heated fat or oil, especially above 200°C, may unite to form long chains or polymers (28). If unsaturated, the molecules may give rise to cyclic compounds. The fat becomes more viscous with use, and the more viscous the frying medium, the greater the absorption of fat by the fried food (31). Hydrolytic and oxidation products formed in the hot fat during frying tend to lower interfacial tension between fat and water, and this favors pene-tration of fat into the food (28). The lowered surface tension plus the increased viscosity of the fat causes it to foam. Addition of silicones (dimethyl polysi-loxanes) to the fat reduces foaming by inhibiting rancidity of the fat and so limiting the accumulation of oxidation products at the high temperature used in frying (8).

For heating frying fats, stainless steel containers are preferable to those made of iron for two reasons. In addition to iron's being a prooxidant, fat is more easily removed from the smooth surface of a stainless steel pan. Foods stick to metal (iron) because of the pits in the surface and one reason that oiling a baking pan prevents sticking is that it partly fills and coats the pits.

HAZARDS IN USING FATS FOR FRYING

There are certain hazards in using fats for frying. Because fat does not boil, it may be hotter than it appears. A burn from hot fat may be severe because of the high temperature and the tendency of the fat to cling to the skin. Another hazard in using fat, and especially for deep fat frying, is the danger of fire. When cold, wet food comes in contact with hot fat, the water as it sinks is converted into steam, the bubbles of which may cause the fat to overflow the container. The surface of the uncooked food should be as dry as possible, overloading the kettle should be avoided, and the wire basket or slotted spoon that holds the food should be lifted momentarily to prevent overflow. Use of a deep kettle reduces the hazard. Fat splashed on the unit may ignite, and thus set the contents of the container on fire. Should this happen, a lid should be put on the pan and the heat turned off. The kettle should be removed from a hot electric unit. A deep fat fryer with thermostat control minimizes this hazard and also frees one to concentrate on the food rather than on maintaining the temperature of the fat.

When butter is heated to sauté food, spattering does not occur even though butter contains appreciable water. A surfactant (see Chapter 16) present in butter keeps the water in the form of an emulsion so that the water does not separate from the fat. Instead, the butter foams as the water boils away. Most margarines contain an antispattering agent, usually lecithin (12).

Cleaning the pan after foods have been fried presents problems. Stainless steel pans are easiest to clean, because hot suds only are required. The fat and the gummy material on the exterior of an aluminum pan can be removed by scouring with steel wool or other aluminum cleanser. Iron utensils may be soaked in ammonia to dissolve the gummy film of polymerized fat, which can then be washed away.

REFERENCES

1. Bennion, M., and F. Hanning. 1956. Decomposition of lard in the frying of French-fried potatoes and of fritter-type batters. *J. Home Econ.* **48:** 184–188. Effects of the two products on smoke point and on discoloration of fat; effects of ingredients in the batter on smoke point and on fat absorption.
2. Blunt, K., and C. M. Feeney. 1915. The smoking temperature of edible fats. *J. Home Econ.* **7:** 535–541. Analysis of the main factors which affect the smoking point of fats.
3. Brignoli, C. A., J. E. Kinsella, and J. L. Weihrauch. 1976. Comprehensive evaluation of fatty acids in foods. V. Unhydrogenated fats and oils. *J. Am. Dietet. Assoc.* **68:** 224–230. Compilation of data.
4. Carpenter, D. L., and H. T. Slover. 1973. Lipid composition of selected margarines. *Amer. Oil Chem. Soc. J.* **50:** 372–376. Fatty acids in the oils used.
5. Chemical Rubber Company. 1980–1981. *Handbook of Chemistry and Physics.* 61st edition. R. C. Weast, ed. Cleveland: CRC Press.
6. Coenen, J. W. E. 1976. Hydrogenation of edible oils. *Amer. Oil Chemists' Soc. J.* **53:** 382–389. Details of the process.
7. Denton, M. C., E. Wengel, and L. Pritchett, 1920. Absorption of fat by fried batters and doughs, and causes of variations. *J. Home Econ.* **12:** 111–127. Variations in doughnut type batters which affect fat absorption.
8. Freeman, I. P., F. B. Padley, and W. L. Sheppard. 1973. Use of silicones in frying oils. *Amer. Oil Chemists' Soc. J.* **50:** 101–103. Antifoaming agents.
9. Glass, R. L. 1966. Food rancidity: Its nature and prevention. *Bakers Digest* **40:** 34–35, 38–39. Clear, concise presentation.
10. Goddard, V. R., and L. Goodall. 1959. Fatty acids in food fats. U.S. Dept. Agr. Home Economics Research Report No. 7.
11. Griffith, T., and J. A. Johnson. 1957. Relation of browning reaction with storage stability of sugar cookies. *Cereal Chem.* **34:** 159–169. Effects of glucose.
12. Harris, B. H., A. K. Epstein, and F. J. Kahn. 1941. Fatty interface modifiers. Composition, properties, and uses in the food industry. *Oil and Soap* **18:** 179–182. Antispattering and other roles of surfactants.

13. Hoerr, C. W. 1960. Morphology of fats, oils, and shortenings. *J. Am. Oil Chemists' Soc.* **37**: 539–546. Polymorphic forms of crystals in fats.

14. Hoerr, C. W., and D. F. Waugh. 1955. Some physical characteristics of rearranged lard. *J. Am. Oil Chemist's Soc.* **32**: 37–41. Effects of molecular rearrangement on crystal formation and the functional properties of lard.

15. Hoerr, C. W., and J. V. Ziemba. 1965. Fat crystallography points way to quality. *Food Eng.* **37**(5): 90–95. Tailoring fats for different food uses.

16. Husted, H. H. 1976. The interesterification of edible oils. *Amer. Oil Chemists' Soc. J.* **53**: 390–392. Nature of the process; advantages.

17. Institute of Shortening and Edible Fats and Oils. 1974. *The Chemistry of Foods Fats and Oils.* Washington, D.C.: The Institute. 18 pp. Clear, simple presentation of the chemistry of fats and oils.

18. Keppler, J. G., M. M. Horikx, P. W. Meijboom, and W. H. Feenstra. 1967. Isolinoleic acids responsible for the formation of hardening flavor. *Amer. Oil Chemists' Soc. J.* **44**: 543–544. Identity of the compounds.

19. Kreulen, H. P. 1976. Fractionation and winterization of edible fats and oils. *Amer. Oil Chemists' Soc. J.* **53**: 393–396. Nonchemical modification of edible lipids.

20. Lowe, B., S. Pridham, and J. Kastelic. 1960. The free fatty acid and the smoke point of some fats. *J. Home Econ.* **50**: 778–779. Data for fats produced by modern methods of processing.

21. Luce, G. T. 1967. Acetylated monoglycerides as coatings for selected foods. *Food Technol.* **21**: 1462–1463, 1466, 1468. Unique properties.

22. Lutton, E. S. 1957. On the configuration of cocoa butter. *J. Am. Oil Chemists' Soc.* **34**: 521–522. Triglyceride make up of the fats in chocolate.

23. May, W. A., R. J. Peterson, and S. S. Chang. 1978. Synthesis of some unsaturated lactones and their relationship to deep-fat fried flavor. *J. Food Sci.* **43**: 1248–1252. An attempt to pin-point the source of the deep-fat fried flavor.

24. McComber, D., and E. M. Miller. 1976. Differences in total lipid and fatty acid composition of doughnuts as influenced by lecithin, leavening agent, and use of frying fat. *Cereal Chem.* **53**: 101–109. Absorption of frying fat.

25. Ottenstein, D. M., L. A. Wittings, G. Walker, V. Mahadevan, and N. Pelick. 1977. *Trans* fatty acid content of commercial margarine samples determined by gas-liquid chromatography on OV-275. *Amer. Oil Chemists' Soc. J.* **54**: 207–209. Seven retail samples analyzed.

26. Robertson, J. A. 1972. Sunflower: America's neglected crop. *Amer. Oil Chemists' Soc. J.* **49**: 239–244. Fatty acid make-up.

27. Roth, H., and S. P. Rock. 1972. The chemistry and technology of frying fats. 1. Chemistry. *Bakers Digest* **46**(4): 38–45, 66. Autoxidation reviewed; technical.

28. Roth, H., and S. P. Rock. 1972. The chemistry and technology of frying fats. 2. Technology. *Bakers Digest* **46**(5): 38–40, 41–44. Changes in fats brought about by frying.

29. Sanders, J. H. 1959. Processing of food fats—a review. *Food Technol.* **13**: 41–45. Brief outline of main steps in preparing shortenings from vegetable oils; alkali refining, hydrogenation, deodorization, plasticizing, interesterification, and winterizing discussed.

30. Sherwin, E. R. 1976. Antioxidants for vegetable oils. *Amer. Oil Chemists' Soc. J.* **53**: 430–436. Rancidity; types and function of antioxidants.

31. Stern, S., and H. Roth. 1959. Properties of frying fat related to fat absorption in doughnut frying. *Cereal Sci. Today* **4:** 176–179. Relation between fat absorption and development of viscosity.
32. Wagenknecht, A. C., and F. A. Lea. 1956. The action of lipoxidase in frozen raw peas. *Food Research* **21:** 605–610. Oxidation of fat and chlorophyll in frozen peas catalyzed by lipoxidase.
33. Weihrauch, J. L., C. A. Brignoli, J. A. Reeves III, and J. L. Iverson. 1977. Fatty acid composition of margarines, processed fats and oils. A new compilation of data for tables of food composition. *Food Technol.* **31**(2): 80–85, 91. Data for the main oils and for edible fats.
34. Weiss, T. J. 1970. *Food Oils and Their Uses.* Westport, Conn.: Avi Publishing Co. p. 126.

FIFTEEN
Pastry

Pastry includes conventional pie crust and the less frequently made puff pastry. Conventional crust is used to make such popular desserts as double-crust fruit pies, single-crust soft pies, and fruit tarts. The single crust may be baked and the cooked filling added; this is usually topped with meringue or whipped cream, as for cream pie. For custard and pumpkin pie the raw filling is cooked in the crust as the latter bakes. Conventional crust is used also in such entrées as meat pie and quiche Lorraine. Puff pastry is used for patty shells, tarts, and as top crust for meat pies.

Pastry crust is one of the simplest of the batters and doughs in terms of the number of ingredients. Making high-quality pastry should be a simple matter, because only four ingredients, flour, fat, salt, and water, are used. That it is not is attested by the wide variation in the quality of pastry one has eaten and the lack of confidence of many cooks.

An important characteristic of good pastry is tenderness. Pastry should cut easily with a fork, and it should disintegrate readily when one bites into it, but it should not crumble. High-quality pastry is flaky. Flakes are due to layers of gluten which have been raised in blisters by steam formed as the crust bakes. If the layers are thick and the blisters few, the pastry will be tough. If the layers are thin and the blisters numerous, the pastry will be tender as well as flaky. Pastry should be crisp, not doughy or soggy. The edge of the pastry crust should be a golden brown and the center a paler brown (4).

The degree to which each characteristic is actually obtained in a pastry depends upon the ingredients, their proportions, and the way they are manipulated. Crusts made from crumbs and softened table fat are simpler to make and are essentially failure-proof, which in part accounts for their popularity.

INGREDIENTS AND THEIR FUNCTIONS

FLOUR

Flour is the main ingredient in pie crust. Two kinds of flour may be used. The kind affects the characteristics of the pastry (3). All-purpose flour, because of its higher protein content, yields more gluten, and the more gluten developed the more cohesive the dough. The result is either a tough or a flaky pastry, depending on how extensively the gluten is distributed. In contrast to all-purpose flour, pastry flour does not yield as much gluten and tends to make a tender but crumbly pastry (3).

SALT

Salt is used to season the flour. Omitting the salt makes no difference in pastry except in taste.

FAT

Fat contributes tenderness, or shortness, to pastry. Part of the toughness (lack of shortness) in pastry comes from the cooked starch paste. A cup of flour is about three-quarters starch. If ¾ cup of starch were combined with 2 table-spoons of water as used in pastry and the mixture then rolled and baked, the product would be hard even without the protein of the flour. If a ball of dough made from flour and water were rolled and baked, it would be tough and hard. The protein in the flour yields gluten wherever the flour is dampened with water and manipulated. When the dough is rolled and baked, the gluten is denatured by heat and this contributes additional toughness.

Fats tenderize pastry by waterproofing the particles of flour (13). Both the protein and the starch in flour have an affinity for water, that is, contain polar groups. In a molecule of fat, the carbonyl $\left(\diagdown C = O \diagup \right)$ groups are polar as are the double bonds in unsaturated fatty-acid radicals. These particular groups in a molecule of fat make it possible for the fat to unite at strategic spots with polar groups on the surface of particles of flour. The remainder of the molecule of fat (the major part of it) with no affinity for the flour (or the water) acts as a mechanical barrier to prevent contact of the water molecules with the protein of the flour. It is in this way that fat waterproofs flour and so limits the development of gluten.

Pure fats have more shortening power than do those which, like butter and margarine, contain moisture. Even with pure fats such as lard, hydrogenated shortenings, and edible oils, the characteristics of pastry depend upon the particular fat used (5,7). A cup of lard (220 grams) weighs more than a cup of hydrogenated shortening (188 grams). Liquid fats have more covering or spreading power than do plastic fats so that a high proportion of flour particles become coated with fat. Softer fats spread more readily and contact more flour particles than do firmer ones. The higher the ratio of liquid to crystals, the greater is the covering power of fat (7). This is influenced by the temperature of the fat as well as by its fatty acid makeup.

In addition to making pastry tender, fats also contribute desirable flakiness by separating the dough into layers. Oils, on the other hand, tend to coat each particle of flour. As a result, water contacts the flour with difficulty, little gluten is developed, and a tender but crumbly or even greasy pastry results. Plastic fats tend to make a more flaky product. Lard is considered a superior fat for making pastry (10).

LIQUID

The liquid used in pastry is usually water, but pastry made with oil by the stir-and-roll method contains milk. Without liquid, the flour particles would not adhere to form a dough. Liquid is needed to hydrate the flour so that during the mixing the gluten can be developed sufficiently to give a certain amount of cohesion to the dough. How extensively gluten is distributed throughout pastry and, of course, the amount of gluten, determine whether pastry is (1) crumbly and with a tendency to be too brown, (2) compact and tough and browning with difficulty, or (3) crisp, flaky, and tender. To produce the third type, gluten should be distributed throughout the mass of the dough in hundreds of small areas. A third purpose of the liquid in pastry dough is to provide steam to leaven it and so actually produce the flakes.

PROPORTIONS OF INGREDIENTS

SALT

As for biscuits, muffins, and most other quick breads, ½ teaspoon of salt per cup of flour is usually recommended.

FAT

The proportion of fat customarily recommended varies from ¼ to ⅓ cup for each cup of flour. In one study (11) pastry made with plastic fat was nearest optimum in quality when the volume of fat was one-fourth the volume of flour. When liquid fat was used, the optimum volume was less (3.5 tablespoons per cup of flour). When less than ¼ cup of plastic fat is used, it is difficult to stir in the water and make a dough without at the same time developing so much gluten as to make the pastry tough. When more than ⅓ cup of fat is used for each cup of flour, the pastry tends to be crumbly and greasy. Within the recommended range, the smaller the proportion of fat, the greater is the likelihood of the development of too much gluten as the dough is worked after the addition of water. If cut into the flour adequately, one-fourth cup of lard per cup of flour will give tender, flaky pastry.

LIQUID

Only a minimum of water should be used, but that little is necessary if the pastry is to be flaky. If pastry has too little water, it tends to be crumbly and browns very quickly, as does understirred pastry made with the optimum amount of water. Two tablespoons of water per cup of flour are sufficient to make the dough adhere and contribute flakiness with minimum risk of the pastry being tough. With the small amount of liquid used in pastry, errors in measuring in percent can be large and so make a great difference in the quality of the pastry. A difference of ½ teaspoon (3 milliliters) of water per cup of flour can make a noticeable difference in the tenderness of the pastry. When more than 2 tablespoons of water per cup of flour are used, the chances of developing too much gluten in the dough and so making the pastry tough are great (6). The smaller the proportion of fat to flour, the more important it is to avoid excess water; otherwise, the pastry is likely to be tough.

MANIPULATION OF INGREDIENTS

One cause for lack of confidence in making pastry is that considerable skill is required for the manipulation of ingredients. Even though ingredients are in correct proportion, how and how much they are manipulated determine whether pastry will be tender or tough, flaky or mealy (6,12,15). The proportions suggested above put the minimum demands on skill in making pastry. Until one's technique is perfected, however, it is difficult to achieve in pastry the particular combination of tenderness and flakiness desired.

In a certain respect tenderness and flakiness in pastry are opposing characteristics which is probably the reason it is difficult to achieve both in the same pastry. Gluten toughens pastry, yet to obtain flaky pastry some gluten is necessary. The secret, of course, is in its distribution. Even though two samples of pastry contain the same amount of gluten, they may differ in tenderness, owing to differences in the distribution. If the flakes are large and exist as a few thick layers, the pastry will be tough; if the layers are numerous and tissue-paper thin, the pastry will be crisp yet tender.

CUTTING FAT INTO THE FLOUR

The first step in making pastry is to sift the salt with the flour to distribute the salt evenly. A plastic fat may be distributed throughout the flour by cutting it in with a pastry blender, a pastry fork, two knives, or two spatulas manipulated with a cutting motion like the blades of scissors. The technique is the same as that employed for biscuits. (See Chapter 12.) Kitchen scissors may be used, or the fat may be cut in by the fingers. If the fingers are used, one must be careful to work fast and keep contact between fat and fingers brief to avoid melting the fat. The purpose of this cutting is to subdivide the fat and to increase its surface area so that more of the flour particles make contact with it. The mixture resembles coarse cornmeal when the fat is cut into the flour sufficiently. Some of the pieces of flour are embedded in the fat, but between small chunks of fat are layers of flour particles untouched by fat. Where pieces of flour are in contact with fat or embedded in it, the water cannot reach the flour. The finer the fat is cut, the more flour particles are waterproofed and the less likely is an excessive development of gluten which would result in a tough pastry. Gluten in the pastry in the photomicrograph in Figure 15-1 was stained to show its distribution.

STIRRING THE DOUGH

Water is added to the flour-fat mixture all at once and in such a way as to distribute the water over the mixture as evenly as possible. The mixture should be stirred *at once* and with a wide circular motion. Otherwise, part of the

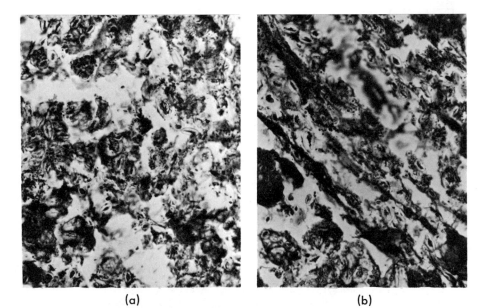

(a)   (b)

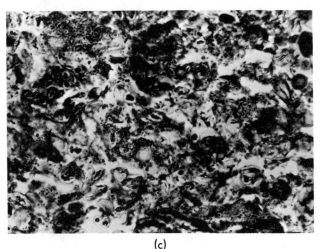

(c)

FIGURE 15-1. Photomicrographs of raw pastry dough stained to show gluten: (a) standard dough, gluten in delicate strands with indistinct edges; (b) dough with excess manipulation, gluten in distinct strands; (c) dough with excess water, large amounts of gluten but strands indistinct. Magnification × 200. (From S. Hirahara and J. Simpson, *Journal of Home Economics* **53:** 684, copyright © 1961, American Home Economics Association, Washington, D.C.)

dough will absorb more than its share of water. Some very wet, sticky spots result, whereas some flour gets no water. When this happens, spots that are too damp are overworked to get the spots that are too dry worked into the dough; the excessive stirring makes tough pastry. Stirring should be discontinued when the dough adheres in large lumps.

INTERRELATION BETWEEN INGREDIENTS AND MANIPULATION

To achieve the desired characteristics in pastry, the kind of ingredients, their proportions, and the extent to which they are manipulated are interrelated. Different conditions necessitate varying the amount of manipulation before and after the water is added.

EFFECTS OF KIND OF FAT AND TYPE OF FLOUR

When oil is used instead of plastic fat, the flour is more readily waterproofed. In this case the dough needs to be manipulated more after the liquid is added to develop enough gluten to make the pastry flaky and not too tender. The warmer a plastic fat, the more flour it can contact and the more tender is the pastry. Pastry flour, because it is low in gluten, tends to make a pastry that is so tender it is mealy (3). Dough made from pastry flour not only can tolerate more mixing but needs more after the water is added to develop some cohesiveness in the dough.

EFFECTS OF PROPORTIONS OF FAT AND WATER

When a high proportion of fat is used, the fat should be cut into the flour less or the dough should be manipulated more after the water is added so the pastry will be flaky and not too tender. When a low proportion of fat to flour is used, the fat should be cut into the flour more to limit the development of gluten. When a slight excess of water is added, stirring the dough should be kept to a minimum to prevent excessive development of gluten and tough crust. When the water is skimped, the dough not only tolerates more stirring, but requires more to prevent its being too tender and crumbly and lacking flakiness. Limiting the amount of water and the manipulation of the dough after the water is added can compensate for a low ratio of fat to flour, too.

EFFECT OF THE EXTENT TO WHICH FAT IS CUT INTO THE FLOUR

The extent to which the fat is cut into the flour determines the tolerance of the dough to mixing after the water is added. The thicker the layers of flour between the pieces of fat, the thicker are the layers of gluten developed in the dough subsequently. The less the fat is cut into the flour, the trickier it is to distribute the water evenly throughout the dough without developing so much gluten that the pastry is tough. The more the fat is cut in at this point and the better it is distributed, the smaller are the areas of flour not waterproofed by fat and so free to be dampened by water. It is in this flour that gluten is developed. Obviously, the more the fat is cut into the flour, the more the dough can be handled after the water is added without developing so much gluten that the dough is excessively cohesive and the pastry tough. In fact, the more such dough is stirred at this point, the more flaky as well as tender is the pastry. For example, pastry made by cutting the fat in with 100 strokes and incorporating the liquid with 60 strokes is at least as flaky and as tender as pastry made by cutting the fat into the flour with 50 strokes and incorporating the water with 30 strokes. If minimum proportions of both fat and liquid are used, and if, in addition, the fat is cut into the flour extensively, the dough has a high tolerance to handling after the water is added.

The discussion above applies to the standard method of combining ingredients in making pastry. Other methods for making pastry have been developed (14). When ingredients are combined by the water-paste method, for example, an attempt is made to control the amount and distribution of gluten in another way. In this method all of the liquid is combined with enough of the fat-flour mixture to tie up most of the water. This lumpy paste in which gluten develops is combined with the remainder of the fat-flour mixture. Tender, flaky pastry can be made by this method, but no better than by the standard method, when the precautions outlined above are observed. For pastry made by the stir-and-roll method, melted fat or oil is used and milk is the liquid. The two are combined and then stirred into the flour to form a dough. Ingredients combined by this method require more manipulation to develop enough gluten so the pastry will be flaky and not excessively tender.

ROLLING AND SHAPING THE PASTRY

After pastry dough is stirred sufficiently in the bowl, it is shaped into a ball. Then it is rolled to a desirable thickness (slightly less than ⅛ inch) on a clean, flat surface. A minimum of flour should be used on the rolling surface, because this flour increases the toughness of pastry (12). A pastry cloth under the dough facilitates rolling, but the cloth is difficult to launder and keep sanitary. Rolling pastry between two sheets of waxed paper eliminates the need for flour. Lifting the rolling pin as it approaches the edge of the circle of dough prevents the formation of a beveled edge. In addition to flattening the ball of dough into a sheet large enough to fit into a pie pan, rolling flattens out the small masses of gluten into very thin layers. The lumps of fat are also spread into layers. A cut down through a sheet of rolled raw dough properly stained would show thin layers of gluten with embedded starch grains alternating with and superimposed upon layers of fat. The thinner and more numerous the layers, the flakier and more tender is the pastry.

After the dough is rolled into a sheet, it should be transferred, without stretching, to a pie pan, and the excess dough trimmed away. For a single-crust pie, the pastry may be baked on either the inside or the outside of the pie pan. Pricking the dough helps prevent steam pockets forming between crust and pan.

BAKING PASTRY

A hot oven (425°F [218°C]) is usually recommended for baking pastry. A moderately hot oven is also satisfactory if the baking time is lengthened. The baking time is influenced, too, by the material from which the pan is made. A pan made of highly emissive dark or dull metal or glass favors rapid and

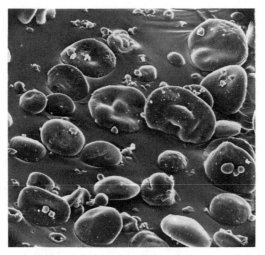

FIGURE 15-2. Incompletely pasted (gelatinized) starch grains isolated from pastry. Low moisture and high fat sharply restrict the pasting of starch in pie crust. (From R. C. Hoseney, W. A. Atwell, and D. R. Lineback, *Cereal Foods World* **22**(2): 57, 1977. Reprinted by permission.)

uneven browning of the crust. Lowering the temperature approximately 25°F (15°C) and increasing the baking time a few minutes will yield a more evenly browned crust.

During baking, the fat melts and the gluten begins to set. Starch grains appear little altered in appearance due to the low level of moisture (8). (See Fig. 15-2.) Part of the water in the layers of gluten in which the starch grains are embedded is converted to steam. Steam from layers of dough which are separated by layers of fat forms pockets around the fat and puffs up the layers of gluten. When these are coagulated by heat, the bubbles break, and layers of gluten with embedded starch grains, the whole coated with layers of fat, are left. Pockets of steam which form in dough as it bakes make the pastry porous and flaky. Some of the steam pockets show as large blisters in the crust; others are quite small.

It is interesting to watch pastry as it bakes if an oven with a glass window is available. After the pastry has been in the oven for approximately five minutes, the dough becomes quite agitated. A pocket of steam forms in a particular area and lifts the dough until the dough no longer can stand the strain, at which point the inflated dough collapses and steam escapes. Thousands of miniature explosions, side by side, superimposed on each other, in unison, and in sequence, occur in the dough during the next five minutes in the oven. Gradually the number of explosions decreases and the agitation of the dough ceases as most of the water boils away. At this point the dough begins to set and the surface begins to brown. If all has gone well, the result is a light, crisp, tender product that can be handled, yet cuts easily with a fork and collapses with slight pressure in the mouth—in short, a perfect pastry.

CHARACTERISTICS OF PASTRY

TENDERNESS VERSUS TOUGHNESS

Tenderness in pastry is determined by the amount and the distribution of gluten. The amount of gluten developed in the pastry is a composite of many factors. These include the kind of flour, the temperature of the ingredients, the kind of fat, the proportion of fat to flour and of liquid to flour, the extent to which the fat is cut into the flour, and the extent to which the dough is stirred after the water is added. If pastry is too tender, it is mealy. Factors that contribute to mealiness include use of an oil or warm plastic fat, use of pastry flour, cutting the fat in excessively, using too little water, and undermanipulating the dough after the water is added. Tough pastry is the result of too little fat, too much water, cutting fat into the flour insufficiently, or too much manipulation of the dough after the water is added. Use of flour on the board or pastry cloth makes pastry tougher. Because pastry is crisp, an objective way to assess its tenderness (really the crispness or friability) is to measure the force used to break the pastry by an instrument known as a shortometer (1) (Fig. 15-3). Because pastry is not homogeneous, the breaking strength of a number of samples must be measured to arrive at an average figure representative of the pastry.

FIGURE 15-3. Shortometer used to measure the breaking strength and so assess the tenderness of pastry. (Photograph by Zoe Ann Holmes.)

FLAKINESS

Flakiness in pastry is due to layers of gluten with embedded starch grains separated by fat and puffed up by steam. Plastic fats favor the development of flakiness. The better the fat is distributed, the finer the flakes. Some manipulation of the dough after the water is added is necessary to develop gluten. Flaky pastry that is tender is desired, but it should not be so tender that it will not hold together. Small, thin sheets of gluten distributed throughout the pastry make crisp, flaky, yet tender pastry. (See Fig. 15-4.) The same amount distributed less widely might give a tough crust. Puff pastry differs from conventional pastry in the greater numbers of layers of gluten separated by layers of fat (9).

CRISPNESS

Crispness in pastry results when sufficient water is evaporated from the layers of dough during baking. It is influenced by how thick the dough is rolled, how long the pastry is baked, and whether the crust is an upper or a lower one. Making a pie that has a crisp lower crust is a real achievement, especially if the filling is fluid when it is poured into the unbaked crust as it is for custard and pumpkin pie. Having the baking temperature too low at first or allowing the pie to stand before it is put to bake is likely to give a soggy crust. Keeping the amount of water in the pastry crust to a minimum reduces the tendency of the lower crust to be soggy. If the filling is warm (not hot!) so that it does not take too long to begin to thicken, the lower crust is less likely to be soggy. Increasing the proportion of egg in a filling lowers the setting temperature. Another way to eliminate a soggy crust in custard pie, and not as fantastic as it sounds, is to bake the crust in one pan and the filling in another and transfer the cooked filling to the baked crust. The baked filling needs to be cooled before an attempt at transfer is made. Brushing the surface of the unbaked pastry crust with slightly beaten egg white and placing it in a hot oven for a few minutes to coagulate the protein and waterproof the crust before adding the filling reduces sogginess. For fruit pies, the juice may be thickened before it is poured into the unbaked pie crust.

PUFF PASTRY

Puff pastry (see Fig. 15-5) differs from conventional pie crust in the way the fat is incorporated and in the ratio of fat to flour (1:2 v/v). Fat is distributed in the dough by repeated folding and rolling it inside the latter. First a stiff dough is made with the flour, water, and a small part of the fat. The dough is chilled, then rolled into a rectangle approximately ¼-inch thick, on half of which the remainder of the fat is spread. The dough is folded to encase the fat, and then this fat-dough sandwich is folded into thirds. After it has chilled, the dough is again rolled into a rectangle ¼-inch thick. This folding, chilling, and rolling is repeated three or four times before the dough is cut and baked. The many foldings give paper-thin layers of dough separated by layers of fat. Butter, freed

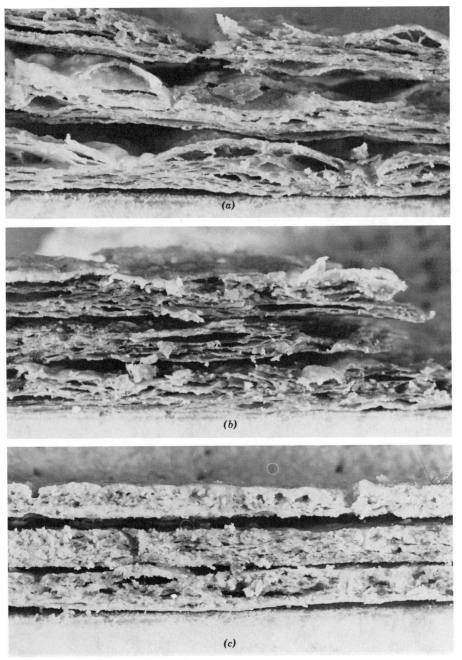

FIGURE 15-4. Pastry (3-layer stacks) varying in flakiness from (a) most to (c) least. (From D. Preonas, A. I. Nelson, and M. P. Steinberg, "Continuous Production of Pie Dough," *Bakers Digest* **41**(6): 34–40. Reprinted with permission from the December, 1967, issue of *Bakers Digest*, Chicago, Ill.)

FIGURE 15-5. Effects of folding on volume of puff pastry: (a) under-; (b) optimum; and (c) over-folding. (Adapted from J. T. Colburn and G. R. Pankey, *Bakers Digest* **38**(2): 72, 1964.)

of milk solids and water, is a satisfactory fat for making puff pastry, as are certain margarines (2). It is essential that the fat spreads to form continuous layers without extensive penetration into the layers of dough. Steam collects at these layers of fat and "puffs" the pastry (9).

REFERENCES

1. Bailey, C. H. 1934. An automatic shortometer. *Cereal Chem.* **11:** 160-163. Instrument devised to measure the breaking strength of pastry.
2. Colburn, J. T., and G. R. Pankey. 1964. Margarines, roll-ins, and puff pastry shortenings. *Bakers Digest* **38**(2): 66–68. Desirable characteristics of fats for puff pastry.
3. Denton, M. C., B. Gordon, and R. Sperry. 1933. Study of tenderness in pastries made from flour of varying strengths. *Cereal Chem.* **10:** 156–160. Breaking strength of pastries made from low-, from medium-, and from high-protein flour.
4. Finished foods—a third report. Pie crusts—from recipe and mix. *J. Home Econ.* **54**: 767–771 (1962). Desirable characteristics, factors for success, defects and their causes.
5. Fisher, J. D. 1933. Shortening value of plastic fats. *Ind. Eng. Chem.* **25:** 1171–1173. Breaking strength of pastries made with different fats; congealing points of fat and shortening value.
6. Hirahara, S., and J. I. Simpson. 1961. Microscopic appearance of gluten in pastry dough and its relation to the tenderness of baked pastry. *J. Home Econ.* **53:** 681–686. Standard pastry dough, dough with excess manipulation, and dough with excess water compared; photomicrographs of raw dough.
7. Hornstein, L. R., F. B. King, and F. Benedict. 1943. Comparative shortening value of some commercial fats. *Food Research* **8:** 1–12. An attempt to account for differences in the shortening value of fats.
8. Hoseney, R. C., D. R. Lineback, and P. A. Seib. 1978. Role of starch in baked foods. *Bakers Digest* **52**(4): 11–14, 16, 18, 40. Scanning electron micrographs of starch in baked products, including pastry.
9. Lagendijk, J., and J. van Dolfsen. 1965. Classification of puff-pastry fats and margarines based on dough firmness. *Cereal Chem.* **42:** 255–263. Nature of the fat and characteristics of the pastry.

10. Lowe, B., P. M. Nelson, and J. H. Buchanan. 1938. *The physical and chemical characteristics of lard and other fats in relation to their culinary value.* Iowa Agr. Exp. Sta. Res. Bull. **242:** 1–52. Iodine value and refractive index of fats and the breaking strength of pastry.
11. Matthews, R. H., and E. H. Dawson. 1963. Performance of fats and oils in pastry and biscuits. *Cereal Chem.* **40:** 291–302. Three oils, lard, and two hydrogenated vegetable oils compared.
12. Noble, I. T., H. McLaughlin, and E. G. Halliday. 1936. Factors influencing the apparent shortening value of a fat. *Cereal Chem.* **11:** 343–346. Effects of manipulation and of flour used to roll the dough on the breaking strength of shortbread.
13. Platt, W., and R. S. Fleming. 1923. The action of shortening in the light of the newer theories of surface phenomena. *Ind. Eng. Chem.* **15:** 390–394. An attempt to relate the tenderizing effects of fat in pastry to fundamental work by Harkins and co-workers on the orientation of molecules at film interfaces.
14. Rose, T. S., M. E. Dressler, and K. A. Johnston. 1952. Effect of fat and water incorporation on the average shortness and uniformity of tenderness of pastry. *J. Home Econ.* **44:** 707–709. Comparison of pastry made by the water-in-fat emulsion and by the conventional method.
15. Swartz, V. N. 1943. Effects of certain variables in techniques on the baking strength of lard pastry wafers. *Cereal Chem.* **20:** 121–126. Effects of increasing the water, of increasing the mixing time after the water was added and of having ingredients at room *vs.* refrigerator temperature.

SIXTEEN
Emulsions

An emulsion is defined as a dispersion or suspension of one liquid in another, with the molecules of the two liquids immiscible or mutually antagonistic. Both mayonnaise and French dressing are food emulsions, but there are many other examples. Shortened cake batters, cream puffs, cheese sauce and cheese soufflé, cream, cream cheese, egg yolk, and even cream soups and gravies contain fat in emulsified form.

NATURE OF AN EMULSION

PHASES

An emulsion has three phases, or parts. One, the dispersed phase, consists of suspended droplets. In foods these are usually oil, although not always. The second phase is the continuous phase (also referred to as the "dispersions medium"). In foods, this is usually water. If oil and water are mixed, they separate at once and with a definite, sharp line. As Aeschylus has Clytemnestra say,

> Pour oil and vinegar into the same jar,
> You would say they stand apart unlovingly.*

To keep droplets of one liquid suspended in another in which it is immiscible requires a third substance, the molecules of which have some affinity for both of the liquids. The affinity must be partial and unequal. Such a substance is called an emulsifier. Emulsifiers belong to a group of compounds called surfactants.

FUNCTIONS OF AN EMULSIFIER

If a liquid like oil is added to water, with which it is immiscible, and the mixture is beaten, the blades of the beater shear the liquids and they form droplets. Surface tension accounts for the tendency of liquids to form droplets. Molecules in the surface of a liquid do not have the same freedom of movement as those in the interior (1). The diagram in Figure 16-1 shows the reason for this. The *net* attractive force on a molecule in the main body of a liquid

*From Agamemnon of Aeschylus, Louis MacNeice, translator, Faber and Faber, Ltd., publishers, London.

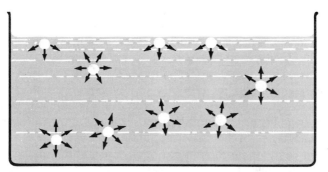

FIGURE 16-1. Forces acting on molecules in the interior and on the surface of a liquid. (Reproduced from Paul Becker, *Principles of Emulsion Technology,* by permission of Reinhold Book Corporation, a subsidiary of Chapman-Reinhold, Inc., New York, 1955.)

surrounded on all sides by the same kind of molecules is zero. But the pull on molecules in the *surface* of a liquid is unbalanced and toward the interior of the liquid. This inward pull on molecules in the surface confers on them the character of an elastic skin. The formation of droplets of liquid, illustrated in Figure 16-2, is due to this net inward attraction on molecules in the surface.

Because oil and water are immiscible, force, usually applied through the moving blades of a beater, is required to form droplets of the two liquids and keep them intermingled (1). This intermingled state will continue only so long as beating or shaking continues. Once it stops, the droplets of each of the immiscible liquids coalesce, because the molecules of each liquid have great affinity for each other and little or none for molecules of the other liquid. The

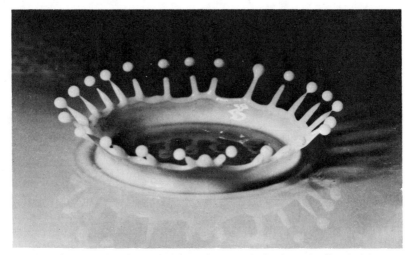

FIGURE 16-2. Photomicrograph at 1/100,000 of a second of a drop of milk splashing onto a flat surface. The beads of liquid of the "crown" form because of surface tension. (From Harold Edgerton, MIT, Cambridge, Mass.)

oil, being lighter, will rise to the top and the heavier water will settle to the bottom of the container. Thus there is a separation of the liquids into two phases. The plane where the two phases meet is known as the "interface."

An emulsifier aids in the formation of an emulsion by (1) decreasing the surface tension of one liquid more than the other and (2) preventing the coalescence of the droplets of the other liquid. The liquid with the lower surface tension will spread more readily and become the continuous phase. At the same time, molecules of the emulsifier must collect at the oil/water interface to prevent coalescence of the dispersed phase.

A number of different compounds can serve as emulsifying agents (1,9) but they have this characteristic in common. One part of the molecule must have a combination of atoms so that it has an affinity for and will dissolve in oil, that is, it is nonpolar. The other part of the molecule must be polar in nature and so be able to unite with water.

To understand how an emulsifier prevents coalescence of droplets of immiscible liquids, consider one droplet of oil which has been sheared by the blades of a beater from a spoonful of oil which has been added. Before the droplet of oil has a chance to reunite with other droplets, molecules of an emulsifier line up around the circumference of the oil droplet. The fat-soluble part of each molecule of the emulsifier is oriented toward and in fact dissolved in the outer layer of fat molecules in the droplet. Figure 16-3 shows a diagram of such a droplet (1). The water-soluble portion of each molecule is oriented toward and dissolved in the continuous phase of water surrounding the droplet of oil. Molecules of emulsifier pack closely enough around the droplet of oil to form a layer one molecule thick. The protective film around emulsified oil droplets consists of at least three layers—the outermost layer of fat molecules,

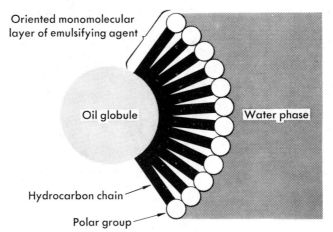

FIGURE 16-3. Diagram showing the orientation of emulsifying agent in an oil-in-water emulsion. (Reproduced from J. R. Hartman, *Colloid Chemistry*, 1947, by permission of Houghton Mifflin Company, Boston.)

the layer of emulsifier, and the innermost layer of water molecules. This protective layer of emulsifier prevents droplets of oil already emulsified from uniting with oil as it is added. Should two oil droplets already emulsified collide, the protective film prevents their coalescence. In a number of instances dispersed droplets in an emulsion are surrounded by a layer of electric charges which further serves to stabilize the emulsion.

EMULSIFYING AGENTS

NATURALLY OCCURRING

Naturally occurring emulsifiers include the phospholipids, lecithin (phosphatidyl choline), and phosphatidyl ethanolamine. Phospholipids are derivatives of fat in which, instead of a fatty acid, phosphoric acid is esterified with glycerol at one of the terminal carbon atoms. The particular fatty-acid radicals attached to the other two carbon atoms of the glycerol depend on the source of the phospholipid. Usually one of the two fatty acids is unsaturated. Attached to the phospholipid molecule at one of the hydroxyl groups of the phosphoric acid residue is either choline, which gives rise to lecithin, or ethanolamine or serine, which give rise to phosphatidyl ethanolamine or phosphatidyl serine, the last two phospholipids called cephalins.

Formulas for lecithin and for phosphatidyl ethanolamine are

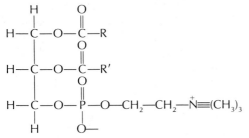

Lecithin (phosphatidyl choline)

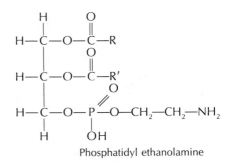

Phosphatidyl ethanolamine

Usually R denotes an unsaturated-fatty-acid radical, oleic, linoleic, or linolenic. R′ usually stands for a saturated-fatty-acid radical. Stearic acid predominates in the phospholipids of animal origin, and palmitic in those from plants. Molecules of phospholipids contain both nonpolar fatty-acid radicals and the polar phosphoric acid radical with the nitrogen-containing fragment.

Gelatin and egg white, both proteins, are fair emulsifiers, but egg yolk is superior to either. Egg yolk is approximately one-third fat. But the constituents in the yolk which make it a superior emulsifier are the lipoproteins. The importance of egg yolk as a source of emulsifying agent is indicated by the ratios of egg and fat in cream puffs compared to popovers and in a rich compared to a lean cake formula:

	Popovers	Cream Puffs	Lean Cake	Rich Cake
Fat	1 tbsp	½ cup	¼ cup	1½ cups
Egg	2	6	1	6

MANUFACTURED SURFACTANTS

Glyceryl monostearate is one fabricated emulsifier which has been in use for many years. The stearic acid radical is nonpolar and the remainder of the glycerol with the two hydroxyl groups is polar. Soap is another manufactured surfactant. It markedly lowers the surface tension of water, and by emulsifying fat increases its cleansing power. A number of edible surfactants have been introduced in recent years (7). Some are organic acid (acetic, citric, lactic, and tartaric) esters of monoglycerides. Those surfactants which tend to form alpha crystals made possible mixes for shortened cakes which can be combined without creaming the fat. (See Chapter 21.) Glyceryl lactylpalmitate is widely used in cakes and cake mixes and a citric acid ester is used as an antispattering agent in margarine. Other surfactants are fatty-acid esters of alcohol other than glycerol, that is, propylene glycol and sorbitan. Surfactants in this group include sorbitan fatty esters known as SPANS, which forms water-in-oil emulsions, and polyoxyethylene sorbitan fatty esters, known as TWEENS, which forms oil-in-water emulsions. In shortened cake the TWEENS tends to give moistness while the SPANS improves grain, texture, and volume. Another manufactured substance approved in 1959 by the Food and Drug Administration as a stabilizer in salad dressing is carboxymethyl cellulose.

COMMON EMULSIONS

FRENCH DRESSING

Proportions of ingredients typical of French dressing are ½ to ¾ cup of oil, ¼ cup of vinegar or lemon juice, ½ teaspoon each of paprika and mustard, plus salt and sugar for flavor. This type of dressing is made by shaking the oil and acid (lemon juice or vinegar) in the presence of the paprika and mustard.

The emulsion that forms is temporary. The ¾ cup of oil yields the upper limit of fat droplets which can be accommodated by the ¼ cup of acid, and

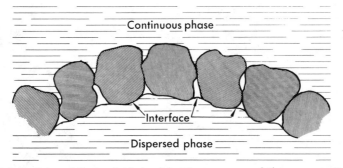

FIGURE 16-4. Particles of finely divided solid acting as an emulsifying agent. (From A. W. Thomas, *Journal of the American Leather Chemists Association* **22:** 171, 1927. Reprinted by permission.)

less than ½ cup of oil would yield so few droplets that the emulsion would be even more temporary. The emulsion that is formed by shaking the oil and the acid is stabilized by the solids of the two powders which collect at the interface between the oil and the acid, as shown in Figure 16-4. Aside from providing solid particles, mustard contains a surface-active constituent which lowers markedly the surface tension of the water (5) and the interfacial tension between the water and the oil (12). Mustard promotes the formation of an oil-in-water emulsion so the oil becomes the disperse phase and the water the continuous phase (3).

The fat droplets in a French-type dressing are large because they are formed by shaking the oil and vinegar. When shaking ceases, the droplets of fat soon coalesce, because the protective film of emulsifier is too weak to protect the dispersed phase. Some French-type dressings do not separate into two phases because the emulsion has been stabilized either by a vegetable gum or by gelatin. These act by making the aqueous phase so viscous that the fat globules are unable to rise. Vegetable gums used for this purpose include agar, acacia, carrageenan, karaya, and tragacanth. Gums are also used in cream cheese, another food with a high fat (33 percent) and high moisture content (55 percent).

MAYONNAISE

Basic proportions of ingredients for mayonnaise are one egg yolk and ⅛ cup of vinegar or lemon juice (plus seasonings) per cup of oil. Mayonnaise is an example of a permanent emulsion. The technique for making a permanent emulsion is more complicated than that for making a temporary one (10). In making mayonnaise, the acid plus seasoning and egg yolk are combined. The shape of the bowl, which should be narrow and deep (Fig. 16-5), and the blades of the beater used to incorporate the oil are important in making a good emulsion. In addition, both mustard and egg yolk lower interfacial tension between water and oil. The livetin fraction of egg yolk proteins (13) and the

FIGURE 16-5. Oil is more effectively divided into small droplets by the blades of the beater if a small bowl with a narrow base is used when making mayonnaise. (Photograph by Wilbur Nelson.)

micelles appear to be the most effective surface-active agents. As each portion of the oil is added, the mixture is beaten sufficiently to break up the fat into small droplets. It is important that small portions of oil be added at first and that each portion of oil be thoroughly emulsified before the next is added. Beating can be either continuous or intermittent. After some of the oil has been emulsified, the next portions are more readily emulsified. To avoid breaking the emulsion, no more oil should be added at one time than the quantity that is already emulsified.

Mayonnaise thickens as more oil is beaten into it. The question arises as to why adding fluid oil to egg yolk and acid, both fluid, results in a product as thick as mayonnaise. First, consider what happens to the oil. By the cupful, it pours. When separated into droplets which are surrounded by a film of emulsifier, the oil is immobilized and loses its fluidity. As more oil is incorporated, the droplets become more numerous and the interfacial area between oil and acid increases. The following example will serve to illustrate the magnitude of the increase in surface area when oil is emulsified (1). Assume a cylinder with a diameter of 1 square centimeter which contains 10 milliliters of oil and a quantity of water. The interfacial area between the oil and water is 1 square centimeter. If this oil is emulsified in the water as droplets 0.1 micrometer in diameter, the interfacial area has increased 3 million fold (to 300 square meters). This is shown graphically in Figure 16-6. The water in the

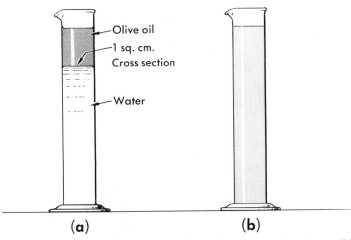

FIGURE 16-6. Increase in interfacial area when an emulsion is formed. (a) Ten milliliters of oil in contact with water with an interfacial area of 1 square centimeter. (b) Ten milliliters of oil emulsified in water as droplets 0.1 micron in diameter with an interfacial area 300 meters square. (Reproduced from Paul Becker, *Principles of Emulsion Technology*, by permission of Reinhold Book Corporation, a subsidiary of Chapman-Reinhold, Inc., New York, 1955.)

mayonnaise, which separates the droplets of oil, is reduced to a very thin film, much of it bound to the surface of the fat droplets. The flow of any unbound water in these films is impeded by the droplets of fat. The more oil added and the more finely it is divided, the thicker the mayonnaise. In fact, it may become stiff enough to cut and hold a sharp edge. One egg yolk contains sufficient emulsifier to coat the fat droplets from 2 or possibly 3 cups of oil.

Electron micrographs of mayonnaise made with only egg yolk as the emulsifier showed droplets of fat surrounded by layers of electron-dense particles. (See Fig. 16-7.) Their size suggested that they came from the low density lipoprotein micelles of the yolk, but lipovitellins may have contributed some of the electron-dense particles observed (2).

COOKED DRESSING

Cooked salad dressings are acidified liquids (water, milk, or fruit juice) thickened with starch alone or with egg. Such products involve basic principles of starch cookery (given in Chapter 8) or of egg cookery (Chapter 19). The amount of fat included in cooked dressings is so small as to be readily emulsified by the proteins present. When cooked salad dressing is added to mayonnaise in amounts to reduce the vegetable oil content below 65 percent, the product must be labeled salad dressing.

Simple but attractive salads in which the dressings discussed above may be used are shown in Figure 16-8.

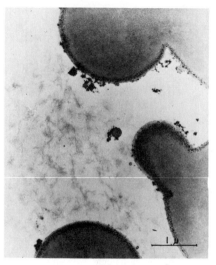

FIGURE 16-7. Scanning electron micrograph of layers of electron-dense particles around droplets of fat from mayonnaise. (From C. M. Chang, W. D. Powrie, and O. Fennema, *Canadian Institute of Food Science and Technology J.* **5:** 136, 1972. Reprinted by permission.)

OTHER EMULSIONS

The importance of a good emulsion in cream puff batter is emphasized in Chapter 12 (on quick breads). For a discussion of cake batters as an emulsion see Chapter 21, for cream and milk as emulsions see Chapter 17, and for the function of emulsifiers in ice creams see Chapter 5.

The emulsifier present in butter and those added to margarines when they are manufactured prevent spattering when these fats are heated.

BROKEN EMULSIONS

Under certain circumstances the protective film around the dispersed phase is disturbed and a supposedly permanent emulsion separates into two phases. A number of factors may cause an emulsion to break. Allowing the surface of the emulsion to dry will cause it to break, as does allowing an emulsion to freeze. Drying and freezing disrupt either the continuous phase of water around the droplets of fat or the film of emulsifier. Adding salt to the emulsion may sometimes cause it to break because salt increases the surface tension of water. Violent or continuous jarring may break an emulsion when a product is shipped. Stability of salad dressings is of concern in precooked frozen foods. Salad dressings withstand freezing and frozen storage better if the oil used does not crystallize at low temperature, if relatively high levels of either egg yolk or salt are used, and if waxy rather than regular starch is used as thickening agent (4).

A broken emulsion may be re-formed by adding it slowly to liquid (one

(a)

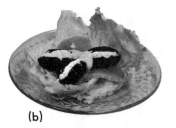
(b)

(c)

(d)

Fruit

(a)

(b)

(c)

(d)

Vegetable

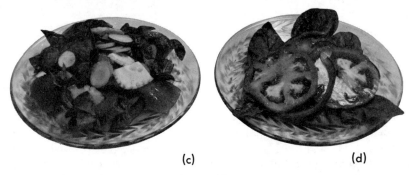

FIGURE 16-8. Simple but attractive salads. (Top) Fruit: (a) apple; (b) orange slices and prunes stuffed with cream cheese; (c) sliced orange and thinly sliced onion; (d) grapefruit and orange sections. (Bottom) Vegetable: (a) potato; (b) cabbage; (c) tossed vegetable; (d) sliced tomato and green pepper on spinach leaves. (Photographs by Wilbur Nelson.)

tablespoon of water for mayonnaise made with one cup of oil), beating the mixture after each addition, or the broken emulsion may be gradually stirred into a stable emulsion. When a good emulsion is emulsifying a broken one, the force involved can be felt as a drag on the spoon or spatula used to combine the two.

VINEGAR

A brief discussion of vinegar is included in this chapter because this ingredient is commonly used in salad dressings. Cider, wine, malt, and distilled vinegar are four common types. The characteristic constituent of vinegar (literally, *vin aigre*, "sour wine") is acetic acid, which is produced by fermentation (8). Vinegar is fermented in two stages. First, a sugar solution is converted to alcohol by yeast and then this alcoholic brew is converted to an acetic acid solution. Microorganisms responsible for the second stage in the conversion of sugars to acetic acid are those of the *Acetobacter* group. Cider vinegar is made from apple juice, wine vinegar from grape juice, malt vinegar from malted grain, the starch in the last converted to sugar by malt, or sprouted barley. Distilled vinegar is made by fermentation of a dilute solution of alcohol. Other acids besides acetic form during fermentation, and these react with the alcohol to yield esters which contribute aroma to the vinegar. Vinegar from each source has a charcteristic flavor. Vinegars on the market are standardized at 5 percent (50 grains) or 4 percent (40 grains) acetic acid. Lemon juice is approximately 5 percent citric acid and so is comparable to vinegar in acidity. The pH of distilled vinegar tends to be lower than that of other forms (6).

REFERENCES

1. Becher, P. 1955. *Principles of Emulsion Technology*. New York: Reinhold Publishing Co. 149 pp. Technical information on the theory of emulsion formation in understandable terms.
2. Chang, C. M., W. D. Powrie, and O. Fennema. 1972. Electron microscopy of mayonnaise. *Canad. Inst. Food Sci. Technol. J.* **53**(3): 134–137. Electron micrographs of protective layer surrounding droplets of emulsified oil.
3. Corran, J. W. 1934. Emulsification by mustard. *Spice Mill* **57**: 175–177. Effectiveness of mustard demonstrated.
4. Hansen, H., and L. R. Fletcher. 1961. Salad dressings stable to frozen storage. *Food Technol.* **15**: 256–262. Factors which increase stability of emulsions to freezing.
5. Kilgore, L. B. 1932. The mustard and the mayonnaise. *Glass Packer* **11**: 621–623. Level of mustard in mayonnaise to give a stable emulsion.
6. Kintner, T. C., and M. Mangel. 1952. Variation in hydrogen ion concentration and total acidity in vinegar. *Food Research* **17**: 456–459. Cider, wine, malt, peach, pear, apricot, and distilled vinegars compared.

7. Lauridsen, J. B. 1976. Food emulsifiers: Surface activity, edibility, composition, and application. *Amer. Oil Chemists' Soc. J.* **53:** 400–407. Formulas for common synthetic surfactants shown graphically; uses.

8. Mayer, Ernst. 1963. Historic and modern aspects of vinegar making. *Food Technol.* **17:** 582–584. Fermentation process in the production of vinegar.

9. Pratt, C. D., and W. W. Hays. 1952. Food emulsifiers bring new highs in uniformity. *Food Eng.* **24:** 109–112. Types of emulsifiers and their uses.

10. Robinson, S. K. 1924. Practice in mayonnaise manufacture. *Am. Food J.* **19:** 185–187. Practical pointers on the making of mayonnaise.

11. Snell, H. M., A. G. Olsen, and R. E. Kremers. 1935. Lecitho-protein. The emulsifying ingredient in egg yolk. *Ind. Eng. Chem.* **27:** 1222–1223. Identification of the effective emulsifier in egg yolk.

12. Ury, R. 1962. Unpublished data. Class in Experimental Food Studies, Oregon State University.

13. Vincent, R., W. D. Powrie, and O. Fennema. 1966. Surface activity of yolk, plasma and dispersions of yolk fractions. *J. Food Sci.* **31:** 643–648. Surface activity and emulsifying capability of various egg yolk fractions.

FILMS

1. *Liquids in Solution.* 11 min. Color. "Basic Chemistry Series." Miscible and immiscible liquids; formation of emulsions. McGraw-Hill.

2. *Song of the Salad.* Color. One hundred and six frames. H. J. Heinz Co.

SEVENTEEN
Milk

Milk is used as an ingredient in a variety of food products. Many of the problems encountered in the use of milk for making such products as scalloped potatoes, cream of tomato or cream of asparagus soup, cheese sauce, macaroni and cheese, cottage cheese, or even yeast bread dough stem from the proteins in the milk. Before discussing some of the problems involved in the preparation of such foods, a brief discussion of the structure and reactions of proteins in general is presented.

PROTEINS IN FOODS

AMINO ACIDS

STRUCTURE

Proteins are made up of amino acids (11), which are organic acids with the characteristic carboxyl group (—C—OH). The simplest amino acid has attached to this carboxyl carbon one carbon atom, designated the alpha carbon. To this carbon is joined, besides the two atoms of hydrogen, an amino group (—NH$_2$), the feature that distinguishes an amino acid from a fatty acid. The formula for the simplest amino acid, glycine, is

The structure of glycine is similar to that of acetic acid except that an amino group has replaced one of the hydrogens in the methyl group of acetic acid.

For other amino acids one of the hydrogens of glycine is replaced by one carbon atom (as in a methyl group) or by a chain of carbon atoms, all of which can be represented by the symbol R. Thus the type formula

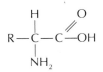

can represent any amino acid. The particular combination of atoms that constitutes the R differentiates one amino acid from another.

KINDS

There are more than twenty different amino acids, with as many different R
groups. The following page shows the structural formulas for nine, knowledge
of which is essential for understanding the behavior of the protein molecules
of milk (as well as those of foods to be discussed in subsequent chapters).

PROTEIN MOLECULES

PEPTIDE BONDS

When the carboxyl of one amino acid unites with the amino group of another,
with the elimination of one molecule of water,

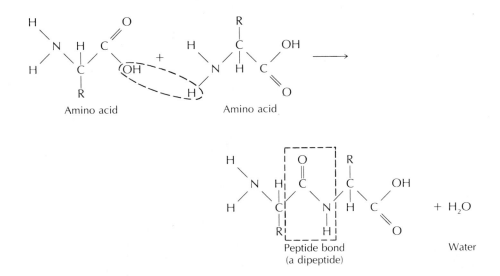

the bond that unites the two amino acids is called a "peptide bond" and the
substance formed a "dipeptide." Union of three amino acids gives a tripeptide;
a number of amino acids so united form a particular kind of polymer, a polypeptide.

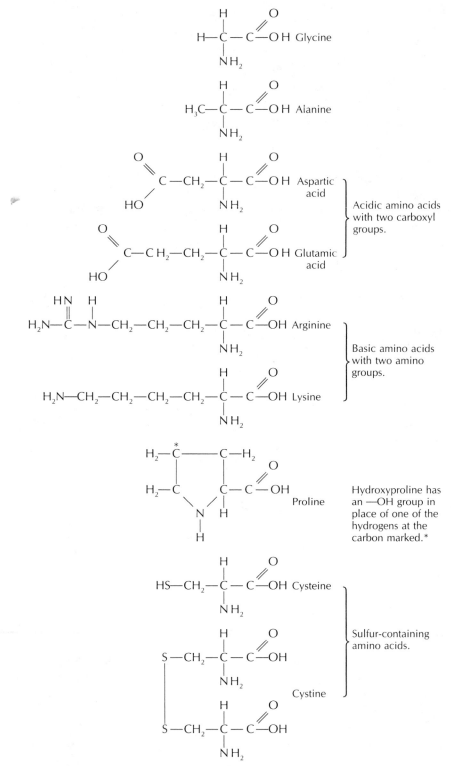

Protein molecules are polypeptides and the peptide bond represents the primary linkage. A fragment of a polypeptide is shown here:

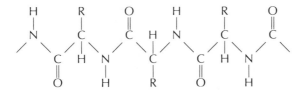

The main chain of atoms, which consists of repeating units of —C—C—N—, is known as the "backbone" of the protein molecule. Projecting alternately from either side of the main chain, like balls of fringe, are the R groups. One protein molecule differs from another in the particular R groups (amino acids) it contains and in the order in which they are united in the polypeptide.

UNIQUE R GROUPS

These R groups in large degree determine the behavior of proteins in food preparation. Glutamic and aspartic acids contain two carboxyl groups, only one of which participates in the formation of a peptide bond. Lysine and arginine each contain more than one basic amino ($—NH_2$) group, only one of which is involved in peptide bond formation. Protein molecules which contain a number of such basic or acidic amino acid residues are sensitive to changes in acidity. Such molecules may, depending on hydrogen-ion concentration, carry a surplus of negative charges due to ionization of carboxyl groups ($—COO^-$), a surplus of positive charges which involve the amino groups ($—NH_3{}^+$), or the number of negative and positive charges may balance each other. In the last instance, the protein molecule is said to be at its "isoelectric point." Proline is included in the foregoing list of nine amino acids because the ring structure in this amino acid, and in hydroxyproline, imposes certain restrictions on the shape of protein molecules which contain these amino acids. The unique feature of cystine is the disulfide group ($—S—S—$), which may be broken by reducing agents. This frees sulfhydryl groups ($—SH$) as in cysteine. Such a reaction possibly accounts for the excessive slackness and stickiness of some yeast bread doughs.

HELICAL CONFORMATION

Due to the bonding angles between the various atoms along the polypeptide backbone, the molecules of many proteins coil like a spring or spiral staircase in a conformation known as a "helix" (11,26). Helping to hold the polypeptide in this arrangement are hydrogen bonds, which form when a carbonyl group

$\left(\diagdown \atop \diagup \right. \!\!\! C\!\!=\!\!O \left. \vphantom{\diagdown} \right)$ at one point along the molecule approaches an imido

group $\left(\diagdown \atop \diagup \right. \!\!\! N\!\!—\!\!H \left. \vphantom{\diagdown} \right)$ farther along the polypeptide backbone. (See Fig. 17-1.)

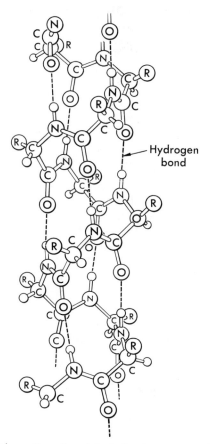

FIGURE 17-1. A drawing of a portion of an alpha-helix of a protein molecule. (From R. B. Corey and L. Pauling, "The Configuration of Polypeptide Chains of Proteins" in *Proceedings of the International Wool Textile Research Conference,* Volume B. *Chemical Physics and Physical Chemistry of Wool and Proteins.* Copyright © 1955 by the Commonwealth Scientific and Industrial Research Organization, Melbourne, Australia. Reprinted by permission.)

An imaginary line between the two atoms linked by a hydrogen bond would parallel the major axis of the helix, as shown in Figure 17-1. Certain molecules do not assume the helical shape typical of most proteins. This is true of protein molecules in which more than 8 percent of the amino acid residues are proline or hydroxyproline. The carbon atom where the bond angle would normally occur to give rise to the helix is a part of the ring of proline. This limits the flexibility of the protein molecule and causes it to assume a special type of helix. The main proteins of milk contain a fairly high proportion of proline residues, as do some of the proteins that make up gluten. Another proline- and hydroxyproline-rich protein is collagen, one of the important proteins of meat.

FIBRILLAR VERSUS GLOBULAR PROTEINS

The helix of a protein molecule may be extended, or it may be folded back on itself, the bend disrupting the helix, and arranged in such a way as to give the molecule a compact shape. Protein molecules compact in shape are categorized as globular proteins. Many proteins of concern in food preparation are of this type. Myosin in meat is a linear or rod-shaped molecule.

Maintenance of the compact shape of globular protein molecules is ascribed to bonds between reactive spots on adjacent R groups which project from the backbone. Bonding forces which may be involved in maintaining protein molecules in their characteristic shape include hydrogen bonds between neighboring hydroxyl and carboxyl groups or between hydroxyl and amino groups. Or the attractive force may be due to salt bridges (ionic bonds) which form between the —COO⁻ groups of an acidic amino acid radical and the $-NH_3^+$ group of a basic amino acid radical, thus:

$$-NH_3^+ \quad {}^-OOC-$$

Amino acid side chains that consist of carbon and hydrogen only are repelled by water and sometimes forced into association. Such association is termed a "hydrophobic bond." Too, the shape of globular protein molecules may be stabilized by van der Waals forces, which also act as bonding forces between molecules of fat in crystals. Covalent bonds may also serve to stabilize the structure of protein molecules. These include the disulfide bond (—S—S—) which links two cysteine residues. Or two R groups along the polypeptide backbone may be esterified to phosphoric acid, which serves as a cross link.

PROTEINS AS COLLOIDS

Most protein molecules are large because they contain a number of amino acid residues. On the basis of their size and great surface area, protein molecules belong to the class of particles called "colloids" (20). Particles, either molecules or groups of them that come within a size range from 0.001 to 0.1 micrometer, are so designated. Particles of colloidal size are unable to form true solutions; instead, they form colloidal dispersions in water. Such dispersions are also referred to as "sols." Because of the size of the particles involved, colloidal sols are likely to be unstable. Two factors which help to keep colloidal particles dispersed as a sol are the presence of layers of water molecules bound to the surface of the colloidal particles and the repulsion between like charges on the particles which serves to keep them apart. Casein, the main protein of milk, does not bind water readily. It is easily destabilized, particularly by acid, which leads to the formation of a gel (clabbered milk) by the protein or of curds if the gel is broken by stirring. Destabilization of the protein sol in milk is desired when cheese is made, but in making scalloped potatoes and cream of tomato soup it is to be avoided.

DENATURATION

When the three-dimensional arrangement of the helix or the polypeptide chain is altered, a protein molecule is said to be "denatured." Most globular proteins denature readily. When the bonds that maintain the unique spatial arrangement of the protein molecule are disrupted, it is free to unfold or extend. Sometimes such a change is desired in food preparation; in other cases efforts are made to prevent denaturation of the proteins in foods.

These bonds may be disrupted in a number of ways. Heating a protein that is dispersed in water may break hydrogen bonds, as may a high concentration of salt. Protein molecules whose conformation is stabilized by salt bridges are sensitive to changes in acidity. Certain protein molecules can be denatured by spreading them in thin films as in a foam. (See the section on milk foams in this chapter and also the discussion of egg foams in Chapter 19.) Although breaking disulfide bonds (which are covalent) by reducing agents is not always classed as denaturation, such a change may alter the conformation of a protein molecule, at times with unwanted results. The poor quality of yeast bread from dough that contains dead yeast cells is attributed to the detrimental effects of the reducing agents from the yeast on the disulfide bonds in the gluten. The compactness of a loaf of whole wheat bread is attributed to the action on gluten of glutathione, a reducing agent found in the germ.

Unfolding of the protein molecule as it is denatured exposes reactive groups along the polypeptide chain. Rebonding between reactive groups on the same or on adjacent denatured protein molecules may follow. When this rebonding takes place and enough molecules unite so that the protein is no longer dispersed as a sol, the protein is said to be "coagulated." When all the liquid is trapped in the network of capillary spaces formed by protein molecules, the result is a gel. A gel is an elastic solid, the water of a sol immobilized by a network of colloidal particles. In milk such a gel is called a "clot." If the liquid separates from the coagulated protein, the protein is said to be "precipitated." When this happens to the gel or clot of milk, the precipitate is referred to as a "curd" (a shrunken gel) and the aqueous phase "whey".

MILK

COMPOSITION

The composition of different forms of milk is found in Table 17-1. The values are for 100 grams, or slightly less than ¼ pound. This weight of fluid milk measures somewhat more than ⅓ cup (6⅔ tablespoons or 100 milliliters).

Because milk has a high percentage of water, it is used as the source of water in foods such as cakes, bread, and cream soups. Milk is less sweet than its approximate 5 percent sugar content might lead one to expect, because of the low sweetness of lactose. Milk is a good source of high quality protein.

Table 17-1 Composition of different forms of milk (per 100 grams)

Milk	Water (%)	Calories[a]	Protein (g)	Fat (g)	Carbohydrate (g)	Calcium (mg)	Phosphorus (mg)	Iron (mg)	Vitamin A Value (I.U.)	Thiamine (mg)	Riboflavin (mg)	Niacin (mg)	Ascorbic Acid (mg)
Whole milk	87.69	64	3.28	3.66	4.65	119	93	.05	138	.038	.161	.084	1.47
Low fat (2%) milk	89.21	50	3.31	1.92	4.80	122	95	.05	205[b]	.039	.165	.086	.95
Skim milk	90.80	35	3.41	.18	4.85	123	101	.04	204[b]	.036	.140	.088	.98
Dried nonfat, instant	3.96	358	35.10	.72	52.19	1,231	985	.31	2,370	.413	1.744	.891	5.58
Evaporated, whole	74.04	134	6.81	7.56	10.04	261	202	.19	243	.047	.316	.194	1.88
Cream													
Half and half	80.57	130	2.96	11.50	4.30	105	95	.07	434	.035	.149	.078	.86
Light whipping	63.50	292	2.17	30.91	2.96	69	61	.03	1,127	.024	.125	.042	.61
Sour, cultured	70.95	214	3.16	20.96	4.27	116	85	.06	790	.035	.149	.067	.86
Yogurt, plain	87.90	61	3.47	3.25	4.66	121	95	.05	123	.029	.142	.075	.53

[a]1 kilocalorie = 4.185 kilojoules.

[b]Vitamin A added (2000 I.U. per quart).

SOURCE: U.S. Dept. Agr. Handbook No. 8-1. Composition of Foods. Dairy and Egg Products. Raw, Processed, Prepared. Revised 1976.

The cow converts feed protein to food protein with an efficiency of 31 percent, the highest conversion for any animal protein (27).

The minimum fat content of whole milk is set by law in each state and varies from 3.0 to 3.8 percent. Federal standards propose a minimum fat content of 3.25 percent. Certain breeds (Jersey and Guernsey) secrete milk with a fat content near 5 percent. Glycerides of milk fat differ from others of animal origin in that they contain short-chain (C_4-C_{10}) saturated fatty acids. These may give rise to desirable flavors in such products as cheese and to off-flavors in rancid butter or dried whole milk. The color of the fat is influenced by the carotenoids in the feed. Milk is a poor source of the mineral iron, a good source of phosphorus, and an excellent source of calcium.

Milk contains vitamin A (carried by the fat) and some thiamine (derived from bacteria which thrive in the rumen). It is a good source of niacin and an excellent source of riboflavin. The latter, which gives the greenish fluorescence to whey (the watery part of milk from which much of the protein has been removed), is influenced by the feed of the cow and by the flow of milk. Riboflavin in milk is easily destroyed if the milk is exposed to bright sunlight. The ascorbic acid content of milk varies with the feed of the cow and the procedures used to prepare different forms of milk for the market.

DISPOSITION OF CONSTITUENTS IN MILK

SOLUTION

As is true of most foods, milk is complex from the standpoint of its physical organization (16). For one thing, milk is a solution. Dissolved in the 87 parts of water per 100 of milk is the milk sugar, lactose. Four water-soluble vitamins are in solution in milk: thiamine, riboflavin, niacin, and ascorbic acid. Part of the minerals in milk are in solution. Included are chlorides and citrates and potassium, magnesium, and sodium ions. Part of the calcium phosphate is in solution.

COLLOIDAL DISPERSION

Dispersed in the aqueous phase, colloidally rather than in solution, are calcium and magnesium phosphates, citrates, and milk proteins (16). The latter include the caseins, precipitated by acidifying the milk, and the whey or serum proteins. Caseins account for approximately 80 percent of the milk proteins. The three major fractions of casein are alpha$_s$-, beta-, and kappa-casein, with gamma-casein a minor component. α_s-casein accounts for slightly more than one-half, β-casein from one-fourth to one-third, κ-casein up to 15 percent, and γ-casein 3–5 percent of the entire casein complex (40). The caseins of milk are associated with each other and with part of the salts of milk in structures called micelles (23). (See Fig. 17-2.) These essentially spherical micelles are responsible for the opalescent whiteness of milk. This micellar complex is often referred to as calcium phosphocaseinate.

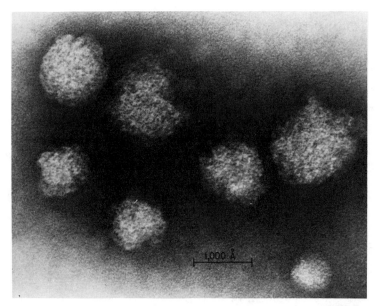

FIGURE 17-2. Casein micelles from cow's milk. (Courtesy of R. S. Carroll, USDA, Regional Research Center, Philadelphia. From *Fundamentals of Dairy Chemistry,* B. H. Webb, A. H. Johnson, and A. J. Alvord, editors, p. 443, 1974. Avi Publishing Company. 250 Post Road East, Westport, Conn., publisher.)

Exactly how the caseins are arranged in the micelle is still unclear, although this has been the subject of much research and various models have been proposed. Molecules of the caseins, because of their high content of prolyl amino acid residues (8 to 16 percent) were thought to exist as random coils. Recent evidence indicates, however, that monomers of casein assume a compact, ellipsoidal shape, with a length to diameter ratio of 4:1, for example, for α_s-casein (32). Acidic amino acid residues are clustered near one end of the molecule and apolar groups in the remainder. When a monomer assumes its ellipsoidal shape, part of the nonpolar groups are oriented to a hydrophobic interior and the charged, acidic portion to one end, making possible both hydrophobic and polar-type bonding. The micelles are made of approximately spherical subunits, the volume of which is less than half the volume of the micelle in which they are found, indicating that the micelle is porous. The casein molecules are assembled in the subunits of the micelle in such a way that the κ-casein with its carbohydrate-rich and acidic end can protect the α_s-casein from precipitation by the calcium of the milk (2, 37). Hydration and net charge on the surface possibly account for the stability of the micelle (29).

The whey proteins, roughly one-fifth of the total proteins in milk, contain two major fractions: the globulins, which are dispersible in dilute salt solution; and the albumins, which account for approximately 68 percent of the total whey proteins. To make a complicated naming picture even more contusing, the major constituent of the lactalbumin fraction of milk is called beta-lacto-globulin (16). The factor in unscalded milk which is thought to be responsible for the low volume and the inferior quality of yeast bread is believed to be a part of the globulin fraction of the whey proteins of milk. Some of the whey proteins are enzymes.

EMULSION

Milk typifies not only a solution and a colloidal dispersion (a sol), but it is also an emulsion. The fat in milk is present as small droplets or globules with an average diameter of 3 to 6 microns (18). Fat globules may range in size from less than one to 10 microns, the size influenced by the breed of cow. Jersey and Guernsey cows secrete larger fat globules than do Holsteins. Fat droplets in milk are prevented from coalescing by a thin coating of emulsifier (a few millimicrons thick) around the fat globules at the liquid-fat interface. (See Chapter 16 for a discussion of emulsions.)

The layer of emulsifier around the fat globules of milk is more complex (18) than is the alignment of solid particles of mustard and paprika around droplets of oil in French dressing or the orientation of lecithoprotein around fat droplets in mayonnaise. The structure suggested for this membrane is envisioned diagrammatically in Figure 17-3.

Four phospholipids, including lecithin, participate in the formation of the fat globule membrane in milk (28). These are oriented with their nonpolar groups in the fat globules and their hydrophilic groups in the aqueous phase of the milk to form a film one molecule thick around the fat globules (18). Evidence suggests that near the periphery of the fat globules high-melting triglycerides are segregated, the fatty-acid chains of which intermesh with those of the nonpolar prongs of the phospholipid molecules. Molecules of vitamin A and of cholesterol are interspersed among the molecules of phospholipids. Protein also contributes to the membrane. The innermost layer of protein molecules is envisioned with the polypeptide backbone parallel to the surface of the fat globule. Hydrophilic side chains of this layer are oriented toward the hydrophilic groups of the phospholipids and the hydrophobic R groups oriented away from the fat globule. A second layer of protein molecules parallel to the first has its hydrophobic side chains pointed inward and the hydrophilic ones pointed outward. Fat globules at the pH of fresh milk are known to carry a negative charge, which helps to keep them dispersed. Protein found in the fat globule membrane of nonhomogenized milk differs from the proteins in the aqueous phase of milk (5).

Although the fat is emulsified in freshly drawn milk so that the droplets are suspended throughout the milk, they do not remain so. The fat globules associate in clusters which become so large that the forces binding them to the water phase are insufficient to counteract the effect of the difference in density between the oil phase and the water phase. A globulin, one of the

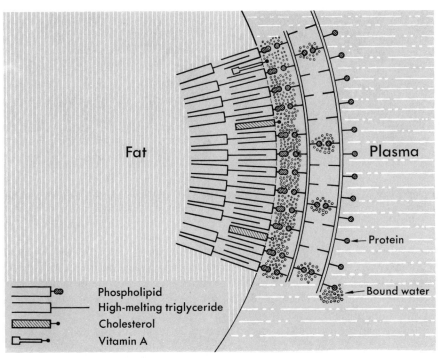

FIGURE 17-3. Diagram of the structure of the fat globule membrane in milk. (From Nicolai King, *The Milk Fat Globule Membrane,* 1955. Reprinted by permission of the Commonwealth Agricultural Bureau, Bucks, U.K.)

serum proteins, promotes clustering. When whole milk stands, clusters of fat droplets, being lighter, rise to the top of the milk, a process known as "creaming" (4). Cream is milk that is extra rich in emulsified fat droplets. Fat droplets contribute viscosity to milk and cream: the greater the number, the more viscous is the product. In goat's milk the fat globules are so small that they are unable to float to the top of the milk. As a result, goat's milk does not cream. Carotene dissolved in the fat globules gives the creamy tint to milk and cream.

HOMOGENIZATION

To eliminate creaming, milk is homogenized. Milk is forced under pressure through fine orifices which reduce the fat globules to an average diameter of less than 2 micrometers (5). (See Fig. 17-4.) The higher the pressure used to force the milk through the orifices, the smaller the fat globules. With the formation of many smaller fat droplets, the surface of the fat increases enormously. As the fat droplets are subdivided by homogenization, the original emulsifying material is supplemented by proteins from the aqueous phase of the milk. These differ from the original protein and consist of casein subunits and serum proteins (5,13). The small size of the fat droplets and their greater density because of adsorbed casein eliminate visible creaming (23). Differ-

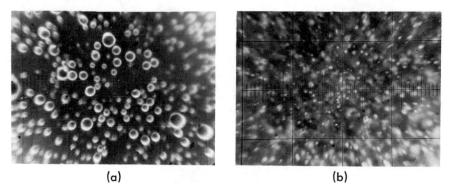

(a)   (b)

FIGURE 17-4. Fat globules in (a) nonhomogenized milk and (b) homogenized milk. Smallest gradation on the scale is 2 microns. Photomicrographs taken with dark field illumination. (Courtesy of CP Division, St. Regis, Chicago, Ill.)

ences in the behavior in cooking of homogenized milk compared to unhomogenized are believed to stem, in part at least, from the increased surface of the fat globules in the homogenized milk and from the spreading of the casein on this surface. Homogenized milk is whiter, more opaque, and more viscous than unhomogenized milk with the same fat content. The sense of richness when one drinks homogenized milk is associated with its greater viscosity.

PASTEURIZATION OF MILK

Very little milk is marketed raw because milk may be a carrier of microorganisms from individuals suffering from typhoid and scarlet fever, diphtheria, septic sore throat, and tuberculosis. Cows, too, are susceptible to tuberculosis, and milk from cows suffering from Bang's disease may cause undulant fever in humans, a chronic and debilitating disease characterized by intermittent fever. So most market milk is "pasteurized," a mild heat treatment which eliminates pathogenic bacteria that might be present. To effect pasteurization, milk may be heated to 62°C (145°F) and held at that temperature for 30 minutes or heated to 72°C (161°F) and held for 15 seconds. The latter does less harm to the flavor. As a result of pasteurization, a number of bacteria besides pathogens are destroyed, but some nonpathogens do remain in the milk. For this reason, the milk is cooled immediately after pasteurization to 10°C (50°F) or preferably below to prevent the rapid growth and multiplication of bacteria that remain. The enzyme, phosphatase, serves as a built-in indicator by which the adequacy of pasteurization may be gauged. Pasteurized milk gives a negative test for phosphatase. So sensitive is this test that the presence of 0.1 percent raw milk added to pasteurized milk can be detected, as can the fact that the pasteurization temperature was off by one degree Fahrenheit. The enzyme lipase is inactivated by pasteurization, which prevents homogenized milk from becoming rancid.

Milk is graded on the basis of bacterial count (number of bacteria per milliliter of milk). Grade A milk must have a low bacterial count (a maximum of 20,000 per milliliter). Most of the fluid milk on the retail market is Grade A. To keep the bacterial count low, milk and milk products must be stored at refrigerator temperature.

Milk may be fortified with vitamins A and D. For the former, the level is 2000 International Units per quart. Vitamin D milk must have 400 United States Pharmacopoeia (U.S.P.) Units added per quart.

TYPES OF DAIRY PRODUCTS

FLUID MILK

Fluid whole milk which contains at least the minimum fat content specified by the state, and fluid milks with lower fat content are usually available in homogenized form. When the fat content of milk is reduced below the minimum set by law, the milk is designated "skim milk." For those milks which are practically fat-free, the term "nonfat" is used. Cream may be separated from milk by gravity (letting the milk stand undisturbed) or by centrifuging in a cream separator. Milks are now marketed with the fat content specified. Milk with 2 percent fat is routinely available.

CREAM

The heavier the cream, the higher is the proportion of fat droplets to milk. The fat content increases from half and half with approximately 10 percent fat, to coffee cream with approximately 18 percent fat, to light whipping cream with a minimum butterfat content of 30 percent, and to heavy whipping cream with a minimum fat content of 35 percent.

EVAPORATED MILK

Evaporated milk is prepared from whole milk by preheating it to facilitate evaporation of moisture and then removing 60 percent of the water under vacuum. The resultant concentrate is then homogenized, sealed in a tin, and sterilized. Carrageenan, a vegetable gum, added to evaporated milk before it is sterilized, stabilizes the α_s- and β-caseins against precipitation by either calcium ions or by the high temperature even more effectively than does the κ-casein present in the milk (12). The effectiveness of the carrageenan (kappa form) is attributed to the ester sulfate groups and the 3,6-anhydrogalactose units in the molecule (21). The distinctive flavor and tan color of evaporated milk result from the reaction between the proteins and the lactose of milk at the high sterilization temperature. Evaporated milk does not cream, and because it has been sterilized it keeps indefinitely as long as the can is unopened. Once the seal is broken, the contents become contaminated with microorganisms and the milk should be refrigerated and handled as fresh milk. To reconstitute evaporated milk, usually equal parts of the concentrate and water are used. Vitamin D is added to evaporated milk in an amount to give 400 U.S.P. Units per quart.

CONDENSED MILK

The market form of milk called "condensed" is made from whole milk by removing half the water. Sugar is added in sufficient quantity (approximately 44 percent) to preserve the milk, which is then canned. The milk is not sterilized, but because of the high concentration of sugar it keeps well.

FRESH-MILK CONCENTRATE

A fresh-milk product which has been sterilized at a high temperature for a short time, concentrated, and canned · septically has been marketed. It will keep for six weeks at refrigerator temperature. The short heating time (3 seconds) at the high temperature (270°F) reduces the bacterial count to less than one per milliliter without giving the milk a cooked flavor (6).

DRIED MILK SOLIDS

Whole milk, skim milk, and buttermilk are available in the form of dried powders. Dried cream and whey (a by-product of cheese making) are also available. Milk used to make dried milk is pasteurized. That destined for the manufacture of cottage cheese gets no additional heating. For the bread-making industry, which uses the bulk of the dried milk produced, the milk is heated sufficiently (usually to 85°C or 185°F, for 20 minutes) to inactivate the loaf-depressant factor. Milk to be dried for general purposes receives a less severe heat treatment before it is dried (9).

To evaporate the moisture from milk, it is first condensed under reduced pressure. This concentrate is then blown as a fine spray into a preheated vacuum chamber. The resulting powders have a moisture content of approximately 2 to 3 percent. To reconstitute these powders, 4½ ounces of dried whole milk or 3½ ounces of nonfat dry milk solids are made to a volume of one quart with water. Reconstituting milk powder is unnecessary for a number of products. This is especially true of batters and doughs, where the milk powder may be sifted with the dry ingredients and water (equivalent to the amount of milk specified) added when the milk normally would be.

Dried milk solids added to water as a fine powder tend to lump. To eliminate this difficulty some milk powder is exposed to water vapor, which causes the fine pieces to clump or agglomerate in much the same way that flour is agglomerated. Water can then more easily find its way in the interstices that separate adjacent particles. The particles in instant-dispering milk powder are not only larger, but the exposure to moisture has brought to the surface of the individual particles lactose, the more water-soluble constituent of the dried milk solids. This, too, facilitates reconstituting the dried milk powder (3).

BUTTER

Butter is obtained from cream by a process called "churning." The cream is agitated or whipped, which disrupts the membranes around the fat droplets. As the fat droplets continue to coalesce, the milk eventually separates into two phases, the butterfat, and the aqueous phase with its dissolved and dispersed constituents. The membranes around some of the fat droplets remain. The clumps of fat are removed from the milk and the butterfat washed in several changes of cold water to remove the milk. Butter is usually salted and is worked to remove excess water. However, butter contains approximately 15 percent water, a part of which is emulsified. The minimum fat content of butter is 80 percent. The high moisture content of butter makes it liable to hydrolytic rancidity if it is stored in a warm place. One fatty acid so released is butyric, a molecule with a short chain. It is volatile and has an unpleasant odor.

BUTTERMILK

Buttermilk is the fluid left when cream or milk is churned and the fat is removed. The milk may be sweet or sour. Buttermilk is similar to skim milk except that it contains phospholipids and protein from the fat globule membranes.

SOUR MILK

Two commonly available forms of sour milk on the retail market are cultured buttermilk and yogurt. They are made from pasteurized skim milk. For yogurt, additional solids are added to the milk or the solids are concentrated by evaporating part of the water. After the milk is inoculated with a culture of *Streptococcus thermophilus* and *Lactobacillus bulgaricus,* it is incubated. The sour taste is due mainly to the lactic acid produced from lactose. Fermentation of the citrate in milk yields acetaldehyde, diacetyl, and acetic acid. Incubation time and temperature influence the contribution of the two organisms to the fermentation process and determine whether the product will be predominantly sour or have an agreeable balance between sour taste and aroma (19). Individuals who are unable to tolerate milk because of the lactose are able to consume fermented milks.

SOUR CREAM

Sour cream is light cream cultured as is yogurt. Half-and-half sour cream produced in the same manner is available.

FILLED AND IMITATION DAIRY PRODUCTS

These range from filled milk in which part or all of the milk fat has been replaced by fat of plant origin to nondairy creamers or coffee whiteners made with sodium caseinate or soy protein and vegetable oil.

MILK FOAMS

FOAM FORMATION

A foam consists of bubbles of gas trapped in a liquid, with the liquid as the continuous phase and the gas bubbles as the dispersed phase. In edible foams the gas is usually air and the liquid phase chiefly water. If a sealed jar half filled with water is shaken, bubbles of air are formed in the water, but the foam so formed is transient. The foam disappears as soon as shaking ceases, mainly because of the high surface tension of the water. Water foams readily when it contains a substance such as soap or detergent that lowers its surface tension. A foam is formed in foods usually by whipping or beating a liquid. If the surface tension of the liquid is low enough, the blades of the beater can pull the liquid around the pockets of air.

EVAPORATED MILK FOAMS

Molecules of protein in milk lower the surface tension of the water. A foam forms when fluid milk is beaten, but the bubbles are large and they rise to the surface of the milk and soon disappear.

It is one thing for a liquid to foam and quite another for the foam to be stable. A viscous liquid can more easily retain bubbles of air that are incorporated. When the contents of milk solids are increased as in evaporated milk, the increased viscosity enables the milk to better retain gas bubbles. Evaporated milk whips best if it has been chilled to the point where ice crystals have formed from part of the water in the milk. This serves to further increase the concentration of solids as well as make the milk more viscous. Addition of acid in the form of lemon juice increases the viscosity of the milk through its effect on the dispersibility of the proteins. Whipped evaporated milk yields a glossy foam with fine cells and a large volume (three times the unwhipped volume). The milk thickens as more air cells are whipped into it. The film of liquid around the air cells gets thinner and the many air cells impede flow, much as mayonnaise thickens as more oil is beaten into it. Although a whipped evaporated milk foam becomes very thick, it does not set. Such a foam must be served or used promptly. Upon standing, the milk drains from around the bubbles of air; they coalesce and then rise to the surface. In less than an hour the milk regains its fluid state, leaving little sign that it was once a foam. Chilling a whipped evaporated milk foam makes it last longer.

DRIED MILK FOAMS

If dried milk solids are combined with much less water than would be needed to reconstitute the milk, the viscosity of the milk concentrate is sufficient to retain bubbles of air whipped into it. Nonfat dry milk yields a more stable foam than does dry whole milk. A whipped milk foam made with nonfat dry milk resembles beaten egg white more than it does either whipped evaporated milk or whipped cream. Some of the protein in the milk is denatured in the

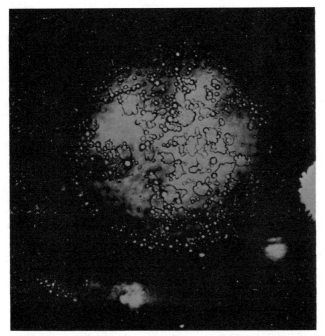

FIGURE 17-5. Photomicrograph of one air cell in whipped cream, showing partially clumped fat globules that stiffen and give permanence to the foam. (From A. C. Dahlberg and J. C. Hening, New York Agricultural Experiment Station Bulletin No. 113, 1925. Reproduced by permission.)

foam so that the foam sets although the structure is fragile. Upon standing, liquid drains from around the gas cells, leaving behind fragile films of denatured protein. Lemon juice beaten into a milk foam increases its stability. Increasing the viscosity of a milk concentrate by dispersing in it either gelatin or one of a number of vegetable gums (algin, karaya, locust bean, or tragacanth) gives a more stable foam. Addition of lemon juice or calcium sucrate also increases the viscosity of milk and improves the foam.

WHIPPED CREAM

In contrast to milks, cream with a high enough fat content whips to a fine, stable foam. Like evaporated milk, and for the same reasons, cream thickens when air is whipped into it. But in whipped cream the foam also stiffens. A whipped-cream foam is stabilized by a rigid but fragile structure formed by clumping of fat globules on the surface of the gas bubbles. (See photomicrograph in Figure 17-5.)

As cream is whipped, air cells are incorporated in the liquid, which also contains fat droplets with their film of emulsifier. As more and more air bubbles are incorporated, the aqueous film around the air bubbles, and in which the fat droplets are floating, becomes thinner and thinner. This has the effect of orienting the fat droplets in the film of water around the air bubbles. As more air bubbles are incorporated, fat globules are partially denuded of emulsifier (18). Some of the softer fat extrudes from a globule and makes contact with fat of another globule, and the two adhere. Thus the emulsified fat droplets begin to clump (10). As a result, a whipped-cream foam stiffens and has more permanence than do milk foams, although some drainage occurs. Presence of the enzyme which promotes clustering of fat globules and creaming also favors foam formation. This enzyme is denatured by the heat of pasteurization so pasteurized cream does not whip as readily as raw cream (1). The more severe heat treatment used to prolong the shelf life of ultra-pasteurized whipping cream increases whipping time.

The slight clumping of fat droplets, which is responsible for the stiffening of whipped cream, is the first step in the breaking of the emulsion, as in making butter. For this reason the amount of beating must be carefully controlled, and it is important to recognize when to stop whipping the cream. The cream whipped to maximum volume is soft and glossy, but leakage will be greater than it would be were the cream whipped to maximum stiffness (24). Only a few turns of the blades of the beater make the difference between optimum and overbeaten whipped cream. When too much air is beaten in, the whipped cream begins to take on a curdled appearance. The fat freed by breaking the emulsion causes the foam to collapse. Sugar added to whipped cream before it reaches maximum stiffness delays the clumping of fat. There is somewhat less danger of overbeating cream once the sugar is added, however. The whipped cream must be beaten longer to make it equally stiff.

A number of factors influence the ease with which a cream whips (1). An important one is the concentration of fat globules. Cream that contains less than 30 percent fat has too few fat globules to whip to a stiff, stable foam without the addition of a whipping aid. Figure 17-6 illustrates the effect of the percentage of fat on the volume, stiffness, and stability of whipped cream (10). Gelatin, vegetable gums, lemon juice, or calcium sucrate may be used to increase the viscosity of too thin cream and help to compensate for a deficiency in fat globules. Cream which contains 30 percent fat should whip and that with 35 percent fat should whip to a thick, stable foam in 30 seconds. Cream with 30 percent fat contains a sufficient number of fat globules to surround and give permanence to the air bubbles (10).

Success in the formation of a foam from milk or cream depends in part upon the temperature of the liquid. All forms of milk whip better when they are chilled (7° to 10°C or 45° to 50°F) (1), because this makes them more viscous. Even heavy whipping cream will not whip when it is too warm (21°C or 70°F). At this temperature or above, the cream is not thick enough to retain the air bubbles pulled in by the blades of the beater. Also, the milk fat is so near the melting point that when two fat globules are thrown together by the action of the beater, the droplets, instead of merely adhering, coalesce. Thus cream that is too warm when whipped will separate into butter and buttermilk without a stable foam ever forming.

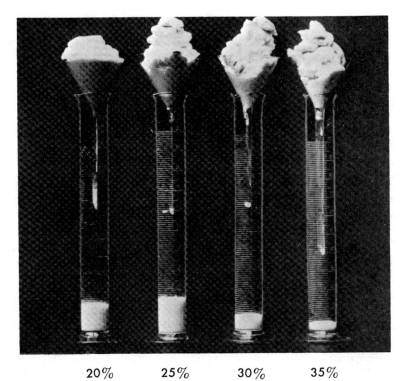

20%   25%   30%   35%

FIGURE 17-6. Effects of percentage of fat on the volume and stability of whipped cream (cream pasteurized and aged 24 hours at 4.4° C (40° F). (From A. C. Dahlberg and J. C. Hening, New York Agricultural Experiment Station Bulletin No. 113, 1925. Reproduced by permission.)

Larger globules of fat cluster more readily than smaller ones. For this reason cream does not whip so well after it has been homogenized (1). Homogenized milk or cream should be scalded to cause the smaller fat globules to coalesce and then chilled before it is whipped.

Instant-foaming whipped-cream substitutes are available. Such pressure-packed whips contain water, vegetable protein, oil, emulsifier, flavoring, and one or more gases. Carbon dioxide and nitrous oxide are usually used as propellants. The mixture and the gases are packed in the dispenser under pressure. When the dispenser is opened, the pressure is released and the expanding gases inflate the liquid as it is expelled. Instant-foaming pressure-packed cream is also available.

MILK COOKERY

Colloidal proteins remain dispersed in water in part because the molecules are hydrated. Molecules of water are bound to polar groups on the surface of the molecule of protein by means of hydrogen bonds. Other water molecules bond to this first layer of tightly bound water molecules and these in turn bond to a third layer. In this way layer after layer of less and less firmly bound water is built up until a shell of water surrounds each protein molecule. In addition to these protective spheres of bound water, some proteins remain in colloidal dispersion because the particles carry like charges and so repel each other. This is true for the casein micelles of milk. A number of factors may bring about destabilization of the collodially dispersed proteins of milk. In fact, destabilization of the protein is desired in some instances.

EFFECTS OF HEAT ON SERUM PROTEINS

Heat denatures the serum proteins of fresh milk and they precipitate (23). Inactivation of phosphatase by the mild heat treatment used to pasteurize milk has been mentioned. The enzyme lipase, a protein, is inactivated during pasteurization also. Were it not, this enzyme would rapidly bring about hydrolytic rancidity in homogenized milk (5,18). The factor (or factors) in unheated milk which causes slackness and stickiness in yeast bread dough and low loaf volume (see Chapter 13) requires more drastic treatment for denaturation than do most of the other serum proteins of milk.

In the preparation of a number of food products milk is preheated before it is combined with other ingredients. When milk is heated, the denatured and coagulated serum proteins settle to the bottom of the container, carrying some of the colloidal calcium phosphate which is precipitated by heat too. Settling of this precipitate is one of the reasons why milk scorches so readily when the container is placed directly on the hot unit. A pan with a thick bottom and moderate heat or a double boiler should be used.

EFFECT OF HEAT ON SKIN FORMATION

When milk is heated in an uncovered utensil, a skin forms on the surface. This is attributed to evaporation of water from the surface and concentration of casein which occludes some milk fat and calcium salts. If milk is heated uncovered for some time and the skin removed as it forms, appreciable amounts of milk solids are removed from the milk. Another disadvantage of the formation of a skin is that it tends to hold steam and thus makes the milk more likely to boil over. A foam on the surface of hot milk minimizes the formation of a skin. It is for this reason that hot cocoa and hot chocolate are served topped with marshmallow or whipped cream or the beverage itself is whipped to induce a foam.

EFFECT OF HEAT ON CASEIN

Unlike the globular serum proteins of milk, the colloidally dispersed casein micelles are relatively insensitive to heat at the pH of fresh milk. Moderate heat as used in cooking fresh milk fails to alter the stability of the casein micelles enough for the protein to precipitate. In fact, sweet fluid milk may be held for four hours at the boiling point before the casein complex is destabilized so that clotting occurs. The high temperature used to sterilize evaporated milk may destabilize the casein micelles, however.

EFFECT OF HEAT ON HOMOGENIZED MILK

The effect of homogenization on the behavior of milk in food preparation has been the subject of a number of studies. In scalloped potatoes or in cooked cereal, homogenized milk is more likely to curdle than is nonhomogenized milk (15). White sauce made with homogenized milk is thicker than that made with nonhomogenized milk (see Fig. 17-7). A curdled appearance in white sauce made with homogenized milk is due to lakes of fat that rise and collect on the surface of the white sauce. Failure of the added fat to blend with the white sauce is attributed to its inability to penetrate the new film of emulsifier formed by homogenization (36). To prevent this defect in white sauce made with homogenized milk, the amount of added fat should be minimal; alternately, the lakes of fat may be beaten into the sauce with a rotary beater. Beating disperses the fat and gives to the sauce a very smooth, velvety consistency.

Stirred custards made with homogenized milk are thicker and not so sweet as those made with unhomogenized milk. Baking time is longer for custards made with homogenized milk, owing to slower heat penetration. The gel that forms is firmer, and less liquid drains from the gel (7). According to another study, however, baked custards made from homogenized milk are less firm (17). According to a third report, more liquid separates from baked custard made with homogenized milk (15). Manipulative techniques in preparing the custards possibly account for the conflicting results. (See section on custards in Chapter 19.)

EFFECT OF HEAT ON COLOR AND FLAVOR

The browning of evaporated milk brought about by heat was mentioned earlier. The high temperature used to process the milk and the concentration of lactose favor the sugar-amine reaction leading to the brown color (25). Both hydrogen sulfide and methyl sulfide derived from the proteins, mainly beta-lactoglobulin, contribute to the flavor of heated milk. Heating milk fat gives δ-decalactone, a compound with a buttery, coconutlike flavor characteristic of foods cooked in butter (25).

EFFECT OF POLYPHENOLIC COMPOUNDS ON MILK PROTEINS

When milk is heated with foods that contain appreciable quantities of certain polyphenolic substances, the milk may curdle. These polyphenolic compounds are sometimes referred to as "tannins." Foods that contain such compounds produce an astringent, puckery sensation in the mouth. The precipitation of the proteins in milk by polyphenolic compounds is attributed to dehydration. The curdling of cream of asparagus soup and of scalloped

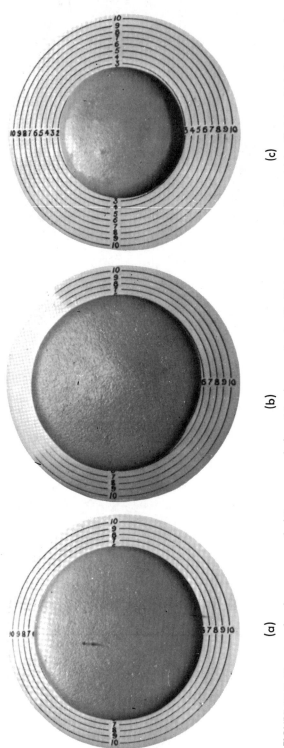

(a)

(b)

(c)

FIGURE 17-7. Line spread and appearance of white sauce made from (a) unhomogenized milk; (b) homogenized milk; and (c) milk into which the sauce fat was homogenized. (From A. M. Towson and G. M. Trout, *Food Research* **11:** 266, copyright © 1946 by Institute of Food Technologists.)

potatoes is attributed to the presence of polyphenolic constitutents in these foods. Salt in high concentration can cause milk proteins to precipitate, for example, cured ham baked in milk.

EFFECTS OF ACID ON CASEIN

At the pH of fresh milk (6.6), casein micelles are dispersed as a fairly stable colloidal sol. If raw milk is left to stand in a warm place, acid accumulates. Lactic acid-forming bacteria convert lactose of the milk to lactic acid, $CH_3CHOHCOOH$. Pasteurization destroys these bacteria, so pasteurized milk usually sours in this way only after it has been re-inoculated with a culture of lactic-acid-forming bacteria. Lowering of the pH of milk as acid accumulates disrupts the stability of the micellar complex and may result in coagulation of the milk. The acid that is formed removes calcium salts from the casein micelles. It also depresses the ionization of acidic amino acid residues of the caseins. One-fifth of the amino acid residues in casein are dicarboxylic (glutamic and aspartic acids). The isoelectric point of casein, the pH value at which the net charge on the polymer is zero and the point at which it is least soluble, is 4.6. However, the caseins of milk do not remain colloidally dispersed when the pH of the milk goes below pH 5.2 (16). At this point the colloidally dispersed calcium phosphocaseinate is converted to a gel. Neutral casein, which gives the gel its structure, is formed as follows:

$$\underset{\substack{\text{(Colloidally} \\ \text{dispersed micelles)}}}{\text{Calcium phosphocaseinate}} + \underset{\substack{\text{(Hydrogen} \\ \text{ions)}}}{H^+} \rightarrow \underset{\text{(Gel)}}{\text{Neutral casein}} + Ca^{++}$$

When the gel forms, molecules of casein presumably unite at strategic spots to form capillary spaces which trap the liquid. The gel that forms is an elastic solid. When a gel is formed from milk by acid, the milk is designated as "clotted" or "clabbered" milk. If this clabbered milk or clot or coagulum is broken by stirring or cutting, the liquid seeps out and the gel separates into two phases, the watery part of the milk called "whey" and the casein-rich part called "curds." Heating the clabbered milk will shrink the clot and cause more of the whey to separate from the curd. The major portion of the serum proteins are expelled in the whey.

On occasion, milk which when cold shows no signs of clotting may do so when heated. The κ-casein which stabilizes the micelle is unaffected by a temperature of 100°C for 5 minutes in a neutral medium. But lowering the pH or addition of sodium chloride makes κ-casein more labile to heat, and lowers its protective or stabilizing action on the micelles (41). Three-fourths of the κ-casein is precipitated when heated at pH 6.2.

Milk comes in contact with acid in other ways than in the souring of milk by lactic acid-forming bacteria. When either milk or cream is served with a fruit such as peaches or berries, acids from the fruit lower the pH of the milk or cream and cause it to become perceptibly thick or even to curdle. When lemon juice is added to milk to make milk sherbet, the mixture should be frozen at once; otherwise it will clot and stirring will then break or separate the mixture into curds and whey. Milk sometimes curdles when cream of tomato soup is made. The pH of processed tomatoes may be as low as 4.0. A number of techniques have been recommended to protect casein from the acid and so prevent curdling of tomato soup. Included are adding the tomato to the milk rather than the opposite, having both the milk and tomato hot when they are combined and serving the soup promptly, and thickening either the tomato juice or milk before they are combined.

If stewed tomatoes are thickened with a paste made from flour and milk or cream, the acid from the tomatoes causes the milk to curdle as soon as the cold paste is combined with the hot tomatoes. As cooking continues, however, the curds disappear. The great surplus of acid from the high proportion of tomato to milk causes a reversal of charge on the protein molecules of the milk, making it possible for them to be again colloidally dispersed.

Milk or cream used to make caramels sometimes curdles. Acid from brown sugar, the dehydrating effect of the high concentration of sugar, and the high temperature in the boiling syrup all no doubt contribute to the instability of the casein.

EFFECT OF RENNIN ON CASEIN MICELLES

The micelles of casein in milk can be destabilized by the enzyme rennin. Rennin (chymosin) is the active ingredient in rennet tablets. This enzyme is responsible for the first stage in the clotting of milk. It causes cleavage of a specific linkage, the phenyl alanine-methionine peptide bond (14,35), splitting off the carbohydrate-rich, acidic portion of the molecule from the primarily hydrophobic remainder, designated para-κ-casein (35).

$$\kappa\text{-casein} \xrightarrow{\text{Rennin}} \underset{\text{(hydrophobic)}}{\text{para-}\kappa\text{-casein}} + \underset{\text{(soluble)}}{\text{acidic glycopeptide}}$$

With loss of the acidic portion of the molecule, the remainder of the κ-casein no longer stabilizes the micelles which can then approach each other and unite, possibly by hydrophobic bonding (33), to form a three-dimensional network which traps the aqueous phase of the milk. Unlike the effect of acid, rennin does not displace calcium from the micelle, so the curd of milk formed by the action of rennin is calcium phosphocaseinate. The gel formed by rennin is tough and rubbery compared to that formed by acid, which tends to be less elastic and more fragile.

Temperature is critical if milk is to be coagulated as a result of the action of rennin. If the temperature of the milk is above 60°C (140°F), the enzyme will be inactivated. The enzyme-altered casein will not unite to form a gel unless the temperature of the milk is above 15°C (59°F), considered evidence that hydrophobic bonds are involved (33). The optimum temperature for this second phase in the coagulation is 40°C (104°F). Milk should not be over-heated even though it is cooled to 40°C before the rennin is added, because the gel, if it forms, will be weak. This is attributed in part to a heat-induced complex between β-lactoglobulin and κ-casein which makes the latter immune to attack by rennin (30,39). Cutting or stirring breaks the gel or clot and heating shrinks it. Both cause the gel to separate into curds and whey.

HANDLING MILK AND FOODS MADE WITH MILK

KEEPING QUALITY AND SAFETY

The shelf-life of fluid milk can be prolonged by keeping it at a low temperature. For example, milk which would be usable after 5 days at 7°C (45°F), the highest temperature recommended in a refrigerator, would keep nearly three times that long if stored at 2°C (35°F).

Milk and foods which are made with high proportions of milk, such as whipped cream, sauces, puddings, and soft pie fillings, are not only nourishing for humans but provide good media for the growth of microorganisms as well. Foods such as those listed have been implicated in a number of cases of food poisoning because microorganisms known as *Staphylococci* were permitted to grow in the food. These microorganisms are widely distributed and food may become contaminated by contact with work surfaces, utensils, and hands. If such food is held in a warm place, these microorganisms grow and in the process develop a metabolic product which is toxic to humans. Consumption of the food that contains the enterotoxin results in gastrointestinal upsets of variable severity and duration. Prompt cooling of such foods, at least to 10°C (50°F) and preferably 4°C (40°F), will limit the growth of these (and most other) microorganisms and so prevent the production of the enterotoxin. Even so, such foods should be eaten soon after they are prepared for best quality.

EFFECT OF LIGHT ON RIBOFLAVIN

The riboflavin content of milk can make a significant contribution to the diet. The lability of this vitamin when milk in clear glass containers was exposed to sunlight has been known for many years (34). Milk exposed to fluorescent light of an intensity of 300 foot-candles at a temperature of 4.4°C (40°F) for 48 hours lost approximately 11 percent of its riboflavin in glass or regular plastic containers and 3 percent in paper or gold-tinted plastic containers (31). Loss was low in all containers at a light intensity of 150 foot-candles and a temperature of 1.7°C (35°F).

REFERENCES

1. Babcock, C. J. 1922. *The whipping quality of cream.* U.S. Dept. Agr., Bull. No. 1075. 22 pp. Basic information about factors which affect the quality of whipped cream.

2. Bloomfield, V. A., and R. J. Mead, Jr. 1975. Structure and stability of casein micelles. *J. Dairy Sci.* **58:** 592–601. Facts pertaining to micellar structure.

3. Bockian, A. H., G. F. Stewart, and A. L. Tappel. 1957. Factors affecting the dispersibility of "instant dissolving" dry milks. *Food Research* **22:** 69–75. Why "instant" milks disperse so readily.

4. Brunner, J. R. 1974. Physical equilibra in milk: the lipid phase. In *Fundamentals of Dairy Chemistry.* B. H. Webb, A. H. Johnson, and J. A. Alford, eds. Westport, Conn.: Avi Publishing Co., Inc. Pp. 487–495.

5. Brunner, J. R. 1976. Homogenization. In *Principles of Food Science.* Part I. *Food Chemistry.* O. R. Fennema, ed. New York: Marcel Dekker, Inc. Pp. 648–649.

6. Calbert, H. E., and A. M. Swanson. 1956 (Aug.). Process innovations improve fresh milk concentrate. *Food Eng.* **28:** 46–47, 172, 175. Production of a concentrate which will keep under refrigeration for weeks.

7. Carr, R. E., and G. M. Trout. 1942. Some cooking qualities of homogenized milk. I. Baked and soft custard. *Food Research* **7:** 360–369. Effects of type of milk on heat penetration, cooking time, firmness or thickness, and stability of custards.

8. Cheryan, M., P. J. Van Wyk, N. F. Olson, and T. Richardson. 1975. Secondary phase of enzymatic milk coagulation. *J. Dairy Sci.* **58:** 477–481. Effects of temperature and pH on the clotting phase.

9. Choi, R. P. 1959. Dry milk-processing for specific uses. *Cereal Sci. Today.* **4:** 39–42. Manufacture and uses of different forms of dried milk.

10. Dahlberg, A. C., and J. C. Hening. 1925. *Viscosity, surface tension and whipping properties of milk and cream.* New York State Exp. Sta. Tech. Bull. No. 113. 42 pp. Factors affecting the quality of whipped cream.

11. Doty, P. 1957. Proteins. *Sci. American* **197** (3): 173–178, 180, 182, 184. Amino acids, polypeptides, and protein molecules; illustrated.

12. Hansen, P. M. T. 1968. Stabilization of α_s-casein by carrageenan. *J. Dairy Sci.* **51:** 192–195. Why this hydrocolloid is added to evaporated milk.

13. Henstra, S., and D. G. Schmidt. 1970. On the structure of the fat-protein complex in homogenized cow's milk. *Neth. Milk and Dairy J.* **24:** 45–51. Evidence for subunits of casein micelles in new fat globule membranes.

14. Hill, R. D. 1969. Synthetic peptide and ester substrates for rennin. *J. Dairy Sci.* **36:** 409–415. The labile peptide linkage.

15. Hollender, H., and K. G. Weckel. 1941. Stability of homogenized milk in cookery practice. *Food Research* **6:** 335–343. Problems in the use of homogenized milk in scalloped potatoes, cereal and custard.

16. Jenness, R., and S. Patton. 1959. *Principles of Dairy Chemistry.* New York: Wiley. 446 pp. A good source of information on various aspects of milk.

17. Jordan, R., E. S. Wegner, and H. A. Hollender. 1954. Nonhomogenized *vs.* homogenized milk in baked custard. *J. Am. Dietet. Assoc.* **30:** 1126–1130. Effects of two formulas, three temperatures for preheating milk, and three baking temperatures.

18. King, N. 1955. *The Milk Fat Globule Membrane and Some Associated Phenomena.* Farnham Royal, Bucks, England: Commonwealth Agricultural Bureau. 99 pp. Monograph summarizing information about the nature of the fat globule membrane.

19. Kroger, M. 1976. Quality of yogurt. *J. Dairy Sci.* **59:** 344–350. Microbiological activity and flavor; body.

20. Krutch, J. W. 1953. The crystal and the colloid. In *The Best of Two Worlds.* New York: W. Sloane Associates. Pp. 143–155. An essay on the nature of the crystal and the colloid.

21. Lin, C. F., and P. M. T. Hansen. 1968. Stabilization of calcium caseinate by carrageenan. *J. Dairy Sci.* **51:** 945. Effective groups on the hydrocolloid.

22. *Milk and its products. Facts for consumer education.* 1954. U.S. Dept. Agr., Agr. Infor. Bull. No. 125. 31 pp. Nutritive value, market information and care in the home.

23. Morr, C. V. 1975. Chemistry of milk proteins in food processing. *J. Dairy Sci.* **58:** 977–984. Chemical basis for changes; a review.

24. Nielsen, V. H. 1968. Improving the whipping quality of cream. *Am. Dairy Rev.* **30:** 66, 76, 78. Factors that influence the quality of whipped cream.

25. Patton, S. 1958. Review of the organic chemical effects of heat on milk. *J. Agr. Food Chem.* **6:** 132–135. Color and flavor developed in milk by heat and the flavor of heated milk fat.

26. Pauling, L., R. B. Corey, and R. Hayward. 1954. The structure of protein molecules. *Sci. American* **191** (1): 51–59. Development of the knowledge of the structure of protein molecules; many excellent illustrations.

27. Pimentel, D., W. Dritschilo, J. Krummel, and J. Kutzman. 1975. Energy and land constraints in food protein production. *Science* **190:** 754–761. Options for use of resources to meet the world's food needs.

28. Rhodes, D. N., and C. H. Lea. 1958. On the composition of the phospholipids of cows' milk. *J. Dairy Res.* **25:** 60–69. Composition of the phospholipids of the milk fat globule membrane.

29. Rose, D. 1965. Protein stability problems. *J. Dairy Sci.* **48:** 139–146. A review.

30. Sawyer, W. H. 1969. Complex between β-lactoglobulin and κ-casein. A review. *J. Dairy Sci.* **52:** 1347–1355. Effects of heating milk on its coagulation by rennin.

31. Singh, R. P., D. R. Heldman, and J. R. Kirk. 1975. Kinetic analysis of light-induced riboflavin loss in whole milk. *J. Food Sci.* **40:** 164–167. Effects of container, temperature, and intensity of light.

32. Slattery, C. W. 1976. Review: Casein micelle structure; An examination of models. *J. Dairy Sci.* **59:** 1547–1556. Evidence for and against various proposed models.

33. Slattery, C. W., and R. Evard. 1973. A model for the formation and structure of casein micelles from subunits of variable composition. *Biochim. Biophys. Acta* **317:** 529–538. Porous micellar model proposed.

34. Stamberg, O. E., and D. R. Theophilus. 1945. Photolysis of riboflavin in milk. *J. Dairy Sci.* **28:** 269–275. Early report on destruction by light.

35. Swaisgood, H. 1975. Primary sequence of kappa-casein. *J. Dairy Sci.* **58:** 583–591. Amino acid sequence and resultant chemical and physical properties.

36. Towson, A. M., and G. M. Trout. 1946. Some cooking qualities of homogenized milk. II. White sauces. *Food Research* **11:** 261–273. Effect of milk on thickness of sauce and apparent curdling due to poor incorporation of added fat.

37. Waugh, D. F., and R. W. Noble, Jr. 1965. Casein micelles. Formation and structure. *Am. Chem. Soc. J.* **87:** 2236–2257. A model for the casein micelle.

38. Wegner, E. S., R. Jordan, and H. A. Hollender. 1953. Homogenized and non-homogenized milk in the preparation of selected food products. *J. Home Econ.* **45:** 589–591. Cocoa, chocolate, and rennet custard compared.

39. Wheelock, J. V., and A. Kirk. 1974. The role of β-lactoglobulin in the primary phase of rennin action on heated casein micelles and heated milk. *J. Dairy Res.* **41:** 367–372. Why heating milk interferes with the action of rennin.

40. Whitney, R. Mc., J. R. Brunner, K. E. Ebner, H. M. Farrell Jr., R. V. Josephson, C. V. Morr, and H. E. Swaisgood. 1976. Nomenclature of the proteins of cow's milk. Fourth Revision. *J. Dairy Sci.* **59:** 795–815. Nomenclature updated.

41. Zittle, C. A. 1969. Influence of heat on κ-casein. *J. Dairy Sci.* **52:** 12–16. As affected by pH and NaCl.

FILM

1. *The Colloidal State.* 16 min. Coronet. Particle size, types of dispersions, precipitation of casein by acid and rennin.

EIGHTEEN

Cheese

Cheese is the curd of milk, basically a gel of casein from which more or less of the whey has been removed by heating, stirring, and pressing. More than 400 varieties of natural cheeses are made, with names which range from Abertam to Zomma (2). Figure 18-1 shows some of the more common varieties. Only a cheese expert or a connoisseur of cheese would be familiar with all. One is entitled to wonder how the curd from milk could give rise to so many varieties.

TYPES OF NATURAL CHEESE

One factor that contributes to the great variety of cheeses is the kind of milk used. In this country cow's milk is used almost exclusively, but the milk from sheep is used to make French Roquefort, goat's milk is used to make Norwegian gjetost, and buffalo milk was used for Italian mozzarella. Whole milk is usually used, but some cheese is made from cream as well as milk, some is made from skimmed milk, and some from whey. The type of curd is a second factor that contributes to differences among cheeses. For cream cheese and for old-fashioned cottage cheese, the curd is formed by acidifying the milk. For most, however, the curd is made by rennin. (See Chapter 17.) Whether the cheese is ripened and, if it is, the kind of microorganisms used constitutes a third distinguishing factor (1). The temperature to which the cheese is exposed as it ripens, the humidity in the air, and the length of the ripening period also confer unique characteristics on cheese of different types. In addition to the kind of milk, the type of curd, and the amount and conditions of ripening, cheeses may differ in consistency from soft to semisoft, hard to very hard, to grating cheese. Softness of cheese depends mainly on moisture content, but to some extent on the ripeness.

UNRIPENED CHEESE

Unripened cheese is ready to eat as soon as it is made. Cottage cheese, cream cheese, and Neufchâtel are examples of unripened cheese. These are characterized by high moisture content. Cottage cheese has the highest (maximum of 80 percent), followed by Neufchâtel with a maximum of 65 percent. Neufchâtel (milk fat-content less than 33 percent but not less than 20 percent) is a leaner cousin of cream cheese. The latter has a minimum fat content of 33

1—Wheel of Swiss
2—American (Cheddar style)
3—Romano
4—American (longhorn style)
5—Gorgonzola
6—Cottage
7—Asiago
8—Brick
9—American (daisy style)
10—Provolone
11—Blue
12—Kumminost
13—Muenster
14—Gjetost
15—Primost
16—Bel Paese
17—Sardo
18—Cream
19—Process Cheese Food
20—Process American
21—Parmesan
22—Limburger
23—Edam (cannonball)
24—Baby Edam
25—Sapsago
26—Hand
27—Brie
28—Sectors of Blue
29—American (10-lb. print)
30—Apple
31—Baby Gouda
32—Process Cheese Spread
33—Camembert
34—Port du Salut (Oka)
35—Nokkelost
36—Block Edam
37—Nordlands-Ost

FIGURE 18-1. Commonly used cheeses. (Courtesy of the National Dairy Council.)

percent and a maximum moisture content of 55 percent. If dry curd cottage cheese is creamed, the minimum fat content is 4 percent. Any of the following ingredients may be added to cream cheese to give it its characteristic consistency: algin, carob bean gum, gelatin, gum karaya, gum tragacanth, or guar gum. These ingredients are permitted in amounts not to exceed 0.5 percent of the weight of the finished cheese.

Not all unripened cheese is soft. Gjetost and mysost, made from whey, are unripened cheeses that are firm because of their low moisture content. Lactose makes them sweet. Unripened cheese low in moisture may be stored for some time, in contrast to high-moisture cheese, which must be consumed soon after it is made.

SOFT RIPENED CHEESE

Ripened cheeses vary in consistency from soft to very hard. Three soft ripened cheeses are Brie, Camembert, and Limburger. All three have a moisture content of approximately 50 percent. All three are surface-ripened cheeses, the first two by white or grayish-white molds which together with bacteria grow on the surface, followed by the growth of yellow and reddish molds which impart a creamy yellow translucency to the interior of the cheese. Yeasts and a species of bacteria are the curing agents for Limburger cheese. Limburger is creamy white on the interior and has a characteristic high aroma.

SEMISOFT RIPENED CHEESE

Semisoft ripened cheeses have a moisture content that ranges from 35 to 45 percent. Bel Paese, Brick, and Muenster are semisoft cheeses ripened primarily by bacteria. Gorgonzola, Roquefort, and Stilton, also semisoft, are cured by blue mold as well as by bacteria. Blue cheeses are mellow and have a piquant flavor. The flavor is due in part to hydrolysis of fat and liberation of free fatty acid (caproic, caprylic, and capric).

FIRM AND HARD RIPENED CHEESE

Both firm and very hard ripened cheeses are cured by bacteria. Cheddar, Edam, Gouda, Gruyère, and Swiss are examples of firm ripened cheeses. The holes in Swiss cheese are due to gas formed by bacteria as the cheese ripens. Very hard or grating cheeses include Parmesan, Romano, and Sap Sago. These are characterized by a low moisture content.

Detailed information about some of the more commonly used varieties of cheese is given in Table 18-1.

MAKING CHEDDAR CHEESE

The bulk of the cheese used in the United States is cheddar, known also as American or American cheddar. Of the nearly 2 billion pounds of cheese annually manufactured in this country, more than half is American cheddar. The main cheese-producing states are Wisconsin, New York, Missouri, Illinois, and Minnesota.

Table 18-1   Characteristics of some popular varieties of natural cheeses

Kind or Name	Place of Origin	Kind of Milk used in Manufacture	Ripening or Curing Time	Flavor	Body and Texture	Color	Retail Packaging	Uses
Soft, Unripened Varieties								
Cottage, plain or creamed	Unknown	Cow's milk skimmed; plain curd, or plain curd with cream added	Unripened	Mild, acid	Soft, curd particles of varying size	White to creamy white	Cup-shaped containers, tumblers, dishes	Salads, with fruits, vegetables, sandwiches, dips, cheese cake
Cream, plain	U.S.A.	Cream from cow's milk	Unripened	Mild, acid	Soft and smooth	White	3- to 8-oz. packages	Salads, dips, sandwiches, snacks, cheese cake, desserts
Neufchâtel (Nū-shä-tĕl′)	France	Cow's milk	Unripened	Mild, acid	Soft, smooth similar to cream cheese but lower in milkfat	White	4- to 8-oz. packages	Salads, dips, sandwiches, snacks, cheese cake, desserts
Ricôtta (Rǐ-co′-ta)	Italy	Cow's milk, whole or partly skimmed, or whey from cow's milk with whole or skim milk added. In Italy, whey from sheep's milk	Unripened	Sweet, nut-like	Soft, moist or dry	White	Pint and quart paper and plastic containers, 3 lb. metal cans	Appetizers, salads, snacks, lasagne, ravioli, noodles and other cooked dishes, grating, desserts

Variety	Place of Origin	Kind of Milk Used	Ripening or Curing Time	Flavor	Texture	Color	Shape	Uses
Firm, Unripened Varieties								
Gjetost[a] (Yĕt'ôst)	Norway	Whey from goat's milk or a mixture of whey from goat's and cow's milk	Unripened	Sweetish, caramel	Firm, buttery consistency	Golden brown	Cubical and rectangular	Snacks, desserts, served with dark breads, crackers, biscuits or muffins
Mysost (Müs-ôst) also called Primost (Prēm'-ôst)	Norway	Whey from cow's milk	Unripened	Sweetish, caramel	Firm, buttery consistency	Light brown	Cubical, cylindrical, pie-shaped wedges	Snacks, desserts, served with dark breads
Mozzarella (Mô-tsa-rel'la) also called Scamorza	Italy	Whole or partly skimmed cow's milk. In Italy, originally made from buffalo's milk.	Unripened	Delicate, mild	Slightly firm, plastic	Creamy white	Small round or braided form, shredded, sliced	Snacks, toasted sandwiches, cheeseburgers, cooking, as in meat loaf, or topping for lasagne, pizza, and casseroles
Soft, Ripened Varieties								
Brie (Brē)	France	Cow's milk	4 to 8 weeks	Mild to pungent	Soft, smooth when ripened	Creamy yellow interior; edible thin brown and white crust	Circular, pie-shaped wedges	Appetizers, sandwiches, snacks, good with crackers and fruit, dessert
Camembert (Kăm'ĕm-bâr)	France	Cow's milk	4 to 8 weeks	Mild to pungent	Soft, smooth; very soft when fully ripened	Creamy yellow interior; edible thin white, or gray-white crust	Small circular cakes and pie-shaped portions	Appetizers, sandwiches, snacks, good with crackers, and fruit such as pears and apples, dessert

Table 18-1 Characteristics of some popular varieties of natural cheeses (*continued*)

Kind or Name	Place of Origin	Kind of Milk used in Manufacture	Ripening or Curing Time	Flavor	Body and Texture	Color	Retail Packaging	Uses
Limburger	Belgium	Cow's milk	4 to 8 weeks	Highly pungent; very strong	Soft, smooth when ripened; usually contains small irregular openings	Creamy white interior; reddish yellow surface	Cubical, rectangular	Appetizers, snacks, good with crackers, rye or other dark breads, dessert
Semisoft, Ripened Varieties								
Bel Paese[b] (Bĕl Pä-ā′-zē)	Italy	Cow's milk	6 to 8 weeks	Mild to moderately robust	Soft to medium firm, creamy	Creamy yellow interior; slightly gray or brownish surface sometimes covered with yellow wax coating	Small wheels, wedges, segments	Appetizers, good with crackers, snacks, sandwiches, dessert
Brick	U.S.A.	Cow's milk	2 to 4 months	Mild to moderately sharp	Semisoft to medium firm, elastic, numerous small mechanical openings	Creamy yellow	Loaf, brick, slices, cut portions	Appetizers, sandwiches, snacks, dessert
Muenster (Mŭn′stēr)	Germany	Cow's milk	1 to 8 weeks	Mild to mellow	Semisoft, numerous small mechanical openings. Contains more moisture than brick	Creamy white interior; yellow tan surface	Circular cake, blocks, wedges, segments, slices	Appetizers, sandwiches, snacks, dessert

Name	Country	Kind of milk	Ripening time	Flavor	Body and texture	Color	Shape and style	Uses
Port du Salut (Por dü Så-lü')	France	Cow's milk	6 to 8 weeks	Mellow to robust	Semisoft, smooth, buttery, small openings	Creamy yellow	Wheels and wedges	Appetizers, snacks, served with raw fruit, dessert
Firm Ripened Varieties								
Cheddar	England	Cow's milk	1 to 12 months or more	Mild to very sharp	Firm, smooth, some mechanical openings	White to medium-yellow-orange	Circular, cylindrical loaf, pie-shaped wedges, oblongs, slices, cubes, shredded, grated	Appetizers, sandwiches, sauces, on vegetables, in hot dishes, toasted sandwiches, grating, cheeseburgers, dessert
Colby	U.S.A.	Cow's milk	1 to 3 months	Mild to mellow	Softer and more open than Cheddar	White to medium-yellow-orange	Cylindrical, pie-shaped wedges	Sandwiches, snacks, cheeseburgers
Caciocavallo (Kä'chō-kä-val'lō)	Italy	Cow's milk. In Italy, cow's milk or mixtures of sheep's, goat's, and cow's milk	3 to 12 months	Piquant, similar to Provolone but not smoked	Firm, lower in milkfat and moisture than Provolone	Light or white interior; clay or tan colored surface	Spindle or tenpin shaped, bound with cord, cut pieces	Snacks, sandwiches, cooking, dessert; suitable for grating after prolonged curing
Edam (Ē'dăm)	Netherlands	Cow's milk, partly skimmed	2 to 3 months	Mellow, nut-like	Semisoft to firm, smooth; small irregularly shaped or round holes; lower milkfat than Gouda	Creamy yellow or medium yellow-orange interior; surface coated with red wax	Cannon ball shaped loaf, cut pieces, oblongs	Appetizers, snacks, salads, sandwiches, seafood sauces, dessert

Table 18-1 Characteristics of some popular varieties of natural cheeses (continued)

Kind or Name	Place of Origin	Kind of Milk used in Manufacture	Ripening or Curing Time	Flavor	Body and Texture	Color	Retail Packaging	Uses
Gouda (Gou'-dä)	Netherlands	Cow's milk, whole or partly skimmed	2 to 6 months	Mellow, nut-like	Semisoft to firm, smooth; small irregularly shaped or round holes; higher milk fat than Edam	Creamy yellow or medium yellow-or-ange interior; may or may not have red wax coating	Ball shaped with flattened top and bottom	Appetizers, snacks, salads, sandwiches, seafood sauces, dessert
Provolone (Prō-vō-lō'-nē) also smaller sizes and shapes called Provolette, Provoloncini	Italy	Cow's milk	2 to 12 months or more	Mellow to sharp, smoky, salty	Firm, smooth	Light creamy interior; light brown or golden yellow surface	Pear shaped, sausage and salami shaped, wedges, slices	Appetizers, sandwiches, snacks, soufflé, macaroni and spaghetti dishes, pizza, suitable for grating when fully cured and dried
Swiss, also called Emmentaler	Switzerland	Cow's milk	3 to 9 months	Sweet, nut-like	Firm, smooth with large round eyes	Light yellow	Segments, pieces, slices	Sandwiches, snacks, sauces, fondue, cheeseburgers
Very Hard, Ripened Varieties								
Parmesan (Pärme-zän) also called Reggiano	Italy	Partly skimmed cow's milk	14 months to 2 years	Sharp, piquant	Very hard, granular, lower moisture and milkfat than	Creamy white	Cylindrical, wedges, shredded, grated	Grated for seasoning in soups, or vegetables, spa-

Name	Origin	Kind of milk	Ripening time	Flavor	Body/texture	Color	Shape/style	Uses
					Romano			ghetti, ravioli, popcorn, used extensively in pizza and lasagne
Romano (Rō-mä'-nō) also called Sardo Romano Pecorino Romano	Italy	Cow's milk. In Italy, sheep's milk (Italian law)	5 to 12 months	Sharp, piquant	Very hard granular	Yellowish-white interior, greenish-black surface	Round with flat ends, wedges, shredded, grated	Seasoning in soups, casserole dishes, ravioli, sauces, breads, suitable for grating when cured for about one year
Sap Sago[a] (Săp'-să-gō)	Switzerland	Skimmed cow's milk	5 months or more	Sharp, pungent clover-like	Very hard	Light green by addition of dried, powdered clover leaves	Conical, shakers	Grated to flavor soups, meats, macaroni, spaghetti, hot vegetables; mixed with butter makes a good spread on crackers or bread

Blue-Vein Mold-Ripened Varieties

Name	Origin	Kind of milk	Ripening time	Flavor	Body/texture	Color	Shape/style	Uses
Blue, spelled Bleu on imported cheese	France	Cow's milk. In France, cow's milk or sheep's milk or mixtures of these	2 to 6 months	Tangy, peppery	Semisoft, pasty, sometimes crumbly	White interior, marbled or streaked with blue veins of mold	Cylindrical, wedges, oblongs, squares, cut portions	Appetizers, salads, dips, salad dressing, sandwich spreads, good with crackers, dessert

Table 18-1   Characteristics of some popular varieties of natural cheeses (continued)

Kind or Name	Place of Origin	Kind of Milk used in Manufacture	Ripening or Curing Time	Flavor	Body and Texture	Color	Retail Packaging	Uses
Gorgonzola (Gôr-gŏn-zō'-la)	Italy	Cow's milk. In Italy, cow's milk or goat's milk or mixtures of these	3 to 12 months	Tangy, peppery	Semisoft, pasty, sometimes crumbly, lower moisture than Blue	Creamy white interior, mottled or streaked with blue-green veins of mold. Clay colored surface	Cylindrical, wedges, oblongs	Appetizers, snacks, salads, dips, sandwich spread, good with crackers, dessert
Roquefort[a] (Rŏk'-fert) or (Rŏk-fôr')	France	Sheep's milk	2 to 5 months or more	Sharp, slightly peppery	Semisoft, pasty, sometimes crumbly	White or creamy white interior, marbled or streaked with blue veins of mold	Cylindrical, wedges	Appetizers, snacks, salads, dips, sandwich spreads, good with crackers, dessert
Stilton[a]	England	Cow's milk	2 to 6 months	Piquant, milder than Gorgonzola or Roquefort	Semisoft, flaky; slightly more crumbly than Blue	Creamy white interior, marbled or streaked with blue-green veins of mold	Circular, wedges, oblongs	Appetizers, snacks, salads, dessert

[a]Imported only.

[b]Italian trademark—licensed for manufacture in U.S.A.; also imported.

SOURCE: U.S. Dept. Agriculture. Marketing Bulletin No. 17. *Cheese Buying Guide for Consumers.* 1961.

FORMING THE CURD

In the making of cheddar cheese, pasteurized whole milk is cooled to 30–31°C (86°–88°F) and lactic acid starter is added (2). The milk is held long enough to develop sufficient acidity and then rennin or another proteolytic enzyme is added. Once rennin derived from veal was used exclusively, but to extend the scarce supply a blend of rennin with swine pepsin, with a clotting enzyme obtained from a mold, or from another source is used (6). The enzyme initiates the first step in the conversion of the colloidally dispersed calcium phosphocaseinate micelles to cheese. (See section on effects of rennin on casein micelles.) The gel or clot that forms subsequently traps the water and the fat globules of the milk in the protein network.

After the gel is formed it is cut into small cubes to permit the whey to drain from the curds. The curds are salted and a food coloring is added to give the typical yellow of most cheddars, in contrast to the creamy white of uncolored Swiss cheese. The curds are warmed slightly to shrink them, which causes more whey to be expelled. Whey contains much of the lactose, the proteins not precipitated by acid or enzyme, and water soluble vitamins and minerals. Additional liquid is released as the curds are handled to shape the cheese and again when the curd is pressed. Even so, the moisture content of even a firm cheese such as American cheddar is approximately 37 to 38 percent.

RIPENING

When cheese is first formed, it is tough, rubbery, and bland tasting. Before it is put on the market, freshly made cheese, characterized as "green," is put into storage for a time to ripen. During this holding period, enzymes, either those from milk or those elaborated by molds or bacteria, bring about hydrolysis of part of the calcium phosphocaseinate. Lower polymers such as proteoses and peptones as well as amino acids are formed. This breakdown of the calcium phosphocaseinate of cheese as it ages makes the proteins more dispersible. Salt added to the curds keeps the cheese from ripening too fast and improves the texture of the ripened cheese. The curd of green cheese gradually loses its rubberiness as it ages. A fully ripened cheese has a crumbly or mealy texture.

Equally important is the effect of ripening on the flavor of cheese. Free fatty acids from the hydrolysis of the milk fat and H_2S liberated from cysteine residues of beta-casein must be in balance for good flavor (4,5). So too must be the ratio of fatty acids to acetate (0.55:1.0) (8). If short chain fatty acids equal or exceed the acetate, the cheese may have a fruity or rancid flavor. But the breakdown products of fat as well as those from lactose, citrates, and proteins and the products of their interaction are essential for converting a bland-tasting "green" cheese into a flavorful, ripened cheese. Salt in the curd promotes the formation of desirable flavor components (10).

Federal regulations require that cheese made from unpasteurized milk be ripened for not less than 60 days at a temperature no lower than 35°F. During this holding period pathogenic bacteria which might be present in the milk die. This regulation applies, of course, only to cheese that enters interstate commerce. Some cheeses are marketed with the age stamped on them; others are labeled mild, mellow, sharp, or very sharp, terms which indicate progressively longer aging periods. Providing storage space while cheese ripens adds to the cost.

White deposits found occasionally on fully ripened cheeses are sometimes mistaken for mold. They may be crystals of the amino acid tyrosine. This accumulates as the proteins in the cheese are hydrolyzed. Tyrosine, because of its low solubility, precipitates if enough accumulates.

PASTEURIZED PROCESS CHEESE

Any natural cheese can be made into process cheese. A high proportion of the cheese marketed is in the form of process cheese. The natural cheese is grated or shredded, and an emulsifier, usually disodium phosphate, is added; the cheese is then blended and heated to pasteurize it. The moisture content of a process cheese can be only 1 percent greater than the maximum allowed for the natural form. More moisture is allowed in cheese spread, and for cheese food even more is permitted. The minimum fat content is lower for process than for natural, lower still for cheese food, and lowest for cheese spread. Thus the cheese in cheese food is more dilute than in process cheese and still more dilute in cheese spread. The money spent for these items buys less cheese but more convenience, such as greater spreadability. The intimate blending of constituents in process cheese diminishes the strength of the cheese flavor. Too, the emulsifier contributes a taste of its own. Advantages of cooking with cheese in processed form are that it blends readily with liquid and is less likely to curdle or become stringy or matted if it is overheated.

COMPOSITION OF CHEESES

Table 18-2 gives the composition of a few of the varieties of cheeses commonly used. Figures are based on 100 grams, or slightly less than ¼ pound.

Cheese retains a high proportion of most of the nutrients of the milk from which it was made and supplies these in a more concentrated form. Cheese is a rich source of high-quality protein, has a high percentage of fat (cottage cheese excepted), and is an excellent source of calcium and phosphorus (cottage and cream cheese excepted) (3,6). Cheese is an excellent source of riboflavin, and if made from whole milk, contributes vitamin A to the diet. Primost and Gjetost are high in lactose.

USES OF CHEESE

Cheese is a versatile food found in menus from appetizers to desserts. As appetizers, cheese may appear as dips, spreads, or wedges. Cheese soufflé, fondue, or omelet or cheese in casserole dishes or as sandwiches make a main

Table 18-2 Composition of cheeses (per 100 grams)

Cheese	Water (%)	Calories[a]	Protein (g)	Fat (g)	Carbohydrate (g)	Calcium (mg)	Phosphorus (mg)	Iron (mg)	Vitamin A Value (I.U.)	Thiamine (mg)	Riboflavin (mg)	Niacin (mg)	Ascorbic Acid (mg)
Natural													
Blue	42.41	353	21.40	28.74	2.34	528	387	.31	721	.029	.382	1.016	0
Brick	41.11	371	23.24	29.68	2.79	674	451	.43	1,083	.014	.351	.118	0
Cheddar	36.75	403	24.90	33.14	1.28	721	512	.68	1,059	.027	.375	.080	0
Cottage, creamed	78.96	103	12.49	4.51	2.68	60	132	.14	163	.021	.163	.126	Trace
Cream	53.75	349	7.55	34.87	2.66	80	104	1.20	1,427	.017	.197	.101	0
Gjetost	13.44	466	9.65	29.51	42.65	400	444	b	b	b	b	.813	0
Limburger	48.42	327	20.05	27.25	.49	497	393	.13	1,281	.080	.503	.158	0
Parmesan, grated	17.66	456	41.56	30.02	3.74	1,376	807	.95	701	.045	.386	.315	0
Swiss	37.21	376	28.43	27.45	3.38	961	605	.17	845	.022	.365	.092	0
Process, pasteurized													
American	39.16	375	22.15	31.25	1.60	616	745	.39	1,210	.027	.353	.069	0
American cheese food	43.15	328	19.61	24.60	7.29	574	459	.84	913	.029	.442	.140	0
American cheese spread	47.65	290	16.41	21.23	8.73	562	712	.33	788	.048	.431	.131	0

[a]1 kilocalorie = 4.185 kilojoules.
[b]Lack of data.

SOURCE: U.S. Dept. Agr. Handbook No. 8-1. *Composition of Foods. Dairy and Egg Products. Raw, Processed, Prepared.* Revised 1976.

course. Cottage, cream, and Neufchâtel cheeses are used in salads, as are shredded or grated hard cheese. Cheeses which are preeminently for dessert include Bel Paese, Brie, Camembert, Port du Salut, and Roquefort. Camembert, Edam, Gouda, and Liederkranz are popular for cheese trays with crackers and fruit.

CHEESE IN COOKING

The bulk of the cheese used in cooking is American cheddar or some modification of it. Problems in melting cheese and in blending cheese with liquid are discussed below.

MELTING CHEESE

As cheese is heated, it softens until it becomes a viscous liquid thin enough to flow. This softening is due in part to the fat in the cheese. At the temperature of the refrigerator the fat in cheese is solid; at room temperature it softens, and as the temperature of the cheese is warmed above this, fats in the cheese liquefy. The more fat in the cheese the more readily the cheese liquefies. When cheese is heated beyond a certain temperature, coagulation and shrinkage of the protein offset the tendency of the cheese to soften because of the melting of the fat. The fat may separate from the curd.

The presence of water in cheese permits the curd to shrink due to evaporation of moisture. Cheese melted in the oven or under the broiler may shrink and toughen because of loss of moisture to the air and because of the effect of heat on the protein. Too long exposure to hot, dry atmosphere is one of the greatest indignities that cheese suffers at the hands of cooks.

BLENDING CHEESE WITH LIQUID

Often cheese is combined with liquid as in cheese sauce, macaroni and cheese, and cheese soufflé. The higher the moisture and fat content of the cheese, the more readily it blends with liquid (9). To take advantage of the high fat content, the temperature of the liquid is important. If it is not hot enough to melt the fat, the cheese will not blend with the liquid. If the liquid is too hot, the cheese shrinks excessively and moisture is forced from the curd. An overheated cheese sauce is watery and either stringy and matted or grainy. More highly ripened cheese (9), because the protein of the curd is more readily dispersed, blends better with liquid. The riper the cheese, the higher the temperature it can tolerate. Cheese does not disperse well at a pH below 5.6; it tends to string and mat (9). A Swiss fondue for dipping is a special type of cheese sauce made by melting grated Swiss cheese in dry white wine heated in a chafing dish until it is bubbling hot. The boiling point of the alcohol in the wine is low enough so that the cheese does not become overheated. The sauce is eaten by dipping cubes of French bread or other edibles into it.

A final factor favoring the blending of cheese with liquid is the presence of emulsifier in the cheese. It is for this reason that process cheese presents less of a problem in making cheese dishes. A cheese sauce made from process cheese is less likely to curdle. The texture of a cheese sauce made from process cheese is very smooth, although it has an adhesive, tacky, rubbery consistency which some find objectionable. Cheese sauce made with natural cheese seems grainy by comparison, but the cheese flavor is more pronounced. Using part process and part natural cheese gives advantages of both.

Hard cheese is usually grated before an attempt is made to incorporate it in liquid. It is impossible to grate process cheese; instead, this type should be cut into very thin slices or shredded to facilitate blending. Process cheese, if thinly sliced, blends readily with white sauce if the liquid is hot enough. Grated sharp cheese blends readily, too, because the cheese is in such small pieces and is fully ripened. Ordinarily, mild, less highly ripened grated cheese blends more slowly than does sharp cheese.

REFERENCES

1. Anon. 1961. Cheese buying guide for consumers. U.S. Dept. Agr., Marketing Bull. No. 17. 18 pp. Brief account of the making of natural and process cheese; buying points, use and care in the home. Popular varieties.
2. Anon. 1978. *Cheese varieties and descriptions.* U.S. Dept. Agr. Handbook No. 54. 151 pp. A listing of varieties of cheese with descriptions.
3. Blunt, K., and E. Summer. 1928. The calcium of cheese. *J. Home Econ.* **20:** 587–590. Analysis of cottage, cheddar, and Swiss cheese (commercial source).
4. Harper, W. J., A. Carmona, and T. Kristoffersen. 1971. Protein degradation in cheddar cheese slurries. *J. Food Science* **36:** 503–506. Beta-casein as the source of characteristic flavor.
5. Kristoffersen, T. 1967. Interrelationship of flavor and chemical changes in cheese. *J. Dairy Sci.* **50:** 279–284. Constituents in the flavor of ripened cheese.
6. McCammon, R. B., W. J. Caulfield, and M. M. Kramer. 1933. Calcium and phosphorus of cheese under controlled conditions. *J. Dairy Sci.* **16:** 253–263. Analyses of cheese, both acid and rennin curds produced under laboratory conditions.
7. Nelson, John H. 1975. Impact of milk clotting enzymes on cheese technology. *J. Dairy Sci.* **58:** 1739–1750. Proteolytic enzymes in current use.
8. Ohren, J. A., and S. L. Tuckey. 1969. Relation of flavor development in cheddar cheese to chemical changes in the fat of the cheese. *J. Dairy Sci.* **52:** 598–607. Role of fat in cheese flavor.
9. Personius, C. J., E. Boardman, and A. R. Ausherman. 1944. Some factors affecting the behavior of cheddar cheese in cooking. *Food Research* **9:** 308–311. Effect of fat content, moisture content and ripening on the melting characteristics and the blending of cheese with liquid.
10. Thakur, M. K., J. R. Kirk, and T. I. Hedrick. 1975. Changes during ripening of unsalted cheddar cheese. *J. Dairy Sci.* **58:** 175–180. Effect of salt on flavor and texture.

NINETEEN
Eggs

In addition to being cooked and served in a variety of ways, eggs perform a number of functions in products in which they are used as ingredients. Eggs furnish an emulsifier in mayonnaise, cream puffs, and cheese soufflé, and act as a gelling agent in custards, as a coating material for croquettes, as a thickening agent in soft pie fillings, and as structural material in shortened cakes. When whipped to a foam, eggs serve as a means of incorporating air in meringues, sponge and angel cakes, and in shortened cakes as well.

STRUCTURE

SHELL

The egg is unique in a number of ways, not least of which is its elaborate structure. (See Fig. 19-1.) The shell of an egg, constituted mainly of crystals of calcium carbonate deposited in an organic matrix, surrounds and supports the part that is used for food. An egg shell is brittle and rigid, but it is not impervious (42). It contains thousands of pores so small that they are invisible and a few just large enough to be seen without magnification. Spots of color which appear on the white of a colored Easter egg are evidence of the porosity of the shell. Shells of some eggs are white and those of others brown. Pigmentation of the shell depends on the breed of the hen and has no bearing on the quality of the egg. Eggs with white shells are preferred in some areas, whereas in other markets those with brown shells are first choice.

SHELL MEMBRANES

Inside the shell of an egg are two shell membranes, one of which adheres tenaciously to the shell. These membranes are made mainly of keratin (a protein also found in human hair), together with mucin (42). After an egg is laid the contents shrink more than the shell and the two membranes are separated by a small air cell. This usually appears at the large end of an egg.

ALBUMEN

The egg proper consists of the white, known as the albumen, and the yolk. The albumen is present in three layers, an outermost layer of thin white, a layer of thick white, and another layer of thin white which lies adjacent to the yolk (42). Some hens secrete a higher ratio of thick to thin white than do

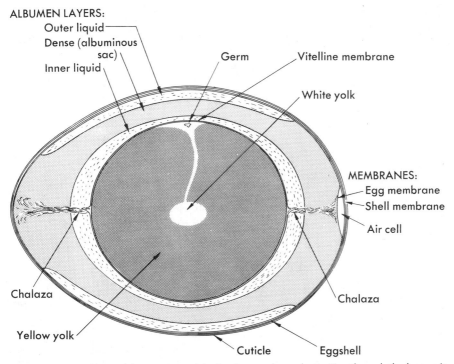

ALBUMEN LAYERS:
  Outer liquid
  Dense (albuminous sac)
  Inner liquid

Germ

Vitelline membrane

White yolk

MEMBRANES:
  Egg membrane
  Shell membrane
  Air cell

Chalaza

Chalaza

Yellow yolk

Cuticle   Eggshell

FIGURE 19-1. Diagram of the structure of the hen's egg, shown by section through the long axis. (From A. L. Romanoff and A. J. Romanoff, *The Avian Egg,* copyright © 1949 by John Wiley & Sons, Inc., New York, p. 112. Reprinted by permission.)

others. Storage conditions also affect the thickness of the albumen and the ratio of thick to thin egg white. (See the discussion of changes during storage, this Chapter.)

YOLK

Separating the egg white from the yolk, and enclosing the latter, is the yolk sac, called the "vitelline membrane." Projecting from either side of the yolk are ropelike structures called chalazae. These serve to anchor the yolk in the thick white and keep it centered in the egg, but permit the yolk to rotate.

An egg yolk consists of a small sphere of white yolk surrounded by yellow yolk. In some eggs thin bands of white yolk alternate with thicker bands of yellow around this central core. The germ spot on the surface of the yolk is attached to the white yolk in the center by the tubelike latebra. The color of an egg yolk is influenced mainly by the xanthophyll content of the ration fed the hen. Because most carotenoid pigments deposited in the yolk have no vitamin A value, more highly colored egg yolks are not necessarily richer in vitamin A.

COMPOSITION

The shell of the egg contributes 11 percent of its weight, the white 58 percent and the yolk 31 percent. The composition of egg white and yolk differ markedly as the figures in the following table show (49):

	Egg White	Egg Yolk
Water	88.0%	48.0%
Protein	11.0	17.5
Fat	.2	32.5
Minerals	.8	2.0

Eggs are an important source of high-quality protein. The laying hen ranks second to the milk cow as an efficient converter of feed protein to food protein (40).

EGG WHITE

The chief constituents in egg white, aside from water, are proteins which are secreted into the oviduct as the mature yolk traverses it, after which the egg is encapsuled by the shell (49). The main protein in egg white, more than half the total, is ovalbumin (39,50). This protein (or group of closely related protein molecules) is readily denatured by heat, a characteristic of interest when eggs are used in food preparation. Conalbumin, which like ovalbumin is coagulated by heat, accounts for about 14% of the total protein in egg white. A third protein, ovomucoid, makes up 12 percent of the total. Ovomucoid is not coagulated by heat. These three glycoproteins (or protein fractions), ovalbumin, conalbumin, and ovomucoid, account for more than 80 percent of the protein in egg white. In addition, egg white contains approximately 7 percent globulins, including lysozyme, a protein which can dissolve (lyse) the cell walls of certain bacteria. Egg white also contains ovomucin (less than 2 percent of the total protein) which contributes to the thickness of thick white and a small quantity of the protein avidin. The latter is of interest because of its ability to bind and make unavailable biotin. Avidin is easily denatured when eggs are cooked. Also present is a small amount of a protein to which the riboflavin of the egg white is bound.

EGG YOLK

Egg yolk is roughly half water and half solids. Proteins account for approximately one-third, and fats two-thirds, of the latter. The main protein in egg yolk is vitellin (39,50). In addition, egg yolk contains phosvitin (a protein unusually high in phosphorus), and livetin (high in sulfur). The fat in an egg yolk consists of triglycerides, phospholipids, and cholesterol. Vitellin is present in egg yolk as a lipoprotein complex and is referred to as lipovitellin. The main phospholipid is lecithin (phosphatidyl choline) with some phosphatidyl ethanolamine and small amount of phosphatidyl serine. Fatty acids found in the triglycerides of egg yolk are oleic, palmitic, stearic, and linoleic, in that order.

Much effort has been expended to learn the disposition of the fat and the protein in egg yolk (10,50). The literature is confusing and what follows is an attempt to summarize current understanding. Of the proteins, only livetin, a small fraction of the total in egg yolk, is dispersed in the aqueous phase. And little of the fat in egg yolk is free. Instead, the fat and most of the protein are located in particles which are suspended in the aqueous phase (plasma) of the yolk. Three types of particles have been identified—a few large spheres, granules which make up slightly more than one-fifth of the solids, and the more numerous and smaller micelles which account for approximately three-fourths of the yolk solids. The micelles contain almost 90 percent of the triglycerides as a microemulsion, the proposed structure of which is analogous to that for the fat globule membrane of milk (Fig. 17-3). Envisioned at the core of the micelle is a droplet of fat which is surrounded by a phospholipid-protein layer. Many of the functional properties of egg yolk in baking are attributed to these micelles (45). The larger granules contain the remainder of the fat, also in emulsified form. Cholesterol is found in the granules (21).

CONSTITUENTS IN THE WHITE AND IN THE YOLK OF AN EGG

Quantities of various nutrients found in an egg white and in an egg yolk (medium size) are listed in Table 19-1. Egg yolk is higher in calories than the

Table 19-1   Composition of egg white and egg yolk

	Unit	Egg White	Egg Yolk
Weight	g	29	15
Calories		15	52
Protein	g	3.2	2.4
Fat	g	Trace	4.6
Carbohydrate	g	.2	.1
Calcium	mg	3	21
Phosphorus	mg	4	85
Iron	mg	Trace	.8
Vitamin A value	I.U.	0	510
Thiamine	mg	Trace	.03
Riboflavin	mg	.08	.07
Niacin	mg	Trace	Trace
Ascorbic acid	mg	0	0

SOURCE: U.S. Dept. Agr. Agriculture Handbook No. 456. *Nutritive Value of American Foods in Common Units.* U.S. Dept. Agr., ARS. 1975.

FIGURE 19-2. Micrometer or gauge for measuring the height of thick egg white, shown in position over an egg. (Courtesy of the United States Department of Agriculture.)

white because the former contains more fat and less water. An egg white contains somewhat more protein than the yolk. The calcium of an egg is in the shell rather than in the edible part. The yolk is an excellent source of iron and of riboflavin, and the white contains an appreciable amount of the latter. The vitamin A and the thiamine of egg are found in the yolk.

QUALITY OF EGGS

A freshly laid egg has a high proportion of thick white which resists spreading when the egg is broken from the shell. Thick white appears to be a weak, transparent gel in which are embedded parallel, translucent bands (Fig. 19-7). There is general agreement that ovomucin contributes to the physical properties of thick white, but the role of lysozyme is still at issue. One theory is that the gel-like character of thick white is the result of interaction between lysozyme and ovomucin (9,12). An opposing theory attributes the thickness to ovomucin alone (41). The height of thick egg white, that is, its resistance to spreading, can be measured objectively by a micrometer as shown in Figure 19-2. The yolk of a fresh egg is upstanding and it remains centered in the white. Few eggs are consumed on the day they are laid. Unless eggs are handled properly the quality deteriorates rapidly during storage.

CHANGES DURING STORAGE

A number of changes take place in eggs during storage. The air cell enlarges because of a loss of moisture. More important from the standpoint of maintaining quality is loss of carbon dioxide, which permits the egg white to become more alkaline. The pH of the white may rise from about 7.6 in a freshly laid egg to as high as 9.0 to 9.7 in a few days (42). The white becomes thinner, so it spreads more when the egg is broken out. One reason proposed for the thinning of egg white is that the rise in pH when the egg loses CO_2 allows the electrostatic complex between lysozyme and ovomucin to break (12). An opposing theory is that reaction of lysozyme with ovomucin disrupts the ovomucin gel and thinning results (41). Breaking of disulfide bonds in ovomucin has been suggested as a factor in the thinning of egg white (8). In addition to thinning, the white may eventually become yellow and even cloudy. The vitelline membrane which confines the yolk stretches, and the yolk flattens. The thinner white is no longer able to keep the yolk centered in the egg.

HANDLING EGGS TO MAINTAIN QUALITY

The temperature of an egg when it is laid is that of the body of the hen, 40°C (105°F). To maintain the high quality of a freshly laid egg it must be cooled promptly, preferably to 4.4°C (40°F), and held in a cool place. The effect of storage temperature on the quality of egg albumen (16) is shown graphically in Figure 19-3. Most of the eggs on the market are infertile. Were an egg

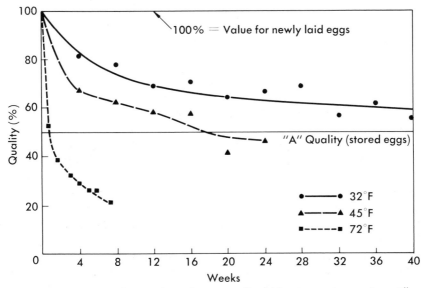

FIGURE 19-3. Albumen index (quality) of eggs as affected by storage temperature. Albumen quality declines rapidly in eggs held at room temperature. (From E. H. Dawson, C. Miller, and R. A. Redstrom, United States Department of Agriculture Bulletin No. 164, 1956.)

fertile, it would need to be cooled at least to below 20°C (68°F) or the embryo would begin to develop.

Storage of eggs in a closed container retards the loss of both moisture and carbon dioxide, as does submerging the eggs in a solution of waterglass (sodium silicate). This is a viscous liquid that plugs the pores of the shells. Eggs so treated and stored in a cool place will keep from four to six months and may be higher in quality than eggs only a few days old which have been improperly handled. Coating eggs with mineral oil (16) fills the pores and makes the shell less permeable to water vapor and carbon dioxide and so delays deterioration in quality of eggs during storage. Thermostabilizing eggs (dipping in warm mineral oil for a few minutes) is particularly effective in maintaining quality of stored eggs.

CANDLING EGGS

Candling is the method used to assess the quality of an egg without removing it from the shell. The appearance of the egg is observed as it is rotated with a strong light behind it (49). The electronic eye is replacing the human eye for this examination. Factors which are used as an index to the grade of an egg when it is candled are size and position of the air cell, clearness of white, position and mobility of the yolk and the shadow cast by it, and the condition of the shell. On the basis of the above characteristics eggs may be assigned to U.S. quality grades AA, A, B, and C. Break-out characteristics of eggs for the different grades (49) are shown in Figure 19-4. It should be noted that the quality of eggs for any one grade may be high, medium, or low. And due to difficulties inherent in assessing quality of eggs by candling, 20 percent of the eggs may actually grade lower than the label indicates.

FUNCTIONAL PROPERTIES OF EGGS OF DIFFERENT GRADES

The grade of an egg is more important for some uses to which eggs are put than for others. Eggs of AA grade are essential for high quality in fried or poached egg (17). A fried or poached egg of high quality is compact, and the yolk is centered in and covered by a thick layer of coagulated white. (See Fig. 19-5). The lower the grade of the egg the flatter is the cooked product, the thinner the coating of white over the top of the yolk, and the more ragged the edges of the white. If the egg is of lower grade, the yolk moves off center in eggs hard cooked in the shell, just as it does in those poached or fried. Differences in scrambled eggs, muffins, shortened cakes, and soft pie fillings due to the quality of egg are not detectable. However, the volume, tenderness, and acceptability of angel food cake is less when made with eggs of lower quality (16). Off-flavor associated with storage eggs of lower quality is more noticeable in soft cooked eggs than in either custard or angel food cake, no doubt because other ingredients partially mask the off flavor of the eggs.

RESISTANCE OF EGGS TO SPOILAGE

Eggs are unique among foods of animal origin in that, with minimum precautions, they may be kept in common storage for an appreciable time without spoiling (although deteriorating in *quality*) even though the shell may be fairly heavily contaminated. A number of factors contribute to the superior keeping quality of eggs. Although the shell of an egg is porous, the pores normally are filled with organic material which hinders the entrance of microorganisms into the egg unless the surface is damp. The two membranes inside the shell, and particularly the inner one, act as the first effective line of defense against microbial invasion of the egg proper (33). Equally important, the white itself contains substances with antibacterial action (19). The most effective germicidal agent in the white is lysozyme, which lyses (dissolves) the cell membranes of some bacteria. The lower the pH of the egg the more effective is lysozyme, an added reason for preventing loss of carbon dioxide from eggs. Avidin, which binds biotin, a nutrient needed by certain microorganisms, thus curtails their growth. A third constituent in the white of an egg which enables it to resist microorganisms that might invade it is conalbumin, which unites with iron and makes it unavailable. Thus microorganisms for which iron is essential are unable to grow. Should salmonella penetrate the inner membrane, however, these food poisoning microorganisms can multiply in the white (1).

Once an egg is broken from the shell, the contents are heavily contaminated and the natural defenses of the egg no longer are able to cope with the load of microorganisms. Eggs out of the shell are highly perishable, must be kept cold at all times, and used promptly.

PRESERVING EGGS BY FREEZING AND DRYING

Eggs, in addition to storage in the shell, may be preserved either by freezing or by drying. Egg whites freeze satisfactorily without preliminary treatment. Egg yolk and blended whole egg untreated are not satisfactory after frozen storage. The egg, after thawing, is thick, pseudo-plastic, and lumpy. The undesirable consistency is attributed to aggregation of lipoproteins, possibly due to change in the structure of water brought about by freezing (11,26). Addition of salt, sugar, or corn syrup to egg yolk prior to freezing yields thawed yolk with near normal fluidity (34). Once thawed, frozen eggs should be used promptly.

Whole egg, egg yolk, and egg white are available in dried form, the latter as freeze, foam-spray, and spray dried. Eggs in dried form are used extensively in packaged mixes. Recipes using dried eggs are available. Pasteurization of the broken-out eggs prior to drying eliminates the possibility of their being carriers of the food poisoning bacteria of the salmonella group. The sensitivity of salmonella to heat parallels that of the α-amylase of the yolk, so the ade-

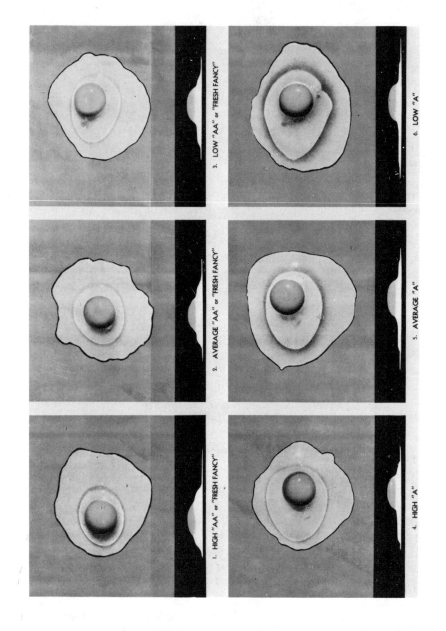

1. HIGH "AA" or "FRESH FANCY"
2. AVERAGE "AA" or "FRESH FANCY"
3. LOW "AA" or "FRESH FANCY"
4. HIGH "A"
5. AVERAGE "A"
6. LOW "A"

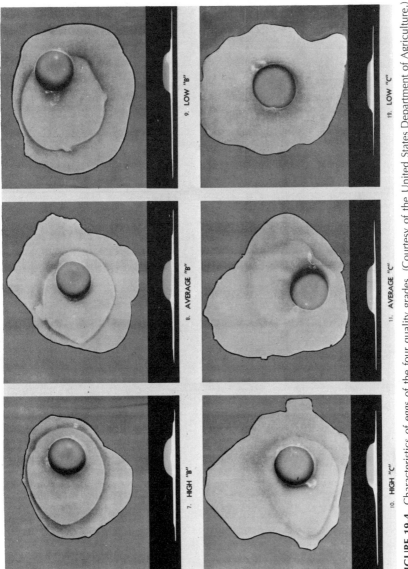

FIGURE 19-4. Characteristics of eggs of the four quality grades. (Courtesy of the United States Department of Agriculture.)

FIGURE 19-5. A poached egg of high quality has an upstanding yolk and a thick, compact white. (Courtesy of the Poultry and Egg National Board.)

quacy of pasteurization of egg yolk or whole egg can be assessed by testing for residual α-amylase, using the starch-iodine method (37).

SIZE OF EGGS

Eggs vary markedly in size and are classed according to one of six sizes, jumbo, extra large, large, medium, small, and peewee. Successive sizes differ in weight by three ounces per dozen. The smallest eggs, peewee, which weigh 15 ounces per dozen, are half as large as jumbo, which weigh 30 ounces per dozen. When a recipe calls for an egg, it is understood that the egg will be one of medium size. Such eggs weigh 21 ounces per dozen. Each medium egg white has a volume of 30 milliliters and the yolk a volume of 18 milliliters, giving a total of 48 milliliters for a medium-sized whole egg.

USES OF EGGS IN COOKING

Eggs are often cooked and served as the main protein dish in a meal, and they are important also in the making of a number of prepared dishes. Eggs are a means of introducing air into many baked products, especially sponge and angel cakes. They provide emulsifier for shortened cakes, cream puffs, cheese soufflés, and mayonnaise. They serve as a thickening agent in soft pie fillings, in cooked salad dressing, and in stirred custard, and as a gelling agent in baked custard. Eggs supply liquid in batters and doughs, essential for the pasting of starch, and are a source of steam to leaven cream puffs, popovers, and angel and sponge cake. They act as a structural ingredient to give rigidity to the crumb of quick breads, cakes, and soufflés. The important role of eggs in baking is attributed in large measure to the low density lipoprotein micelles (30,45).

EFFECT OF HEAT ON EGG PROTEINS

As is true of many proteins, those in egg (ovomucoid in the white excepted) are denatured by heat, after which coagulation occurs. Ovalbumin, the main protein in egg white, is readily denatured by heat. But denaturation of the ovomucin-lysozyme complex may be the first step in the coagulation of egg white (20). To account for the change in egg white from a thick, transparent liquid to an opaque, white coagulum when it is cooked, it has been suggested that the input of energy may have disrupted the crystalline hydrates of water which surround nonpolar side chains on the exterior of protein molecules. According to the theory the unmasked molecules then aggregate by hydrophobic bonding. (31).

Egg yolk, a thick liquid, no longer flows when cooked; it becomes solid, but with a mealy texture. The range in temperatures over which coagulation takes place varies with the rate of heating. In the case of ovalbumin an increase in temperature of 10 degrees increases the rate of coagulation more than 600 times. At high temperatures the rate of coagulation is so rapid that it is almost instantaneous. Eggs exposed to heat of high intensity are overcoagulated before they can be removed. The proteins of egg whites are more sensitive to coagulation by heat than are those of the yolk. In undiluted egg white, coagulation may begin near 60°C (140°F), with the white no longer able to flow near 65°C (149°F). Coagulation of the yolk begins near 65°C (149°F), and the yolk no longer flows when the temperature nears 70°C (158°F) (35). Heating undiluted egg much beyond this temperature shrinks and toughens the coagulum of the white. When diluted as for custard or in the presence of sugar, the coagulation temperature is elevated.

BASIC METHODS OF EGG COOKERY

SOFT- AND HARD-COOKED EGGS IN THE SHELL. Cooking an egg in the shell is probably the simplest method of all. A pan with one pint of boiling water for each egg is required with the heat turned off as soon as the eggs go in. The pan should be kept in a warm place. To cook a number of eggs, less water may be used and the heat adjusted to maintain the water at simmering temperature.

The eggs are left in the hot water until they are coagulated to the stage of doneness desired. For a soft-cooked egg the white should be the consistency of soft, quivery jelly and the yolk a thick liquid. This requires from 3 to 5 minutes. An additional 2 minutes should be allowed if eggs are at refrigerator temperature.

Eggs hard cooked in the shell need to stay in the water until the white becomes an opaque tender gel and until the yolk becomes a pale yellow and has a mealy rather than a pasty consistency. Heat is transmitted from hot water around the egg to the yolk through the coagulating white by conduction. To get the yolk hot enough to coagulate, the surrounding white must be heated somewhat beyond its coagulation temperature. At best, the white is somewhat overcooked by the time the yolk is fully cooked. The yolk can be hard cooked with minimum damage to the white if the water in which the egg is cooked is not above 85°C (185°F). In this way the white is not excessively overheated before heat is conducted to the yolk. If the temperature of the water is too low, cooking time is excessively long, the white is so tender it is difficult to remove the shell without tearing the white, and the yolk is waxy and the color of an uncooked egg. It takes less time to hard-cook eggs in the shell in boiling water (12 minutes compared to 25-35 minutes in water at simmering temperature), but the white of an egg hard cooked in boiling water is rubbery and tough.

The white of an egg which has been boiled may discolor, the browning a result of the reaction between glucose and amine groups of certain proteins of the white (4). The longer the egg remains at elevated temperature and the more alkaline the egg, the greater the discoloration. Cracking may be a problem when eggs are cooked in the shell. In one study, fewer shells cracked when eggs were put in water already boiling instead of in cold water brought to a boil subsequently (28). The shells were easier to remove, too. For some reason, more shells cracked when a hole was drilled in the large end of the egg.

Occasionally a greenish-gray layer may be observed on the surface of the yolk of an egg which has been hard cooked in the shell. The iron sulfide responsible for this discoloration is attributed to a reaction between the iron of the yolk and hydrogen sulfide liberated from sulfur-containing proteins. The alkalinity of the white which is in contact with the yolk favors the reaction (5). The discoloration is similar to that on the tines of a silver fork used to eat eggs, except that on the fork the deposit is silver sulfide.

The higher the temperature of the water and the longer the egg is heated, the more hydrogen sulfide liberated. The surface of the yolk of an egg hard cooked in boiling water will be darker than that of an egg cooked in water at simmering temperature. Loss of carbon dioxide and the resultant increase in the alkalinity of the egg favor the production of hydrogen sulfide, as does slow cooling of hard-cooked egg in the shell. When an egg is done, it should be placed in water to cool and the shell removed. The resultant lower temperature and pressure near the outside of the egg help draw hydrogen sulfide away from the surface of the yolk. To hard-cook an egg with the minimum discoloration of the yolk, a fresh egg should be cooked in water at simmering temperature, followed by removal of the shell and prompt cooling. Egg yolk alone with the vitelline membrane intact may be hard cooked in hot water.

It is sometimes difficult to remove the shell from a hard-cooked egg without some of the white adhering. This is likely to happen if the egg is fresh (less than 48 hours old) or if the shell has been dipped to prevent the loss of carbon dioxide. Ease of removing the shell from a hard-cooked egg is associated with a high pH (8.7 or above). In fact, the white of a fresh egg (less than 2 hours old) made alkaline by exposure to ammonia vapor for 10 minutes parts with the shell cleanly (47). Cooling the egg in ice water for 1 minute followed by 10 seconds reheating facilitates removal of the shell (23).

POACHED EGG. An egg to be poached is turned from the shell and promptly put to cook in hot water as for egg soft cooked in the shell. The egg is left in the hot water until the white is jellylike and uniformly coagulated and the yolk semiliquid and covered by a thick coating of white. Ideally, a poached egg should be compact with no ragged edges (see Fig. 19-5). This necessitates an egg of top quality. The technique used to put the egg in the water influences somewhat how much the white will spread. Use of an egg poacher eliminates spreading of the white.

FRIED EGG. To prevent a fried egg from spreading and to coagulate it in a reasonable time, the pan needs to be preheated. However, popping, spattering, and bubbling of the white, due to the formation of steam, occur when an egg contacts fat or a utensil that is too hot. A frying temperature of 137°C has been suggested (2). When an egg is fried in just enough fat to prevent its sticking to the pan, heat must move from the surface of the egg in contact with the frying pan up through the egg, a slow process. If the pan is too hot, the under surface of the egg will be overcoagulated and toughened before heat reaches the upper surface. A tough, brown edge on a fried egg is coagulated, dehydrated, shrunken, and partially scorched protein. This "cracked" protein is flavorful, however. The egg may be turned or a small amount of water may be added and a lid placed on the pan so that steam may speed cooking of the upper surface. When more fat is used in the pan to fry an egg, heat penetration is faster. Cooking may be speeded by basting the top of the egg with hot fat. The white of a fried egg should be thick and compact. It should be uniformly coagulated and tender. The yolk should be unbroken and covered with a layer of coagulated white.

SCRAMBLED EGG. For scrambled egg, the yolk and white are blended with or without the addition of a small amount (1 tablespoon) of milk or cream per egg. The mixture is then heated to effect coagulation of the proteins. The secret of making scrambled egg that is moist (but not watery), tender, and fluffy is to heat the mix slowly and scrape the egg from the edges and bottom of the pan as it coagulates. This prevents the cooked part from being overcoagulated and allows the uncoagulated part to contact the hot pan. Once the coagulum forms, the egg should be removed from the heat. If scrambled eggs are over-heated, excessive shrinkage of the coagulum squeezes out liquid temporarily. The heat soon evaporates this, with the result that the product is shrunken, tough, and dry. Cooking scrambled eggs in a double boiler gives better control over the intensity of heat applied to cook the eggs. A glass double boiler makes it possible to have a better view of the cooking progress. If scrambled eggs are not served promptly, they either cool or, if kept hot, they are likely to be overcooked. They can be held for a short time over hot water if the partially cooked eggs are combined with a medium white sauce (⅓ to ½ cup for 6 eggs).

A French or plain omelet differs from scrambled egg in the way it is cooked. The mixture for a French omelet is cooked in an oiled frying pan. Instead of scraping the coagulum from the frying pan as it forms, it is lifted from the pan only enough to allow uncooked egg to come in contact with the pan. A French omelet, unlike a puffy omelet (see section on puffy omelet near the end of this chapter), is flat, in one piece, and of the size and shape of the pan. It is customary to roll a French omelet as it is turned from the pan onto the serving plate, so the coagulum should be soft and flexible. One egg will yield a French omelet 6 inches in diameter.

In one study, the loss of thiamine from eggs cooked by four methods (in the shell, fried, poached, and scrambled) averaged 15 percent. Loss of riboflavin ranged from 1.5 percent for scrambled to 16.5 percent for poached, and averaged 7.7 percent for the four methods (46). Another study found no loss of riboflavin from eggs hard cooked in the shell, approximately 10 percent for scrambled, 16 percent for fried eggs, and up to 24 percent in baked meringues (25).

CUSTARDS

The ingredients in custard are egg, sugar, and milk, plus salt and vanilla for flavor. The egg, sugar, and salt are blended before the milk is added. The milk is usually scalded (heated to approximately 85°C, or 185°F) because this improves the flavor and may shorten the cooking time. The coagulable protein from one whole egg or two egg yolks is sufficient to thicken or gel one cup of milk. Less than 1 percent of the gel is due to proteins from the milk. However, salts supplied by the milk are essential for gelation of a custard mixture (35).

When a custard mixture of one egg and one cup of milk is baked, it no longer flows. Molecules of egg protein, mainly ovalbumin, which are denatured by heat, unite to form a network which enmeshes the fluid milk and so forms a gel. Heating undiluted egg causes a gel to form too, but a custard is a more fragile gel.

The baking utensil that contains the custard mix is placed in a pan of hot water and put into a moderate oven (177°C, or 350°F) for the custard to bake. Alternately, the custard mixture may be cooked on a surface unit, usually in the top of a double boiler. The mixture should be cooked surrounded by hot water (85°–90°C, or 185°–194°F) but not over boiling water. To equalize the temperature, the custard should be stirred continuously as it cooks. The product is referred to as a soft custard. A soft custard does not become as firm as a baked custard because stirring breaks up the gel as it forms. It does thicken, however. A soft custard is a base for Spanish cream which is caused to gel by the addition of gelatin.

The temperature to which a custard must be heated for it to thicken (or gel) is influenced by a number of factors. The temperature is higher than that required to coagulate the egg because the protein of the egg is diluted with milk. Whether sugar was omitted or doubled in a standard recipe made no difference in gel strength or firmness (sensory) of a baked custard, but sugar did make the custard more translucent and the crust more tender (51). Acid, on the other hand, lowers the setting temperature. Because of the acid supplied by the fruit, baked custard which contains slices of dried figs or dates gets done sooner than one without fruit. The higher the proportions of egg to milk, the lower the temperature at which the custard sets. But two egg yolks in the place of one egg raises the coagulation temperature.

When a stirred custard is cooked, there are advantages to having the temperature rise slowly, especially after the mix reaches 75°C (167°F). A custard heated slowly begins to thicken at a lower temperature, thickens gradually over a wider temperature range, and is done at a lower temperature (35). If the mix is heated rapidly, it must be heated to a higher temperature before it begins to thicken and a difference of only 1 to 3 degrees may separate the beginning of thickening and the appearance of curds. Ten to 12 minutes for the temperature of the mix to rise from 75°C (167°F) to 83°–85°C (181°–185°F), near which temperature the custard should be done, provides an adequate margin of safety between the initiation of thickening and the appearance of curds. The temperature of the mix within this range may remain stationary or even drop momentarily as the proteins coagulate. A baked custard from the same mix as a soft custard can tolerate a somewhat higher internal temperature. The effect of homogenized milk on heat penetration in custard was discussed in Chapter 17.

A custard heated beyond gelation temperature is likely to curdle, as is one held at gelation temperature for a time. For this reason, once a custard has reached the consistency desired, the utensil that contains it should be placed in cold water at once. Overheating a custard shrinks the gel. An overheated stirred custard separates into curds and whey. The texture and consistency of a curdled custard can be improved by removing it from the heat and beating it as soon as the curds appear. An overheated baked custard becomes porous, the pores filled with watery serum. This expulsion of liquid from a gel is an example of syneresis. Stirred custard is more sensitive to overheating than is a baked one.

A soft custard is done when it forms a thick, velvety coating on the spoon

FIGURE 19-6. A soft cooked custard is done when it forms a thick, velvety coating on a spoon. (Photograph by Wilbur Nelson.)

or other utensil used to stir it. (See Fig. 19-6). A stirred custard should be smooth and have the consistency of whipping cream. It will thicken somewhat as it cools. A baked custard is done when a silver knife inserted in the center comes out free of milky fluid. An alternate way to assess the doneness of a baked custard is to tilt the container to see whether the milk at the center still flows. A baked custard of high quality is a tender gel, uniformly coagulated and with no signs of porosity.

Baking a custard pie filling in an unbaked pie shell demands unreconcilable conditions. If the pie is baked at the high temperature recommended for the crust, the filling is likely to be porous and to weep. If baking temperature is low, delay in setting the filling permits absorption of liquid by the crust. Either way a soggy lower crust is likely. The only sure way to avoid this is to bake crust and filling separately and then transfer baked, cooled filling to the crust. This has hazards, too, and requires steady nerves and some dexterity.

A quiche Lorraine is a baked entrée made with unsweetened custard filling poured over cheese and cooked bacon bits in an unbaked pastry shell. The quiche is then baked as for a custard pie.

SOFT PIE FILLING

Egg yolk is used in cooked salad dressing and in many soft pie fillings to supplement the thickening power of the starch. The usual practice in making pie filling is to incorporate the yolk into the cooked starch paste. Unless the filling is heated sufficiently after the yolk is added, the filling will thin as it stands in the baked pie shell. Eggs contain α-amylase, the enzyme content of the yolk being much higher than that of the white (29). Heating whole egg 3.5 minutes at 60°C inactivates less than half of the enzyme; heating the yolk, approximately one-fourth. Addition of sugar (10 percent) to yolk held at 63°C lowers inactivation to about 6 percent (37). The higher the proportion of sugar in a pie filling, the higher the temperature needed to prevent thinning. Heating a cream pie filling which has approximately one-third as much sugar as liquid (v/v) to 85°C will prevent thinning, whereas a butterscotch filling in which the ration of sugar to liquid is twice as high must be heated to a higher temperature.

EGG FOAMS

FOAM-FORMING PROPERTIES OF EGG WHITE PROTEINS

General information on foams and foam formation is found in Chapter 17. Egg white is a viscous liquid of colloidally dispersed proteins in water. The liquid may be converted into a foam by beating or whipping air bubbles into it. The ease with which egg white can be whipped to a fine foam with small air cells is attributed to the presence of globulins, ovomucin, and conalbumin (13,38). Duck eggs, deficient in globulins, do not foam well, nor do hen's eggs from which globulins have been removed (36). Laminations observed in thick egg white (as shown in Fig. 19-7) are attributed to ovomucin (18). When egg white is first beaten, layers of ovomucin are sheared from the white. These coil to form hollow tubes, with the appearance of fibers. Egg white beats to a better foam when these fibers do not exceed 300 to 400 microns in length. Perhaps rapid initial beating of egg white, which results in a foam with larger volume, does so because it shears layers of ovomucin to an optimum length. Molecules of ovomucin not only contribute viscosity to egg white, but when spread in a monomolecular layer at the interface between air in the bubbles and the thinning films of liquid around them, they uncoil, exposing reactive R-groups. Molecules of such surface-denatured proteins unite through reactive R-groups and so stabilize the foam. Excessive beating (and denaturation), however, results in a foam that is inelastic. Ovomucin is less concentrated in the drainage from egg white foam than in the unbeaten white and together with conalbumin, lysozyme, and globulins is retained in the drained foam (13). The lysozyme content of egg white may influence its foaming potential; whites higher in lysozyme yielded foams with lower volumes when whipping times were the same (44).

Finally, coagulation of protein when an egg foam is cooked gives permanence to the foam. Egg white and particularly the ovalbumin is readily coagulated by heat.

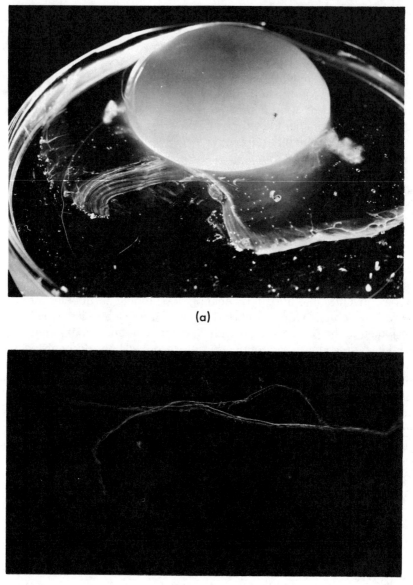

(a)

(b)

FIGURE 19-7. Structure of thick egg white. (a) Cross section of thick white. Whole egg placed in distilled water; layering revealed by cutting thick white. Oblique illumination. (b) Blending or beating egg white shears off layers that curl to give "fibers," usually several centimeters long. Dark field illumination. (From R. H. Forsythe and D. H. Bergquist, *Poultry Science* **30:** 305, 1951. Reprinted by permission.)

STAGES TO WHICH EGG WHITES ARE BEATEN

As air is beaten into egg whites, the mass becomes foamy, but it remains transparent and can still flow. If beating is stopped at this stage, the liquid drains from around the large air cells and the bubbles coalesce. If beating continues, large air cells incorporated at the foamy stage are subdivided and additional air is introduced. As the number of air cells increases, the film of liquid around each becomes thinner and thinner. The result is that egg white thickens as it is beaten.

As beating continues the foam gets thicker, finer, and whiter. Soon it begins to form peaks as the beater is withdrawn. The peaks become more definite and more permanent as beating continues. They progress from soft peaks with rounded tops (see Fig. 20-3) to stiff peaks with sharp points. This gradual stiffening of the foam is attributed to surface denaturation of protein (36).

Egg whites are beaten to different stages for incorporation into various products. It is important to have clearly in mind the stage to which the egg white should be beaten before starting. Equally important is the ability to recognize when the beaten egg has reached the stage desired. Once the optimum stage is reached for the particular product, the foam should be used promptly; otherwise it will stiffen upon standing *without additional beating*.

Up to a point the volume of an egg foam increases with continued beating. Should the foam be beaten beyond the stiff peak (but still shiny) stage, it takes only a few additional revolutions of the blades of the beater to make the foam stiff, dry, and opaque and curdled in appearance. The surface-denatured protein in the film is rendered insoluble and the film around the air cells is no longer elastic (7). The protein in such an overbeaten foam behaves as though it had been cooked. Liquid drains from the film and the bubbles coalesce (Fig. 19-8). Thus coagulation of egg proteins can be caused by both beating and heating.

Once egg whites are beaten, they should be combined with other ingredients *at once*. If egg white foam beaten no more than to the soft-peak stage stands for more than a few seconds, the foam stiffens and loses its elasticity. When it is combined with other ingredients, air cells are ruptured.

FACTORS AFFECTING EGG WHITE FOAMS

A number of factors influence the quality of an egg foam. The utensils used to produce the foam are important. The bowl should be large enough to allow for the expansion in volume. If it is too large, however, especially at the base, the blades of the beater will whip more air than egg.

A good foam can be obtained by beating eggs with either a rotary beater or a wire whip, but the construction of the implement is important. The finer the wire or the thinner the blade, the smaller are the cells and the finer is the

I

II

(a)

(b)

(c)

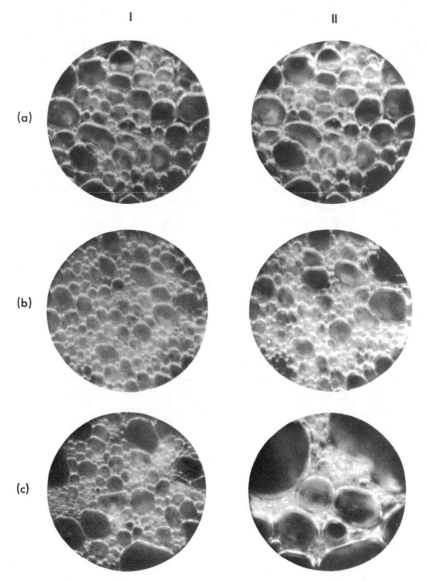

FIGURE 19-8. Effects of extent of beating on the structure and the stability of egg white foams. Photomicrographs in column I are of foams taken 2 minutes after beating stopped. Note the finer cells in Ib (foam beaten for 2 minutes) compared with the underbeaten foam in Ia and with the overbeaten foam in Ic. Coalescence of cells after foams stood for 10 minutes (column II) is especially marked in the overbeaten foam in IIc. Magnification × 27. (From Mark Barmore, Colorado Agricultural Experiment Station Technical Bulletin 9, 1934.)

foam. When the beating is done by hand, thin whites whip faster and give foams slightly larger in volume than do thick whites (43). There is some advantage in using a hand beater for thin whites because the likelihood of overbeating them is not so great. If the egg white is very viscous, it is difficult to shear it fast enough with a hand-operated beater to get the best volume. When the blades of the beater are propelled by electric rather than muscle power, thick whites whip to a foam with good volume and fine texture (3) and are somewhat less likely to be overbeaten than are thin whites.

Egg whites whip more readily at room temperature (21°C, or 70°F) than at refrigerator temperature (43). The volume of the foam is greater and the texture finer. Egg whites are too viscous to whip readily when cold. Egg whites that have been frozen and then thawed whip as well or better than unfrozen (3).

Reconstituted dried egg whites require a much longer time to whip than do fresh egg whites. Prior to drying, egg whites are pasteurized to eliminate salmonella microorganisms. The heating needed to make the eggs safe to eat greatly increases the whipping time (32). This has been attributed to damage to the lysozyme-ovomucin complex (20), but another reason may be the lability of conalbumin to heat (14). Heat denaturation of the lysozyme-ovomucin complex, which results in a dry foam that tends to break as the blades of the beater are incorporating additional air bubbles, has been suggested also as a factor contributing to the longer beating time for dried egg whites (20).

The presence of fat, even in small amounts, interferes with the foaming of egg whites and reduces the foam volume (3,43). The directions on packages of angel food cake mix specify use of a bowl other than plastic because of the difficulty of removing traces of fat which cling tenaciously to a plastic surface. Should a yolk be broken when the white and yolk are being separated, it is difficult to remove traces of the yolk from the white. To identify the foam depressant(s) in egg yolk, three yolk fractions, lipovitellenin, lipovitellin, and livetin, were isolated and each added separately to egg whites used to make angel food cake. The two lipoproteins but not the livetin reduced cake volume (15). Data from the study appeared to suggest that the lipoproteins interfered with the foaming potential of ovomucin and lysozyme.

Salt is used for flavor in recipes that contain egg white. Acid, usually cream of tartar or lemon juice, is used to make the foam more stable (7). Both ingredients delay the formation of a foam. For this reason, egg whites are beaten to the foamy stage before acid and salt are added. In addition to delaying foam formation, acid reduces somewhat the volume of the beaten egg white.

Dilution of egg white with water, up to 40 percent of the volume of the egg, increases the volume of the foam as much as would an equivalent volume of egg. Addition of liquid to eggs used to make omelet and sponge cake makes both products more tender too. However, water added to egg whites used in meringues increases leakage.

If sugar is added to egg white before beating is started, extensive beating is needed to produce a foam (24). Once formed, the foam is stable and very fine although the volume may be less. The shininess of egg white foam with added sugar is due in part to the prevention of coagulation of the protein with the accompanying opaqueness. Once sugar is added to egg white beaten to the foamy stage, to the soft-peak, or even to the stiff-peak stage, beating can continue longer without the foam being overbeaten. After sugar has been beaten into a foam, it can stand for some time without becoming coagulated and losing its elasticity. The foam can be manipulated and spread without rupturing the air cells.

EGG YOLK FOAMS

Although egg white foams are far more common, yolk too may be converted into a foam. Two foods in which egg yolk foams are used are puffy omelet and sponge cake (Chapter 20). Yolks require more extensive beating than do the whites. Yolks become lighter in color and thicker as air bubbles are beaten in, but yolk proteins are not surface-denatured and the foam does not stiffen or set as does one made from egg whites. Even so, egg yolk foam should be used without undue delay because the larger gas bubbles tend to rise to the surface and liquid drain to the bottom of the foam.

MERINGUES

Meringues are egg white foams into which sugar has been incorporated. There are two kinds of meringues, soft ones used as toppings for cream, lemon, and chocolate pies, and hard meringues used as confections or to make a base for the filling in lemon angel pie. Soft meringues are made with a minimum of 2 tablespoons (30 ml) of sugar per egg white, with 2½ tablespoons (38 ml) per egg white possibly giving a meringue superior in appearance and one which cuts more readily (22). Because an average egg white measures 2 tablespoons (30 ml), the water in the egg white is converted into a fairly concentrated syrup.

To make meringue, egg whites are beaten to the foamy stage and then salt is added. Beating is continued until the foam barely flows in the bowl, at which point portions of sugar are added without delay and beaten into the foam. After the last portion of sugar is added, the meringue is beaten until it is fine grained and fairly thick, but will still form peaks with rounded tops. A meringue is more stable when sugar is beaten rather than folded in.

Meringues may be of poor quality because of faulty manipulation. If the egg white is overbeaten before sugar is added, the volume of the meringue will be low and it will have a curdled look. If the meringue is underbeaten after the sugar is added, it will have a low volume, will shrink unduly, and will have a slick and shiny surface. Meringues beaten until they are very stiff after the sugar is added have fine cells, but the surface looks dull after the meringue is baked.

Soft meringues are spread on soft pie fillings and baked. The object of baking is to coagulate the protein and stabilize the foam without causing undue shrinkage. Baking may cause defects in soft meringues, two of which are difficult to avoid. One, usually referred to as "weeping," is the accumulation of liquid where the meringue and the filling meet. This is attributed to leakage from the meringue due to undercoagulation of the foam (27). Leakage is likely to be least when the meringue is baked on a hot filling (60°–77°C, or 140°–170°F). The second defect, the appearance of amber-colored droplets of syrup on the surface of baked meringues, is attributed to overcoagulation of the protein in the foam (27). Beading is more likely to occur on meringues baked on hot fillings. If a meringue is baked on a hot filling to minimize leakage, beading can be minimized by baking the meringue in a hot oven for a short time (425°F, or 218°C, for 4½ minutes). Too, a baking temperature of 425°F gives more tender and less sticky meringues. The incorporation of a whipping aid or a vegetable gum (algin or guar) failed to decrease the percent sag and greater compactness of meringues baked in a microwave oven (6).

A soft meringue of high quality is fluffy, slightly moist, and tender. The surface should be a light brown with little contrast in color between peaks and depressions. The surface should be fine grained and have a glossy sheen.

Hard meringues contain ¼ cup (60 ml) of sugar per egg white. The egg whites are beaten to the soft peak stage, the sugar is added, and beating is continued until the foam forms stiff peaks. The meringue mixture may be spooned onto an oiled baking sheet. Hard meringues are baked at a lower temperature (250°F or 120°C) and for a longer time (60 minutes or more) than are soft meringues. Hard meringues should be dry, crisp, and tender. They should look puffy and be a delicate brown.

PUFFY OMELET

To make a puffy omelet, the egg yolks with the added liquid should be beaten first and until they are very *thick* and light lemon in color. The yolks will not stiffen as do the whites, but they should be beaten thoroughly. Then the whites are beaten until they are stiff but not dry. Without delay the two foams should be combined with a gentle folding technique until the mixture is homogeneous. This mixture is unstable and will separate into a more dense layer below and a lighter foamy layer above unless it is cooked promptly.

The oiled pan in which the mixture is cooked should be preheated. It should not be too hot, however, because this produces a hard layer on the surface of the omelet next to the cooking utensil. Omelets may be cooked on a surface unit or in the oven. When an omelet that is cooking on a surface unit begins to set around the edges, the pan may be covered and the heat lowered to complete cooking. It will cook faster covered, but should the omelet touch the lid it is likely to fall when the lid is removed. Alternately the omelet can be placed under the broiler for a short time to coagulate the uppermost layers. Heat penetrates the omelet mainly by conduction. The slow transfer of heat by conduction is doubly slow in puffy omelet because of the air bubbles which act as insulators. Baking a puffy omelet in an uncovered pan in a slow oven (325°F or 163°C) presents less of a problem than cooking it on a surface unit.

A puffy omelet should be light and puffy, uniformly cooked throughout, and have no islands of unblended white. It should be tender, slightly moist, and a delicate uniform brown.

SOUFFLÉ AND FONDUE

A fondue is a less concentrated protein dish than a soufflé, as the following listing of ingredients shows:

Ingredients	Cheese Fondue	Cheese Soufflé
Milk	1 cup	½ cup
Grated cheese	1 cup	1 cup
Eggs	3–4	3–4
Salt	½ tsp	½ tsp
Butter	1 tbsp	2 tbsp
Bread	1 cup, cubed	—
Flour	—	2 tbsp

Quantities of cheese, eggs, and salt are the same in both the fondue and the soufflé, but the fondue has twice as much milk as the soufflé. The milk for a fondue is thickened with bread cubes instead of being made into a white sauce with flour. The hot milk-bread mixture for a fondue is blended with the egg yolk, the cheese is added and blended, and then the beaten egg whites are folded in. A very thick white sauce is used in a soufflé. The white sauce need not be cooked beyond the point of maximum thickness as it will finish cooking as the soufflé bakes. Egg yolks with their emulsifiers are added to the white sauce before the cheese to aid in blending. The white sauce should be warm enough to melt the fat in the cheese when the latter is added. Egg whites beaten to form stiff peaks which remain shiny are folded into the whitesauce-egg-cheese mixture. If the sauce is too thick or the egg white foam too stiff from standing or from overbeating, extensive folding is needed to blend the two and much air is lost from the beaten whites.

Both soufflé and fondue are baked in a moderate oven (350°F, or 177°C). The casserole which contains the mix is placed in a pan of hot water to protect the contents, especially that part next to the baking utensil, from a too rapid rise in temperature before the heat has time to penetrate to the interior. As these products bake, heat expands the air bubbles incorporated via the egg foam and both the soufflé and the fondue rise. Heat coagulates proteins of both egg yolk and egg white and these help to give structure to the soufflé and fondue. A high proportion of egg is needed to provide enough structure to

FIGURE 19-9. A perfect soufflé, handsome yet fragile, light, tender and steaming hot. (From *Sunset,* August 1962. Darrow M. Watt, Photographer, 188 Felton Drive, Menlo Park, CA.)

keep the product from falling as it cools. A very thick white sauce base helps too. Baking should be timed so that the product can be served as soon as it comes from the oven. Some shrinkage may be expected in both a soufflé and a fondue when they are removed from the oven, but they should not collapse. A soufflé should be fluffy and light, slightly moist, and tender. The top should be a delicate brown. (See Fig. 19-9.) A Swiss fondue differs from the type of fondue discussed above. (See Chapter 18.) A soufflé used as an entree may contain cooked meat, fish, poultry, or vegetables instead of cheese. Made with cooked fruit or melted chocolate, soufflé is suitable as a dessert.

REFERENCES

1. Adler, H. E. 1965. Salmonella in eggs—An appraisal. *Food Technol.* **19:** 623–625. A review of the hazards.
2. Andross, M. 1940. Effect of cooking on eggs. *Chem. & Ind.* **59:** 449–454. One of the early studies of simple egg cookery.
3. Bailey, M. I. 1935. Foaming of egg whites. *Ind. Eng. Chem.* **27:** 973–976. A study of some factors which influence foam formation.

4. Baker, R. C., and J. Darfler. 1969. Discoloration of egg albumen in hard-cooked eggs. *Food Technol.* **23:** 77–79. Factors responsible.

5. Baker, R. C., J. Darfler, and A. Lifshitz. 1967. Factors affecting the discoloration of hard-cooked egg yolks. *Poultry Sci.* **46:** 664–672. Compound responsible and factors favoring its formation.

6. Baldwin, R. E., R. Upchurch, and O. J. Cotterill. 1968. Ingredient effects on meringue cooked by microwaves and by baking. *Food Technol.* **22:** 1573–1576. Attempts to eliminate disadvantages of cooking soft meringues by microwaves.

7. Barmore, M. A. 1934. *The influence of chemical and physical factors on egg white foams.* Colorado Agr. Exp. Sta. Bull. No. 9. 58 pp. Effects of beating time, addition of acid, type of beater, and traces of egg yolk on stability of egg white foams.

8. Beveridge, T., and S. Nakai. 1975. Effects of sulfhydryl blocking on the thinning of egg white. *J. Food Sci.* **40:** 864–868. An attempt to account for the thinning of egg white.

9. Brooks, J., and H. P. Hale. 1959. The mechanical properties of the thick white of the hen's egg. *Biochim. Biophys. Acta* **32:** 237–250. Proposed structure of thick egg white.

10. Chang, C. H., W. D. Powrie, and O. Fennema. 1977. Microstructure of egg yolk. *J. Food Sci.* **42:** 1193–1200. Current concepts summarized.

11. Chang, C. H., W. D. Powrie, and O. Fennema. 1977. Studies on the gelation of egg yolk and plasma upon freezing and thawing. *J. Food Sci.* **42:** 1658–1665. Factors involved.

12. Cotterill, O. J., and A. R. Winter. 1955. Egg white Lysozyme. 3. The effect of pH on the lysozyme-ovomucin interaction. *Poultry Sci.* **34:** 679–686. Possible role of lysozyme in the consistency of thick white.

13. Cunningham, F. E. 1976. Properties of egg white drainage. *Poultry Sci.* **55:** 738–743. Proteins essential for foaming.

14. Cunningham, F. E. 1965. Stabilization of egg-white proteins to pasteurizing temperatures above 60°C. *Food Technol.* **19:** 1442–1447. Heat lability of egg white proteins.

15. Cunningham, F. E., and O. J. Cotterill. 1972. Performance of egg white in the presence of yolk proteins. *Poultry Sci.* **51:** 712–714. An attempt to pinpoint the foam depressant in yolk.

16. Dawson, E. H., C. Miller, and R. A. Redstrom. 1956. *Cooking quality and flavor of eggs as related to candled quality, storage conditions and other factors.* U.S. Dept. Agr. Inf. Bull. No. 164. 44 pp. Relationship of candled characteristics of eggs and their functional properties in cooking; research from three state experiment stations summarized graphically.

17. *Egg Buying Guide for Consumers.* 1954. U.S. Dept. Agr., Home and Garden Bull. No. 26. 8 pp. Official grades for eggs, weight classes and tips on buying.

18. Forsythe, R. H., and D. H. Bergquist. 1951. The effect of physical treatments on some properties of egg white. *Poultry Sci.* **30:** 302–311. The "structure" of thick white and the effect of its breakdown during foam formation.

19. Garibaldi, J. A. 1960. Factors in egg white which control growth of bacteria. *Food Research* **25:** 337–344. Bactericidal action of various components of egg white.

20. Garibaldi, J. A., J. W. Donovan, J. G. Davis, and S. L. Cimino. 1968. Heat

denaturation of the ovomucin-lysozyme electrostatic complex—a source of damage to the whipping properties of pasteurized egg white. *J. Food Sci.* **33:** 514–524. An attempt to account for the longer whipping time.

21. Garland, T. D., and W. D. Powrie. 1978. Chemical characterization of egg yolk myelin figures and low density lipoproteins isolated from egg yolk granules. *J. Food Sci.* **43:** 1210–1214. Composition of the granules.

22. Gillis, J. N., and N. K. Fitch. 1956. Leakage of baked soft meringue topping. *J. Home Econ.* **48:** 703–707. Effects of level of sugar, beating time before sugar is added, and baking time.

23. Hale, K. K., Jr., and W. M. Britton. 1974. Peeling hard cooked eggs by rapid cooling and heating. *Poultry Sci.* **53:** 1069–1077. One suggestion for alleviating the problem.

24. Hanning, F. M. 1945. Effect of sugar or salt upon denaturation produced by beating and upon the ease of formation and the stability of egg white foams. *Iowa State Coll. J. Sci.* **20:** 10–12. Beating time, foam volume, and drainage from egg foams with and without sugar; effect of salt.

25. Hanning, F. M., B. Schick, and H. J. Seim. 1949. Stability of riboflavin in eggs to cooking. *Food Research* **14:** 203–208. Effect of light (sun and artificial) and of hard cooking, scrambling, frying, and baking (angel food cake, custard, and soft meringues).

26. Hasiak, R. J., D. V. Vadehra, R. C. Baker, and L. Hood. 1972. Effect of certain physical and chemical treatments on the microstructure of egg yolk. *J. Food Sci.* **37:** 913–917. Photomicrographic evidence.

27. Hester, E. E., and C. J. Personius. 1949. Factors affecting the beading and leakage of soft meringues. *Food Technol.* **3:** 236–240. Temperature of the filling, baking time and temperature, addition of acid and quality of egg investigated.

28. Irmiter, T. F., L. E. Dawson, and J. R. Reagen. 1970. Methods of preparing hard cooked eggs. *Poultry Sci.* **49:** 1232–1236. Boiling- *vs.* cold-water start.

29. Kaga, T. 1923. Uber die fermente in Huhnerei. *Biochem. Z.* **141:** 439. Amylase in egg yolk.

30. Kamat, V. B., G. A. Lawrence, C. J. Hart, and R. Yoell. 1973. Contribution of egg yolk lipoproteins to cake structure. *J. Sci. Food Agric.* **24:** 77–88. Role of micelles and granules in sponge and pound cakes.

31. Karmas, E., and G. R. DeMarco. 1970. Denaturation thermophiles of some proteins. *J. Food Sci.* **35:** 725–727. Beef muscle and egg albumen compared.

32. Kline, L., T. F. Sugihara, M. L. Bean, and K. Ijichi. 1965. Heat pasteurization of raw liquid egg white. *Food Technol.* **19:** 1709–1718. Effect of different temperatures on salmonella and on foaming of egg white.

33. Lifshitz, A., R. C. Baker, and H. B. Naylor. 1964. The relative importance of chicken egg exterior structures in resulting bacterial penetration. *J. Food Sci.* **29:** 94–99. Shell, outer and inner membranes compared.

34. Lopez, A., C. R. Fellers, and W. D. Powrie. 1954. Some factors affecting gelation of egg yolk. *J. Milk and Food Technol.* **17:** 334–339. Effect of temperature and additives.

35. Lowe, B. 1955. *Experimental Cookery.* New York: Wiley. 573 pp.

36. MacDonnell, L. R., R. E. Feeney, H. L. Hanson, A. Campbell, and A. T. Sugihara. 1955. The functional properties of egg white proteins. *Food Technol.* **9:** 49–53. The role of globulins, ovomucin and ovalbumin in egg white foams.

37. Murthy, G. K. 1970. Thermal inactivation of alpha-amylase in various liquid egg products. *J. Food Sci.* **35:** 352–356. Whole egg and yolk compared; effects of added salt and sugar.

38. Nakamura, R., and Y. Sato. 1964. Studies on the foaming properties of chicken egg white. X. On the role of ovomucin (B) in egg white foaminess. *Agr. Biol. Chem.* **28:** 530–534. Protein essential for foaming.

39. Parkinson, T. L. 1966. The chemical composition of eggs. *J. Sci. Food Agric.* **17:** 101–111. Summary of data on the protein content.

40. Pimentel, D., W. Dritschilo, J. Krummel, and J. Kutzman. 1975. Energy and land constraints in food protein production. *Science* **190:** 754–761. Options for use of resources to meet the world's food needs.

41. Robinson, D. S., and J. B. Monsey. 1972. Changes in the composition of ovo-mucin during the liquefaction of egg white: The effects of ionic strength and magnesium salts. *J. Sci. Food Agric.* **23:** 893–904. Possible role of lysozyme in the thinning of egg white.

42. Romanoff, A. L., and A. J. Romanoff. 1949. *The Avian Egg.* New York: Wiley. 918 pp. A comprehensive treatment of the subject.

43. St. John, J. L., and I. H. Flor. 1931. A study of whipping and coagulation of eggs of varying quality. *Poultry Sci.* **10:** 71–82. Thick *vs.* thin, fresh *vs.* aged, and warmed *vs.* chilled whites, and the effect of egg yolk.

44. Sauter, E. A., and J. E. Montoure. 1972. The relation of lysozyme content of egg white to volume and stability of foam. *J. Food Sci.* **37:** 918–920. Lysozyme content and foaming properties.

45. Schultz, J. R., and R. H. Forsythe. 1967. The influence of egg yolk lipoprotein-carbohydrate interactions on baking performance. *Bakers Dig.* **41** (1): 56–57, 60–62. Proposed structure of egg yolk lipoprotein micelles and their function.

46. Stamberg, O. E., and C. F. Petersen. 1946. Riboflavin and thiamin loss in cooking eggs. *J. Am. Dietet. Assoc.* **22:** 315–317. Cooked in the shell, fried, poached, and scrambled compared.

47. Swanson, M. H. 1959. Some observations on the peeling problem of fresh and shell treated eggs when hard cooked. *Poultry Sci.* **38:** 1253–1254. pH of egg white and ease of peeling.

48. Urbain, O. M., and J. N. Miller. 1930. Relative merits of sucrose, dextrose and levulose as used in the preservation of eggs by freezing. *Ind. Eng. Chem.* **22:** 355–357. Effectiveness of the three sugars in maintaining flow properties of frozen yolks.

49. U.S. Dept. Agriculture. 1978. *Egg Grading Manual.* U.S. Dept. Agr., Handbook No. 75. 64 pp. Brief account of the formation of an egg, its structure and composition; egg grades and grading.

50. Vadehra, D. V., and K. R. Nath. 1973. Eggs as a source of protein. CRC *Critical Reviews in Food Technology* **4:** 193–309. Composition and functional properties.

51. Wang, A. C., K. Funk, and M. E. Zabik. 1974. Effect of sucrose on the quality characteristics of baked custard. *Poultry Sci.* **53:** 807–813. Effects on firmness, gel strength, flavor, translucence, and tenderness of crust.

FILM

1. *How to Cook Eggs.* Color. Fifty frames. Poultry and Egg National Board.

TWENTY

Sponge and Angel Cake

Sponge and angel food cakes are sometimes referred to as "foam" cakes. Justification for so classifying sponge and angel cakes is that a foam is formed first by beating egg whites and then adding the sugar, after which flour is incorporated into the watery film around the air cells. This designation may be misleading because almost all batters and doughs and the baked products from them are foams. A less misleading term for cakes of this type would be "meringue" cakes, because basically the batters are meringues into which cake flour has been incorporated.

DESIRABLE CHARACTERISTICS

A flat or slightly rounded top is desired in a cake of this type. The top crust should look rough, have the appearance of macaroons, and be an even, delicate brown. Crumb of angel cake should be snowy white, that of sponge cake a golden yellow; it should be slightly moist rather than either dry or sticky. Small, uniform cells with thin cell walls are desired. The crumb should be resilient yet tender. The cake should be light and have a delicate flavor (8).

INGREDIENTS AND THEIR FUNCTIONS

Both sponge and angel cake have a high proportion of egg, sugar, and water to cake flour. The ingredients supply approximately ½ cup (120 ml) more of water per cup of flour than do those for shortened cake. Fat is not used in cakes of this type, except in chiffon cake, which is made with salad oil (Table 20-1).

EGGS

Angel cake is made from egg whites; sponge and chiffon cakes usually are made of whole eggs, although a formula for sponge cake made with yolks only is available. Eggs are an important ingredient in sponge and angel cakes, both because of the quantity involved and the functions they perform. Receipes are formulated for eggs of medium size and should either peewee or extra large eggs be substituted by number, the volume of egg would be decreased or increased by nearly 30 percent. Eggs should be measured to assure the right amount.

Table 20-1   Formulas for meringue-type cakes

Ingredients	Sponge	Angel	Chiffon
Cake flour	1 cup	1 cup	1⅛ cups
Sugar	1 cup	1¼ to 1½ cups	¾ cup
Egg yolk	½ cup	—	³⁄₁₆ cup
Egg white	¾ cup	1¼ to 1½ cups	½ cup
Salt	¼ tsp	¼ tsp	½ tsp
Cream of tartar	¾ tsp	1 to 1¼ tsp	¼ tsp
Vanilla	1 tsp	1 tsp	1 tsp
Water	3 tbsp	—	⅜ cup
Salad oil	—	—	¼ cup
Baking powder	—	—	1½ tsp

Eggs serve as a means of incorporating air into the batter which, in angel food cake, provides approximately half the leaven (1). The coagulated egg protein contributes markedly to the structure of cakes of this type. Eggs furnish water, which is essential if flour is to form a batter. Part of the water serves as a source of leaven when converted to steam. Water is essential for gelatinization of the starch which helps set the cake crumb. When egg yolk alone is beaten as for sponge cake, the plasma fraction plus the low density lipoproteins contribute to aeration. The high density granules which inhibit aeration do help to retain the incorporated air (13).

Eggs of low quality give a cake of reduced volume (5). Frozen egg whites, unless they have been pasteurized, whip to a foam more readily than fresh and yield cakes of high quality (4,14). Thin frozen whites are somewhat superior to thick. Eggs are usually pasteurized before they are dried and this heating prolongs the beating time (18). Both dried egg whites and dried whole egg tolerate—in fact, require—far more beating than fresh ones to produce a fine, stable foam. Whipping reconstituted dried whole egg at 60°C (140°F) facilitates the formation of a foam (11). The poor whipping ability of dried whole eggs is attributed in part to some disruption of the emulsion in the yolk and liberation of the fat which is detrimental to foam formation (12). Even in fresh eggs traces of fat from yolk broken when an egg is separated may retard foaming of the egg white and reduce the beaten volume. The deleterious effects of a small amount of yolk in the whites on the volume and acceptability of angel food cake can be in part counteracted by the addition of 2 percent freeze-dried egg white, the effectiveness of the addition possibly due to replacement of ovoglobulin, ovomucin, or the lysozyme-ovomucin complex tied up by the yolk (17).

SUGAR

Sugar with fine granulation is preferred for meringue-type cakes. Sugar is a tenderizing agent used to counterbalance the effects of eggs and flour. For a

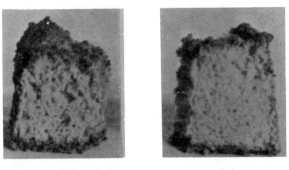

(a) (b)

(c) (d)

FIGURE 20-1. Effects of varying amounts of cream of tartar on grain and volume of angel cake. (From Emily Grewe and A. M. Child, *Cereal Chemistry* **7**: 247, 1930. Reprinted by permission.)

cake made near sea level, the weight of the sugar should not exceed the weight of the eggs by more than 25 percent. For higher altitudes (where the boiling point of water is low), the weight of sugar should be reduced or the flour increased (1). Otherwise, elevation of the coagulation temperature of egg proteins by the sugar and limited gelatinization of the starch will prevent the batter from setting (6,15). The advantage of using the maximum amount of sugar the batter will tolerate is that the cake is more tender.

ACID

Meringue-type cakes are not really successful unless the batter contains acid (9). (See Fig. 20-1.) Acid changes the pale yellowish green flavonoid pigment in egg white to colorless form. Angel food cake made with acid is snowy white compared to the pale yellow of one without acid. Acid also makes the grain of the cake finer. This favorable effect of acid on angel cake is attributed to its stabilizing action on the protein which collects at the air-liquid interface in the foam (1). Presumably, acid enables the films of protein in the air cells of the foam, which serve as the basis for the cells of the cake, to last until the heat penetrates the cake enough to set the structure of the crumb. Although the addition of acid to an egg white foam reduces its volume somewhat, cakes from such foams have larger volumes because the batter shrinks less during baking. Cakes made with acid are more tender than those without.

Recipes for meringue-type cakes specify either lemon juice or cream of tartar. Cream of tartar is superior to either citric or acetic acid, when the amount of acid added is sufficient to bring the pH of the batter to 6.0 or lower (1). The pH of angel food cake batter is near 5 compared to a pH of 8 to 9 for egg white.

FLOUR

Flour, like the proteins of egg, contributes structure to meringue-type cakes. Because of its composition and fine granulation, cake flour must be used for sponge and angel cakes if they are to be of top quality. For cakes of this type the proportion of flour should be less than half that of the eggs on a weight basis; otherwise, the cake will be tough.

MANIPULATION OF ANGEL FOOD CAKE

Angel food cake requires fewer ingredients than do other types of meringue cakes. Manipulation presents fewer problems, too. Even so, the technique used to manipulate ingredients for angel food cake may make the difference between success and failure.

MAKING THE MERINGUE

The egg whites, preferably at 21°C (70°F) (14), are beaten to the foamy stage, as shown in Figure 20-2. Salt and acid are added and beating is continued until the foam forms soft peaks but is still soft enough to flow in the bowl. (See Fig. 20-3.) When the egg foam reaches this stage, a portion of the sugar should be added *promptly*. Beating (slow speed) each addition of sugar into the egg white dissolves the sugar and stabilizes the foam, which at this point consists of air cells surrounded by films of syrup containing egg proteins. If sugar is added too soon, the egg whites must be beaten longer, but there is less danger of overbeating the foam. If egg whites are overbeaten and the foam is made inelastic before the sugar is added, the cells break during subsequent manipulation. Leaven is lost and the gas cells are unable to expand as they should during baking. A cake compact and small in volume results.

After the last portion of sugar is added the foam should be beaten until it is fine grained. Cells in the baked cake are always somewhat coarser than they were in the meringue from which the cake was made. If the meringue is underbeaten, the cells of the cake will be large, the cell walls thick, the crumb gummy, and the volume of the cake small. If the meringue is overbeaten, the cells become very small, the foam inelastic, and the cake compact and lower in volume although fine grained. If the meringue is beaten to the optimum stage, the cells of the cake will be desirably small, the cell walls thin, the crumb tender, and the volume large. Up to a point, the more the meringue

FIGURE 20-2. Egg whites are beaten to the foamy stage before salt and cream of tartar are added. (Photograph by Wilbur Nelson.)

FIGURE 20-3. Egg whites beaten to the soft peak stage. They are still glossy and moist-looking and will flow in the bowl if it is tipped. Prompt addition of sugar at this stage is essential to keep the foam from becoming stiff and inelastic. (Photograph by Wilbur Nelson.)

is beaten the larger will be the volume of the cake. However, a point is reached where denaturation of protein in the film makes it inelastic and so offsets any increase in the amount of air incorporated. Overbeaten meringues lose additional air when flour is incorporated. The character of the meringue when incorporation of the flour begins is crucial in determining the quality of the cake.

INCORPORATION OF FLOUR

The objective in folding the flour into meringue is to distribute the particles of flour uniformly in the syrupy film around the air cells. This requires deft handling. A flexible spatula or French whip may be used. Making a meringue of the egg white and part of the sugar strengthens the foam and minimizes loss of volume as flour is folded in. Too, flour can be distributed more readily if part of the sugar has been sifted with it. Sifting portions of the flour-sugar mixture over the surface of the foam and folding it into the foam *promptly* facilitates even distribution of the flour. Delay in folding may result in uneven distribution of the flour. Folding (see Figs. 20-4 and 20-5) should be gentle and should be discontinued as soon as the flour is evenly distributed. The less the batter is folded after the flour is added, the less the flour is hydrated; the longer the batter is folded, the more water the injured starch grains absorb and the tighter the batter. Undermanipulation at this stage gives a tender cake but one with coarse cells and uneven texture; overmanipulation makes for finer cells but a cake that is tougher, more compact, and smaller in volume. See Figure 20-6 for the effects of manipulation on cake quality.

FIGURE 20-4. A spatula is used to fold the sifted flour and sugar into the egg white foam into which part of the sugar has been beaten. In this view the spatula has moved across the bottom of the bowl, with the edge—not the flat surface—leading, and is ready to move up through the batter (see Figure 12-1). (Photograph by Wilbur Nelson.)

FIGURE 20-5. In this view, the spatula has just moved across the upper layers of the batter, flat edge parallel with the surface, and, edge leading, will move next down to the bottom of the bowl. (Photograph by Wilbur Nelson.)

MANIPULATION OF SPONGE CAKE

Making sponge cake involves more complicated procedures than making angel cake. Thus there are more opportunities for mistakes in technique. A number of different routines have been worked out for combining the ingredients for sponge cake. The one outlined below gives good results in the hands of the inexperienced. The yolks are beaten first because this foam does not set upon standing as does that from beaten egg white. The yolks should be beaten until they are *thick* and a light lemon color. A portion of the sugar may be beaten into this foam. The egg whites are beaten and made into a meringue with part of the sugar, as for angel food cake. The flour which has been sifted with the remainder of the sugar is folded into the beaten egg yolks. Excessive folding at this stage should be avoided. Otherwise the mixture will be so stiff that it is difficult to combine the egg yolk-flour mixture and the beaten egg white without loss of air. Finally, the yolk-flour mixture and the beaten whites are combined by folding until no streaks of white are visible. Folding should be continued no longer than is necessary to accomplish this. Otherwise the flour will absorb too much liquid from the foam and it will begin to collapse.

Alternate methods for combining the ingredients for sponge cakes include (1) combining the beaten egg yolk and beaten white before the flour is folded in, (2) making the sugar into a syrup (boiling point 118°C, or 245°F) which is beaten into the beaten whites before the whites and beaten yolks are combined and the flour is folded in, and (3) beating the whole egg until it is very stiff and then beating in the sugar and finally folding in the flour. When the last method is used, the salt should be sifted with the flour rather than added to the eggs (3).

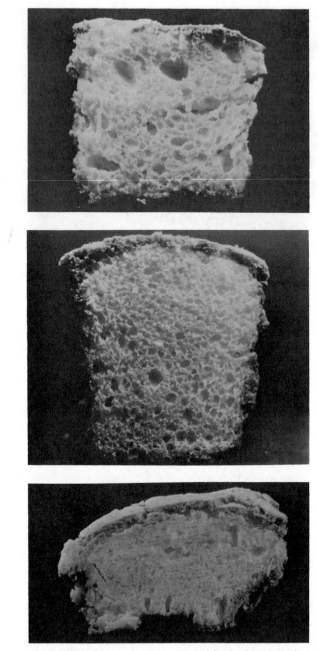

(a)

(b)

(c)

FIGURE 20-6. Extent of folding flour and sugar into angel food cake. (a) Undermanipulation gives uneven grain, coarse texture, and low volume. (b) Optimum and gentle folding gives moderately fine grain, light spongy texture, and good volume. (c) Overmanipulation and rough handling results in close texture and small volume. (From E. G. Halliday and I. T. Noble, *Hows and Whys of Cooking,* University of Chicago Press, 1946. Reprinted by permission of Isabel Noble.)

BAKING

BAKING PAN

Meringue-type cake batters should be transferred to the baking pan and baked at once; otherwise, the batter tends to layer, with the largest air cells rising to the top. Angel or sponge cake batter may be baked in loaf pans as well as in the usual tubular angel food cake pan. The tube in the latter provides support for the cake as well as more surface for heating it. Sponge cake batter baked in a shallow pan is used for jelly roll. Angel food cakes baked in aluminum or tinned pans have thinner, lighter brown crusts than do those baked in glass or enameled iron (16). It is essential to remove all trace of fat from the pan so that the cake batter can adhere as it rises and bakes. If the pan has been used for other purposes, it should be cleaned thoroughly. Hot water with some ammonia is particularly effective.

BAKING TIME AND TEMPERATURE

During baking the batter is inflated by the expansion of air bubbles beaten into the egg whites, supplemented by steam that forms from part of the liquid. It has been observed that air bubbles begin to expand as the temperature approaches 40°C, and diffusion of gases begins when the batter reaches 45°C or slightly above and ends when the temperature nears 88°C (2). When the coherent film of batter around the gas cells gets hot enough to set, gases escape from the bubbles and texture of the cake crumb is established. Explosive rupture of material around the gas bubbles was observed in cake batter made with chlorinated flour but not in batter made with nonchlorinated flour (2). Starch grains isolated from angel food cake showed extensive folding and deformation, indicative of a fairly advanced stage of gelatinization (Fig. 20-7).

Preferably, meringue-type cakes are baked in a preheated oven. The low baking temperature formerly recommended for meringue-type cakes was based on the reasoning that high temperatures should be avoided because these cakes contained a high proportion of eggs. The assumption was that a high oven temperature meant a high internal temperature in the cake. Actually, there is very little difference in internal temperature regardless of baking temperature (1). Also, the effect of the sugar on the coagulation temperature of the egg protein was not considered. In one study cakes baked at 350°F (177°C) rather than 325°F (163°C), 300°F (149°C), or 280°F (138°C) were bigger and seemed more moist and more tender. The superior quality of the cakes baked at higher temperatures is attributed to more rapid setting of the batter and absorption of less water by the starch of the flour. The effects of even higher baking temperatures have been evaluated, resulting in the recommendation of a baking temperature of 400°F (204°C) or 425°F (218°C) (9). Approximate baking times are 30 and 25 minutes, respectively, compared to 40 minutes at 350°F (177°C). Cakes baked at the higher temperature have greater volume and are more tender but tend to brown excessively. Also, a few minutes

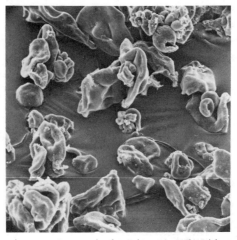

FIGURE 20-7. Scanning electron micrograph of starch grains isolated from angel food cake. (From R. C. Hoseney, W. A. Atwell, and D. R. Lineback, *Cereal Foods World* **22**(2): 57, 1977. Reprinted by permission.)

overbaking does far more harm at the higher baking temperatures. A piece of brown paper placed on a rack above the cake near the end of the baking period reduces excess browning of the top crust. More recently, angel cakes made from one-step packaged mix and baked at 177° or 191°C (350° and 375°F) were judged better in quality and had greater volume than cakes baked at 204° or 218°C (400° or 450°F) (7).

Some shrinkage should be expected near the end of the baking period and as the cake cools. Because of the elastic character of baked meringue-type cakes, the pan should be upturned and the cake left to hang and stretch as it cools to room temperature before it is loosened and removed from the pan. Elasticity of the crumb makes the cake hard to cut. A sharp knife with a serrated edge and a sawing motion should be used. Dampening the blade facilitates cutting.

REFERENCES

1. Barmore, M. A. 1936. *The influence of various factors, including altitude, in the production of angel food cake.* Colorado Exp. Sta. Tech. Bull. 15. 54 pp. Experimental data on the factors which contribute to success.
2. Bell, A. V., K. G. Berger, J. V. Russo, G. W. White, and T. L. Weathers. 1975. A study of the micro-baking of sponges and cakes using cine and television microscopy. *J. Food Technol.* **10:** 147–156. An inside view of sponge, pound, and high-ratio cakes as they bake.
3. Briant, A. M., and A. R. Willman. 1956. Whole-egg sponge cake. *J. Home Econ.* **48:** 420–421. Directions for making sponge cake from unseparated eggs.

4. Clinger, C., A. Young, I. Prudent, and A. R. Winter. 1951. The influence of pasteurization, freezing, and storage on the functional properties of egg white. *Food Technol.* **5:** 166–170. Angel food cake was the test material.

5. Dawson, E. H., C. Miller, and R. A. Redstrom. 1956. *Cooking quality and flavor of eggs as related to candled quality, storage conditions and other factors.* U.S. Dept. Agr. Inf. Bull. No. 164. 44 pp. Relationship between the candled characteristics of eggs and their functional properties in cooking; research at three experiment stations summarized graphically.

6. Derby, R. I., B. S. Miller, B. F. Miller, and H. B. Trimbo. 1975. Visual observation of wheat-starch gelatinization in limited water systems. *Cereal Chem.* **52:** 702–713. Levels of water from 32 to 60 percent compared.

7. Elgidaily, D. A., K. Funk, and M. E. Zabik. 1969. Baking temperature and quality of angel cakes. *J. Am. Dietet. Assoc.* **54:** 401–406. Four temperatures compared, using a one-stage packaged mix.

8. Finished foods—a second report. 1961. Cake-mix cakes—foam type. *J. Home Econ.* **53:** 759–762. Characteristics, factors for success, defects and their causes.

9. Grewe, E., and A. M. Child. 1930. The effect of potassium acid tartrate as an ingredient in angel cake. *Cereal Chem.* **7:** 245–250. A neat experiment to assess the functions of cream of tartar in angel cake.

10. Hoseney, R. C., A. W. Atwell, and D. R. Lineback. 1977. Scanning electron microscopy of starch isolated from baked products. *Cereal Foods World* **22**(2): 56–60. Extent of gelatinization of starch in starch-water and flour-water systems, in doughs, and starch isolated from baked products.

11. Jordan, R., and M. S. Pettijohn. 1946. Use of spray-dried whole-egg powder in sponge cakes. *Cereal Chem.* **23:** 265–277. How to handle dried egg to obtain maximum foam volume.

12. Joslin, R. P., and B. E. Proctor. 1954. Some factors affecting the whipping characteristics of dried whole egg powders. *Food Technol.* **8:** 150–154. Cause of the poor whipping ability and attempts to improve it.

13. Kamat, V. B., G. A. Lawrence, C. J. Hart, and R. Yoell. 1973. Contribution of egg yolk lipoproteins to cake structure. *J. Sci. Food Agric.* **24:** 77–88. The role of egg yolk protein fractions in foam formation.

14. Miller, E. L., and G. E. Vail. 1943. Angel food cake from fresh and frozen egg whites. *Cereal Chem.* **20:** 528–535. Thick and thin frozen whites compared, beaten at four different temperatures; five baking temperatures compared.

15. Pyke, W. E., and G. Johnson. 1940. *Preparing and baking yellow sponge cakes at different altitudes.* Colorado Exp. Sta. Tech. Bull. 27. 22 pp. Problems involved in balancing recipes for different altitudes.

16. Reed, S. J., E. V. Floyd, and M. S. Pittman. 1937. Effect of pan on temperature of baking and tenderness of angel food cake. *J. Home Econ.* **29:** 188–192. Heat penetration in cakes, browning, and tenderness as affected by the baking pan.

17. Sauter, E. A., and J. E. Montoure. 1975. Effects of adding 2% freeze-dried egg white to batters of angel food cakes made from whites containing egg yolk. *J. Food Sci.* **40:** 869–871. The beneficial effects of added white as related to the level of contamination.

18. Slosberg, H. M., H. L. Hanson, G. F. Stewart and B. Lowe. 1948. Factors influencing the effects of heat treatment on the leavening power of egg white. *Poultry Sci.* **27:** 294–301. Angel food cake the test material.

TWENTY-ONE
Shortened Cakes

Shortened cakes are those that contain fat. Batters for shortened cakes are emulsions. In addition, both the batter and the baked cake are foams, the former a mobile and the latter a rigid one. Some of the ingredients in shortened cakes form true solutions and others are colloidally dispersed. Particles of flour are suspended in the liquid. The kind of ingredients, their proportions, and how they are manipulated are interrelated. These plus how the cake is baked contribute to the quality of the finished product.

A high-quality shortened cake has a flat or slightly rounded top. The crust should be fine grained and a uniform golden brown. The grain (cells) should be small and uniform, the cell walls thin, and the crumb resilient, soft, and velvety. The cake should be light, tender, and slightly moist. It should taste acceptably sweet and otherwise have a good flavor (15).

INGREDIENTS AND THEIR FUNCTIONS

FLOUR

Cake batter must contain ingredients that confer on it the ability to hold gas bubbles and that make the baked cake rigid but still compressible. Flour is one such ingredient. One structural material supplied by flour is a small amount of protein which is coagulated by heat. The main component, however, is starch, which, when it is pasted during baking, is essential for the structure of cake crumb (21,24). The material in the crumb of cake which once surrounded the gas cells in the batter is made in part of gelatinized starch grains. Size of the gas cells in shortened cake depends upon how much the batter expands during baking before the cells rupture. This in turn is influenced in part by the size of the particles of flour. Flour is pin-milled in the final step in the reduction of wheat endosperm to particles of a size optimum for making cakes. Pin-milling may improve baking performance by dislodging starch grains from the matrix of protein of the endosperm, thus making them available to water (13). Excessive damage to starch grains is avoided (25); otherwise, the grains absorb excess water, making the batter too viscous and reducing volume of the cake. Cake flour, because of the small size of the particles, yields a cake with small cells, which contributes to fine grain and velvety texture (30). Volume of the cake is greater, too (39). Cake flour is treated with chlorine which bleaches the pigments, lowers the pH, and improves its baking performance. Whether

FIGURE 21-1. For shortened cake made by the conventional method the sugar is worked into the fat until the mass is light and fluffy and moist-appearing, a technique called creaming. (Photograph by Wilbur Nelson.)

the chlorine acts on starch only or on other constituents is still a question, but higher levels of sugar and fat can be used with chlorine-treated flour. Cakes have larger volume, finer grain, and better texture (23,35).

FAT

One function of plastic fat in shortened cakes is that it serves as a means of incorporating air into the batter. Most hydrogenated shortenings are marketed containing from 10 to 12 percent gas by volume. This gas is distributed throughout the fat as bubbles from 2 to 10 micrometers in diameter (32). When cakes are made by the conventional method, fat is worked with a spoon or spatula to incorporate additional air bubbles (Fig. 21-1). This technique is called creaming. Air bubbles are suspended in the liquid fat which surrounds the crystals, but the crystals are essential if a plastic fat is to retain air bubbles.

All fats do not cream equally well. The form in which the crystals of a plastic fat exist influences how well that fat creams. Those plastic fats, the crystals of which are stable in the beta prime form, are superior for creaming. Such fats incorporate air bubbles 1 micrometer or less in diameter. The smaller and more numerous the crystals, the finer and more numerous are the bubbles of trapped air. Such fats when creamed have the consistency of whipped

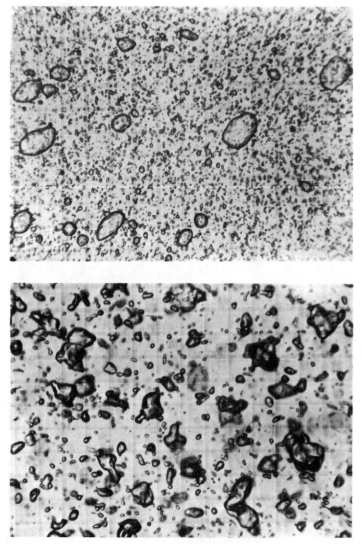

FIGURE 21-2. Rearranged lard with fine crystals (top) incorporates more and smaller air cells than does ordinary lard with coarse crystals (bottom). Original magnification × 194. (From C. W. Hoerr and D. F. Waugh, *Journal of the American Oil Chemists' Society* **32:** 38, 1955. Reprinted by permission.)

cream. Butter that is not aerated needs more creaming than hydrogenated shortening. Regular lard does not cream as well as most plastic fats because of the presence of large crystals.

The illustrations in Figure 21-2 show the effects of the size of crystals of fat on the number, size, and distribution of air bubbles incorporated in the fat (9). The sample at the bottom is of ordinary lard, that on top, of rearranged lard, crystals of which are shown in Figure 14-3. Because of their small crys-

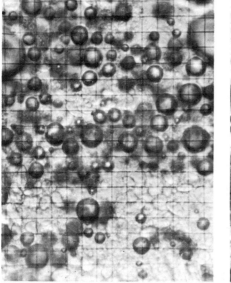
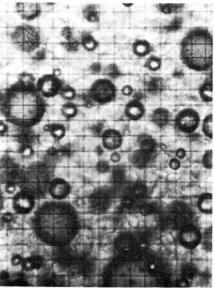

Beta prime   **Intermediate**

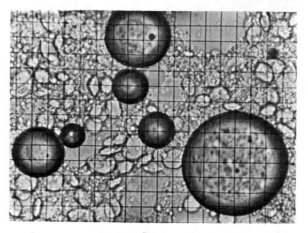

Beta

FIGURE 21-3. Photomicrographs of cake batter that show the effects of the type of crystals in a fat on the number, size, and distribution of air cells in a cake batter. Original magnification approximately × 200. Grid lines represent approximately 18 microns. (From C. W. Hoerr, *Journal of the American Oil Chemists' Society* **37:** 544, 1960. Reprinted by permission.)

tals, rearranged fats cream well. Size of the crystals and the creaming quality of a fat in turn affect the number, size, and distribution of gas cells in cake batter, as shown in Figure 21-3.

A fat with a wide plastic range is best for creaming. One disadvantage of using butter for shortened cakes is its narrow plastic range. A drop in temperature of a few degrees makes it too hard to cream and a rise in temperature of a few degrees makes it too soft. Hydrogenated vegetable shortenings maintain desirable plasticity over a wide range in temperature.

Aside from incorporating air, fat has another important function in shortened cakes. During baking, crystals in plastic fat melt, so fat makes cake batter more fluid and more mobile. With too little fat, the batter is not mobile enough to "give" with the expansion and oscillation of gas bubbles. An excess of fat makes the batter too fluid and too mobile. Optimum mobility is desired in cake batter because of its effect on the grain and on the textural qualities of the crumb (7). Fat helps determine whether the walls of dough in cake batter will explode with the pressure of expanding gases or merely expand. Fats help determine whether the crumb will be fragile or tough and thus act as tenderizing agents in cakes as they do in pastry.

Liquid shortening used in packaged cake mixes which are combined single stage, that is, without creaming, are not responsible for aerating the batter. See the discussion below.

EMULSIFIERS

Hydrogenated shortenings on the market contain a level of emulsifier (glyceryl monostearate plus some distearate) adequate for making shortened cake but not high enough to lower the smoke point unduly if the fat is used for frying. The presence of emulsifier is essential for those cakes with a high ratio of sugar and liquid to flour. The level of emulsifier in most hydrogenated shortenings is approximately 3 percent. Butter retains emulsifier from the cream but not enough to make the best cake. Addition of the optimum level of glyceryl monostearate to butter results in a superior cake (17,22). Cakes made with half butter for flavor and half hydrogenated shortening for superior creaming and emulsifying properties, a procedure that is feasible at home, yielded a cake more like one made from commercial shortening. Increasing the mixing time improved the all-butter cake made without emulsifier (17).

The presence of emulsifier in plastic shortening used for cake making results in a finer dispersing of fat throughout the batter. Batter that contains emulsifier is thinner, has a higher specific gravity, and has greater mobility. It appears that somewhat less air is incorporated when emulsifier is present, but the air is more finely dispersed. The smaller air cells that form in the presence of emulsifier make the grain of the cake finer. When gas cells are few, they become too large because carbon dioxide is evolved. As a result, they may migrate to the surface of the batter (18), especially during the early part of the baking. Loss of leaven and of cake volume results. Batter with emulsifier is glossy and less likely to curdle. The photomicrographs in Figure 21-4 illustrate the effects of glyceryl monostearate on cake batter made with butter (22). Figure 21-4a shows a photomicrograph of batter which contains no emulsifier other than that which the butter contains normally. The fat is stained and appears in diffuse dark gray clumps. The round, dark-rimmed air bubbles appear to be associated with the fat. The batter shown in part b has added 6 percent glyceryl monostearate (based on the weight of the fat). In this

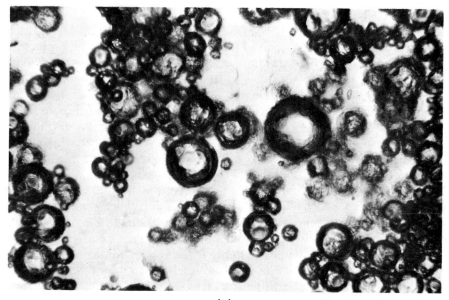

(a)

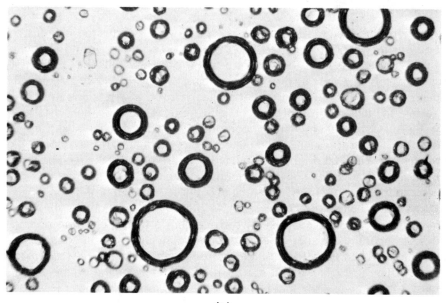

(b)

FIGURE 21-4. Effect of added emulsifier on the dispersion of gas cells in cake batter. (a) Batter made with butter without added emulsifier. The fat is stained and appears dark. The spheres with black outlines are gas bubbles. Other ingredients appear white. (b) Batter made with butter to which 6 percent glyceryl monostearate was added. Gas cells are evenly distributed. Fat is so well dispersed that little contrast exists between it and the other ingredients. Original magnification ×120. (From Martha Jooste and Andrea Mackey, *Food Research* **17:** 188. Copyright © 1952 by Institute of Food Technologists.)

batter the fat is so finely dispersed that it appears as a faint gray mist. The effect of the emulsifier on the quality of the cake is shown in Figure 21-5. Compare cakes 1 and 3 in each of the four series, A through D. Addition of emulsifier improved volume, grain, and texture of the cakes, as shown in the lower cake in each series.

There are surface active compounds now available that are even more effective than saturated monoglycerides such as glyceryl monostearate in dispersing the fat, but especially in aerating cake batter (6,38). These include unsymmetrical diglycerides such as 1-acetyl-3-monostearin, propylene glycol monostearate, and lactylated monoglycerides. These additives have in common the tendency to exist in the α-crystalline form. In a cake batter such compounds become oriented at the interface between fat and water and form a tough film that effectively seals off the fat from direct contact with the aqueous phase. Such a film is shown in Figure 21-6 (20,38). When this sealing occurs, the proteins in the batter (from milk and eggs) can foam and the batter can be aerated by beating rather than by creaming the air into the fat. Without these special surfactants, the fat would block foaming of the protein. These surfactants can be used with liquid as well as plastic fats, and they make possible packaged cake mixes that can be combined in one stage.

SUGAR

Sugar performs several functions in shortened cake besides the obvious one of making it sweet (2). Sugar facilitates the incorporation of air into plastic fats as they are creamed. As the spoon, spatula, or beater rolls the sharp-edged sugar crystals into the fat, air which adheres to faces of the crystals is introduced as small bubbles into the fat. Sugar must be in crystalline form to be effective for this purpose. The finer (and more numerous) the crystals, the greater is the number of air cells incorporated. Powdered sugar lacks the sharp edges on crystals (present in granulated sugar) which are essential for pulling bubbles of air into fat during creaming. Sugar also elevates the temperature at which the egg proteins coagulate during baking. It delays the pasting of the starch grains too (3,24). The gas cells in batter with a high proportion of sugar expand more before the batter sets. No doubt this accounts for the coarse grain and open texture of cakes which contain a high proportion of sugar. Because sugar thus weakens the structure of shortened cakes, it contributes to tenderness. When 60 percent of the sucrose in white layer cake was replaced by the solids in high fructose corn syrup, darkening of the crumb resulted unless a leaven was used that lowered the pH of the crumb (36).

EGGS

The protein of eggs, in addition to aiding in the aeration of single-stage cake batter, also serves as a means of incorporating air into cake batter made by conventional creaming, especially when the eggs are separated and the beaten whites are folded into the batter at the end. When the protein coagulates

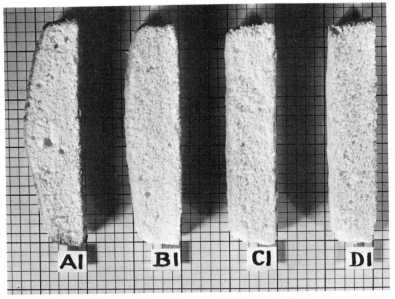

Butter cakes with no emulsifier added.

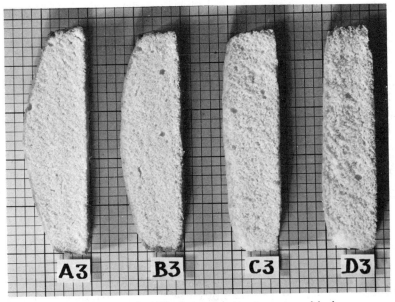

Butter cakes with 6% glyceryl monostearate added.

FIGURE 21-5. Effects of baking temperature and of emulsifier on the quality of shortened cakes. Oven temperature: A—425° F; B—375° F; C—325° F; D—300° F. (From Martha Jooste and Andrea Mackey, *Food Research* **17**: 192, 193. Copyright © 1952 by Institute of Food Technologists.)

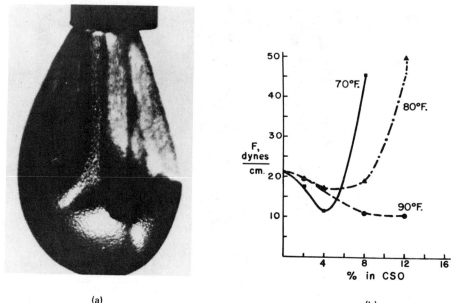

(a)   (b)

FIGURE 21-6. Function of an alpha-tending surfactant. (a) Formation of an interfacial film between a droplet of water and cottonseed oil (CSO). Withdrawal of part of the water resulted in partial collapse of the film of surfactant, which emphasized its integrity. (b) Effects of concentration and temperature on the strength of the interfacial film formed by the surfactant. (From J. C. Wootton, N. B. Howard, J. B. Martin, D. E. McOsker, and J. C. Holme, *Cereal Chemistry* **44:** 337, 1967. Reprinted by permission.)

during baking, it contributes to the structure of the baked cake and acts as a toughening ingredient. Eggs also supply liquid to batters and doughs. In addition, egg yolk is a rich source of emulsifying agents. The size of the eggs used will make a difference in the cake. For experimental work the amount of egg used in a cake is weighed or measured.

LEAVEN

Air which is creamed into the fat, that clinging to the particles of sifted flour, and air introduced by means of the egg and by stirring the batter provide the gas cells in cake batter which eventually become the grain of the baked cake. These air cells provide focal points for the collection of steam which forms during baking and for the carbon dioxide liberated from the soda by the acid in the baking powder. A true pound cake is leavened by air and steam only; other shortened cakes are leavened by carbon dioxide in addition. The amount of baking powder required in a shortened cake depends upon how much air is creamed into the fat, on the number of eggs included, and on whether the egg is added whole or is separated and the beaten white folded in at the end of the mixing. Compared with a two-egg cake, a four-egg cake which also contains more fat, needs less additional leaven from baking powder.

If double-acting baking powder is used in a recipe formulated for single-acting powder, the cake may be overinflated. The cells tend to be coarse and the crumb fragmented. All baking powders yield the same amounts of carbon dioxide, but nearly three-fourths of that from single-acting baking powder is released in the cold batter, whereas less than half that from double-acting baking powder is so released. Cakes made with different types of baking powder differ in taste, too, because they contain different salt residues. A cake made with SAS-phosphate baking powder has a more alkaline crumb than does one made with soda and cream of tartar. The more acidic the cake batter, up to a point, the finer the grain, the more velvety the crumb, the whiter and sweeter is the cake (9). The emulsion is less stable in a batter that is neutral or slightly alkaline (1).

Heat penetration is slower in cake batter that contains an excess of soda as in devil's food cake. This fact, in addition to the effect of the excess soda on the batter, accounts in part at least for the coarse grain. The color of chocolate and devil's food cake is due to the pigments supplied by the cocoa or chocolate. These change color with a change in hydrogen-ion concentration. At a pH of 5.0 they are yellow. With increase in alkalinity the hue shifts to various shades of brown and finally to a mahogany red at pH 7.5 (16).

LIQUID

Liquid in shortened cake batter performs a number of important functions (37). It dissolves the salt and sugar and makes possible the ionization of soda and acid in the baking powder so that they can react. Liquid disperses the fat and the flour and hydrates the protein and starch in the latter. The liquid also provides some steam to leaven the cake. Fluid milk is usually used, but water and milk solids may be substituted, the latter sifted with the dry ingredients. Fruit juices may serve as the liquid with or without the addition of soda to neutralize the acid. Liquid is needed to gelatinize the starch and so set the structure.

SALT

Salt is used for flavor. The proportion of salt to flour is somewhat less than for quick breads, possibly because of the high proportion of sugar or because cake recipes were first formulated for butter, which is usually salted.

PROPORTIONS OF INGREDIENTS

BALANCING INGREDIENTS IN A CAKE FORMULA

Shortened cakes vary from a lean, one-egg cake to a rich pound cake. In all recipes regardless of the richness, the ingredients need to be in balance. Structural or toughening ingredients, eggs and flour, are balanced with tenderizing ingredients, fat and sugar. Liquid ingredients, milk, egg, and fat, are balanced with the dry ingredient, flour. An increase in one source of leaven necessitates a decrease in another.

Table 21-1   Formulas for muffins, three conventional cakes, and one quick-mix cake

Ingredient	Muffins	Conventional Cakes			Quick-Mix
		One Egg	Two Eggs	Four Eggs	
Flour[a]	3 cups	3 cups	3 cups	3 cups	2¼ cups
Salt	1 tsp	1 tsp	1 tsp	1 tsp	1 tsp
Baking powder	6 tsp	4½ tsp	3¾ tsp	3½ tsp	3 tsp
Sugar	3-6 tbsp	1½ cups	1½ cups	1½ cups	1½ cups
Fat	3-6 tbsp	¼ cup	½ cup	1 cup	½ cup
Egg	1½	1	2	4	2
Milk	2 cups	1¼ cups	1 cup	½ cup	1 cup

[a]Cake flour, except for muffins, where all-purpose flour is used.

A number of such balancings are illustrated in the conventional one-, two-, and four-egg cake formulas given in Table 21-1. Formulas for muffins and for a quick-mix cake are included. The quantity of flour is the same in all three conventional cakes. The proportion of sugar (approximately 100 percent of the weight of the flour) does not vary in this series. Each additional cup of fat is balanced in the formula by inclusion of one egg and by reduction of milk by ¼ cup. The weight of the egg approximates that of the fat. The egg supplies protein to counterbalance the fat, but of equal importance is the liquid which helps preserve the sugar/liquid ratio. If this is too high, gelatinization of starch is retarded and uptake of water by the starch does not occur at the critical point in baking when grain and texture of the cake crumb should be established (4,24). In high-ratio cakes the sugar may equal 130 percent of the weight of the flour. An increase in sugar in a cake formula would necessitate a corresponding increase in liquid. Such a formula would in turn call for a higher level of emulsifier. An increase in egg is accompanied by a decrease in baking powder. In each of the conventional cake formulas, the volume of milk and fat approximates the volume of sugar.

Although ingredients in a cake recipe should be balanced, the balance need not be exact. For example, a three-egg cake recipe may be changed to a four-egg cake and the fat increased by somewhat more or somewhat less than ¼ cup without the cake being a failure. It is this tolerance for some variation which makes possible a very large number of combinations of proportions and innumerable "new" cake recipes. A balanced two-egg cake may have an ingredient either increased or decreased by up to 25 percent without making the cake a failure (12). Cake volume is likely to be increased with small increases of sugar, baking powder, or egg. When proportions of any of the three are decreased, volume is reduced. Increase in either the fat or the liquid reduces the cake volume. Any alteration in proportions which tends to make the volume greater tends to make the grain of the cake larger and the texture coarser. An increase in the proportions of either fat or sugar makes the crumb of cake more fragile and more tender, whereas a decrease in the proportions of either has a toughening effect. When the proportion of any one ingredient is altered by more than 25 percent without a compensating decrease or increase in another ingredient, the quality of the product is likely to be poor and the result a failure. Unbalanced proportions in a cake may be the result of a faulty recipe, errors in measuring, or deliberate alteration of proportions.

QUICK-MIX CAKES

For cakes not made by the conventional method but where most or all of the ingredients are combined in one or at most two steps, a special formula is used (26). A formula typical of a cake of this kind is like that for a balanced two-egg cake, except that the flour is reduced from 3 to 2¼ cups. Such high-sugar-ratio cake batters are thus richer and more fluid (29). The sugar in the quick-mix cake in Table 21-1 equals 139 percent of the weight of the flour. The proportion of liquid in the cake is near the upper limit. Should the eggs be larger than average, the cup used to measure the milk larger than standard, or the flour have been exposed to humid air and picked up moisture, the cake may be a failure. Shortening with emulsifier is recommended for cakes of this type; otherwise, the liquid in the formula needs to be reduced. The fluid batter of a cake of this type makes it possible to disperse the ingredients more readily than in the case of a conventional formula. Packaged cake mixes can be combined so easily because they have a high ratio of liquid (and sugar) to flour, and the special emulsifier in the fat facilitates the incorporation of air in the aqueous phase of the batter (20, 38). Such high-ratio cakes are moist and tender.

ADJUSTMENTS FOR ALTITUDE

For making cakes at high altitudes, the baking powder should be decreased because there is less air pressure to be overcome as the cake rises. A higher proportion of egg can be used at higher altitudes without making the cake tough. Also, because water vaporizes at a lower temperature at high altitudes, the liquid in the cake may need to be increased. A reduction in the proportion of sugar may be advisable. Alteration in the proportions of ingredients usually is not necessary below an elevation of 3000 feet. At higher altitudes a cake may become overinflated and collapse during baking unless the recipe is modified. Recipes for cakes to be baked at different altitudes are available (14).

COMBINING INGREDIENTS FOR SHORTENED CAKES

OBJECTIVES

Regardless of the method used to combine ingredients for shortened cakes, one of the objectives is to distribute the salt and the baking powder evenly throughout the flour. This is accomplished by sifting together these dry ingredients or in some cases by adequate stirring. Good distribution of baking powder is essential if the cake is to have small cells and fine grain. A second objective is to disperse the fat. This is facilitated in conventional cakes by combining the egg with the creamed fat. The egg contributes emulsifier which, together with that in the fat, aids in dispersing the fat in the liquid. Aeration of the batter is accomplished in conventional cakes mainly by creaming the fat with sugar or in packaged mixes by stirring the batter. Folding beaten eggs into the batter near the end of the mixing is a third means of introducing air into cake batter. Finally, the batter is manipulated to dampen all ingredients and dissolve some without losing either too much of the liberated carbon dioxide or making the batter too viscous by overstirring.

METHODS

For combining ingredients for shortened cake a great variety of methods is possible, many of which will produce a successful product. By varying only the order in which the main ingredients are combined, more than 600 routines are possible. Commonly used methods include the muffin and muffin-meringue, conventional and conventional-sponge, pastry-blend, and the quick mix.

MUFFIN. A simple and rapid way to combine ingredients for shortened cake is by the muffin method. Eggs and milk are blended and these, together with the melted fat, are stirred into the sifted dry ingredients. Batter for cake made in this way tends to be thin. It can be stirred more than muffin batter because of the higher proportions of fat and sugar. The volume of the cake tends to be smaller than if the cake were made by the conventional method. Cells of cake made by the muffin method tend to be large and the crumb coarse because of the poor dispersal of ingredients. The cake is likely to be less tender than it might be otherwise and the crust appears sugary. However, the quality of a lean, one-egg cake made by the muffin method may be nearly as good as one made by the conventional method and less time and work are needed to combine ingredients. The quality of the cake may be quite acceptable if it is eaten while still warm. Cakes made by the muffin method stale more rapidly because of the poor dispersion of fat.

Cakes made with oil but combined by a method known as muffin-meringue compare favorably with cakes made from plastic fats combined by the conventional method (see below) (27). The muffin-meringue differs from the muffin method in that part of the sugar is beaten into the egg or the egg white and this meringue is folded into the remainder of the ingredients, which have been combined by the muffin method.

CONVENTIONAL. The first step in combining cakes by the conventional method is to cream the sugar with the fat. When creaming is done by hand, the sugar is usually added in small portions and is worked in thoroughly after each addition. When a mixer is used, the sugar may be added all at once.

Creaming produces an air-in-fat foam. Fats cream best at temperatures from 24°C (75°F) to 26°C (79°F). Below 20°C (68°F) the ratio of crystals to oil is too high for optimum creaming, that is, the fat is too firm. At temperatures above 30°C (86°F) the ratio of crystals to oil is too low to retain the air bubbles. Cake batter made at higher temperatures is not well aerated and tends to be thin.

The more the fat-sugar mixture is creamed, the more air is incorporated. Both sugar crystals and air bubbles are suspended in the liquid portion of the fat. When the creamed mass is light and fluffy, the eggs are added, usually one at a time, and blended with the creamed sugar and fat. At this point the mass should be fluffy and well aerated, essential for optimum volume and grain. Under-creaming of the fat and sugar can be compensated for by stirring the eggs into the creamed mass more. By hand it is unlikely that the mixture will be overmanipulated up to this point. When creaming is done by an electric mixer, both sugar and egg may be added to the fat before creaming begins. The creamed mass is not only an air-in-oil foam but is also an emulsion of water in oil.

After the eggs are incorporated sufficiently into the fat-sugar foam, portions of both the liquid and the sifted dry ingredients (usually one-half) are added and these are stirred (not beaten) into the creamed mass. This is repeated with the second half of the liquid and dry ingredients. Stirring should begin promptly once dry ingredients and liquid are added or the batter will tend to be lumpy. The batter is stirred until the flour is dampened. If a mixer is used, it should be set at low speed. How much the batter needs to be stirred beyond this to give it correct flow properties depends upon the richness of the batter. The richer the batter (more fat or sugar), the more it needs to be stirred. This is one reason cake batter tolerates and even needs more stirring than muffin batter. The fat is now dispersed as lakes or even more diffusely in the aqueous phase of the batter. Air cells are now in the aqueous phase of the batter too.

The extent to which the batter is stirred as well as how much the fat and sugar are creamed will influence grain, texture, and volume of the cake. If creaming of a conventional cake is skimped, cells are few and large, cell walls thick, and volume small because the batter is insufficiently aerated. If the batter is understirred, ingredients are poorly dispersed and the batter is unable to withstand the pressure of expanding gases during baking. Such batter produces a cake of low volume with coarse, thick-walled cells and a crumbly crumb. Batter overmanipulated at the final mixing stage will be too viscous and the gas cells unable to expand as they should during baking. Such batter gives a cake with a fine grain, but the cells have a tendency to form tunnels. The tight grain of the cake plus the loss of carbon dioxide during the excessive manipulation yield a cake of lowered volume. The appearance of the crust is one clue to how much the batter was stirred. If the crust has large pores, appears glazed, and browns excessively, the batter was probably understirred. Cake with a dull crust that does not brown well or one with a peaked top due to tunnels may indicate overstirring.

CONVENTIONAL-SPONGE. A modification of the conventional method known as the conventional-sponge or conventional-meringue is similar to the conventional method. The difference is that the egg, or the egg white, is beaten with part of the sugar and this foam is folded into the batter at the end of the mixing period. This method of combining ingredients for shortened cake is especially recommended for those made from lard or other soft fats. If egg is added to creamed sugar and lard, the foam breaks and much of the air is lost from the creamed mass. This is attributed to a drop in temperature when the sugar dissolves in the liquid from the egg. This causes some of the liquid glycerides of the lard to crystallize and much of the creamed air is lost as a consequence. Placing the container of creamed lard and sugar in a pan of warm water (not so warm as to melt the crystals in lard) before the eggs are added will minimize or prevent the drop in temperature. Adding the eggs after the flour is incorporated accomplishes the same thing, especially when part of the sugar is already dissolved in the egg.

PASTRY-BLEND METHOD. In the pastry-blend method, fat and flour are blended until they are fluffy. Sugar, salt, baking powder, and half the milk are combined with the fat-flour blend, followed by the egg and the remainder of the milk. This method gives a good dispersion of the fat and a cake with fine grain and texture.

QUICK-MIX METHOD. Finally, cakes may be combined by a method known by such names as "quick-mix," "single-stage," "dump," or "one bowl." Packaged cake mixes are combined by this method. A conventional cake formula combined by a quick-mix method will not yield a successful cake. A quick-mix method puts special demands on the proportions of ingredients (29) and on the emulsifier. A so-called high-ratio formula is required. Such a formula for a two-egg cake to be made by the single-stage method is given in Table 21-1. The ingredients, and especially the fat, should be at room temperature. To make a cake by the single-stage method, the fat and all or part of the milk and the flavoring are added to the sifted dry ingredients. The mixture is stirred for a specified time or alternately for a specified number of strokes. Then the unbeaten egg, together with any milk remaining, is added. Stirring is continued again for a specified time or number of strokes. The fluidity of the batter of a quick-mix cake accounts for the fact that the ingredients can be dispersed adequately by stirring without preliminary creaming of fat and sugar. Presence of emulsifier in the fat in high-ratio cakes favors extensive dispersion of air cells in the batter in the absence of creaming.

BAKING

A stable, shortened cake batter, unlike that for meringue-type cake, can stand covered in the baking pan for some time without appreciable loss in quality. However, it is not advisable to allow the batter to stand in the bowl and transfer it later, because of loss of carbon dioxide. The baking pan should be approximately half full of batter.

CHANGES EFFECTED BY BAKING

A number of changes take place simultaneously in cake batter as it bakes. Air bubbles creamed into the fat are released to the aqueous phase, beginning before the fat is completely melted and clearing it by the time the temperature reaches 40°C (5). Additional carbon dioxide is liberated from the baking powder and this collects in the air bubbles. As the cake batter heats, the constituents are set into motion, due in part to convection currents and in part to the pressure of accumulating and expanding gases. Batter next to the sides and bottom of the baking pan heats first, that in the center last (28). This induces convection currents in the batter. Movement of the batter is a slow-motion version of the movement of currents of hot air in the oven. It is too slow to be observed. However, evidence of these currents in cake can be demonstrated by putting batter of two colors in the same pan, one on top of the other. Alternately, the top and bottom surfaces of cake batter may be dyed (33). Convection currents set up in the cake as it bakes will distribute the dyed layers in a fashion similar to that shown in Figure 21-7.

Heat enlarges gas cells during baking, most rapidly at 80°C (5). Internal pressure inside a cake causes violent movement in the batter, especially during the middle third of the baking period. Gas cells, lubricated by mobile lakes of fat, are pushed about. The longer the gas cells in a batter are jostled, the greater the chances of their colliding and coalescing, with what was once two smaller bubbles becoming one larger one. Liberation of carbon dioxide plus expansion of gas cells as they are heated cause the cake to rise. Steam forms, contributing to the leavening. The cake is likely to fall if the oven is opened and the temperature of the batter drops at this stage.

FIGURE 21-7. Partial cross section of a layer cake, showing the flow pattern of white and colored batters caused by convection currents during baking. (From H. B. Trimbo, S. Ma, and B. S. Miller, *Bakers Digest* **40**(1): 42, 1966. Reprinted by permission.)

When the batter is being inflated, its stability is critical if it is to yield cake crumb of high quality. Emulsifier confers greater elasticity on the film of protein around gas bubbles. Polyvalent ions supplied by milk, eggs, flour, and leaven contribute to stability of the batter, too (20).

For the best grain and texture the gas cells must expand, but not too much, before they break. The expansion and rupture are a composite of pressure inside the gas cell and resistance to expansion due to coagulation of protein and gelatinization of the starch. The aqueous protein film around the gas bubbles must give with the expanding gases until just the right moment, at which critical juncture coagulation of protein and especially uptake of water by the gelatinizing starch grains immobilizes the batter. When a cake batter reaches maximum internal temperature (near boiling), the starch grains undergo major swelling, but gelatinization may be incomplete due to insufficient water aggravated by the level of sugar (13). As the batter sets, the cells, without collapsing, rupture and leak leavening gases, and the emulsion breaks, with part of the fat appearing at the air/cake crumb interface (31). Evaporation of moisture from the surface during the early part of the baking period keeps the surface cool, but eventually the crust gets hot enough to brown.

HEAT PENETRATION DURING BAKING

A high baking temperature (at least 365°F [185°C] or even higher temperature of 375°F. [190°C]) gives cakes with greater volume and finer crumb. At lower temperatures, heat penetration is slower and the batter expands more and is agitated longer before it sets. This allows the gas cells to expand excessively and the batter to be overstretched before the crumb is set by coagulation of protein and gelatinization of starch. As a result, the grain of the cake is larger and the texture not so fine. Improvement in volume and in cell structure with increase in oven temperature is illustrated with cakes in Figure 21-5 (22). A preheated oven is recommended for cakes because of more rapid heat penetration. Baking temperature also affects the contour of the cake. Expansion in the interior after batter on the surface began to set accounts for the rounded top and the slightly humped top of cakes baked at 425°F (218°C) and 375°F (185°C), respectively.

Heat penetration in cake batter is influenced by factors in addition to the baking temperature (10). (See Chapter 3 for a discussion of heat and its transfer.) The emissivity of the baking pan, which depends upon the material and its finish, is one factor (8,11). Cakes baked in dark or dull pans will bake more quickly and the volume of the cake will be larger, the cells smaller, and the texture of the crumb fine and velvety. On the other hand, slower-baking pans, those that are bright and shiny, will give cakes with smaller volume and coarser grain. Two-thirds of the heating accomplished in an oven is effected by radiant energy. A bright, shiny surface deflects much of this radiant energy and so slows down the baking rate. Fast-baking pans, although they do produce a superior cake in most respects, do not give the best-looking ones. The top tends to be humped, and browning is less uniform. For appearance, choose a shiny pan at the expense of interior quality and volume. However, the combination of a reflective baking pan and a household oven as currently engineered represents an inefficient utilization of energy (28).

Tunnels are more likely to occur in shortened cake baked at a high temperature, in one baked in an 8-inch rather than a 9-inch pan, and in cake with a low sugar/flour ratio (34).

REFERENCES

1. Ash, D. J., and J. C. Colmey. 1973. The role of pH in cake baking. *Bakers Digest* **47**(1): 36–39, 42, 64. Factors influencing pH; effects on color, flavor, and stability of emulsion.
2. Baxter, A. J., and E. E. Hester. 1958. The effect of sucrose on gluten development and the solubility of the proteins of soft wheat flour. *Cereal Chem.* **35**: 366–374. An attempt to account for the effects of sucrose on baked products made with flour.
3. Bean, M. M., and W. T. Yamazaki. 1978. Wheat starch gelatinization. 1. Sucrose: Microscopy and viscosity effects. *Cereal Chem.* **55**: 936–944. Effects of concentration on the initial stage and the extent of gelatinization of wheat starch grains.
4. Bean, M. M., W. T. Yamazaki, and D. H. Donelson. 1978. Wheat-starch gelatinization in sugar solutions. 2. Fructose, glucose, and sucrose: Cake performance. *Cereal Chem.* **55**: 945–952. Effects of concentration as well as kind of sugar.
5. Bell, A. V., K. G. Berger, J. V. Russo, G. W. White, and T. L. Weathers. 1975. A study of the micro-baking of sponges and cakes using cine and television microscopy. *J. Food Technol.* **10**: 147–150. Temperature rise and gaseous diffusion and expansion.
6. Birnbaum, H. 1978. Surfactants and shortening in cake making. *Bakers Digest* **52**(1): 28, 30, 32, 34–35, 38. Surfactants for liquid and plastic shortenings.
7. Carlin, G. T. 1944. A microscopic study of the behavior of fats in cake batters. *Cereal Chem.* **21**: 189–199. Structure of shortened cake batters, effects of emulsifier, fate of air cells and formation of crumb structure during baking.
8. Charley, H. 1950. Effects of baking pan material on heat penetration during baking and on quality of cakes made with fat. *Food Research* **15**: 155–168. Volume and crumb characteristics of cakes baked in pans varying in emissivity.
9. Charley, H. 1951. Heat penetration during baking and quality of shortened cakes varying in pH value. *Food Research* **16**: 181–186. Effects of two levels of cream of tartar and two levels of baking soda.
10. Charley, H. 1952. Effects of size and shape of the baking pan on the quality of shortened cakes. *J. Home Econ.* **44**: 115–118. Effects of pan depth; effects of the shape of pans with the same capacity.
11. Charley, H. 1956. Characteristics of shortened cake baked in a fast- and in a slow-baking pan at different oven temperatures. *Food Research* **21**: 302–305. An attempt to compensate for the pan effect by alterations in baking temperature.

12. Davies, J. R. 1937. The effect of formula and procedure variables upon cake quality. *Cereal Chem.* **14:** 819–833. Liquid, fat, sugar, and baking powder varied; also mixing time, amount of batter in pan, and baking temperature.

13. Derby, R. I., B. S. Miller, B. F. Miller, and H. B. Trimbo. 1975. Visual observation of wheat-starch gelatinization in limited water systems. *Cereal Chem.* **52:** 702–713. Variations in water from 33 percent to 60 percent; effect of sugar on available water.

14. Dyar, E., and E. Cassel. 1948. *Mile-high cakes.* Colorado Agr. Exp. Sta. Bull. 404-A. 27 pp. Recipes for different altitudes.

15. Finished foods—A first report. 1961. Cake-mix cakes—shortening type. *J. Home Econ.* **53:** 281–284. Factors contributing to success; defects and their causes.

16. Grewe, E. 1930. Effect of variation of ingredients on color of chocolate cake. *Cereal Chem.* **7:** 59–66. Hydrogen-ion concentration and the color of chocolate cakes.

17. Guy, E. J., and H. E. Vettel. 1973. Effects of mixing time and emulsifier on yellow cakes containing butter. *Bakers Digest* **47**(1): 43–46, 48. Character of the crumb with and without emulsifier.

18. Handelman, A. R., J. F. Conn, and J. W. Lyon. 1961. Bubble mechanics in thick foams and their effects on cake quality. *Cereal Chem.* **38:** 294–305. Technical treatment of the fate of gas bubbles in cake batter.

19. Hoerr, C. W., and D. F. Waugh. 1955. Some physical characteristics of rearranged lard. *J. Am. Oil Chemists' Soc.* **32:** 37–41. Effects of rearrangement on creaming quality of lard and on aeration of cake batter.

20. Howard, N. B. 1972. The role of some essential ingredients in the formation of layer cake structure. *Bakers Digest* **46**(5): 28–30, 32, 34, 36–37, 64. Aeration, stability, and thermal setting of batter.

21. Howard, N. B., D. H. Hughes, and R. G. K. Strobel. 1968. Function of starch granule in the formation of layer cake structure. *Cereal Chem.* **45:** 329–338. Its role in thermal setting of the batter.

22. Jooste, M. E., and A. O. Mackey. 1952. Cake structure and palatability as affected by emulsifying agents and baking temperatures. *Food Research* **17:** 185–196. Effects of glyceryl monostearate on batters made with butter and with hydrogenated vegetable shortening; effects of baking temperature; photomicrographs of batter and photographs of cakes.

23. Kulp, K. 1972. Some effects of chlorine treatment of soft wheat flour. *Bakers Digest* **46**(3): 20–29, 32. Possible reasons for the beneficial effects.

24. Miller, B. S., and H. B. Trimbo. 1965. Gelatinization of starch and white layer cake quality. *Food Technol.* **19:** 640–648. Interrelations of sugar, water, and gelatinization of starch as cake bakes.

25. Miller, B. S., H. B. Trimbo, and K. P. Powell. 1967. Effects of flour granulation and starch damage on the cake making qualities of soft wheat flour. *Cereal Sci. Today* **12:** 245–247, 250–252. Effect of pin-milling.

26. Miller, E., and B. Allen. 1918. Problems in cake making. *J. Home Econ.* **10:** 542–547. Functions of ingredients, relations of proportions to optimum manipulation, and single-stage cake mixer method first described.

27. Ohlrogge, H. B., and G. Sunderlin. 1948. Factors affecting the quality of cakes made with oil. *J. Am. Dietet. Assoc.* **24:** 213–216. Comparison of twelve methods of mixing cakes made with liquid fat.

28. Peart, V., S. T. Kern, and D. P. DeWitt. 1980. Optimizing oven radiant energy use. *Home Econ. Research J.* **8:** 242–251. Order in which areas of layer cake baked in a conventional and in a biradiant oven achieve doneness.
29. Pyke, W. E., and G. Johnson. 1940. Relation of mixing method and a balanced formula to quality and economy in high-sugar-ratio cakes. *Food Research* **5:** 335–359. Principles underlying balancing ingredients in shortened cakes, with emphasis on cakes at high altitude.
30. Shellenberger, J. A., F. W. Wichser, and R. C. Lakamp. 1950. Cake properties in relation to flour particle size. *Cereal Chem.* **27:** 106–113. Effect of size of particles on cake quality; illustrated.
31. Shepherd, I. S., and R. W. Yoell. 1976. Cake emulsions. In *Food Emulsions.* S. Friberg, ed. New York: Marcel Dekker. Pp. 215–275. An overview of the subject.
32. Thompson, S. W., and J. E. Gannon. 1956. Observations on the influence of texturation, occluded gas content, and emulsifier content on shortening performance in cake making. *Cereal Chem.* **33:** 181–189. Cake quality affected by the interaction of occluded gas, emulsifier content, and manipulation.
33. Trimbo, H. B., S. Ma, and B. S. Miller. 1966. Batter flow and ring formation in cake making. *Bakers Digest* **40**(1): 40–42, 44–45. A study of convection currents in the batter as it bakes.
34. Trimbo, H. B., and B. S. Miller. 1973. The development of tunnels in cakes. *Bakers Digest* **47**(5): 24–27, 71. Contributing factors: mechanism of formation.
35. Tsen, C. C., K. Kulp, and C. J. Daly. 1971. Effect of chlorine on flour proteins, dough properties, and cake quality. *Cereal Chem.* **48:** 247–255. Advantages of chlorine treatment.
36. Volpe, T., and C. Meres. 1976. Use of high fructose syrups in white layer cake. *Bakers Digest* **50**(2): 38–41. Effects on cake quality.
37. Wilson, J. T., and D. H. Donelson. 1963. Studies on the dynamics of cake-baking. I. The role of water in the formation of layer cake structure. *Cereal Chem.* **40:** 466–481. Influence of proportions of liquid on volume and contour of cake and on crumb quality.
38. Wootton, J. C., N. B. Howard, J. B. Martin, D. E. McOsker, and J. Holme. 1967. The role of emulsifiers in the incorporation of air in layer cake batter systems. *Cereal Chem.* **44:** 333–343. Surfactants for aerating cake batter made by the single stage.
39. Yamazaki, W. T., and D. H. Donelson. 1972. The relationship between flour particle size and cake volume potential among Eastern soft wheats. *Cereal Chem.* **49:** 649–653. Importance of particle size.

FILM

1. *The Inside Story of Cake Baking.* 30 min. Color. Swift & Co. Sterling-Movies U.S.A., Inc., New York, N.Y.

TWENTY-TWO
Meat

The word "meat" in its broadest sense means any food taken for nourishment. In common usage, however, the term refers to those parts of animals that are used for food. In this chapter meat refers to the flesh of beef animals, of sheep, and of pigs. Most of the beef on the market comes from unsexed, young male animals called steers, some comes from young females called heifers, a limited amount of lower quality comes from mature females (cows), whereas veal comes from immature animals. Pork is not differentiated by age and sex of the pig.

CONSUMPTION OF MEAT

The annual per capita consumption of meat in this country forecast for the year 1979 was 146 pounds (108). This included 78 pounds of beef, 65 pounds of pork, just under 2 pounds of veal, and somewhat more than 1 pound of lamb and mutton. Worldwide, 25 percent of the supply of dietary protein comes from livestock, but in the United States 69 percent of dietary protein is of animal origin (91). To support this high consumption of meat, we feed to livestock more than 90 percent of the plant proteins which could be eaten directly by humans. Where population is dense and the amount of arable land and the supply of moisture is limited, a country cannot afford to feed animals food which is fit for human consumption. Animals get protein from plants, concentrate it, and resynthesize proteins with combinations of amino acids more suitable for humans. In the process much potential human food is wasted. Where the food supply is limited, humans must garner from plants the proteins and other nutrients instead of feeding animals to do this for them, wasting potential human food in the process.

COMPOSITION

The approximate composition of some common cuts of meat is given in Table 22-1. Meats contain from 15 to 20 percent protein. They are valued for the quantity of this nutrient which they provide in the diet. The proteins in meats, like those in eggs and milk, are of high quality. The fat content of meat, which ranges from 5 percent to as much as 40 percent, varies with the type of animals and with the breed, feed, and age of the animal. Calories supplied by meat vary with the content of fat. Most of the calcium in the body of an animal is

Table 22-1 Composition of selected cuts of meat (100-gram edible portion, raw)

Cut of Meat	Water (%)	Calories[a]	Protein (g)	Fat (g)	Carbohydrates (g)	Calcium (mg)	Phosphorus (mg)	Iron (mg)	Vitamin A (I.U.)	Thiamine (mg)	Riboflavin (mg)	Niacin (mg)	Ascorbic Acid (mg)
Pork, medium fat[b]	56.3	308	15.7	26.7	0	9	175	2.3	(0)	.76	.18	4.1	—
Lamb, choice grade[c]	61.0	263	16.5	21.3	0	10	147	1.2	—	.15	.20	4.8	—
Beef, choice grade													
Arm from chuck	64.2	223	19.4	15.5	0	12	180	2.9	30	.08	.17	4.7	—
Flank	71.7	144	21.6	5.7	0	13	201	3.2	10	.09	.19	5.2	—
T-bone	47.5	397	14.7	37.1	0	8	135	2.2	70	.06	.13	3.5	—
Round bone sirloin	55.7	313	16.9	26.7	0	10	155	2.5	50	.07	.15	4.1	—
Rib, 11th-12th	43.0	444	13.7	42.7	0	8	124	2.1	90	.06	.12	3.3	—
Round	66.6	197	20.2	12.3	0	12	203	3.0	20	.09	.18	4.8	—
Hamburger, lean	68.3	179	20.7	10.0	0	12	192	3.1	20	.09	.18	5.0	—
Hamburger, regular	60.2	268	17.9	21.2	0	10	156	2.7	40	.08	.16	4.3	—
Liver, beef	69.7	140	19.9	3.8	5.3	8	352	6.5	43,900[d]	.25	3.26	13.6	31
Liver, calf	70.7	140	19.2	4.7	4.1	8	333	8.8	22,500[d]	.20	2.72	11.4	36
Liver, pork	71.6	131	20.6	3.7	2.6	10	356	19.2	10,900[d]	.30	3.03	16.4	23
Heart, beef	77.5	108	17.1	3.6	.7	5	195	4.0	20	.53	.88	7.5	2
Heart, pork	77.4	113	16.8	4.4	.4	3	131	3.3	30	.43	1.24	6.6	3

SOURCE: U.S.D.A. Agr. Handbook No. 8. *Composition of Foods. Raw, Processed, Prepared.* Revised 1963.

[a] 1 kilocalorie = 4.185 kilojoules.

[b] Composite of trimmed ham, loin, shoulder, and sparerib.

[c] Composite of trimmed leg, loin, rib, and shoulder.

[d] Values vary widely.

NOTES: Dash means lack of data.

found in the bones, so the edible portion of meat is low in this mineral. Lean muscle meats are excellent sources of phosphorus and of iron. Liver is an especially rich source of iron and a concentrated source of vitamin A. Meats are excellent sources of niacin and riboflavin and are good sources of thiamine. Pork is richer in thiamine than is beef. Lean meats are deficient in ascorbic acid. The water content of lean meat is approximately 75 percent.

STRUCTURE OF MEAT

A cut of meat consists of lean tissue, which, aside from water, is chiefly protein, with some fatty tissue and bone. The lean part of meat consists of one or more muscles, each of which is made up of many bundles of muscle fibers. Thus muscle fibers are the basic structural unit of the lean of meat.

MUSCLE FIBERS

Muscle fibers are very long, thin structures ensheathed by a delicate, transparent membrane, the sarcolemma. The latter contains a jellylike, viscous protein sol, the sarcoplasm (1). Muscle fibers are analogous to the small juice-filled sacs which constitute the flesh of an orange except that muscle fibers are much longer and thinner, and cylindrical in shape. Muscle fibers are microscopic in size; they vary in diameter from 10 to 100 micrometers (54) and in length from a few millimeters to several centimeters (2). Fibers of beef (semitendinosus) imaged by a scanning electron microscope are shown in Figure 22-1. Minerals, vitamins, enzymes, and the pigment myoglobin are in the sarcoplasm within the fibers.

Embedded in this undifferentiated sarcoplasmic protein matrix of the muscle fibers are threadlike structures, the myofibrils, 1 to 2 micrometers in diameter (2,54,61). Longitudinal striations seen in muscle fibers viewed with the light microscope (Fig. 22-2) are due to these myofibrils. Visible the length of the muscle fiber are alternating dark and light bands known as cross striations (54). These are due to the way the myofibrils are structured. Myofibrils are made of substructures called myofilaments. The latter are of two types: thick (diameter, 100 angstroms); and thin (diameter, 50 angstroms). Rows of thick myofilaments alternate with rows of thin myofilaments the length of the myofibril. The long axis of both the myofibrils and the myofilaments parallels the long axis of the muscle fiber. A thin longitudinal section of a muscle fiber much magnified by an electron microscope (Fig. 22-3) shows the myofilaments which make up the myofibrils (54). The striations (banding) observed in Figure 22-3 are the result of the differential staining of components of the muscle fiber, which are present in an orderly, repeat pattern. The narrowest, darkest bands have been designated the Z-lines, from either side of which emerge rows of thin filaments. Two neighboring Z-lines mark the outer limits of one sarcomere, in the center of which are found rows of thick filaments. Rows of thick and thin filaments are interspersed in such a way that each thick filament is surrounded by six thin filaments and each thin filament is surrounded by

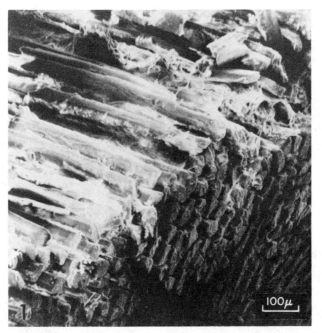

FIGURE 22-1. A three-dimensional view of muscle (beef semitendinosus) fibers embedded in connective tissue, imaged at low magnification by scanning electron microscopy. (Courtesy of S. B. Jones, USDA Eastern Regional Research Center, Philadelphia. Reprinted from *Food Technology* **31**(4): 82, 1977. Copyright © by Institute of Food Technologists.)

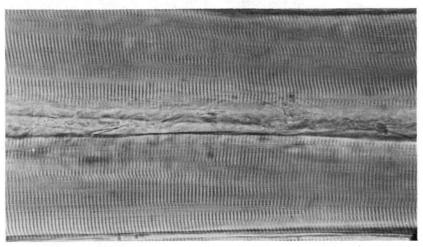

FIGURE 22-2. Microscopic view of a longitudinal section of two muscle fibers from uncooked round of beef showing longitudinal and cross striations. Magnification × 450. (From Belle Lowe and Joseph Kastelic, Iowa Agricultural Experiment Station Research Bulletin 465, 1961. Reprinted by permission.)

FIGURE 22-3. Transmission electron micrograph of a thin longitudinal section of a muscle fiber. The darker bands which alternate with lighter ones are due to overlap of thick and thin filaments. Original magnification × 24,000. (Courtesy of H. E. Huxley, from *Scientific American* **199**(5): 69, 1958.)

three thick filaments. On either side of the center of each sarcomere are two wide, dark bands where the thin filaments which project from the Z-lines overlap the thick filaments in the middle of the sarcomere (8,55,80). The width of these two bands as well as the length of the sarcomere (i.e., the extent to which thick and thin filaments overlap as they slide past each other) varies, depending on whether the muscle in the live animal is relaxed or contracted and after slaughter on whether the muscle is pre-rigor, in rigor, or post-rigor and the conditions under which rigor occurred and was resolved. The space along the myofibril which is occupied by the rows of thick filaments is designated the A-band, and the space in the middle of the A-band free of thin filaments is the H-zone. The lighter staining space between neighboring A-bands which is bisected by the Z-line is designated the I-band.

Thick filaments approximately 1.5 μm long are made chiefly of the protein myosin, each molecule of which consists of a long, thin rod (the "tail") terminating at one end in a pair of small structures which constitute the globular-shaped "head." A thick filament consists of bundles of these myosin molecules joined head end to tail end, head ends oriented outward in both directions from the center of the filament and with the heads (also referred to as "feet" or cross-linkages) projecting from the surface of the filament in a six-fold screw axis. Thin filaments, somewhat shorter than thick filaments, are made chiefly of the protein actin, individual molecules of which are approximately spherical in shape. Monomers of actin can unite like beads on a string to form polymers, two strands of which are twisted in a helix to form a thin filament. Closely associated with the thin filaments are two regulatory proteins, tropomyosin and troponin. Evidence suggests that α-actinin is present in or near the Z-line (105). The arrangement of the structural components of a muscle fiber are shown schematically in Figure 22-4. A surface view of a longitudinal fracture of a muscle fiber as viewed by a scanning electron microscope is shown in Figure 22-5b. The image, a topographical view of the surface, shows A-bands, I-bands, and Z-lines.

According to Huxley's sliding filament theory, the thin actin filaments slide from each end of a sarcomere toward its center as a muscle contracts. A polypeptide at the end of the myosin head first extends and then unites momentarily with a thin filament, and finally contracts, thereby inching the thin filaments on either side toward the center of the sarcomere. Repetition of the cycle results in shortening of the sarcomere and contraction of the muscle (29,56). When a muscle relaxes, the actomyosin complex breaks, the thin filaments are free to slide back to their original position, and the sarcomeres return to their relaxed length, a condition that prevails in the muscles immediately after an animal is slaughtered.

CONNECTIVE TISSUE

Muscle fibers, bones, and fat of meat are held in place by connective tissue. Surrounding individual muscle fibers are wispy layers of connective tissue

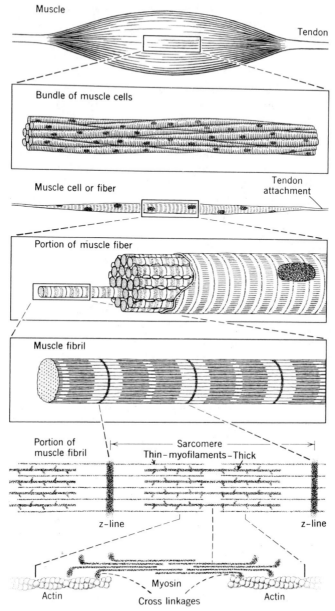

FIGURE 22-4. Structural components of muscle, shown schematically.

called endomysium. This endomysial tissue merges with the perimysium, connective tissue with thicker fibers which surrounds and unites bundles of muscle fibers (Fig. 22-6). Bundles of fibers, in turn, give rise to muscles that are surrounded by epimysial connective tissue. Connective tissue consists chiefly of an undifferentiated matrix called ground substance, made mainly of mu-

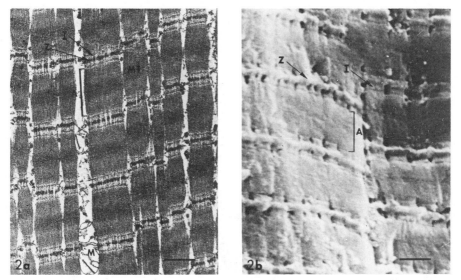

FIGURE 22-5. Two views of the fine structure of aged beef muscle (semitendinosus) fibers. (a) Transmission electron micrograph. (b) Scanning electron micrograph. A, A-band; I, I-band; Z, Z-line. Bar represents 1 micrometer. (Courtesy of S. B. Jones, USDA Eastern Regional Research Center, Philadelphia. Reprinted from *Food Technology* **31**(4): 83, 1977. Copyright © by Institute of Food Technologists.)

copolysaccharides in which fibers of collagen and elastin are embedded. Collagen fibers are composed of fibrils which, in turn, are made of molecules of tropocollagen (3,111). The latter consist of three polypeptides wound about each other in a manner analogous to a three-ply thread, with a right-hand twist. The individual polypeptides are coiled, too, but to the left in a helix characteristic of protein molecules with a high proline content. Glycine accounts for one-third of the amino acid residues in collagen and proline and hydroxyproline one-fourth. Lysine and hydroxylysine are present, too.

Collagen fibers thus consist of an ordered assembly of long chains of tropocollagen molecules. Collagen fibers predominate over those of elastin in connective tissue of most muscles, two exceptions being the semitendinosus of the round (Fig. 22-12a) and the latissimus dorsi of the chuck, muscles involved in pulling the legs backward (7).

Although collagen fibers are flexible, they do not stretch as do those of elastin. Collagenous connective tissue is found in tendons that attach muscle to bone, in the skin, in the bones, and in the dentine of the teeth. A collagen-rich tendon may be observed at the end of muscles in the leg of a chicken. Connective tissue which contains collagen fibers is pearly white in contrast to yellow connective tissue in which elastic fibers predominate. The neck ligament from the beef animal is made mainly of elastic fibers. This structure may be seen in the meat from the shoulder region of the animal. Collagen fibers can be disintegrated in hot water, whereas those of elastin are affected little if any. From the standpoint of tenderizing meat during cooking, it is fortunate

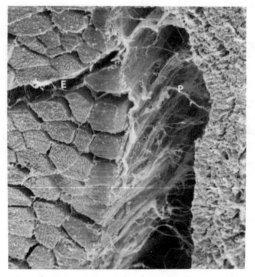

FIGURE 22-6. Scanning electron micrograph of raw beef semitendinosus muscle fractured perpendicular to the muscle fiber axis, showing (e) endomysial and (p) perimysial connective tissue. (Courtesy of S. B. Jones, USDA Eastern Regional Research Center, Philadelphia. Reprinted from *Journal of Food Science* **43:** 1182, 1978. Copyright © by Institute of Food Technologists.)

that collagen fibers predominate over elastic fibers in the connective tissue in muscle.

FAT

When an animal eats more food than it needs to maintain itself and provide the energy which it needs to live and move about, the surplus is converted into fat which begins to accumulate in body tissues. Fat is deposited in the connective tissue within the muscle, where it is known as "marbling," around and between muscles, under the skin, and in other connective tissue which contains special fat storage cells. Globules of fat may be packed so tightly in these cells that they appear angular. Fat is deposited in the connective tissue around organs in the abdominal cavity. An example is the kidney, where a moderate coating of fat cushions and protects this organ. Age, feed, and amount of exercise that an animal gets influence the fat content of the meat. Meat from well-fed animals with limited exercise and past the period of most rapid growth tends to contain more fat. Pigs accumulate fat more readily than do other meat-producing animals. A moderately well-fed pig may have a thick layer of fat-filled cells over the entire surface of the body.

IDENTIFICATION OF MEAT

A high proportion of the money spent for food goes for meat. Knowing the best method and technique for cooking meat to make it most palatable is important. To choose an appropriate cooking method, however, one must be able to identify meats. This involves the ability to distinguish beef, veal, lamb, or pork by sight and to know the part of the animal from which the meat comes. Both factors have a bearing on the most suitable cooking methods.

TYPES OF MEAT

Color of the lean and character and amount of fat are the two best indices for identification of the animal from which the meat comes. The color of beef when freshly cut is a dark, purplish red. This changes to a bright, cherry red when the meat is exposed to oxygen. The change in color from purplish red to bright red is reversible. With prolonged exposure to oxygen, the pigment is oxidized and loses its bright red color. Veal, too young to have accumulated as much pigment as the older beef animals, is grayish-pink and the bones have a pinkish tinge. The lean of lamb is a darker, deeper red than beef. The paler rose-pink of fresh pork is due at least in part to the high proportion of white, myoglobin-free muscle fibers interspersed among the red, myoglobin-rich ones (15). The species difference in this regard is illustrated by the whale which is so richly endowed with oxygen-storing red muscle fibers that it can stay submerged without breathing for many minutes (1), whereas the rabbit has a high proportion of white glycolytic muscle fibers that provides not only rapid take-off but also early oxygen depletion, and thus a biochemical basis for the "scared rabbit" reputation.

The fat of pork with its higher unsaturated fatty acid content is much softer than that from either beef or lamb (see Table 14-1). Lamb fat is the hardest of all, in fact, is quite brittle. It is usually whiter than beef fat, which tends to be more yellow especially if the animal has been fattened for market by grazing.

In addition to the color of the lean and the character of the fat, the size and contour of a cut are also a clue to the source of the meat. The size and shape clearly differentiate a loin chop of lamb, a center cut pork chop, and a T-bone steak from beef.

CUTS OF MEAT

Identification of a cut of meat is more important than identification of the animal source for choosing an appropriate cooking method. Distinguishing features of a cut of meat are the size, shape, and location of bone, the size and shape of muscles found in the cut, and the amount and distribution of fat. Bone, if present, is one of the best identifying features. For this reason, familiarity with the skeletal structure of meat animals is essential (81).

The skeletal structure of beef, veal, lamb, and pork is basically the same, as shown by the charts in Figure 22-7, which depict the bones in the four meat animals. Not only are bones and muscles similar in shape in cuts from analogous parts of different animals, but the meat is likely to be comparable in tenderness, too.

Before meat leaves a packing plant the carcass is reduced to pieces of manageable size. To subdivide a carcass it is split first into right and left sides down the center of the backbone. This is usually done in the packing plant

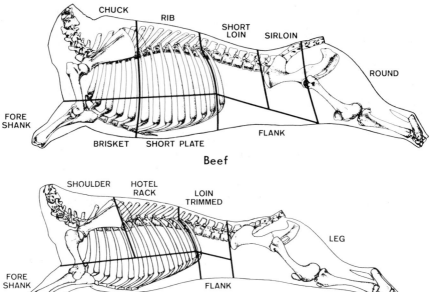

Beef

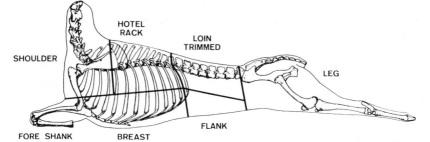

Veal

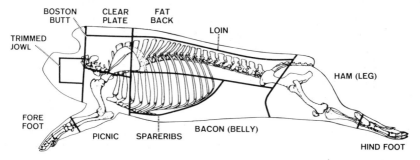

Lamb

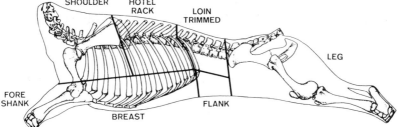

Pork

FIGURE 22-7. Primal cuts of beef, veal, lamb, and pork, showing bone structure. (Courtesy of the National Live Stock and Meat Board.)

for pork, veal, and beef. Sides of beef and veal are further divided between the 12th and 13th ribs into fore and hind quarters. These are then cut into wholesale, or primal, cuts.

PRIMAL CUTS OF BEEF. Primal cuts of beef from the fore quarters (starting at the head end of the animal) include the chuck and rib above, and the brisket and plate below (Fig. 22-7). The chuck contains the neck bones, the shoulder blade, part of the backbone, the upper part of the first five ribs, the arm bone, and the muscles attached to these bones. The rib wholesale cut contains part of the backbone and the upper part of the ribs. The brisket contains the breast bone and the lower ends of the first five ribs. The foreshank is attached to the brisket. The plate contains the lower ends of ribs 6 to 12.

From the hind quarter and adjoining the rib cut is the short loin, which contains the mid-section of the backbone, and below it the flank, which is boneless. To the rear of the short loin is the sirloin, which contains part of the hip bone and the tail bone. The final wholesale cut of beef is the round, which includes the rump. The latter is a triangular-shaped piece that contains the remainder of the tail bone and the aitch (or rump) bone. The round is named for the round bone (femur) it contains.

PRIMAL CUTS OF VEAL AND LAMB. Primal cuts of veal and lamb (Fig. 22-7) differ from primal cuts of beef in the following way. The shoulder of veal or lamb corresponds to the chuck of beef and the hotel rack to the rib of beef. Breast of veal or lamb includes the parts called brisket and short plate in beef. The leg of veal or lamb comprises the equivalent of both round and sirloin of beef.

PRIMAL CUTS OF PORK. Primal cuts of pork (Fig. 22-7) differ somewhat from those of beef, veal, and lamb. Beginning at the head end of the pork carcass, primal cuts include the jowl, the Boston butt, which corresponds to the upper part of the shoulder of lamb and veal or the chuck of beef, and the picnic (shoulder) of pork, which corresponds to the lower part of the shoulder of lamb or veal or to the chuck of beef. The picnic includes the fore shank of the pig. The loin of pork includes almost all of the backbone, the upper part of most of the ribs, and part of the hip bone. Sliced off the outside of the loin and parallel to the backbone is a layer of fatty tissue known as "fat back." Similar tissue sliced off the upper part of the exterior of the Boston butt is known as "clear plate." Both fat back and clear plate consist of connective tissue in which fat is deposited. Both are used as sources of lard. The lower part of most of the ribs of pork, called spare ribs, is peeled away from the walls of the abdominal cavity. Fresh, the latter is called "side pork" and when cured and smoked, "bacon." Ham corresponds to round of beef and to the leg of lamb and veal minus the sirloin part of the last two.

RETAIL CUTS. When a carcass of meat is subdivided into both primal and retail cuts, an attempt is made to separate thicker from thinner pieces and tender meat

FIGURE 22-8. Orientation of muscle fibers in different parts of a beef animal, shown schematically. (Courtesy of the Ohio Art Company, Brian, Ohio.)

from less tender. Whenever possible the cut is made across the grain of the muscle, that is, perpendicular to the long axis of the muscle fibers. The first two objectives are easier to accomplish than the third, because muscles run in more than one direction, especially in certain parts of an animal. This is illustrated in the diagram in Figure 22-8. Partly on this account, meat from the chuck is less desirable than that from the round.

Pork usually and beef and veal frequently reach the retailer already divided into primal cuts. The entire carcass of lamb is usually sold to the retailer. In the meat market these large cuts are further subdivided into pieces of marketable size suitable for preparing in the home kitchen. These are the retail cuts. A specific cut may be known by different names in different parts of the country.

In many instances the retail cut is named for the primal cut from which it came. Thus sirloin steak comes from the sirloin, round steak from the round, and rib roast from the rib of beef. Loin chops come from the loin and sliced ham from the ham of pork, rib chops from the rib, and loin chops from the loin of lamb.

Some cuts of meat are named for the bones that they contain. In an attempt to simplify identification of cuts of meat on the basis of bones, the following charts have been devised (81). Shown in Figure 22-9 are the seven basic retail cuts of meat and their location on the carcass. In Figure 22-10 are shown the seven basic shapes of the bones by which these basic retail cuts may be identified. The round arm bone is found in the lower part of the shoulder or chuck. Cuts which contain this bone are known as shoulder arm steaks, shoulder arm chops, or shoulder arm pot roasts. Cuts from the upper

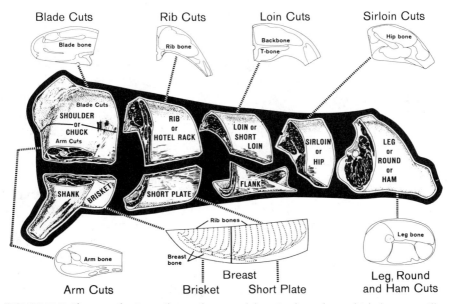

FIGURE 22-9. The seven basic retail cuts of meat and the primal cuts from which they come illustrated with a side of beef). (Courtesy of the National Live Stock and Meat Board.)

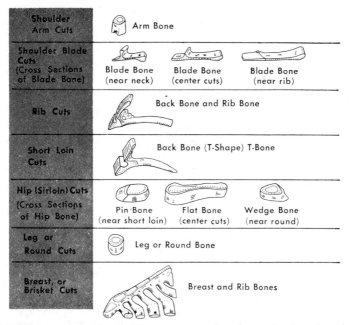

FIGURE 22-10. Bones serve to identify the seven groups of retail cuts. Cuts from the sirloin contain either the pin bone, the flat bone, or the round bone, and the last may appear round on one side of the cut. (Courtesy of the National Live Stock and Meat Board.)

part of the shoulder or chuck contain cross sections of the blade bone. Cuts from this part of the animal are called blade or 7-bone steaks, chops, or pot roasts. Rib chops, steaks, or roasts contain the backbone and the rib bone. Cuts from the short loin contain cross sections of the backbone or vertebrae which are usually but not always T-shaped. These cuts are called club, T-bone, porterhouse steaks, or simply loin steaks. Cuts of meat from the sirloin or the hip of the animal contain cross sections of the hip bone which vary in shape. The hip bone shows up in cuts nearest the short loin as the pin bone, in the center as the flat bone, and nearest the leg as the wedge bone. Cuts from the leg or round contain a round bone. These cuts can be distinguished from those of the shoulder arm where the bone is round, too, by the size and the shape of the muscles in the two cuts. (See Fig. 22-11). Cuts from the breast or brisket contain the breast bone (or sternum) and the ends of the rib bones.

Although bones may aid in distinguishing one retail cut from another, shape, size, and location of muscles serve as identifying features, too. Many cuts contain cross sections of several muscles (Figs. 22-11, 22-12), and the same muscle, differing somewhat in size, shape, and location, may appear in consecutive cuts. The longissimus dorsi (Fig. 22-12b) appears in cuts, made perpendicular to the backbone, from chuck, rib, and loin. The psoas major muscle is found in cuts from the loin. The biceps femoris muscle originates in the sirloin, is a prominent muscle in the rump, and forms part of the bottom round (Fig. 22-12a). A publication is available which reproduces from tracings minor as well as major muscles found in 39 retail cuts of beef (107).

The variety of popular names under which the same retail cut of beef is marketed is often confusing to the consumer at the meat display counter. To bring some order out of this confusion, recommended names for 314 retail cuts of beef, pork, and lamb have been proposed for adoption by retailers (59). The list is called the Uniform Meat Identity Standards. Information recommended for the label on each retail cut includes (1) the kind of meat, (2) the wholesale cut from which it comes, and (3) the name recommended for the cut.

TENDERNESS OF MEAT

Tender meat, in contrast to that which is hard to cut and hard to chew, is much prized. Toughness is one of our most vivid sensory impressions when we eat meat. Meats differ greatly in tenderness, some cuts being very tender and others extremely tough, even from the same carcass.

VARIATIONS IN TENDERNESS

Many of the muscles from the upper half of an animal along the backbone are more tender than those from the lower half. Cuts from the chuck are more tender than those from the brisket, those from the rib more tender than those from the plate of beef. Muscles from the rib are more tender than those from the chuck; muscles from the loin are more tender than those from the round.

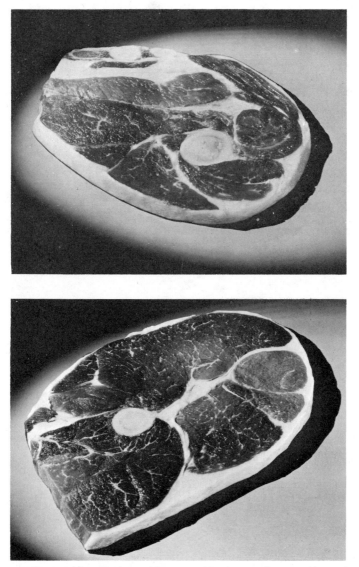

FIGURE 22-11. Shapes of the muscles and location of fat distinguish a round bone shoulder arm cut (top) from round steak from the round (bottom). (Courtesy of the National Live Stock and Meat Board.)

Cuts from the lower part of the legs, from the neck, and from the flank of beef are toughest of all.

Although a carcass is divided to separate more-tender from less-tender parts, different muscles within a cut are not equally tender. Figure 22-12 shows by diagram the muscles in the round and in the loin of beef. Numbers in the diagrams indicate the amount of force required to shear individual muscles

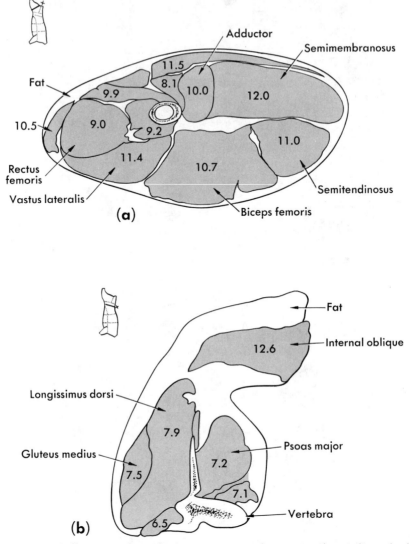

FIGURE 22-12. Different muscles within a cut vary in tenderness. Numbers indicate the force needed to shear the cooked meat: (a) round; (b) short loin. (From J. M. Ramsbottom and E. J. Strandine, *Food Research* **13:** 322, 1948. Copyright © by Institute of Food Technologists.)

after the meat was cooked (93). Muscles of the loin, except the internal oblique, are more tender (have lower shear values) than the most tender muscle of the round. Differences in tenderness among the other muscles of the loin are not great. The two muscles for which cuts from the short loin are prized are the *longissimus dorsi* (backstrap) and the *psoas major* (tenderloin). In round steak the *semimembranosus* (top round) is only slightly tougher than the *semitendinosus* or the *biceps femoris* (bottom round). The *rectus femoris* and the three smaller muscles next to the bone have somewhat lower shear values. Marked differences among three muscles of the rib of beef have been documented (87).

BASIS OF TOUGHNESS

The underlying cause of the toughness in meats and why meats differ so markedly have been the subject of a great number of studies. Fat deposited in connective tissue within the muscle, which appears as white flecks, marbling, was once thought to contribute to tenderness, but desirable as intramuscular fat may be for other reasons it is of questionable value in predicting tenderness in meat (22,84). There is general agreement, however, that well-marbled meat tastes juicier, doubtless because the melted fat lubricates the lean. Early work emphasized the relation between collagen content and toughness of meat (95). Although intramuscular connective tissue may be a major contributor to toughness in some cuts, in others the myofibrillar component may be more important. The former has been characterized as background toughness and the latter as actomyosin toughness (74,76). Recognition of these two separate factors has enabled workers to zero in on the contributions of each.

CONNECTIVE TISSUE TOUGHNESS.   Later studies emphasized that tenderness of meat was related to the solubility of collagen, not just to the collagen content (27) and that solubility of collagen decreased with advancing age of the animal (47,48). Collagen in the connective tissue of younger animals was not only more readily soluble, but the sudden release of hydroxyproline occurred at a lower temperature (40). The more heat-labile cross-links of collagen fibers from younger animals are believed to be replaced by more thermally-stable links in older animals (3). The tendency of meat from older animals to be tougher may thus reflect the changing ratio of heat-stable to heat-labile cross-links of collagen (101). This may account for the fact that veal is more readily tenderized by cooking than beef even when veal is higher in collagen. Although the percentage of soluble collagen in five different muscles of beef was found in one study to be related to the contribution of the connective tissue component to toughness (27), in another study differences observed in the number or nature of the cross-links in the collagen of active versus less-active muscles failed to account for the former being judged as less tender and the latter more tender (101). A preponderance of one of three isomorphic forms of collagen has been identified in the perimysium of tougher muscles, but its significance has not yet been established (4). Regardless of the underlying cause, the connective tissue component of muscle may be the major contributor to toughness in meat from a mature animal, and especially in muscles which have done much work. But meat from a young animal and from muscles which get comparatively little exercise may become tough, depending on how the carcass is handled after slaughter.

ACTOMYOSIN TOUGHNESS. Muscles potentially tender because connective tissue contributes little to toughness may become tough because of the condition of the myofibrillar component. Immediately after an animal is slaughtered the warm flesh is soft and pliable. In a few hours, depending on the particular animal, its physiological state, and certain environmental conditions, the meat goes into rigor. Muscles become rigid and inelastic. Cross-links form between the myosin and the actin filaments to the extent that they have overlapped (56), and these cross-links are locked in place during rigor. Rigidity is attributed to shortening of sarcomeres which occurs during onset of rigor, and the loss of extensibility maintains that rigidity (39).

TENDERIZING BY AGING

Meat in rigor (approximately 24 hours postmortem in the case of beef) is tougher than it was immediately after the animal was slaughtered. If the carcass is held for a few days, rigor will pass and the muscles again become soft and pliable. For optimum tenderness, meat must be allowed to age after the passage of rigor. In one study, 8 out of 20 muscles of beef had reached maximum tenderness when aged 5 to 8 days, but the remaining 12 muscles required 11 days or more, leading to the recommendation of an aging period of 11 days as optimum for both tenderization and overall palatability of the four major wholesale cuts of beef (chuck, rib, loin, and round) (103). Pork needs less time to develop rigor and rigor disappears sooner, with one day of aging judged adequate (45). Normally, sufficient time elapses for aging to effect appreciable tenderization of meat before meat reaches the consumer. To control the growth of microorganisms the meat is held at temperatures of 1° to 3.3°C (34° to 38°F) and the humidity held to approximately 70 percent. Aging of meat may be effected also by holding at higher temperature for a shorter time, usually around 21°C (70°F) for two days. The humidity is kept high (85 to 90 percent) to minimize evaporation; ultraviolet light in the aging room controls bacterial growth. Such fast-aged meat is sold in retail outlets.

Changes that take place in the myofibrils after the animal is slaughtered but before rigor develops influence the extent to which meat is tenderized by aging. Rapid chilling of pre-rigor meat by exposure to temperature below 15°C may bring about "cold-shortening" of the muscles. An excised muscle induced to shorten by rapid chilling to the extent of 35 to 40 percent of its resting length is at peak toughness (76). Viewed microscopically, a cold-shortened muscle resembles one that has contracted (104). All fibers in a muscle are not subject to cold-shortening, even those lying side by side. When a fiber shortens actively, adjoining fibers are passively shortened and appear crumpled and wavy. And a fiber that cold-shortens does not do so over its entire length. In areas where shortening is severe, breaks may occur across muscle fibers (112). When a muscle shortens near 35 percent of its resting length, the sarcomeres are shortened to the approximate length of the myosin filaments (31), and this overlap of thick and thin filaments makes possible extensive cross-linking between myosin and actin filaments and also eliminates areas along the fiber (the I-bands) where resistance to shear should be less (75).

A muscle cooled while still attached to bone will be more tender than if it had been excised (94), but muscles left on the carcass are not equally restrained from shortening. If a carcass is suspended by the aitch bone rather than by the achilles tendon (the usual practice), more of the muscles are maintained near their relaxed length in the live animal and tenderness of a number of the muscles is improved (52). Holding a carcass at elevated temperature (16°C) for 16 to 20 hours postmortem rather than chilling it immediately increased tenderness of longissimus muscle 47 percent and also avoided the irregular shape of a carcass hung by the aitch bone (102). Hanging a carcass by the aitch bone rather than the conventional way, however, made more difference in the tenderness of nine major muscles of beef than did conditioning the carcass at 16°C for 20 hours prior to chilling (50). In general, muscles with less connective tissue show greater response in tenderness and in length of sarcomeres to the way a carcass is hung than do muscles in which connective tissue is prominent (52). Electrical stimulation of a carcass improves tenderness and makes boning of the warm carcass possible without causing undue toughness (26), and possibly shortens the aging time needed to tenderize the meat (98).

Just how aging tenderizes meat is still being investigated. Aging does not significantly increase the solubility of collagen (47). Some lengthening of the sarcomeres occurs (104). Weakening and eventual disintegration of Z-lines accompany aging (31), as does weakening of the lateral adhesion of the myofibrils (32). The ease with which aged muscle can be stretched and the breaks that occur, mainly at the junction of the Z-line and the I-band, suggest that aging weakens myofibrillar structure (30). A muscle stretched to twice its resting length (at which point little if any overlap of actin and myosin filaments should exist) and held in that position during onset and resolution of rigor was still tenderized by aging, a result that appears to rule out weakening of rigor linkages between actin and myosin filaments as a cause of tenderization (34). Aging brings about an increase in the α-actinin that can be extracted from muscle (18). The possibility that cathepsins (enzymes) present in meat contribute to the tenderization that accompanies aging is still questioned, although evidence has been presented that these enzymes can effect changes resembling those that occur during aging (36). And a protein endogenous to muscle has been shown to disintegrate the Z-line when calcium ions are present (11). When the individual proteins that make up the myofibrils were treated with a calcium-activated protease from muscle, it was concluded that its attack on α-actinin was responsible for the disintegration of the Z-line (90). Regardless of how aging alters myofibrils to make meat more tender, the ease with which myofibrils were fragmented when tissue from loin steaks was homogenized was reported to be a better index to tenderness than either the length of the sarcomeres or the solubility of the collagen (28).

MEAT TENDERIZERS

Meat that is tough may be tenderized by treatment with certain enzymes which catalyze the hydrolysis of one or more of the proteins of muscle (1). Proteolytic enzymes are available which will attack the sarcolemma and the muscle fibers; others will attack either the collagen or elastin as well (79). Enzymes from tropical plants which are effective meat tenderizers are bromelain from pineapple, ficin from figs, and proteases from the latex of the green papaya fruit (64), including papain, chymopapain (the main enzyme), and a peptidase. Bromelain is more active toward collagen than toward the proteins of the myofibrils, but the reverse is true for papain, ficin, and the fungal enzyme, Rhozyme P-11 (63). All three papaya enzymes can hydrolyze the proteins of the myofibrils extensively, but connective tissue is attacked only after it has been heated to disrupt the triple helix. All three enzymes are unaffected by heating to 60°C, but chymopapain is the most stable of the three at 70°C (64).

A preparation of papaya enzymes as a dry powder diluted with salt and referred to as papain has been on the market as a meat tenderizer for some time. Sprinkled on the surface of meat, it must then be forked into the interior to be effective. It is essentially inactive in meat at room temperature, is increasingly active as meat is heated from 55° to 75°C (131° to 167°F), and is very active after meat reaches 80°C (176°F) (1). Once meat is heated to the optimum temperature, digestion of the proteins will continue. A temperature a few degrees higher (85°C, or 185°F) will inactivate the enzyme. Tenderization of meat by enzymes appears to be different from that effected by either aging or cooking. Meats tenderized by enzymes tend to have a mushy consistency due to the loss of structure of the muscle fibers.

INSPECTION

Meat is inspected to ensure that it is wholesome and fit for human consumption. The Federal Meat Inspection Act of 1906 makes inspection mandatory for all meat packing plants that slaughter and process meat to be marketed in interstate commerce. Federal inspection is done by or under the supervision of a trained veterinarian under the auspices of the Food Safety and Quality Service of the United States Department of Agriculture. The live animal, the carcass and certain parts where disease is likely to be evident, and the packing plant all are scrutinized, the meat for signs of disease and the plant from the standpoint of sanitation. Carcasses which pass federal inspection are identified on each wholesale cut by a round, purple stamp bearing the legend "U.S. INSP'D & P'S'D" together with the official number of the packing plant. (See Fig. 22-13.) A harmless purple fluid is used to stamp meat that passes inspection. The wording, "U.S. Inspected and Passed by Department of Agriculture," is used on labels of processed meats which pass inspection. The Wholesome Meat Act of 1967 made inspection of all meat mandatory including that slaugh-

FIGURE 22-13. Meat inspection stamps. The stamp on the left, used on fresh and cured meats, shows that the meat was inspected and passed as clean, wholesome food. The stamp on the right is used on canned and packaged meat products. The number indicates the meat packing establishment. (Courtesy of the United States Department of Agriculture.)

tered and marketed within a state. Inspection may be done under federal or state auspices. If the latter, the same standards apply as for federally inspected meat.

GRADES OF MEAT

QUALITY GRADES

Meat which has been inspected for wholesomeness may be graded for quality and for yield. Because of the great variation among beef carcasses in the quality of the lean, eight quality grades have been established: Prime, Choice, Good, Standard, Commercial, Utility, Cutter, and Canner (109). Presumably these grades reflect differences in the palatability of the meat, although there is some question as to their predictive value (13). The four top-quality grades, Prime through Standard, are reserved for the two youngest maturity classes (A and B) of beef. These younger animals have pinker, less ossified bones and the color and texture of the lean differ from that in more mature animals. C, D, and E maturity carcasses are graded Commercial or lower.

Both marbling and firmness and texture of the lean are considered when a quality grade is assigned to a carcass. Marbling, abundant in beef graded Prime, is slightly less so in Choice grade beef. (See Fig. 22-14.) Beef graded Good is somewhat leaner than that of the two top grades, and Standard grade beef has little if any marbling. Commercial grade beef may have marbling comparable with that in Prime or Choice beef, but it comes from mature animals. Utility, Cutter, and Canner grades of beef are used in ground beef and in fabricated meat products. The shield-shaped mark (Fig. 22-15) indicating the quality grade is repeated as a ribbon on the length of wholesale cuts in such a way that a grade mark appears on most retail cuts. Much of the beef on the market is of Choice grade. Grades established for veal are Prime, Choice, Good, Standard, Utility, and Cull. Little veal is marketed. Quality

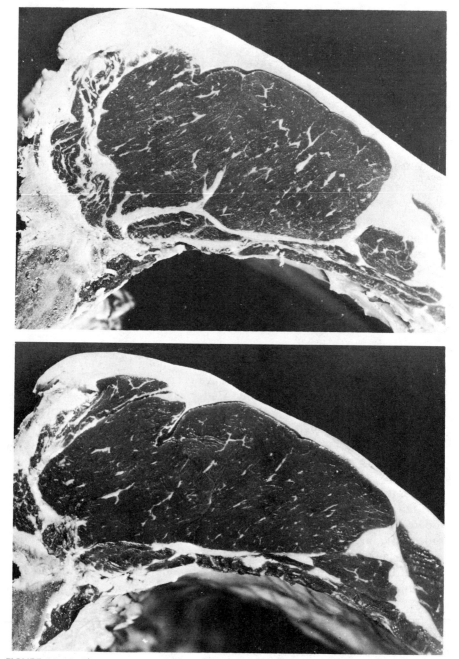

FIGURE 22-14. The two commonest grades of beef found on the market. Choice grade beef (above) is well marbled and has a good covering of exterior fat. Beef of Good grade (below) is leaner, with little fat intramuscularly and externally. (Courtesy of the United States Department of Agriculture.)

FIGURE 22-15. The grade of meat is indicated by a shield-shaped stamp. (Courtesy of the United States Department of Agriculture.)

grades for lamb are Prime, Choice, Good, Utility, and Cull. Pork on the market carries no grade mark for quality. A high proportion of beef and lamb on the market has been graded for quality, although grading, unlike inspection, is voluntary. In addition to these federal grades for quality, individual meat packers may use their own grading system along with brand names to indicate the grade of their products. Thus Swift's Premium, Armour's Star, and Wilson's Certified all denote a top-grade product from the respective packers.

YIELD GRADES

Meat that is officially graded for quality is graded for yield, also (110). Thickness and fullness of muscle and the amount of fat (both external and in the body cavity) that must be trimmed away are considered when a yield grade is assigned. Yield grades for beef are numbered 1 through 5. Carcasses, the round, loin, rib, and chuck of which yield the highest proportion of boneless, closely trimmed meat qualify for yield grade 1, those with the lowest proportion for yield grade 5.

COLOR OF MEAT

FRESH MEAT

Differences in the color of lean meats are due mainly to differences in concentration of the pigment myoglobin, which accounts for approximately three-fourths of the total pigment of red meat, the remainder due to the hemoglobin of the blood (37). Beef contains more myoglobin than does either veal or pork. The more exercised muscles tend to be deeper in color. For example, the heel of the round is a deeper color than cuts from the loin or rib of beef. Pork shoulder steak is a deeper color than is a chop from the loin.

At times puzzling changes may occur in the color of fresh meat, especially noticeable in lean beef. The change in color is due to a change in the pigment myoglobin. Molecules of myoglobin (and hemoglobin) contain the iron porphyrin compound, heme. Heme is made of four pyrrole groups united to form a porphyrin ring as shown:

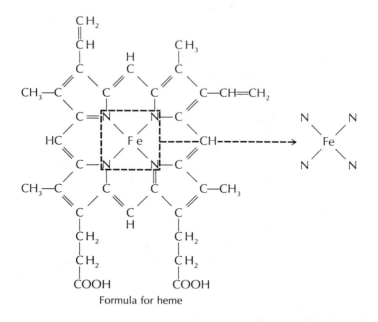

Formula for heme

Resonance of the conjugated double bonds in the porphyrin ring gives rise to the color of meat pigments. In the center of the porphyrin ring is an atom of iron linked covalently to the nitrogens of the four pyrrole groups. In the molecule of myoglobin the nitrogen of the protein moiety, a globin, is attached to the ferrous iron at the fifth coordination site (82), as shown:

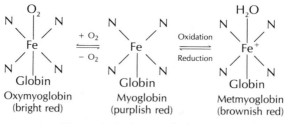

| Oxymyoglobin (bright red) | Myoglobin (purplish red) | Metmyoglobin (brownish red) |

Pigment in fresh, uncooked meats

Myoglobin, like hemoglobin, can unite temporarily and reversibly with oxygen, as shown above. In the live animal the myoglobin of muscle takes from hemoglobin of the blood the oxygen which the latter transports from the lungs to the tissues where it is needed. As soon as an animal stops breathing, its supply of oxygen is cut off and the tissues are depleted of oxygen. Myoglobin in unoxygenated form with the iron in the ferrous state gives to freshly cut beef its purplish-red color. Upon exposure to air the pigment in the cut surface of meat becomes oxygenated to form oxymyoglobin, which is a bright cherry red color. This difference in color of the pigment, depending on whether or not it is oxygenated, explains why the outer layer of ground meat on display for sale at a meat counter may be a bright red, whereas the interior is purplish-red. It also accounts for the fact that a slice of beef which has been partly covered by another may be two colors, purplish-red where the two overlapped and bright red on the exposed part.

When oxygen pressure is high, the pigment is maintained in the oxygenated form. Exposed to low levels of oxygen, the oxygen-myoglobin complex dissociates, the iron is oxidized to the ferric state, and brownish-red metmyoglobin is the result, as shown above. Reducing conditions which continue for a time in the meat will convert any metmyoglobin formed back to myoglobin. Thus in raw, uncured meat three forms of the pigment may exist in dynamic equilibrium (37). For prepackaged meats to retain a bright red color, the packaging film must be permeable to oxygen (92).

The pH of muscle influences the color of meat. At death the tissues are slightly alkaline, but lactic acid derived from glycogen accumulates in muscle postmortem. The final pH affects both the water-holding capacity of muscle and its color. The abnormally pale flesh from stress-susceptible pigs and the dark-cutting flesh of some beef animals are associated with abnormally low and high pH values, respectively (60).

CURED MEAT PIGMENT

Myoglobin has the ability to unite loosely not only with oxygen but also with nitric oxide, which occurs when meats such as bacon, ham, and corned beef are cured. The nitric oxide myoglobin is a light red (pink) rather than the purplish-red of myoglobin. When meat is exposed to low heat during curing, part of the nitric oxide myoglobin is changed to a more stable complex, the iron still in the ferrous state. The pigment is now considered to be nitric oxide myochrome (70), as shown:

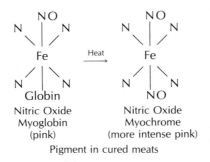

Pigment in cured meats

Although heat is not detrimental to the color of cured meat, exposure to light when the meat is in contact with oxygen will cause the color to fade.

Light accelerates the dissociation of nitric oxide from the pigment after which oxidation takes place (92). The iron is changed from the ferrous to the ferric form. Slices of ham are turned with the liner uppermost in meat display counters to protect the pigment and the color of the meat from the harmful effects of light. Photo-induced fading can be prevented by vacuum packaging in an oxygen-impervious wrap (92). Under certain circumstances oxidation of the porphyrin ring rather than of the iron may result in the formation of yellowish or greenish fluorescing compounds. The iridescence sometimes observed in cured ham and dried beef is attributed to the refraction of light by structural components of the meat rather than to changes in the pigment.

The advisability of using nitrite in curing meat has been questioned because of the possibility that nitrites may give rise to nitrosamines, suspected of being carcinogens (120). Nitrite, however, not only supplies nitric oxide which stabilizes the color but also alters flavor and, more importantly from a health standpoint, limits the growth of *Clostridium botulinum* and the production of toxin in meats which have not been heated sufficiently to be sterile (24).

COOKING MEAT

Meats are usually served cooked for a number of valid reasons. Heat destroys microorganisms which may have contaminated the surface. In addition to making the meat safer to eat, cooking also changes the color, alters the water-holding capacity, affects the tenderness, and develops the flavor and especially the characteristic aroma of meat. Some methods of cooking yield a more flavorful product than others. Heat brings about changes in the fat, the protein and, in the case of cured meats, the sugar which contribute to cooked meat flavor. The presence of sugar in cured meats and of glycogen in liver accounts for the ease with which these meats brown and even scorch if the cooking temperature is too high.

EFFECTS ON MEAT PIGMENT AND COLOR

Meat may be cooked for esthetic reasons. Heat brings about changes in the pigment which alter the color of the meat. The color of beef is changed more by cooking than is the less highly pigmented pork. Much of the pigment in the interior of a cut of raw beef is present as reduced and unoxygenated purplish-red myoglobin. When the meat is heated, the pigment is converted first to oxymyoglobin, as evidenced by the bright red color of the meat when cut (9). And with further heating the protein moiety of the pigment is denatured, the ferrous iron is oxidized, and the meat takes on the grayish-brown color of denatured globin hemichrome. Although the exact constitution of the pigment in cooked meat is still questioned, its attributes are not inconsistent with the structure as shown (38):

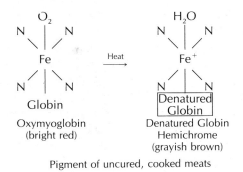

Pigment of uncured, cooked meats

Because heat brings about a change in the color of the pigment in meat, the color of cooked meat, especially tender cuts of beef, is used as an index to doneness, that is, the extent to which the meat proteins have been coagulated. The three stages of doneness to which tender cuts of beef may be cooked are characterized as rare, medium, and well done. For rare beef the internal temperature is 60°C (140°F). Rare meat is plump and juicy. The interior of rare beef is bright red and the surface is covered with a thin brown layer containing denatured globin hemichrome. Beef cooked to an internal temperature of 71°C (160°F) has reached the medium-done stage. The meat is less juicy and not so plump in appearance as rare meat. The interior of beef at the medium-done stage is pink rather than the bright red of rare beef because more of the myoglobin has been denatured, and the surface layer of brown is deeper. Tender beef heated to an internal temperature of 77°C (170°F) is considered well done. The meat no longer looks plump. It is less juicy than that cooked to the medium-done stage, although it need not be dried out. Meat cooked to the well-done stage is a uniform brown throughout.

The color of well-done meat from different animals is influenced by the amount of pigment in the raw meat. Well-done beef is darker than well-done pork. Pork loin changes from a pale, grayed pink to a near white. Pork shoulder steak and uncured ham, a dull rose red when raw and a deeper color than the loin, are grayish brown when cooked. Veal changes from pink to brownish gray. Cooking intensifies the color of the pigment in cured meats. On occasion, leftover meat which has been cooked to the well-done stage may take on the color of what appears to be oxymyoglobin.

Lamb and many cuts of beef are cooked to the well-done stage. Pork comes from young animals, and the meat is usually tender. However, for a number of years the recommended internal temperature for fresh pork was 85°C (185°F). This is higher than the well-done stage for tender cuts of beef. Flesh of pigs may be infected with the parasitic worm, *Trichinella spiralis,* which causes trichinosis in humans. These worms, which are embedded in the muscles of the animal, are microscopic in size, and their presence may go undetected when the meat is inspected. The high internal temperature formerly recommended for fresh pork was deemed essential to make the meat safe to eat. A temperature of 58.3°C (137°F) is lethal for the parasite, however, so the high temperature formerly recommended seems excessive. The minimum internal temperature of 65°C (149°F) now recommended for fresh pork loin provides an adequate margin of safety (116). This temperature is midway between the rare and medium stages of doneness for tender cuts of beef. Pork roasted to this lower internal temperature is juicier and more tender but less flavorful than that heated to a higher internal temperature.

Although cooking tender cuts of meat to a specified internal temperature to assess doneness is more precise than is cooking so many minutes per pound or per inch of thickness, two similar cuts cooked to the same internal temperature may vary somewhat in doneness, as assessed by color of the lean, if they are heated at different rates either in different media or in the same medium but at different temperatures (22). For example, 1-inch steaks cooked on a broiler rack in an oven at 177°C (350°F) to an internal temperature of 80°C (176°F) had the gray color of well-done beef, whereas steaks braised in steam to an internal temperature of 85°C (185°F) were still slightly pink (22). Cooking time for the former was approximately an hour and for the latter approximately 15 minutes.

Although doneness of tender beef may be assessed reasonably well by the color of the meat, tough cuts may not be tender when they reach an internal temperature of 77°C (170°F), the well-done stage for tender beef. So color is not a good criterion for doneness of less tender meat. The character of the connective tissue in a cut of meat influences how and how long the meat should be heated to make it tender. Collagen fibers in tough cuts should be sufficiently solubilized by cooking that the meat is fork-tender and the muscle fibers and bundles of fibers can be separated with relatively little pressure of the teeth.

EFFECTS ON MEAT PROTEINS AND TENDERNESS

Early studies emphasized the beneficial effects of low cooking temperature and low internal temperature on cooking losses, shrinkage, and tenderness of meat. Advantages of a low cooking temperature were attributed to the resultant longer cooking time (21). Later it was pointed out that what is considered a high cooking temperature depends on how the heat is transferred, with 400°F (204°C) judged high for roasting but low for broiling, and 250°F (121°C) judged low for roasting but 212°F (100°C) considered high for braising (22). Greater tenderness of beef cooked at lower temperatures (i.e., heated more slowly) has been verified by a number of workers, and the time the meat is held near 60°C has been proposed as a decisive factor (10).

Recent literature on meat cookery and tenderness is almost as voluminous as is that on the underlying causes of the toughness of meat. And the potential for altering the inherent tenderness or toughness of meat by cooking is great. Both the rate of heat penetration in the meat as affected by the temperature of the cooking medium and the final internal temperature have been investigated by a number of workers for their effects on the connective tissue and the fibrillar proteins and on the water-holding capacity of meat, all of which influence tenderness. The great number of papers on how cooking affects tenderness of meat is symptomatic of the complexity of the issue. The tenderness of cooked meat is evaluated by taste panel, by the force needed to shear the tissue, by tensile strength, and by the force required to compress the tissue.

Heating may either increase or decrease the tenderness of meat. Connective tissue is tenderized when meat is cooked. In one study, a decrease in shear observed when muscle (semitendinosus of the round) was held for some time at temperatures within the range of 55° to 65°C was attributed to the shrinkage or melting of collagen (72). There is some evidence that proteolytic activity occurs when the tissue is held for some time near 60°C (67,86). Tenderness of meat (top round) has been related to the time the internal temperature of the meat stayed in the 55°C to 60°C range (117). And the greater tenderness of meat (beef semitendinosus) when it was heated at 93°C instead of 149°C was attributed to the longer (3½ times) cooking time needed to bring the meat to an internal temperature of 70°C (88).

Shrinkage of collagen when meat is first put to cook causes the muscles to hump, particularly noticeable in less tender cuts. Heating beyond this stage will eventually convert collagen to water-dispersible gelatin. This change can markedly increase the tenderness of tough cuts of meat. The more collagen converted to gelatin, the weaker the collagen fibers; the less force required to separate the structural components of the meat, the more tender it is.

The time required to convert collagen to gelatin varies with the temperature. Conversion is negligible at 60°C (140°F) and requires considerable time when the temperature of the meat is no higher than 65°C (149°F). Between 65°C (149°F) and 80°C (176°F) conversion is more rapid (118). Over this range in temperature the rise in internal temperature in tough cuts of meat is retarded, as the flattening of the heating curve in Figure 22-16 illustrates (20). If muscle is heated at a temperature just above 75° to 80°C, shear declines (72), with transformation of collagen to gelatin the likely cause. Cooking tough cuts of meat in liquid at a low temperature (not above a slow boil) requires a relatively long time to convert enough of the collagen to gelatin so that fibers separate with ease. As the internal temperature increases the time required to convert collagen to gelatin decreases. Conversion is faster at 100°C (212°F) than it is at 85°C (185°F) and faster still at 121°C (250°F), the temperature in a pressure saucepan operating at 15 pounds (103 kPa) steam pressure. Cooking liquid around tough cuts of meat which have been cooked until tender often solidifies in a gel after it cools. The gelatin which forms from the insoluble collagenous connective tissue is responsible for gelling the broth after it has cooled.

$$\text{Gelatin sol} \rightleftharpoons \text{Gelatin gel}$$
$$\text{(Hot)} \qquad\qquad \text{(Cold)}$$

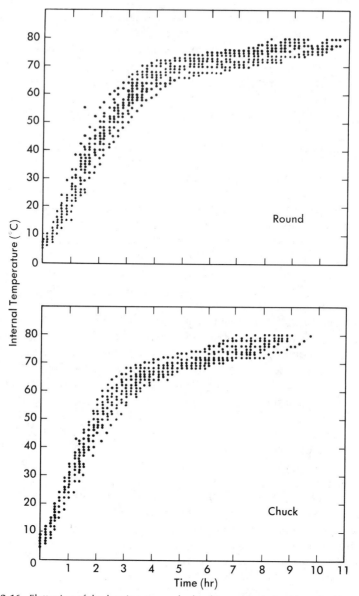

FIGURE 22-16. Flattening of the heating curves for beef (round and chuck) cooked in an oven at 125° C (257° F). (Courtesy of Sylvia Cover and Texas Agricultural Experiment Station, *Food Research* **6:** 236. Copyright © 1941 by Institute of Food Technologists.)

Ease in separation of fibers and bundles of fibers is not the only consideration when less-tender cuts of meat are cooked. The effects of heat on muscle fiber proteins should be considered, too. Less-tender meat may need more extensive heating to solubilize connective tissue fibers than is desirable from the standpoint of tenderness of the muscle fibers. Two stages in the temperature-dependent toughening of meat have been identified (33). The first increase in the force needed to shear the tissue occurred early in the heating sequence when the temperature of the tissue (neck muscle) rose from 40°C to 50°C. This increase in shear was accompanied by a sharp decrease in the solubility of myosin. A marked decrease in the hydration of the proteins of muscle when they were heated from 40°C to 50°C had been reported (44) earlier. Hardening of meat tissue has been observed when muscle was heated at temperatures between 65°C and 75°C (72). Identified as the second phase of toughening (33), meat heated in this temperature range had an additional increase in the force needed to shear it. Shortening of muscle fibers induced by shrinkage of collagen and the resultant loss of meat juice may account for this second stage in heat-induced toughening (33), although the effects of heat on the proteins of muscle fibers directly may be involved. Proteins of the muscle fibers are not equally sensitive to heat. α-actinin, the most labile, is made insoluble at 50°C, myosin at 55°C, actin at 70° to 80°C, and tropomyosin above 80°C (19). Denaturation and coagulation of sarcoplasmic proteins occur over a wide range in temperatures (40°C to 90°C) (33). The firming of meat tissue as it is heated is attributed to denaturation (unfolding) of the protein molecules of the muscle fibers and the subsequent formation of hydrogen, hydrophobic, and finally disulfide linkages between peptide chains (12).

The effect of heating on the water-holding capacity of muscle is an important factor relating to tenderness. Moisture, most of which in raw tissue is free water but held in the capillary spaces formed by the structural components of muscle (119), is lost as the proteins coagulate and the tissue shrinks. Liquefied fat is squeezed from fat storage areas as connective tissue is shrunken by heat. The crispness of cooked bacon is due to loss of moisture and to the effects of heat on the proteins of the lean and of the connective tissue that held the fat. Losses of fat and water contribute to shrinkage and loss of weight when meat is cooked. In an uncovered utensil, part of the loss of weight is due to evaporation. Some of the moisture collects with the fat in the cooking utensil and these make up the drippings. Cooking makes meat less juicy even when the meat is covered with water.

The loss of weight as meat is cooked is considered a rough index to the water-holding capacity of the tissues. Loss of weight and of water from longissimus and biceps femoris steaks were reported to increase with each increase in internal temperature (61°, 68°, 74°, and 80°C) (96). The increase from 74° to 80°C made the greatest difference in retention of water and in dimensions of the steaks. Softness and juiciness of the steaks decreased as internal temperature increased. Beef longissimus sealed in plastic and heated in a water bath programmed for a rise in temperature of 0.1°C per minute to a maximum of 60°C (rare) and held at that temperature for a total heating time of 10 hours contained twice as much uncoagulated protein as did samples of the muscle heated to 80°C in 1 hour and held at that temperature for an additional hour. Weight loss for the sample held at 60°C averaged 21.9 percent compared with a loss of 38.7 percent for samples held at 80°C (68). These results led to the suggestion that greater retention of juices due to reduced coagulation of myofibrillar proteins as well as alteration of the collagen fibers may account for the greater tenderness of meat cooked for a long time at a low temperature.

EFFECTS ON THE FINE STRUCTURE OF MUSCLE

The way cooking alters the fine structure of muscle and the relationship of the latter to tenderness have been studied using the light microscope, and, more recently and in greater detail, the transmission electron microscope which gives a greatly magnified view through the tissue, and the scanning electron microscope which gives a three-dimensional image or topographical view of the tissue.

Early work using the light microscope showed dimensional changes in muscle fibers brought about by heat. A gradual decrease in the width of muscle fiber fragments occurred up to 45°C and a rapid decrease from 45°C to 62°C, at which point the decrease was essentially complete. Shrinkage in length did not begin until 55°C, was very rapid and extensive between 55°C and 65°C, and continued but was less marked between 65°C and 80°C (51). Longitudinal shrinkage was accompanied by a loss of the brilliant birefringence characteristic of the raw tissue.

Changes in the fine structure of beef longissimus shown by transmission electron microscopy included initiation of shortening of sarcomeres and some degradation of structure of the Z-line when the tissue was heated to 50°C (99). Heated to 60°C, the thin filaments had begun to disintegrate and the thick filaments to coagulate, possibly accounting for the loss of birefringence observed when tissue was heated to this temperature. At 70°C changes in both thick and thin filaments were more marked. At 80°C and especially at 90°C filaments had become amorphous but banding that corresponded to the original sarcomeres remained (99). The transmission electron micrographs of Figure 22-17 illustrate changes in the fine structure of beef semitendinosus muscle heated to internal temperatures of 63°C, 68°C, and 73°C (69). Disappearance of material from the I-band and coagulation of material in the A-band are evident in tissue heated to 63°C. Some disorder appears in the Z-line. Reduction in the length of the sarcomeres is due mainly to shrinkage of the I-band. At 68°C, additional shortening of the I-band had occurred, but some actin filaments still remained. Heating to 73°C resulted in further shortening of the sarcomeres, some disruption of the Z-disks, and some breaks where the filaments of the I-band joined the Z-line. Changes in the fine structure of longissimus muscle heated to the three internal temperatures were more marked than were those in the semitendinosus. The progressive toughening of the muscle, measured by shear, as the internal temperature increased was attributed to the contracted and possibly hardened material of the A-band (69).

Changes in the fine structure of beef semimembranosus muscle, as imaged by a scanning electron microscope, were slight when the tissue was held at

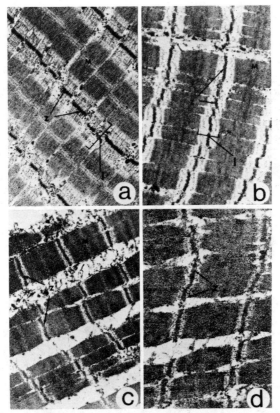

FIGURE 22-17. The effects of heating on the structure of aged beef muscle (semitendinosus) shown by transmission electron microscopy: (a) unheated; (b) heated to 63° C; (c) heated to 68° C; and (d) heated to 73° C. Magnification × 9260 for a, b, and c and 13,900 for d. I, I-band; M, M-line; Z, Z-line. (Reprinted from R. C. Leander, H. B. Hedrick, M. F. Brown, and J. A. White, *Journal of Food Science* **45:** 5, 1980. Copyright © by Institute of Food Technologists.

50°C for 45 minutes (62). When held at 60°C, the A-bands appeared more compact and breaks were observed at the junction of the A- and I-bands which left rigid blocks corresponding to the A-bands of the raw tissue. Little change in length of the sarcomeres was evident. When the tissue was held at 90°C, the sarcomeres had shortened and extensive detachment of Z-disks had occurred, but banding of the sarcomeres persisted.

Some changes in the connective tissue of meat when it was heated have been reported. Viewed by the light microscope, shrinkage of endomysial connective tissue was observed first near 50°C and was complete near 70°C, at which temperature changes in the perimysial fibers were first observed (99). Increases in both interfiber and interfibrillar spaces have been demonstrated in beef longissimus heated to 60°C (17). The endomysial sheath, closely associated with the muscle fibers in the raw state, appeared detached and wavy

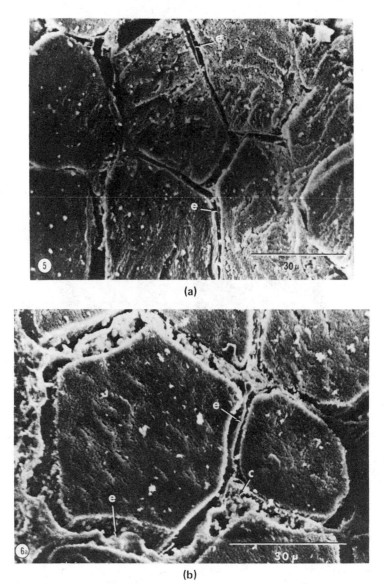

(a)

(b)

FIGURE 22-18. Effects of heating on the ultrastructure of beef longissimus muscle fibers, shown by scanning electron micrographs of cross-sectional fractures: (a) unheated ($\times$ 730); (b) heated to 70°C internal temperature ($\times$ 900). (Reproduced from C. S. Cheng and F. C. Parrish, *Journal of Food Science* **41:** 1452, 1976. Copyright © by Institute of Food Technologists.)

after the tissue was heated to 70°C (Fig. 22-18), indicative of shrinkage of the muscle fibers. Granular material appeared between the endomysial connective tissue and the fibers of longissimus muscle heated to 70°C, but was more evident when the internal temperature was 80°C. Degradation of perimysial connective tissue of longissimus and psoas major muscles of beef began near

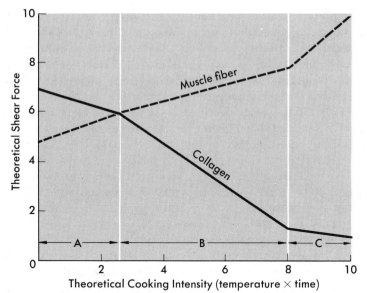

FIGURE 22-19. Effects of cooking on tenderness of meat. (From H. H. Wang et al., *Food Research* **19:** 320. Copyright © 1954 by Institute of Food Technologists.)

70°C and occurred rapidly at 80°C (17), but perimysial connective tissue in semitendinosus of beef still retained some of its fibrous character even after it had been heated at 90°C for 45 minutes (14).

The preceding discussion indicates that although heat may tenderize meat through its action on collagen, it may also toughen through its effect on coagulation and shrinkage of muscle fibers. These opposing effects are illustrated graphically in Figure 22-19. If tender cuts are heated only to the collagen melting temperature (near 60°C) or slightly above, coagulation of muscle fiber proteins will be incomplete, excessive shrinkage of muscle fibers will be avoided, and less of the meat juices will be lost. The meat will be as tender as cooked meat can be. Meat with background toughness because of collagen fibers is entirely different. Heating such meat at low temperature for a long time will eliminate connective tissue toughness and will minimize toughening caused by overcoagulation of muscle fiber proteins (68). However, even meat that originally was tender can be made rubbery, tough, and stringy by overheating. Toughness is due to the effects of high temperature on proteins of the muscle fibers and stringiness to almost complete conversion of collagen to gelatin.

EFFECTS ON FLAVOR

The effects of cooking on the flavor of meat is another consideration. Evidence suggests that cooking decomposes one or more precursors in the lean of meat to give the basic cooked meat taste. Less tender cuts which get much exercise have more extractives and thus are more flavorful. Lactones and sulfur-containing compounds, including sulfides, mercaptans, and cyclic compounds such as pyrazine, are thought to make important contributions to the flavor of cooked meats (16). Hydrogen sulfide, a prominent component, has been shown to be formed from the amino acid cystine (77). None of the numerous compounds isolated has been identified as uniquely meaty (114). Less tender cuts cook in less time in a pressure saucepan, but the flavor is not so well developed (43). Components identified in the aroma of beef cooked (in water) by microwave radiation have been characterized as less desirable than those identified in the aroma of beef heated conventionally (73). Apparently, long cooking is needed to develop a full, meaty flavor. The aroma from the heated adipose tissue differentiates beef from pork from lamb (49). Precursors of the aroma appear to be water soluble because when the fats were extracted with water before they were heated, they had only a basic meaty odor, not the aroma characteristic of the kind of meat (115).

The odorous compound in the fat of uncastrated male pigs, particularly noticeable in cooked, uncured pork, has been identified as the volatile steroid 5-α-androst-16-ene-3-one (85). Women can detect the odor better than men (92 percent vs. 56 percent of the subjects tested), and with the same odor thresholds women found the odor more unpleasant than did men (41).

Cooked meat reheated after being refrigerated is susceptible to oxidative rancidity referred to as warmed-over flavor. The phospholipid, phosphatidyl ethanolamine, with its high content of long chained polyunsaturated fatty acids is the major precursor of the warmed-over aroma, but the polyunsaturated fatty acids of the triglycerides are involved, too (58). Lamb is less susceptible to warmed-over flavor than is beef. Pork, with its high content of unsaturated fatty acids (Table 14-1), is the most susceptible of the three. The reaction that leads to warmed-over flavor is initiated by ferrous iron freed by cooking, not heme pigment as once thought (57). Nitrite, a good acceptor of free radicals, inhibits warmed-over flavor, so cured meats are less susceptible to oxidative rancidity. And in beef such oxidative rancidity was less the higher the cooking temperature and the longer the cooking time (53). The production of antioxidants as the meat browned was suggested as the cause. The aroma of cooked pork was judged better when it was reheated in a microwave rather than in a conventional oven (89).

EFFECT ON NUTRITIVE VALUE

Cooking does not appreciably lower the nutritive value of the proteins of meat (42). Retention of the B-vitamins (thiamine, riboflavin, niacin, and pantothenic acid) when meat is cooked is good (23,65,106). Losses of thiamine tend to be somewhat greater. Retention of the B-vitamins is somewhat greater in rare compared to well-done meat (23). When meat is cooked by moist heat, an appreciable quantity of each vitamin is found in the cooking liquid (78). Whether lamb roasts were cooked slowly in a microwave or in a conventional oven made no difference in the retention of thiamine and riboflavin (83).

Retentions of the two vitamins were essentially the same when top rounds of beef were cooked slowly in a portable oven broiler and in a conventional electric oven (65).

METHODS

Methods of cooking meat are classed as either dry- or moist-media methods. Actually, changes which take place in the interior of a piece of meat occur in a watery medium regardless of the cooking method used. Methods are described as moist or dry media on the basis of the medium which surrounds the meat as it cooks. Dry-media cooking encompasses those methods in which the meat is cooked without added water and with no lid on the pan so that moisture from the meat can evaporate. The meat is exposed to radiant energy or is in contact with hot air, a hot frying pan, or hot fat from which heat is conducted rather than with hot water or steam. Roasting, broiling, panbroiling, and frying are classed as dry-media methods for cooking meat. Dry-media methods are usually recommended for tender cuts of meat where coagulation of meat fiber proteins to the preferred stage of doneness is the object. Ground meat may be cooked by dry-media methods.

Moist-media cooking includes those methods in which the meat is cooked in a covered utensil (saucepan, pressure saucepan, foil wrap, or plastic bag), whether water is added or the meat is cooked in the steam or liquid which is released from the meat as the proteins coagulate. Braising and cooking in water are moist-media cookery methods. Pot roasting and breading are forms of braising. Less-tender cuts of meat are usually cooked by moist-media methods, especially on a surface unit. In this way the meat may be cooked long enough to be tenderized without danger of its cooking dry and scorching.

Tender cuts of meat are usually cooked by dry-media methods and tough cuts by moist-media methods, but there are exceptions. Tender cuts may be cooked by moist-media and some tough cuts can be tenderized by dry-media methods. For example, a tough cut of beef may be made tender by roasting if the oven temperature is kept very low (80°C, or 176°F) and the cooking time is long (several hours) (22).

ROASTING. Roasting is one of the simplest methods of cooking meat. The cut is placed with the fat side up on a rack, unless the bone will support it, and in a shallow pan. A meat thermometer, if available, is placed in the cut with the bulb in the center of the largest muscle not touching bone or fat. The oven need not be preheated but may be set to bake and turned on when the roast is put to cook. An oven temperature of 163°C (325°F) is satisfactory for all except very small cuts, for which a higher temperature (177°C or 350°F) is recommended, or for very large cuts, for which a lower temperature (149°C or 300°F) gives more uniform doneness.

Roasts are cooked to the degree of doneness desired as indicated by the internal temperature or for the time specified in a timetable. Timetables for roasting give the approximate cooking time in minutes per pound. Differences in the size and shape of the cut, in the temperature of the meat when it is put to cook, and small differences in oven temperature will influence the roasting time. Frozen roasts need not be thawed before they are put to cook, but the cooking time may be increased 50 percent, so thawing saves energy. The fat content of meat influences the roasting time, which is longer for muscle low in fat or with coarse, uneven marbling (25). Use of a meat thermometer is a more accurate way to assess doneness. Allowance should be made for the fact that, because of conduction from hotter outer layers, the temperature will continue to rise 5 to 10 degrees after the meat is removed from the oven, especially in larger roasts.

In one study which compared beef ribs roasted at an oven temperature of 225°F (107°C) with the customarily recommended 325°F (163°C), cooking losses were usually lower for the former even though the cooking time was longer. As might be anticipated, cooking losses increased as the internal temperature increased from 60°C to 70°C to 77°C (6). Roasts cooked at the lower temperature and those heated to the rare stage at the higher oven temperature were judged more tender than the others. Roasting meat in a microwave rather than in a conventional oven reduced cooking time markedly but increased cooking losses and shrinkage (46,66,121). Roasts should be removed from a microwave oven some time (20 to 30 minutes) before the meat reaches the internal temperature desired to allow for the increase in temperature that follows (46,97). Roasts carve better if allowed to stand a few minutes after they are cooked.

Roasting is a good method for cooking large, tender cuts of meat. Beef rib or rump roast, leg or loin of veal, loin or shoulder of pork, ham, or leg or shoulder of lamb are frequently roasted. Cuts from the round or chuck of Choice or Good grade beef may be roasted, especially if the oven temperature is reduced to 300°F (149°C) or lower so that meat is heated a longer time to reach the stage of doneness desired.

BROILING.   Broiling is cooking by radiant energy. On an electric range the door to the broiler or oven is left partly open so the thermostat will not turn the current off; on a gas range the door is usually closed. Meat to be broiled is placed on a rack in the broiler pan and the oven regulator set at "broil." The broiler pan is adjusted so that the meat is from 2 to 5 inches from the source of heat. The shorter distance is used for thin cuts of meat, ¾ to 1 inch thick, whereas those 1 to 2 inches thick are placed farther from the heat. Broiled meat is more uniformly done the farther the cut is placed from the source of the heat. Also, less spattering and smoking occur and the oven or broiler is not so hard to clean. The aroma of meat broiled nearer the unit may be somewhat greater, owing to "cracking" of proteins and decomposition of fat by heat.

When the meat is approximately half done and the top surface is brown, it is then salted, turned, and broiled on the other side. Salt on raw meat draws liquid from tissues to the surface by osmosis, and this moisture delays browning. Tongs, rather than a fork that pierces the lean, are recommended for turning the meat. Cooking is continued until the desired stage of doneness is reached. Doneness can be observed by making a slit near the bone and noting the color of the juice. A more accurate way of assessing doneness of broiled meat is with a meat thermometer, but one can be used only on thicker cuts.

The approximate total cooking time for broiling cuts of meat of different thicknesses to both rare and medium-done stages are given in timetables for cooking meats. Most cuts require an additional 5 minutes to progress from rare to medium done. A half-inch difference in thickness of a cut to be broiled makes a difference of approximately 5 minutes in broiling time. Thicker cuts yield plumper and juicier cooked meat. A broiled steak 1½ to 2 inches thick, cut into two servings, is superior to two ¾- to 1-inch broiled steaks. Broiled meat should be served immediately once it has reached the desired doneness.

Tender steaks and chops, ground meat, and cubed meat for kabobs are suitable for broiling. Broiling is a faster method of cooking than is roasting because the transfer of energy (chiefly radiant) is more rapid. The estimated cooking time for a 2-to-3-pound loin roasted to the rare stage in a hot oven is 5 to 10 minutes longer than that for a 2-inch porterhouse steak weighing 2½ to 3½ pounds broiled to the rare stage.

A recent study compared roasting top round (semimembranosus) in an oven at 350°F (176°C) versus broiling (350°F or 176°C at the top surface) of top round to internal temperatures of 60°C and 71°C (5). Roasting required twice as much time as did broiling but used less than half the kilowatts of electricity. Cooking losses were greater from steaks that were broiled and greater in steaks heated to the higher temperature. Roasted steaks were ranked juicier and more tender than those broiled to the same temperature, but neither the method nor the doneness had a marked effect on the shear force. Steaks heated to 60°C by roasting appeared not as well done as did those heated to 60°C by broiling. Steaks which were roasted needed less attention and the oven had less spatter.

PANBROILING. In panbroiling, energy is transferred from a surface unit to the meat primarily by conduction from the heated frying pan or griddle, although some radiant energy gets through the utensil. Meat is placed in a cold skillet or griddle and the heating unit is adjusted to moderate so that the meat cooks slowly. It is turned occasionally, and any fat that accumulates is poured off so the meat will continue to panbroil rather than panfry. When the meat appears to be done, the color of the meat may be checked by making a cut in the thickest part or in the meat next to the bone. Cuts which are suitable for panbroiling have a fair amount of fat and include those recommended for broiling. Ground beef patties and pork chops are often panbroiled.

PANFRYING AND DEEP FAT FRYING. Meat may be cooked in fat by panfrying or by deep fat frying. Panfried meat is cooked in a small amount of added fat or in the fat which accumulates as the meat cooks. The temperature is adjusted so that the fat is hot enough to brown the meat but no so hot that the fat decomposes and smokes. The meat is turned occasionally. Panfried meat is crisp and flavorful at some sacrifice in tenderness and juiciness. Thin cuts of tender meat or tough cuts tenderized by slashing or cubing are best for pan-frying.

For deep fat frying, enough fat is used to cover the meat completely, thus ensuring a rapid transfer of heat into the meat. Fat used to fry meat is preheated to a temperature of 177°C (350°F) to 190°C (375°F).

BRAISING. Braising is the more commonly used of the two methods of moist-media cookery. The meat may first be browned on a surface unit of the range. A heavy utensil is used. If the cut is lean or the meat has been floured, a small amount of fat in the utensil is essential for browning the meat. The temperature should be high enough that the meat browns, but not so high that the fat smokes. The meat is turned to brown on all sides. A small quantity of liquid may be added at the beginning and during cooking to keep the meat from becoming dry. The utensil is covered with a tight-fitting lid and the surface unit adjusted to keep the cooking liquid between simmering temperature and a gentle boil. Alternately, braised meat may be cooked in an oven set at 121°C (250°F) to 149°C (300°F).

The feasibility of using a portable oven broiler to cook less tender cuts has been studied (65). Top round of beef in a covered dish cooked to 88°C in an oven broiler with the heat setting low had greater cooking losses, but was more tender (shear value and panel scores) than was top round cooked in an electric oven preheated to 135°C (275°F). Flavor, juiciness, and retention of thiamine and riboflavin were essentially the same for the two methods. The meat will cook in less time in a pressure saucepan, but the meat fibers tend to be tough and stringy and the flavor of the meat is not fully developed. A comparison of top round of beef braised in an oven at 149°C (300°F) and in a pressure saucepan at 115°C (10 psi or 69 pKa) with samples of the same muscle cooked in deep fat or roasted in an oven at 149°C (300°F) showed that cooking losses were greatest from meat cooked in a pressure saucepan and least from meat that was roasted. The method of cooking made little difference in flavor, tenderness, and overall acceptability (100). Doneness of braised meat can be tested by piercing it with a fork. The cooking liquid from braised meat is very flavorful and can be used for making gravy or sauce.

Rolled shoulder of lamb or veal and large pieces of meat from the chuck and the heel of the round of beef are usually cooked by braising. When vegetables are cooked with the meat, the product is called pot roast. Smaller cuts of meat which are suitable for braising include pork liver, kidney, flank steak, short ribs, and round and shoulder arm steak of beef. The last two cuts of beef when braised are called Swiss steak. Shoulder chops of lamb and shoulder steaks of pork and veal, veal loin and rib chops and veal round steaks (called "cutlets") are cooked successfully by braising. Pork chops, although tender cuts, are usually braised with or without water added. Cubed stew meat from beef, veal, or lamb is braised also. Flank steak is often stuffed, rolled parallel to the grain of the fibers, and cooked by braising. When the meat is carved, it can be cut across the grain of the fibers.

COOKING IN WATER.   Large pieces of less-tender meat may be cooked in water to cover. The meat may or may not be browned before it is covered with water or broth. The utensil is covered and the meat simmered until it is tender when tested with a fork. If the meat is to be served cold, allowing it to cool in the broth is recommended to make it juicy and flavorful. Cooling should be hastened by placing the uncovered utensil in cold water. Cuts cooked in liquid include heart, tongue, kidney, smoked ham shank or picnic, corned beef, and heel of round. Meat for stew may be cooked by this method as well as by braising. Meat (and bone) for soup is cooked in water. The bone contributes no flavor but the gelatin obtained from it contributes body to the soup stock. Pieces of neck and the heel of round make especially flavorful soup stock and stews. Vegetables should be added to stews as well as to "boiled" dinners only after the meat is nearly done.

Soup stock may be clarified for esthetic purposes. The cool stock is blended with egg white and then heated. The fine particles which float in the broth and make it cloudy are trapped by the coagulating egg which may be strained out. Chilling meat broth to be used as soup stock hardens the fat so it can be removed easily. The layer of fat which hardens on the surface of the broth protects it from contamination by bacteria. The fat should be removed just before the broth is used. Soup stock as in vegetable soup should not have a film of fat floating on the surface.

COOKING FROZEN MEAT

Frozen steaks can go directly into the broiler or skillet, to be cooked without preliminary thawing. At least partial thawing of large tender cuts of meat like roasts may be desirable to shorten the time the cut remains in the oven. Frozen meat should be thawed in the wrapper and, preferably, in the refrigerator. Tough cuts may be thawed in the water in which the meat is to be cooked. The cooking time for frozen meat is longer than for unfrozen cuts of the same kind and size to allow for the thawing of the cut.

STORAGE OF MEAT

Cells of raw meat continue some of the life processes of the live animal. Metabolic changes which take place in the cells of meat tissue are temperature-dependent. The lower the holding temperature, the slower are the reactions and the longer is the time the meat can be kept. A low storage temperature also slows the multiplication of bacteria on the surface of the meat. The high percentage of water in fresh meat favors the multiplication of bacteria and is one reason meats spoil so readily. Fresh meat should be cooked within three or four days of the date of purchase. Hamburger meat is highly perishable because grinding enormously increases the surface area that may be contaminated by microorganisms. Hamburger should be cooked within a day or two after purchase, or frozen in cookable portions and stored at $-18°C$ (0°F). Freezing raw meat denatures the protein somewhat even under the best of circumstances. Thawing and refreezing compound the damage.

The cells of cooked meat are actually dead; hence, although the bacterial population is temporarily reduced by cooking, the cooked meat is highly perishable. Cooked meat should be cooled promptly and then refrigerated. Even then it should be used within four days for best quality.

REFERENCES

1. American Meat Institute Foundation. 1960. *The Science of Meat and Meat Products*. San Francisco: W. H. Freeman & Co. Pp. 37–44, tenderizing agents; pp. 73–85, proteins in meat; pp. 88–95, pigments in meat.
2. Bailey, A. J. 1972. The basis of meat texture. *J. Sci. Food Agric.* **23:** 995–1007. A review.
3. Bailey, A. J., C. M. Peach, and L. J. Fowler. 1970. Chemistry of collagen cross-links. Isolation and characterization of two intermediate cross-links in collagen. *Biochem. J.* **117:** 819–831. Lysine-derived reducible and permanent cross-links.
4. Bailey, A. J., D. J. Restall, T. J. Sims, and V. C. Duance. 1979. Meat tenderness: Immunofluorescent localization of isomorphic forms of collagen in bovine muscles varying in texture. *J. Sci. Food Agric.* **30:** 203–210. Collagen types and tenderness of muscle.
5. Batcher, O. M., and P. A. Deary. 1975. Quality characteristics of broiled and roasted beef steaks. *J. Food Sci.* **40:** 745–746. Cooking times, cooking losses, press fluid, shear, and panel scores.
6. Bayne, B. H., M. B. Allen, N. F. Large, B. H. Meyers, and G. E. Goertz. 1973. Sensory and histological characteristics of beef rib roasts heated at two rates to three end point temperatures. *Home Economics Research J.* **2:** 29–34. Oven temperatures of 107°C and 163°C and end points of 60°C, 70°C, and 77°C compared.
7. Bendall, J. R. 1967. The elastin content of various muscles of beef animals. *J. Sci. Food Agric.* **18:** 553–558. Muscles grouped for high, medium, and low elastin content.
8. Bendall, J. R. 1966. Muscle as a contractile machine. In *Physiology and Biochemistry of Muscle as Food.* E. J. Briskey, R. G. Cassens, and J. C. Trautman, eds. Madison: University of Wisconsin Press. Pp. 7–16. Organization of muscle fibers.
9. Bernofsky, C. J., B. Fox, Jr., and B. S. Schweigert. 1959. Biochemistry of myoglobin. VII. The effects of cooking on the myoglobin of beef muscle. *Food Research* **24:** 339–343. Changes in the pigment of meat induced by heat.

10. Bramblett, V. D., R. L. Hostetler, G. E. Vail, and H. N. Draudt. 1959. Qualities of beef as affected by cooking at very low temperatures for long periods of time. *Food Technol.* **13:** 707–711. Five muscles of the round cooked at 63°C versus 68°C.

11. Busch, W. A., M. H. Stromer, D. E. Goll, and A. Suzuki. 1972. Ca^{2+}-specific removal of Z-lines from rabbit skeletal muscle. *J. Cell Biol.* **52:** 367–381. An endogenous enzyme that can degrade the myofibrils.

12. Buttkus, H. 1974. On the nature of the chemical and physical bonds which contribute to some structural properties of protein foods: A hypothesis. *J. Food Sci.* **39:** 484–489. Bonding involved when protein foods are cooked.

13. Campion, D. R., J. R. Crouse, and M. E. Dikeman. 1975. Predictive value of USDA beef quality grade factors for cooked meat palatability. *J. Food Sci.* **40:** 1225–1228. Low predictive value for young steers.

14. Carroll, R. J., F. P. Rorer, S. B. Jones, and J. R. Cavanaugh. 1978. Effect of tensile stress on the ultrastructure of bovine muscle. *J. Food Sci.* **43:** 1181–1187. Connective tissue and muscle fibers of raw and heated (90°C) beef semitendinosus viewed by transmission and scanning electron microscopy.

15. Cassens, R. G., and C. C. Cooper. 1971. Red and white muscle. *Advances in Food Research* **19:** 1–74. Characterization of the two types; importance to meat science.

16. Chang, S., and R. J. Peterson. 1977. Symposium: The basis of quality in muscle foods. Recent developments in the flavor of meat. *J. Food Sci.* **42:** 298–305. Summary of current knowledge.

17. Cheng, C. S., and F. C. Parrish. 1976. Scanning electron microscopy of bovine muscle: Effects of heating on ultrastructure. *J. Food Sci.* **41:** 1449–1454. Micrographs of longissimus muscle, raw and heated to 60°, 70°, and 80°C.

18. Cheng, C. S., and F. C. Parrish. 1978. Molecular changes in the salt-soluble myofibrillar proteins of bovine muscle. *J. Food Sci.* **43:** 461–463, 487. Postmortem changes related to aging.

19. Cheng, C. S., and F. C. Parrish. 1979. Heat-induced changes in myofibrillar proteins of beef longissimus muscle. *J. Food Sci.* **44:** 22–25. Effects of internal temperature on proteins of thick and thin filaments and of Z-disks.

20. Cover, S. 1941. Effect of metal skewers on cooking time and tenderness of beef. *Food Research* **6:** 233–238. Rate of heat penetration and tenderness of beef; heating curves during cooking.

21. Cover, S. 1943. Effects of extremely low rates of heat penetration on tenderizing of beef. *Food Research* **8:** 388–394. Oven temperatures of 80°C (176°F) and 125°C (357°F) compared.

22. Cover, S., and R. L. Hostetler. 1960. *Beef tenderness by new methods: An examination of some theories.* Texas Agr. Expt. Sta. Bull. No. 947. 24 pp. A review of theories; data on the effect of dry *vs.* moist heat and on the degree of doneness as it affects tenderness of loin and round steaks.

23. Cover, S., B. A. McLaren, and P. B. Peters. 1944. Retention of the B-vitamins in rare and well-done beef. *J. Nutrition* **27:** 363–375. Rib roasts of beef analyzed for thiamine, riboflavin, niacin, and pantothenic acid.

24. Crosley, N. T., and R. Sawyer. 1976. N-nitrosamines: A review of chemical and biological properties and their estimation in foodstuffs. *Advances in Food Research* **22:** 1–71. A summary.

25. Cross, H. R. 1977. Effect of amount, distribution and texture of marbling on cooking properties of beef longissimus. *J. Food Sci.* **42:** 185–188. Cooking time of 192 longissimus steaks differing widely in marbling.

26. Cross, H. R. 1979. Effects of electrical stimulation on meat tissue and muscle properties. A review. *J. Food Sci.* **44:** 509–514. Summary of papers on the topic; future outlook.

27. Cross, H. R., Z. L. Carpenter, and G. C. Smith. 1973. Effects of intramuscular collagen and elastin on bovine muscle tenderness. *J. Food Sci.* **38:** 998–1003. Five muscles compared.

28. Culler, R. D., F. C. Parrish, Jr., G. C. Smith, and H. R. Cross. 1978. Relationship of myofibrillar fragmentation index to certain chemical, physical and sensory characteristics of bovine longissimus dorsi. *J. Food Sci.* **43:** 1177–1180. Sarcomere length, soluble collagen, and myofibrillar fragmentation as indices to tenderness.

29. Davies, R. E. 1963. A molecular theory of muscle contraction: Calcium-dependent contractions with hydrogen bond formation plus ATP-dependent extension of part of the myosin-actin cross bridge. *Nature* **199:** 1068–1074. Biochemical reactions involved in shortening of the sarcomeres.

30. Davey, C. L., and M. R. Dickson. 1970. Studies on meat tenderness. 8. Ultrastructural changes in meat during aging. *J. Food Sci.* **35:** 56–60. Myofibrillar changes and loss of tensile strength.

31. Davey, C. L., and K. V. Gilbert. 1967. Structural changes in meat during aging. *J. Food Technol.* **2:** 57–59. Effects on the Z-line.

32. Davey, C. L., and K. V. Gilbert. 1969. Studies in meat tenderness. 7. Changes in the fine structure of meat during aging. *J. Food Sci.* **34:** 69–74. Effects on lateral adhesion; role of calcium ions.

33. Davey, C. L., and K. V. Gilbert. 1974. Temperature-dependent cooking toughness in beef. *J. Sci. Food Agric.* **25:** 931–938. Two phases of heat-induced toughening.

34. Davey, C. L., and A. E. Grafhaus. 1976. Structural changes in beef muscle during aging. *J. Sci. Food Agric.* **27:** 301–306. Another attempt to learn what happens when meat is aged.

35. Davey, C. L., H. Kuttel, and K. V. Gilbert. 1967. Shortening as a factor in meat aging. *J. Food Technol.* **2:** 53–56. Relation of shortening to tenderness.

36. Eino, M. F., and D. W. Stanley. 1973. Surface ultrastructure and tensile properties of cathepsin and collagenase treated muscle fibers. *J. Food Sci.* **38:** 51–55. Evidence that cathepsin effects changes resembling those from aging.

37. Fox, J. B., Jr. 1966. The chemistry of meat pigments. *J. Agr. Food Chem.* **14:** 207–210. Fresh and cured meat pigments and the color of meat.

38. Giddings, G. G. 1977. Symposium: The basis of quality in muscle foods. The basis of color in muscle foods. *J. Food Sci.* **42:** 288–294. A review; technical.

39. Goll, D. E., N. Arakawa, M. H. Stromer, W. A. Busch, and R. M. Robson. 1970. Chemistry of muscle proteins as a food. In *The Physiology and Biochemistry of Muscle as a Food*. E. J. Briskey, E. J. Cassens, and B. B. Marsh, eds. Madison: University of Wisconsin Press. Vol. 2, pp. 755–800. Onset and resolution of rigor.

40. Goll, D. E., W. G. Hoekstra, and R. W. Bray. 1964. Age associated changes in bovine muscle connective tissue. 2. Exposure to increasing temperature. *J.*

Food Sci. **29:** 615–621. Solubility of connective tissue from muscles of veal, steer, cow, and old cow.

41. Griffiths, N. M., and R. L. S. Patterson. 1970. Human olfactory response to 5-a-androst-16-ene-3-one—principal component of boar taint. *J. Sci. Food Agric.* **21:** 4–6. Odor thresholds of men versus women.

42. Griswold, R. M. 1951. Effect of heat on the nutritive value of proteins. *J. Am. Dietet. Assoc.* **27:** 85–95. A review article.

43. Griswold, R. M. 1956. The effect of different methods of cooking beef round of commercial and prime grades. I. Palatability and shear force values. *Food Research* **20:** 160–170. Braising, cooking in a pressure saucepan, and roasting at two oven temperatures.

44. Hamm, R., and F. E. Deatherage. 1960. Changes in hydration, solubility and charges of muscle proteins during heating of meat. *Food Research* **25:** 587–610. An early study of the effects of heat on muscle proteins.

45. Harrison, D. L., J. A. Bowers, L. L. Anderson, H. J. Tuma, and D. K. Kropf. 1970. Effect of aging on palatability and selected related characteristics of pork loin. *J. Food Sci.* **35:** 292–294. Aging for 1, 4, 8, and 12 days.

46. Headley, M. E., and M. Jacobson. 1960. Electronic and conventional cookery of lamb roasts. *J. Am. Dietet. Assoc.* **36:** 337–340. Cooking time, cooking losses, and palatability.

47. Herring, H. K., R. G. Cassens, and E. J. Briskey. 1967. Factors affecting collagen solubility in bovine muscle. *J. Food Sci.* **32:** 534–538. Maturity of the animal, state of contraction, and postmortem aging considered.

48. Hill, F. L. 1966. The solubility of intramuscular collagen in meat animals of various ages. *J. Food Sci.* **31:** 161–166. Cattle, pigs, and sheep differing in maturity.

49. Hornstein, I., and P. F. Crowe. 1963. Meat flavor; Lamb. *J. Agr. Food Chem.* **11:** 147–149. Source of the characteristic aroma of meats.

50. Hostetler, R. L., Z. L. Carpenter, C. C. Smith, and T. R. Dutson. 1975. Comparison of postmortem treatments for improving tenderness of beef. *J. Food Sci.* **40:** 223–226. Two methods of hanging a carcass with and without preliminary conditioning at 16°C prior to chilling.

51. Hostetler, R. L., and W. A. Landmann. 1968. Photomicrographic studies of dynamic changes in muscle fiber fragments. 1. Effects of various heat treatments on length, width, and birefringence. *J. Food Sci.* **33:** 468–470. Changes attributed to coagulation of proteins of the muscle fibers.

52. Hostetler, R. L., B. A. Link, W. A. Landmann, and H. A. Fitzhugh, Jr. 1973. Effect of carcass suspension method on sensory panel scores for some major bovine muscles. *J. Food Sci.* **38:** 264–267. Nine muscles varying in connective tissue compared.

53. Huang, W. H., and B. E. Green. 1978. Effect of cooking method on TBA numbers of stored beef. *J. Food Sci.* **43:** 1201–1203, 1209. Beef semitendinosus heated by roasting, braising, in a pressure saucepan, in a microwave oven, and by canning.

54. Huxley, H. E. 1958. The contraction of muscle. *Sci. American* **199**(5): 67–82. The structure of striated muscle; electron micrographs and diagrams.

55. Huxley, H. E. 1969. The mechanism of muscular contraction. *Science* **164:** 1356–1366. Details of the sliding filament theory.

56. Huxley, H. E. 1971. The structural basis of muscular contraction. *Proc. Royal Soc. B.* **178:** 131–149. The Croonian lecture on the topic.

57. Igene, J. O., J. A. King, A. M. Pearson, and J. I. Gray. 1979. Influence of heme pigments, nitrite and non-heme iron on the development of warmed-over flavor (WOF) in cooked meat. *J. Agr. Food Chem.* **27:** 838–842. Identification of major prooxidants.

58. Igene, J. O., and A. M. Pearson. 1979. Role of phospholipids and triglycerides in warmed-over flavor development in meat model systems. *J. Food Sci.* **44:** 1285–1290. Sources of warmed-over flavor.

59. Industrywide Cooperative Meat Identification Standards Committee. 1973. *Uniform Meat Identity Standards.* National Live Stock and Meat Board. A proposal for standardizing the names and labeling of retail cuts of meat.

60. Janicki, M. A., J. Kortz, and J. Rozyczka. 1967. Relationship of color with certain chemical and physical properties of porcine muscle. *J. Food Sci.* **32:** 375–378. The pH, water-holding capacity, and color.

61. Jones, S. B. 1977. Ultrastructural characteristics of beef muscle. *Food Technol.* **31**(4): 82–85. Beef semitendinosus muscle imaged by a scanning electron microscope.

62. Jones, S. B., R. J. Carroll, and J. R. Cavanaugh. 1977. Structural changes in heated bovine muscle: A scanning electron microscope study. *J. Food Sci.* **42:** 125–131. Beef semitendinosus muscle heated at 50°, 60°, and 90°C.

63. Kang, C. K., and E. E. Rice. 1970. Degradation of various meat protein fractions by tenderizing enzymes. *J. Food Sci.* **35:** 563–565. Effects of collagenase, bromelain, trypsin, ficin, and Rhozyme P-11 on myofibrillar, sarcoplasmic and stroma proteins.

64. Kang, C. K., and W. D. Warner. 1974. Tenderization of meat with papaya latex proteases. *J. Food Sci.* **39:** 812–818. Stability of the proteases to heat; substrates.

65. Korschgren, B. M., and R. E. Baldwin. 1978. Sensory qualities, cooking losses, shear values, and B-vitamins of beef roasts cooked by slow heat. *Home Economics Research J.* **7:** 116–120. Top rounds braised in a portable oven broiler versus a household electric oven.

66. Korschgren, B. M., R. E. Baldwin, and S. Snider. 1976. Quality factors in beef, pork, and lamb cooked by microwaves. *J. Am. Dietet. Assoc.* **69:** 635–639. Low- and high-powered ovens compared.

67. Laakkonen, E., J. W. Sherbon, and G. H. Wellington. 1970. Low-temperature, long-time heating of bovine muscle. 3. Collagenase activity. *J. Food Sci.* **35:** 181–183. Evidence for a collagenase-like enzyme in the water-soluble fraction.

68. Laakkonen, E., G. H. Wellington, and J. W. Sherbon. 1970. Low-temperature, long-time heating of bovine muscle. 1. Changes in tenderness, water-holding capacity, pH and amount of water-soluble components. *J. Food Sci.* **35:** 175–177. Effect of programmed, slow rise in internal temperature.

69. Leander, R. C., H. B. Hedrick, M. F. Brown, and J. A. White. 1980. Comparison of structural changes in beef longissimus and semitendinosus muscle during cooking. *J. Food Sci.* **45:** 1–6, 12. Transmission and scanning electron microscopy of muscle fibers and connective tissue heated at 177°C to internal temperatures of 63°, 68°, and 73°C.

70. Lee, S. H., and R. G. Cassens. 1976. Nitrite binding sites on myoglobin. *J. Food Sci.* **41:** 969–970. Evidence for the dinitrosyl structure of cooked cured meat pigment.

71. Lijinsky, W., and S. S. Epstein. 1970. Nitrosamines as environmental carcinogens. *Nature* **225:** 21–23. Sources and possible hazards.

72. Machlik, S. M., and H. N. Draudt. 1963. The effect of heating time and temperature on the shear of beef semitendinosus muscle. *J. Food Sci.* **28:** 711–718. Muscle heated at one degree intervals between 50°C and 90°C.

73. MacLeod, G., and B. M. Coppock. 1976. Volatile flavor components of beef boiled conventionally and by microwave radiation. *J. Agr. Food Chem.* **24:** 835–842. Identification and characterization of the compounds.

74. Marsh, B. B. 1977. Symposium: The basis of quality in muscle foods. The basis of tenderness in muscle foods. *J. Food Sci.* **42:** 295–297. A readable summary of current concepts.

75. Marsh, B. B., and W. A. Carse. 1974. Meat tenderness and the sliding-filament hypothesis. *J. Food Technol.* **9:** 129–139. An attempt to account for the effects of shortening of the sarcomeres on tenderness.

76. Marsh, B. B., and N. G. Leet. 1966. Studies in meat tenderness. III. The effects of cold-shortening on tenderness. *J. Food Sci.* **31:** 450–459. The concepts of background and actomyosin toughness.

77. Meschi, E. P., E. L. Pippen, and H. Lineweaver. 1964. Origin of hydrogen sulfide in heated chicken muscle. *J. Food Sci.* **29:** 393–399. Identification of the sulfur-containing precursor.

78. Meyer, B. H., W. F. Hinman, and E. G. Halliday. 1947. Retention of some vitamins of the B-complex in beef during cooking. *Food Research* **12:** 203–211. Niacin and pantothenic acid retention in braised, broiled, and fried beef.

79. Miyada, D. S., and A. L. Tappel. 1956. The hydrolysis of beef proteins by various proteolytic enzymes. *Food Research* **21:** 217–225. Enzymes and their substrates.

80. Murray, J. M., and A. Weber. 1974. The cooperative action of muscle proteins. *Scientific American* **230**(2): 58–71. The assemblage of protein molecules in the muscle fiber; their interaction during contraction; illustrated.

81. National Live Stock and Meat Board. 1978. *Lessons on Meat.* 86 pp. Identification, care and storage, cooking, and carving of meat.

82. Nobbs, C. L., H. C. Watson, and J. C. Kendrew. 1966. Structure of deoxymyoglobin. *Nature* **209:** 339–341.

83. Noble, I., and L. Gomez. 1962. Vitamin retention in meat cooked electronically. Thiamine and riboflavin in lamb and bacon. *J. Am. Dietet. Assoc.* **41:** 217–220. Meat cooked in microwave range at "Lo" setting and in conventional oven at 149°C.

84. Parrish, F. C., Jr., D. G. Olson, B. E. Minor, and R. E. Rust. 1973. Effect of degree of marbling and internal temperature of doneness on beef rib steaks. *J. Animal Sci.* **37:** 430–434. Three degrees of marbling and three internal temperatures compared.

85. Patterson, R. L. S. 1965. 5 a-androst-16-ene-3-one: Compound responsible for boar taint. *J. Sci. Food Agric.* **19:** 31–37. Identification of the compound.

86. Paul, P., L. Buchter, and A. Wierenga. 1966. Solubility of rabbit muscle proteins after various time-temperature treatments. *J. Agr. Food Chem.* **14:** 490–492. Longissimus dorsi muscle heated at 5 degree intervals from 40°C to 80°C for up to 10 hours.

87. Paul, P. C., R. W. Mandigo, and V. H. Arthud. 1970. Textural and histological differences among three muscles of the same cut of beef. *J. Food Sci.* **35:** 505–510. Longissimus dorsi, spinalis dorsi, and trapezius of beef rib compared.

88. Penfield, M., and B. M. Meyers. 1975. Changes in tenderness and collagen of beef semitendinosus muscle heated at two rates. *J. Food Sci.* **40:** 150–154. Heated at 93°C and 149°C to end points of 40°, 50°, 60°, and 70°C.

89. Penner, K. K., and J. A. Bowers. 1973. Flavor and characteristics of conventionally and microwave reheated pork. *J. Food Sci.* **38:** 553–555. Flavor, moistness, and TBA values.

90. Penny, I. F. 1974. The action of a muscle proteinase on the myofibrillar proteins of bovine muscle. *J. Sci. Food Agric.* **25:** 1273–1284. Possible substrates for the enzyme.

91. Pimentel, D., W. Dritschilo, J. Krummel, and J. Kutzman. 1975. Energy and land constraints in food protein production. *Science* **190:** 754–761. Options for use of resources for meeting the world's food needs.

92. Ramsbottom, J. M., P. A. Goeser, and H. W. Schultz. 1951. How light discolors meat: What to do about it. *Food Ind.* **23**(2): 120–124, 222. Effect of display lighting on visual perception of meat color; instability of cured meat pigments to light.

93. Ramsbottom, J. M., and E. J. Strandine. 1948. Comparative tenderness and identification of muscles in wholesale cuts of beef. *Food Research* **13:** 315–330. Tenderness (shear force) of 50 of the most important muscles of beef.

94. Ramsbottom, J. M., and E. J. Strandine. 1949. Initial physical and chemical changes in beef as related to tenderness. *J. Animal Sci.* **8:** 398–410. Effects of early postmortem changes.

95. Ramsbottom, J. M., E. J. Strandine, and C. H. Koonz. 1945. Comparative tenderness of representative beef muscles. *Food Research* **10:** 497–509. Histological rating for content of connective tissue and tenderness of raw and cooked tissue of 25 muscles of beef.

96. Ritchey, S. J., and R. L. Hostetler. 1964. Relationship of free and bound water to subjective scores for juiciness and softness and to changes in weight and dimensions of steaks from two beef muscles during cooking. *J. Food Sci.* **29:** 413–419. Steaks from longissimus and biceps femoris heated to four internal temperatures from rare to well done.

97. Ruyack, D. F., and P. Paul. 1972. Conventional and microwave heating of beef: Use of plastic wrap. *Home Economics Research J.* **1:** 98–103. Cooking times and losses, shear, penetrometer, and taste panel scores.

98. Savell, J. W., G. C. Smith, and Z. L. Carpenter. 1978. Beef quality and palatability as affected by electrical stimulation and cooler aging. *J. Food Sci.* **43:** 1666–1668. Effects on aging time and tenderness.

99. Schmidt, J. G., and F. C. Parrish, Jr. 1971. Molecular properties of postmortem muscle. 10. Effect of internal temperature and carcass maturity on structure of bovine longissimus. *J. Food Sci.* **36:** 110–119. Light, phase, and transmission electron microscopic views of muscle heated to temperatures from 50°C to 90°C.

100. Schock, D. R., D. L. Harrison, and L. Anderson. 1970. Effect of dry and moist heat treatments on selected beef quality factors. *J. Food Sci.* **35:** 195–198. Top round cooked by deep fat frying, roasting, and braising in a household oven and in a pressure saucepan.

101. Shimokomaki, M., D. F. Edsen, and A. J. Bailey. 1972. Meat tenderness: Age related changes in bovine intramuscular collagen. *J. Food Sci.* **37:** 892–896. Stable and labile cross-links as influenced by age and by activity of muscle.

102. Smith, G. C., T. C. Arango, and Z. L. Carpenter. 1971. Effects of physical and mechanical treatments on the tenderness of beef longissimus dorsi. *J. Food Sci.* **36:** 445–449. Methods of hanging the carcass and elevated cooling temperatures compared.

103. Smith, G. C., G. R. Culp, and Z. L. Carpenter. 1978. Postmortem aging of beef carcasses. *J. Food Sci.* **43:** 823–826. Aging time for optimum tenderness of four major wholesale cuts of beef.

104. Stromer, M. H., and D. E. Goll. 1967. Molecular properties of post-mortem muscle. 3. Electron microscopy of myofibrils. *J. Food Sci.* **32:** 386–389. Effects of aging time and temperature on microscopic appearance.

105. Suzuki, A., D. E. Goll, I. Singh, R. E. Allen, R. M. Robson, and M. H. Stromer. 1976. Some properties of purified skeletal muscle α-actinin. *J. Biol. Chem.* **251:** 6860–6870. Substantiating evidence that α-actinin is present in the Z-line.

106. Tucker, R. E., W. F. Hinman, and E. G. Halliday. 1946. The retention of thiamine and riboflavin in beef cuts during braising, frying and broiling. *J. Am. Dietet. Assoc.* **22:** 877–881. Heel of round, chuck, round steak, and loin compared.

107. Tucker, H. Q., H. M. Voegeli, and G. M. Wellington. 1952. *A Cross Sectional Muscle Nomenclature of the Beef Carcass.* 41 pp. East Lansing: Michigan State College Press. Reproduction of tracings of the muscles in 39 retail cuts.

108. United States Department of Agriculture. Economics, Statistics, and Cooperatives Service A. *National Food Review.* NFR-9. Winter 1980. P. 51. Per capita consumption of major foods.

109. United States Department of Agriculture, Food Safety and Quality Service. 1975. Official United States Standards for Grades of Carcass Beef. Pp. 1–20.

110. United States Department of Agriculture, Food Safety and Quality Service. 1978. USDA Yield Grades for Beef. Marketing Bulletin No. 45. 20 pp.

111. Veis, A. 1970. Collagen. In *The Physiology and Biochemistry of Muscle as Food.* Vol. 2, pp. 455–470. E. J. Briskey, R. G. Cassens, and B. B. Marsh, eds. Madison: University of Wisconsin Press. Chemical makeup of collagen.

112. Vogle, C. A. 1969. Some observations on the histology of cold-shortened muscle. *J. Food Technol.* **4:** 275–281. Optical, transmission, and scanning electron microscopy of muscle cold shortened (2°C) compared with muscle held at 18°C.

113. Wang, H., E. Rasch, V. Bates, J. F. Beard, J. C. Pierce, and O. J. Hankins. 1954. Histological observations on fat loci and distribution in cooked beef. *Food Research* **19:** 314–322. Hydrolysis of collagen and dispersion of fat in cooked beef; effect of cooking on tenderness.

114. Wasserman, A. E. 1972. Thermally produced flavor components in the aroma of meat and poultry. *J. Agr. Food Chem.* **20:** 737–740. A review.

115. Wasserman, A. E., and A. M. Spinelli. 1972. Effects of some water-soluble components on aroma of heated adipose tissue. *J. Agr. Food Chem.* **20:** 171–174. Essential for development of aroma characteristic of meats from different animals.

116. Webb, N. L., N. B. Webb, D. Cedarquist, and L. J. Bratzler. 1961. The effects of internal temperature and time of cooking on pork loin roasts. *Food Technol.* **15:** 371–373. Palatability and safety of pork loin roasted to end point temperatures below 85°C (185°F).

117. Williams, J. R., and D. L. Harrison. 1978. Relationship of hydroxyproline sol-

ubilized to tenderness of bovine muscle. *J. Food Sci.* **43:** 464–467, 492. Beef top round cooked in oven film bags at 94°C and 194°C to internal temperatures of 70°C and 80°C.

118. Winegarden, M. W., B. Lowe, J. Kastelic, E. A. Kline, A. R. Plagge, and P. S. Shearer. 1952. Physical changes in connective tissue of beef during heating. *Food Research* **17:** 172–184. Effect of heating on connective tissue and its relation to tenderness of cooked meat.

119. Wismer-Pedersen, J. 1971. Water. In *The Science of Meat and Meat Products*, pp. 177–191. J. F. Price and B. S. Schweigert, eds. San Francisco: W. H. Freeman and Co. Free and bound water in meat; its importance.

120. Wolff, T. A., and A. E. Wasserman. 1972. Nitrates, nitrites and nitrosamines. *Science* **177:** 15–18. Food sources of nitrites; their role in curing meats.

121. Ziprin, Y. A., and A. F. Carlin. 1976. Microwave and conventional cooking in relation to quality and nutritive value of beef and beef soy loaves. *J. Food Sci.* **41:** 4–8. Cooking time, cooking losses, and thiamine retention.

SLIDES AND FILMS

1. *101 Meat Identification Slides.* One hundred and one slides of retail cuts. Color. National Live Stock and Meat Board.

2. *How to Cook Meat by Moist Heat.* Color. Fifty-three frames. National Live Stock and Meat Board.

3. *How to Cook Meat by Dry Heat.* Fifty-two frames. National Live Stock and Meat Board.

TWENTY-THREE
Poultry

Poultry includes ducks, geese, guineas, and pigeons as well as turkeys and chickens. The last two account for the bulk of the poultry consumed. The annual per capita consumption of ready-to-cook chicken has increased from 18.7 pounds in 1947/1949 to an estimated 52 pounds in 1979 (23,24). During the same time the per capita consumption of ready-to-cook turkey has increased from 3.3 to 10.0 pounds. This is a 3-fold increase in the consumption of poultry in the last 30 years. The greatest expansion in an agricultural enterprise in recent years has been in the broiler-fryer category of poultry. Availability of a dependable supply of ready-to-cook poultry on a year around basis due to streamlined production and marketing procedures no doubt accounts for the spectacular increase in the use of poultry. Poultry and egg products together constitute one of the largest sources of farm income.

MARKET CLASSES OF POULTRY

The different classes of poultry are marketed on the basis of age. Age influences tenderness and fat content and so dictates the cooking methods that are appropriate. Signs of youth in poultry are smooth leg skin, supple wing joint, pliable keel or breast bone, and the presence of pin feathers. Young birds have no hairs on the skin and little subcutaneous fat. The weight of the bird varies with age. Rock Cornish hens are marketed at less than 7 weeks of age and at ready-to cook weights of less than 2 pounds. Broiler-fryer chickens are marketed at 8 weeks or more and at ready-to-cook weights of 1½ to 2½ pounds. Roasters weigh in at 2½ to 4½ pounds at 2½ to 5 months of age. A capon (unsexed male) may weigh from 4 to 8 pounds and is usually marketed under 8 months of age. Birds nearing 1 year or older, called hen, laying hen, or fowl, may weigh from 2½ to 5½ or more pounds when ready to cook. Very young broiler-fryer turkeys, under 4 months of age, weigh from 4 to 8 pounds ready-to-cook. Fully grown young turkeys suitable for roasting may weigh from 6 to 24 pounds. Broiler-fryer ducklings, less than 2 months of age, and roasting duckling, under 4 months of age, weigh from 2½ to 5 pounds. The ready-to-cook weight of goose may vary from 4 to 12 pounds, of pigeon from ½ to 1 pound, and of guinea from ¾ to 1½ pounds.

PREPARING POULTRY FOR THE MARKET

Poultry is marketed ready-to-cook, i.e., head, feet, and entrails are removed. Birds are customarily fasted for 8 hours prior to slaughter. They are killed by a method that minimizes struggle. The jugular vein is cut so that the bird bleeds well. As an aid in removing the feathers the bird is scalded, that is, dipped in hot water briefly. A dip in water at a temperature as low as 52° to 54°C (126° to 130°F) will loosen the feathers on chickens and turkeys without damaging the outer layer of skin (the cuticle). However, water at 59° to 60°C (138° to 140°F) and a scalding time of 45 seconds may be used (21). (This is a few degrees lower than the minimum temperature [66°C] recommended for water used to rinse dishes.) Although this removes the cuticle and allows the flesh to show through the transparent skin below (particularly noticeable in frozen poultry), the higher temperature facilitates removal of feathers as well as pin feathers (feathers which have not quite emerged). Any time-saving technique is important in an enterprise where profit is measured in fractions of a cent per pound. Feathers are removed from the scalded poultry by a machine equipped with rubberlike projections which rub or brush the feathers from the skin. Ducks and geese are scalded in water at 66° to 71°C (150° to 160°F) for 1½ to 2½ minutes. Water above 71°C (160°F) damages the skin of poultry.

Evisceration of the bird usually follows scalding and picking. The abdominal cavity is slit and the entrails removed. Head, feet, and oil gland are removed from the drawn bird. The weight after drawing is approximately three-fourths that of the live bird.

The bird is chilled either before or after the entrails are removed. The latter is preferable from the standpoint of flavor. Also, prompt cooling is essential to control growth of bacteria which contaminate the flesh once the skin is broken. Equally important is the fact that the time of onset of rigor, its duration, and the tenderness of the meat once rigor has passed are influenced by the way the bird is cooled (7). Muscle from poultry cooled in ice water is more tender than that from poultry held in water at higher temperature, and more tender than that cooled in air (8). Prompt cooling from body temperature to 15°C before the pH is lowered to 6.3 by accumulation of lactic acid is essential if toughening of the muscles is to be avoided (7,16).

Poultry, like meats in general, is tough if it is cooked before or while the meat is still in rigor. Poultry goes into and out of rigor more rapidly than other meats. A minimum of 4 to 5 hours should elapse from the time a chicken is slaughtered until it is cooked. For turkey, at least 12 hours should elapse. Weakening of the z-line of breast muscle and lengthening of the sarcomeres of leg muscle of chicken were observed as the result of aging (13). Aging poultry longer than 24 hours results in no additional tenderizing (7).

Eviscerated birds are marketed whole, disjointed or, less commonly, as halves or quarters. The bird left whole usually costs a few cents less per pound, and disjointing is easy to do. Hairs found on poultry are not loosened by

FIGURE 23-1. This mark on poultry indicates that the bird has been inspected for wholesomeness. (Courtesy of the United States Department of Agriculture.)

scalding. If the bird is bought whole, hairs can be removed by singeing over an open flame of a gas burner or a piece of burning paper. Newsprint should not be used because the carbon in printer's ink leaves black smudges on the skin.

INSPECTION AND GRADING

Practically all poultry is now marketed in ready-to-cook form. This means that the consumer has few if any clues as to the health of the bird and the wholesomeness of the meat. In a live bird signs of health (bright eyes, red comb, sleek feathers, and good posture) are easily recognized. Since 1971 inspection of all poultry has been mandatory. A label or tag bearing a round purple stamp that says "Inspected for Wholesomeness by the United States Department of Agriculture" (see Fig. 23-1) assures the consumer of the health of the bird and the sanitary conditions in the plant in which it was slaughtered (22). Inspection is done under a trained veterinarian.

Poultry which has been graded for quality as well as inspected for wholesomeness is available (22). Characteristics which are considered in assigning the grade are shape and meatiness, distribution of fat, and general appearance of the bird. Breaks in the skin, bruises, and pin feathers lower the grade. Quality grades for poultry are A, B, and C. Grade A and grade B fryers are shown in Figure 23-2. A shield-shaped mark similar to the grading (or grade) mark for meats shows the quality of an inspected bird (see Fig. 23-3). Poultry may be inspected without being graded but not the reverse. A combination grading (or grade) and inspection mark showing the market class may be used as a wing-tag.

The surface of some uncooked poultry may harbor salmonellae, microorganisms which cause one type of food poisoning. Rinsing the bird inside

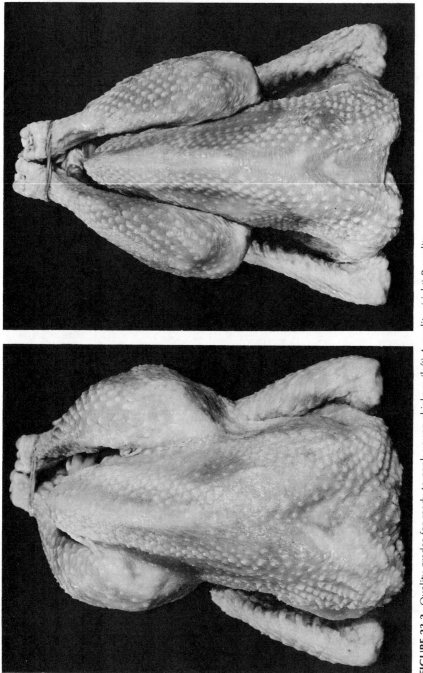

FIGURE 23-2. Quality grades for ready-to-cook young chicken: (left) A quality; (right) B quality. (Courtesy of the United States Department of Agriculture.)

FIGURE 23-3. The USDA grade shield for use on poultry that has been graded for quality as well as inspected for wholesomeness. (Courtesy of the United States Department of Agriculture.)

Any surface with which the bird has come in contact should be washed thoroughly in warm, soapy water. Cutting boards should be rinsed with dilute chlorine bleach or other sanitizer. Otherwise, food prepared subsequently may be contaminated. Hazards are great, for example, if ingredients such as those for a salad, uncooked before they are eaten, come in contact with contaminated surfaces.

COMPOSITION

Poultry is comparable to beef, lamb, and pork in composition and nutritive value. The proteins in poultry, approximately one-fifth the edible portion, are of high quality. Poultry is a good source of iron and phosphorus. Poultry, like all lean meat, is a good source of B-vitamins. Dark meat of chicken is richer in riboflavin than the light, but light meat is richer in niacin. The fat content varies with the age of the bird from under 5 percent in young chicken to near 25 percent in mature fowl. A feeding ration high in corn favors the deposition of fat. The fat content also varies with the type of poultry. It is higher in duck than in chicken and higher still in goose. Dark meat has more fat and more connective tissue than white; it also contains the pigment myoglobin missing from white meat. Xanthophyll and carotene in the feed are responsible for the yellow color of the fat of poultry.

COOKING POULTRY

Principles for cooking poultry are basically those for cooking meat. The cooking method is selected on the basis of the tenderness of the poultry and its fat content, both influenced mainly by the age of the bird. Older and tougher birds are appropriately cooked by methods suitable for tough cuts of meat and young tender birds by methods recommended for tender cuts.

Young tender poultry can be cooked by broiling. Halves, quarters, or pieces are placed on a broiler rack, skin side down to prevent the flesh from sticking to the rack. The surface which is uppermost may be basted with melted fat or oil to keep the meat from drying out, because young birds tend to have little fat. When broiler halves were heated to an internal temperature of 95°C (203°F) in the breast muscle, at broiling temperatures of 350°F (177°C), 375°F (190°C), and 400°F (204°C), the lowest temperature gave broilers somewhat closer to optimum doneness (12). As was pointed out in the chapter on meat, doneness is influenced not only by the temperature attained but also by the length of the heating period.

Because of the small amount of fat present, frying and deep fat frying are particulary suitable methods for cooking young tender poultry. Coating serving-sized pieces with flour or dipping in batter before frying yields a crisp crust. Pieces coated with flour and rolled in fat and placed in a shallow baking pan may be oven-fried at 350° to 400°F. Broiled and fried poultry should be turned with tongs rather than a fork to avoid loss of juices.

Somewhat older but still immature birds are suitable for roasting. They are still tender but have more fat than a fryer or broiler. Capons (unsexed males) are usually roasted. During cooking the bird, breast side up on a rack, needs to be basted with drippings which accumulate in the roasting pan or with melted table fat, rendered chicken fat, or salad oil. An oven temperature of 325°F (163°C) is most often recommended for roasting poultry. The body cavity and crop may be stuffed and the bird trussed just before it is put in to cook. A foil wrap on a large bird such as turkey prolongs roasting time and in one study resulted in less juicy meat than in an open pan, the cooking method preferred by the taste panel (6). In another study, however, dark muscle cooked in foil had more moisture than that cooked in an open pan, in ovenproof film, or paper bag, and light meat had more moisture cooked in open pan or in foil (14). Cooking time was longest in a paper bag, more browning occurred, and dark meat was more tender cooked in either an open pan or paper bag. The four treatments made no difference in tenderness of light meat.

For older tougher birds moist-media methods allow time to tenderize the meat without its becoming dry. Stewing (simmering) whole birds in water and braising disjointed ones are common practices. Smothering and fricasseeing are modifications of braising. Braising may be done in a covered pan on a surface unit or in an oven at 325°F.

Fatty tissue from the body cavity and under the skin, especially of older birds, may be cut into small pieces and rendered over low heat to expel the fat. This may be used to baste broiled or roasted poultry, as fat in the stuffing, to make sauce for creamed chicken, to brown chicken for braising, or as part of the fat for frying. The crisp tissue that remains can be used in the same way as bacon bits.

DONENESS OF POULTRY

Poultry is cooked to the well-done stage. Cooking times given in timetables serve as a guide to the length of time to cook poultry. A flexible knee joint in a bird stewed whole or one that is roasted is a sign that the meat is tender. The internal temperature may be used as an index to doneness, too, if thigh or breast muscle is large enough to cover the bulb of a thermometer. In one study, optimum doneness was achieved by roasting turkey halves at 325°F (163°C) to an end-point temperature of 95°C (203°F) in the thigh muscle or 90°C (194°F) in the breast muscle (11). The meat was considered underdone when the internal temperature was 5 degrees lower than specified in either muscle. On the other hand, stuffed whole turkeys weighing 16 to 21 pounds as purchased were considered neither undercooked nor overdone when they were roasted in an oven at 325°F (163°C) to an end-point temperature in the thigh of 85°C (185°F) (15). In a third study, whole stuffed turkeys roasted at 325°F (163°C) to an end-point temperature in the thigh of 82°C (180°F) were considered overall more desirable than were those foil-wrapped and cooked either at 450°F (232°C) to an end-point temperature of 82°C (180°F) in the thigh or at 200°F (93°C) to a temperature in the thigh of 73°C (163°F) (4). In the last study birds were of three weight classes which ranged from 12 to 24 pounds.

For stuffed roasted birds, the ultimate criterion of doneness is adequate heating of the stuffing. This is essential to eliminate the possibility of bacterial food poisoning. A number of cases of food poisoning of bacterial origin have been traced to poultry products. Poultry may act as the carrier for two types of food-poisoning microorganisms: salmonellae, and staphylococci. In the case of salmonellae, the microorganisms themselves are the cause of the food poisoning, whereas the staphylococci it is the toxin produced that is harmful. Furthermore, the toxin is not inactivated by heat, as are the microorganisms. An end-point temperature of 74°C (165°F) in the stuffing has been recommended as adequate for inactivating pathogens (5). The temperature need not go quite that high before the bird is removed from the oven. If the bird is held for 20 to 30 minutes before it is served, the temperature in the stuffing will continue to rise 5 to 10°F. This holding period facilitates carving, too. Multiplication of microorganisms, including food-poisoning types, is particularly rapid within the temperature range of 10° to 49°C (50° to 120°F), called (10) the dangerous incubation zone. As the bird is roasted and again as the cooked bird cools, it should be within this temperature range for not more than four hours. Leftover cooked poultry and stuffing, removed from the body cavity, should be chilled promptly and stored at 4.4°C (40°F) or below.

FROZEN POULTRY

Frozen poultry to be broiled, fried, or roasted should be thawed at least partially and in the refrigerator preferably. Thawing time varies from 1 day for a small (4-pound) bird to 3 days for a turkey that weighs 20 pounds. Unstuffed, frozen poultry may be thawed at room temperature if the bird in its plastic wrap is overwrapped with a double-walled paper bag which keeps the thawed exterior cool. Thawed this way a 4 to 6 pound bird thaws in approximately 15 hours and a 12 to 20 pound bird in up to 20 hours at 70°F (21°C) or above (17). Thawing of frozen poultry sealed in the freezing wrap may be speeded also by placing the sealed package in changes of cold (not warm) water. Approximate thawing times in cold water are 1 to 2 hours for a 4-pound chicken and 8 hours for a 20-pound turkey.

Once frozen poultry has thawed, it should be cooked promptly. Thawed poultry should not be refrozen. When frozen young chickens are cooked, discoloration may occur in the meat next to the larger bones (9). Freezing and thawing release hemoglobin from the red cells in the bone marrow. The porosity of bones in young chickens allows seepage of the pigment into the flesh next to the bones. Heating denatures the pigment and this is responsible for the discoloration. Darkening is not a problem in older birds because the bones are more dense. No completely satisfactory way to prevent this discoloration in frozen young birds has been found.

FLAVOR OF COOKED POULTRY

Volatile carbonyls are responsible for the "chickeny" aroma of cooked poultry (18). Without them, the sulfur compounds that are present give only a "meaty" or beeflike aroma. Hydrogen sulfide is a prominent constituent (19). The lipids of cooked chicken and especially cooked turkeys are susceptible to oxidative rancidity which gives rise to a warmed-over flavor (25). Two aldehydes, one of which is unsaturated, and which are typical end products of the oxidation of fats have been identified as contributors of warmed-over flavor in cooked poultry (20). Turkey reheated by microwaves is reported to have less warmed-over flavor than that reheated conventionally (1).

B-VITAMINS IN COOKED POULTRY

Whether turkey was cooked by microwaves or in a conventional oven made no difference in the thiamine content and no significant difference in the riboflavin content (2). Chicken breasts cooked by microwaves retained more vitamin B_6 than did chicken cooked conventionally, but loss of weight was greater (26). Another study reported more vitamin B_6 on a cooked weight basis in turkey breast cooked by microwaves rather than in a conventional oven, but no difference when the B_6 was calculated on a dry weight basis (3).

YIELD

The edible portion of turkey and of roasting chicken and hen is approximately three-fourths (73 percent) of the ready-to-cook weight. In broiler-fryer chickens the percentage of bone and refuse averages somewhat higher (32 percent). One pound of ready-to-cook poultry will yield approximately two servings.

REFERENCES

1. Bowers, J. 1972. Eating quality, sulfhydryl content and TBA values of turkey breast muscle. *J. Agr. Food Chem.* **20:** 706–708. Fresh cooked and that reheated conventionally and by microwaves compared.

2. Bowers, J., and B. A. Fryer. 1972. Thiamin and riboflavin in cooked and frozen reheated turkey. *J. Am. Dietet. Assoc.* **60:** 399–401. Heating in a microwave and a gas oven compared.

3. Bowers, J., B. A. Fryer, and P. P. Engler. 1974. Vitamin B$_6$ in turkey breast muscle cooked in microwave and conventional ovens. *Poultry Sci.* **53:** 844–846. Cooking time, cooking loss, moisture, and B$_6$ content.

4. Bramblett, V. D., and K. W. Fugate. 1967. Choice of cooking temperature for stuffed turkeys. Part I. Palatability factors. *J. Home Econ.* **59:** 180–185. Three oven temperatures and two internal temperatures in the thigh compared.

5. Castellani, A. G., R. R. Clarke, M. I. Gibson, and D. F. Meisner. 1953. Roasting time and temperature required to kill food poisoning microorganisms introduced experimentally into turkeys. *Food Research* **18:** 131–138. Factors affecting attainment in stuffing of temperature lethal for food poisoning microorganisms.

6. Deethardt, D., L. M. Burrill, K. Schneider, and C. W. Carlson. 1971. Foil-covered vs. open-pan procedures for roasting turkey. *J. Food Sci.* **36:** 624–625. Juiciness, tenderness, flavor, and cooking losses reported.

7. De Fremery, D. 1966. Relationship between chemical properties and tenderness of poultry muscle. *J. Agr. Food Chem.* **14:** 214–217. Relation of post morten handling of poultry, metabolic changes and tenderness of poultry.

8. Dodge, J. W., and W. J. Stadelman. 1959. Post mortem aging of poultry and its effect on the tenderness of breast muscle. *Food Technol.* **13:** 81–83. Cooling in air and in water at the same temperature and in ice water compared.

9. Ellis, C., and J. G. Woodruff. 1959. Prevention of darkening in frozen broilers. *Food Technol.* **13:** 533–538. Review of causes and treatment to prevent darkening; illustrated.

10. Esselen, W. B., A. S. Levine, and M. J. Brushway. 1956. Adequate roasting procedures for frozen stuffed poultry. *J. Am. Dietet. Assoc.* **32:** 1162–1166. Heat penetration and cooking times for frozen, thawed, and fresh birds roasted at two oven temperatures.

11. Goertz, G. E., K. Cooley, M. E. Ferguson, and D. L. Harrison. 1960. Doneness of frozen and defrosted turkey halves roasted to several end point temperatures. *Food Technol.* **14:** 135–138. Flavor, tenderness, juiciness, and doneness of birds roasted to different end point temperatures.

12. Goertz, G. E., D. Meyer, B. Weathers, and A. S. Hooper. 1964. Effect of cooking temperature on broiler acceptability. *J. Am. Dietet. Assoc.* **45:** 526–529. Three broiler temperatures and three oven temperatures compared.

13. Hay, J. D., R. W. Currie, F. H. Wolfe, and E. J. Sanders. 1973. Effects of postmortem aging on chicken muscle fibrils. *J. Food Sci.* **38:** 981–986. Electron micrographs of breast and leg muscles 0, 3, 48, and 162 hours postmortem.

14. Heine, N., J. Bowers, and P. G. Johnson. 1973. Eating quality of half turkey hens cooked by four methods. *Home Economics Research J.* **1:** 210–214. Open pan, oven-proof film, foil wrap, and paper bag compared.

15. Hoke, I. M., and M. K. Kleve. 1966. Heat penetration, quality and yield of turkeys roasted to different internal thigh temperatures. *J. Home Econ.* **58:** 381–384. Three end-point temperatures compared.

16. Kahn, A. W. 1971. Effect of temperature during post-mortem glycolysis and dephosphorylation of high energy phosphates on poultry meat tenderness. *J. Food Sci.* **36:** 120–121. Importance of temperature when muscle goes into rigor.

17. Klose, A. A., and H. H. Palmer. 1968. Thawing turkeys at ambient air temperature. *Food Technol.* **22**(10): 108–112. Thawing of plastic-bagged birds overwrapped in double-walled paper bag at 55°, 70°, and 85°F.

18. Minor, L. J., A. M. Pearson, L. E. Dawson, and B. S. Schweigert. 1965. Chicken flavor: The identification of some chemical components and the importance of sulfur compounds in the cooked volatile fraction. *J. Food Sci.* **30:** 686–696. Contribution of carbonyls and sulfur compounds.

19. Pippen, E. L., and E. P. Mecchi. 1969. Hydrogen sulfide a direct and potentially indirect contributor to cooked chicken aroma. *J. Food Sci.* **34:** 443–446. Importance of H_2S.

20. Ruenger, E. L., G. A. Reineccius, and D. R. Thompson. 1978. Flavor compounds related to the warmed-over flavor of turkey. *J. Food Sci.* **43:** 1198–1200. Two aldehydes identified.

21. Shannon, W. G., W. W. Marion, and W. J. Stadelman. 1957. Effect of temperature and time of scalding on the tenderness of breast meat of chicken. *Food Technol.* **11:** 284–285. Interrelation of scalding time and temperature and tenderness.

22. United States Department of Agriculture. Consumer and Marketing Service. *Inspection, Labeling, and Care of Meat and Poultry.* Agr. Handbook 416. 1971. 46 pp.

23. United States Department of Agriculture. Economic Research Service. *National Food Situation.* NFS-127. February, 1969. P. 18. Per capita consumption of food commodities.

24. United States Department of Agriculture. Economics, Statistics and Cooperatives Service A. *National Food Review.* NFR-9. 1980 (Winter). P. 51. Per capita consumption of major foods.

25. Wilson, B. R., A. M. Pearson, and F. B. Shorland. 1976. Effect of total lipids and phospholipids on warmed-over flavors in red and white muscle from several species as measured by thiobarbituric acid analysis. *J. Agr. Food Chem.* **24:** 7–11. Chicken, turkey, beef, pork, and mutton analyzed.

26. Wing, R. W., and J. C. Alexander. 1972. Effect of microwave heating on vitamin B_6 retention in chicken. *J. Am. Dietet. Assoc.* **61:** 661–664. Microwave and conventional oven compared.

TWENTY-FOUR
Fish

Fish provide an estimated 5 percent of the available food protein worldwide (13). Several thousand species of fish exist but only about 200 are of commercial importance. The typical consumer is familiar with only a few of these varieties, judged by the limited use of fish in this country. The per capita consumption of fish has increased from 10.3 pounds in 1960, to 11.8 pounds in 1970, to an estimated 13.7 pounds in 1979 (19). Somewhat over 50 million tons of fish are harvested from the sea annually with less than half used for human consumption (2). Most varieties of fish are underutilized; a few varieties are heavily exploited. Almost half the catch is made of anchovies, herrings, and sardines. Fish could well occupy a more prominent place in the diet (12) in view of the fact that nearly three-fourths of the earth's surface is covered with water. However, the fossil energy required to get fish to the consumer is high (13).

TYPES OF FISH

To bring some order to the great number of species (18), fish are sometimes classed on the basis of anatomical differences as fish with vertebrae and fins or as shellfish. Fin fish can be grouped further into lean (fat content under 5 percent) and fat fish (fat content 5 to 20 percent). Bass, flounder, halibut, perch, and sole are examples of lean fish. Fat fish include albacore, herring, mackerel, salmon (Chinook and red), shad, sardines, smelt, and tuna. Fin fish are also classified on the basis of the kind of water in which they spend their adult lives as either fresh or salt water types.

These attempts at classifying fin fish are of little help to the consumer who cannot be expected to know the characteristics of 200 or more species, many offered in a variety of forms. To compound confusion, some species of fish are known by more than one common name, and the same name is used for more than one species. Work has been initiated to formulate a simple, usable system for identifying fish (11). This includes categorizing fin fish for retail purposes on the basis of edibility characteristics considered important to the consumer and providing an organized system of naming, with a unique market name for each product. Of eight edibility characteristics tentatively proposed, two—flavor and flakiness—were considered of primary importance. For each edibility factor, a 5-point scale from most to least has been proposed. Thus fish could be categorized on the basis of edibility from mild and flaky to strong and nonflaky, with 23 combinations of strength of flavor and extent of flakiness in between.

Shellfish have, instead of a skeleton, a hard shell on the outside of the soft tissues. The crustaceans, one group of shellfish, are encased in a chitinous armor which, being segmented, gives the creatures power of locomotion. Crabs, crayfish, lobsters, prawn, and shrimp are such. Mollusks constitute another group of shellfish. These creatures have a soft, unsegmented body in a calcified shell. Most mollusks are bivalves. Included are abalone, clams, mussels, oysters, and scallops. The snail is a mollusk although not a bivalve. Other mollusks include octopus, squid, and periwinkle.

COMPOSITION AND NUTRITIVE VALUE

Composition of representative fishes is given in Table 24-1. As the table shows, fish are an excellent source of protein. Fish are interchangeable with meat in both quantity and quality of protein. Shellfish have a slightly sweet taste due to glycogen, which in meat and poultry is found in the liver only. Salt water fish contain iodine. Fish are an excellent source of phosphorus but low in iron compared with red meats. Fish, like meats, are low in calcium. Canned salmon is the exception because the fish is processed long enough to solubilize the bones. Fish with vertebrae tend to be lower in thiamine, riboflavin, and niacin than are red meats. The fat in most fish is highly unsaturated.

PURCHASING FISH

MARKET FORMS

Fresh fin fish can be purchased in the round (whole fish as landed), drawn (entrails removed), dressed (minus entrails, head, tail, fins and scales), as steaks (cross section from ½ to 1 inch thick), and as fillets (slices parallel to the backbone). Market forms of canned fish and of shellfish are given in the A.H.E.A. *Handbook of Food Preparation.*

FRESHNESS IN FISH

Both the appearance and the odor of a fish are clues as to its freshness (14). The skin of a fresh fish is shining and iridescent and is covered with a thin, transparent layer of slime. The eyes are full and bright, the pupil jet black, and the cornea transparent. Gills are bright pink. The flesh, once rigor has passed, is soft and flabby but it does not pit when pressed with the finger as does fish that is no longer fresh. The flesh is translucent when cut and shimmering rather than dull and milky appearing. A fresh fish has a not unpleasant odor described as seaweedy in contrast to the "dead-fish" odor of one too long out of water.

Table 24-1 Composition of representative fish (100-gram edible portion, raw)

	Water (%)	Calories[a]	Protein (g)	Fat (g)	Carbohydrate (g)	Calcium (mg)	Phosphorus (mg)	Iron (mg)	Vitamin A Value (I.U.)	Thiamine (mg)	Riboflavin (mg)	Niacin (mg)	Ascorbic Acid (mg)
Vertebrates													
Albacore (tuna)	66.2	177	25.3	7.6	0	26	—	—	—	—	—	—	5
Bass, striped	77.7	105	18.9	2.7	0	—	212	—	—	—	—	—	—
Carp	77.8	115	18.0	4.2	0	50	253	.9	170	.01	.04	1.5	1
Cod	81.2	78	17.6	.3	0	10	194	.4	0	.06	.07	2.2	2
Flounder, sole	81.3	79	16.7	.8	0	12	195	.8	—	.05	.05	1.7	—
Haddock	80.5	79	18.3	.1	0	23	197	.7	—	.04	.07	3.0	—
Halibut	76.5	100	20.9	1.2	0	13	211	.7	440	.07	.07	8.3	—
Herring, Pacific	79.4	98	17.5	2.6	0	—	225	1.3	100	.02	.16	3.5	3
Mackerel, Atlantic	67.2	191	19.0	12.2	0	5	239	1.0	(450)[b]	.15	.33	8.2	—
Ocean perch, Atlantic	79.7	88	18.0	1.2	0	20	207	1.0	—	.10	.08	1.9	—
Salmon, pink	76.0	119	20.0	3.7	0	—	—	—	—	.14	.05	—	—
Sardine, Pacific	70.7	160	19.2	8.6	0	33	215	1.8	—	—	—	—	—
Trout, lake	70.6	168	18.3	10.0	0	—	238	.8	—	.09	.12	2.7	—
Tuna, yellowfin	71.5	133	24.7	3.0	0	—	—	—	—	—	—	—	—
Shellfish													
Abalone	75.8	98	18.7	.5	3.4	37	191	2.4	—	.18	.14	—	—
Clams, assorted	81.7	76	12.6	1.6	2.0	69	162	6.1	100	.10	.18	1.3	10
Lobster, Northern	78.5	91	16.9	1.9	.5	29	183	.6	—	.40	.05	1.5	—
Oyster, Eastern	84.6	66	8.4	1.8	3.4	94	143	5.5	310	.14	.18	2.5	—
Shrimp	78.2	91	18.1	.8	1.5	63	166	1.6	—	.02	.03	3.2	—

SOURCE: U.S.D.A. Agr. Handbook No. 8. *Composition of Foods. Raw, Processed, Prepared.* Revised 1963.

[a] 1 kilocalorie = 4.185 kilojoules

[b] Value imputed from similar food.

NOTE: Dash means lack of data.

KEEPING QUALITIES OF FRESH FISH

Fish is a highly perishable food, and marketing a top-quality product presents many problems. No doubt this is one factor that contributes to the low per capita use of fish. Spoilage occurs very rapidly in fish that is not drawn promptly because of powerful digestive enzymes which perforate the intestines and attack the walls of the body cavity. Evidence indicates that the flesh of freshly caught fish is sterile (14). Bacterial spoilage does not begin until the fish has gone into and passed out of rigor. Rigor takes place sooner and is of shorter duration in fish than in mammals. The onset of rigor can be delayed and the period of rigor prolonged by minimizing the struggling that the fish does and by prompt chilling once the fish is dead. Either will prolong the period of freshness. Halibut has a long rigor and it stores better than most fish.

Marine microorganisms are in the slime, the gills, and the intestinal tract of fish (14). Most marine bacteria that cause fish to spoil grow best at 10 to 20°C (50 to 68°F). In fact most can grow at 0°C (32°F) and some flourish at −7.5°C (18.5°F). Nevertheless, lowering the temperature of fish from 10°C to 0°C delays the beginning of the rapid growth phase for the microorganisms that are present and cuts the spoilage rate by a factor of 5 to 6 (17). Even so, as a rule fish can be kept in good condition by icing for not more than a week to 10 days. (When fresh fish is purchased, it should be refrigerated (near 0°C) promptly.) If fish is to be kept for more than a few days, other means of preservation must be utilized.

STRUCTURE AND COMPOSITION OF FIN FISH MUSCLE

GROSS STRUCTURAL FEATURES

Two types of muscle are found in vertebrate fish. The main one, the great lateral muscle, makes up the bulk of the edible part of most such fish. On the outside of the lateral muscle in many fish is found a small superficial muscle which fans out on each side of the lateral line (6,8). This muscle, which is dark reddish brown, is rich in myoglobin in contrast to the main muscle, which is practically devoid of it. The lateral muscle of most fish is essentially colorless. Salmon is an exception, but the pink color is due not to myoglobin but to a carotenoid, astaxanthin. A high proportion of fat is found in the superficial dark muscle. The fatty acids in the fat of fish are more highly unsaturated than are those of warm-blooded animals. When fish are stored, rancidity develops, particularly in the dark muscle, catalyzed by iron from the heme pigment.

FINE STRUCTURE OF FISH MUSCLE

The fine structure of the muscles of vertebrate fish is similar to that of warm-blooded animals. The muscles are made of muscle fibers and connective tissue. The muscle fibers which are defined by a sarcolemma are made of actin, myosin, and tropomyosin plus sarcoplasmic protein (6), all of which are found in warm-blooded animals. Some of the myofibrils which are embedded in the sarcoplasm of the fibers of fish muscle are cylindrical in shape as are those in red meats. Others, especially those just inside the sarcolemma, are flat and ribbonlike in cross section. Both types of myofibrils appear to be made up of overlapping thick and thin filaments just as in red meats.

The muscle fibers of fish, unlike those of meat, which are thin and hairlike, are short (usually not more than 3 centimeters or approximately 1 inch long) and thick (6). These short fibers, which are arranged in parallel layers, are embedded at either end in sheets of connective tissue called (7) "myocommata." (See Fig. 24-1.) The layers of muscle fibers are called "myomeres." The structural proteins, actin and myosin, make up about two-thirds of the total protein of the muscle of fish (6). This is a higher proportion than in red meats. Values of 3 to 5 percent are given for the connective tissue content of bony fish (7,8), much lower than that in the most tender cut of beef.

INSTABILITY OF FISH TO FROZEN STORAGE

In addition to the differences cited above, the muscle of fish differs from that of warm-blooded animals in the ability to withstand frozen storage. Fast freezing and thawing of fish cause no undue damage (6). It is during frozen storage that undesirable changes in texture occur. The uncooked fish loses its springiness and becomes friable. Cooked, the fish is dry, tough, stringy, and tasteless. The instability of fish muscle to frozen storage and the undesirable textural changes that take place are believed to be associated with the myofibrillar proteins rather than with those of the sarcoplasm or the connective tissue. Specifically the myosin of fish appears to be the labile component (4). Much work has been done and many words have been written on the instability of fish to frozen storage. To date no satisfactory explanation is forthcoming. Damage to the texture of frozen fish diminishes the lower the temperature at which the frozen product is stored. Fish purchased frozen should be stored at 0°F and thawed just before it is cooked.

COOKING FISH

Fish is cooked to alter the texture, develop flavor, and destroy microorganisms. The observation made in 1943 that fish cookery had received little attention from scientific workers (1) still applies today. Little information of a technical nature is available on the cooking of vertebrate fish and even less on shellfish. The effect of cooking on the shrinkage of fish and meat, as measured by the loss of weight, has been reported (8). Fish (six varieties tested) have been reported to shrink less and less rapidly than beef when 2-ounce samples were cooked by steaming. Percentage loss of soluble salts more or less paralleled

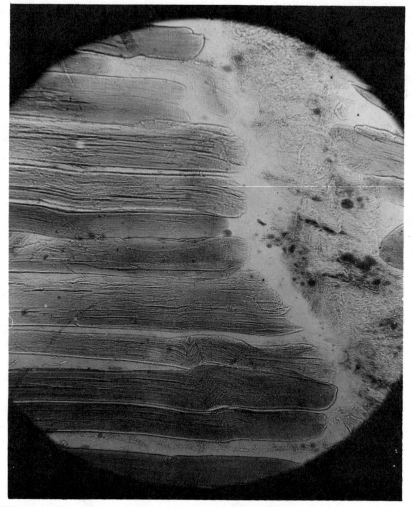

FIGURE 24-1. Photomicrograph of muscle tissue of salmon. Ends of fibers from one myomere (left) with the intervening layer of connective tissue called myocommata separating it from another myomere, the ends of a few fibers of which are seen on the right. Original magnification × 112. (From H. Charley and G. E. Goertz, *Food Research* **23:** 21. Copyright © 1958 by Institute of Food Technologists.)

the loss of water. Baking caused greater shrinkage than steaming and the loss in weight did not level off as it did in the case of steaming. One study showed the muscle fibers of fish more susceptible to heat than were those of chicken or beef (15). Heated to 60°C, little change was observed in the scanning electron microscopic appearance of longissimus dorsi of beef or semitendinosus of chicken, but the dorsal muscle of rainbow trout showed extensive damage. Breaks across the fibers, particularly at the z-discs, and disruptions of fibrils in the H-zone were observed.

A limited number of studies have been concerned with the effects of cooking on the nutritive value of fish (9). The cooking method (baking, broiling, steaming, or boiling) made no difference in the nutritive value of the protein of cod. Appearance, flavor, and texture of the cooked fish were not assessed.

Two studies have been reported in which the internal temperature of the fish rather than an arbitrary cooking time was used as the criterion of doneness. In one study, 1-inch salmon steaks were baked at four oven temperatures to an internal temperature of 75°C (167°F) (3). The oven temperatures used were 350°F (177°C), 400°F (204°C), 450°F (232°C), and 500°F (260°C). In addition, steaks were baked at an oven temperature of 400°F (204°C) to four internal temperatures as follows: 70°C (158°F), 75°C (167°F), 80°C (176°F), and 85°C (185°F). Palatability of the cooked fish was not affected by oven temperature. Much spattering occurred at the two higher baking temperatures. Baking time at the highest oven temperature was half that at the lowest of the four. Salmon steaks baked to the highest internal temperature were judged higher in flavor but lower in moistness than steaks baked to the two lower internal temperatures. Steaks baked to the lowest internal temperature ranked low in flavor and in desirability and were judged underdone. Interestingly, the last steak to be done, regardless of treatment, tended to be ranked highest in flavor and desirability which emphasizes the importance of serving fish promptly once it is cooked. When 2-pound cuts of salmon were baked at the same four temperatures used for the 1-inch steaks (4), a 100-degree difference in baking temperature made a significant difference in evaporation and total cooking losses. Oven temperature made no difference in the palatability of the baked fish. Spattering and charring in the oven at the two higher temperatures were more pronounced than in the case of the 1-inch steaks.

METHODS

Methods used to cook fish include broiling, baking, frying, steaming, and poaching. The latter is done in simmering liquid (water, stock, or milk). Slices of lemon may be added to the poaching water. Such herbs as basil, bay leaf, capers, caraway, chives, dill, fennel, marjoram, or parsley, judiciously used, complement the flavor of fish. Moist-media methods such as poaching are particularly appropriate for lean fish. Fat fish are self-basting so broiling or baking are good methods. Steaks, fillets, or whole fish may be poached. Steaks or whole fish, with or without stuffing, may be baked. Removal of the backbone gives a pocket for stuffing and makes carving easier.

ASSESSING DONENESS

The muscle fibers of raw fish are not tough and the amount of connective tissue is small, so tenderizing is not an objective of cooking fish. Not only is the amount of connective tissue less in fish than in red meats, but it appears to be degraded more readily when heated than is that of warm-blooded animals. Fish collagen contains a lower proportion of hydroxyproline than does that in red meats (7). When fish collagen in the myocommata is degraded to gelatin, the myomeres (layers of muscle fibers) separate readily and give rise to the flakes of cooked fish. Fish is done as soon as heat has coagulated the muscle fiber proteins (and solubilized the collagen) so that the flesh can be separated into flakes. Loss of translucency of the flesh is another sign of doneness. Fish cooked beyond this stage shrinks excessively and becomes tough and dry because of excessive coagulation of the muscle fiber proteins. Based on practical observations, the same appears true for shellfish. Oysters, for example, should be heated only until the gills ruffle. Additional cooking toughens the muscle.

In the study referred to above, the one-inch salmon steaks which weighed approximately one-half pound required an average of 23 minutes to reach an internal temperature of 75°C (167°F) in an oven at 400°F (204°C) (3). The internal temperature of the salmon steaks was approximately that of the well-done stage for beef. Two-pound cuts of salmon baked at the same temperature required approximately one hour (4). A timetable for cooking fish and shellfish is given in the A.H.E.A. *Handbook of Food Preparation*.

When lobster is cooked, it undergoes a pronounced change in color. The dull olive green of the shell changes to bright pink. When heat denatures the protein of the green carotenoid-protein complex, the bright pink astaxanthin is freed. A comparable but less pronounced change in color occurs in shrimp when they are cooked.

SANITATION AND HEALTH ASPECTS OF SHELLFISH

If crabs and lobsters are bought fresh, they should be alive and active. Crustaceans are usually cooked by plunging the live animal into boiling water where it remains for a few minutes. It should be cooled at once in ice water and then refrigerated. Oysters and clams bought in the shell should be alive, too, indicated by shells that close when the mollusk is tapped.

The production of safe and wholesome shellfish, and in particular oysters, which are often eaten raw, requires stringent sanitary controls. Oysters, which require salt water but are unable to tolerate the concentration of salt in undiluted sea water, grow in protected bays and inlets near the mouths of rivers. There, surface water from the land drains into the ocean and dilutes the salt water to an acceptable level. If the water contains untreated sewage, contamination of the oysters with pathogenic microorganisms will occur. In the past, outbreaks of typhoid fever have been traced to oysters so contaminated. An oyster filters large volumes of water, as much as 5 quarts a day by one 18 months old. In this filtering process many microorganisms are retained. For oysters to be safe to eat requires high standards for the water in the beds where they are cultivated. Sanitary control of the growing areas and of the harvesting and processing of shellfish are under the control of the state in which the shellfish originates, with the U.S. Public Health Service cooperating (20). Inspection of shellfish growing areas and licensing of shellfish shucking plants have eliminated many of the hazards of contamination of shellfish with pathogenic microorganisms.

Clams, mussels, oysters, and scallops may be unsafe to eat during the months from May to October. Paralytic shellfish poisoning may result from eating mollusks which have fed on toxic marine plankton. Three species of dinoflagellates which thrive in abnormally warm sea water, especially of the West Coast, are the source of a neuromuscular poison, saxitoxin (16), similar in its effects to curare. Mollusks should not be taken from sea water in which these plankton have proliferated.

REFERENCES

1. Baker, L. C. 1943. The nation's food. VI. Fish as food. 4. The cooking of fish. *Chem. & Ind.* **62:** 356–359. A summary of previous work.
2. Chapman, W. M. 1966. Resources of the ocean and their potentialities for man. *Food Technol.* **20:** 895–898, 900–901. The world's fishery resources.
3. Charley, H. 1952. Effects of internal temperature and of oven temperature on the cooking losses and the palatability of baked salmon steaks. *Food Research* **17:** 136–143. Oven temperatures of 350° to 500°F and internal temperatures of 70° to 85°C compared.
4. Charley, H., and G. E. Goertz. 1958. The effects of oven temperature on certain characteristics of baked salmon. *Food Research* **23:** 17–24. Four oven temperatures compared; photomicrographs of raw and cooked muscle fibers.
5. Connell, J. J. 1961. The relative stabilities of the skeletal muscle myosins of some animals. *Biochem. J.* **80:** 503–509. Frog, chicken, and seven species of fish compared.
6. Connell, J. J. 1964. Fish muscle proteins and some effects on them of processing. In *Symposium on Foods: Proteins and Their Reactions.* Westport, Conn.: Avi Publishing Co. Pp. 255–293.
7. Dyer, W. J., and J. R. Dingle. 1961. Fish protein with special reference to freezing. In *Fish as Food.* Georg Bergstrom, ed. Vol. I, pp. 275–320. Structure of fish muscle, behavior of fish proteins, and theories of freezing damage.
8. Hamoir, G. 1955. Fish proteins. *Advances in Protein Chemistry* **10:** 227–282. A review article; technical.
9. McCance, R. A., and H. L. Shipp. 1933. *The chemistry of flesh foods and their losses on cooking.* Med. Research Council Spec. Rept. Ser. No. 187. 146 pp. Cooking losses of meats and fish compared.
10. Marks, A. L., and H. W. Nilson. 1946. *Effect of cooking on the nutritive value of the proteins of the cod.* Commercial Fisheries Rev. 8, No. 12. 6 pp. Baking, broiling, simmering, and boiling compared.
11. National Marine Fisheries Service. 1978 (March). A Model Retail Plan for Seafood Species. U.S. Department of Commerce, National Oceanic and Atmospheric Administration, Washington, D.C.
12. Pariser, E. R., and O. A. Hammerle. 1966. Some cultural and economic limitations on the use of fish as food. *Food Technol.* **20:** 629–632. Food prejudices and taboos as they affect the consumption of fish.

13. Pimentel, D., W. Dritschilo, J. Krummel, and J. Kutzman. 1975. Energy and land constraints in food protein production. *Science* **190:** 754–761. Options for meeting the world's food needs.

14. Reay, G. A., and J. M. Shewan. 1949. The spoilage of fish and its preservation by chilling. *Advances in Food Research* **2:** 343–392. A review.

15. Schaller, D. R., and W. D. Powrie. 1972. Scanning electron microscopy of heated beef, chicken, and rainbow trout muscle. *Can. Inst. Food Science Technol. J.* **5:** 184–190. Effects of heating to 60°C and 97°C recorded.

16. Schantz, E. J., J. M. Lynch, G. Vayvada, K. Matsumoto, and H. Rapoport. 1966. The purification and characterization of the poison produced by *Gonyaulax catenella* in Axenic culture. *Biochemistry* **5:** 1191–1195. Paralytic poisoning from saxitoxin in shellfish.

17. Spencer, R., and C. R. Baines. 1964. The effect of temperature on the spoilage of wet white fish. *Food Technol.* **18:** 769–773. Fluctuations in temperature of fish from catch to consumer and effects on quality.

18. United States Congress. 79th, 1st Session. 1945. *Fishery Resources of the United States.* Senate Document No. 51. 135 pp. Major and minor aquatic species, illustrated; distribution, utilization and conservation.

19. United States Department of Agriculture. *National Food Review.* Economics, Statistics, and Cooperatives Service A. 1980 (Winter). NFR-9, p. 51. Per capita consumption of major foods.

20. United States Public Health Service. Division of Environmental Engineering and Food Production. 1965. *National Shellfish Sanitation Programs; Manual of Operation.* Parts I and II. PHS Pub. No. 33. Sanitary control of the growing, harvesting, and processing of shellfish.

TWENTY-FIVE
Gelatin

The uses of gelatin as an agent to increase the viscosity of cream which is otherwise too thin to whip and as a stabilizer to prevent the growth of large crystals in ice cream have been pointed out in previous chapters. The present chapter will consider the use of gelatin as the setting agent in such foods as molded gelatin desserts, either plain or with fruit, in molded vegetable salads and aspics, and in gelatin whips, sponges, and creams. Gelatin is a most effective gelling agent. As little as 1 part gelatin can set or immobilize 99 parts of water by weight.

CHEMISTRY

The effectiveness of gelatin as a gelling agent stems from its unique amino acid makeup. Gelatin molecules contain high proportions of three groups of amino acids. Approximately one-third of the amino acid residues are either glycine or alanine, nearly one-fourth are basic or acidic, and approximately one-fourth are either proline or hydroxyproline. The high proportion of polar residues confers on gelatin molecules great affinity for water. Because of the high proportion of proline and hydroxyproline residues, gelatin molecules are unable to coil in the helical shape characteristic of many proteins. Instead they are long and thin, a characteristic that is advantageous in gel formation.

MANUFACTURE OF GELATIN

As was pointed out in Chapter 22, gelatin is a protein derived from collagen fibers found in collagenous connective tissue. Two main sources of connective tissue used in the manufacture of gelatin are (1) demineralized bones and skin or (2) hide from which hair and grease have been removed (5). Such collagen-rich material is given a preliminary soaking in either acid or alkali, the latter more commonly. This preliminary soaking treatment removes impurities and facilitates the conversion of collagen to gelatin. The conversion is effected by heating the pretreated tissue in water until the cross links which hold the three gelatin chains in the collagen helix are broken (3). Gelatin molecules so formed are dispersed in the hot water. Some moisture is evaporated and the concentrated colloidal sol is cooled and allowed to gel in a thin layer, which is then dried. The dried product is marketed for home use in either granular or pulverized form.

USE OF GELATIN IN FOODS

DISPERSING DRIED GELATIN

The pulverized form of gelatin used in flavored packaged mixes can be dispersed by adding boiling water and stirring because the pieces of gelatin are so fine. Pieces of granular gelatin are too large for directly applied hot water to disperse them readily. Instead, the granules are soaked for a short time in three to four volumes of cold liquid. This preliminary hydration of the granules facilitates the dispersion of the gelatin molecules as a sol by hot water. To effect the dispersion, hot water may be added to the hydrated gelatin. The water should be hot enough so that the final temperature is at least 35°C (95°F). Alternately, the hydrated granules may be converted to a concentrated sol by heating over hot water. It is difficult to disperse this concentrated sol of gelatin in the cold liquid specified in some recipes. Cold liquid in small portions should be added to the concentrated gelatin sol (not warm sol to cold liquid!). Each portion should be stirred in thoroughly before the next one is added. Otherwise the gelatin will solidify in rubbery strands and lumps instead of forming a uniform sol.

Polar groups on a gelatin molecule supply many potential spots where water molecules may bond to the gelatin. Other water molecules may bond to this first adsorbed layer and thus build up shells or spheres of water around each gelatin molecule. Gelatin molecules are sufficiently hydrated to account for their dispersion as a colloidal sol. They differ in this respect from casein, another gel former, the molecules of which are dispersed as a sol in part because they are hydrated but also because they carry like charges and so repel each other. Many proteins are denatured by heat, but gelatin, like casein, which is also high in proline, is not.

GELATION OF A GELATIN SOL

As a sol of gelatin cools, it becomes more viscous. However, more than thickening is involved in conversion of a sol to a gel. Rigidity appears rather rapidly after a preliminary cooling and holding period. Rigidity is a characteristic of a gel just as fluidity is a characteristic of a sol. When gelation occurs, the dispersion of colloidal gelatin becomes an elastic solid.

The mechanism for the formation of a gel from a gelatin sol is unknown. A number of suggestions have been put forward, however (4). Crystal formation is believed to be involved because x-ray diagrams have demonstrated the presence of crystalline areas in gelatin gels (2). It is theorized that small sections of a number of gelatin molecules unite by lateral association to form these crystallites. Individual molecules join in more than one crystallite to form a highly ramified three-dimensional network which immobilizes the liquid (2). (See Fig. 25-1.) The fluid sol is converted into an elastic "solid" or gel. Longer gelatin molecules are advantageous in gel formation as they are more likely to make contact with and bond to other molecules to form the crystalline

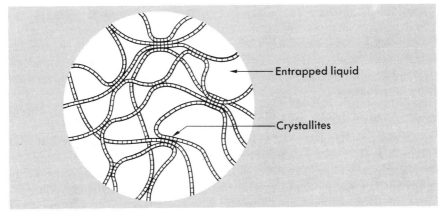

FIGURE 25-1. Network of gelatin molecules in a gel, shown schematically.

areas. Molecules or ions in the liquid can diffuse from one part of a gel to another as can be demonstrated by stabbing a gelatin gel with a tooth pick previously dipped in food coloring. Held for a time in the refrigerator, the gel will be uniformly colored throughout.

The forces responsible for binding gelatin molecules in the fragile architecture of the gel are not known. Both hydrogen bonds and van der Waals forces (2) have been suggested because of the nature of the gelatin molecules and the ease with which the gel liquefies and reforms with change in temperature. Blocking of polar groups in side chains along the gelatin molecule does not interfere with the formation of a gel so these apparently are not involved in gel formation. Blocking of the peptide groups does prevent gel formation (1). Presumably this indicates that the peptide linkage is involved in some manner in gelation.

After a gelatin sol has been chilled in a refrigerator or in a *cold* room, a gel forms. Once a sol is converted to a gel, it can without liquefying stand a temperature somewhat higher than that required for the gel to form in the first place. However, most edible gelatin gels when placed in a warm room (approximately 28°C or 82°F), will liquefy or melt. Although a sol must be cooled for a gel to form, slow cooling is advantageous. The gel that results can be raised to a higher temperature before it liquefies. Presumably slow cooling permits better orientation of gelatin molecules for gel formation. Once a gel forms and then is liquefied, it gels faster the second time than it did originally. This suggests that gelation may occur in two stages, a period of preliminary orientation of the molecules in the sol and the final establishment of the network. The first is a relatively slow process and the latter takes place rapidly once it starts. Acid prolongs the setting time of a gelatin sol and lowers the liquefying temperature of a gel.

The faster a sol is cooled the sooner it sets, but more is involved in gel formation than just lowering the temperature. Time is required for the network to be established. Once a gel is formed, rigidity increases with time. The most rapid increase in firmness takes place during the first day.

As a gel ages some of the liquid may escape from the network. An increase in the number or strength of the attractive forces between the gelatin molecules or diminished attraction between gelatin molecules and water are possible causes of syneresis.

PROPORTIONS OF GELATIN

The amount of gelatin needed to gel a liquid varies from 1 to 2 percent. With 1 tablespoon or 7 grams of gelatin per pint, proportions frequently used, the percentage is 1½. Enough gelatin should be used so that the gels resist melting at normal serving temperatures. The proportion may be increased if the gel is to be served on a warm day. Too much gelatin makes a stiff, rubbery gel. Ideally, the gel should be just firm enough to hold its shape, yet tender and quivery. The amount of gelatin may need to be increased slightly in a tart jelly because acid lowers the temperature at which a gel liquefies as well as the temperature required for the gel to form. Acid also affects the clarity of a gelatin dispersion. The isoelectric point of alkaline-processed gelatin is near 4.7 to 5.0. When such gelatin is dispersed in water, the sol is cloudy. Increments of acid added to the water increases the clarity of the sol.

FRUIT AND VEGETABLE JELLIES

If fruits or vegetables are to be combined with gelatin, the sol should be cooled and allowed to stand until it is the thickness of thick egg white and until the gel is just ready to form. At this stage the gelatin sol is thick enough to keep the vegetable or fruit from floating. Uncooked fruit is especially likely to float because it is buoyed up by the pockets of intercellular gas in the fresh tissue. Raw pineapple should not be used with gelatin because a gel will not form. This fruit contains the enzyme bromelain which not only converts collagen to gelatin (see Chapter 22) but also hydrolyzes molecules of gelatin.

WHIPS, SPONGES, AND CREAMS

Before a sol is beaten for whips, sponges, and creams, it should cool to 50°F or 10°C and stand until it has reached the consistency of thick egg white. Whipping a gelatin sol at this stage will yield a foam at least double the volume of the original sol. After it is whipped, gelatin molecules in the fluid of the foam will set the liquid. A whip or a sponge is thus a combination of a foam and a gel. A sponge differs from a whip in that beaten egg whites are incorporated in the former. For creams, whipped cream is folded into the gelatin foam. Gelatin is used to set the custard for Spanish cream.

UNMOLDING GELATIN GELS

The container in which the gelatin sol is to set may be oiled *lightly* with salad oil for ease in unmolding. When the container with the gel is dipped momentarily in lukewarm water, the oil becomes more fluid. Hot water should not be used, because this will melt the gel. Even after the container is dipped in warm water the gel will not leave it readily as air pressure of 15 pounds per square inch is holding the gel to the mold. Loosening the gel at one side of the container will allow air to come between the gel and the container, and the gel will then slide free.

REFERENCES

1. Bello, J., and J. R. Vinograd. 1958. The biuret complex and the mechanism of gelation. *Nature* **181**: 273–274. Importance of the peptide groups in the formation of a gel by gelatin.
2. Ferry, J. D. 1948. Protein gels. *Advances in Protein Chemistry* **4**: 40–47. Interpretation of gelation as network formation.
3. Gross, J. 1961. Collagen. *Sci. American* **204**(5): 121–130. Chemistry and structure of collagen: illustrated.
4. Harrington, W., and P. von Hippel. 1961. The structure of collagen and gelatin. *Advances in Protein Chemistry* **16**: 122–127. Properties of gelatin gels.
5. Idsen, B., and E. Braswell. 1957. Gelatin. *Advances in Food Research* **7**: 236–249. Manufacture of gelatin.

TWENTY-SIX
Legumes

Legumes (beans, peas, and lentils) are the dried seeds from plants which belong to the Leguminosae family, hence the name given to foods of this group (13). Legumes supply 20 percent of the dietary protein worldwide (29). Soybeans, one legume, yield a high return of protein, based on the arable land and the fossil energy used to produce them. A number of varieties of common beans (*Phaseolus vulgaris*) are used in this country, although legumes are not used as extensively here as in many parts of the world. A per capita consumption of 5.9 pounds of dried beans and 6.6 pounds of peanuts was forecast for 1979 (37). Safflower, sesame, and sunflower seeds, grown mainly for their oils, yield meals high in protein, with lysine a limiting amino acid (4).

VARIETIES OF LEGUMES USED FOR FOOD

There are several varieties of legumes used for food for which grade standards have been established (36), including the following beans: small white (called "navy" in the Great Lakes region), medium white (Great Lakes), light and dark red and white kidney, marrow, yelloweye, great northern, butternut, pinto, small white and large white (Pacific coast), western red kidney, pink (California small pink), small red (red Mexican, California red, Idaho red), bayo, cranberry, and blackeye. The last, referred to as cow peas, actually belong to the bean family but of the genus *Vigna*. The others belong to the *Phaseolus* genus. Included in the standards are those for limas and baby limas (*Phaseolus lunatus*).

Two varieties of peas (*Pisum sativum*) are commonly used. The smooth-coated pea when mature yields the split pea of commerce and the wrinkled or sweet garden pea is harvested when immature and is considered a green vegetable in menu planning. Other legumes in addition to beans and peas include the chick pea (*Cicer arientinum*), also known as garbanzos, lentils (*Lens culinaris*), peanuts (*Arachis hypogaea*), and soybeans (*Glycine max*).

Principal types of dry beans are shown in Figure 26-1.

COMPOSITION AND NUTRITIVE VALUE

The composition of representative legumes is given in Table 26-1. Included for comparative purposes are two cereals, rolled oats and whole wheat cereal, and also nuts and round steak. The high moisture content of the last should

FIGURE 26-1. Principal types of dry beans: (top) white; (bottom) colored. (Courtesy of the United States Department of Agriculture.)

be kept in mind when the other foods, all of which are dried, are compared with it. When cooked, the 100 grams of dried legumes will measure approximately one and one-fourth cups, and the cereals will yield somewhat less than three cups. The approximate measures for 100 grams of nuts are one cup for English walnuts (halves), just under one cup for pecan halves, a generous

Table 26-1 Composition of legumes and representative cereals, nuts, and lean meats (100-grams dry-weight edible portion)

Food	Water (%)	Calories[a]	Protein (g)	Fat (g)	Carbohydrates (g)	Calcium (mg)	Phosphorus (mg)	Iron (mg)	Vitamin A Value (I.U.)	Thiamine (mg)	Riboflavin (mg)	Niacin (mg)	Ascorbic Acid (mg)
Legume													
Beans, common white[b]	10.9	340	22.3	1.6	61.3	144	425	7.8	0	.65	.22	2.4	—
Beans, common red[b]	10.4	343	22.5	1.5	61.9	110	406	6.9	20	.51	.20	2.3	—
Beans, pinto, calico, red Mexican[b]	8.3	349	22.9	1.2	63.7	135	457	6.4	—	.84	.21	2.2	—
Beans, lima[b]	10.3	345	20.4	1.6	64.0	72	385	7.8	Trace	.48	.17	1.9	—
Lentils[b]	11.1	340	24.7	1.1	60.1	79	377	6.8	60	.37	.22	2.0	—
Peanuts, roasted	1.8	582	26.2	48.7	20.6	72	407	2.2	—	.32	.13	17.1	0
Peas, split[b]	9.3	348	24.2	1.0	62.7	33	268	5.1	120	.74	.29	3.0	—
Soybeans[b]	10.0	403	34.1	17.7	33.5	226	554	8.4	80	1.10	.31	2.2	—

Nuts													
Almonds, dried	4.7	598	18.6	54.2	19.5	234	504	4.7	0	.24	.92	3.5	Trace
Pecans	3.4	687	9.2	71.2	14.6	73	289	2.4	130	.86	.13	.9	2
Walnuts, black	3.1	628	20.5	59.3	14.8	Trace	570	6.0	300	.22	.11	.7	—
Walnuts, English	3.5	651	14.8	64.0	15.8	99	380	3.1	30	.33	.13	.9	2
Cereal													
Rolled oats	8.3	390	14.2	7.4	68.2	53	405	4.5	(0)	.60	.14	1.0	(0)
Wheat cereal, whole meal	10.4	338	13.5	2.0	72.3	45	398	3.7	(0)	.51	.13	4.7	(0)
Beef, round, choice, 89% lean	66.6	197	20.2	12.3	0	12	203	3.0	20	.09	.18	4.8	—

Source: U.S. Dept. Agr. Handbook No. 8. *Composition of Foods. Raw, Processed, Prepared.* Revised 1963.

[a] 1 kilocalorie = 4.185 kilojoules.

[b] Mature seed.

NOTES:

Dash means lack of data

Zero in parentheses indicates values too small to measure.

three-fourth cup for black walnuts (broken kernels), and a skimpy three-fourth cup for whole kernel almonds.

As a group, legumes contain approximately twice as much protein as cereals and, on a per-serving basis, about half as much protein as lean meat. Mature soybeans are higher than most legumes in protein. Quality of protein is as important as quantity. Legumes are better than cereals as a source of the essential amino acids isoleucine, leucine, phenylalanine, threonine, and valine. In particular, their especially high content of lysine, an essential amino acid in which cereals are low, makes legumes good supplements for cereals. The sulfur-containing amino acids of dried legumes, methionine and cystine, appear to be poorly utilized (14). Cereals supplement legumes for these two amino acids, so beans and rice and beans and corn are nutritious combinations. Other supplementary combinations are navy beans and Brazil nuts (1) and navy beans and sesame seed protein (6). Soybeans are not only higher in protein than other legumes, but they are also richer in essential amino acids. Soy flours and grits and soy protein concentrates and isolates are widely used. Protein isolated from soybeans is spun into fibers, and this textured vegetable protein is used to fabricate processed meats (5) and as a meat extender (34).

Beans and peas are low in fat (less than 2 percent) and high in carbohydrates (approximately 60 percent). Peanuts and soybeans are exceptions. Peanuts, because of their high fat content, resemble nuts, and soybeans are high in protein as well as fat. Although beans are better sources of calcium than are cereals, their content of this mineral is not noteworthy. Soybeans contain more calcium than other legumes. The phosphorus content of legumes is high. Much of the phosphorus in mature beans, in contrast to the immature, is present as phytic acid, that is, as inositol hexaphosphoric acid (23). Legumes are somewhat better sources of iron and as good or better sources of thiamine than are whole grain cereals. Legumes compare favorably with lean meat as a source of iron and are a better source of thiamine. Most legumes contain somewhat more riboflavin than either rolled oats or whole wheat but less niacin than whole wheat. Lean meat is superior to both whole grain cereals and legumes as a source of riboflavin or niacin. Legumes supply B_6, folacin, pantothenic acid, and biotin, other vitamins of the B-complex (27,32). Ascorbic acid is absent from legumes and the vitamin A value is negligible. The starch content of most legumes is high.

COOKING LEGUMES

Cooking gelatinizes the starch, alters the texture, and improves the flavor, thus making legumes palatable. Moderate heating increases the availability of the proteins of most legumes (3) and eliminates toxic substances from some (21,22). Dried beans contain lectins (hemagglutinins) which are toxic. Raw soybeans and most other beans contain a trypsin inhibitor and raw soybeans contain a growth inhibitor as well. Heating fresh green soybeans in the pod in boiling water for 3 minutes inactivated 90 percent of the trypsin inhibitor (11).

SOAKING

Dried beans, because of their low moisture content, cook faster if they are given a preliminary soaking. A bean consists of two cotyledons encased in a seed coat known to botanists as the testa. The seed coat is quite impermeable to water. This has been demonstrated in the following way (35). The hilum or scar where the bean was attached to the pod was coated with beeswax and the gain in weight when beans so treated were soaked in cold water was compared with that for untreated beans. In 24 hours beans with the hilum waterproofed had gained in weight 0.28 percent, in contrast with untreated beans that gained 79 percent. This effectively demonstrated that water enters the bean at the hilum. From there it seeps around the periphery of the bean and causes the seed coat to wrinkle. These wrinkles are eliminated when the cotyledons swell subsequently and fill the seed coat. How fast dried beans take up water depends on its temperature. The weight of dried beans soaked in water at room temperature (20°C) became stationary after 16 hours compared with 5 hours at 40°C, 4 hours at 50°C, 1.5 hours at 60°C, and 0.8 hour at 90°C (18). Soaking at temperatures of 60°C and above increased the amounts of calcium, magnesium, thiamine, riboflavin, and niacin leached from the beans. Roughly half the oligosaccharides were removed, too. Heating dried beans in boiling water for 2 minutes and then allowing them to soak for 1 hour prior to cooking gives a product as good as that from an overnight soak in cold water (12). When a short soak in hot water is used, the beans should be cooked in the soaking water. Both water-soluble vitamins and minerals are conserved. Lentils and split peas cook satisfactorily without prior soaking. For soaking (and cooking) dried legumes, 2 to 3 cups of water per cup of dried material are used.

A procedure has been developed for processing dried beans to make them quick cooking (31). The treatment involves soaking the dried beans after preliminary vacuum infiltration with a solution made of sodium chloride, sodium tripolyphosphate, sodium bicarbonate, and sodium carbonate.

When soaked beans are held for several hours at elevated temperature (55° to 60°C), autolysis of part of the phytic acid to inositol and inorganic phosphate by the phytase in the beans occurs (9,10,19). This has been investigated because of possible adverse effects of phytic acid on the availabilty of proteins and some minerals in the beans.

COOKING TIME AND DONENESS

Cooking legumes weakens intercellular bonding material so that pressure of a fork or the teeth causes the intact, starch-filled cells to separate. Most dried legumes require gentle boiling for approximately 1½ hours. Lentils, split peas, and blackeye peas cook in less than an hour, however. Soybeans when thor-

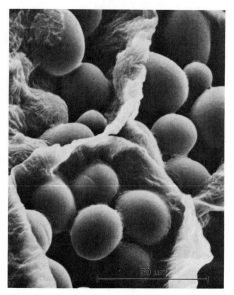

FIGURE 26-2. Scanning electron micrograph of a section through a raw, hydrated lima bean cotyledon, showing starch grains in parts of three cells. (Reprinted from L. B. Rockland and F. T. Jones, *Journal of Food Science* **39:** 343, 1974. Copyright © by Institute of Food Technologists.)

oughly cooked never have the mealy texture of other dried beans. Separation of the cells of cooked beans contrasts with raw beans, where pressure causes fracture across cell walls, exposing the starch-filled interior (30). (See Fig. 26-2.) As legumes are cooked, phytic acid unites with calcium in the pectic substances that bond adjacent cells, making the material soluble (17,24).

The temperature of the water in which the beans are soaked influences the cooking time. For example, dried beans (small white) cooked in the least time after thay had been soaked in water at 90°C rather than at lower temperatures (to 20°C) (18). The high temperature inactivated the enzyme phytase present in the bean which would otherwise eliminate the calcium-sequestering ability of phytic acid by catalyzing its hydrolysis to inositol and inorganic phosphate. Beans soaked in water at 60°, 70°, or 80°C took longest to cook, presumably because the phytic acid was hydrolyzed by phytase and could no longer bind divalent ions. The shorter cooking time (10 minutes) needed to bring about complete separation of the cells of quick cooking lima beans compared with the 45 minutes for water-soaked beans was attributed to chelation of divalent ions in the pectic substances between cells by the salts used to make the beans quick cooking (30). Although soaking dried beans in water at 90°C shortened the cooking time needed to tenderize them, the starch grains remained birefringent longer (18), as did those in beans soaked in salt solution used to make them quick cooking (15). Hard water prolongs the cooking time for dried beans (35). It is possible that both calcium and magnesium ions in hard water cause some interference with the tenderizing of dried beans during cooking because of their reaction with pectic constituents. If the water is extremely hard, the beans may be made uncookable. Addition of soda to the soaking and cooking water will shorten the time appreciably. The amount recommended is ⅛ teaspoon per cup of beans (12). Apparently this small amount of soda has no effect on the loss of thiamine during cooking and the quality of the cooked bean is almost as good as without soda. An excess of soda should be avoided because this makes the beans dark and mushy and because of the possibility of greater loss of thiamine. Stir-frying soaked, dried soybeans in oil for 10 minutes shortened the cooking time more than did adding soda to the cooking water. Retention of thiamine was greater and flavor was judged better, also (28).

Cooking time for dried legumes may be shortened by the use of a pressure saucepan. Actual cooking times for soaked legumes range from 3 to 10 minutes (12). This is in addition to approximately 25 minutes to bring the saucepan slowly to an operating pressure of 15 pounds and return the pressure to zero. Addition of 1 tablespoon of fat per cup of beans is recommended to reduce foaming both in the pressure saucepan and in a saucepan. For the latter leaving the lid ajar for the first few minutes of cooking is an added precaution.

Two ingredients commonly added to beans when they are baked are molasses and tomato juice. Both prolong the time required to make the beans tender (35). This effect is attributed to the calcium in the former and to the acid in the latter. Partially cooking the beans before either ingredient is added is recommended to keep the cooking time reasonably short.

The conditions under which dried beans are stored influence the cooking time. If beans are stored with a high moisture content (11 percent or above) or at high relative humidity, particularly at elevated temperature, cooking time is prolonged (2). Such adverse storing conditions lower the digestibility of the protein and the availability of the sulfur-containing amino acids, too.

SEASONING

Addition of salt to dried legumes (approximately 1 teaspoon per cup) is essential to make them palatable. The salt should be added early in the cooking period for best flavor. Palatability of cooked legumes may be further enhanced by the judicious addition of onion, celery, parsley, carrots, or tomato along with herbs or spices to season.

YIELD OF COOKED LEGUMES

The volume of a pound of dried legumes ranges from 2 to 2½ cups. Legumes increase in volume 2 to 3 times when cooked (25). This means that a pound of dried legumes will yield from 4 to 7 cups cooked.

Preparing entrées of legumes is more time-consuming than is cooking meat, but legumes are a nutritious and relatively inexpensive meat substitute. Legumes give variety to the diet and could well occupy a more prominent place.

FLATUS AFTER INGESTING LEGUMES

The flatus experienced by many individuals from 5 to 7 hours after ingesting beans contains elevated levels of hydrogen and especially of carbon dioxide. Hydrogen is elevated in the breath, too (8). The increase in hydrogen comes from two oligosaccharides, raffinose and stachyose, which, because of a lack of α-galactosidase in the upper intestinal tract, are attacked by microorganisms in the lower intestines. The component of dried beans which gives rise to the carbon dioxide has not been identified (26). Investigating the possibility of eliminating part of the raffinose and stachyose, one-third of these oligosaccharides were extracted from soybeans when they were boiled for 20 minutes in a 10:1 ratio of water to beans (20). Loss of protein was 1 percent. Lowering the ratio of water to beans 3:1 reduced the extraction of oligosaccharides to 7.7 percent, but did not materially decrease the amount of protein extracted. Boiling the beans for 1 hour in the larger volume of water extracted more than half the oligosaccharides and 2.6 percent of the protein. Adding soda (0.5 percent) increased extraction of the oligosaccharides but almost tripled the loss of protein. Whole wheat cereal causes flatus, also, with the constituent(s) responsible located in the two milling fractions, shorts and red dog (16).

REFERENCES

1. Antunes, A. J., and P. Markakis. 1977. Protein supplementation of navy beans with Brazil nuts. *J. Agr. Food Chem.* **25:** 1096–1098. Effectiveness of methionine-rich nuts.
2. Antunes, P. L., and V. Sqarbieri. 1979. Influence of time and conditions of storage on technological and nutritional properties of a dry bean (*Phaseolus vulgaris* L.) variety Rosinha G$_2$. *J. Food Sci.* **44:** 1703–1706. Temperatures of 12°, 25°, and 37°C and relative humidities of 52 percent, 65–70 percent, and 76 percent compared.
3. Bates, R. P., F. W. Knapp, and P. E. Araujo. 1977. Protein quality of green-mature, dry mature, and sprouted soybeans. *J. Food Sci.* **42:** 271–272. Protein efficiency ratio of the three forms, raw and heated.
4. Betschart, A. A., C. K. Lyon, and G. O. Kohler. 1975. Sunflower, safflower, sesame, and castor protein. In *Food Protein Sources,* N. W. Pirie, ed. Cambridge University Press. Pp. 79–104. A review.
5. Bird, K. M. 1974. Plant proteins: Progress and problems. *Food Technol.* **28**(3): 31–32, 36, 39. Textured vegetable protein.
6. Boloorforooshan, M. and P. Markakis. 1977. Protein supplementation of navy beans with sesame seed. *J. Food Sci.* **44:** 390–397. Effect on protein efficiency ratio.
7. Burr, H. K., S. Kon, and H. J. Morris. 1968. Cooking rates of dry beans as influenced by moisture content and temperature and time of storage. *Food Technol.* **22:** 336–338. Effects of the three variables on cooking time of three varieties of dried beans.

8. Calloway, D. H., C. A. Hickey, and E. L. Murphy. 1971. Reduction of intestinal gas-forming properties of legumes by traditional and experimental food processing methods. *J. Food Sci.* **36:** 251–255. Flatus-forming legumes.

9. Chang, R., B. M. Kennedy, and S. Schwimmer. 1979. Effects of autolysis on the nutritional qualities of beans (*Phaseolus vulgaris*). *J. Food Sci.* **44:** 1141–1143. Effects on availability of phosphorus and on protein efficiency ratio.

10. Chang, R., S. Schwimmer, and H. K. Burr. 1977. Phytate: Removal from dry whole beans by enzymatic hydrolysis and diffusion. *J. Food Sci.* **42:** 1098–1101. Effect of incubation at 60°C.

11. Collins, J. L., and B. F. Beatty. 1980. Heat inactivation of trypsin inhibitor in fresh green soybeans and physiological responses of rats fed the beans. *J. Food Sci.* **45:** 542–545. Time required in boiling water.

12. Dawson, E. H., J. C. Lamb, E. W. Toepfer, and H. W. Warren. 1952. *Development of rapid methods of soaking and cooking dried beans.* U.S. Dept. Agr. Bull. No. 1051. 53 pp. Methods of soaking, type of water, addition of soda, and cooking temperature studied.

13. Deschamps, I. 1958. Peas and beans. In *Plant Protein Foodstuffs.* A. M. Altschul, ed. New York: Academic Press. Pp. 717–735. Types of legumes, botanical information, and use.

14. Evans, R. G., D. H. Bauer, K. A. Sisak, and P. A. Ryan. 1974. The availability for the rat of methionine and cystine contained in dry bean seed (*Phaseolus vulgaris*). *J. Agr. Food Chem.* **22:** 130–133. Evidence of poor utilization.

15. Hahn, D. M., F. T. Jones, I. Akhavan, and L. B. Rockland. 1977. Light and scanning electron microscope studies on dry beans: Intracellular gelatinization of starch in cotyledons of large lima beans (*Phaseolus lunatus*). *J. Food Sci.* **42:** 1208–1212. Quick cooking and conventional dried beans compared.

16. Hickey, C. A., E. L. Murphy, and D. H. Calloway. 1972. Intestinal-gas production following ingestion of commercial wheat cereals and milling fractions. *Cereal Chem.* **49:** 276–282. Milling fractions responsible for flatus.

17. Isherwood, F. A. 1955. Texture in fruits and vegetables. *Food Mfg.* **30:** 399–402, 420. Textural changes in plant material including the role of phytin.

18. Kon, S. 1979. Effect of soaking temperature on cooking and nutritional quality of beans. *J. Food Sci.* **44:** 1329–1334. Temperatures from 20°C to 90°C compared.

19. Kon, S., A. C. Olson, D. F. Frederick, S. B. Eggling, and J. R. Wagner. 1973. Effects of different treatments on phytate and soluble sugars in California small white beans (*Phaseolus vulgaris*). *J. Food Sci.* **38:** 215–217. Enzymes activated at 55°C.

20. Ku, S., L. S. Wei, M. P. Steinberg, A. I. Nelson, and T. Hymowitz. 1976. Extraction of oligosaccharides during cooking of soybeans. *J. Food Sci.* **41:** 361–364. Attempts to reduce oligosaccharides in cooked beans.

21. Liener, I. 1979. Significance for humans of biologically active factors in soybeans and other food legumes. *J. Am. Oil Chemists' Soc.* **56:** 121–129. Toxic substances present.

22. Liener, I. E. 1976. Legume toxins in relation to protein digestibility. A review. *J. Food Sci.* **41:** 1076–1081. Trypsin inhibitor and lectins in legumes.

23. Makower, R. U. 1969. Changes in phytic acid and acid-soluble phosphorus in maturing pinto beans. *J. Sci. Food Agric.* **20:** 82–84. Immature and mature beans compared.

24. Mattson, S. 1946. The cookability of yellow peas. *Acta Agriculturae Suecana* **2:** 185–231. Technical documentation of the causes and prevention of hard-cooking peas.

25. Meiners, C. R., N. L. Derise, H. C. Lau, M. G. Crews, S. J. Ritchey, and E. W. Murphy. 1976. The content of nine mineral elements in raw and cooked mature dry legumes. *J. Agr. Food Chem.* 1126–1130. Ten legumes analyzed.

26. Murphy, E. L., H. Horsley, and H. K. Burr. 1972. Fractionation of dry bean extracts which increase carbon dioxide egestion in human flatus. *J. Agr. Food Chem.* **20:** 813–817. An attempt to identify the source of CO_2 in flatus.

27. Ogunmodide, B. K., and V. A. Oyenuga. 1970. Vitamin B content of cowpeas (*Vigna unguiculata* Walp). II. Pyridoxine, pantothenic acid, biotin and folic acid. *J. Sci. Food Agric.* **21:** 87–91. Three varieties of cowpeas tested.

28. Perry, A. K., C. Peters, and F. O. Van Duyne. 1976. Effect of variety and cooking method on cooking times, thiamine content and palatability of soybeans. *J. Food Sci.* **41:** 1330–1334. Use of soda in the cooking water; stir-frying in oil.

29. Pimentel, D., W. Dritschilo, J. Krummel, and J. Kutzman. 1975. Energy and land constraints in food protein production. *Science* **190:** 754–761. Options for use of resources to meet the world's food needs.

30. Rockland, L. B., and F. T. Jones. 1974. Scanning electron microscope studies on dry beans: Effects of cooking on the cellular structure of cotyledons of rehydrated large lima beans. *J. Food Sci.* **39:** 342–346. Water-soaked and salt-soaked beans compared.

31. Rockland, L. B., and E. A. Metzler. 1967. Quick cooking lima and other dry beans. *Food Technol.* **21:** 344–348. Salts used in the treatment.

32. Rockland, L. B., C. F. Miller, and D. M. Hahn. 1977. Thiamine, pyridoxine, niacin and folacin in quick-cooking beans. *J. Food Sci.* **42:** 25–28. Quick-cooking versus conventional dried beans.

33. Sefa-Dedeh, S., D. W. Stanley, and P. W. Voisey. 1979. Effects of storage time and conditions on the hard-to-cook defect of cowpeas (*Vigna unguiculata*). *J. Food Sci.* **44:** 790–796. Three temperatures and three relative humidities compared.

34. Shaner, K. M., and R. E. Baldwin. 1979. Sensory properties, proximate analysis and cooking losses of meat loaves extended with chickpea meal or textured plant protein. *J. Food Sci.* **44:** 1191–1193. Effects on flavor and juiciness.

35. Snyder, E. B. 1936. *Some factors affecting the cooking quality of the pea and Great Northern type of dry beans.* Neb. Agr. Exp. Sta. Research Bull. 85. 31 pp. Early and fundamental work on the problems involved in the cooking of dry beans.

36. United States Department of Agriculture. Bureau of Agricultural Economics. *Handbook of Official U.S. Standards for Beans.* 34 pp. Varieties and grades.

37. United States Department of Agriculture. *National Food Review.* Economics, Statistics and Cooperatives, Service A. 1980 (Winter). NFR-9, p. 51. Per capita consumption of major foods.

TWENTY-SEVEN
Fruits

Fruits are valued for their attractive color, for their pleasing aroma due mainly to aldehydes, alcohols, and esters, for their sweet-tart taste, for their crisp, crunchy texture from water-inflated cells, and for the nutrients that they contribute to the diet.

Most fruits consist of the pulpy, edible material which develops around and adheres to the seeds after a plant has flowered. The edible part may surround a core as in an apple (Fig. 27-1) or a hard stone as in apricots and peaches. A number of seeds may be enclosed in one ovary as in currants and gooseberries. The edible material may be surrounded by a hard rind as in muskmelon or by a leathery rind as in oranges and lemons. The fleshy fruit of the strawberry consists of the enlarged receptacle of the flower (Fig. 27-2). Both blackberries and raspberries are composed of the edible material around several ovaries from a single flower (Fig. 27-3). Pineapple, a multiple fruit, develops from several flowers, as do figs. Rhubarb, actually a stem, is considered a fruit.

Fruits are eaten raw, after freezing or in dried form. In addition, fresh, frozen, or dried fruits may be cooked in a variety of ways. Elementary knowledge of the structure of plant material is basic to an understanding of the changes which take place in fruits before they are served. Much of the information that follows applies to vegetables as well as to fruits. In some cases the distinction between the two is a fine one. Tomatoes illustrate this. Served as juice for breakfast they do duty as a fruit, but for dinner they may be served as a vegetable. Used raw in salad, they are likely to be considered a vegetable. Botanically, cucumbers and squash are fruits, but in menu planning they are looked upon as vegetables.

STRUCTURE OF PLANT TISSUE

Fruits and vegetables, like cereals, are made of cells not all of which are alike. For example, the peel of an apple and the fleshy part underneath the skin are different because of differences in the structure of cells which make up the two types of tissue. Fruits and vegetables contain, in varying amounts, tissues of the following types: dermal, or protective; vascular, or food- and water-conducting; supporting; and parenchyma, or ground tissue. Parenchyma cells make up most of the edible parts of vegetables and fruits (15). (See Fig. 27-4.)

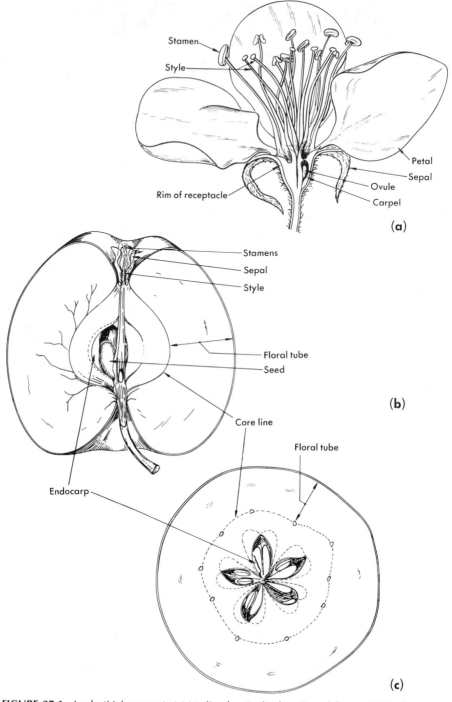

FIGURE 27-1. Apple (*Malus* genus). (a) Median longitudinal section of flower. (b) Median longitudinal section of mature apple. (c) Cross section of mature apple. (From *The Botany of Crop Plants* by W. W. Robbins. Copyright © 1917 by P. Blakiston's Son and Company. Used by permission of McGraw-Hill Book Company.)

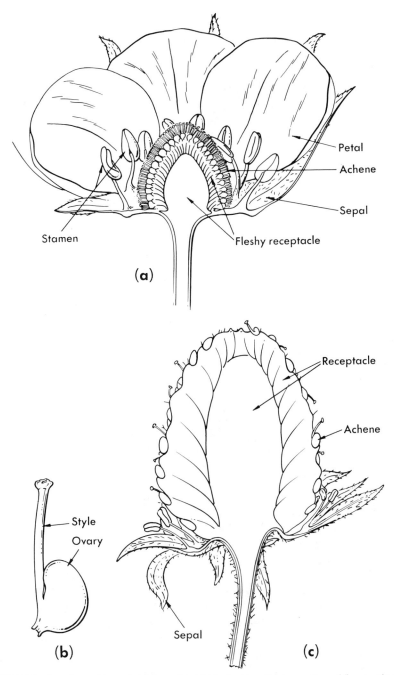

FIGURE 27-2. Strawberry (*Fragaria chiloensis*). (a) Median lengthwise section of flower. (b) Single achene. (c) Median lengthwise section of the aggregate fruit. (From *The Botany of Crop Plants* by W. W. Robbins. Copyright © 1917 by P. Blakiston's Son and Company. Used by permission of McGraw-Hill Book Company.)

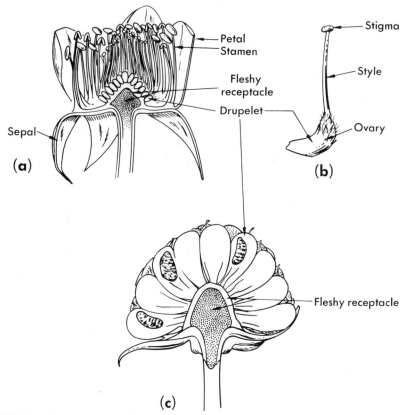

FIGURE 27-3. American red raspberry (*Rubus strigosus*). (a) Median lengthwise section of flower. (b) Single immature pistil. (c) Median lengthwise section of fruit. (From *The Botany of Crop Plants* by W. W. Robbins. Copyright © 1917 by P. Blakiston's Son and Company. Used by permission of McGraw-Hill Book Company.)

Typically polyhedral in shape, parenchyma cells include those in which food is either synthesized or stored. Most of the cells of green leaves are examples of synthesizing cells, but the parenchyma cells that predominate in the edible part of an apple or potato store sugar and starch.

CELLULOSE AND THE CELL WALL

All plant cells, including parenchyma cells, are defined by a cell wall whose function is to give support to the contents of the cell (33). Young cells have a primary cell wall only, but a secondary cell wall forms inside the primary cell wall as tissue begins to mature. Cell walls are porous and permeable to water. The major constituent of the cell wall is cellulose (28), a β-D-glucose polymer (see Starch Chemistry, Chapter 8). It gives to the cell wall part of its toughness and pliability. Cellulose is deposited in cell walls as fibers (25). These fibers are made of smaller structures, called "microfibrils," which are

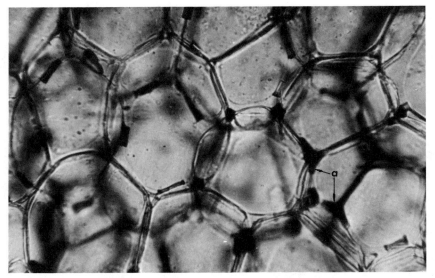

FIGURE 27-4. Microscopic view of parenchyma cells from living plant tissue (onion). Dark areas (a) are intercellular spaces filled with air. (Photograph by H. B. Currier, 1946. From T. E. Weier and R. Stocking, *Advances in Food Research* **2:** 299. Copyright © 1949 by Academic Press Inc.)

made of cellulose molecules. These fibers are deposited in a feltlike manner in the cell wall. The connecting interstices contain a noncrystalline matrix of hemicelluloses and pectic substances.

As is true of a number of topics in food science, the literature on hemicelluloses is confusing. The term "hemicellulose," as it is frequently used, is as nonspecific as is the term "tannin." Hemicelluloses include polymers of the pentose (5-carbon) sugar xylose together with some glucuronic acid (the organic acid derived from glucose). Other hemicelluloses are polymers of the pentose, arabinose, along with galacturonic acid (the acid derived from galactose). The former, called "xylans," are the main type of hemicellulose. The latter are called arabans. Hemicelluloses are not as highly polymerized as is cellulose and they are more vulnerable to degradation by alkali. When plant tissue is cooked in alkaline water (soda added), it becomes mushy due to the action of soda on the hemicelluloses of the cell wall.

The walls of parenchyma cells are relatively thin. In contrast, the walls of cells in outer or protective tissue which contain a higher proportion of celluloses and hemicelluloses are thick. The skin of apple, pear, tomato, and cucumber and the rind of lemons and oranges are examples of such protective tissue. Cells that make up vascular tissue have thick cell walls high in cellulose, too. These are long slender cells united end to end to form hollow tubes whose function is to conduct either water or food throughout the plant. The walls of certain of these cells and of cells which form supporting tissue in plants contain, in addition to cellulose, molecules of a group of substances known as "lignin." Lignin, an aromatic substance derived from benzene, is the constituent that makes wood woody. It is deposited between crystallites of cellulose chiefly in secondary cell walls after growth ceases. The human digestive tract is unable to hydrolyze this material nor does cooking have any effect on it. Edible parts of fruits do not usually contain heavily lignified tissue. However, the gritty deposits in pears called sclereids contain appreciable quantities of lignin.

PECTIC SUBSTANCES

Pectic substances are found in the primary cell wall in the interstices between deposits of cellulose and hemicelluloses. Pectic substances also serve as intercellular cement between walls of adjoining cells. The intercellular area between adjacent cells is known as the middle lamella. Pectic substances are polymers of D-galacturonic acid united by the α-1,4-glycosidic linkage. A limited number of residues of the sugar rhamnose interrupt the galacturonic acid chain. Formulas for galactose, galacturonic acid, and for a fragment of a pectin molecule are given below.

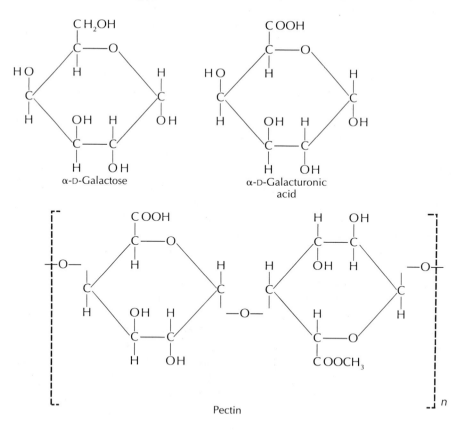

α-D-Galactose

α-D-Galacturonic
acid

Pectin

It is customary to classify pectic substances into one of three groups: pectic acids, pectinic acids (pectins), and protopectin. In pectic acids the carboxyl groups on the galacturonic acid residues in the polymer are not esterified. Pectic acids form salts, as do other acids. Pectic acids are deposited in plant tissue as calcium or magnesium pectates. Pectinic acids (also called pectins) have methyl ester groups esterified to some of the carboxyl groups along the galacturonic acid polymer as shown. If more than a negligible proportion of the carboxyl groups are esterified, the pectinic acid is designated as pectin. Pectins are dispersible in water. Like the pectic acids, pectins form salts called "pectinates." Pectins are used with sugar and acid to make fruit jellies such as apple and grape. Low methoxyl pectins are those pectinic acids in which a majority of the carboxyl groups are free rather than esterified. Protopectin is the name given to the insoluble pectic substances found in immature plant tissue. Despite much work, the nature of protopectin and the reasons for its insolubility remain to be elucidated. Protopectin may be converted to water-dispersible pectin when plant tissue is heated in simmering or boiling water. Because of this, firm plant tissue may be softened by cooking. Apples and the spongy white albedo of citrus fruits are particularly rich in pectic constituents and are used commercially as sources of pectin. Low methoxyl pectins can with divalent ions such as the calcium of milk form gels in the absence of sugar and acid.

CYTOPLASM

Inside the nonliving cell wall lies a protoplasmic membrane, also called plasmalemma, which encloses the protoplasm of the cell. (See Figs. 27-5 and 27-6.) Just inside this membrane, in a narrow layer around the periphery of the cell, is the cytoplasm. The jellylike cytoplasm is colloidal in character and free to move about within the cell. Embedded in the cytoplasm are organized bodies called "plastids." Fat droplets and pigments soluble in fat are contained within the plastids. In cells of certain plants the plastids serve as a storage place for starch, each starch-filled plastid constituting a starch grain. Cells of the potato as well as those of the endosperm of wheat and corn are packed full of such starch-filled plastids (grains). (See Figs. 9-2 and 28-4.) Also distributed throughout the protoplasm are the mitochondria in which enzymes are located. The nucleus of the cell is embedded in the cytoplasm.

VACUOLE

A unique feature of most parenchyma cells is that a major part (up to 90 percent) of the interior is occupied by one or more vacuoles or saclike spaces, shown schematically in Figures 27-5 and 27-6. Each is separated from the cytoplasm by a vacuolar membrane (also called a "tonoplast"). The vacuoles contain cell sap. Both the protoplasmic and the vacuolar membranes are semipermeable and osmotically active. They are made of a protein-lipid complex.

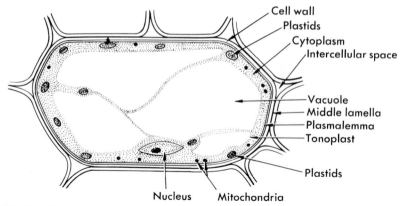

FIGURE 27-5. Diagram showing the main components of a parenchyma cell.

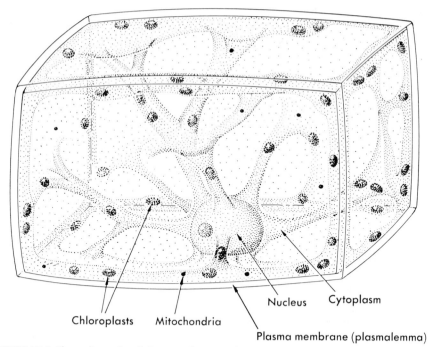

FIGURE 27-6. Three-dimensional diagram of a green plant cell. The proportion of vacuolar space is much greater and the cytoplasm occupies much less space than can be shown by a diagram. (From V. A. Greulach and J. E. Adams, *Plants: An Introduction to Modern Botany.* Copyright © 1967 by John Wiley & Sons, Inc., New York, p. 114. Reprinted by permission.)

INTERCELLULAR AIR SPACES

At the point where three or more cells adjoin, the fit may not be perfect. Instead, small spaces are left which become filled with intercellular air (15). (See Figs. 27-4, 27-5 and 27-7.) These microscopic pockets of gas refract rays of light which hit them much as the pits in frosted glass make what was once clear glass appear milky white. These gas-filled spaces are mainly responsible for the opaqueness (chalky white cast) of uncooked plant tissue in contrast to the translucency of the cooked tissue. In some plant tissue the volume of intercellular gas is appreciable, in others negligible. Tissues from plums and potatoes contain relatively few intercellular air spaces (26). In apple, however, gas-filled spaces between the cells may occupy 20 to 25 percent of the volume and account for the fact that apples float in water. Bobbing for apples in a tub of water on Halloween is possible because the fruit is buoyed up by this intercellular air. Otherwise, the fruit would sink.

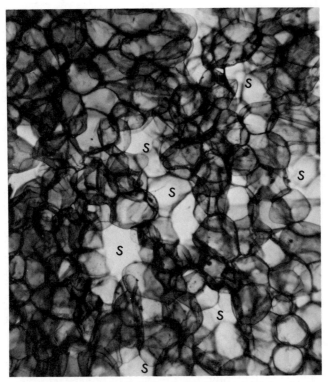

FIGURE 27-7. Photomicrograph of the flesh of an apple (Gravenstein) showing parenchyma cells and large intercellular spaces (s). Tangential section. Original magnification × 40. (Courtesy of R. M. Reeve.)

COMPOSITION OF FRUITS

WATER

Fruits tend to be juicy because of their high content of water, percentages of which vary from 75 to 90 (see Table 27-1). Dissolved in the water, the bulk of which is found in the vacuoles, are soluble substances like sugars, salts, organic acids, water-soluble pigments, and vitamins. Substances unable to dissolve in water are colloidally dispersed in it.

CARBOHYDRATES

Fruits contain appreciable amounts of carbohydrates. In fact, aside from water, carbohydrates are the main constituents in fruits. Included are sugars and starches in addition to celluloses, hemicelluloses, and pectic substances. An immature fruit such as an apple may contain a fair amount of starch. This disappears and sugar accumulates as the fruit ripens. As bananas ripen the decrease in starch and the increase in sugar is even more pronounced. If an unripe banana is chilled or held in a cool place too long, hydrolysis of starch is retarded and the banana does not ripen normally (5,18). On the other hand, bananas do not develop full yellow color if ripened at a high temperature (13). The sugar content of most fruits increases as they ripen. The sweetness of melons, oranges, peaches, and strawberries when they are fully mature is due to the high level of sugar.

Celluloses, in addition to giving strength and support to plant cells and tissues, contribute to the textural qualities for which fruits and vegetables are prized. In addition, fruits and vegetables provide bulk in the diet because digestive juices lack enzymes capable of hydrolyzing the β-glucosidic linkage in cellulose (see Chapter 8).

Quantities of the different forms of pectic substances in fruits vary with the fruit and with its maturity (35). Mature but firm fruit contains a high proportion of insoluble protopectin. As ripening proceeds, the cells adhere less tightly and the tissues soften. Textural changes in ripening fruits have been attributed to the action of pectin-degrading enzymes, pectinesterase and polygalacturonase. A number of workers have attempted to account for the marked difference in the texture of ripe, firm-fleshed cling peaches compared with soft-fleshed freestones. In an early study, no polygalacturonase was found in freestone peaches even though the intrinsic viscosity of the pectin decreased markedly as the fruit ripened (21). An increase in water-soluble pectin was reported in freestone peaches as they ripened, whereas the conversion of protopectin to soluble pectin was negligible in clings (23). Differences in pectinesterase activity failed to account for differences in texture between peaches of the two types (27). Recently, the presence of polygalacturonase has been reported in ripening peaches (24). Clings contain only exopolygalacturonase which splits monomers from the reducing end of the chain, and this makes little difference in the size of the polymer or in its solubility. Freestones, on

Table 27-1 Composition of raw fruits (100-gram edible portion)

Fruit	Water %	Calo-ries[a]	Protein (g)	Fat (g)	Carbo-hydrates Total (g)	Fiber (g)	Cal-cium (mg)	Phos-phorus (mg)	Iron (mg)	Vitamin A Value (I.U.)	Thia-mine (mg)	Ribo-flavin (mg)	Niacin (mg)	Ascorbic Acid (mg)
Apples	84.8	56	.2	.6	14.1	1.0	7	10	.3	90	.03	.02	.1	7
Apricots	85.3	51	1.0	.2	12.8	.6	17	23	.5	2700	.03	.04	.6	10
Avocados	74.0	167	2.1	16.4	6.3	1.6	10	42	.6	290	.11	.20	1.6	14
Bananas	75.7	85	1.1	.2	22.2	.5	8	26	.7	190	.05	.06	.7	10
Grapefruit	88.4	41	.5	.1	10.6	.2	16	16	.4	80	.04	.02	.2	38[b]
Lemons	90.1	27	1.1	.3	8.2	.4	26	16	.6	20	.04	.02	.1	53[c]
Muskmelon	91.2	30	.7	.1	7.5	.3	14	16	.4	3400[d]	.04	.03	.6	33
Oranges	86.0	49	1.0	.2	12.2	.5	41	20	.4	200	.10	.04	.4	50[b]
Peaches	89.1	38	.6	.1	9.7	.6	9	19	.5	1330[d]	.02	.05	.0	7
Pears	83.2	61	.7	.4	15.3	1.4	8	11	.3	20	.02	.04	.1	4
Strawberries	89.9	37	.7	.5	8.4	1.3	21	21	1.0	60	.03	.07	.6	59

SOURCE: U.S.D.A., Agr. Handbook No. 8. *Composition of Foods. Raw, Processed, Prepared.* Revised 1963.

[a]1 kilocalorie = 4.185 kilojoules.
[b]Weighted value for the season.
[c]Fruit marketed in summer.
[d]Yellow-fleshed varieties.

the other hand, contain both *exo-* and *endo*polygalacturonase. The latter hydrolyzes the chain at random, reducing the size of the molecule markedly and increasing its dispersibility.

Changes in the pectic substances which normally accompany ripening of juicy, soft-fleshed varieties may be altered if fruit picked before it is fully ripe is held at 8°C or lower for 2 weeks or more. A condition known as woolly breakdown occurs. A delay in the elaboration of pectinesterase and a deficiency of polygalacturonase result in insoluble low methyl ester pectic molecules which, by retaining water in the cell walls, may be responsible for the dry, woolly condition (12).

PROTEIN, FAT, AND MINERALS

Fruits contain relatively small amounts of protein, enough for the life processes of the plant but not enough to make a significant contribution to the daily needs of the human body for this nutrient. One serving of most fruits contains 1 gram or less of protein. The amount of fat in most fruits is low, avocados and olives excepted. Fruits are low in calcium and phosphorus and most are not particularly good sources of iron.

VITAMINS

Most fruits are low in the B-vitamins. Citrus fruits, including oranges, lemons, and grapefruit, are excellent sources of ascorbic acid, as are two more seasonal fruits, cantaloupe and strawberries. Yellow fruits such as apricots, cantaloupe, and peaches are fairly good sources of carotene, the precursor of vitamin A.

ORGANIC ACIDS

Dissolved in the cell sap are a number of organic acids. Together with the sugars present these contribute to the taste of fruits. Common acids in fruits are citric, in high concentration in citrus fruits and the main acid in tomatoes; malic, the chief acid in apples and peaches; malic and tartaric in grapes; malic and oxalic in rhubarb; citric and malic in pineapple; and citric and benzoic in cranberries.

Among the fruits, limes and lemons have the lowest pH (are most acid) with a pH of 2.0 to 2.2. Cranberries are a tart fruit, with a pH near 2.7. Within the range of pH 3.0 to 3.4 are red currants, plums, gooseberries, prunes, apples, grapefruit, rhubarb, apricots, blackberries, and strawberries. The average pH for peaches, raspberries, blueberries, oranges, and pears falls within the range of 3.5 to 3.9. The pH of bananas (average 4.6) and figs is higher than that of most fruits (2), except watermelon, with a pH near 6.

PIGMENTS

CHLOROPHYLL AND CAROTENOIDS

Meals would be drab and uninteresting were it not for the colorful pigments in fruits and vegetables. Both green chlorophyll and yellow carotenoids are found in the plastids of the cells dissolved in the fat. Few mature fruits contain chlorophyll in appreciable quantities except avocados, greengage plums, and gooseberries. When the last two are canned, they lose some of their color although they were never very green. Vegetables, especially green leafy ones, are richer sources of chlorophyll than are fruits. Discussion of chlorophyll and the retention of green color is deferred to the next chapter.

Yellow apricots, muskmelon, oranges, peaches, and pineapple contain carotenoid pigments, as do red grapefruit, tomatoes, watermelon, and rose hips. Alteration of the color of fruits due to changes in the carotenoid pigments is slight and usually goes unnoticed. Carotenoid pigments are discussed in the next chapter, on vegetables.

FLAVONOID PIGMENTS

Flavonoid pigments are found in fruits and vegetables (8). These are water soluble and are found in the cell sap rather than in the plastids. Flavonoid pigments include the anthocyanins (literally, "blue flower"), the anthoxanthins (literally, "yellow flower"), formerly called "flavones," and a third group, which contains a number of related phenolic compounds, many erroneously categorized as "tannins."

Flavonoids are phenolic compounds related to flavone for which one group of water-soluble pigments was named originally. Flavone has the formula

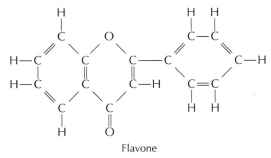

Flavone

Structurally pigments of both the anthocyanin and the anthoxanthin groups contain two 6-membered rings of carbon linked by a 3-carbon unit. The basic structure of an anthocyanin pigment is shown here:

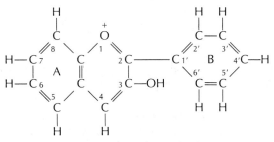

Basic structure for anthocyanin pigments

The unit on the left is designated the A ring, that on the right the B ring. The central ring differentiates the two groups.

Individual pigments within each of the two groups differ in accordance with the side groups attached and their position of attachment on the molecule. Pigments in both groups typically have hydroxyl (—OH) groups attached at positions 5 and 7 on the A-ring. In anthocyanins a sugar residue is attached at position 3 and frequently at position 5. Sugar is attached most frequently at position 7 and less commonly at positions 5 and 3 in the anthoxanthins. The sugar moiety contributes to the solubility of these pigments in water. A pigment from which the sugar residue has been hydrolyzed is known as an "aglycone"; an aglycone of an anthocyanin is called an "anthocyanidin." Attached to the molecule at positions 3', 4', or 5' may be —OH groups or, in the case of anthocyanins, methoxyl (CH_3O—) groups.

ANTHOCYANINS. Individual anthocyanins may be red, purple, or blue (10). The color depends upon the particular groups attached to the basic structure and on the position of the carbon to which they are attached. An increase in the number of hydroxyl groups shifts the hue of the pigment from red toward blue, as does the presence of a diglycoside. Thus the aglycone pelargonidin with one —OH group at position 4' has a reddish hue, cyanidin with —OH groups at positions 3' and 4' is blue, and delphinidin, with —OH groups at positions 3', 4', and 5', is bluer still. The red color of strawberries is due mainly to a glucoside of pelargonidin.

Glycosides of cyanidin, the commonest aglycone, are likely to be found in plants that are woody rather than herbaceous. The pigment is removed from plant tissue, usually by dilute hydrochloric acid, so the aglycone is obtained as the chloride. The formula for cyanidin chloride is

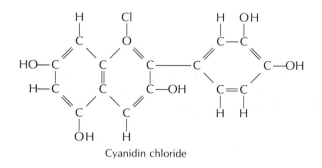

Cyanidin chloride

Fruits which contain cyanidin glycosides include blackberries, blueberries, boysenberries (a cross of blackberry, raspberry, and loganberry), sweet cherries (Windsor and Bing varieties), sour cherries, ripe gooseberries, pomegranates, and the skin of Jonathan and Stayman winesap apples and of Flame Tokay grapes. Most fruits which have been analyzed contain more than one anthocyanin pigment. Cranberries contain a cyanidin glycoside but also one of peonidin, which is like cyanidin except the molecule contains a methoxyl group at position 3′. The presence of such a group shifts the hue of the pigment toward the red end of the spectrum. The pigments in concord grapes are derivatives of delphinidin, cyanidin and malvidin (like delphinidin except that methoxyl groups have replaced the hydroxyls at positions 3′ and 4′), giving a predominantly blue hue.

ANTHOXANTHINS. The anthoxanthins are more widely distributed in plants than are the anthocyanins (8). Anthoxanthins found in fruits and vegetables include flavones, flavonols, and the flavanones. Differences in the central ring which contains the 3-carbon fragment (shown below with the A- and B-rings in skeleton) differentiate pigments of the three subgroups thus:

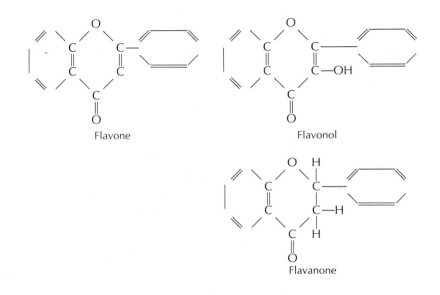

Flavone

Flavonol

Flavanone

One of the commonest anthoxanthins is the flavonol quercetin. Its formula is

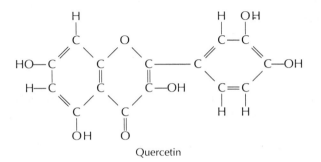

Quercetin

Most anthoxanthins occur as glycosides. One such glycoside is the flavanone naringin, the 7-rhamnoglucoside of naringenin. (Naringin is the bitter substance in grapefruit peel.) Naringenin has the formula shown below.

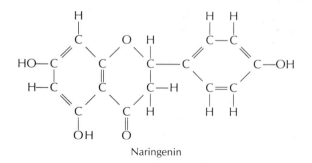

Naringenin

Anthocyanin and anthoxanthin pigments frequently occur in the same plant tissue. In some plant material the color of an anthocyanin pigment is intensified and also shifted to a bluer hue by the presence of an anthoxanthin, an effect referred to as co-pigmentation (3). Structures for co-pigments between anthocyanins and flavanols such as quercetin and rutin have been proposed (34).

EFFECTS OF ACIDITY ON THE COLOR OF FLAVONOIDS. Both anthocyanins and anthoxanthins are amphoteric compounds, with the ability to react with both acids and bases (8,10). Anthoxanthins may change from a yellow color in alkaline medium to creamy white in neutral, to colorless in acid media, the condition that prevails in the cell sap. Anthocyanins exist in a form that is red in acid media as in the vacuole of the cell. Many pigments of this group shift to the purple anhydro or color base as the acidity of the medium decreases and the pH approaches 7 (34). In alkaline medium a further shift to the blue occurs. Such changes led an early worker to characterize these pigments as "vegetable chameleons." The amphoteric character of anthocyanin pigments is illustrated below with cyanidin (10).

Shift in hue to purple or blue may be observed on the surface of dumplings made from baking powder biscuit dough which is cooked in stewed blueberries or blackberries. (A greenish hue sometimes observed is believed to be due to a mixture of yellow anthoxanthins and blue anthocyanins.) The same change may be observed when unrinsed utensils which contain juice from these fruits come in contact with alkaline dishwater. Not all anthocyanin-containing fruit juices show this marked change in hue with change in pH. The groups attached to the basic structure and their position of attachment determine the response of the pigment to a change in environment. A free hydroxyl group at position 4' and a minimum of four hydroxyl groups are essential for the formation of the salt of the color base and the blue color.

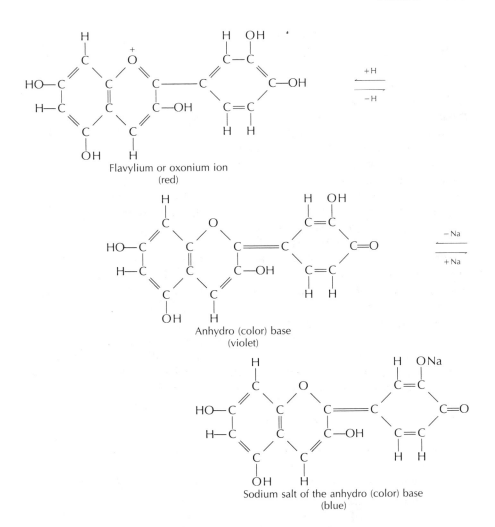

Flavylium or oxonium ion
(red)

Anhydro (color) base
(violet)

Sodium salt of the anhydro (color) base
(blue)

EFFECTS OF METAL IONS ON THE COLOR OF FLAVONOIDS. Both anthocyanin and anthoxanthin pigments react with metals. The products formed may bring about undesirable changes in the appearance of fruits and vegetables. An anthocyanin with two or three free hydroxyl groups on adjacent carbons may unite with aluminum, tin, or iron to form a blue, greenish-blue, or slate-blue complex. For this reason contact of anthocyanin-containing fruits with utensils made of iron, tin, or, to a lesser extent, of aluminum should be avoided.

Corrosion of the tin can (actually iron coated with tin) and alteration of the color of an anthocyanin-containing food from red to purple to blue hue occur when such canned foods are stored (16). Because of this, cans coated with lacquer are used for such foods. Discoloration is reduced, but small openings in the lacquered lining permit localized corrosion of the can. The anthocyanin pigment combines with the metal ions as they are removed from the can by the acid present in the food. The pigment thus frees the acid for continued reaction with the can, but in restricted areas. Hydrogen gas is liberated, the can bulges, and in time the can is perforated. By the time the can begins to leak, the color of the food is altered. The lower the acidity of the food, the more likely is the can to be perforated because it is the color base of the pigment that reacts with the metal (as shown in the preceding reaction).

Discoloration of an anthocyanin pigment by contact with metal is troublesome, but occasionally this characteristic may be used to advantage. For example, acid added, usually in the form of lemon juice, to loganberry or blackberry juice shifts the color toward the red. If a bluish punch is desired, pineapple juice added with lemon juice will prevent the shift in color. The small amount of iron dissolved in the pineapple juice from equipment used to prepare it for canning prevents the pigment from shifting to the red form. When either strawberry juice or cranberry juice is used as a base for punch, the punch is less likely to change in hue with addition of other ingredients because of the structure of the anthocyanin pigments involved.

Anthoxanthin pigments as well as anthocyanins react with or chelate metals. Sites where metal ions such as those of iron may unite with the pigment are at the two hydroxyl groups at positions 3' and 4', at the carbonyl ($-C=O$) group at position 4 and the hydroxyl group at position 3, or at the carbonyl group and the hydroxyl group at position 5. Products so formed may be bluish, greenish, or reddish. Anthoxanthins which have a hydroxyl group at either position 3 or 5 and a carbonyl at position 4 can unite with either tin or aluminum ions to form a bright-yellow complex. Cooking water from yellow-skinned onions cooked in an aluminum pan is bright yellow due to this complex (8).

Strawberry preserves undergo a change in color during storage. The bright red of the anthocyanin pigment in fresh preserves becomes duller and takes on a rusty brown tinge (29). The greater susceptibility to deterioration of color with certain varieties may be due to the higher content of phenolic compounds (1). Presence of oxygen and of reducing sugars and a high pH favor the breakdown of the pigment. Degradation of the anthocyanin is hastened by oxidation of the ascorbic acid present. Storage of the preserves in a warm place accelerates the loss of bright color. Some processors of strawberry preserves hold the berries as frozen stock and make preserves only when they are needed for the market. In this way they maintain a continuous supply of a product of good color.

FLAVANOLS.   Aside from the anthocyanins and the anthoxanthins, an assortment of phenolic compounds is present in fruits and vegetables. Browning of fruits, to be discussed in a subsequent section of this chapter, is attributed to the presence of one or more of these phenolic substrates. Catechin is one such, the formula of which is

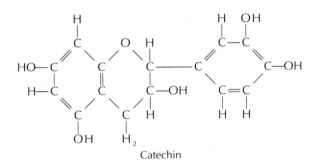

Catechin

Related to catechin is another group of compounds, the pro- or leucoanthocyanins. As the leuco prefix implies, compounds of this group are colorless.

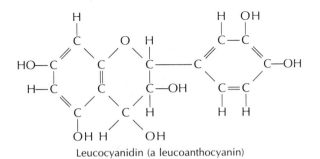

Leucocyanidin (a leucoanthocyanin)

When a colorless proanthocyanin is heated in the presence of acid (and oxygen), the corresponding anthocyanidin is formed. This type of reaction is believed to be responsible for the pinkish hue of some canned pears (19). Leucocyanidin (see above) is the most commonly occurring proanthocyanin. It is now thought that proanthocyanins in foods comprise the bulk of the compounds which in the past have been referred to as "tannins." Astringency in foods (which, to a limited extent, is desirable) is attributed to compounds in this class (8).

AROMA

Fruits have appetite appeal because of their pleasing aroma. Aroma is usually at its best when fruit is at the peak of maturity and before senescence has begun. Most fruits, except bananas and pears which profit from a brief cold storage before they finish ripening, are highest in quality when harvested at this stage. The odor of a particular fruit is due to a complex mixture of volatile constituents. An odor is difficult to analyze because many of the components are unsaturated and highly unstable. These include esters, aldehydes, alcohols, ketones, and terpenes. Too, the amount of any one constituent is usually small. By means of gas chromatography coupled with other analytical techniques, constituents in the aroma of a number of fruits have been isolated and identified. Sensory evaluation of these compounds has been used to identify those that contribute to a general fruity odor and those that contribute to the specific character of the aroma. For example, three esters, amyl acetate, propionate, and butyrate, have been shown to possess "bananalike" aroma. Constituents that contribute to the "fruity" component of banana flavor were identified as butyl and hexyl acetate and butyl and amyl butyrate (20). Information about the aroma of a number of fruits has been summarized (14).

POSTHARVEST CHANGES IN RAW FRUIT

Even after fruits and vegetables are harvested, the cells do not die for some time. Energy is required by plant cells, however, if they are to stay alive and the tissues remain edible. This energy they obtain from the oxidation of energy-rich nutrients, mainly carbohydrates, stored in the cells. Oxygen is normally used and carbon dioxide is given off as these stored constituents are utilized for energy. If this process, called respiration, can be slowed, the cells can live longer. Low storage temperature (but above freezing) is the technique commonly used to slow down respiration and so prolong the storage period during which fruits and vegetables have acceptable quality. If the oxygen content of the atmosphere around a fruit is reduced to a low level or if the carbon dioxide content of the surrounding air is raised to a high level, such alterations in the atmosphere which surrounds a fruit will retard respiration and so slow the rate of ripening of a fruit. Regulation of the concentration of oxygen and carbon dioxide in the surrounding atmosphere (within the limits tolerable by living plant tissue) to control respiration is now employed to prolong the storage life of certain fruits and vegetables. This technique, called *controlled atmosphere storage,* was first successfully applied to apples.

MOISTURE CONTENT

When a fruit or vegetable is yet a part of a growing plant, it gives off water in the form of vapor. This loss of water is compensated for by the uptake of water through the roots of the plant. Harvested fruits or vegetables stored in the open or in an uncovered container continue to lose moisture to the air and, cut off from a source of water, become dehydrated. The plant tissue assumes a limp and lifeless appearance. As long as cells of plant tissue remain alive the water content may increase or decrease rather markedly and rapidly without doing irreparable harm. Both vacuolar and protoplasmic membranes of living cells are semipermeable and osmotically active. Water may be drawn into cells when fruit or vegetable tissue is surrounded by water because of the solutes that are present. These solutes lower the vapor pressure of the water within the cell, permitting the entrance of water from around the tissue. The pressure required within the cell to prevent this entrance of water is known as osmotic pressure.

Actually, water molecules both enter and leave the cell, but the net flow is into the cell because of the concentration of solutes in the cell sap. Such

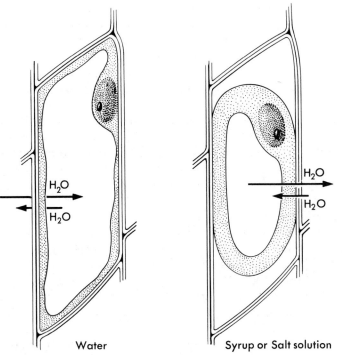

FIGURE 27-8. A turgid cell on the left. The water-filled vacuole exerts pressure on the cytoplasm, pressing it against the restraining cell wall. On the right, the loss of water from the vacuole allows the elastic cytoplasm to relax. Such a partially hydrated cell is limp instead of turgid. Loss of water (as vapor) to the air has a similar effect. (From V. A. Greulach and J. E. Adams, *Plants: An Introduction to Modern Botany*. Copyright © 1967 by John Wiley & Sons, Inc. Reprinted by permission.)

vacuole-filled cells (see Fig. 27-8) exert pressure on each other, and this gives to plant tissues their crispness. A lettuce leaf which is flabby due to loss of water from the vacuoles of the cell will rapidly refresh and become crisp when placed in cold water or even in air saturated with water vapor. Nutrients lost as a result of wilting are not regained, however.

Water may be drawn from cells by osmosis if plant tissue is placed in water that contains a solute in greater concentration outside the cell than inside. (See the diagram in Figure 27-8.) Sugar, acid, and salt especially cause withdrawal of water from cells with resulting loss in turgor. Salt sprinkled on the surface of a slice of cucumber draws moisture from the cells, which collects as beads of liquid, and the slice becomes flabby. Sugar sprinkled on sliced, raw fruit may cause the withdrawal of enough water from the cells to partly or completely cover the fruit with syrup.

DISCOLORATION

Under certain conditions a number of fruits, including apples, avocados, bananas, cherries, peaches, and pears, change from a creamy white to an unattractive brown or gray color. Bruising or other injury to the tissue disrupts the structural arrangement and disposition of constituents within the cells and allows the contents to make contact. This may lead to discoloration of uncooked fruit tissue. So may cutting the fruit.

For browning to take place, a phenolic compound known as a "substrate" must be present in the raw tissue. There are a number of phenolic compounds that can serve as substrates for enzymatic browning of fruits (7). Besides catechin and its derivatives, these include tyrosine, caffeic acid, chlorogenic acid, dopamine, and the aglycones of certain flavonoids. Phenolic substances with *ortho*-dihydroxy or vicinal (on adjacent carbons) trihydroxy groups are susceptible to discoloration catalyzed by phenol oxidase enzymes. Oxygen, either from the air in contact with the cut surface or from intercellular spaces within the tissue, must come into contact with the substrate.

For discoloration to occur rapidly, an enzyme must be present in the tissue of raw fruit to catalyze the reaction. Enzymes which catalyze the oxidation (ortho-diphenol: oxygen oxido-reductase) are known by a number of trivial names—phenol oxidase, polyphenol oxidase, phenolase, or polyphenolase. The action of polyphenolase enzymes in the conversion of green to black tea was discussed in Chapter 7. Phenol oxidase enzymes, each of which may be specific for certain substrates, are present in many fruits and vegetables. If phenolic substrate and oxygen are in contact for several days, browning will take place even though phenol oxidase enzymes have been denatured by heating. Thus browning may be observed in canned fruits, such as pears and peaches, which stand above the surface of the liquid in inadequately vented jars.

The chemical changes that take place in the conversion of the colorless substrate in the intact fruit to the colored reaction products in injured tissue are complex. A shift from a quinol to a quinone form of the molecule (see discussion of Antioxidants, Chapter 14), catalyzed by the enzyme, appears to be the first step. Then nonenzymatic oxidation and polymerization yield condensation products that are responsible for the discoloration.

Prevention of browning by elimination of the substrate is not practical. Apples, bananas, cherries, peaches, and pears, all contain one or more substrates for phenol oxidase enzymes. One variety of peach, Sunbeam, is an exception. It has been developed and propagated because it is deficient in substrate. There is some indication that the stage of ripeness of a fruit may influence its susceptibility to discoloration. In one study, browning was less in bananas at the green-tip stage of ripeness than it was in riper fruit (32).

Browning can be prevented by avoiding contact of oxygen with the substrate. Coating the fruit with sugar or covering it with syrup keeps atmospheric oxygen away from the surface. However, there is still the problem of intercellular oxygen. Sugar also reduces the concentration of oxygen dissolved in the syrup or water around the fruit.

A number of means are available to limit the activity of the phenol oxidase enzymes. The activity of the enzyme is temperature dependent, with the optimum near 43°C (109°F). If food is kept cold, browning is slowed, but, even in frozen storage, fruits brown unless they are treated to prevent it. Enzymes are proteins, easily denatured by heat as in blanching or cooking. The activity of phenol oxidase, like that of all enzymes, is pH dependent. Altering the hydrogen-ion concentration of the fruit may effectively block its action. The cut surface of fruit may be coated with acid. Lemon or other citrus fruit juice may be used, as may a solution of cream of tartar. Concentrated sugar solution also depresses enzyme activity. Sugared sliced peaches do not brown as readily as unsugared.

A solution of ascorbic acid is effective in preventing browning. It is possible that it acts as a reducing agent for the oxidized intermediate of a phenolic compound and thus prevents subsequent changes in the substrate, which would result in the formation of colored products. In addition, ascorbic acid is believed to act on some functional group in the enzyme (6). In the work on bananas referred to above (32), fruit at the green-tip stage contained more of the substrate dopamine but also more ascorbic acid, which presumably blocked the initial step in the conversion of the substrate to dark melanin.

Treatment of fruits with sulfur dioxide effectively prevents browning. The sulfurous acid formed ($SO_2 + H_2O \rightarrow H_2SO_3$) is a strong reducing agent. It combines with quinones formed from phenolic compounds and so blocks further changes in the molecule. In addition, the sulfurous acid gradually reduces the effectiveness of the enzyme (17). Instead of exposing fruit to sulfur dioxide fumes, it may be sulfured by dipping in a dilute solution of sodium bisulfite. If the sliced fruit is then immersed for a short time in a solution of dipotassium phosphate (K_2HPO_4), the odor of sulfur is less pronounced and the fruit remains crisp and does not brown subsequently (11). Calcium in the dip (0.1 percent from $CaCl_2$) acts synergistically with either SO_2 (0.3 percent) or ascorbic acid (1.0 percent). After a 3-minute dip, slices of Golden Delicious apples did not brown in several weeks when held at 1°C (22).

Sodium chloride can inhibit the activity of phenol oxidase enzymes, but a concentration too high for palatability is needed. It is the chloride ion that is effective. A dilute salt solution will retard development of brown color for a limited time. Peaches prepared in quantity for canning may be placed in dilute salt solution as they are peeled and held until they are canned.

PREPARATION OF FRUIT FOR SERVING

RAW

Fruit should be washed thoroughly and drained before it is served. If a fruit such as an apple is to be served raw and with the skin on, washing with mild soap or detergent followed by thorough rinsing aids in removing from the waxy epidermis not only soil and microorganisms but traces of poison spray. It is probably good practice to discard the paring from the stem and blossom ends because these areas are hard to clean thoroughly.

A sharp knife with a thin blade should be used to cut the skin from an orange or grapefruit, to section grapefruit, and to slice an orange. A blade of 4 to 5 inches is a good length. A sawing motion both for paring and for slicing fruit permits the blade to move through the fruit without bruising it and with a minimum loss of juice.

COOKED

Fresh fruit may be cooked by stewing, making into sauce, or baking. Fruit may be cooked whole or in halves or quarters. Cooked, it may be served as stewed fruit or it may be sieved and served as sauce. In either case, the fruit should be put to cook in boiling water to shorten the cooking time. The amount of water depends upon the juiciness of the fruit, the ratio of fruit to the size of the pan, and the amount of liquid which will evaporate from the pan. Fruit is done when it is tender and translucent.

If apples are to be made into sauce, the core and skin may be left on the apples. Only the stem and the parings in the depression at both stem and blossom ends need be removed. The skin may add color to the sauce. When the cooked apple is put through a sieve, inedible parts are removed. When apples are made into sauce in this way, waste averages somewhat less than when apples are pared and cored in advance. Applesauce should be juicy but not runny, the texture should be fine grained rather than too smooth or too coarse, and it should have a mellow apple flavor. Some varieties of apples form sauce more readily than others. Ease of saucing appears more closely related to solubility of the pectic material in the middle lamella than to such structural features as cell size or amount of intercellular air spaces. However, tissue of apples that sauce readily appears to be blown apart by expanding bubbles of gas (26).

Both pears and apples may be baked. A hot oven and a covered baking dish for apples give a product with a clearer, brighter color and better flavor. A lid on the container shortens baking time although apples tend to lose their shape when they are baked in a covered utensil. Desirable texture and flavor in baked apples are associated with high acidity, but such fruit is more likely to lose its shape. The red Delicious apple, which is low in acid, holds its shape exceedingly well when baked, but the cooked product is rather tasteless.

A number of fruits, including grapefruit, sliced bananas, apple rings, and pineapple slices, may be broiled, or fruit may be dipped in batter and deep fat fried.

CHANGES IN FRUIT CAUSED BY COOKING

CRISPNESS

When fruits and vegetables are heated, the cell membranes are denatured and lose their selective permeability. The passage of water and solutes across cell membranes is no longer governed by osmosis. Instead, both water molecules and solutes pass into and out of cells by diffusion. This process is slow, compared with the passage of molecules across a semipermeable membrane. Apple slices cooked in water lose some water to the surrounding liquid and solutes from the cell sap diffuse into the cooking water. The cells of cooked tissue are no longer taut with water and the tissues become limp. The flabbiness of cooked as well as wilted plant tissue is due to loss of water from the cell sap, but cells killed by heat can never again become turgid.

While fruit is still cooking it may float, buoyed up by steam generated within the tissue. Removed from the heat, it will sink. As intercellular gas has been replaced by water, cooked fruit is translucent compared to raw.

TENDERNESS

When fruits and vegetables are cooked, they not only lose crispness but they also become tender. Conversion of insoluble pectic compounds in the middle lamella to water-dispersible form reduces adhesion between cells (28). As a result the tissue is more easily pierced with a fork or crushed by the teeth. Constituents in the cell wall, except lignin, which is unaltered by cooking, are softened.

Sugar, especially in high concentration, slows down the tenderization by cooking because it interferes with the solubilizing of pectin. In fact, sugar is used in fruit jellies as a precipitant of pectin. (See Chapter 29.) Sugar in high concentration also dehydrates celluloses and hemicelluloses. The increased translucency of fruit cooked in syrup is due to alteration of the refractive index of cell wall constituents. Were prepared fruit put to cook in syrup instead of water, withdrawal of water from layers of cells on the surface would shrink and toughen the exterior of the pieces. It is for this reason that soft berries which tend to disintegrate on cooking are put to cook in concentrated sugar syrup. Preserved fruits are firm and hold their shape because of the heavy syrup in which they are cooked. If raw fruit is too firm, cooking in water to partially tenderize it before the sugar is added may be indicated. To obtain preserved fruit which is plump as well as firm and not shriveled, the concentration of syrup should be increased gradually during cooking.

In cooked fruit both cytoplasm and cell membranes are denatured. Sugar in the surrounding syrup passes from cell to cell to the interior of each piece, much as molecules of a copper sulfate crystal in the bottom of a beaker of water eventually diffuse and color the water uniformly. Diffusion continues until the concentration of sugar in the syrup and in the fruit reaches equilibrium. This requires some time, because diffusion is a much slower process than the passage of water in osmosis. Sugar diffuses more rapidly through the outer layers of cells of fruit cooked in water than in fruit, the outer layers of which have been toughened by cooking in concentrated syrup.

DRIED FRUIT

COOKING

Removal of water from fruit when it is dried makes the product tougher. Compare the tenderness of a fresh plum with that of a prune (a dried plum). When dried fruit is prepared for serving, the water removed from the cells by drying is returned by soaking and the tissues are softened by cooking. The cells in dried fruits are no longer alive. Hot water is used to soak the dried fruit to speed hydration of cell constituents. Usually, 1 hour is sufficient to allow water to diffuse into the interior of the fruit. The fruit is then simmered to soften the tissue. Sugar is added to dried fruit after the tissue is tenderized, because its presence in the cooking liquid only delays rehydration and tenderization. Cooked dried fruits improve if they are held at least overnight to allow sugar to diffuse into the fruit.

Tenderized dried fruits are an attempt by the producer to market a quicker-cooking product to compete for the consumer's food dollar with other quick-cooking, time-saving products available. Such dried fruits have a high percentage of moisture so they need little if any soaking and a relatively short cooking period. The more moisture a dried product contains the less time it takes to "refresh" it (to quote the producer).

STORING

Treating fruit such as apples, apricots, peaches, and pears with sulfur dioxide prior to drying yields a product that is bright and clear in color. Such fruits keep their bright colors if they are stored properly (4). Cool storage is recommended; otherwise the fruit will darken. Contact of the fruit with humid air should be prevented. The concentration of sugars in dried fruit is high. In a moist atmosphere, sugar from the fruit together with organic acids will dissolve in the moisture of the surface. If the fruit dries subsequently, this sugar will crystallize on or near the surface. This gives the dried fruit a dull, unappetizing appearance.

REFERENCES

1. Abers, J. E., and R. E. Wrolstad. 1979. Causative factors of color deterioration in strawberry preserves during processing and storage. *J. Food Sci.* **44:** 75–78. Leucoanthocyanins, flavanols, and total phenols in two varieties.
2. A.H.E.A. 1975. *Handbook of Food Preparation.* Buying guide, pp. 86–90; hydrogen-ion concentration, p. 21; timetable, pp. 96–99.
3. Asen, S., R. N. Stewart, and K. H. Norris. 1972. Co-pigmentation of anthocyanins in plant tissue and its effect on color. *Phytochemistry* **11:** 1139–1144. Co-pigmentation by the flavonol quercetin.
4. Barger, W. R., W. T. Pentzer, and C. K. Fisher. 1948. Low temperature storage

retains quality of dried fruit. *Food Ind.* **20:** F 1-4. (March). Effects of storage temperature and humidity on quality of dried fruit.

5. Barnell, H. R. 1943. Studies in tropical fruit. XV. Hemicellulose metabolism in banana fruit during ripening. *Ann. Bot., London* **7:** 297–323. Effects of storage temperature on ripening of bananas.

6. Baruah, P., and T. Swain. 1952. The effect of l-ascorbic acid on the *in vitro* activity of polyphenoloxidase from potato. *Biochem. J.* **55:** 392–399. Function of ascorbic acid in prevention of enzymatic browning.

7. Baruah, P., and T. Swain. 1959. The action of potato phenolase on flavonoid compounds. *J. Sci. Food Agr.* **10:** 125–129. Substrates which participate in oxidative browning reactions.

8. Bate-Smith, E. C. 1954. Flavonoid compounds in foods. *Advances in Food Research* **5:** 261–300. Classification, structure, properties, and distribution of flavonoid pigments; a review.

9. Bate-Smith, E. C. 1954. Astringency in foods. *Food* **23:** 124–129. Nature of astringency, compounds responsible, and importance in certain foods.

10. Blank, F. 1947. The anthocyanin pigments in plants. *Bot. Rev.* **13:** 241–247. Structures, reactions, colors; a review.

11. Bolin, H. R., F. S. Nury, and B. J. Finkle. 1964. An improved process for preservation of fresh peeled apples. *Bakers Digest* **38:** 46–48. Use of dipotassium phosphate with sodium bisulfite as a browning inhibitor.

12. Buescher, R. W., and R. J. Furmanski. 1978. Role of pectinesterase and polygalacturonase in the formation of woolliness in peaches. *J. Food Sci.* **43:** 264–266. One explanation for chilling injury.

13. Charles, R. J., and M. A. Tung. 1973. Physical, rheological and chemical properties of banana during ripening. *J. Food Sci.* **38:** 456–459. Ripening at 16° and 25°C compared.

14. Charley, H. 1972. Fruits and Vegetables. In *Food Theory and Applications.* P. C. Paul and H. H. Palmer, eds. John Wiley & Sons, Inc. Pp. 306–308.

15. Crafts, A. S. 1944. Cellular changes in certain fruits and vegetables during blanching and dehydration. *Food Research* **9:** 442–452. Microscopic appearance of fresh tissue, changes caused by steaming and drying, with photomicrographs.

16. Culpepper, C. W., and J. S. Caldwell. 1927. The behavior of anthocyan pigments in canning. *J. Agr. Research* **35:** 107–132. Effect of pigment on corrosion and pitting of the can.

17. Embs, R. J., and P. Markakis. 1965. The mechanism of sulfite inhibition of browning caused by polyphenol oxidase. *J. Food Sci.* **30:** 753–758. Reaction with quinones and inhibition of the enzyme.

18. Haard, N. F., and D. Timbie. 1973. Chilling injury in green banana fruit: Changes in peroxidase isoenzymes in soluble and particulate pools. *J. Food Sci.* **38:** 642–645. Failure to ripen and associated changes in the fruit.

19. Luh, B. S., S. J. Leonard, and D. S. Patel. 1960. Pink discoloration of canned Bartlett pears. *Food Technol.* **14:** 53–56. An attempt to link the pinkness of overheated canned pears to leucoanthocyanin content.

20. McCarthy, A. I., J. K. Palmer, C. P. Shaw, and E. E. Anderson. 1963. Correlation of gas chromatographic data with flavor profiles of fresh banana fruit. *J. Food Sci.* **28:** 379–384. Components in banana flavor as analyzed by a flavor panel and by gas chromatography.

21. McCready, R. M., and E. A. McComb. 1954. Pectic constituents in ripe and unripe fruit. *Food Research* **19**: 530–535. Changes in esterification and in polymerization of pectic substances in ripening peaches, pears, and avocado.

22. Ponting, J., D. R. Jackson, and G. Waters. 1972. Refrigerated apple slices: Preservative effects of ascorbic acid, calcium and sulfite. *J. Food Sci.* **37**: 434–436. Inhibition of enzymic browning.

23. Postlmayr, H. L., B. S. Luh, and S. J. Leonard. 1956. Characterization of pectin changes in freestone and clingstone peaches during ripening and processing. *Food Technol.* **10**: 618–625. Soluble and insoluble pectic substances, viscosity of syrup and texture of canned fruit.

24. Pressey, R., and J. K. Avants. 1978. Difference in polygalacturonase composition of clingstone and freestone peaches. *J. Food Sci.* **43**: 1415–1417, 1423. Pectic enzymes and texture.

25. Preston, R. D. 1957. Cellulose. *Sci. Amer.* **197**(3): 157–162, 164–166, 168. Chemistry of cellulose and structure of cellulose fibers; illustrated.

26. Reeve, R. M., and L. R. Leinbach. 1953. Histological investigation of texture in apples. I. Composition and influence of heat on structure. *Food Research* **18**: 592–603; II. Structure and intercellular spaces. *Food Research* **18**: 604–617. An attempt to account for differences in the textural quality of varieties of apples.

27. Shewfelt, A. L. 1965. Changes and variations in the pectic constitution of ripening peaches as related to product firmness. *J. Food Sci.* **30**: 573–576. Three pectic fractions in freestones and clings at four stages of ripeness.

28. Sterling, C. 1963. Texture and cell-wall polysaccharides in foods. In *Recent Advances in Food Science—3. Biochemistry and Biophysics in Food Research.* J. M. Leitch and D. N. Rhodes, eds. London: Butterworths. Pp. 259–276. A review article; comprehensive and technical.

29. Tinsley, I., and A. H. Bockian. 1960. Some effects of sugar on the breakdown of pelargonidin-3-glucoside model systems at 90°C. *Food Research* **25**: 161–173. Summary of factors which affect the destruction of anthocyanin in strawberry preserves; data on the effect of sugars on the pigment.

30. United Fruit and Vegetable Association. *Fruit and Vegetable Facts and Pointers.* Washington, D.C.: The Association. Set of reports of 79 fresh fruits and vegetables; botany, history, varieties, production, grades, marketing, storage, consumption.

31. United States Department of Agriculture. 1961. *Tips on Selection of Fruits and Vegetables.* Marketing Bull. 13. 44 pp.

32. Weaver, C., and H. Charley. 1974. Enzymatic browning of ripening bananas. *J. Food Sci.* **39**: 1200–1202. Dopamine, ascorbic acid, polyphenol oxidase, and discoloration.

33. Whaley, W. G., H. H. Mallenhauer, and J. H. Luch. 1960. The ultra structure of the meristematic cell. *Am. J. Bot.* **47**: 401–450. Structure of the developing plant cell; excellent electron micrographs; technical.

34. Williams, M., and G. Hrazdina. 1979. Anthocyanins as food colorants: Effects of pH on the formation of anthocyanin-rutin complexes. *J. Food Sci.* **44**: 66–68. Proposed structures for co-pigment complexes.

35. Woodmansee, C. W., J. H. McClendon, and G. F. Somers. 1959. Chemical changes associated with the ripening of apples and tomatoes. *Food Research* **24**: 503–514. Analysis of pectic constituents, acids and alcohol-insoluble solids.

TWENTY-EIGHT
Vegetables

Vegetables are more varied in form than are fruits. Practically every part of a plant is represented by one or more vegetables. Spinach and cabbage are leaves; asparagus and celery are stems; carrots, parsnips, and sweet potatoes are roots; broccoli and cauliflower are flowers, although broccoli also includes leaves and stems; cucumber, pepper, squash, and tomato are fruits; beans, peas, and corn are seeds; onions are bulbs; white potatoes are tubers.

A per capita consumption of 97 pounds of fresh vegetables, excluding potatoes, and 66 pounds of processed were forecast for 1979 (71). Although the consumption of potatoes has increased recently, the 123 pounds per capita forecast for 1979 is far short of the 195 pounds consumed in 1910. Potatoes yield more food energy and more protein per acre of land than corn and rank second to corn in yield of food energy per unit of fossil energy expended (52).

STRUCTURE AND COMPOSITION

The structure of vegetables is similar to that of fruits (see Structure of Plant Tissue, Chapter 27). Individual vegetables vary in composition as do fruits. Table 28-1 gives the composition of some of the more commonly used vegetables. Like fruits, vegetables are characterized by a low concentration of fat and by a high moisture content. Except for beans and peas, most are low in protein.

CARBOHYDRATES

Vegetables show a somewhat greater range in carbohydrate content than do fruits. Beans, corn, peas, and potatoes, all of which store starch, are high in carbohydrate (Fig. 28-1). Immature, they contain sugar; but as they mature the sugar is replaced by starch. Tubers of sunchokes (Jerusalem artichokes) accumulate the carbohydrate inulin, a polymer of fructose, instead of starch. Of the nonstarchy vegetables given in Table 28-1, beets, carrots, and onions are intermediate in carbohydrate content and the other vegetables contain approximately 5 percent.

The cells of vegetables contain more cellulose than do those of fruits, and lignin is often present in appreciable amounts in vascular and supporting tissue. In some vegetables vascular tissues are distributed throughout, but in others they are more localized. In carrots and parsnips water-conducting cells

Table 28-1 Composition of commonly used vegetables (100-gram, edible portion, raw)

Vegetable	Water (%)	Calories[a]	Protein (g)	Fat (g)	Carbohydrate Total (g)	Fiber (g)	Cal-cium (mg)	Phos-phorus (mg)	Iron (mg)	Vitamin A (I.U.)	Thia-mine (mg)	Ribo-flavin (mg)	Niacin (mg)	Ascorbic Acid (mg)
Beans, lima, immature	67.5	123	8.4	.5	22.1	1.8	52	142	2.8	290	.24	.12	1.4	29
Beans, snap	90.1	32	1.9	.2	7.1	1.0	56	44	.8	600	.08	.11	.5	19
Beets	87.3	43	1.6	.1	9.9	.8	16	33	.7	20	.03	.05	.4	10
Broccoli	89.1	32	3.6	.3	5.9	1.5	103	78	1.1	2,500[b]	.10	.23	.9	113
Cabbage	92.4	24	1.3	.2	5.4	.8	49	29	.4	130	.05	.05	.3	47[c]
Carrots	88.2	42	1.1	.2	9.7	1.0	37	36	.7	11,000[d]	.06	.05	.6	8
Cauliflower	91.0	27	2.7	.2	5.2	1.0	25	56	1.1	60	.11	.10	.7	78
Corn, sweet	72.7	96	3.5	1.0	22.1	.7	3	111	.7	400[e]	.15	.12	1.7	12

Lettuce, head	95.5	13	.9	.1	2.9	.5	20	22	.5	330	.06	.06	.3	6
Onions, mature	89.1	38	1.5	.1	8.7	.6	27	36	.5	40[f]	.03	.04	.2	10
Peas, green, immature	78.0	84	6.3	.4	14.4	2.0	26	116	1.9	640	.35	.14	2.9	27
Potatoes	79.8	76	2.1	.1	17.1	.5	7	53	.6	Trace	.10	.04	1.5	20[g]
Spinach	90.7	26	3.2	.3	4.3	.6	93	51	3.1	8,100	.10	.20	.6	51
Sweet potato	70.6	114	1.7	.4	26.3	.7	32	47	.7	8,800	.10	.06	.6	21
Tomatoes	93.5	22	1.1	.2	4.7	.5	13	27	.5	900	.06	.04	.7	23[g]

SOURCE: U.S.D.A. Agr. Handbook No. 8. *Composition of Foods. Raw, Processed, Prepared.* Revised 1963.

[a]1 kilocalorie = 4.185 kilojoules.

[b]For leaves, 16,000 I.U. per 100 grams, for flowers, 3000 I.U.; for stalks, 100 I.U.

[c]Freshly harvested, 51 mg per 100 g; stored, 42 mg per 100 g.

[d]Value varies with variety and maturity.

[e]Yellow varieties.

[f]Yellow-fleshed varieties.

[g]Year-round average.

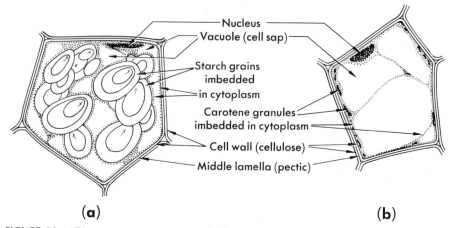

Nucleus
Vacuole (cell sap)
Starch grains imbedded in cytoplasm
Carotene granules imbedded in cytoplasm
Cell wall (cellulose)
Middle lamella (pectic)

(a) **(b)**

FIGURE 28-1. Diagram (a) comparing starch-filled potato cell ($\times$ 300) with (b) carrot cell ($\times$ 500); the latter is mainly vacuole crisscrossed with thin strands of cytoplasm. (From R. M. Reeve, *Food Industries,* December 1942, p. 53. Reprinted by permission of Food Engineering.)

are situated in the center of the vegetable, in the inner core called the "xylem." Surrounding the xylem is the part of the vegetable called the "phloem," in which the food-conducting and storage cells are found. A carrot cut in half lengthwise reveals this gross structure. Cells of the phloem are not usually lignified, but those of the xylem, and of the supporting tissue especially, may be.

Older vegetables particularly may have a fairly high proportion of lignified tissue. The lower part of the stalks of broccoli and asparagus and the stems and midribs especially of older leaves of spinach and kale are places where lignified tissue may be expected (39). Parsnips and beets which are mature, particularly those grown under adverse conditions, may contain some lignified fibers which resist cooking. These remain in cooked vegetables as long, tough strings.

MINERALS AND VITAMINS

As a group, vegetables are richer in minerals and vitamins than are fruits. Thin, dark-green leafy vegetables are high in iron, riboflavin, ascorbic acid, and carotene (pro-vitamin A). Vegetables are a good source of thiamine. Thin green leaves other than those of the goosefoot family supply appreciable quantities of calcium. The calcium in spinach and other plants of this family is unavailable because the oxalic acid present binds the calcium in an insoluble form.

ORGANIC ACIDS

Vegetables contain a number of organic acids, metabolic products of the cells. Formulas for ten organic acids found in vegetables and fruits follow.

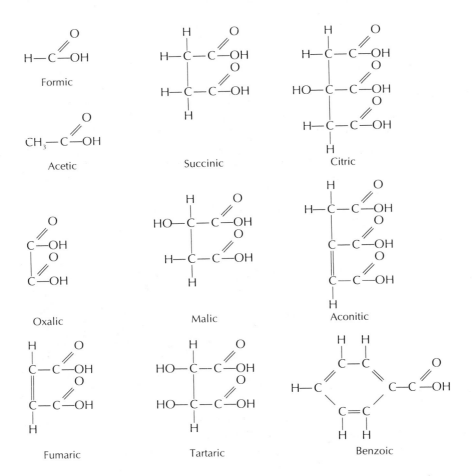

In acetic acid, a methyl group (CH_3—) has replaced the hydrogen in the formic acid. Oxalic acid consists of two carboxyl groups. Succinic acid has two carboxyl groups joined by a —CH_2—CH_2— fragment. Fumaric acid differs from succinic in that the two middle carbons are joined by a double bond. Malic acid is like succinic except that a hydroxyl (—OH) group has replaced a hydrogen on one of the two central carbon atoms; tartaric acid has an —OH group on each of the two middle carbons. Both citric and aconitic are tri-carboxylic acids, the latter with a double bond between two of the carbons. Benzoic acid consists of a benzene ring to which is attached a carboxyl group. All of the organic acids above are soluble in water and two of them, formic and acetic, are volatile.

The concentration of acid is lower in vegetables than it is in fruits. Tomatoes, vegetables with the highest concentration of acid, have a pH which ranges from 4.0 to 4.6 or above. The pH of a number of vegetables falls within the range of pH 5.0 to 5.6. Potatoes, peas, and corn are higher (pH 6.1–6.3)(1).

QUALITY CHARACTERISTICS OF RAW VEGETABLES

Vegetables are valued in the diet for their texture, flavor, color, and nutritive value. They should be handled, stored, and cooked in such ways as to preserve these attributes (61). The quality of a vegetable when it is cooked and served is conditioned by its quality in the raw state.

There are certain earmarks of high quality in vegetables that one should learn to recognize (46,70). In general, vegetables should look clear and bright and be firm and free from rot and other dead tissue. Other desirable characteristics depend on the vegetable. Stalks of *asparagus* should be rounded instead of ridged and the tips should be compact. *Snap beans* should have thick, meaty walls rather than spongy ones and the pods should be straight. They should be crisp enough to break easily and with a snap. Heads of *cabbage* should be firm, with the outer leaves close together near the base. The leaves should look translucent rather than opaque and greenish rather than white. A white core rather than a yellowish one is another sign of quality. Stalks of *celery* should be thick, succulent, fine grained, and brittle. A large heart with the stalks fitting together compactly is an indication of high quality, as is the absence of deep ridges on the outside of the stalks. *Broccoli* stalks should be small, with translucent skin and small, dark-green leaves with short stems. The buds are closed and their surface covered with a satiny bloom. *Cauliflower* should be pearly white and compact with bright green leaves. *Onions* should have thin, dry skins and thin, firm necks. Green, brittle pods of *peas* that are well filled but not bulging are desired. *Potatoes* should be symmetrical and have shallow eyes. A russet skin is a characteristic of the variety, but a green color under the skin means that the potato was stored in light. Such green tissue may contain, in addition to chlorophyll, more than the trace normally present in potatoes of a group of glycoalkaloids frequently referred to as solanine (50). These glycoalkaloids, mainly α-solanine and α-chaconine, impart a bitter taste and a burning sensation, and they are toxic as well. Sprouts are a potent source of these toxic compounds. Green areas should be cut away before the potato is cooked. *Root vegetables* should have clear, bright skins. They should be plump and free from whiskers. *Spinach* leaves should be dark green and glossy with succulent stems. *Tomatoes* should be a clear, bright red. The surface should be glossy and smoothly curved rather than angular. Of course, the variety of the vegetable influences to some extent the character of a particular sample. Danvers carrots differ from Chantenay; Blue Lake green beans differ from Kentucky Wonder.

STORAGE TO MAINTAIN QUALITY

The stage of maturity of a vegetable when it is harvested will influence color, flavor, texture, and nutritive value (61). Ideally most vegetables are harvested while still immature and before lignin has accumulated in the cell walls. Decrease in the sugar content of vegetables as they mature has been mentioned.

This is particularly noticeable in starchy vegetables. New potatoes, new peas, and corn are quite sweet compared with their mature counterparts. Plant tissues, even after harvest, are still alive. Metabolic processes continue within the cells, and tissues soon begin to deteriorate. The sugar content of an immature vegetable may drop rapidly once it is harvested. Roasting ears put to cook a few minutes after they are picked will taste sweet because of the sugar present. Held for an hour or two after picking, kernels of sweet corn may have already lost much of their sweetness and after a few hours may no longer taste sweet. The genetics of some sweet corn is such as to delay the conversion of sugar to starch in the harvested ear. The sugar content of garden peas decreases even faster than does that of corn. The higher the holding temperature, the greater is the loss. If vegetables must be stored, conditions should be such as to slow changes that lead to deterioration (53). To maintain the sweet taste of fresh vegetables, they should be cooled promptly and stored in a refrigerator.

On the other hand, holding mature, starchy potatoes in cold storage results in the accumulation of sugar. For this reason potatoes immediately out of cold storage cannot be used successfully for potato chips. The high concentration of sugar makes them brown unduly and unevenly. Potatoes used to make chips should be brought from cold storage and held at a higher temperature (70°C) so that the cells can metabolize the accumulated sugar. Some varieties of potato recover from cold storage better than others.

Sweet potatoes, unlike white potatoes, are held for several days in a warm place to cure. During this curing and subsequent storage, α-amylase activity increases especially in moist-fleshed varieties. The content of dextrins is higher and the size of the dextrin molecules smaller in those varieties that are moist rather than dry when cooked (74).

One undesirable postharvest change in vegetables, mediated by the action of enzymes, is the accumulation of lignin. The petioles of spinach, the stems of broccoli, and the spears of asparagus may become tough and stringy due to lignin if the vegetables are stored improperly. In the case of asparagus, just cutting the spears results in the elaboration of an enzyme in the cut area which may lead to the formation of lignin (54). Enzyme activity is highly temperature dependent. Storage just above freezing retards enzyme action and delays loss of quality as well as spoilage of most vegetables.

Although many vegetables maintain high quality longer when stored at temperatures just above freezing, some vegetables of tropical or subtropical origin are damaged if stored at temperatures above freezing but below approximately 10°C (35). Abnormal respiration may result in pitting, russetting, loss of color, or leatheriness. Vegetables that are susceptible to chilling injury and thus should be stored in a cool but not a cold place, include peppers, cucumbers, eggplant, snap beans, sweet potatoes, tomatoes, and winter squash.

In addition to lowering the temperature, respiration in the tissue may be reduced further by modification of the atmosphere in contact with the vegetable. How little oxygen and how much carbon dioxide the tissues will tolerate before the controlled atmosphere does more harm than good must be worked out for each vegetable. Levels of carbon dioxide that are too high result in browning of leaves of lettuce along the midribs and near the base and darkening of cauliflower. This may occur when vegetables are enclosed in transparent wrap impermeable to carbon dioxide. Yellowing of broccoli, which occurs within 2 or 3 days at room temperature, is best retarded by storage near 0°C (37). For extended storage, a low level of oxygen (but not below 0.5–1.0 percent) or a high level of carbon dioxide (10 percent) retards yellowing.

Loss of moisture from vegetables, which results in wilting, should be prevented during storage (19). Most vegetables should be rinsed and drained thoroughly before they are stored (onions, potatoes, and winter squash are exceptions). Storage in a vegetable crisper or in a plastic bag helps prevent dehydration. A small piece of vegetable will become dehydrated in a vegetable crisper because so much water vapor is needed to saturate the empty space.

PREPARATION FOR COOKING

WASHING

Because the parts of plants used as vegetables grow in or near the soil, washing is even more important than it is for fruits. Vegetables need to be washed thoroughly to remove particles of soil and microorganisms that are in the soil. Vegetables may be contaminated with *Escherichia coli.*Their presence suggests that the food may have come into at least indirect contact with sewage, because these bacteria thrive in the human intestinal tract. Several changes of clean water do the job as well as running water, the use of which tends to be wasteful. Vegetables should be lifted from the water rather than the water poured or drained off, in which case soil remains in the container with the vegetable. Lukewarm water cleanses better than cold. A vegetable brush aids in cleaning the surface of such vegetables as celery and potatoes.

WASTE IN PREPARATION

As with fruits, certain parts of vegetables are considered unpalatable, if not inedible, and these are discarded. Vegetables usually need trimming, but unnecessary waste should be avoided. Table 28-2 gives the average percentage of waste from a few vegetables. Part of the waste is inherent in the vegetable. Percent of inedible material is low (9 percent) in onions and high (62 percent) in peas. The percentage of waste may be used to find the amount that should be subtracted from the weight as purchased (A.P.) to give the yield of edible portion (E.P.). The edible portion of peas costs somewhat more than twice as much as the same weight of vegetable as purchased. Figures given in Table 28-2 are averages for vegetables of typical quality. The percentage of waste for a particular sample of any one vegetable may vary from this average value,

Table 28-2 Waste from
representative vegetables
as purchased

Vegetable	Waste
Asparagus	47%
Broccoli, untrimmed	39
Cabbage, untrimmed	20
Carrots, with tops	41
Carrots, without tops	18
Onions, mature	9
Peas (in pods)	62
Potatoes	19
Tomatoes, peeled	18

SOURCE: U.S.D.A. Agr. Handbook No. 102.
*Food Yields Summarized by Different Stages of
Preparation.* Revised 1975.

the amount depending on the quality of the vegetable. For example, the waste from trimmed broccoli on the market near growing areas is usually much less than the 39 percent given in the table.

The amount of waste varies not only with the vegetable but also with the tool and with the technique used to remove inedible parts. Potatoes serve as an example. The least waste from potatoes probably occurs when they are boiled in the skin, or jacket, as it is called. Heating solubilizes the material which joins the innermost layer of cells of the skin to the outermost layer of cells of the edible portion of the potato. This permits a sharper separation of the skin from the edible portion and gives a minimum of waste.

Cooking a potato in the skin may impart an undesirable flavor to the edible part, however. Also, it may be inconvenient to skin the potato after it is cooked, especially while it is still hot. As an alternative, scraping a potato keeps the weight of waste low as does paring it with a floating-blade peeler. Typical figures for waste from potatoes pared with a knife are 17 to 18 percent versus 11 to 12 percent with a floating-blade peeler (28). Thus the use of a paring knife may increase the waste 50 percent over that when a floating-blade peeler is used. The correct way to use a peeler is with a ballistic or whittling motion, without so much pressure that the cutting blade is unable to rotate freely on the pin. The peeler is so constructed as to limit the amount of edible portion that can be removed along with the skin. The distance between the two blades of the peeler determines the depth or thickness of the paring so that as a peeler wears it takes deeper and deeper bites.

Much waste occurs if the individual who prepares the vegetable fails to identify the most nutritious parts. Leaves of broccoli, sometimes discarded, are richer in nutrients than the stems or stalks which are cooked (60). Weight for weight, the tender, dark-green leaves are nutritionally the richest part of the broccoli plant. The tender green leaves at the base of a head of cauliflower should not be wasted. Furthermore, these delicate green leaves give needed contrast to the whiteness of the flower. Leaves of celery can be chopped and used as seasoning in vegetable soup, stews, dressing, or as part of the greens in a tossed vegetable salad. There is no point, however, trying to cook parts of a vegetable that cannot be tenderized. Lignified parts of a vegetable such as the butt ends of asparagus stalks and broccoli stems cannot be tenderized. These should be removed before the vegetable is put to cook.

COOKING METHODS

Vegetables are sometimes served raw; more frequently, they are cooked. Vegetables are heated to bring about changes in texture and flavor which are considered desirable. Heating also destroys a number of microorganisms that are present on the surface of vegetables.

A number of factors may influence the choice of cooking method for a vegetable. These include the presence in the vegetable of water-soluble nutrients, of pigments, of acids, and of certain flavor constituents. Of course the menu is a factor, too. Vegetables may be baked, boiled, steamed, or panned. Potatoes, either as chips or French fries, are cooked in deep fat as are onion rings dipped in batter. (See Chapter 14 for discussion of deep fat frying.) Most vegetables are low in calories. Added butter, bacon fat, sour cream, and sauces are not.

BAKING

Vegetables may be baked in the skin as are potatoes or in the shucks as are roasting ears of corn, a method of cooking used by the American Indians. For the latter, the husks are opened enough to remove the silks and the entire ears are soaked in water. This keeps the husks from burning before the kernels are done. Or the shucks may be removed and the ear recovered with aluminum foil. Most young, tender root vegetables may be baked in the skin, as may tomatoes. Onions may be so cooked or the skin may be removed and the onions wrapped in foil before they are baked. For scalloped potatoes, the skin of the potato is removed and the prepared vegetable is baked in a covered casserole which keeps the moisture in as does a skin. The advantage of baking a vegetable is that no added water comes into contact with it to leach out water-soluble nutrients. The disadvantage is that heat penetration during baking is slow. Also, more fuel is required.

BOILING IN THE SKIN

When a vegetable is boiled in the skin, enough water to cover is used, as is a lid on the pan. The large amount of cooking water does not add unduly to the loss of nutrients during cooking because the skin on the vegetable is intact. Beets in their skins (with approximately 2 inches of tops left on so that water-soluble nutrients and pigments do not leach out into the cooking water) may be cooked by this method. So may small Danish squash, for which the cooking time is a few minutes less than it is for baking the squash when it is cut in half. Baking time can be shortened by placing the squash with the cut surface down on the baking sheet or pan, rather than up. Corn may be cooked by boiling on the cob. Potatoes, both white and sweet, may be boiled in the skins.

BOILING PREPARED VEGETABLES

Putting prepared vegetables in just enough boiling, salted water to prevent scorching and cooking with a lid on the pan is a basic method of cooking vegetables. The water should be brought back to a boil as rapidly as possible and then the heat lowered to maintain a slow boil. The aim is to have the vegetable just done when only a few drops of cooking water are left in the pan. This method minimizes losses of soluble nutrients to the cooking water. A pan with a tight-fitting lid is needed, as is careful adjustment of the intensity of heat; otherwise, the vegetable may scorch.

Not all vegetables boiled in this way have the best color or flavor, however. Green vegetables which need more than 5 to 7 minutes to become tender may lose some of their bright green color when cooked by this method. Vegetables of the cabbage group (broccoli, Brussels sprouts, cabbage, rutabagas, and turnips) may have an unpleasant aroma (see discussion of sulfur compounds in vegetables, this chapter) when they are cooked by this method unless the vegetable is shredded or sliced so that it will be done within 5 to 7 minutes. For the best color and aroma these vegetables may be put to cook in enough boiling, salted water to approximately cover the vegetable with the lid left off the pan. In this way the volatile acids escape along with steam and nonvolatile acids are diluted. This method of cooking minimizes undesirable changes in the color and flavor of these vegetables as they are cooked. Loss of water-soluble nutrients may be somewhat greater, but the more rapid warm-up in excess boiling water may reduce destruction of ascorbic acid.

STEAMING

When prepared vegetables are cooked by steaming, energy is transmitted by steam to the product suspended in a perforated container above vigorously boiling water. Most vegetables can be steamed, but the cooking time is usually somewhat longer than for boiling. The advantage of steaming over boiling is that only that water from the steam that condenses comes in contact with the vegetable. Cooking in a pressure saucepan is actually steaming, although the temperature is elevated because of the steam pressure built up in the pressure saucepan. The pressure saucepan is usually operated at 15 pounds steam pressure, and the cooking temperature is 121°C (250°F) compared with approximately 100°C (212°F) in a steamer. This elevation of temperature in a pressure saucepan causes a sharp reduction in cooking time.

PANNING OR STIR-FRYING

This method may be used to cook leafy vegetables and succulent vegetables that can be shredded. Shredded beets, carrots, or cabbage may be cooked by panning, as may spinach. In panning, the vegetable is cooked to a large extent in steam from water which seeps out of the cut tissues. A heavy pan with a tight-fitting lid is essential for panning. A small amount of fat in the bottom of the pan keeps the vegetable from sticking until enough of the cell sap can be drawn from the vegetable to start the cooking. The secret of success in panning is to have the pieces of vegetable thin so that heat will penetrate rapidly and the cooking time will be short. The heating unit should be set high enough to start cooking promptly and then lowered, not so much that cooking stops, but so that water will not evaporate from the utensil. The vegetable should be stirred for the first minute or two of the cooking period, but evaporation should be kept to a minimum. Panning as a method for cooking vegetables has all the advantages of cooking in a small amount of water plus a shorter cooking time because the vegetable is shredded or cut into thin slices.

TEXTURE OF VEGETABLES AND THE EFFECTS OF COOKING

CRISPNESS

A raw vegetable of high quality is crisp in texture, owing to the pressure that turgid cells exert on one another. When pieces of crisp, raw vegetable are put to cook in boiling water, heat denatures the cytoplasm and the cell membranes. Cells no longer retain water; instead, they lose water by diffusion through the now permeable membranes. The limpness of cooked vegetables in contrast to the crispness of raw ones is due to this loss of water. Loss of water from cells killed by heat causes most vegetables (even though cooked in enough water to cover) to weigh less than they did raw. Starchy vegetables are an exception. A vegetable cooked by microwaves loses more water than does one boiled conventionally, even when the same volume of cooking water is used for each (57). This loss of water upon cooking is reflected in the somewhat diminished size of the cells from the phloem of carrot boiled on a conventional range and the greater shrinkage and pronounced folding of the cell walls of tissue cooked by microwaves (Fig. 28-2).

TENDERNESS

The walls of cells in plant tissue serve as structural elements. Cell walls are distributed to provide support for the plant in accordance with basic mechanical engineering principles (65). Adhesion of the walls of adjacent cells contributes to the textural qualities of raw vegetables. Cementing material (pectic substances and hemicelluloses) between cells makes them adhere so that the raw vegetable resists the pressure of the teeth in chewing. The crunchy texture

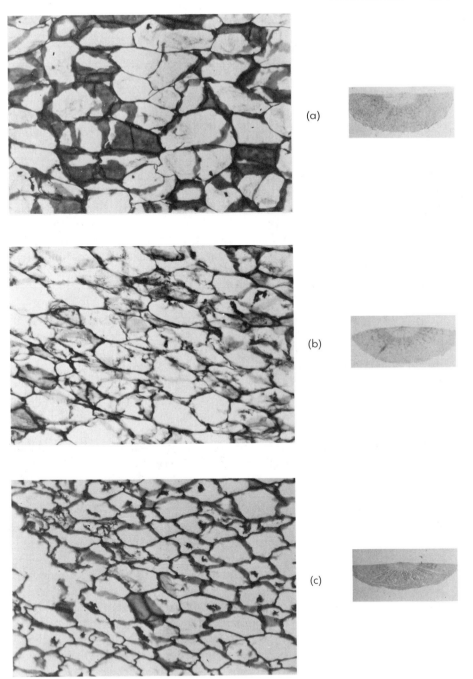

(a)

(b)

(c)

FIGURE 28-2. Cross section (× 2) and parenchyma cells (× 41) of the phloem of carrot: (a) raw; (b) boiled conventionally; (c) cooked by microwave energy. (Reprinted from Elaine Schrumpf and Helen Charley, *Journal of Food Science* **40:** 1025, 1975. Copyright © by Institute of Food Technologists. Reprinted by permission.)

of raw vegetables and fruits contrasts pleasingly with the soft texture of milk, eggs, cheese, meats, and cooked starches.

For the sake of tenderness, somewhat less structural integrity is desired in cooked vegetables than in raw. However, vegetables should not be cooked until they lose completely those textural qualities for which they are valued. Cooking converts insoluble pectic substances into ones that are dispersible in hot water (63,64,75) and alters other skeletal material associated with the cell walls (17). If the cooking period is too brief, the vegetable may not be tender because the cells adhere too much. Too much alteration of structural constituents may result in a mushy product which disintegrates with little or no pressure. How much the texture of a vegetable is altered by cooking is influenced by the standard of doneness used by the cook. Too often, vegetables are overcooked before they are served. Ideally, cooking should stop while enough cementing material remains to cause the cells to adhere, but not so much that it is hard to bite or chew the vegetable. Vegetables are done when they are pierced with a fork, but not too readily. Oriental cooks have mastered the art of ending the cooking of vegetables before the texture is ruined by overcooking.

A range in cooking time for vegetables is usually given (see timetable in the A.H.E.A. *Handbook of Food Preparation*). The size of the pieces influences the cooking time needed to tenderize a vegetable. Potatoes cut into quarters or carrots that are sliced cook in less time than the whole vegetable. A young, tender vegetable may take less time to cook than the minimum given in the timetable, whereas a mature one may need more than the maximum. Being able to estimate the time needed to cook a vegetable requires enough experience to judge the maturity or quality of the particular sample.

A vegetable cooks in a pressure saucepan in much less time than by conventional boiling at atmospheric pressure. For example, diced carrots reached the just done stage in 19 minutes by boiling (100°C) but needed only 50 seconds in a pressure saucepan at 121°C (10). Because vegetables cook so fast in a pressure saucepan, only a few seconds' difference in cooking time makes a great difference in the doneness of the vegetable. And conventional boiling may result in more uniform doneness among different tissues than does microwave cooking (57). When the outer layer of stems of broccoli cooked by microwaves was still slightly tough, tissue in the center was so tender as to seem slightly overcooked. Tissue in the core of carrots was slightly tough, whereas that in the outer cylinder tended to be spongy. That tissues respond differently to cooking has been documented by scanning electron microscopy of phloem and xylem tissue of carrots cooked by boiling, steaming, and in a pressure saucepan (17). Longer cooking times are needed to tenderize most vegetables at higher elevations, the actual increase depending upon the vegetable, on whether it is fresh or frozen, and on how the vegetable is cooked (microwave oven, conventional range, or pressure saucepan) (9).

Vegetables such as asparagus and broccoli present special problems. The lower half of the stem cf either requires longer cooking time than the upper half. Buds of broccoli require even less cooking than the upper part of the stem. Getting all parts of the vegetable equally done is not easy. It is pointless to try to cook parts of a vegetable that contain appreciable quantities of lignin, for they cannot be tenderized by cooking. Nonlignified parts will be over-cooked and those that contain lignin will never become tender. A frozen vegetable cooks in less time than a corresponding raw one, due in part to the freezing process and to the fact that the vegetable was blanched before it was frozen. Most frozen vegetables should be put to cook without thawing because this minimizes loss of ascorbic acid.

Acid added to the water in which vegetables are cooked may slow the breakdown of some of the structural components (66). For example, thin slices of vegetable may be simmered for an hour in vegetable soup without the slices losing identity and shape when tomato juice is added along with the vegetables. Without the acid from the tomato, the slices would disintegrate into cells or groups of cells after an hour of cooking.

Calcium ions in high concentration in the cooking water may influence the texture of cooked plant tissue. The divalent calcium ions react with pectic or pectinic acids in the middle lamella to form insoluble calcium pectates or pectinates. The calcium in molasses added to parboiled dried beans for baked beans lengthens the cooking time required to tenderize them. For a number of years calcium chloride has been added to commercially canned tomatoes as a firming agent (38). Tomatoes contain the enzyme pectin methyl esterase. The demethylated pectin formed in the middle lamella by the action of this enzyme on the pectic substances reacts with calcium ions to form insoluble calcium pectate. This leads to firming of the tomatoes.

Calcium ions affect the textural quality of peas. This vegetable contains phytic acid (inositol hexaphosphate) in the interior of the cell. Cooking disrupts the structural compartmentalization within the cell and cell contents come in contact with the middle lamella. The phytic acid unites with calcium from calcium pectate to form insoluble calcium phytate (phytin). The resulting in-creased solubility of pectic material in the middle lamella leads to tenderiza-tion of the peas when they are cooked. However, peas stored so that the enzyme phytase which they contain can hydrolyze phytic acid to inositol and phosphoric acid, neither of which binds calcium, remain firm or hard even with prolonged cooking (29).

TEXTURE OF COOKED POTATOES

Potatoes, because of their high content of starch, absorb water as they cook in contrast to most vegetables that lose weight even when cooked in excess water. The texture of cooked potatoes varies from mealy to waxy (soggy). The former have a glistening appearance and a granular, dry feeling on the tongue.

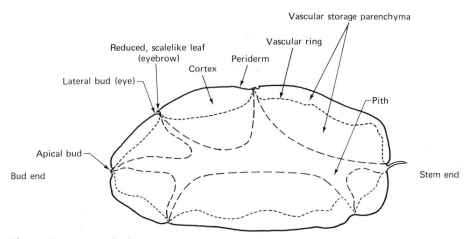

Figure 28-3. Longitudinal section of a potato tuber (*Solanum tuberosum*). (From D. L. Hsu and Marion Jacobson, *Home Economics Research J.* **13:** 28, 1974. Reprinted by permission.)

Waxy potatoes appear translucent and feel pasty and wet. Much effort has been expended to account for the difference in cooking quality of potatoes. A number of factors appear to be involved. Soil, climate, fertilizer, genetic factors (variety), and composition of the tuber have been investigated. Some varieties of potato do tend to be mealy when they are cooked; others tend to be soggy. The starch content, which varies from one part of the tuber to another (see Figures 28-3 and 28-4) as well as among tubers, appears to be a factor. As a potato is heated, starch grains packed inside the cells swell severalfold. Swelling of potato starch occurs at a relatively low temperature (Fig. 8-10). An early theory was that these swollen granules exerted pressure within the cells, causing rounding and cell separation when cementing pectic material in the middle lamella was weakened by cooking (56). No swelling of potato cells was observed, however, when slices of potato tissue were heated on a microscope slide. To account for the association of mealiness and high starch content of the tuber, it has been suggested that because calcium ions are needed for the deposition of starch molecules in the granule, fewer calcium ions are free to react with and so insolubilize pectic substances in the middle lamella (11). Regardless of the cause, cells tend to separate in a cooked potato that is mealy, and they tend to adhere in a nonmealy potato. (See Fig. 28-5.)

   Although it is not known precisely why one potato will be mealy when cooked and another nonmealy, it is possible to predict fairly well how a potato will cook by measuring its specific gravity (6,26). For this purpose, potatoes are placed in a brine made with one cup of salt and 11 cups of water (Fig. 28-6). A potato that floats in brine of this strength is less dense (has lower specific gravity) and the chances are good that the cells of this potato will adhere after it is cooked. This characteristic is desirable in a potato to be used for salad or

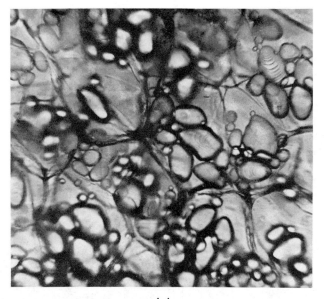

(a)

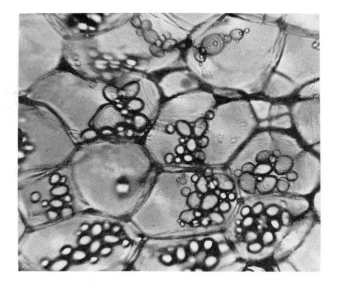

(b)

Fig. 28.4. Starch granules in the parenchyma cells of potato. (a) Numerous, large granules in the larger parenchyma cells of the internal phloem (c in Fig. 28–2). (b) Fewer granules in the pith or "water core" (d in Fig. 28–2). Original magnification × 150. (From R. M. Reeve, *American Potato Journal* 44:44, 1967 and *Economic Botany* 21:296, 1967. Used by permission of the New York Botanical Garden.)

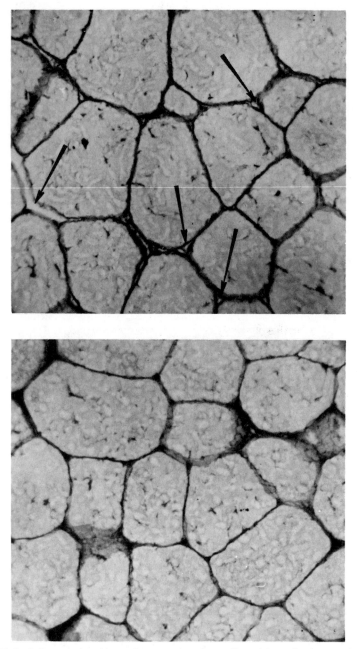

FIGURE 28-5. Cell separation (shown by arrows) and rounding of the cells characterize a mealy cooked potato (top). In a waxy or "soggy" potato (bottom) the cells adhere and remain angular. (From C. Sterling, "Texture of Cell-wall Polysaccharides in Foods" in *Recent Advances in Food Research-3—Biochemistry and Biophysics in Food Research,* J. M. Leitch and D. N. Rhodes, editors. Copyright © 1963 by Butterworths, London, p. 274. Reprinted by permission.)

FIGURE 28-6. Specific gravity of a potato is an index to its cooking quality. Floaters (in brine made of 1 cup of salt and 11 cups of water) are likely to be waxy when cooked, sinkers likely to be mealy. (Courtesy of Andrea Mackey and the Oregon Agricultural Experiment Station.)

scalloped potatoes. On the other hand, if the potato sinks, this means that the potato is dense and such potatoes tend to be mealy when cooked. For mashed potatoes this is a desirable characteristic, and many people consider it so for baked potatoes. Sinkers, with high specific gravity, have more starch than do floaters. This lends support to the theory that higher starch content and lower cell adhesion are related. Attempts have been made to market potatoes separated on the basis of specific gravity. The relation between specific gravity and texture of cooked potatoes is illustrated in Figure 28-7.

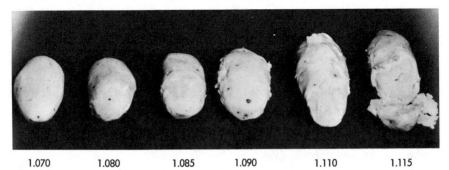

| 1.070 | 1.080 | 1.085 | 1.090 | 1.110 | 1.115 |

FIGURE 28-7. Texture of cooked potatoes that vary in specific gravity. Floaters with low specific gravity on the left to sinkers with high specific gravity on the right. (Courtesy of Andrea Mackey and the Oregon Agricultural Experiment Station.)

It may be desirable to have potato cells separate, but they should not disintegrate. Pastiness in mashed potatoes is due to rupture of the cells of the potato and release of starch grains. Excessive manipulation of potatoes after they are mashed will rupture cells and give a pasty, unpalatable product.

Potatoes baked in foil compared favorably in mealiness, color, and flavor with those baked unwrapped. If held for some time (1 hour) before they were served, both deteriorated. Piercing the foil minimized the damage (15). Aside from one experimental variety of potato which was outstanding in quality whether cooked in a conventional or a microwave oven, potatoes baked conventionally (60 minutes at 205°C) were ranked better than those baked (5 minutes) in a microwave oven (43).

FLAVOR OF VEGETABLES AND THE EFFECTS OF COOKING

Information about the constituents responsible for the flavor and, especially, the aroma of a number of vegetables is available (31). Much work has been done with those vegetables that have a distinct aroma. Included are onions, garlic, and chives, of the genus *Allium,* and broccoli, cabbage, cauliflower, cress, kale, mustard, and turnip, of the genus *Brassica,* the latter belonging to the Cruciferae family. The distinctive aroma of these vegetables comes from sulfur-containing precursors.

MILD VEGETABLES

Cooking should bring out or enhance the flavor of vegetables. Improper methods or overcooking may result in a loss of flavor or may develop an undesirable one (68). Loss of flavor in mild vegetables such as carrots and peas is primarily a decrease in sweetness, due to sugar dissolving in the cooking water. Contact of the vegetable with water should be kept to a minimum. Both a minimum of water and a short cooking time help maintain the sweet taste of vegetables.

Development of an undesirable flavor is more to be guarded against than is loss of flavor. The flavor of even mild vegetables such as carrots and peas will become strong if the cooking time is prolonged. As an extreme case, one has only to compare the flavor of fresh cooked peas with that of canned peas or cooked carrots with canned carrots to note the effects of prolonged cooking and high temperature on the flavor of originally mild vegetables. If canned vegetables are to keep, they must be overcooked, but this does spoil the fresh flavor. Even slight overcooking of mild vegetables does some damage to the flavor. The risk of loss of nutritive value is greater, also.

SULFUR COMPOUNDS IN VEGETABLES

Two groups of vegetables, one from the lily family and the other from the mustard family, are noted for the sulfur compounds they contain. Garlic, onions, chives, and leeks, members of the lily family, contain derivatives of the sulfur-containing amino acid cysteine. The main derivative in garlic, (+)-S-allyl-L-cysteine sulfoxide, known by the trivial name alliin, was identified first. Also present in raw garlic is an enzyme known as alliinase or cysteine sulfoxide lyase. Damage of the cells by slicing, mincing, or chewing brings enzyme and substrate into contact. The enzyme converts the (+)-S-allyl-L-cysteine sulfoxide to ammonia, pyruvic acid, and diallyl thiosulfinate (allicin), the last a volatile compound with a not unpleasant odor. The reaction is shown (5) as

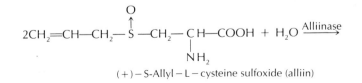

$$(+)-S\text{-Allyl}-L-cysteine\ sulfoxide\ (alliin)$$

Diallyl thiosulfinate   Ammonia   Pyruvic acid
(allicin)

The allicin is unstable and decomposes to give diallyl disulfide, the main constituent in garlic odor, which is potent and unpleasant, even offensive to many.

Onions, chives, and leeks contain (+)-S-methyl- and (+)-S-propyl-L-cysteine sulfoxide, but little if any of the allyl compound. Present also is a sulfoxide lyase which catalyzes the breakdown of these sulfoxides to dimethyl, dipropyl, and methylpropyl thiosulfinates. The dipropyl derivative is characterized as having a typical onionlike odor. The ratio of propyl to methyl derivatives decreases from the stronger onions to the mild chives, to the still milder leeks (13). The thiosulfinates are unstable, and their decomposition products include aldehydes, alcohols, and dimethyl, dipropyl, and methylpropyl di- and trisulfides.

More abundant in onions than the methyl and propyl cysteine sulfoxides and possibly important as a flavor precursor (58) is (+)-S-propenyl-L-cysteine sulfoxide

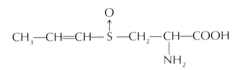

This sulfoxide has been identified as the chief substrate for the cysteine sulfoxide lyase and the precursor of the lachrymator in onion (59). When the

tissue is cut, the enzyme catalyzes the breakdown of this sulfoxide to ammonia, pyruvic acid, and, instead of a thiosulfinate, either thiopropanal sulfoxide

$$CH_3{-}CH_2{-}CH{=}S{=}O$$

or propenyl sulfenic acid

$$CH_3{-}CH{=}CH{-}\overset{\overset{\textstyle O}{\uparrow}}{S}{-}H$$

which rapidly rearranges to the thiopropanal sulfoxide. The latter has been identified as the lachrymator in freshly cut onion tissue (12). The lachrymator is unstable and decomposes rapidly. Substances formed by the action of the lyase on the propenyl sulfoxide have been proposed as contributors to the biting sensation on the tongue, the bitterness, and part of the odor of minced or chewed onion tissue, as well as being responsible for the tear-eliciting effect (58).

The (+)-S-propenyl-L-cysteine sulfoxide has been proposed as the main, if not the only, precursor of compounds that have the characteristic odor of cooked onions (59), but both propyl and propenyl di- and trisulfides have been identified in the aroma of boiled onions and dimethyl thiophene in that of fried onions (7). Much of the odor of onions can be volatilized by cooking. It is a question of how much onion aroma one wants to retain. For little or none, the vegetable should be cooked in enough water to cover in an uncovered pan. To retain as much as possible of the onion aroma, the vegetable should be cooked in a pan with a lid and in a minimum of water. The choice of cooking method might be influenced by whether the raw onions are mild or strong.

Onions increase in sweetness when they are cooked. The reason for this is still unclear, although it has been attributed to the production of *n*-propanethiol, a compound reputed to be many times sweeter than sucrose (77).

Vegetables that belong to the mustard family, the Cruciferae, constitute a second group high in sulfur-containing compounds. Included are broccoli, Brussels sprouts, cabbage, cauliflower, kale, kohlrabi, mustard, rutabaga, turnip, cress, radish, and horseradish, all except the last three members of the *Brassica* genus. Instead of propyl, propenyl, or allyl, however, only (+)-S-methyl-L-cysteine sulfoxide

$$CH_3{-}\overset{\overset{\textstyle O}{\uparrow}}{S}{-}CH_2{-}\underset{\underset{\textstyle NH_2}{|}}{CH}{-}COOH$$

is present. Two vegetables of the cabbage group, cauliflower and broccoli, contain high concentrations of this sulfoxide. Values of 2380 micrograms per gram of vegetable have been reported for cauliflower, compared with 304 for cabbage. Buds of broccoli averaged 2406 micrograms per gram, the leaves somewhat less and the stems least of all. Even so, the stems contained 850 micrograms per gram (45).

Cysteine sulfoxide lyase, once considered absent from these vegetables, has been demonstrated in some, its inactivity attributed to its high optimum pH. The flavor of these vegetables when raw comes not from the decomposition of the cysteine sulfoxide but from another group of sulfur-containing compounds found in the Cruciferae. In the intact vegetable these are present as glucosides of the isothiocyanates, the latter known as mustard oils. Mustard oils are volatile, pungent, and sometimes produce a biting or burning sensation on the tongue. Mustard oil glucosides or glucosinolates are represented by the following type formula:

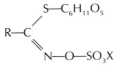

The X represents different bases attached to the sulfate ion. Among the R groups identified in vegetables of the mustard family are p-hydroxy benzyl, phenylethyl, and allyl. One glucosinolate, sinigrin, is found in cabbage, black mustard, and horseradish. When tissue is damaged by cutting, shredding, or chewing, the enzyme glucosinolase (myrosinase) comes in contact with the precursor. The sinigrin is hydrolyzed to glucose, potassium acid sulfate, and allyl isothiocyanate (a mustard oil) as follows (2):

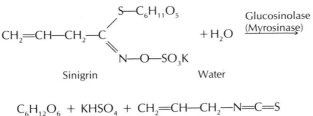

Allyl isothiocyanate and other mustard oils give an agreeable pungent aroma to grated or shredded raw cabbage.

When cabbage and other *Brassica* are cooked, volatile and odorous compounds are produced from the sulfur-containing cysteine sulfoxide and mustard oil precursors. One-fourth of the total sulfur in the volatiles from cooked cabbage was reported to be in the form of H_2S, formed from the allyl isothiocyanate which resulted from the hydrolysis of sinigrin when the vegetable was cooked (62). Increasing the cooking time from 5 to 7 minutes doubled the evolution of H_2S from cooked cabbage. Cauliflower yielded almost twice as much H_2S as cabbage, both cooked to the just-done stage. Dimethyl disulfide formed by hydrolysis of (+)-S-methyl-L-cysteine sulfoxide was identified in an early study as another important constituent in the aroma of cooked cabbage (16). In a later work little of the disulfide was found, but dimethyl sulfide constituted somewhat more than one-fourth of the total volatiles from cabbage which had been boiled for 10 minutes (42). Allyl isothiocyanate and allyl cyanide increased in the volatiles as the cooking time increased up to 20 minutes at which time breakdown of the sinigrin appeared to be complete. Two intensely unpleasant sulfur-containing compounds, one identified as dimethyl trisulfide, increased in the aroma of broccoli, Brussels sprouts, cabbage, and cauliflower as the cooking time was prolonged (44). Interaction of H_2S with an unstable intermediate in the decomposition of the sulfoxide was proposed as the source of the trisulfide.

Broccoli, Brussels sprouts and cauliflower, because of their higher content of cysteine sulfoxide, have the potential for becoming more malodorous than cabbage when overcooked. Cooking conditions for Brassica should be such as to minimize the production of volatile sulfur-containing compounds from the nonvolatile precursors. A short exposure of the vegetable to heat is recommended. The water should be boiling when the vegetable is put to cook, it should be returned to the boil as rapidly as possible, and the vegetable should be cooked no longer than necessary to make it just tender. Enough water almost to cover the vegetable will dilute the acids from the vegetable and also permit it to be cooked in an uncovered pan. This allows the volatile acids to escape with the steam. Production of hydrogen sulfide and other sulfides is kept to a minimum when vegetables of the cabbage family are cooked in this way. An uncovered pan also permits the escape of volatile sulfides which, if retained, would give the vegetable a disagreeable odor (22,24).

Asparagus is another sulfur-containing vegetable of interest, not for its aroma when cooked, but because of the odorous compounds that appear in the urine of some individuals soon after they have eaten asparagus. Two S-methyl thioesters have been identified as the main contributors of the odor, but the precursor(s) in the asparagus that give rise to these compounds remain to be identified (76).

PIGMENTS IN VEGETABLES AND THE EFFECTS OF COOKING

The bright colors of vegetables contribute to the esthetic pleasure of eating. Too often these vivid hues are muted before the vegetables are served. Some knowledge of the structure and the basic reactions of plant pigments is essential for an understanding of the changes that take place in the color of vegetables and how these can be kept to a minimum. For a discussion of flavonoid pigments which are found in vegetables as well as fruits, see Chapter 27.

CHLOROPHYLL

Green vegetables especially may undergo pronounced changes in color. The pigment involved is chlorophyll. A molecule of chlorophyll has four pyrrole groups, each a five-membered ring made of four carbon atoms and one of nitrogen (33). The four pyrrole groups are united to form a porphyrin ring as in myoglobin. Instead of the atom of iron in the molecule of myoglobin, chlorophyll contains magnesium. Phytol alcohol is attached by ester linkage to one of the pyrrole groups, methyl alcohol to a second. The phytyl residue with 20 carbon atoms in the chain is the part of the molecule which confers on chlorophyll its solubility in fat and fat solvents. Two forms of chlorophyll, chlorophyll a, which is an intense blue green, and chlorophyll b, which is a duller yellow green, are found in land plants. The two chlorophylls are present in an approximate ratio of 3 parts chlorophyll a to 1 part chlorophyll b. Chlorophyll b has a formyl group at the position marked with an asterisk instead of the methyl group in chlorophyll a, as shown on next page.

Magnesium is rather easily displaced from the molecule of chlorophyll when it is heated in the presence of organic acids. Hydrogen replaces the magnesium and a pale greenish-gray compound known as pheophytin a, or an olive green pheophytin b, results.

Removal of the phytyl group from the molecule of chlorophyll is catalyzed by the enzyme chlorophyllase, found in some vegetables. Hydrolysis of the ester linkage yields a compound, known as a chlorophyllide, which is water soluble. A limited amount of chlorophyllide produced during storage of certain green vegetables prior to cooking possibly accounts for the light-green tint of the cooking water from them. Under certain circumstances in the handling or processing of plant materials, both magnesium and the phytyl residue may be eliminated from the chlorophyll molecule. In this case the resulting compound, known as a pheophorbide, resembles pheophytin in color. This reaction takes place during brining of cucumber pickle stock (32).

When a green vegetable is first put to cook in boiling water, the green color becomes brighter. Greater translucency of plant tissue due to expulsion of intercellular air has been suggested as a possible cause (41). As cooking continues, compartmentalization within the cell is disrupted. Constituents, including organic acids, diffuse from the vacuoles throughout the cell and into the cooking water. As the acids contact the chlorophylls the latter are converted to their respective pheophytins. No longer masked by the intense green chlorophyll, the yellow and orange pigments present in green plant tissue now show along with the green. This combination together with the pheophytins gives the vegetable a muddy olive green hue.

Green vegetables that are lower in acid retain a higher percentage of chlorophyll and of their green color when they are cooked than do more acid

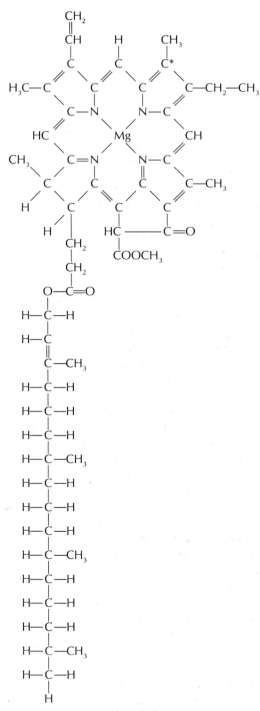

Chlorophyll a†
Chlorophyll b has a —CHO group at the carbon marked*
instead of the —CH₃ group.

†From V. A. Greulach and J. E. Adams, An Introduction to Modern Botany, 2nd edition. Copyright © 1967 by John Wiley & Sons, Inc. Used by permission of authors and publisher.

vegetables. In one study frozen spinach and frozen peas, both with a pH of 6.7, retained two-thirds to three-fourths of their chlorophyll when the vegetables were cooked to optimum doneness, whereas green beans with a pH of 6.0 retained only one-fourth. As the pH of the cooking water for green beans was elevated from 6.2 to 7.0 by addition of buffer, the retention of chlorophyll increased (69).

Because acids are present in plant tissue along with chlorophyll, the problem is how to minimize their effect during the cooking of vegetables. This may be accomplished by cooking the vegetable in an uncovered pan to eliminate volatile acids and by using enough water to cover the vegetable to dilute those acids which are not volatile (22,23,24). The major portion of the volatile acids is eliminated during the first few minutes the vegetable is in contact with the boiling water. Having the water boiling when the vegetable is put to cook and leaving the lid off the pan for at least the first few minutes are recommended for better retention of color.

Destruction of chlorophyll increases with cooking time. In the study referred to above, retention of chlorophyll in broccoli dropped from 82.5 percent when the cooking time was 5 minutes to 31.3 percent when the cooking time was 20 minutes. At the end of 5 minutes' cooking the retention of chlorophyll *a* was 78.7 percent, that of chlorophyll *b* 90.3 percent. After 20 minutes' cooking, retentions were 18.4 and 57.6 percent, respectively. Thus chlorophyll *a* is more readily converted to pheophytin than is chlorophyll *b*, to the greater detriment of color (69).

If a green vegetable is such that it will cook in a very short time, the color will be retained even when the vegetable is cooked in a small amount of water in a covered pan. In one study, broccoli cooked no longer than 5 minutes retained a good color regardless of the method used (21). The short cooking time needed to cook panned cabbage accounts for its greenness. Shredded, panned green beans retain a good color for the same reason. Both broccoli and green beans cooked for the short time required in an electronic oven retained their color better than did the same vegetables cooked in a small amount of water in a covered pan, but those cooked by stir-frying retained even more color (18). Overcooking in a pressure saucepan, a matter of seconds, is detrimental to the color of the green vegetables. If the time required to cook a green vegetable is longer than 5 to 7 minutes, enough chlorophyll will be converted to pheophytin to affect the color of the vegetable unless precautions are taken to minimize the effects of the acid. The better retention of color of frozen green vegetables during cooking is due to elimination of the major part of the plant acids as the vegetable was blanched prior to freezing.

Should a green vegetable be cooked in water that contains sodium bicarbonate, any soda not required to neutralize the acids in the cooking water will react with the chlorophyll. In this case the phytyl and methyl groups are displaced and bright-green water-soluble chlorophyllin is formed. The sodium salt of chlorophyllin gives to cooked green vegetables an intense and artificial-

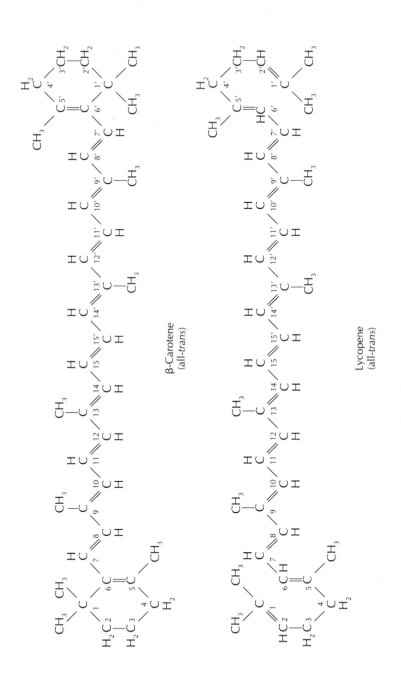

β-Carotene
(all-*trans*)

Lycopene
(all-*trans*)

appearing greenness. Vegetables cooked with soda tend to have a mushy texture, due to breakdown of hemicelluloses in the cell walls. Green vegetables cooked in just enough of a dilute solution (0.1–0.3 percent) of ammonium bicarbonate to prevent scorching kept their green color, and retention of ascorbic acid was unaffected by the bicarbonate. Calcium acetate added to the cooking water counteracted undue softening of the tissues (48).

CAROTENOIDS

Carotenoids include the yellow, orange, and red-orange fat-soluble pigments (20). They are found in the chloroplasts of green leaves, where they are masked by the high concentration of chlorophyll and in such yellow vegetables as sweet potatoes, winter squash, and carrots. The red pigment in tomatoes is a carotenoid, lycopene. Carotenoid pigments are of two types, carotenes and xanthophylls. Carotenes, which include α- and β-carotene and lycopene, are hydrocarbons with 40 carbon atoms in the molecule. Xanthophylls contain, in addition to carbon and hydrogen, one or more atoms of oxygen.

β-Carotene is the most common carotenoid. A molecule of β-carotene has a central chain of carbon atoms that unites the 6-membered ring structures at either end of the molecule, shown on page 514. The molecule is symmetrical, that is, the two halves are alike. In the human body a molecule of β-carotene can give rise to two molecules of colorless vitamin A. α-Carotene differs from β-carotene in that the position of the double bond in one of the rings is shifted to carbons 4' and 5'. α-Carotene has only half the vitamin A value of β-carotene. In lycopene the rings at either end of the molecule are open and the molecule has two more double bonds than either α- or β-carotene, as also shown.

Lutein is one xanthophyll widely distributed in green leaves. It has the same structure as α-carotene except that an —OH group has replaced a hydrogen at carbon 3 and another —OH a hydrogen at carbon 3'. Another xanthophyll, cryptoxanthin, found in yellow corn, has the same structure as β-carotene except that one —OH group has replaced a hydrogen at carbon 3'. Zeaxanthin, more widely distributed than cryptoxanthin, is 3,3'-dihydroxy-β-carotene. A molecule of cryptoxanthin yields one molecule of vitamin A. Lutein and zeaxanthin have no vitamin A value.

The red-orange color of β-carotene is due to the large number of conjugated double bonds (double bonds alternating with single bonds) in the molecule. Normally the central portion of the molecule is in the all-*trans* form as shown, which makes this part of the molecule linear. The double bonds are capable of resonance and are responsible for the hue of the carotenoid pigments. The more vivid hue of lycopene is due to the two additional double bonds in the molecule. Watermelon, pink grapefruit, and rose hips (the fruit of the rose), in addition to tomatoes, contain lycopene.

Isomerization of the molecule occurs when these unsaturated carotenoids are heated in the presence of acid. The all-*trans* form of the pigment changes over to a *cis* configuration. The bend occurs at a double bond, in which case the molecule is no longer linear. (See Chapter 14, on fats.) This change in shape reduces resonance in the molecule and so the intensity of the color. β-Carotene in the *cis* form, for example, changes from the typical red-orange to a paler yellow-orange.

A change in the color of a vegetable that contains carotenoid pigments is not as noticeable as is that which often occurs in a green vegetable. Fat-soluble carotenoids are not lost to the cooking water, but appreciable amounts may dissolve in the table fat used to season a vegetable such as carrots. When slices of sweet potato or carrot have been in contact with boiling water for 2 or 3 minutes, the hue shifts slightly toward yellow. The β-carotene in the raw vegetable is localized in the chromoplasts and in carrots the highly concentrated pigment is deposited as crystals in a variety of shapes throughout the cytoplasm of the cells. These carotene bodies may be observed under the microscope in freehand sections of raw carrot. A brief exposure to boiling water causes the β-carotene to dissolve in the lipids which appear as droplets near the periphery of the cell. A change in physical state of the pigment thus accounts for the initial change in hue (55).

Longer heating, and especially overcooking, may result in a *trans→cis* shift and some loss in intensity of color (10). The longer the vegetable is cooked and the higher the temperature, the greater is the change in hue. Because of the quantity of carotene present, cooked carrots are still bright and attractive. In the case of rutabagas, cooking intensifies the color. This is attributed to the presence of *cis*-lycopene in the raw vegetable. During cooking some of the molecules isomerize to the more colorful *trans* form (27).

ANTHOCYANINS

These water-soluble cell sap pigments can be leached from a vegetable by the cooking water. Cooking in a steamer or in a pressure saucepan or by panning, all of which limit the contact of the vegetable with water, are better methods than boiling in water to prevent loss of anthocyanins from vegetables due to solution. If the vegetable is boiled, a small amount of cooking water reduces solution of the pigments of this group. Red cabbage is one anthocyanin-containing vegetable which is cooked, especially in certain regions of the United States. The pigment in red cabbage is actually purple in the raw tissue. It is confined to the outer layers of cells of the cabbage leaf. Unless the cooking water is acidified, the pigment will change to a dull and unappetizing blue. It is to prevent this that slices of sour apple are sometimes included with red cabbage when it is cooked. Certain minerals react with anthocyanin pigments to give a blue-colored complex. Red cabbage shredded with a nonstainless-steel blade, such as a floating-blade peeler, turns blue very rapidly from the reaction between the iron of the peeler and the pigment of the cabbage. Addition of acid shifts the pigment to the flavylium ion (see the discussion on Changes in Color of Flavonoid Pigments, Chapter 27) and a red color.

BEET PIGMENTS

Until recently the purplish-red color of beets was attributed to anthocyanins, but atypical ones that contained nitrogen. Beets are now known to contain two groups of related pigments, one purplish red and the other yellow, known collectively as betalaines (40). The term betacyanin(e)s has been used to denote the red pigments and betaxanthin(e)s the yellow pigments in beets. The major red pigment is betanin(e), which when hydrolyzed yields the aglycone betanidin, a derivative of indole. The chief yellow pigment is vulgaxanthin I.

Regardless of the structure, the pigments in beets behave in some respects as though they were in fact anthocyanins. Pared and sliced beets cooked in a large amount of water lose much pigment and become pale and anemic looking. If the skin, roots, and 1 or 2 inches of stem are left on the beets, they may be boiled in water to cover without undue leaching of the pigments. If beets are quartered, sliced, or diced, they should be cooked in a small amount of water with a lid on the pan. Cooking in a steamer or in a pressure saucepan or shredding and panning also prevent leaching of beet pigments during cooking. Acid does not affect the color of the betacyanin(e)s in beets dramatically as it does the color of many anthocyanins (72). Betanine has been considered recently as a possible replacement for certain red food colorings that have been banned (49).

ANTHOXANTHINS

Normally, these water-soluble pigments are colorless in plant tissue and so go unnoticed in vegetables as well as in fruits. In alkaline medium they turn creamy white to yellow. Onions, cauliflower, turnips, and white cabbage all contain flavonols. If the last three vegetables are cooked in a covered pan for a long time, as is customary in some parts of the country, hydrogen sulfide will be liberated from the sulfur-containing compounds in these vegetables. The flavonols are closely related chemically to anthocyanins except that the former are in a higher state of oxidation. Hydrogen sulfide is a reducing agent, and this compound presumably reduces the molecules of the flavonols present in the vegetable to anthocyanins. The pinkish tint in overcooked cabbage, cauliflower, and turnips is attributed to the conversion of a small amount of colorless and more highly oxidized pigment to a colored, less oxidized anthocyanin.

DISCOLORATION OF RAW VEGETABLES

Discoloration of potatoes is more of a problem than for most vegetables if for no other reason than that potatoes are prepared so frequently. The discoloration observed on the surface of raw white potatoes which have been pared is not localized in any one area of the potato. It appears first as a pinkish discoloration which intensifies to a brownish color and finally to a dark gray. The discoloration is attributed to the formation of melanin from the amino acid tyrosine in the potato, the reaction catalyzed by phenolase enzyme in the potato (47). The speed and intensity of discoloration vary markedly from tuber to tuber. Surface discoloration of raw potato usually disappears when the potato is cooked.

STEM END BLACKENING OF COOKED POTATOES

Stem end blackening which is observed in some potatoes is another example of discoloration due to phenolic compounds. Diffuse gray-blue-black areas appear, usually in the stem rather than the bud end of the potato, and in the cooked rather than the raw (73). This discoloration which appears after the potato cools is believed to be due to a complex between the iron from the potato and *ortho*-dihydroxy phenols, probably chlorogenic acid. The colorless substrate in the potato unites with ferric iron to form the colored complex (4). Enzymes in the raw potato maintain reducing conditions that keep the iron in the ferrous state. These are inactivated during cooking.

Some lots of potatoes are more susceptible to stem end blackening than are others. Soil and climate appear to influence the susceptibility of potatoes to this type of discoloration. An appreciable amount of citrate in the potato ties the iron and so helps prevent stem end blackening (4). If the pH of the cooking water is 5 or less, stem end blackening can be minimized in potatoes that are susceptible. Adding ½ teaspoon of cream of tartar per pint of cooking water when the potatoes are half-done or ½ teaspoon per pound to mashed potatoes are procedures recommended for potatoes that are susceptible to stem end blackening (8).

NUTRITIVE VALUE AND PALATABILITY OF COOKED VEGETABLES

Vegetables lose nutrients when they are cooked, mainly by solution to the cooking water, but destruction of certain nutrients may occur, also. Sugars, water-soluble vitamins, and minerals may dissolve in the cooking water which is often discarded. Minerals are not destroyed during cooking, nor are starches and sugars, unless the vegetable is scorched, but both thiamine and ascorbic acid may be altered when a vegetable is cooked. Heat changes thiamine to a form that can no longer function as a vitamin in the body. Losses of 5 to 18 percent have been reported. Ascorbic acid not only dissolves in the cooking water but it is also susceptible to oxidation during cooking. The molecule so altered can no longer participate in the reactions in the body where it is needed. Oxidizing enzymes in plant tissue catalyze the oxidation of ascorbic acid when oxygen is present. The greatest destruction occurs during the first two or three minutes of the cooking period (25) while the cooking water is being returned to a boil. To minimize destruction, water should be boiling when a vegetable is put in to cook, not only to inactivate the ascorbic acid oxidase but also to expel oxygen from the tissues and to eliminate dissolved oxygen from the cooking water. Water should be returned to the boil promptly. Once the vegetable is heated, little oxidation occurs, but loss due to solution continues as long as the vegetable is in contact with the cooking water.

Contact of the vegetable with the cooking water should be kept to a minimum to reduce loss of nutrients due to solution (24,68). Using a small amount of cooking water when a vegetable is boiled is recommended for this reason. Alternately, a vegetable may be boiled in the skin where feasible (51). The vegetable should be cooked only until it is barely done. Steaming either in a steamer or in a pressure saucepan reduces contact of the vegetable with water. Overcooking in the latter is measured in seconds rather than minutes.

A number of studies have been concerned with the effects of the method of cooking on the retention of nutrients in vegetables. Because it is doubly vulnerable, retention of ascorbic acid has been used frequently as an index to the effects of the method of cooking on other nutrients. In one study, no marked difference was found in the retention of ascorbic acid in vegetables cooked in a steamer, in a pressure saucepan, or in a small volume of water in a saucepan, but retention was much less when cooking was done in enough water to cover the vegetable. Broccoli retained only 33 percent of its ascorbic acid when cooked in excess water, whereas retentions ranged from 67 to 82 percent for the other three methods (23). Retention of thiamine and of ribo-flavin in cabbage and in peas cooked in water to cover was less than when these vegetables were cooked in a small amount of water in a covered pan, in a steamer, or in a pressure saucepan (68). Whether frozen peas were cooked by microwaves or by conventional boiling made little difference in retention of ascorbic acid, of thiamine, or of riboflavin (67). Retention of folacin was essentially the same whether frozen vegetables were cooked in a microwave oven or on a conventional range. Retentions varied from 78 to 105 percent for frozen green beans, peas, and spinach, but only 51 to 59 percent for frozen broccoli (34). Retention of ascorbic acid was greater when broccoli, cabbage, and cauliflower were cooked by microwaves rather than in a pressure sauce-pan (22). Another study, however, found little difference in retention when beans, broccoli, cabbage, cauliflower, peas, and spinach were cooked by these two methods (36).

The method of cooking that gives the greatest retention of nutrients may not yield the most acceptable cooked vegetable from the standpoint of ap-pearance or flavor. This is true especially of sulfur-containing and of green vegetables that need more than 5 to 7 minutes of cooking to make them tender. A small amount of water in a covered utensil favors the retention of nutrients but confines acids that favor decomposition of chlorophyll and of sulfur-con-taining compounds. Broccoli, cabbage, and cauliflower, in one study, were mildest when boiled in water to cover in an uncovered pan, strongest cooked in a pressure saucepan, and intermediate when cooked by microwaves (22). The color of broccoli and cabbage was greenest when these vegetables were cooked in water to cover in an uncovered pan. But in another study (14) the flavor of broccoli was judged equally good whether the vegetable was cooked by microwaves or in a small amount of water, but the color was greener when the vegetable was cooked by microwaves. In yet another study, broccoli cooked by stir-frying was greenest and that cooked by microwaves greener than that cooked in a small amount of water in a covered pan (18). Frozen broccoli had color that was equally good when cooked in a covered or an uncovered pan, but overcooking in a pressure saucepan for only 30 seconds had a detrimental effect on both color and flavor (3). Peas cooked in a pressure saucepan were more palatable than those boiled in a covered or an uncovered pan or those cooked in a steamer (68). Frozen peas cooked by microwaves had somewhat better color than did those cooked in a small amount of water in a covered pan, but the skins were not so tender, and if overcooked for only 30 seconds, the peas were hard and shriveled (67). Thus it is obvious that there is no one method that is best for all vegetables for both palatability and retention of nutrients. A sensible approach is to emphasize conservation of nutrients but not to the point that the vegetable is so unpalatable that it will not be eaten.

Basic rules for cooking vegetables are summarized:

1. Start the vegetable to cook in boiling, salted water.
2. Return water to a boil as fast as possible.
3. Cook in barely enough water to prevent scorching and with a lid on the pan (unless color or flavor will be damaged).
4. Cook the vegetable only until barely done.
5. Serve promptly.

REFERENCES

1. A.H.E.A. 1975. *Handbook of Food Preparation.* Yields of vegetables per market unit, p. 86; timetable for cooking, p. 96; pH of foods, p. 21.
2. Bailey, S. D., M. L. Bazenet, J. L. Driscoll, and A. I. McCarthy. 1961. The volatile sulfur components of cabbage. *J. Food Sci.* **26:** 163–170. Constituents in the odor of fresh cabbage.
3. Barnes, B., D. K. Tressler, and F. Fenton. 1943. Effect of different methods of cooking on the vitamin C content of quick frozen broccoli. *Food Research* **8:** 13–26. Three methods of cooking, amounts of water and cooking times compared.
4. Bate-Smith, E. C., J. C. Hughes, and T. Swain. 1958. After-cooking darkening of potatoes. *Chem. & Ind.* Pp. 627–628. Interaction of factors which influence darkening.
5. Bernhard, R. A. 1964. Sweet smell of success. *Food Technol.* **18:** 999. Odorous substances in onions.
6. Bettelheim, F., and C. Sterling. 1955. Factors associated with potato texture. I.

Specific gravity and starch content. *Food Research* **20:** 71–80. Eight varieties compared.

7. Boelens, M., P. J. de Valois, H. J. Wobben, and A. van der Gen. 1971. Volatile flavor compounds from onion. *J. Agr. Food Chem.* **19:** 984–991. Freshly cut, boiled, and fried onions analyzed.

8. Bowman, F., and F. Hanning. 1949. Procedures that reduce darkening of cooked potatoes. *J. Agr. Research* **78:** 627–636. Effect of acid on the texture, flavor and color of potatoes that tend to darken after cooking.

9. Bowman, F., E. Page, E. E. Remmenga, and D. Trump. 1971. Microwaves *vs.* conventional cooking of vegetables at high altitude. *J. Am. Dietet. Assoc.* **68:** 427–433. Thirteen fresh and nine frozen vegetables in saucepan, pressure saucepan, and by microwaves.

10. Borchgrevink, N. C., and H. Charley. 1966. Color of cooked carrots related to carotene content. *J. Am. Dietet. Assoc.* **49:** 116–121. Comparison of carrots cooked in a saucepan and in a pressure saucepan and overcooked in a pressure saucepan.

11. Bretzloff, C. W. 1970. Some aspects of cooked potato texture and appearance. II. Potato cell size stability during cooking and freezing. *Am. Potato J.* **47:** 176–182. Photomicrographs of tissue heated to 60°, 80°, and 90°C and cooled to 80° and 27°C.

12. Brodnitz, M. H., and J. V. Pascale. 1971. Thiopropanal S-oxide: A lachrymatory factor in onions. *J. Agr. Food Chem.* **19:** 269–272. Identification of the lachrymator.

13. Carson, J. F., and F. J. Wong. 1961. The volatile flavor component of onions. *J. Agr. Food Chem.* **9:** 140–143. An attempt to identify the constituents in the aroma of onions.

14. Chapman, V. J., J. O. Putz, G. L. Gilpin, J. R. Sweeney, and J. N. Eisen. 1960. Electronic cooking of fresh and frozen broccoli. *J. Home Econ.* **52:** 161–165. Effects on texture, color, and ascorbic acid content; cooking times varied.

15. Cunningham, H. H., and M. V. Zaehringer. 1972. Quality of baked potatoes as influenced by baking and holding methods. *Am. Potato J.* **49:** 271–279. Effects of wrapping in foil.

16. Dateo, G. P., R. C. Clapp, D. A. M. MacKay, E. J. Hewitt, and T. Hasselstrom. 1957. Identification of the volatile sulfur components of cooked cabbage and the nature of the precursors in fresh vegetable. *Food Research* **22:** 440–447. Source of cooked cabbage aroma.

17. Davis, E. A., J. Gordon, and T. E. Hutchinson. 1976. Scanning electron microscope studies on carrots: Effects of cooking on the phloem and xylem. *Home Econ. Research J.* **4:** 214–224. Microstructure of carrot tissue steamed, boiled, and pressure cooked.

18. Eheart, M. S., and C. Gott. 1965. Chlorophyll, ascorbic acid, and pH changes in green vegetables cooked by stir-fry, microwave, and conventional methods and a comparison of chlorophyll methods. *Food Technol.* **19:** 867–870. Green beans and broccoli were the vegetables tested.

19. Ezell, B. D., and M. S. Wilcox. 1962. Loss of carotene in fresh vegetable as related to wilting and temperature. *J. Agr. Food Chem.* **10:** 124–126. Wilted and crisp vegetables compared at temperatures of 32°, 50°, and 70°F.

20. Frank, S. 1956. Carotenoids. *Sci. American* **194**(1): 80–84. Relation of carotene to chlorophyll and possible role in photosynthesis.

21. Gilpin, G. L., J. P. Sweeney, V. J. Chapman, and J. N. Eisen. 1959. Effects of cooking methods on broccoli. II. Palatability. *J. Am. Dietet. Assoc.* **35:** 359–363. Color, texture, flavor, and chlorophyll content.

22. Gordon, J., and I. Noble. 1959. Comparison of electronic *vs.* conventional cooking of vegetables. *J. Am. Dietet. Assoc.* **35:** 241–244. Color, flavor and ascorbic acid content of vegetables of the cabbage family cooked by conventional boiling, in a pressure saucepan and in an electronic range.

23. Gordon, J., and I. Noble. 1959. Effect of cooking method on vegetables. Ascorbic acid retention and color difference. *J. Am. Dietet. Assoc.* **35:** 578–581. Eleven vegetables cooked by four different methods.

24. Gordon, J., and I. Noble. 1964. "Waterless" *vs.* boiling water cooking of vegetables. *J. Am. Dietet. Assoc.* **44:** 378–382. Flavor, color and ascorbic acid content of five vegetables of the cabbage family.

25. Gould, S., D. K. Tressler, and C. G. King. 1936. Vitamin C content of vegetables. V. Cabbage. *Food Research* **1:** 427–434. Concentration in the raw vegetable and changes during cooking.

26. Greenwood, M. L., M. H. McKendrick, and A. Hawkins. 1952. The relationship of the specific gravity of six varieties of potatoes to their mealiness as assessed by sensory methods. *Am. Potato J.* **29:** 192–196. Six varieties varying in mealiness compared.

27. Hanson, S. W. 1954. The effect of heat treatment on some plant carotenoids. In *Color in Foods.* K. T. Farrell, J. R. Wagner, M. S. Peterson, and G. MacKinney, eds. Quartermaster Food and Container Institute. Surveys Progr. Military Subsistence Problems, Series I, No. 5. Pp. 136–159.

28. Heiner, M. K. 1943. Simplifying home preparation of potatoes. *J. Home Econ.* **35:** 646–652. Effects of organization of work center, of tools, and of procedures on time-cost and waste.

29. Isherwood, F. A. 1955. Texture in fruits and vegetables. *Food Mfg.* **30:** 206–216. Effects of starch, of enzymes, and of cell wall constituents on texture.

30. Jadhav, S. J., D. K. Salunke, R. E. Wyse, and R. R. Dalvi. 1973. Solanum alkaloids: Biosynthesis and inhibition by chemicals. *J. Food Sci.* **38:** 453–455. Formulas for the alkaloids and effect of ultraviolet light on their synthesis.

31. Johnson, A. E., H. E. Nursten, and A. A. Williams. 1971. Vegetable volatiles: A survey of components identified. *Chem. & Ind.* Part 1. 556–565. Part 2. 1212–1224. Data for 20 vegetables.

32. Jones, I. D., R. C. White, and E. Gibbs. 1963. Influence of blanching or brining treatments on the formation of chlorophyllides, pheophytins, and pheophorbides in green plant tissue. *J. Food Sci.* **28:** 437–439. Changes in chlorophyll in snap beans, okra, turnip greens, and pickling cucumbers.

33. Kamen, M. D. 1958. A universal molecule of living matter. *Sci. American* **199**(2): 77–78, 80, 82. Relation of chlorophyll, hemoglobin, and cytochromes.

34. Klein, B. P., H. C. Lee, P. A. Reynolds, and N. C. Wangles. 1979. Folacin content of microwave and conventionally cooked frozen vegetables. *J. Food Sci.* **44:** 286–288. Broccoli, green beans, peas, and spinach studied.

35. Kozukue, N. B., and K. Agata. 1972. Physiological and chemical studies of chilling injury in pepper fruit. *J. Food Sci.* **37:** 708–711. Metabolic changes responsible for the symptoms.

36. Kylen, A. M., V. R. Charles, B. H. McGroth, J. M. Schleter, L. C. West, and F. O. Van Duyne. 1961. Microwave cooking of vegetables. *J. Am. Dietet. Assoc.*

39: 321–326. Ascorbic acid and palatability of seven fresh and three frozen vegetables.

37. Lipton, W. J., and C. M. Harris. 1974. Controlled atmosphere effects on the market quality of stored broccoli (*Brassica oleraceae* L. Italica group). *J. Am. Soc. Hort. Sci.* **99:** 200–205. Effects of temperature and levels of O_2 and CO_2 on yellowing of broccoli.

38. Loconti, J. D., and Z. I. Kertesz. 1941. Identification of calcium pectate as the tissue firming compound formed by treatment of tomatoes with calcium chloride. *Food Research* **6:** 490–508. Effectiveness of calcium chloride treatment of canned tomatoes.

39. Longree, K., and F. Fenton. 1950. Objective and subjective studies on factors affecting toughness and stringiness of kale (*Brassica oleracea acephalia*). *Food Research* **15:**471-489. Effects of variety and maturity on texture of cooked kale.

40. Mabry, T. J., and A. S. Dreiding. 1968. The betalains. In *Recent Advances in Phytochemistry*. T. J. Mabry, R. E. Alston, and V. C. Runeckles, eds. Pp. 145–160. A review.

41. Mackinney, G., and C. A. Weast. 1940. Color changes in green vegetables. *Ind. Eng. Chem.* **32:** 392–395. Changes in chlorophyll when green vegetables are heated.

42. MacLeod, A. J., and G. M. MacLeod. 1970. Effects of variations in cooking methods on the flavor volatiles of cabbage. *J. Food Sci.* **35:** 744–750. Conventional boiling and microwave-cooking with and without added water.

43. Maga, J. A., and J. A. Twomey. 1977. Sensory comparison of four potato varieties baked conventionally and by microwaves. *J. Food Sci.* **42:** 541–542. Appearance and flavor compared.

44. Maruyama, F. T. 1970. Identification of trimethyl sulfide as a major aroma component of cooked brassicaceous vegetables. *J. Food Sci.* **35:** 540–543. Broccoli, Brussels sprouts, cabbage, and cauliflower studied.

45. Morris, C. J., and J. F. Thompson. 1956. The identification of (+)-S-methyl-L-cysteine sulfoxide in plants. *J. Am. Chem. Soc.* **78:** 1605–1608. Concentration in cabbage and other crucifers.

46. Morrison, W. W. 1961. *Tips on selecting fruits and vegetables*. U.S. Dept. Agr., Marketing Bull. No. 13. 44 pp. From apples to watermelon; from artichokes to watercress.

47. Muneta, P. 1977. Enzymatic blackening of potatoes: Influence of pH on dopachrome oxidation. *Am. Potato J.* **54:** 387–393. Conversion of tyrosine to melanin reviewed.

48. Odland, D., and M. S. Eheart. 1974. Ascorbic acid retention and organoleptic quality of green vegetables cooked by several techniques using ammonium carbonate. *Home Econ. Research J.* **2:** 241–250. Color and texture of broccoli, Brussels sprouts, cabbage, kale, and green beans.

49. Pasch, J. H., and J. H. von Elbe. 1978. Sensory evaluation of betanine and concentrated beet juice. *J. Food Sci.* **43:** 1624–1625. Possible replacement for Red No. 2 and No. 4 food dyes.

50. Patil, B. C., D. K. Salunke, and B. Singh. 1971. Metabolism of solanine and chlorophyll in potato tubers as affected by light and specific chemicals. *J. Food Sci.* **36:** 474–476. Conditions for accumulation of pigment and alkaloids.

51. Pfund, M. C., and H. W. Nutting. 1942. Iron content of potatoes as influenced

by cooking methods. *Food Research* **7:** 210–217. Baked, boiled unpared and boiled after paring compared.

52. Pimentel, D. W., J. K. Dritschilo, J. Krummel, and J. Kutzman. 1975. Energy and land constraints in food protein production. *Science* **190:** 754–761. Options for use of resources to meet the world's food needs.

53. Platenius, H. 1939. Effect of temperature on the rate of deterioration of fresh vegetables. *J. Agr. Research* **59:** 41–58. Seven vegetables compared at temperatures from 35°F to 80°F; loss of sugar measured.

54. Powers, J. R., and S. R. Drake. 1980. Effect of cut and field-holding conditions on activity of phenylalanine ammonia-lyase and texture in fresh asparagus spears. *J. Food Sci.* **45:** 509–510, 513. Effects of cutting and exposure to light.

55. Purcell, A. E., W. M. Walter, and W. T. Thompkins. 1969. Relationship of vegetable color to physical state of the carotenes. *J. Agr. Food Chem.* **17:** 41–42. Cause of the change in hue of carrots and sweet potatoes early in the cooking period.

56. Reeve, R. M. 1954. Histological survey of conditions influencing texture in potatoes. I. Effects of heat treatment on structure. *Food Research* **19:** 323–332. Potatoes from a mealy and from a non-mealy variety compared.

57. Schrumpf, E., and H. Charley. 1975. Texture of broccoli and carrots cooked by microwave energy. *J. Food Sci.* **40:** 1025–1029. An attempt to account for the effects on texture.

58. Schwimmer, S. 1968. Enzymic conversion of *trans-(+)*-S-1-propenyl-L-cysteine sulfoxide to the bitter and odor-bearing components of onion. *Phytochemistry* **7:** 401–404. Flavor and tear-eliciting components.

59. Schwimmer, S. 1969. Characterization of the S-propenyl-L-cysteine sulfoxide as the principal endogenous substrate of L-cysteine sulfoxide lyase of onion. *Arch. Biochem. Biophys.* **130:** 312–320. An important source of the odor of cooked onions.

60. Sheets, O., O. A. Leonard, and M. Gieger. 1941. Distribution of minerals and vitamins in different parts of leafy vegetables. *Food Research* **6:** 553–569. Calcium, phosphorus, iron, carotene, and ascorbic acid in blade, petiole, midrib, and stem.

61. Simpson, J. I. 1943. Home practices and the nutritive value of fruits and vegetables. *Food Research* **8:** 353–363. Effects of maturity, home storage, preparation and cooking; a review.

62. Simpson, J. I., and E. G. Halliday. 1928. The behavior of sulphur compounds in cooking vegetables. *J. Home Econ.* **20:** 121–126. Effects of cooking time on the evolution of H_2S from cabbage and cauliflower.

63. Simpson, J. I., and E. G. Halliday. 1941. Chemical and histological studies of the disintegration of cell-membrane materials in vegetables during cooking. *Food Research* **6:** 189–206. Effects of steaming on the pectic substances and the cellulose in carrots and parsnips; a chemical and microscopic study.

64. Sterling, C. 1955. Effect of moisture and high temperature on cell walls in plant tissues. *Food Research* **20:** 474–479. Effect of cooking on plant tissue.

65. Sterling, C. 1963. Texture and cell-wall polysaccharides in foods. In *Recent Advances in Food Science—3. Biochemistry and Biophysics in Food Research.* J. M. Leitch and D. N. Rhodes, eds. London: Butterworth. Pp. 259–276. A review.

66. Sterling, C. 1968. Effects of solute and pH on the structure and firmness of cooked

carrots. *J. Food Technol.* **3:** 367–371. Effects of pH 3 to pH 8 and of mono-, di-, and polyvalent ions compared.

67. Stevens, H. B., and F. Fenton. 1951. Dielectric *vs.* stewpan cookery. Comparison of palatability and vitamin retention in frozen peas. *J. Am. Dietet. Assoc.* **27:** 32–35. Palatability and retention of nutrients.

68. Sutherland, C. K., E. G. Halliday, and W. F. Hinman. 1947. Vitamin retention and acceptability of fresh vegetables cooked by four household methods and by an institutional method. *Food Research* **12:** 496–509. Ascorbic acid, thiamine and riboflavin in cabbage, spinach and peas cooked in water to cover, in a minimum of water, in a steamer and in a pressure saucepan.

69. Sweeney, J. P., and M. E. Martin. 1961. Stability of chlorophyll in vegetables as affected by pH. *Food Technol.* **15:** 263–266. Six vegetables varying in pH value compared; effects of cooking time on chlorophylls a and b.

70. United Fresh Fruit and Vegetable Association. *Fruit and Vegetable Facts and Pointers.* Washington, D.C.: The Association. A report on each of 79 fresh fruits and vegetables with information on the history, botany, varieties, growing areas, marketing and storage.

71. United States Department of Agriculture. *National Food Review.* Economics, Statistics, and Cooperatives Service A. NFR-9, Winter 1980, p. 51. Per capita consumption of major foods.

72. Von Elbe, J. H., I. Maing, and C. H. Amundson. 1974. Color stability of betanin. *J. Food Sci.* **39:** 334–337. Effects of pH, heat, oxygen, and light.

73. Wager, H. G. 1955. Why cooked potatoes blacken. *Food Mfg.* **30:** 499–501. Review article on the nature of and possible contributing factors to stem end blackening in cooked potatoes.

74. Walter, W. M., Jr., A. E. Purcell, and A. M. Nelson. 1975. Effects of amolytic enzymes on "moistness" and carbohydrate changes in baked sweet potato cultivars. *J. Food Sci.* **40:** 793–796. Cause of moist and dry textured sweet potatoes.

75. Weier, T. E., and C. R. Stocking. 1949. Histological changes induced in fruits and vegetables by processing. *Advances in Food Research* **2:** 297–342. Microscopic appearance of fresh tissue; effects of heat processing on cell adhesion and on microscopic appearance.

76. White, R. R. 1975. Occurrence of S-methyl thioesters in urines of humans after they have eaten asparagus. *Science* **189:** 810–811. Identification of the odorous compounds.

77. Yamanishi, T., and K. Oriaka. 1955. Chemical studies on the change in flavor and taste of onions by boiling. *J. Home Econ.* (Japan). **6:** 45. Cited in *J. Food Sci.* **33:** 298 (1968). Possible cause of the increase in sweetness when onions are cooked.

TWENTY-NINE
Fruit Pectin Gels (Jellies)

A gel behaves as a solid but an elastic one. Water, which constitutes the bulk of most gels, is immobilized in capillary spaces formed by molecules of the gelling agent. A number of edible gels have been discussed in earlier chapters. Starch-thickened puddings and soft pie fillings are gels. Molecules of amylose which have escaped from gelatinized (and swollen) starch grains unite, as they retrograde, with starch molecules on the surface of the swollen grains. The network so formed traps the water in the interstices. The gelling agent in milk gels is either neutral casein or calcium caseinate, depending on whether the milk was gelled by the action on the colloidally dispersed casein of either acid or rennin. Egg proteins, denatured by heat and aided by ions present in the milk, effect the gel in egg custard. A gelatin sol as dilute as 1 percent may be converted to a gel by lowering the temperature. Under appropriate conditions a colloidal sol of pectin may become a gel, too. This chapter is concerned with some of the conditions under which fruit pectin gels form and the major factors that affect the quality of fruit jellies.

Usually, fruit pectin gels or jellies are made by boiling fruit juice (with or without added pectin and acid) to which has been added the appropriate amount of sugar. Miss Nellie Goldthwaite from the Department of Household Science at the University of Illinois first attempted (1908–1911) to put jelly making on a scientific basis (7,8). No one has been able to improve upon her often quoted description (9) of that "elusive substance, a good fruit jelly."

> Ideal fruit jelly is a beautifully colored, transparent, palatable product obtained by so treating fruit juice that the resulting mass will quiver, not flow, when removed from its mold; a product with texture so tender that it cuts easily with a spoon, yet so firm that the angles so produced retain their shape; a clear product that is neither syrupy, gummy, sticky nor tough; neither is it brittle and yet it will break, and does so with a distinct, beautiful cleavage which leaves sparkling characteristic faces. This is that delicious, appetizing substance, a good fruit jelly.

Such an ideal jelly requires a nice balance among the four main constituents, pectin, acid, sugar, and water, each with a specific function. Pectin is the unique ingredient in this type of product.

FRUIT PECTINS

Pectins are high-molecular-weight pectinic acids or polymers of galacturonic acid (see Chapter 27) with varying proportions of the carboxyl groups esterified with methyl alcohol (18). Those pectinic acids with more than half up to three-fourths of the carboxyl groups so esterified are called pectins; those with fewer carboxyl groups esterified are designated low-methoxyl pectins. The former with the aid of acid are used to make high-sugar pectin jellies; the latter form gels with divalent ions and a lower concentration of sugar or with divalent ions alone, depending upon the extent of methylation. Whether the small amounts of carbohydrates such as arabinose, galactose, rhamnose, and xylose are an integral part of pectin molecules or adventitious material has been an issue for some time. Evidence now points to the fact that a limited number of residues of the sugar rhamnose may be present as part of the polygalacturonic acid backbone of pectic molecules and that galactose and arabinose may be present, attached to this backbone as sidechains (23). The presence of more than a token number of acetyl groups esterified to —OH groups along the polymer inhibits jelly formation (20). The inability of sugar beet pectin to form a gel is attributed to such groups.

PECTIC CONSTITUENTS IN FRUITS

As indicated in Chapter 27, pectic substances are found in the cell walls of plant tissue and also in the middle lamella. The amount of pectic material varies with the fruit and with the particular tissues of a fruit. The skin, the core area, and the albedo (of citrus fruit) are richer sources of pectin than is parenchyma tissue. The cell sap that constitutes cold pressed fruit juice seldom contains pectin. That of blackberries is an exception (8). Apple cider is deficient in pectin, as is commercial grape juice.

The proportion of protopectin, pectin, and pectic acid in a fruit varies with its maturity. Insoluble protopectin predominates in immature fruit. Protopectin yields water-dispersible pectin when fruit tissue is extracted with hot water. As fruits approach maturity, the protopectin content decreases and water-dispersible pectin predominates. The jellying power of pectin is greater, the greater the number of galacturonic acid residues in the molecule. The jelly-forming potential of the pectin is less in overripe fruits than in just-ripe or in slightly immature fruit. Demethylation of pectin occurs in some fruits as they mature, and this alters the conditions under which the pectin is able to form a gel. Complete demethylation gives pectic acid, which is incapable of gel formation. Depolymerization, which lowers drastically the jellying power of pectin, doubtless occurs as fruits become overripe too. A marked drop in jellying power and in viscosity of the pectin sol occurs when only a fraction of the glycosidic bonds in the polymer are hydrolyzed.

FRUITS FOR JELLY MAKING

A number of fruits are good sources of both high-quality pectin and of acid. Such are apples (tart), blackberries, crabapples, cranberries, currants, gooseberries, grapes (Concord and wild), guavas, lemons, loganberries, plums (sour), and raspberries (black and red). Sweet apples, prune plums, oranges, and quinces are good sources of pectin, but the first two are deficient in acid, as are some samples of the last two fruits. Apricots, pomegranate, rhubarb, and strawberries are sufficiently tart but the pectin content is low or of poor quality. Peaches and pears and all overripe fruits are deficient both in pectin and in hydrogen-ion concentration.

PECTIN GEL FORMATION

THEORY

A number of individuals have contributed to the current theory as to how a pectin gel forms (11,17,26). Pectin molecules are hydrophilic because of the great number of polar groups which they contain. The function of water in a fruit pectin gel is to dissolve acid and sugar, both essential for gel formation, and to disperse the pectin. Pectin molecules disperse in water to form colloidal sols, stabilized by the negative charges which result from the ionization of the carboxyl groups (11). When a gel forms, a viscous sol of *pectin* becomes an elastic solid. Molecules of pectin of the sol have united in some fashion to form a three-dimensional network (a gel) in the capillary spaces of which the liquid is now immobilized (26). Although molecules of pectin are essential to give structure to a gel, alone they are unable to immobilize liquid in this fashion. *Acid* is essential (29) to provide hydrogen ions (28). These, it is theorized, neutralize the charges enough so that the dispersed pectin molecules no longer repel one another (11,17). But before crosslinks can form between adjacent pectin molecules *sugar* must be present in sufficient concentration. Sugar effects gelation by lowering the activity of water (22,23).

Still undecided is how molecules of pectin are united at the junction points. One theory, that sugar molecules act as interchain links between adjacent molecules of pectin (26), is considered untenable now (21,26). Linkage by hydrogen bonding between polar groups on the molecules has been proposed (26) but hydrogen bonding between pairs of hydroxyl groups has been ruled out (22). Van der Waals attraction between methoxyl groups has been proposed, too (19,21). A pectin with 100 percent of the carboxyl groups methylated can form a gel without either sugar or acid (22). Because pectin with acetyl groups equal to 1 for each 8 galacturonic acid residues fails to form a gel, steric fit of the molecules at the junction points is considered important (22,23). Regardless of the nature of the linkage, sugar and acid in sufficient concentration can precipitate high methoxyl pectins in such a way as to enable the network to hold the syrup in the interstices. Experimental pectin jellies can be made with water, but fruit juice is desirable for practical jelly making because of the color, flavor, and hydrogen ions which it contains. If the juice is from cooked fruit, it may contain pectin, too.

CONTROL OF THE VARIABLES IN A FRUIT PECTIN JELLY

Production of jelly with the characteristics outlined by Miss Goldwaite requires that the concentration of constituents be balanced in the finished product. The proportions of hydrogen ions, sugar, and pectin determine whether a gel will form and, if so, the temperature at which it begins to set and the quality of the gel. The concentration of each can vary, but within restricted limits. A slight excess of one variable may compensate for a slight deficiency of another. Except for this, failure in jelly making would be far more common.

HYDROGEN-ION CONCENTRATION. Most fruit pectins will form a gel at a hydrogen-ion concentration which falls within the pH range of 2.8 to 3.4. Unless the pH is below 3.5, a gel is unlikely to form. The higher the pH, the longer it takes a gel to set. When the pH is below 2.8, the high hydrogen-ion concentration elevates the temperature at which the jelly sets. If a gel begins to form before the hot mixture is poured, the structure is disrupted and the gel is weakened. Manufacturers circumvent this difficulty by putting the acid in the jelly glass and adding the hot jelly to it.

The hydrogen-ion concentration which is optimum for gel formation depends upon the quality of the pectin, especially its methoxyl content (19), upon the salts present in the fruit extract, and upon the concentration of sugar in the finished jelly. Important as the pH is in making jelly, there is no precise way to measure it in the home, because a pH meter is required. Using fruit high in acidity or combining tart fruit with fruit deficient in acid and selecting fruit that is not overripe are minimum precautions. Comparing the tartness of the pectin extract with that of a mixture of 1 volume of lemon juice to 8 volumes of water provides a rough check. Lemon juice (pH 2.2–2.4) is usually used to supplement the acidity of fruits which are lacking in tartness, although tartaric acid is more effective (7) than citric acid in promoting gel formation because it is more highly ionized. Currants and grapes are particularly good for making jelly in part because of the tartaric acid which they contain.

SUGAR CONCENTRATION. Two ways are available to control the concentration of sugar in finished jelly. The mixture may be boiled to a predetermined weight. This is calculated on the basis of the weight of sugar combined with the fruit pectin extract. Alternately, the boiling point of the jelly may be used as an index to the sugar concentration (and doneness) of the jelly, as is the practice for candies and frostings. (See Chapter 6.) The concentration of sugar required to form a gel may be as low as 40 percent or as high as 70 percent, but it usually falls within the range of 60 to 65 percent. This means that most pectin gels are done when the sugar concentration is sufficient to raise the boiling point of the mixture to 103°–105°C (217°–221°F) (8). The precise concentration which is optimum depends upon the particular pectin molecules involved, the hydrogen-ion concentration of the pectin sol, and the salts which are present. For cranberries to gel the concentration of sugar must be kept below 60 percent (3). This is due in part to the low pH of cranberries (2.7–2.9). Unripe gooseberries, which are equally tart, require less than a 60 percent sugar concentration for gel formation, also.

A 60 percent sucrose solution boils at 103°C (217°F), a 65 percent sucrose solution boils near 104°C (219°F), and one that boils near 105°C (221°F) has a sugar concentration near 68 percent. A 67 percent sucrose solution is saturated at room temperature (20°C, or 68°F). (See Chapter 6.) Inversion of part of the sucrose by acid as the jelly boils plus the presence of pectin prevent the precipitation of sucrose crystals in jelly which has been boiled to 105°C (221°F) or higher. Sucrose crystals may form in jellies made with a commercial pectin concentrate which requires a cooking time too short (1 minute) for sufficient inversion of sucrose to take place.

PECTIN CONCENTRATION.   The concentration of pectin in the finished jelly depends upon how much water is evaporated as the jelly is cooked. The more dilute the pectin in the fruit extract, the more water must be boiled away to concentrate it sufficiently. This means that less sugar should be added to a dilute pectin sol than to a more concentrated one if an excess of sugar in the finished jelly is to be avoided. Of course, the acid is concentrated along with pectin and sugar. The jelly-forming capacity, which depends upon the quality as well as the quantity of pectin, is the issue, and not the absolute amount of pectin.

One way to estimate the amount of pectin in a fruit extract is to precipitate the pectin and note the yield. This can be done by adding 2 to 3 volumes of alcohol to 1 of the pectin sol. Estimating the sugar-carrying capacity of the pectin from the character of the precipitate is little better than guesswork, however. The viscosity of a pectin sol is a better measure of its sugar-carrying and jelly-forming capacity, but even this is not a precise index. The alternative, however, is to make a series of test jellies, varying the proportions of sugar and possibly the amount of acid. Of course, this is impractical when jelly is made in small quantities.

A Jelmeter may be used to measure the viscosity of a pectin sol. (See Fig. 29-1). This device is an adaptation of a viscosimeter (2). It consists of a small test tube to the lower end of which is attached a fine capillary tube. When liquid is confined and allowed to flow through a narrow space like the bore of the capillary, the flow pattern is described as "laminar." As molecules of water flow through the capillary, they move in columns that slide past each other in telescopic fashion. The symmetrical shape of water molecules (essentially spherical) favors this laminar flow. The long, asymmetrical molecules of pectin interspersed among the molecules of water disrupt this flow. As a result, the molecules of dispersing liquid are delayed in their passage through the capillary. A liquid with a slower rate of flow is more viscous. The greater the concentration of pectin molecules and, even more important, the greater the length of the pectin molecules, the more viscous is the pectin sol (18) and the higher its sugar-combining capacity. If the extract needs acid, it should be added before the viscosity is measured. The extract should be at room temperature when the test is made. If the extract is too warm, the flow is speeded; if at refrigerator temperature, it is retarded. In either case, a false reading results.

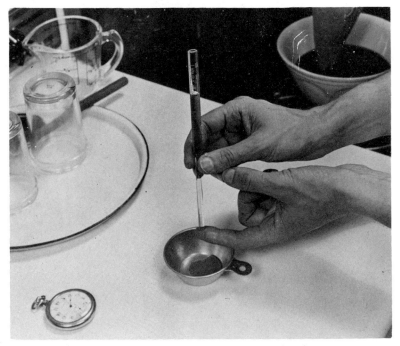

FIGURE 29-1. A jelmeter used to measure the pectin content and thus the sugar-carrying capacity of a fruit pectin extract. (Photography by Wilbur Nelson.)

To make the test, the Jelmeter is filled with the pectin sol. The sol is allowed to flow from the Jelmeter for exactly 1 minute. The upper tube of the Jelmeter is calibrated to read in cups of sugar per cup of fruit pectin extract. The first mark below the top of the Jelmeter, which reads 1¼ cups, is for the most viscous sol. One that is more viscous, that is, flows less than this distance in the time specified should be diluted with water or a juice free of pectin. Otherwise the fruit pectin extract cannot dissolve enough sugar for the jelly-forming potential of the pectin which is present. A pectin sol which flows so fast that it goes below the lowest mark, which indicates ½ cup of sugar per cup of pectin sol, is too low in jellying power to make satisfactory jelly without the addition of pectin concentrate.

The concentration of pectin in the finished jelly is controlled in part by the proportion of sugar added to the fruit pectin extract before evaporation begins. How much the mixture is concentrated by boiling is a second factor. The concentration of pectin required to form a gel varies with the quality of the pectin. A report of a concentration of 0.18 percent in a cranberry jelly (3) is unusually low, but cranberry pectin is high quality and the hydrogen-ion concentration of cranberry juice is high. Pectin is an efficient gel former and the concentration in finished jellies usually varies from 0.5 to 1.0 percent.

ROLE OF DIVALENT IONS

The more highly methylated pectins require sugar for the formation of a gel. The less methylated the pectin, the lower the amount of sugar needed to bring about the formation of a gel, provided divalent ions are present (26). Divalent ions such as calcium cross-link adjacent pectin molecules through carboxyl groups, as shown here:

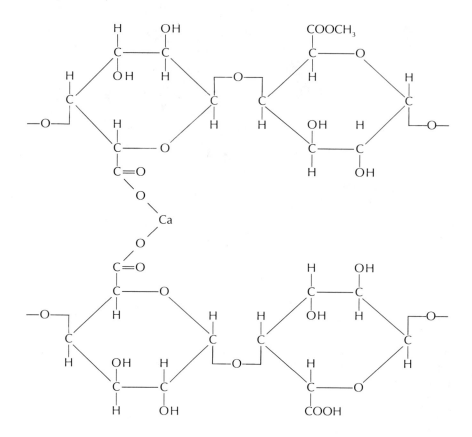

and in this way establish a pectin network. When more than half the carboxyl groups are unmethylated, a gel may be formed by divalent ions in the absence of sugar. Such pectins can convert milk to a gel with the aid of calcium ions present in the milk (12).

SETTING TIME AND TEMPERATURE

The formation of a gel from a pectin sol requires time. Firmness of a gel increases most during the first 48 hours (27). All pectin gels do not begin to set at the same temperature. Highly methylated pectins (approaching 75%) are fast setting, as are those with a low methoxyl content. Those with intermediate methoxyl content (near 50%) are slow setting (18,25). The higher the concentration of sugar, of pectin and, especially, of hydrogen ions, the higher the temperature at which a gel begins to set. The pectin in cranberry sauce sets at such a high temperature (3) that the gel is disrupted if cooking continues for more than a few minutes after the sugar is added. When sugar is combined with warm fruit pectin extract (without boiling), the range of conditions under which a satisfactory gel forms is widened (27).

MAKING FRUIT PECTIN JELLIES

There are three general methods for making fruit pectin jellies. The conventional way is to boil fruit to extract the pectin. Then this strained extract is combined with sugar and the mixture is boiled to concentrate sugar, pectin, and acid. Alternately, sufficient sugar, pectin concentrate, and acid are combined with fruit juice to form a gel. Commercial pectin concentrates are obtained either from apple pomace and parings or from citrus albedo. If the pectin is in powdered form, it is dispersed in the fruit juice before the sugar is added. When liquid pectin is used, sugar is dissolved in the fruit juice first. A short boiling period (usually 1 minute) effects solution of the sugar or dispersion of the pectin (5). Formulas for making jellies with pectin concentrates (both powdered and liquid forms) have been developed (4) and are available in bulletin form (30).

Fruit pectin gels without added pectin concentrate may be made without boiling even for a short time (27). A fruit pectin extract of high viscosity and sufficient tartness should be used. The sugar (1¼ to 1⅓ cups per cup of extract) is stirred into the fruit pectin extract, which is warmed only enough to effect solution. Temperatures as low as 40°C (104°F) have been used (17). All sugar crystals should be dissolved; otherwise, sucrose crystals may form in the jelly. Uncooked fruit purées may be gelled by combining them with sugar and pectin concentrate. Recipes for this type of pectin product have been developed for both fresh (13) and frozen (14) fruits. Uncooked jellies and jams should be stored in a cold place or frozen.

Making jelly by the hot (boiling) method is discussed in detail in the section which follows.

EXTRACTION OF THE PECTIN

For maximum jellying power, fruit which is just ripe or slightly underripe should be selected. However, unripe apples should not be used because the starch that is present makes the jelly cloudy. Some mature fruit may be included for color, aroma, and taste. Soft fruits should be crushed and firm fruits sliced thinly or chopped to facilitate extraction of pectin. If the fruit lacks sufficient tartness (1,6,28) to make jelly, acid is added at this point because it aids in the extraction of pectin with high jellying power. Thin slices of lemon, minus the *yellow* part of the rind, may be cooked along with the fruit. The pulp supplies acid and the albedo pectin. Water is essential for the extraction of pectin but soft, juicy fruits may need little if any additional water. Firm fruits need only enough water to cover (approximately 1 cup per pound). An excess should be avoided because it dilutes the pectin and must be boiled away when the jelly is made.

A simmering temperature is sufficient to extract the pectin from fruit pulp. The cooking time varies with the fruit and with its firmness. Soft fruits require approximately 10 minutes. Firm fruits like apples may need to be cooked 15 to 20 minutes. Long cooking should be avoided because heating the pectin after it has been removed from the tissues hydrolyzes (depolymerizes) it and lowers its jelly-making capacity. For fruits rich in pectin a second extraction may be made. The first should be drained from the pulp, a small amount of water added, and the pulp simmered a second time. Most of the color, the acids, and the salts are removed by the first extraction. The second extraction may yield almost as much pectin as the first, however. The yield of extract averages 1 to 1⅓ cups per pound of fruit (15).

CLARIFICATION

The cooked fruit is first strained to separate pulp from extract. The latter is then clarified by allowing it to drip through a jelly bag made of closely woven cloth or several thicknesses of cheesecloth. Squeezing the pulp increases yield but tends to make the extract cloudy.

TESTING FOR PECTIN

The sugar-carrying capacity of the extract should be tested, preferably with a Jelmeter (see discussion of Pectin Concentration, in this Chapter). Otherwise, ¾ cup sugar per cup of extract should be used. The yield of jelly will be greater, the higher the proportion of sugar to fruit extract.

EVAPORATING THE JELLY

The extract should be combined with an amount of sugar appropriate for the jellying power of the pectin before evaporation begins. Sugar retards depolymerization of the pectin as the jelly cooks. Cooking lots should be kept small (2 to 4 cups) and the heating unit should be large enough and hot enough to maintain a full, rolling boil. Long, slow evaporation hydrolyzes pectin and brings about extensive inversion of sucrose. (See Chapter 6.) The capacity of the container should be four times the volume of the fruit extract to allow for foaming of the jelly as it boils. The clarity of jelly compared to the fruit extract from which it was made is due to material collecting in the foam.

ASSESSING DONENESS

When jelly is made by the hot evaporation method, the boiling point of the mixture may be used as one index to doneness. All fruit pectin extracts do not form the best gels at the same sucrose concentration, however. Although most are done at a sugar concentration represented by a boiling point range of 3° to 5°C or 5° to 9°F above the boiling point of water (i.e., 103°–105°C or 217°–221°F at sea level and with barometric pressure at 760 mm of mercury), some should be boiled somewhat short of this concentration and others may require a slightly higher concentration. The exact concentration of sugar will depend upon the quantity and quality of the pectin and upon the hydrogen-ion concentration of the mixture.

The following test may be used to determine if the concentrations of pectin and hydrogen ions are high enough to form a gel. The pan should be removed from the hot unit momentarily to avoid overcooking the jelly while the test is being made.

A small amount of the hot syrup is rolled in the bowl of a metal spoon to cool it slightly. The mixture is then allowed to drip off the edge of the spoon. Incipient gelation thickens the mixture and causes the heavy drops of liquid to coalesce and break or cut away sharply as they leave the spoon in what is known as the "sheet test." (See Fig. 29-2.) A sheet test is an indication that all the variables which influence gel formation are at least sufficiently concentrated. It is not a guarantee that the jelly has not been cooked beyond the optimum stage, however. The ability to recognize the sheet test when it first appears takes some experience; it is complicated by the fact that all fruit pectins do not sheet in the same fashion. If a jelly fails to give a sheet test when it is boiled to 105°C (221°F), the addition of lemon juice is a way to rule out a deficiency of hydrogen ions as the cause. If a mixture which is sufficiently tart still fails to gel when the boiling point reaches 106.9°C (224°F), equivalent to a 70 percent sucrose solution, this indicates that too much sugar was combined with the original extract for the jellying power of the pectin. Adding 1 teaspoon of liquid pectin per cup of original fruit extract and boiling the mixture for 30 seconds to 1 minute may give a gel.

CHARACTERISTICS OF FRUIT PECTIN JELLIES

The character of a jelly is conditioned first by the nature of the pectin derived from the fruit. Apple pectin forms an elastic jelly; citrus pectin a friable but tender one (18). Some fruit pectins (strawberry, for example) will form a gel but only under restricted conditions (24).

A second major factor that influences the quality of jelly is the proportion of sugar which is combined with the original extract. This influences the balance of ingredients in the finished jelly. When too much sugar is used, one of two things may happen. Pectin (and acid) will be insufficiently concentrated to form a gel if doneness is assessed by the boiling point only. On the other hand, the sugar in the jelly will be too concentrated if the mixture is evaporated until the pectin is concentrated enough for it to give the sheet test. Such gels are sticky and excessively sweet. If the sugar is in great excess, a thick syrup

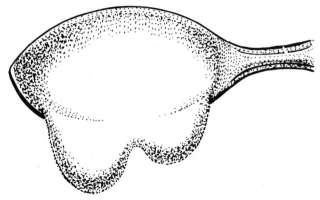

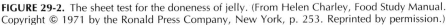

FIGURE 29-2. The sheet test for the doneness of jelly. (From Helen Charley, Food Study Manual. Copyright © 1971 by the Ronald Press Company, New York, p. 253. Reprinted by permission.)

but no gel results. If too little sugar is added to the original extract, the pectin is overconcentrated by the time the sugar reaches a sufficiently high concentration. Excess pectin makes the resulting jelly tough and rubbery. Even when the combining ratio of sugar to fruit pectin is optimum, the gel may be weak or not even form unless sufficient water is evaporated. Evaporation of too much water gives a jelly too stiff to be palatable. The concentration of sugar in jelly is usually sufficient to control any spoilage except mold growth which can be eliminated by covering the surface with melted paraffin to seal out the air. Too much acid in jelly results in syneresis.

CRYSTALS IN JELLY

Sucrose crystals may form in jellies boiled to a high temperature and especially in those which lack tartness. Crystals are likely to form in jellies made with pectin concentrate and a short boil, which gives little opportunity for inversion of sucrose. Glasslike crystals of potassium acid tartrate are likely to form in grape jelly. Chilling the grape pectin extract for 24 to 48 hours and decanting the liquid above the sediment is recommended. Grape jelly made in small lots and used promptly will be free of crystals, because they form slowly. Reducing the concentration of cream of tartar by diluting grape pectin extract with that from other fruit, such as apple, is also recommended to prevent crystal formation.

REFERENCES

1.   A.H.E.A. 1975. *Handbook of Food Preparation.* P. 21. Hydrogen-ion concentration of common foods.
2.   Baker, G. L. 1934. A new method for determining the jellying power of fruit juice extractions. *Food Ind.* **6:** 305, 315. Relation of viscosity and jellying power; use of the pipette from which the Jelmeter evolved.

3. Baker, G. L., and R. F. Kneeland. 1936. Cranberry pectin properties. *Ind. Eng. Chem.* **28:** 372–375. The uniqueness of cranberries as jelly forming fruit.
4. Gilpin, G. L., J. C. Lamb, M. G. Staley, and E. H. Dawson. 1957. Development of jelly formulas for use with fully ripe fruit and added pectin. *Food Technol.* **11:** 323–328. Basic formulas for seven fruits with both dry and liquid pectin concentrates.
5. Gilpin, G. L., J. C. Lamb, and M. G. Staley. 1957. Effect of cooking procedures on quality of fruit jelly. *J. Home Econ.* **49:** 435–438. Cooking times of 1, 2, and 3 minutes and cooking lots of 2, 4, and 6 cups compared.
6. Goldman, M. E. 1949. The pH of fruit juices. *Food Research* **14:** 275–277. Twenty-one fruits tested; range in pH given.
7. Goldthwaite, N. E. 1909. Contributions on the chemistry and physics of jelly-making. *Ind. Eng. Chem.* **1:** 333–340. An early attempt to put jelly making on a scientific basis; importance of acid.
8. Goldthwaite, N. E. 1910. Contributions to jelly-making. *Ind. Eng. Chem.* **2:** 457–462. Scientific jelly making continued; relation of boiling point to doneness.
9. Goldthwaite, N. E. 1917. *The principles of jelly-making.* Univ. Ill. Bull. Vol. XI, No. 31. 18 pp. Theory and practice in making jelly; for homemakers.
10. Halliday, E. G., and G. R. Bailey. 1924. Effect of calcium chloride on acid-sugar-pectin gels. *Ind. Eng. Chem.* **16:** 595–597. The role of calcium ions in the formation of pectin jellies.
11. Hinton, C. L. 1940. The quantitative basis of pectin jelly formation in relation to pH conditions. *Biochem. J.* **34:** 1211–1233. An attempt to account for the effect of pH on the gel formation by pectin; technical.
12. Joseph, G. H. 1953. Better pectins. *Food Eng.* **25:** 71–73, 114. Pectin concentrates including low-methoxyl pectins.
13. Kantrus, E. G. 1951. Frozen jam. *Farm J.* **75:** (June): 114–115. Formulas for uncooked jam from fresh blackberries and red raspberries.
14. Kramer, M. A., and G. Sunderlin. 1953. The gelation of pectin in uncooked jam from frozen red raspberries and strawberries. *J. Home Econ.* **45:** 243–247. Formulas and technique.
15. Lamb, J. C., M. C. Brown, and G. L. Gilpin. 1957. Yield of prepared fruit and juice for jam and jelly making. *J. Home Econ.* **49:** 433–435. Yield from 10 varieties of fruits.
16. McCready, R. M., and M. Gee. 1960. Determination of pectic substances by paper chromatography. *J. Agr. Food Chem.* **8:** 510–513. The non-galacturonide constituents in pectins from different sources.
17. Olsen, A. G. 1934. Pectin studies. III. General theory of pectin jelly formation. *J. Phys. Chem.* **38:** 919–930. Role of acid and sugar; factors which affect setting rate.
18. Olsen, A. G., F. S. Reinhold, E. R. Fehlberg, and N. M. Beach. 1939. Pectin studies. Relation of combining weights to other properties of commercial pectins. *Ind. Eng. Chem.* **31:** 1015–1020. Interrelationship of factors which affect gel formation.
19. Owens, H. S., and W. D. Maclay. 1946. Effect of methoxyl content of pectin on the properties of high-solids gels. *J. Colloid Sci.* **1:** 313–325. Relation between methoxyl content, pH, and character of the gel.
20. Pippen, E. L., R. M. McCready, and H. S. Owens. 1950. Gelation properties of

partially acetylated pectins. *J. Am. Chem. Soc.* **72:** 813–816. Acetylated and deacetylated pectin compared.

21. Pippen, E. L., T. H. Schultz, and H. S. Owens. 1953. Effect of degree of esterification on viscosity and gelation behavior of pectin. *J. Colloid Sci.* **8:** 97–104. Nature of the association between pectin molecules in a gel.

22. Rees, D. A. 1969. Structure, conformation and mechanism in the formation of polysaccharide gels and networks. *Adv. in Carbohydrate Chem. and Biochem.* **24:** 324–326. Pectin-sugars gels included.

23. Rees, D. A. 1972. Polysaccharide gels. A molecular view. *Chem. & Ind.* pp. 630–636. Technical treatment.

24. Ruiz, V. T. 1958. Strawberry pectin jellies. M.S. thesis. Oregon State University Library. 45 pp. Conditions under which satisfactory jellies form.

25. Smit, C. J. B., and E. F. Bryant. 1968. Ester content and jelly pH influences on the grade of pectins. *J. Food Sci.* **33:** 262–264. Percent esterification from 74 to 29 percent compared.

26. Speiser, R., M. J. Copley, and G. C. Nutting. 1947. Effect of molecular association and charge distribution on the gelatin of pectin. *J. Phys. Chem.* **51:** 117–133. Equilibria among the constituents essential for gel formation; high- and low-methoxyl pectin gels.

27. Spencer, G. 1929. The formation of pectin jellies by sugar. *J. Phys. Chem.* **33:** 1987–2011. Sugar and acid requirements for gel formation.

28. St. John, J. L. 1941. What do you mean, pH? *Food Ind.* **13**(12): 65–67, 103. Relation between pH and hydrogen-ion concentration: methods of measuring; pH of common foods.

29. Tarr, L. 1923. *Fruit jellies. I. The role of acids.* Del. Agr. Exp. Sta. Bull. No. 134. 38 pp. Work which led to the concept that hydrogen ion, not total acidity, is the factor in pectin gel formation.

30. United States Department of Agriculture. 1975. *How to Make Jellies, Jams, and Preserves at Home.* H. and G. Bull. No. 56. 34 pp. Recipes and directions.

Index